W9-ASX-341

1172
319
109

Students learn best when they attend and assignments…but learning

MyEconLab *Picks Up Where*

Instructors choose MyEconLab:

"MyEconLab's e-text is great. Particularly in that it helps offset the skyrocketing cost of textbooks. Naturally, students love that."

—Doug Gehrke, Moraine Valley Community College

"MyEconLab offers them a way to practice every week. They receive immediate feedback and a feeling of personal attention. As a result, my teaching has become more targeted and efficient."

—Kelly Blanchard, Purdue University

"Students tell me that offering them MyEconLab is almost like offering them individual tutors."

—Jefferson Edwards, Cypress Fairbanks College

"Chapter quizzes offset student procrastination by ensuring they keep on task. If a student is having a problem, MyEconLab indicates exactly what they need to study."

"MyEconLab helps both students and instructors. There's something there for everyone."

"Someone has already pulled out articles that relate to economics and to the chapter at hand. As much as MyEconLab helps the student, that helps the instructor."

—Diana Fortier, Waubonsee Community College

myeconlab

Get Ahead of the Curve

ectures and Office Hours Leave Off

Students choose MyEconLab:

In a recent study, 87 percent of students who used MyEconLab regularly felt it improved their grade.

"It was very useful because it had EVERYTHING, from practice exams to exercises to reading. Very helpful."

—**student, Northern Illinois University**

"I like how every chapter is outlined by vocabulary and flash cards. It helped me memorize equations and definitions. It was like having a study partner."

—**student, Temple University**

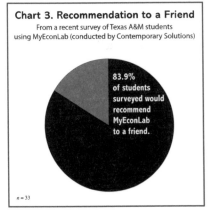

Chart 2. Helpfulness of Study Plan Practice Questions and Feedback
From a recent nationwide survey of students using MyEconLab (conducted by Contemporary Solutions)

90% of students surveyed who used the Study Plan practice questions and feedback felt it helped them to prepare for tests.

n = 227

Chart 3. Recommendation to a Friend
From a recent survey of Texas A&M students using MyEconLab (conducted by Contemporary Solutions)

83.9% of students surveyed would recommend MyEconLab to a friend.

n = 33

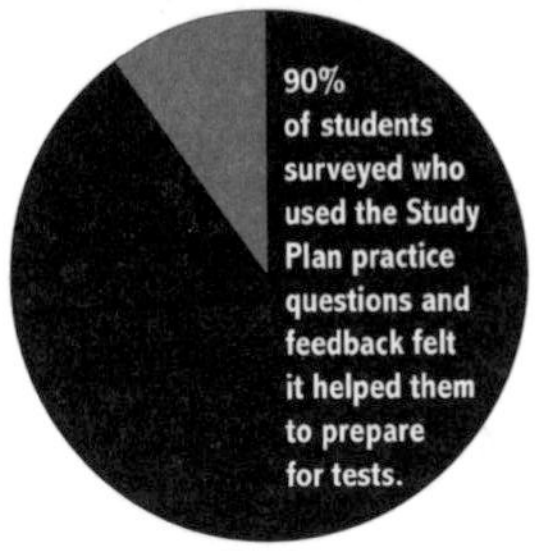

"It made me look through the book to find answers so I did more reading."

—**student, Northern Illinois University**

"It was very helpful to get instant feedback. Sometimes I would get lost reading the book, and these individual problems would help me focus and see if I understood the concepts."

—**student, Temple University**

"I really like the way MyEconLab took me through the graphs step-by-step. The Fast Track tutorials were the most helpful for the graph questions. I used the 1-2-3 buttons all the time."

—**student, Stephen F. Austin State University**

"I would recommend MyEconLab to a friend. It was really easy to use and helped in studying the material for class."

—**student, Northern Illinois University**

"I would recommend taking the quizzes on MyEconLab because it gives you a true account of whether or not you understand the material."

—**student, Montana Tech**

Print and bring this ticket with you

INTERNSHIP OPEN HOUSE

Name
Bersa Shkreta

Payment Status
Free Order

Event

Date+Time Tuesday, November 1, 2011 from 12:00 PM to 2:00 PM (ET)

Type INTERNSHIP OPEN HOUSE 11/1

Location Fenway Room
Emmanuel College
400 The Fenway
Boston, MA 02115

Order Info Ordered by Bersa Shkreta on Oct 27, 2011 at 9:43 AM

5645938871927458001

5645938871927458001

- Please PRINT and bring this ticket to the event entrance.

Do you organize events?
Start selling in minutes with Eventbrite!

www.**eventbrite**.com

microeconomics

Second Edition

R. Glenn Hubbard
Columbia University

Anthony Patrick O'Brien
Lehigh University

Upper Saddle River, New Jersey 07458

Library of Congress Cataloging-in-Publication Data

Hubbard, R. Glenn.
  Microeconomics / R. Glenn Hubbard, Anthony Patrick O'Brien.—2nd ed.
  p. cm.
  Includes bibliographical references and index.
  ISBN-13: 978-0-13-813277-4
  ISBN-10: 0-13-813277-1
  1. Microeconomics. I. O'Brien, Anthony Patrick. II. Title.
  HB172.H83 2008
  338.5—dc22
2007032877

AVP/Executive Editor: David Alexander
Senior Development Editor: Lena Buonanno
VP/Director of Development: Steve Deitmer
Project Manager: Christina Volpe
Editorial Assistant: Valerie Patruno
Marketing Manager: Lori DeShazo
Marketing Assistant: Justin Jacob
Senior Managing Editor, Production: Judy Leale
Project Manager, Production: Suzanne Grappi
Permissions Project Manager: Charles Morris
Senior Operations Supervisor: Arnold Vila
Designer: Blair Brown
Interior Design: Blair Brown
Cover Design: Blair Brown
Cover Illustration/Photo: iStockphoto/Oliver Hoffmann
Illustration (Interior): Fernando Quijano
Director, Image Resource Center: Melinda Patelli
Manager, Rights and Permissions: Zina Arabia
Manager: Visual Research: Beth Brenzel
Manager, Cover Visual Research & Permissions: Karen Sanatar
Image Permission Coordinator: Kathy Gavilanes
Photo Researcher: Rachel Lucas
Composition: GGS Book Services
Full-Service Project Management: GGS Book Services
Printer/Binder: RR Donnelley-Willard
Typeface: 10.5/12 Minion

Credits and acknowledgments borrowed from other sources and reproduced, with permission, in this textbook appear on page C-1.

Copyright © 2008, 2006 by Pearson Education, Inc., Upper Saddle River, New Jersey, 07458.
Pearson Prentice Hall. All rights reserved. Printed in the United States of America. This publication is protected by Copyright and permission should be obtained from the publisher prior to any prohibited reproduction, storage in a retrieval system, or transmission in any form or by any means, electronic, mechanical, photocopying, recording, or likewise. For information regarding permission(s), write to: Rights and Permissions Department.

Pearson Prentice Hall™ is a trademark of Pearson Education, Inc.
Pearson® is a registered trademark of Pearson plc
Prentice Hall® is a registered trademark of Pearson Education, Inc.

Pearson Education LTD.
Pearson Education Singapore, Pte. Ltd
Pearson Education, Canada, Ltd
Pearson Education–Japan

Pearson Education Australia PTY, Limited
Pearson Education North Asia Ltd
Pearson Educación de Mexico, S.A. de C.V.
Pearson Education Malaysia, Pte. Ltd.

10 9 8 7 6 5 4 3 2 1
ISBN-13: 978-0-13-813277-4
ISBN-10: 0-13-813277-1

For Constance, Raph, and Will
—R. Glenn Hubbard

For Cindy, Matthew, Andrew, and Daniel
—Anthony Patrick O'Brien

About the Authors

Glenn Hubbard, policymaker, professor, and researcher.
R. Glenn Hubbard is the dean and Russell L. Carson Professor of Finance and Economics in the Graduate School of Business at Columbia University and professor of economics in Columbia's Faculty of Arts and Sciences. He is also a research associate of the National Bureau of Economic Research and a director of Automatic Data Processing, Black Rock Closed-End Funds, Duke Realty, Information Services Group, KKR Financial Corporation, MetLife, and Ripplewood Holdings. He received his Ph.D. in economics from Harvard University in 1983. From 2001 to 2003, he served as chairman of the White House Council of Economic Advisers and chairman of the OECD Economy Policy Committee, and from 1991 to 1993, he was deputy assistant secretary of the U.S. Treasury Department. He currently serves as co-chair of the nonpartisan committee on Capital Markets Regulation. Hubbard's fields of specialization are public economics, financial markets and institutions, corporate finance, macroeconomics, industrial organization, and public policy. He is the author of more than 100 articles in leading journals, including *American Economic Review, Brookings Papers on Economic Activity, Journal of Finance, Journal of Financial Economics, Journal of Money, Credit,* and *Banking, Journal of Political Economy, Journal of Public Economics, Quarterly Journal of Economics, RAND Journal of Economics,* and *Review of Economics and Statistics.* His research has been supported by grants from the National Science Foundation, the National Bureau of Economic Research, and numerous private foundations.

Tony O'Brien, award-winning professor and researcher.
Anthony Patrick O'Brien is a professor of economics at Lehigh University. He received his Ph.D. from the University of California, Berkeley, in 1987. He has taught principles of economics for more than 15 years, in both large sections and small honors classes. He received the Lehigh University Award for Distinguished Teaching. He was formerly the director of the Diamond Center for Economic Education and was named a Dana Foundation Faculty Fellow and Lehigh Class of 1961 Professor of Economics. He has been a visiting professor at the University of California, Santa Barbara, and the Graduate School of Industrial Administration at Carnegie Mellon University. O'Brien's research has dealt with such issues as the evolution of the U.S. automobile industry, the sources of U.S. economic competitiveness, the development of U.S. trade policy, the causes of the Great Depression, and the causes of black–white income differences. His research has been published in leading journals, including *American Economic Review, Quarterly Journal of Economics, Journal of Money, Credit, and Banking, Industrial Relations, Journal of Economic History,* and *Explorations in Economic History.* His research has been supported by grants from government agencies and private foundations. In addition to teaching and writing, O'Brien also serves on the editorial board of the *Journal of Socio-Economics.*

Preface

When George Lucas was asked why he made *Star Wars*, he replied, "It's the kind of movie I like to see, but no one seemed to be making them. So, I decided to make one." We realized that no one seemed to be writing the kind of textbook we wanted to use in our classes. So, after years of supplementing texts with fresh, lively, real-world examples from newspapers, magazines, and professional journals, we decided to write an economics text that delivers complete economics coverage with many real-world business examples. Our goal was to keep our classes "widget free."

NEW TO THIS EDITION

The core ideas of economics remain unchanged: opportunity costs, comparative advantage, demand and supply, marginal analysis, the role of the entrepreneur in the market system, aggregate demand and aggregate supply, the importance of long-run economic growth to rising living standards, and the role of economic incentives in the design of policy. What does change is the context in which professors present these ideas in class and the policy debates of the time. In the past three years, to take just a few examples, we have witnessed the runaway success of Apple's iPod, companies such as MySpace entering China, renewed debate over policies toward health care, immigration, and the environment, the appointment of a new Federal Reserve chairman, and the bursting of the housing bubble. This new edition helps students understand these changing economic realities.

We were pleased by the success of the first edition and grateful for the many suggestions for improvement we received from instructors and students. In this second edition, we retained the focus of presenting economics in the context of real-world businesses and real-world policy debates that proved so popular. But we have made a number of significant improvements that we hope will make the text an even more effective teaching tool. In addition to the changes listed next, we literally worked through the text line by line, making hundreds of small changes to improve clarity and readability. The second edition includes the following key changes:

*   A more streamlined approach to presenting demand and supply in Chapter 3, "Where Prices Come From: The Interaction of Demand and Supply"
*   A clearer development of consumer surplus and producer surplus in Chapter 4, "Economic Efficiency, Government Price Setting, and Taxes"
*   New coverage of public choice in Chapter 18, "Public Choice, Taxes, and the Distribution of Income."
*   A new feature titled *Economics in Your Life* that relates a key idea in each chapter to the students' personal lives and experiences
*   Updated and new chapter-opening business cases covering such topics as the introduction of the iPod and the end of the housing bubble
*   Dozens of new examples, including several new *Making the Connection* features
*   A new *An Inside Look* newspaper article and analysis in every chapter
*   Many additions to the end-of-chapter *Review Questions* and *Problems and Applications* sections
*   *Review Questions* and *Problems and Applications* sections are now organized according to chapter learning objectives to improve learning assessment

New Streamlined Approach to CHAPTER 3

We have streamlined Chapter 3, "Where Prices Come From: The Interaction of Demand and Supply," to make the chapter more accessible to students encountering demand and supply curves for the first time. The summing of individual demand curves to a market demand curve now appears in Chapter 9, "Consumer Choice and Behavioral Economics." The summing of individual supply curves to a market supply curve appears in Chapter 11, "Firms in Perfectly Competitive Markets."

Chapter 3 now opens with a discussion of Apple and its iPod and iTunes, a company and products that the majority of students are familiar with. We return to the company and its products in the graphs, a *Making the Connection* feature, and the end-of-chapter *An Inside Look* to provide students with continuity as they read and learn about new concepts.

We added a new table, Table 3-3, "How Shifts in Demand and Supply Affect Equilibrium Price (P) and Quantity (Q)." This table provides an important summary of a key topic that many students find challenging.

A Clearer Development of Consumer Surplus and Producer Surplus in CHAPTER 4

Adopters of the first edition praised our use of consumer surplus and producer surplus to analyze the efficiency of competitive markets and the economic effects of price ceilings and price floors. But some instructors and students found our introduction of these important concepts to be a little too terse. In this edition, we proceed more slowly, employing three new graphs in our expanded explanation.

New Public Choice Coverage in CHAPTER 18

Chapter 18, now titled "Public Choice, Taxes, and the Distribution of Income," includes new coverage of public choice. Our goal is to give students some understanding of the economic analysis of government decision making. We include discussion of the voting paradox, the Arrow impossibility theorem, the median voter theorem, rent seeking, and regulatory capture. The new section leads naturally into the discussion of the tax system.

New Personal Dimension: *Economics in Your Life*

Each chapter opens with a discussion of a real-world business that is familiar to students. To pique the interest of students and emphasize the connection between the material they are learning and their own experiences, we have added a personal dimension to the chapter opener with a new feature titled *Economics in Your Life*, which asks students to consider questions about how economics affects their personal lives. At the end of the chapter, we use the concepts covered to answer the questions. Here are examples of the topics we cover in the real-world business case and the new *Economics in Your Life* feature:

Economics in YOUR Life!

Will you buy an iPod or a Zune?

Suppose you are about to buy a new digital music player and that you are choosing between Apple's iPod and Microsoft's Zune. As the industry leader, the iPod has many advantages over a new entrant like Zune. One strategy Microsoft can use to overcome those advantages is to compete based on price. Would you choose a Zune if it had a lower price than a comparable iPod? Would you choose a Zune if the songs sold on Zune Marketplace were cheaper than the songs sold on iTunes? As you read the chapter, see if you can answer these questions. You can check your answers against those we provide at the end of the chapter. Continued on page 89

Chapter 3: "Where Prices Come From: The Interaction of Demand and Supply"

Business case: Apple and the Demand for iPods

Economics in Your Life: Will you buy an iPod or a Zune?

Chapter 11: "Monopolistic Competition: The Competitive Model in a More Realistic Setting

Business case: Starbucks: Growth through Product Differentiation

Economics in Your Life: Opening your own restaurant

Chapter 13: "Oligopoly: Firms in Less Competitive Markets"

Business case: Competing with Wal-Mart

Economics in Your Life: Why can't you find a cheap PlayStation 3?

Updated and New Chapter-Opening Business Cases

As in the previous edition, each chapter-opening business case provides a real-world context for learning, sparks students' interest in economics, and helps unify the chapter. Each case describes an actual company facing a real situation. The company is integrated in the narrative, graphs, and pedagogical features of the chapter. Many of the chapter openers focus on the role of the entrepreneur in developing new products and bringing them to the market. See the fold-out at the back of the book for a complete list of the cases.

New *Making the Connection* Feature

Each chapter includes two to four *Making the Connection* features that present real-world reinforcement of key concepts and help students learn how to interpret what they read on the Web or in newspapers. One-third of the *Making the Connection* features are new to this edition, and most others have been updated. Several *Making the Connection* features discuss health care, which remains a pressing policy issue. Each *Making the Connection* now has at least one supporting end-of-chapter problem to allow students to test their understanding of the topic discussed. See the fold-out at the back of the book for a complete list of the *Making the Connections*.

All New *An Inside Look* Newspaper Articles and Analyses

For this edition, the *An Inside Look* newspaper articles and analyses are all new. Select articles deal with policy issues and are titled *An Inside Look at Policy*. We use articles from sources such as the *Wall Street Journal*, the *Economist*, and *BusinessWeek*. The feature consists of an excerpt of an article, analysis of the article, graph(s), and critical thinking questions. See the fold-out at the back of the book for a complete list of the *Inside Look* articles.

New Review Questions and Problems and Applications—Grouped by Learning Objective to Improve Assessment

At least one-third of the *Review Questions* and *Problems and Applications* are new, and many others have been revised and updated. In this edition, all the end-of-chapter material—summary, review questions, and review problems—is grouped under learning objectives. The goals of this new organization are to help make it easier for professors to assign problems based on learning objectives, both in the book and in MyEconLab and to students efficiently review material that they find difficult. If students have difficulty with a particular learning objective, a professor can easily identify which end-of-chapter questions and problems support that objective and assign them for homework and discuss them in class. Every exercise in a chapter's *Problems and Applications* section is available in MyEconLab. Students can complete these and many other exercises online, get tutorial help, and receive instant feedback and assistance on those exercises they answer incorrectly. Also, student learning will be enhanced by having the summary material and questions and problems grouped together by learning objective, which will allow them to focus on the parts of the chapter they found most challenging. Each major section of the chapter, paired with a learning objective, has at least two review questions and three problems.

As in the first edition, we include one or more end-of-chapter problems that test the students' understanding of the content presented in the *Solved Problem*, *Making the Connection*, and *Don't Let This Happen to You!* special features in the chapter. Professors can cover the feature in class and assign the corresponding problem for homework. The test banks also include test questions that pertain to these special features.

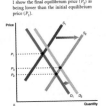

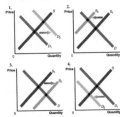

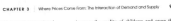

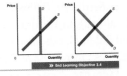

We believe a course is a success if students can apply what they have learned in both personal and business settings and if they have developed the analytical skills to understand what they read in the media. That's why we explain economic concepts by using many real-world business examples and applications in the chapter openers, graphs, *Making the Connection* feature, *An Inside Look* feature, and end-of-chapter problems. This approach helps both business majors and liberal arts students become educated consumers, voters, and citizens. In addition to our widget-free approach, we also have a modern organization and place interesting policy topics early in the book to pique student interest.

We are convinced that students learn to apply economic principles best if they are taught in a familiar context. Whether they open an art studio, do social work, trade on Wall Street, work for the government, or tend bar, students would benefit from understanding the economic forces behind their work. And though business students will have many opportunities to see economic principles in action in various courses, liberal arts students may not. We therefore use many diverse real-world business and policy examples to illustrate economic concepts and to develop educated consumers, voters, and citizens.

Here are several chapters that illustrate our approach:

- **A STRONG SET OF INTRODUCTORY CHAPTERS.** The introductory chapters provide students with a solid foundation in the basics. We emphasize the key ideas of marginal analysis and economic efficiency. In Chapter 4, "Economic Efficiency, Government Price Setting, and Taxes," we use the concepts of consumer surplus and producer surplus to measure the economic effects of price ceilings and price floors as they relate to the familiar examples of rental properties and the minimum wage. (We revisit consumer surplus and producer surplus in Chapter 8, "Comparative Advantage and the Gains from International Trade," where we discuss outsourcing and analyze government policies that affect trade; in Chapter 14, "Monopoly and Antitrust Policy," where we examine the effect of market power on economic efficiency; and in Chapter 15, "Pricing Strategy," where we examine the effect of firm pricing policy on economic efficiency.) In Chapter 7, "Firms, the Stock Market, and Corporate Governance," we provide students with a basic understanding of how firms are organized, how they raise funds, and how they provide information to investors. We also illustrate how in a market system entrepreneurs meet consumer wants and efficiently organize production. To explore how government policy affects business, we cover the outcome of the 2002 Sarbanes-Oxley Act and how companies have responded to the act.

- **EARLY COVERAGE OF POLICY ISSUES.** To expose students to policy issues early in the course, we discuss outsourcing in Chapter 1, "Economics: Foundations and Models," rent control and the minimum wage in Chapter 4, "Economic Efficiency, Government Price Setting, and Taxes," air pollution, global warming, and whether the government should run the health care system in Chapter 5, "Externalities, Environmental Policy, and Public Goods," and government policy toward illegal drugs in Chapter 6, "Elasticity: The Responsiveness of Demand and Supply."

- **COMPLETE COVERAGE OF MONOPOLISTIC COMPETITION.** We devote a full chapter to monopolistic competition (Chapter 12, "Monopolistic Competition: The Competitive Model in a More Realistic Setting") prior to covering oligopoly and monopoly in Chapters 13, "Oligopoly: Firms in Less Competitive Markets," and Chapter 14, "Monopoly and Antitrust Policy." Although many instructors cover monopolistic competition very briefly or dispense with it entirely, we think it is an overlooked tool for reinforcing the basic message of how markets work in a context that is much more familiar to students than are the agricultural examples that dominate other discussions of perfect competition. We use the monopolistic competition model to introduce the downward-sloping demand curve material usually introduced in the monopoly chapter. This helps students grasp the important point that nearly all firms—not just monopolies—face downward-sloping demand curves. Covering monopolistic competition directly after perfect competition also allows for the early discussion of topics such as brand management and the sources of competitive success. Nevertheless, we wrote the chapter so that professors who prefer to cover monopoly (Chapter 14, "Monopoly and Antitrust Policy") directly after perfect competition (Chapter 11, "Firms in Perfectly Competitive Markets") can do so without loss of continuity.

- **EXTENSIVE, REALISTIC GAME THEORY COVERAGE.** In Chapter 13, "Oligopoly: Firms in Less Competitive Markets," we use game theory to analyze competition among oligopolists. Game theory helps students understand how companies with market power make strategic decisions in many competitive situations. We use familiar companies such as Wal-Mart, Target, Coca-Cola, PepsiCo, and Dell in our game theory applications.

- **UNIQUE COVERAGE OF PRICING STRATEGY.** In Chapter 15, "Pricing Strategy," we explore how firms use pricing strategies to increase profits. Students encounter pricing strategies everywhere—when they buy a movie ticket, book a flight for spring break, or research book prices online. We use these relevant, familiar examples to illustrate how companies use strategies such as price discrimination, cost-plus pricing, and two-part tariffs.

- **A CHAPTER DEVOTED TO THE ECONOMICS OF INFORMATION.** In Chapter 17, "The Economics of Information," we explore the important fact that consumers, firms, and governments must make decisions on the basis of incomplete information. Students face uncertainty and make decisions with incomplete information when they buy used cars or health insurance, or when they search for a job. We help students analyze these familiar situations and explore the perspective of the consumer and firm. We also apply the concepts of adverse selection and moral hazard to financial markets.

Please refer to the flexibility chart on **page xliii** of this preface to help select the chapters and order best suited to your classroom needs.

Business Cases and *Inside Look* News Articles

Each chapter-opening case provides a real-world context for learning, sparks students' interest in economics, and helps to unify the chapter. The case describes an actual company facing a real situation. The company is integrated in the narrative, graphs, and pedagogical features of the chapter. Many of the chapter openers focus on the role of the entrepreneur in developing new products and bringing them to the market. For example, Chapter 3 covers Steve Jobs of Apple, Chapter 7 covers Larry Page and Sergey Brin of Google, and Chapter 12 covers Howard Schultz of Starbucks. Here are a few examples of companies we explore in this second edition:

- Can Apple's iPod continue to dominate the market? (**Chapter 3**, "Where Prices Come From: The Interaction of Demand and Supply")

- Why does Barnes & Noble offer a discount on Harry Potter books? (**Chapter 6**, "Elasticity: The Responsiveness of Demand and Supply")

- How does Starbucks differentiate itself from competitors? (**Chapter 12**, "Monopolistic Competition: The Competitive Model in a More Realistic Setting.")

An Inside Look is a two-page newspaper feature that shows students how to apply the concepts of a chapter to the analysis of an article they may read either on the Web or in a newspaper. Select articles deal with policy issues and are titled *An Inside Look at Policy*. Articles are from sources such as the *Wall Street Journal*, the *Economist*, and *BusinessWeek*. The feature presents an excerpt from an article, analysis of the article, graph(s), and critical thinking questions.

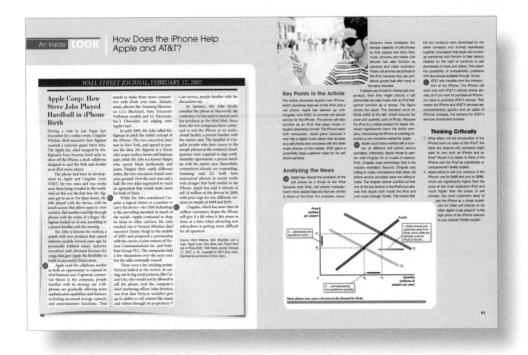

Here are some examples of the articles featured in *An Inside Look*:

- "Apple Coup: How Steve Jobs Played Hardball in iPhone Birth," *Wall Street Journal*, (**Chapter 3**, "Where Prices Come From: The Interaction of Demand and Supply")
- "Borders Slashes Buyer Rewards, Cuts Discounts," *Wall Street Journal*, (**Chapter 6**, "Elasticity: The Responsiveness of Demand and Supply")
- "Can Dunkin Donuts Really Compete with Starbucks?," *Wall Street Journal*, (**Chapter 12**, "Monopolistic Competition: The Competitive Model in a More Realistic Setting.")

Economics in Your Life

After the chapter-opening real-world business case, we have added a personal dimension to the chapter opener with a new feature titled *Economics in Your Life*, which asks students to consider how economics affects their own lives. The feature piques the interest of students and emphasizes the connection between the material they are learning and their own experiences.

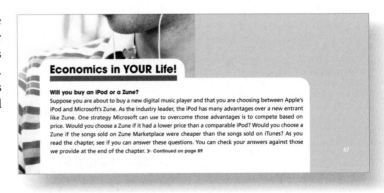

Economics in YOUR Life!

Will you buy an iPod or a Zune?

Suppose you are about to buy a new digital music player and that you are choosing between Apple's iPod and Microsoft's Zune. As the industry leader, the iPod has many advantages over a new entrant like Zune. One strategy Microsoft can use to overcome those advantages is to compete based on price. Would you choose a Zune if it had a lower price than a comparable iPod? Would you choose a Zune if the songs sold on Zune Marketplace were cheaper than the songs sold on iTunes? As you read the chapter, see if you can answer these questions. You can check your answers against those we provide at the end of the chapter. Continued on page 89

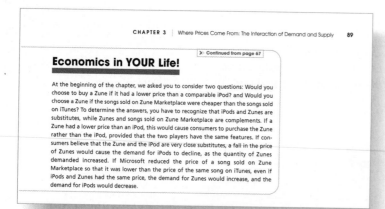

At the end of the chapter, we use the chapter concepts to answer the questions.

Here are examples of the topics we cover in the new "Economics in Your Life" feature:

- Will you buy an iPod or a Zune? (**Chapter 3**, "Where Prices Come From: The Interaction of Demand and Supply")

- Does rent control make it easier to find an affordable apartment? (**Chapter 4**, "Economic Efficiency, Government Price Setting, and Taxes")

- Why can't you find a cheap PlayStation 3? (**Chapter 13**, "Oligopoly: Firms in Less Competitive Markets")

Solved Problems

As we all know, many students have great difficulty handling applied economics problems. We help students overcome this hurdle by including two or three worked-out problems tied to select chapter-opening learning objectives. Our goals are to keep students focused on the main ideas of each chapter and to give students a model of how to solve an economic problem by breaking it down step by step. There are additional exercises in the end-of-chapter *Problems and Applications* section tied to every *Solved Problem*.

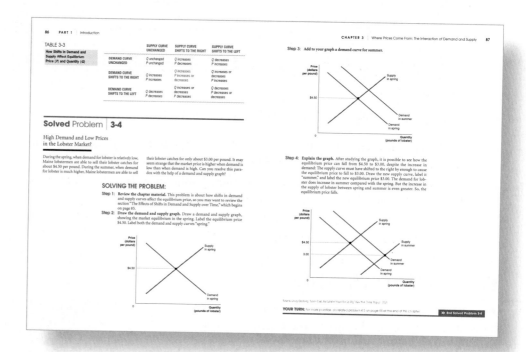

Additional *Solved Problems* appear in the following areas:

- The *Instructor's Manual*
- PowerPoint slides
- The print *Study Guide*
- The *Test Item File* includes problems tied to the *Solved Problems* in the main book.

Don't Let This Happen to You!

We know from many years of teaching which concepts students find most difficult. Each chapter contains a box feature called *Don't Let This Happen to You!* that alerts students to the most common pitfalls in that chapter's material. We follow up with a related question in the end-of-chapter *Problems and Applications* section.

Making the Connection

Each chapter includes two to four *Making the Connection* features that present real-world reinforcement of key concepts and help students learn how to interpret what they read on the Web or in newspapers. Most *Making the Connection* features use relevant, stimulating, and provocative news stories focused on businesses and policy issues. One-third of the *Making the Connection* features are new to this edition, and most others have been updated. Several *Making the Connection* features discuss health care, which remains a pressing policy issue. Each *Making the Connection* has at least one supporting end-of-chapter problem to allow students to test their understanding of the topic discussed. Here are some of the new *Making the Connection* features:

- The Market System in Action: How Do You Make an iPod? (**Chapter 2**, "Trade-offs, Comparative Advantage, and the Market System")

- How Apple Computer Inc. Forecasts the Demand for Consumer Electronics (**Chapter 3**, "Where Prices Come From: The Interaction of Demand and Supply")

- Should the Government Run the Health Care System? (**Chapter 5**, "Externalities, Environmental Policy, and Public Goods")

- How Expanding International Trade Has Helped Boeing (**Chapter 8**, "Comparative Advantage and the Gains from International Trade")

- Why Do Some Firms Like the Hilton Hotels Hide Their Prices? (**Chapter 9**, "Consumer Choice and Behavioral Economics")

- Is Being the First Firm in the Market a Key to Success? (**Chapter 12**, "Monopolistic Competition: The Competitive Model in a More Realistic Setting")

- Should the Government Prevent Banks from Becoming Too Big? (**Chapter 14**, "Monopoly and Antitrust Policy")

- Price Discrimination with a Twist at Netflix (**Chapter 15**, "Pricing Strategy")

- Does Adverse Selection Explain Why Some People Do Not Have Health Insurance? (**Chapter 17**, "The Economics of Information")

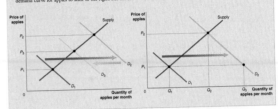

Graphs and Summary Tables

Graphs are an indispensable part of the principles of economics course but are a major stumbling block for many students. Every chapter except Chapter 1 includes end-of-chapter problems that require students to draw, read, and interpret graphs. Interactive graphing exercises appear on the book's supporting Web site. We use four devices to help students read and interpret graphs:

1. Detailed captions

2. Boxed notes

3. Color-coded curves

4. Summary tables with graphs

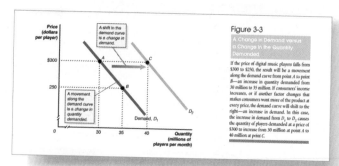

Figure 3-3

A Change in Demand versus a Change in the Quantity Demanded

If the price of digital music players falls from $300 to $250, the result will be a movement along the demand curve from point A to point B—an increase in quantity demanded from 30 million to 35 million. If consumers' income increases, or if another factor changes that makes consumers want more of the product at every price, the demand curve will shift to the right—an increase in demand. In this case, the increase in demand from D_1 to D_2 causes the quantity of players demanded at a price of $300 to increase from 30 million at point A to 40 million at point C.

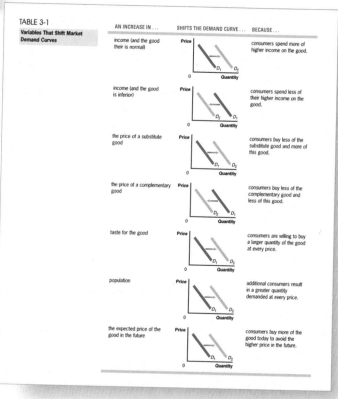

TABLE 3-1

Variables That Shift Market Demand Curves

AN INCREASE IN...	SHIFTS THE DEMAND CURVE...	BECAUSE...
income (and the good their is normal)		consumers spend more of higher income on the good.
income (and the good is inferior)		consumers spend less of their higher income on the good.
the price of a substitute good		consumers buy less of the substitute good and more of this good.
the price of a complementary good		consumers buy less of the complementary good and less of this good.
taste for the good		consumers are willing to buy a larger quantity of the good at every price.
population		additional consumers result in a greater quantity demanded at every price.
the expected price of the good in the future		consumers buy more of the good today to avoid the higher price in the future.

Integrated Supplements

The authors and Prentice Hall have worked together to integrate the text, print, and media resources to make teaching and learning easier. The process of revising the supplements began with the Test Item File Review Board, which consisted of 30 professors who reviewed each question in the first edition's Test Item files. Many of these professors became part of the second edition supplement team. We are grateful to both the members of the Test Item Review Board and our creative and generous supplement authors. They met with us for a two-day meeting to discuss ideas on how to improve the supplements and how to ensure that they are consistent with the main book. Ben Paris, Prentice Hall's Executive Producer of Assessment Programs, evaluated test bank questions and provided the test bank authors guidance on how to write effective questions.

The supplement author team from left to right: Iordanis Petsas, Cathleen Leue, Fernando Quijano, Yvonn Quijano, Ed Scahill, main book authors Glenn Hubbard and Tony O'Brien, Kelly Blanchard, and Ratha Ramoo. Not pictured here are Robert Gillette, Wendine Thompson-Dawson, Rebecca Stein, and Jim Lee.

Resources for the Instructor

Instructor's Manual

Edward Scahill of the University of Scranton prepared the *Instructor's Manual* for microeconomics. This supplement includes chapter-by-chapter summaries, learning objectives, extended examples and class exercises, teaching outlines incorporating key terms and definitions, teaching tips, topics for class discussion, new *Solved Problems*, new *Making the Connections*, new *Economics in Your Life* scenarios, and solutions to all review questions and problems in the book. The *Instructor's Manuals* is available in print and for download from the Instructor's Resource Center. Rebecca Stein of the University of Pennsylvania and the authors prepared the solutions to the end-of-chapter review questions and problems.

Two Test Banks

Ratha Ramoo of Diablo Valley College and Edward Scahill of the University of Scranton prepared two test banks to accompany microeconomics. Each test bank includes 2,000 multiple-choice questions, true/false, short-answer, and graphing questions. There are questions to support each key feature in the book. Test questions are annotated with the following information:

- **Difficulty:** 1 for straight recall, 2 for some analysis, 3 for complex analysis
- **Type:** multiple-choice, true/false, short-answer, essay
- **Topic:** the term or concept the question supports

- **Skill:** fact, definition, analytical, conceptual
- **Learning objective**
- **AACSB** (see description that follows)
- **Page number**
- **Special feature in the main book:** chapter-opening business example, *Economics in Your Life*, *Solved Problem*, *Making the Connection*, *Don't Let this Happen to You!* and *An Inside Look*.

The test banks were checked for accuracy by Thomas C. Kinnaman of Bucknell University; Randy Methenitis of Richland College; Norman C. Miller of Miami University; Brian Rosario of the University of California, Davis; Rachel Small of the University of Colorado, Boulder

AACSB

The Association to Advance Collegiate Schools of Business (AACSB)

The test bank authors have connected select test bank questions to the general knowledge and skill guidelines found in the AACSB standards.

What is the AACSB?

AACSB is a not-for-profit corporation of educational institutions, corporations, and other organizations devoted to the promotion and improvement of higher education in business administration and accounting. A collegiate institution offering degrees in business administration or accounting may volunteer for AACSB accreditation review. The AACSB makes initial accreditation decisions and conducts periodic reviews to promote continuous quality improvement in management education. Pearson Education is a proud member of the AACSB and is pleased to provide advice to help you apply AACSB Learning Standards.

What are AACSB Learning Standards?

One of the criteria for AACSB accreditation is the quality of the curricula. Although no specific courses are required, the AACSB expects a curriculum to include learning experiences in such areas as:

- Communication
- Ethical Reasoning
- Analytic Skills
- Use of Information Technology
- Multicultural and Diversity
- Reflective Thinking

These six categories are AACSB Learning Standards. Questions that test skills relevant to these standards are tagged with the appropriate standard. For example, a question testing the moral questions associated with externalities would receive the Ethical Reasoning tag.

How Can Instructors Use the AACSB Tags?

Tagged questions help you measure whether students are grasping the course content that aligns with the AACSB guidelines noted above. In addition, the tagged questions may help instructors identify potential applications of these skills. This in turn may suggest enrichment activities or other educational experiences to help students achieve these skills.

TestGen

The computerized TestGen package allows instructors to customize, save, and generate classroom tests. The test program permits instructors to edit, add, or delete questions from the test banks; edit existing graphics and create new graphics; analyze test results; and organize a database of tests and student results. This software allows for extensive flexibility and ease of use. It provides many options for organizing and displaying tests, along with search and sort features. The software and the test banks can be downloaded from the Instructor's Resource Center (www.prenhall.com/hubbard).

Acetates

All figures and tables from the text are reproduced and provided as full-page, four-color acetates.

PowerPoint Lecture Presentation

There are two sets of PowerPoint slides, prepared by Fernando and Yvonn Quijano, for instructors to use:

1. A comprehensive set of PowerPoint slides that can be used by instructors for class presentations or by students for lecture preview or review. The presentation includes all the graphs, tables, and equations in the textbook. It displays figures in step-by-step, automated mode, using a single click per graph curve.

2. A comprehensive set of PowerPoint slides with Classroom Response Systems (CRS) questions built in so instructors can incorporate CRS "clickers" into their classroom lectures. For more information on Prentice Hall's partnership with CRS, see the facing page.

Instructors may download these PowerPoint presentations from the Instructor's Resource Center (www.prenhall.com/hubbard).

Instructor's Resource CD-ROM

The Instructor's Resource CD-ROM contains all the faculty and student resources that support this text. Instructors have the ability to access and edit the *Instructor's Manual*, test banks, and PowerPoint presentations. By simply clicking on a chapter or searching for a keyword, faculty can access an interactive library of resources. Faculty can pick and choose from the various supplements and export them to their hard drives.

Classroom Response Systems

Classroom Response Systems (CRS) is an exciting new wireless polling technology that makes large and small classrooms even more interactive because it enables instructors to pose questions to their students, record results, and display the results instantly. Students can answer questions easily, using compact remote-control transmitters. Prentice Hall has partnerships with leading classroom response systems providers and can show you everything you need to know about setting up and using a CRS system. We'll provide the classroom hardware, text-specific PowerPoint slides, software, and support, and we'll also show you how your students can benefit! Learn more at www.prenhall.com/crs.

Blackboard and WebCT Course Content

Prentice Hall offers fully customizable course content for the Blackboard and WebCT Course Management Systems.

Resources for the Student

Study Guide

Wendine Thompson-Dawson of Monmouth College prepared the study guide to accompany microeconomics. The study guide reinforces the textbook and provides students with the following:

- Chapter summary
- Discussion of each learning objective

- Section-by-section review of the concepts presented
- Helpful study hints
- Additional *Solved Problems* to supplement those in the text
- Key terms with definitions
- A self-test, including 40 multiple-choice questions, plus a number of short-answer and true/false questions, with accompanying answers and explanations

Companion Web Site

The free companion Web site, www.prenhall.com/hubbard, gives students access to an interactive study guide that provides instant feedback, economics updates, student PowerPoint slides, and many other resources to promote success in the principles of economics course.

PowerPoint Slides

For student use as a study aide or note-taking guide, PowerPoint slides, prepared by Fernando and Yvonn Quijano, may be downloaded from the companion Web site, at www.prenhall.com/hubbard. The slides include:

- All graphs, tables, and equations in the text
- Figures in step-by-step, automated mode, using a single click per graph curve
- End-of-chapter key terms with hyperlinks to relevant slides

CourseSmart is an exciting new *choice* for students looking to save money. As an alternative to purchasing the print textbook, students can purchase an electronic version of the same content and save up to 50 percent off the suggested list price of the print text. With a CourseSmart etextbook, students can search the text, make notes online, print out reading assignments that incorporate lecture notes, and bookmark important passages for later review. For more information, or to purchase access to the CourseSmart eTextbook, visit www.coursesmart.com.

Vango Notes

Study on the go with VangoNotes (www.VangoNotes.com), detailed chapter reviews in downloadable MP3 format. Now, wherever you are and whatever you're doing, you can study on the go by listening to the following for each chapter of your textbook:

- **Big Ideas:** Your "need to know" for each chapter
- **Key Terms:** Audio "flashcards"—help you review key concepts and terms
- **Rapid Review:** Quick-drill sessions—use it right before your test

VangoNotes are **flexible**: Download all the material (or only the chapters you need) directly to your player. And *VangoNotes* are **efficient**: Use them in your car, at the gym, walking to class, wherever you go. So get yours today, and get studying.

Get Ahead of the Curve

For the Student

MyEconLab is an online course management, testing, and tutorial resource. Instructors can choose how much, or how little time to spend setting up and using MyEconLab.

Each chapter contains two Sample Tests, Study Plan Exercises, and Tutorial Resources. Student use of these materials requires no initial set-up by their instructor. The online Gradebook records each student's performance and time spent on the Tests and Study Plan and generates reports by student or by chapter.

Instructors can assign Tests, Quizzes, and Homework in MyEconLab using five resources:

- pre-loaded Sample Test questions
- Problems similar to the end-of-chapter problems
- Test Bank questions
- Self-authored questions using Econ Exercise Builder

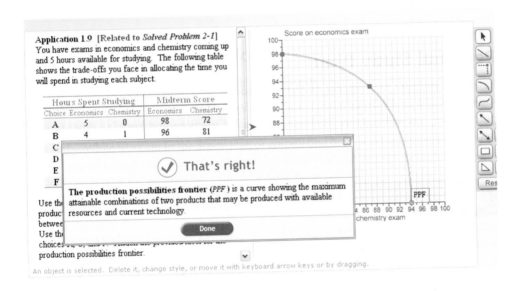

Exercises use multiple-choice, graph drawing, and free-response items, many of which are generated algorithmically so that each time a student works them, a different variation is presented.

MyEconLab grades every problem, even those with graphs. When working homework exercises students receive immediate feedback with links to additional learning tools.

Customization and Communication

MyEconLab in CourseCompass provides additional optional customization and communication tools. Instructors who teach distance-learning courses or very large lecture sections find the CourseCompass format useful because they can upload course documents and assignments, customize the order of chapters, and use communication features such as Digital Dropbox and Discussion Board.

Consultant Board, Accuracy Review Board, and Reviewers

The guidance and recommendations of the following professors helped us develop the revision plans for this new edition and the supplement package. While we could not incorporate every suggestion from every consultant board member, reviewer, or accuracy checker, we do thank each and every one of you, and acknowledge that your feedback was indispensable in developing this text. We greatly appreciate your assistance in making this the best text it could be—you have helped teach a whole new generation of students about the exciting world of economics.

Consultant Board

Kate Antonovics, University of California–San Diego
Robert Beekman, University of Tampa
Valerie Bencivenga, University of Texas–Austin
Kelly Blanchard, Purdue University
Robert Gillette, University of Kentucky
Robert Godby, University of Wyoming
William Goffe, State University of New York–Oswego
Jane S. Himarios, University of Texas–Arlington
Michael Potepan, San Francisco State University
Robert Whaples, Wake Forest University
Jonathan B. Wight, University of Richmond

Accuracy Review Board

Our accuracy checkers did a particularly painstaking and thorough job of helping us proof the graphs, equations, and features of the second edition of the text and the supplements. We are grateful for their time and commitment:

Fatma Abdel-Raouf, Goldey-Beacom College
Mohammad S. Bajwa, Northampton Community College
Hamid Bastin, Shippensburg University
Kelly Blanchard, Purdue University
Don Bumpass, Sam Houston State University
Mark S. Chester, Reading Area Community College
Kenny Christianson, Binghamton University
Ishita Edwards, Oxnard College
Harry Ellis, University of North Texas
Can Erbil, Brandeis University
Marc Fusaro, East Carolina University
Sarah Ghosh, University of Scranton
Maria Giuili, Diablo Valley College
Carol Hogan, University of Michigan–Dearborn
Aaron Jackson, Bentley College
Nancy Jianakoplos, Colorado State University

Thomas C. Kinnaman, Bucknell University
Mary K. Knudson, University of Iowa
Stephan Kroll, California State University–Sacramento
Randy Methenitis, Richland College
Norman C. Miller, Miami University
Michael Potepan, San Francisco State University
Mary L. Pranzo, California State University–Fresno
Brian Rosario, University of California–Davis
Joseph M. Santos, South Dakota State University
Mark V. Siegler, California State University–Sacramento
Rachel Small, University of Colorado–Boulder
Stephen Smith, Bakersfield College
Rajeev Sooreea, Pennsylvania State University–Altoona
Rebecca Stein, University of Pennsylvania
Wendine Thompson-Dawson, University of Utah
Robert Whaples, Wake Forest University

Reviewers

The guidance and thoughtful recommendations of many professors helped us develop and implement a revision plan that expanded the book's content, improved the figures, and strengthened assessment features. We extend special thanks to Joseph Santos of South Dakota State University, Matthew Rafferty of Quinnipiac University, and David Eaton of Murray State University for helping us revise the chapter openers and *Inside Look* features. We are grateful for the comments and many helpful suggestions received from the following reviewers:

ALABAMA

Doris Bennett, Jacksonville State University
Harold W. Elder, University of Alabama–Tuscaloosa
Wanda Hudson, Alabama Southern Community College

ARIZONA

Price Fishback, University of Arizona

ARKANSAS

Jerry Crawford, Arkansas State University

CALIFORNIA

Maneeza Aminy, Golden Gate University

Becca Arnold, Mesa College

Anoshua Chaudhuri, San Francisco State University

Jose Esteban, Palomar College

Craig Gallet, California State University–Sacramento

Maria Giuili, Diablo Valley College

Lisa Grobar, California State University–Long Beach

Dewey Heinsma, Mt. San Jacinto Community College

Jessica Howell, California State University–Sacramento

Greg Hunter, California State University–Pomona

Jonathan Kaplan, California State University–Sacramento

Philip King, San Francisco State University

Lori Kletzer, University of California, Santa Cruz

Stephan Kroll, California State University–Sacramento

David Lang, California State University–Sacramento

Carsten Lange, California State Polytechnic
   University–Pomona

Rose LeMont, Modesto Junior College

Kristen Monaco, California State University–Long Beach

Mary L. Pranzo, California State University–Fresno

Scott J. Sambucci, California State University–East Bay

Stephen Smith, Bakersfield College

Lea Templer, College of the Canyons

Kristin Vangaasbeck, California State
   University–Sacramento

Michael Visser, Sonoma State University

Kevin Young, Diablo Valley College

COLORADO

Dale DeBoer, University of Colorado–Colorado Springs

William G. Mertens, University of Colorado–Boulder

Rachael Small, University of Colorado–Boulder

CONNECTICUT

Matthew Rafferty, Quinnipiac University

DELAWARE

Fatma Abdel-Raouf, Goldey-Beacom College

Ali Ataiifar, Delaware County Community College

FLORIDA

Herman Baine, Broward Community College

Robert L. Beekman, University of Tampa

Eric P. Chiang, Florida Atlantic University

Brad Kamp, University of South Florida

Brian Kench, University of Tampa

Barbara A. Moore, University of Central Florida

Deborah Paige, Santa Fe Community College

Bob Potter, University of Central Florida

Zhiguang Wang, Florida International University

Joan Wiggenhorn, Barry University

GEORGIA

Constantin Ogloblin, Georgia Southern University

Dr. Greg Okoro, Georgia Perimeter College–Clarkston

ILLINOIS

Ali Akarca, University of Illinois at Chicago

Zsolt Becsi, Southern Illinois University–Carbondale

David Gordon, Illinois Valley Community College

Rosa Lea Danielson, College of DuPage

Scott Gilbert, Southern Illinois University

Rajeev K. Goel, Illinois State University

Alan Grant, Eastern Illinois University

Alice Melkumian, Western Illinois University

Jeff Reynolds, Northern Illinois University

Thomas R. Sadler, Western Illinois University

Kevin Sylwester, Southern Illinois University–Carbondale

Wendine Thompson-Dawson, Monmouth College

INDIANA

Robert B. Harris, Indiana University–Purdue
   University–Indianapolis

James K. Self, Indiana University–Bloomington

Arun K. Srinivasan, Indiana University–Southeast Campus

IOWA

John Solow, University or Iowa

Jonathan Warner, Dordt College

KANSAS

Guatam Bhattacharya, University of Kansas

Dipak Ghosh, Emporia State University

Alan Grant, Baker University

Wayne Oberle, St. Ambrose University

Martin Perline, Wichita State University

Joel Potter, Kansas State University

Joshua Rosenbloom, University of Kansas

Shane Sanders, Kansas State University

Bhavneet Walia, Kansas State University

KENTUCKY

David Eaton, Murray State University

Ann Eike, University of Kentucky

Barry Haworth, University of Louisville

Donna Ingram, Eastern Kentucky University

Waithaka Iraki, Kentucky State University

Martin Milkman, Murray State University

David Shideler, Murray State University

LOUISIANA

Sung Chul No, Southern University and A&M College

MARYLAND

Jill Caviglia-Harris, Salisbury University

Dustin Chambers, Salisbury University

Karl Einolf, Mount Saint Mary's University

Bruce Madariaga, Montgomery College

Gretchen Mester, Anne Arundel Community College

MASSACHUSETTS

Michael Enz, Western New England College

Can Erbil, Brandeis University

Lou Foglia, Suffolk University

Aaron Jackson, Bentley College
Ahmad Saranjam, Bridgewater State College
Howard Shore, Bentley College
Janet Thomas, Bentley College
MICHIGAN
Eric Beckman, Delta College
Jared Boyd, Henry Ford Community College
Victor Claar, Hope College
Dr. Sonia Dalmia, Grand Valley State University
Daniel Giedeman, Grand Valley State University
Gregg Heidebrink, Washtenaw Community College
Carol Hogan, University of Michigan–Dearborn
Marek Kolar, Delta College
Susan J. Linz, Michigan State University
James Luke, Lansing Community College
Ilir Miteza, University of Michigan–Dearborn
Norman P. Obst, Michigan State University
Laudo M. Ogura, Grand Valley State University
Michael J. Ryan, Western Michigan University
Charles A. Stull, Kalamazoo College
Michael J. Twomey, University of Michigan–Dearborn
Mark Wheeler, Western Michigan University
Wendy Wysocki, Monroe County Community College
MINNESOTA
Mary Edwards, Saint Cloud State University
Phillip J. Grossman, Saint Cloud State University
David J. O'Hara, Metropolitan State
　University–Minneapolis
Ken Rebeck, Saint Cloud State University
Kwang Woo (Ken) Park, Minnesota State University–Mankato
MISSISSIPPI
Becky Campbell, Mississippi State University
MISSOURI
Chris Azevedo, University of Central Missouri
Ariel Belasen, Saint Louis University
Catherine Chambers, University of Central Missouri
Paul Chambers, University of Central Missouri
Ben Collier, Northwest Missouri State University
John R. Crooker, University of Central Missouri
Mark Karscig, Central Missouri State University
Nicholas D. Peppes, Saint Louis Community College–
　Forest Park
MONTANA
Jeff Bookwalter, University of Montana–Missoula
Agnieszka Bielinska-Kwapisz, Montana State
　University–Bozeman
NEBRASKA
Allan Jenkins, University of Nebraska–Kearney
Kim Sosin, University of Nebraska–Omaha
NEVADA
Bernard Malamud, University of Nevada–Las Vegas

NEW JERSEY
Giuliana Campanelli-Andreopoulos, William Paterson
　University
Donna Thompson, Brookdale Community College
NEW MEXICO
Kate Krause, University of New Mexico
Curt Shepherd, University of New Mexico
NEW YORK
Seemi Ahmad, Dutchess Community College
Chris Annala, State University of New York–Geneseo
John Bockino, Suffolk County Community
　College–Ammerman
Sean Corcoran, New York University
Debra Dwyer, Stony Brook University
Glenn Gerstner, Saint John's University–Queens
Susan Glanz, Saint John's University–Queens
Leonie Stone, State University of New York–Geneseo
NORTH CAROLINA
Marc Fusaro, East Carolina University
Melissa Hendrickson, North Carolina State University
Jeff Sarbaum, University of North Carolina–Greensboro
Catherine Skura, Sandhills Community College
OHIO
Bolong Cao, Ohio University–Athens
Harley Gill, Ohio State University
Leroy Gill, Ohio State University
Steven Heubeck, Ohio State University
Ida A. Mirzaie, Ohio State University
Dennis C. O'Neill, University of Cincinnati
Joseph Palardy, Youngstown State University
Bert Wheeler, Cedarville University
Kathryn Wilson, Kent State University
OKLAHOMA
Ed Price, Oklahoma State University
Abdulhamid Sukar, Cameron University
PENNSYLVANIA
Bradley Andrew, Juniata College
Mohammad Bajwa, Northampton Community College
Howard Bodenhorn, Lafayette College
Milica Bookman, St Joseph's University
Eric Brucker, Widener University
Scott J. Dressler, Villanova University
Satyajit Ghosh, University of Scranton
Anthony Gyapong, Pennsylvania State University–Abington
Andrew Hill, Federal Reserve Bank of Philadelphia
James Jozefowicz, Indiana University of Pennsylvania
Stephanie Jozefowicz, Indiana University of Pennsylvania
Nicholas Karatjas, Indiana University of Pennsylvania
Mary Kelly, Villanova University
Thomas C. Kinnaman, Bucknell University
Christopher Magee, Bucknell University

Judy McDonald, Lehigh University
Ranganath Murthy, Bucknell University
Hong V. Nguyen, University of Scranton
Cristian Pardo, Saint Joseph's University
Rajeev Sooreea, Pennsylvania State University–Altoona
Rebecca Stein, University of Pennsylvania
Sandra Trejos, Clarion University
Ann Zech, Saint Joseph's University
Lei Zhu, West Chester University of Pennsylvania

RHODE ISLAND

Leonard Lardaro, University of Rhode Island
Nazma Latif-Zaman, Providence College

SOUTH CAROLINA

Calvin Blackwell, College of Charleston
Ward Hooker, Orangeburg-Calhoun Technical College
Woodrow W. Hughes, Jr., Converse College
John McArthur, Wofford College

SOUTH DAKOTA

Joseph M. Santos, South Dakota State University
Jason Zimmerman, South Dakota State University

TENNESSEE

Charles Baum, Middle Tennessee State University
Michael J. Gootzeit, University of Memphis

TEXAS

Carlos Aguilar, El Paso Community College
William Beaty, Tarleton State University
Klaus Becker Texas Tech University
Jack A. Bucco, Austin Community College–Northridge and Saint Edward's University
Don Bumpass, Sam Houston State University
Marilyn M. Butler, Sam Houston State University
Cesar Corredor, Texas A&M University
Patrick Crowley, Texas A&M University–Corpus Christi
Mark Frank, Sam Houston State University
Tina J. Harvell, Blinn College–Bryan Campus
Jane S. Himarios, University of Texas–Arlington
James Holcomb, University of Texas–El Paso
Jamal Husein, Angelo State University
Karen Johnson, Baylor University

Kathy Kelly, University of Texas–Arlington
Jim Lee, Texas A&M University–Corpus Christi
Ronnie W. Liggett, University of Texas–Arlington
Kimberly Mencken, Baylor University
Randy Methenitis, Richland College
Charles Newton, Houston Community College–Southwest College
Sara Saderion, Houston Community College–Southwest College
George E. Samuels, Sam Houston State University
Roger Wehr, University of Texas–Arlington
Jim Wollscheid, Texas A&M University–Kingsville
Dr. J. Christopher Wreh, I, North Central Texas College
David W. Yoskowitz, Texas A&M University–Corpus Christi
Inske Zandvliet, Brookhaven College

VERMONT

Nancy Brooks, University of Vermont

VIRGINIA

Philip Heap, James Madison University
George E. Hoffer, Virginia Commonwealth University
Oleg Korenok, Virginia Commonwealth University
Frances Lea, Germanna Community College
John Min, Northern Virginia Community College
Susanne Toney, Hampton University
George Zestos, Christopher Newport University

WASHINGTON

Stacey Jones, Seattle University
Dean Peterson, Seattle University

WISCONSIN

Marina Karabelas, Milwaukee Area Technical College
Elizabeth Sawyer Kelly, University of Wisconsin–Madison
John R. Stoll, University of Wisconsin–Green Bay

DISTRICT OF COLUMBIA

Michael Bradley, George Washington University
Colleen M. Callahan, American University

INTERNATIONAL

Minh Quang Dao, Carleton University–Ottawa, Canada

Previous Edition Class Testers, Accuracy Reviewers, and Consultants

Class Testers

We are grateful to both the professors who class tested manuscript of the first edition and their students for providing clear-cut recommendations on how to make chapters interesting, relevant, and comprehensive:

Charles A. Bennett, Gannon University
Anne E. Bresnock, University of California, Los Angeles and California State Polytechnic University–Pomona
Linda Childs-Leatherbury, Lincoln University, Pennsylvania
John Eastwood, Northern Arizona University
David Eaton, Murray State University
Paul Elgatian, St. Ambrose University
Patricia A. Freeman, Jackson State University
Robert Godby, University of Wyoming
Frank Gunter, Lehigh University
Ahmed Ispahani, University of LaVerne
Brendan Kennelly, Lehigh University and National University of Ireland–Galway
Ernest Massie, Franklin University
Carol McDonough, University of Massachusetts–Lowell
Shah Mehrabi, Montgomery College
Sharon Ryan, University of Missouri–Columbia
Bruce G. Webb, Gordon College
Madelyn Young, Converse College
Susan Zumas, Lehigh University

Accuracy Review Board

We are grateful to the following first edition accuracy checkers for their hard work on the book and supplements:

Kelly Hunt Blanchard, Purdue University
Harold Elder, University of Alabama
Marc Fusaro, East Carolina University
Robert Gillette, University of Kentucky
William L. Goffe, State University of New York–Oswego
Travis Hayes, University of Tennessee–Chattanooga
Anisul M. Islam, University of Houston–Downtown
Faik A. Koray, Louisiana State University
Tony Lima, California State University–Hayward
James A. Moreno, Blinn College
Matthew Rafferty, Quinnipiac University
Jeff Reynolds, Northern Illinois University

Brian Rosario, University of California, Davis
Joseph M. Santos, South Dakota State University
Edward Scahill, University of Scranton
Robert Whaples, Wake Forest University

Consultant Board

We received guidance during the first edition development at several critical junctures from a dedicated consultant board. We relied on the board for input on content, figure treatment, and design:

Susan Dadres, Southern Methodist University
Harry Ellis, Jr., University of North Texas
Robert Godby, University of Wyoming
William L. Goffe, State University of New York–Oswego
Donn M. Johnson, Quinnipiac University
Mark Karscig, Central Missouri State University
Jenny Minier, University of Kentucky
Nicholas Noble, Miami University
Matthew Rafferty, Quinnipiac University
Helen Roberts, University of Illinois–Chicago
Robert Rosenman, Washington State University
Joseph M. Santos, South Dakota State University
Martin C. Spechler, Indiana University–Purdue University–Indianapolis
Robert Whaples–Wake Forest University

Reviewers

The guidance and recommendations of the following professors helped us shape the first edition over the course of three years. We extend special thanks to Joseph Santos of South Dakota State University for helping prepare some of the *Inside Look* features and Robert Gillette of the University of Kentucky, Robert Whaples of Wake Forest University, Nicholas Noble of Miami University, and Lee Craig of North Carolina State University for preparing some of the review questions and problems and applications that appear at the ends of chapters.

ALABAMA

Doris Bennett, Jacksonville State University
Harold W. Elder, University of Alabama–Tuscaloosa
James L. Swofford, University of Southern Alabama

ARIZONA

Doug Conway, Mesa Community College

John Eastwood, Northern Arizona University

Price Fishback, University of Arizona

CALIFORNIA

Renatte Adler, San Diego State University

Robert Bise, Orange Coast Community College

Victor Brajer, California State University–Fullerton

Anne E. Bresnock, University of California, Los Angeles
and California State Polytechnic University–Pomona

David Brownstone, University of California, Irvine

Maureen Burton, California State Polytechnic
University–Pomona

James G. Devine, Loyola Marymount University

Roger Frantz, San Diego State University

Andrew Gill, California State University–Fullerton

Lisa Grobar, California State University–Long Beach

Steve Hamilton, California State University–Fullerton

Ahmed Ispahani, University of LaVerne

George A. Jouganatos, California State
University–Sacramento

Philip King, San Francisco State University–Chico

Don Leet, California State University–Fresno

Rose LeMont, Modesto Junior College

Solina Lindahl, California Polytechnic State University–
San Luis Obispo

Kristen Monaco, California State University–Long Beach

W. Douglas Morgan, University of California, Santa Barbara

Joseph M. Pogodzinksi, San Jose State University

Michael J. Potepan, San Francisco State University

Ratha Ramoo, Diablo Valley College

Ariane Schauer, Marymount College

Frederica Shockley, California State University–Chico

Mark Siegler, California State University–Sacramento

Lisa Simon, California Polytechnic State University–
San Louis Obispo

Rodney B. Swanson, University of California, Los Angeles

Kristin A. Van Gaasbeck, California State
University–Sacramento

Anthony Zambelli, Cuyamaca College

COLORADO

Rhonda Corman, University of Northern Colorado

Dale DeBoer, University of Colorado–Colorado Springs

Murat Iyigun, University of Colorado at Boulder

Nancy Jianakoplos, Colorado State University

Jay Kaplan, University of Colorado–Boulder

Stephen Weiler, Colorado State University

CONNECTICUT

Christopher P. Ball, Quinnipiac University

Donn M. Johnson, Quinnipiac University

Judith Mills, Southern Connecticut State University

Matthew Rafferty, Quinnipiac University

DELAWARE

Fatma Abdel-Raouf, Goldey-Beacom College

Andrew T. Hill, University of Delaware

FLORIDA

Herm Baine, Broward Community College–Central

Martine Duchatelet, Barry University

Hadley Hartman, Santa Fe Community College

Richard Hawkins, University of West Florida

Barbara Moore, University of Central Florida

Augustine Nelson, University of Miami

Jamie Ortiz, Florida Atlantic University

Robert Pennington, University of Central Florida

Jerry Schwartz, Broward Community College–North

William Stronge, Florida Atlantic University

Nora Underwood, University of Central Florida

IDAHO

Don Holley, Boise State University

ILLINOIS

Teshome Abebe, Eastern Illinois University

Ali Akarca, University of Illinois–Chicago

James Bruehler, Eastern Illinois University

Louis Cain, Loyola University Chicago and Northwestern
University

Rik Hafer, Southern Illinois University–Edwardsville

Alla A. Melkumian, Western Illinois University

Christopher Mushrush, Illinois State University

Jeff Reynolds, Northern Illinois University

Helen Roberts, University of Illinois–Chicago

Eric Schulz, Northwestern University

Charles Sicotte, Rock Valley Community College

Neil T. Skaggs, Illinois State University

Mark Witte, Northwestern University

Laurie Wolff, Southern Illinois University–
Carbondale

Paula Worthington, Northwestern University

INDIANA

Kelly Blanchard, Purdue University

Cecil Bohanon, Ball State University

Thomas Gresik, University of Notre Dame

Fred Herschede, Indiana University–South Bend

James K. Self, Indiana University–Bloomington

Esther-Mirjam Sent, University of Notre Dame

Virginia Shingleton, Valparaiso University

Martin C. Spechler, Indiana University–Purdue
University–Indianapolis

Geetha Suresh, Purdue University–West Lafayette

IOWA

Terry Alexander, Iowa State University

Paul Elgatian, St. Ambrose University

KANSAS

Jodi Messer Pelkowski, Wichita State University

Josh Rosenbloom, University of Kansas

KENTUCKY
  Tom Cate, Northern Kentucky University
  Nan-Ting Chou, University of Louisville
  David Eaton, Murray State University
  Robert Gillette, University of Kentucky
  Hak Youn Kim, Western Kentucky University
  Jenny Minier, University of Kentucky
  John Vahaly, University of Louisville
LOUISIANA
  Faik Koray, Louisiana State University
  Paul Nelson, University of Louisiana–Monroe
  Tammy Parker, University of Louisiana–Monroe
  Wesley A. Payne, Delgado Community College
MASSACHUSETTS
  William L. Casey, Jr., Babson College
  Arthur Schiller Casimir, Western New England College
  Michael Enz, Western New England College
  Todd Idson, Boston University
  Russell A. Janis, University of Massachusetts–Amherst
  Anthony Laramie, Merrimack College
  Carol McDonough, University of Massachusetts–Lowell
  William O'Brien, Worcester State College
  Gregory H. Wassall, Northeastern University
  Bruce G. Webb, Gordon College
  Gilbert Wolpe, Newbury College
MARYLAND
  Carey Borkoski, Anne Arundel Community College
  Kathleen A. Carroll, University of Maryland–Baltimore County
  Dustin Chambers, Salisbury University
  Shah Mehrabi, Montgomery College
  David Mitch, University of Maryland–Baltimore County
  John Neri, University of Maryland
  Henry Terrell, University of Maryland
MICHIGAN
  John Nader, Grand Valley State University
  Robert J. Rossana, Wayne State University
  Mark Wheeler, Western Michigan University
MISSOURI
  Jo Durr, Southwest Missouri State University
  Julie H. Gallaway, Southwest Missouri State University
  Terrel Galloway, Southwest Missouri State University
  Mark Karscig, Central Missouri State University
  Steven T. Petty, College of the Ozarks
  Sharon Ryan, University of Missouri–Columbia
  Ben Young, University of Missouri–Kansas City
MINNESOTA
  Monica Hartman, University of St. Thomas
MISSISSIPPI
  Randall Campbell, Mississippi State University
  Patricia A. Freeman, Jackson State University

NEBRASKA
  James Knudsen, Creighton University
  Craig MacPhee, University of Nebraska–Lincoln
  Mark E. Wohar, University of Nebraska–Omaha
NEW HAMPSHIRE
  Evelyn Gick, Dartmouth College
  Neil Niman, University of New Hampshire
NEW JERSEY
  Len Anyanwu, Union County College
  Maharuk Bhiladwalla, Rutgers University–New Brunswick
  Gary Gigliotti, Rutgers University–New Brunswick
  John Graham, Rutgers University–Newark
  Berch Haroian, William Paterson University
  Paul Harris, Camden County College
NEW MEXICO
  Donald Coes, University of New Mexico
NEW YORK
  Erol Balkan, Hamilton College
  Ranjit S. Dighe, City University of New York–Bronx Community College
  William L. Goffe, State University of New York–Oswego
  Wayne A. Grove, LeMoyne College
  Christopher Inya, Monroe Community College
  Clifford Kern, State University of New York–Binghampton
  Mary Lesser, Iona College
  Howard Ross, Baruch College
  Leonie Stone, State University of New York–Geneseo
  Ganti Subrahmanyam, University of Buffalo
  Jogindar S. Uppal, State University of New York–Albany
  Susan Wolcott, Binghamton University
NORTH CAROLINA
  Otilia Boldea, North Carolina State University
  Robert Burrus, University of North Carolina–Wilmington
  Lee A. Craig, North Carolina State University
  Kathleen Dorsainvil, Winston-Salem State University
  Marc Fusaro, East Carolina University
  Salih Hakeem, North Carolina Central University
  Haiyong Liu, East Carolina University
  Kosmas Marinakis, North Carolina State University
  Todd McFall, Wake Forest University
  Shahriar Mostashari, Campbell University
  Peter Schuhmann, University of North Carolina–Wilmington
  Carol Stivender, University of North Carolina–Charlotte
  Vera Tabakova, East Carolina University
  Robert Whaples, Wake Forest University
  Gary W. Zinn, East Carolina University
OHIO
  John P. Blair, Wright State University
  Kyongwook Choi, Ohio University
  Darlene DeVera, Miami University
  Tim Fuerst, Bowling Green University

Ernest Massie, Franklin University
Mike Nelson, University of Akron
Nicholas Noble, Miami University
Rochelle Ruffer, Youngstown State University
Kate Sheppard, University of Akron
Steve Szheghi, Wilmington College
Melissa Thomasson, Miami University
Yaqin Wang, Youngstown State University
Sourushe Zandvakili, University of Cincinnati

OKLAHOMA
David Hudgins, University of Oklahoma

OREGON
Bill Burrows, Lane Community College
Tom Carroll, Central Oregon Community College
Larry Singell, University of Oregon
Ayca Tekin-Koru, Oregon State University

PENNSYLVANIA
Gustavo Barboza, Mercyhurst College
Charles A. Bennett, Gannon University
Howard Bodenhorn, Lafayette College
Milica Bookman, St. Joseph's University
Robert Brooker, Gannon University
Linda Childs-Leatherbury, Lincoln University
Satyajit Ghosh, University of Scranton
Mehdi Haririan, Bloomsburg University
Nicholas Karatjas, Indiana University of Pennsylvania
Brendan Kennelly, Lehigh University
Iordanis Petsas, University of Scranton
Adam Renhoff, Drexel University
Edward Scahill, University of Scranton
Rajeev Sooreea, Pennsylvania State University–Altoona
Sandra Trejos, Clarion University
Peter Zaleski, Villanova University
Susan Zumas, Lehigh University

SOUTH CAROLINA
Calvin Blackwell, College of Charleston
Chad Turner, Clemson University
Madelyn Young, Converse College

SOUTH DAKOTA
Joseph M. Santos, South Dakota State University
Jason Zimmerman, South Dakota State University

TENNESSEE
Bichaka Fayissa, Middle Tennessee State University
Travis Hayes, University of Tennessee–Chattanooga
Christopher C. Klein, Middle Tennessee State University
Milicent Sites, Carson-Newman College

TEXAS
Rashid Al-Hmoud, Texas Tech University
Mike Cohick, Collin County Community College

Cesar Corredor, Texas A&M University
Susan Dadres, Southern Methodist University
Harry Ellis, Jr., University of North Texas
Paul Emberton, Texas State University
Diego Escobari, Texas A&M University
Nicholas Feltovich, University of Houston–Main
Charles Harold Fifield, Baylor University
Richard Gosselin, Houston Community College–Central
James W. Henderson, Baylor University
Ansul Islam, University of Houston–Downtown
Sheila Amin Gutierrez de Pineres, University of Texas–Dallas
James W. Henderson, Baylor University
Ansul Islam, University of Houston–Downtown
Kathy Kelly, University of Texas–Arlington
Thomas Kemp, Tarrant County College–Northwest
Akbar Marvasti, University of Houston–Downtown
James Mbata, Houston Community College
Carl Montano, Lamar University
James Moreno, Blinn College
John Pisciotta, Baylor University
Sara Saderion, Houston Community College–Southwest
Ivan Tasic, Texas A&M University

UTAH
Lowell Glenn, Utah Valley State College
Aric Krause, Westminster College
Arden Pope, Brigham Young University

VIRGINIA
Lee Badgett, Virginia Military Institute
Lee A. Coppock, University of Virginia
Carrie Meyer, George Mason University
James Roberts, Tidewater Community College–Virginia Beach
Araine A. Schauer, Mary Mount College
Sarah Stafford, The College of William & Mary
Michelle Vachris, Christopher Newport University
James Wetzel, Virginia Commonwealth University

WASHINGTON
Robert Rosenman, Washington State University

WASHINGTON, DC
Leon Battista, American Enterprise Institute

WISCONSIN
Pascal Ngoboka, University of Wisconsin–River Falls
Kevin Quinn, St. Norbert College
John R. Stoll, University of Wisconsin–Green Bay

WYOMING
Robert Godby, University of Wyoming

A Word of Thanks

Once again, we benefited greatly from the dedication and professionalism of the Prentice Hall team. Executive Editor David Alexander's energy and support were indispensable. David helped mold the presentation and provided words of encouragement whenever our energy flagged. Developmental Editor Lena Buonanno worked tirelessly to ensure that this text was as good as it could be. We remain literally astonished at the amount of time, energy, and unfailing good humor she brings to this project. As we worked on the first edition, Director of Key Markets David Theisen provided invaluable insight into how best to structure a principles text. His advice helped shape nearly every chapter. Executive Marketing Manager Sharon Koch and Marketing Development Manager Kathleen McLellan helped develop a unique and innovative marketing plan for the first edition, and we sincerely appreciate the upcoming efforts of Lori DeShazo, who is the Executive Marketing Manager for the Second Edition. Steve Deitmer, Director of Development, brought sound judgment to the many decisions required to create this book. Christina Volpe managed the extensive supplement package that accompanies the book. Suzanne Grappi and Blair Brown turned our manuscript pages into a beautiful published book. Ben Paris, executive producer of assessment programs, evaluated test bank questions and provided the test bank authors guidance on how to write effective questions. Valerie Patruno, editorial assistant, was involved in many aspects of the book, including coordinating the review program and assisting with the supplements. Photo researcher Rachel Lucas located photographs that captured the essence of key concepts. We received excellent research assistance from Ed Timmons, David Van Der Goes, and Jason Hockenberry.

A good part of the burden of a project of this magnitude is borne by our families. We appreciate the patience, support, and encouragement of our wives and children. We extend special thanks to Constance Hubbard for her diligent reading of page proofs.

Brief Contents

Contents

CHAPTER 10 Appendix: Using Isoquants and Isocosts to Understand Production and Cost 364

PART 5: Market Structure and Firm Strategy

CHAPTER 11: Firms in Perfectly Competitive Markets 376

PART 7: Information, Taxes, and the Distribution of Income

CHAPTER 17: The Economics of Information   574

CHAPTER 18: Public Choice, Taxes, and the Distribution of Income   598

FLEXIBILITY CHART

The following chart helps you organize your syllabus based on your teaching preferences and objectives:

Core	Policy	Optional
CHAPTER 1: Economics: Foundations and Models *Uses the debate of outsourcing to discuss the role of models in economic analysis.*	**CHAPTER 4:** Economic Efficiency, Government Price Setting, and Taxes	**CHAPTER 1 Appendix:** Using Graphs and Formulas
CHAPTER 2: Trade-offs, Comparative Advantage, and the Market System *Includes coverage of the role of the entrepreneur, property rights, and the legal system in a market system.*	**CHAPTER 5:** Externalities, Environmental Policy, and Public Goods *This chapter may be delayed until after Chapter 14.*	**CHAPTER 4 Appendix:** Quantitative Demand and Supply Analysis *Provides a quantitative analysis of rent control.*
CHAPTER 3: Where Prices Come From: The Interaction of Demand and Supply	**CHAPTER 18:** Public Choice, Taxes, and the Distribution of Income	**CHAPTER 7:** Firms, the Stock Market, and Corporate Governance *Unique chapter that includes coverage of the Sarbanes-Oxley Act.*
CHAPTER 6: Elasticity: The Responsiveness of Demand and Supply		**CHAPTER 7 Appendix:** Tools to Analyze Firms' Financial Information *Covers present value and financial statements.*
CHAPTER 8: Comparative Advantage and the Gains from International Trade *This chapter may be delayed until after Chapter 16.*		**CHAPTER 8 Appendix:** Multinational Firms *Covers the benefits and challenges of operating overseas businesses.*
CHAPTER 10: Technology, Production, and Costs		**CHAPTER 9:** Consumer Choice and Behavioral Economics *Covers utility theory and unique coverage of social influences on behavior and network externalities.*
CHAPTER 11: Firms in Perfectly Competitive Markets		**CHAPTER 9 Appendix:** Using Indifference Curves and Budget Lines to Understand Consumer Behavior *Complete and intuitive coverage for instructors who prefer to cover indifference curves rather than utility theory.*
CHAPTER 12: Monopolistic Competition: The Competitive Model in a More Realistic Setting		**CHAPTER 10 Appendix:** Using Isoquants and Isocosts to Understand Production and Costs *Provides a formal analysis of how firms choose the combination of inputs to produce a given level of output.*
CHAPTER 13: Oligopoly: Firms in Less Competitive Markets *Includes full coverage of game theory and unique coverage of Porter's Five Forces model of competition.*		**CHAPTER 15:** Pricing Strategy *A unique chapter that covers price discrimination, cost-plus pricing, and two-part tariffs.*
CHAPTER 14: Monopoly and Antitrust Policy *This chapter may be covered after Chapter 11.*		
CHAPTER 16: The Markets for Labor and Other Factors of Production *Covers all factors of production in one chapter and includes coverage of discrimination, unions, compensating differentials, and personnel economics.*		
CHAPTER 17: The Economics of Information *Covers asymmetric information and moral hazard.*		

Economics:
Foundations and Models

What Happens When U.S. High-Technology Firms Move to China?

You have probably seen the words "Made in China" on a variety of the products you own, including running shoes, clothing, towels, and sheets. It may not be surprising that relatively simple products are manufactured in China, where workers receive much lower wages than in the United States. Until recently, though, most people would not have expected sophisticated, high-technology products to be designed and manufactured in China. That is why the movement of high-technology manufacturing and even high-technology research and development (R&D) to China has surprised many people. In recent years, U.S. firms such as Oracle, IBM, and Motorola have all opened R&D facilities in China. Harry Shum, who runs Microsoft's research center in Beijing, said, "For us, it's always been about finding the best people. China has 1.3 billion brains. The question is how you make them truly creative, truly innovative. This is the key to China becoming a real superpower in science."

3Com is a leading U.S. high-technology firm. The firm introduced a new network switch for corporate computer systems that not only was manufactured in China but had been designed by Chinese engineers. 3Com was able to charge a much lower price for the switch than competitors that designed and manufactured similar products in the United States. Because the salaries of engineers are so much lower in China, 3Com was able to use four times as many engineers to design its switch than did competing firms employing engineers in the United States. The cost to manufacture the switch was also much lower in China, where the average factory worker earns the equivalent of about $2.10 per hour, including benefits, compared with about $24.00 per hour earned by the average factory worker in the United States.

Many U.S., Japanese, and European firms have been moving the production of goods and services outside their home country, a process called *outsourcing* (sometimes also referred to as *off-shoring*). Articles on outsourcing appear frequently in business magazines and the financial pages of newspapers, and the issue has also been the subject of heated debate among political commentators, policymakers, and presidential candidates. The focus of the debate has been the question "Has outsourcing been good or bad for the U.S. economy?" This question is one of many that cannot be answered without using economics. In this chapter and the remainder of this book, we will see how economics helps in answering important questions about outsourcing, as well as many other issues. Economics provides us with tools for understanding why outsourcing has increased, why some firms are more likely to move production to other countries, and what the effects of outsourcing will be on the wages of U.S. workers, the profits of U.S. firms, and the overall ability of the U.S. economy to produce more and better goods and services. **AN INSIDE LOOK** on **page 18** discusses how developments in China and India are affecting the high-technology sector in the United States.

Sources: Charles Leadbeater and James Wilson, "Do Not Fear the Rise of World-Class Science Asia," *Financial Times*, October 12, 2005, p. 19; Pete Engardio and Dexter Roberts, "The China Price," *BusinessWeek*, December 6, 2004; and Judith Banister, "Manufacturing Earnings and Compensation in China," *Monthly Labor Review*, August 2006, pp. 22–40.

LEARNING Objectives

After studying this chapter, you should be able to:

1.1 Explain these three key economic ideas: *People are* **rational**. *People respond to* **incentives**. *Optimal decisions are made at the* **margin**, page 4.

1.2 Discuss how an economy answers these questions: **What** goods and services will be produced? **How** will the goods and services be produced? **Who** will receive the goods and services? page 8.

1.3 Understand the role of **models** in economic analysis, page 11.

1.4 Distinguish between **microeconomics** and **macroeconomics**, page 15.

1.5 Become familiar with important **economic terms**, page 15.

APPENDIX Review the use of **graphs** and **formulas**, page 24.

Economics in YOUR Life!

Are You Likely to Lose Your Job to Outsourcing?

An estimated 3.3 million jobs in the United States will have been outsourced between 2000 and 2015, according to a report by John McCarthy of Forrester Research, a private research firm. Other estimates of the number of U.S. jobs likely to be outsourced have been in the same range. More than 3 million jobs seems like a large number. Suppose you plan on working as an accountant, a software engineer, a lawyer, a business consultant, a financial analyst, or in another industry where some jobs have already been outsourced. Is it likely that during your career, your job will be outsourced to China, India, or some other foreign country? As you read the chapter, see if you can answer this question. You can check your answer against the one we provide at the end of the chapter.

>> Continued on page 17

I n this book, we use economics to answer questions such as the following:

- How are the prices of goods and services determined?

- How does pollution affect the economy, and how should government policy deal with these effects?

- Why do firms engage in international trade, and how do government policies affect international trade?

- Why does government control the prices of some goods and services, and what are the effects of those controls?

Economists do not always agree on the answers to every question. In fact, as we will see, economists engage in lively debate on some issues. In addition, new problems and issues are constantly arising. So, economists are always at work developing new methods to analyze and answer these questions.

All the questions we discuss in this book illustrate a basic fact of life: People must make choices as they try to attain their goals. We must make choices because we live in a world of **scarcity**, which means that although our wants are unlimited, the resources available to fulfill those wants are limited. You might like to have a 60-inch plasma television in every room of your home, but unless you are a close relative of Bill Gates, you probably lack the money to purchase them. Every day, you must make choices about how to spend your limited income on the many goods and services available. The finite amount of time available to you also limits your ability to attain your goals. If you spend an hour studying for your economics midterm, you have one less hour available to study for your history midterm. Firms and the government are in the same situation as you: They have limited resources available as they attempt to attain their goals. **Economics** is the study of the choices consumers, business managers, and government officials make to attain their goals, given their scarce resources.

We begin this chapter by discussing three important economic ideas that we will return to many times in the book: *People are rational. People respond to incentives. Optimal decisions are made at the margin.* Then we consider the three fundamental questions that any economy must answer: *What* goods and services will be produced? *How* will the goods and services be produced? *Who* will receive the goods and services? Next we consider the role of *economic models* in helping analyze the many issues presented throughout this book. **Economic models** are simplified versions of reality used to analyze real-world economic situations. Later in this chapter, we explore why economists use models and how they construct them. Finally, we discuss the difference between microeconomics and macroeconomics, and we preview some important economic terms.

Scarcity The situation in which unlimited wants exceed the limited resources available to fulfill those wants.

Economics The study of the choices people make to attain their goals, given their scarce resources.

Economic model A simplified version of reality used to analyze real-world economic situations.

1.1 | Explain these three key economic ideas: *People are rational. People respond to incentives. Optimal decisions are made at the margin.*

Three Key Economic Ideas

As you try to achieve your goals, whether they are buying a new computer or finding a part-time job, you will interact with other people in *markets*. A **market** is a group of buyers and sellers of a good or service and the institution or arrangement by which they come together to trade. Most of economics involves analyzing what happens in markets.

Market A group of buyers and sellers of a good or service and the institution or arrangement by which they come together to trade.

Throughout this book, as we study how people make choices and interact in markets, we will return to three important ideas:

1 People are rational.

2 People respond to economic incentives.

3 Optimal decisions are made at the margin.

People Are Rational

Economists generally assume that people are rational. This assumption does *not* mean that economists believe everyone knows everything or always makes the "best" decision. It means that economists assume that consumers and firms use all available information as they act to achieve their goals. Rational individuals weigh the benefits and costs of each action, and they choose an action only if the benefits outweigh the costs. For example, if Microsoft charges a price of $239 for a copy of Windows, economists assume that the managers at Microsoft have estimated that a price of $239 will earn Microsoft the most profit. The managers may be wrong; perhaps a price of $265 would be more profitable, but economists assume that the managers at Microsoft have acted rationally on the basis of the information available to them in choosing the price. Of course, not everyone behaves rationally all the time. Still, the assumption of rational behavior is very useful in explaining most of the choices that people make.

People Respond to Economic Incentives

Human beings act from a variety of motives, including religious belief, envy, and compassion. Economists emphasize that consumers and firms consistently respond to *economic* incentives. This fact may seem obvious, but it is often overlooked. For example, according to an article in the *Wall Street Journal*, the FBI couldn't understand why banks were not taking steps to improve security in the face of an increase in robberies: "FBI officials suggest that banks place uniformed, armed guards outside their doors and install bullet-resistant plastic, known as a 'bandit barrier,' in front of teller windows." FBI officials were surprised that few banks took their advice. But the article also reported that installing bullet-resistant plastic costs $10,000 to $20,000, and a well-trained security guard receives $50,000 per year in salary and benefits. The average loss in a bank robbery is only about $1,200. The economic incentive to banks is clear: It is less costly to put up with bank robberies than to take additional security measures. That banks respond as they do to the threat of robberies may be surprising to the FBI—but not to economists.

In each chapter, the *Making the Connection* feature discusses a news story or another application related to the chapter material. Read the following *Making the Connection* for a discussion of whether people respond to economic incentives even when making the decision to have children.

Making
the
Connection | ## Will Women Have More Babies if the Government Pays Them To?

The populations of the United States, Japan, and most European countries are aging as birthrates decline and the average person lives longer. The governments of these countries have programs to pay money to retired workers, such as the Social Security system in the United States. Most of the money for these programs comes from taxes paid by people currently working. As the population ages, there are fewer workers paying taxes relative to the number of retired people receiving government payments. The result is a funding crisis that countries can solve only by either reducing government payments to retired workers or by raising the taxes paid by current workers.

In some European countries, birthrates have fallen so low that the total population will soon begin to decline, which will make the funding crisis for government retirement programs even worse. For the population of a country to be stable, the average woman must have 2.1 children, which is enough to replace both parents and account for children who die before reaching adulthood. In recent years, the birthrates in a number of countries, including France, Germany, and Italy, have fallen below this replacement level. The concern about falling birthrates has been particularly strong in the small European country of Estonia. In 2001, the United Nations issued a report in which it forecast that, given its current birthrate, by 2050, the population of Estonia would decline from 1.4 million to only about 700,000. The Estonian government responded by using economic incentives in an attempt to increase the birthrate. Beginning in 2004, the government began paying working women who take time off after having a baby their entire salary for up to 15 months. Women who do not work receive $200 per month, which is a substantial amount, given that the average income in Estonia is only $650 per month.

Will women actually have more babies as a result of this economic incentive? As the graph below shows, the birthrate in Estonia has increased from 1.3 children per woman in the late 1990s to 1.5 children per woman in 2006. This is still below the replacement level birthrate of 2.1 children, and it is too early to tell whether the increased birthrate is due to the economic incentives. But the Estonian government is encouraged by the results and is looking for ways to provide additional economic incentives to raise the birthrate further. And Estonia is not alone; more than 45 other countries in Europe and Asia have taken steps to try to raise their birthrates. People may respond to economic incentives even when making the very personal decision of how many children to have.

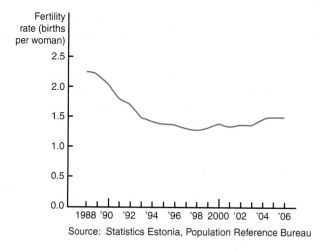

Source: Statistics Estonia, Population Reference Bureau

Source: Marcus Walker, "In Estonia, Paying Women to Have Babies Is Paying Off," *Wall Street Journal*, October 20, 2006, p. A1. Copyright © 2006 Dow Jones. Reprinted by permission of Dow Jones via Copyright Clearance Center; and Sharon Lerner, "The Motherhood Experiment," *New York Times*, March 4, 2007.

YOUR TURN: Test your understanding by doing related problem 1.7 on page 21 at the end of this chapter.

Optimal Decisions Are Made at the Margin

Some decisions are "all or nothing": An entrepreneur decides whether to open a new restaurant. He or she either starts the new restaurant or doesn't. You decide whether to enter graduate school or to take a job instead. You either enter graduate school or you don't. But most decisions in life are not all or nothing. Instead, most decisions involve doing a little more or a little less. If you are trying to decrease your spending and increase your saving, the decision is not really a choice between saving every dollar you earn or spending it all. Rather, many small choices are involved, such as whether to buy a caffè mocha at Starbucks every day or to cut back to three times per week.

Economists use the word *marginal* to mean an extra or additional benefit or cost of a decision. Should you watch another hour of TV or spend that hour studying? The *marginal benefit* (or, in symbols, *MB*) of watching more TV is the additional enjoyment you receive. The *marginal cost* (or *MC*) is the lower grade you receive from having studied a little less. Should Apple Computer produce an additional 300,000 iPods? Firms receive *revenue* from selling goods. Apple's marginal benefit is the additional revenue it receives from selling 300,000 more iPods. Apple's marginal cost is the additional cost—for wages, parts, and so forth—of producing 300,000 more iPods. *Economists reason that the optimal decision is to continue any activity up to the point where the marginal benefit equals the marginal cost—in symbols, where* $MB = MC$. Often we apply this rule without consciously thinking about it. Usually you will know whether the additional enjoyment from watching a television program is worth the additional cost involved in not spending that hour studying, without giving it a lot of thought. In business situations, however, firms often have to make careful calculations to determine, for example, whether the additional revenue received from increasing production is greater or less than the additional cost of the production. Economists refer to analysis that involves comparing marginal benefits and marginal costs as **marginal analysis**.

In each chapter of this book, you will see the special feature *Solved Problem*. This feature will increase your understanding of the material by leading you through the steps of solving an applied economic problem. After reading the problem, you can test your understanding by working the related problems that appear at the end of the chapter and in the study guide that accompanies this book.

Marginal analysis Analysis that involves comparing marginal benefits and marginal costs.

Solved Problem | 1-1

Apple Computer Makes a Decision at the Margin

Suppose Apple is currently selling 3,000,000 iPods per year. Managers at Apple are considering whether to raise production to 3,300,000 iPods per year. One manager argues, "Increasing production from 3,000,000 to 3,300,000 is a good idea because we will make a total profit of $100 million if we produce 3,300,000." Do you agree with her reasoning? What, if any, additional information do you need to decide whether Apple should produce the additional 300,000 iPods?

SOLVING THE PROBLEM:

Step 1: **Review the chapter material.** The problem is about making decisions, so you may want to review the section "Optimal Decisions Are Made at the Margin," which begins on page 6. Remember to think "marginal" whenever you see the word "additional" in economics.

Step 2: **Explain whether you agree with the manager's reasoning.** We have seen that any activity should be continued to the point where the marginal benefit is equal to the marginal cost. In this case, that involves continuing to produce iPods up to the point where the additional revenue Apple receives from selling more iPods is equal to the marginal cost of producing them. The Apple manager has not done a marginal analysis, so you should not agree with her reasoning. Her statement about the *total* profit of producing 3,300,000 iPods is not relevant to the decision of whether to produce the last 300,000 iPods.

Step 3: **Explain what additional information you need.** You will need additional information to make a correct decision. You will need to know the additional revenue Apple would earn from selling 300,000 more iPods and the additional cost of producing them.

YOUR TURN: For more practice, do related problems 1.4, 1.5, and 1.6 on pages 20–21 at the end of this chapter.

≫ End Solved Problem 1-1

1.2 LEARNING OBJECTIVE

1.2 | Discuss how an economy answers these questions: *What* goods and services will be produced? *How* will the goods and services be produced? *Who* will receive the goods and services?

The Economic Problem That Every Society Must Solve

We have already noted the important fact that we live in a world of scarcity. As a result, any society faces the economic problem that it has only a limited amount of economic resources—such as workers, machines, and raw materials—and so can produce only a limited amount of goods and services. Therefore, society faces **trade-offs**: Producing more of one good or service means producing less of another good or service. In fact, the best way to measure the cost of producing a good or service is the value of what has to be given up to produce it. The **opportunity cost** of any activity—such as producing a good or service—is the highest-valued alternative that must be given up to engage in that activity. The concept of opportunity cost is very important in economics and applies to individuals as much as it does to firms or to society as a whole. Consider the example of someone who could receive a salary of $80,000 per year working as a manager at a firm but opens her own firm instead. In that case, the opportunity cost of her managerial services to her own firm is $80,000, even if she does not explicitly pay herself a salary.

Trade-offs force society to make choices, particularly when answering the following three fundamental questions:

1 *What* goods and services will be produced?

2 *How* will the goods and services be produced?

3 *Who* will receive the goods and services produced?

Throughout this book, we will return to these questions many times. For now, we briefly introduce each question.

Trade-off The idea that because of scarcity, producing more of one good or service means producing less of another good or service.

Opportunity cost The highest-valued alternative that must be given up to engage in an activity.

What Goods and Services Will Be Produced?

How will society decide whether to produce more economics textbooks or more HD-DVD players? More daycare facilities or more football stadiums? Of course, "society" does not make decisions; only individuals make decisions. The answer to the question of what will be produced is determined by the choices made by consumers, firms, and the government. Every day, you help decide which goods and services will be produced when you choose to buy an iPod rather than an HD-DVD player or a caffè mocha rather than a chai tea. Similarly, Apple must choose whether to devote its scarce resources to making more iPods or more MacBook laptop computers. The federal government must choose whether to spend more of its limited budget on breast cancer research or on homeland security. In each case, consumers, firms, and the government face the problem of scarcity by trading off one good or service for another. And each choice made comes with an opportunity cost measured by the value of the best alternative given up.

How Will the Goods and Services Be Produced?

Firms choose how to produce the goods and services they sell. In many cases, firms face a trade-off between using more workers or using more machines. For example, a local service station has to choose whether to provide car repair services using more diagnostic computers and fewer auto mechanics or more auto mechanics and fewer diagnostic computers. Similarly, movie studios have to choose whether to produce animated films using highly skilled animators to draw them by hand or fewer animators and more computers. In deciding whether to move production offshore to China, firms may be choosing between a production method in the United States that uses fewer workers and more machines and a production method in China that uses more workers and fewer machines.

Who Will Receive the Goods and Services Produced?

In the United States, who receives the goods and services produced depends largely on how income is distributed. Individuals with the highest income have the ability to buy the most goods and services. Often, people are willing to give up some of their income—and, therefore, some of their ability to purchase goods and services—by donating to charities to increase the incomes of poorer people. Each year, Americans donate more than $250 billion to charity, or an average donation of $2,100 for each household in the country. An important policy question, however, is whether the government should intervene to make the distribution of income more equal. Such intervention already occurs in the United States, because people with higher incomes pay a larger fraction of their incomes in taxes and because the government makes payments to people with low incomes. There is disagreement over whether the current attempts to redistribute income are sufficient or whether there should be more or less redistribution.

Centrally Planned Economies versus Market Economies

Societies organize their economies in two main ways to answer the three questions of what, how, and who. A society can have a **centrally planned economy** in which the government decides how economic resources will be allocated. Or a society can have a **market economy** in which the decisions of households and firms interacting in markets allocate economic resources.

From 1917 to 1991, the most important centrally planned economy in the world was that of the Soviet Union, which was established when Vladimir Lenin and his Communist Party staged a revolution and took over the Russian Empire. In the Soviet Union, the government decided what goods to produce, how to produce them, and who would receive them. Government employees managed factories and stores. The objective of these managers was to follow the government's orders rather than to satisfy the wants of consumers. Centrally planned economies like the Soviet Union have not been successful in producing low-cost, high-quality goods and services. As a result, the standard of living of the average person in a centrally planned economy tends to be quite low. All centrally planned economies have also been political dictatorships. Dissatisfaction with low living standards and political repression finally led to the collapse of the Soviet Union in 1991. Today, only a few small countries, such as Cuba and North Korea, still have completely centrally planned economies.

All the high-income democracies, such as the United States, Canada, Japan, and the countries of western Europe, are market economies. Market economies rely primarily on privately owned firms to produce goods and services and to decide how to produce them. Markets, rather than the government, determine who receives the goods and services produced. In a market economy, firms must produce goods and services that meet the wants of consumers, or the firms will go out of business. In that sense, it is ultimately consumers who decide what goods and services will be produced. Because firms in a market economy compete to offer the highest-quality products at the lowest price, they are under pressure to use the lowest-cost methods of production. For example, in the past 10 years, some U.S. firms, particularly in the electronics and furniture industries, have been under pressure to reduce their costs to meet competition from Chinese firms.

In a market economy, the income of an individual is determined by the payments he receives for what he has to sell. If he is a civil engineer and firms are willing to pay a salary of $85,000 per year for engineers with his training and skills, that is the amount of income he will have to purchase goods and services. If the engineer also owns a house that he rents out, his income will be even higher. One of the attractive features of markets is that they reward hard work. Generally, the more extensive the training a person

Centrally planned economy An economy in which the government decides how economic resources will be allocated.

Market economy An economy in which the decisions of households and firms interacting in markets allocate economic resources.

has received and the longer the hours the person works, the higher the person's income will be. Of course, luck—both good and bad—also plays a role here, as elsewhere in life. We can conclude that market economies answer the question "Who receives the goods and services produced?" with the answer "Those who are most willing and able to buy them."

The Modern "Mixed" Economy

In the nineteenth and early twentieth centuries, the U.S. government engaged in relatively little regulation of markets for goods and services. Beginning in the middle of the twentieth century, government intervention in the economy dramatically increased in the United States and other market economies. This increase was primarily caused by the high rates of unemployment and business bankruptcies during the Great Depression of the 1930s. Some government intervention was also intended to raise the incomes of the elderly, the sick, and people with limited skills. For example, in the 1930s, the United States established the Social Security system, which provides government payments to retired and disabled workers, and minimum wage legislation, which sets a floor on the wages employers can pay in many occupations. In more recent years, government intervention in the economy has also expanded to meet such goals as protection of the environment and the promotion of civil rights.

Mixed economy An economy in which most economic decisions result from the interaction of buyers and sellers in markets but in which the government plays a significant role in the allocation of resources.

Some economists argue that the extent of government intervention makes it no longer accurate to refer to the U.S., Canadian, Japanese, and western European economies as pure market economies. Instead, they should be referred to as *mixed economies*. A **mixed economy** is still primarily a market economy with most economic decisions resulting from the interaction of buyers and sellers in markets, but in a mixed economy the government plays a significant role in the allocation of resources. As we will see in later chapters, economists continue to debate the role government should play in a market economy.

One of the most important developments in the international economy in recent years has been the movement of China from being a centrally planned economy to being a more mixed economy. The Chinese economy had suffered decades of economic stagnation following the takeover of the government by Mao Zedong and the Communist Party in 1949. Although China remains a political dictatorship, production of most goods and services is now determined in the market rather than by the government. The result has been rapid economic growth that in the near future may lead to total production of goods and services in China surpassing total production in the United States.

Efficiency and Equity

Productive efficiency The situation in which a good or service is produced at the lowest possible cost.

Allocative efficiency A state of the economy in which production is in accordance with consumer preferences; in particular, every good or service is produced up to the point where the last unit provides a marginal benefit to society equal to the marginal cost of producing it.

Voluntary exchange The situation that occurs in markets when both the buyer and seller of a product are made better off by the transaction.

Market economies tend to be more efficient than centrally planned economies. There are two types of efficiency: *productive efficiency* and *allocative efficiency*. **Productive efficiency** occurs when a good or service is produced at the lowest possible cost. **Allocative efficiency** occurs when production is in accordance with consumer preferences. Markets tend to be efficient because they promote competition and facilitate voluntary exchange. **Voluntary exchange** refers to the situation in which both the buyer and seller of a product are made better off by the transaction. We know that the buyer and seller are both made better off because, otherwise, the buyer would not have agreed to buy the product or the seller would not have agreed to sell it. Productive efficiency is achieved when competition among firms in markets forces the firms to produce goods and services at the lowest cost. Allocative efficiency is achieved when the combination of competition among firms and voluntary exchange between firms and consumers results in firms producing the mix of goods and services that consumers prefer most. Competition will force firms to continue producing and selling goods and services as long as the additional benefit to consumers is greater than the additional cost of production. In this way, the mix of goods and services produced will be in accordance with consumer preferences.

Although markets promote efficiency, they don't guarantee it. Inefficiency can arise from various sources. To begin with, it may take some time to achieve an efficient outcome. When DVD players were introduced, for example, firms did not instantly achieve productive efficiency. It took several years for firms to discover the lowest-cost method of producing this good. As we will discuss in Chapter 4, governments sometimes reduce efficiency by interfering with voluntary exchange in markets. For example, many governments limit the imports of some goods from foreign countries. This limitation reduces efficiency by keeping goods from being produced at the lowest cost. The production of some goods damages the environment. In this case, government intervention can increase efficiency because without such intervention, firms may ignore the costs of environmental damage and thereby fail to produce the goods at the lowest possible cost.

Just because an economic outcome is efficient does not necessarily mean that society finds it desirable. Many people prefer economic outcomes that they consider fair or equitable, even if those outcomes are less efficient. **Equity** is harder to define than efficiency, but it usually involves a fair distribution of economic benefits. For some people, equity involves a more equal distribution of economic benefits than would result from an emphasis on efficiency alone. For example, some people support taxing people with higher incomes to provide the funds for programs that aid the poor. Although governments may increase equity by reducing the incomes of high-income people and increasing the incomes of the poor, efficiency may be reduced. People have less incentive to open new businesses, to supply labor, and to save if the government takes a significant amount of the income they earn from working or saving. The result is that fewer goods and services are produced, and less saving takes place. As this example illustrates, *there is often a trade-off between efficiency and equity*. In this case, the total amount of goods and services produced falls, although the distribution of the income to buy those goods and services is made more equal. Government policymakers often confront this trade-off.

Equity The fair distribution of economic benefits.

1.3 LEARNING OBJECTIVE

1.3 | Understand the role of models in economic analysis.

Economic Models

Economists rely on economic theories, or *models* (the words *theory* and *model* are used interchangeably), to analyze real-world issues, such as the economic effects of outsourcing. As mentioned earlier, economic models are simplified versions of reality. Economists are certainly not alone in relying on models: An engineer may use a computer model of a bridge to help test whether it will withstand high winds, or a biologist may make a physical model of a nucleic acid to better understand its properties. One purpose of economic models is to make economic ideas sufficiently explicit and concrete so that individuals, firms, or the government can use them to make decisions. For example, we will see in Chapter 3 that the model of demand and supply is a simplified version of how the prices of products are determined by the interactions among buyers and sellers in markets.

Economists use economic models to answer questions. For example, consider the question from the chapter opener: Has outsourcing been good or bad for the U.S. economy? For a complicated issue such as the effects of outsourcing, economists often use several models to examine different aspects of the issue. For example, they may use a model of how wages are determined to analyze how outsourcing affects wages in particular industries. They may use a model of international trade to analyze how outsourcing affects income growth in the countries involved. Sometimes economists use an existing model to analyze an issue, but in other cases, they must develop a new model. To develop a model, economists generally follow these steps:

1 Decide on the assumptions to be used in developing the model.

2 Formulate a testable hypothesis.

3 Use economic data to test the hypothesis.

4 Revise the model if it fails to explain well the economic data.

5 Retain the revised model to help answer similar economic questions in the future.

The Role of Assumptions in Economic Models

Any model is based on making assumptions because models have to be simplified to be useful. We cannot analyze an economic issue unless we reduce its complexity. For example, economic models make *behavioral assumptions* about the motives of consumers and firms. Economists assume that consumers will buy the goods and services that will maximize their well-being or their satisfaction. Similarly, economists assume that firms act to maximize their profits. These assumptions are simplifications because they do not describe the motives of every consumer and every firm. How can we know if the assumptions in a model are too simplified or too limiting? We discover this when we form hypotheses based on these assumptions and test these hypotheses using real-world information.

Forming and Testing Hypotheses in Economic Models

Economic variable Something measurable that can have different values, such as the wages of software programmers.

A *hypothesis* in an economic model is a statement that may be either correct or incorrect about an *economic variable*. An **economic variable** is something measurable that can have different values, such as the wages paid to software programmers. An example of a hypothesis in an economic model is the statement that outsourcing by U.S. firms reduces wages paid to software programmers in the United States. An economic hypothesis is usually about a *causal relationship*; in this case, the hypothesis states that outsourcing causes, or leads to, lower wages for software programmers.

Before accepting a hypothesis, we must test it. To test a hypothesis, we must analyze statistics on the relevant economic variables. In our example, we must gather statistics on the wages paid to software programmers, and perhaps on other variables as well. Testing a hypothesis can be tricky. For example, showing that the wages paid to software programmers fell at a time when outsourcing was increasing would not be enough to demonstrate that outsourcing *caused* the wage fall. Just because two things are *correlated*—that is, they happen at the same time—does not mean that one caused the other. For example, suppose that the number of workers trained as software engineers greatly increased at the same time that outsourcing was increasing. In that case, the fall in wages paid to software engineers might have been caused by the increased competition among workers for these jobs rather than by the effects of relocating programming jobs from the United States to India or China. Over a period of time, many economic variables change, which complicates testing hypotheses. In fact, when economists disagree about a hypothesis, such as the effect of outsourcing on wages, it is often because of disagreements over interpreting the statistical analysis used to test the hypothesis.

Note that hypotheses must be statements that could, in principle, turn out to be incorrect. Statements such as "Outsourcing is good" or "Outsourcing is bad" are value judgments rather than hypotheses because it is not possible to disprove them.

Economists accept and use an economic model if it leads to hypotheses that are confirmed by statistical analysis. In many cases, the acceptance is tentative, however, pending the gathering of new data or further statistical analysis. In fact, economists often refer to a hypothesis having been "not rejected," rather than having been "accepted," by statistical analysis. But what if statistical analysis clearly rejects a hypothesis? For example, what if a model leads to a hypothesis that outsourcing by U.S. firms lowers wages of U.S. software programmers, but this hypothesis is rejected by the data? In that case, the model must be reconsidered. It may be that an assumption used in the model was too simplified or too limiting. For example, perhaps the model used to determine the effect of outsourcing on wages paid to software programmers assumed that software programmers in China and India had the same training and experience as software programmers in the United States. If, in fact, U.S. software programmers have more training and experience than Chinese and Indian programmers, this difference may explain why our hypothesis was rejected by the economic statistics.

The process of developing models, testing hypotheses, and revising models occurs not just in economics but also in disciplines such as physics, chemistry, and biology. This process is often referred to as the *scientific method*. Economics is a *social science* because it applies the scientific method to the study of the interactions among individuals.

| Making the Connection | ### When Economists Disagree: A Debate over Outsourcing |

There is an old saying in the newspaper business that it's not news when a dog bites a man, but it is news when a man bites a dog. In 2004, many newspapers ran a "man bites dog" story concerning economics.

Does outsourcing by U.S. firms raise or lower incomes in the United States?

Most economists believe that international trade—including the trade that results when firms move production offshore—increases economic efficiency and raises incomes. It was news, then, when Paul Samuelson, an MIT economist and a winner of the Nobel Prize in Economics, wrote an article in the *Journal of Economic Perspectives* questioning whether incomes in the United States will be higher as a result of the outsourcing of jobs to India and China. Samuelson presented a model of the effects of outsourcing that can be illustrated with the following hypothetical case: Suppose a bank in New York has been using a company in South Dakota to handle its telephone customer service. The bank then switches to using a company in Bangalore, India, that pays its workers much lower wages. Samuelson argued that even when the workers fired by the South Dakota firm eventually find new jobs, the jobs may pay lower wages. If outsourcing becomes widespread enough, Samuelson argued, it may result in a significant decline in U.S. incomes.

Many economists objected to Samuelson's argument. One economist who wrote a rebuttal to Samuelson was Jagdish Bhagwati, a former student of Samuelson's and a professor of economics at Columbia University. Bhagwati argued that in Samuelson's example, the wages of South Dakota call center workers were reduced by outsourcing, but the costs to the bank were also reduced, which would allow the bank to reduce the prices it charged its customers. In Bhagwati's model, these gains to consumers from lower prices more than offset the loss to workers from lower wages, so the United States experiences a net gain from outsourcing. Samuelson argued, though, that if the United States exports the product—in this case banking services—to other countries, the lower price hurts the exporting firms. In that case, the United States might still be hurt by outsourcing.

This brief summary does not do full justice to the models of Samuelson and Bhagwati, which are too complicated for us to cover in this chapter. We can, however, discuss the sources of the disagreement between these two economists. We have seen that economists sometimes differ about the assumptions that should be used in building a model. That is not the case here: Samuelson and Bhagwati basically agree on the model and the assumptions to be used. Instead, they disagree over how to interpret the relevant economic statistics. Bhagwati argues that the number of U.S. jobs moving to other countries has been relatively small, amounting to about 1 percent of the jobs created in the U.S. economy each year. He also argues that the jobs lost to outsourcing tend to be low-wage jobs, such as telephone customer service or data entry, and are likely to be replaced by higher-wage jobs. Samuelson argues that the impact of outsourcing is greater than Bhagwati believes, and he is less optimistic that newly created jobs in the United States will pay higher wages than the jobs lost to outsourcing.

The debate between Samuelson and Bhagwati demonstrates that economics is an evolving discipline. New models are continually being introduced, and new hypotheses are being formulated and tested. We can expect the debate over the economic impact of outsourcing to continue to be lively.

Sources: Paul A. Samuelson, "Where Ricardo and Mill Rebut and Confirm Arguments of Mainstream Economists Supporting Globalization," *Journal of Economic Perspectives*, Vol. 18, No. 3, Summer 2004, pp. 135–146; Jagdish Bhagwati, Arvind Panagariya, and T. N. Srinivasan, "The Muddles Over Outsourcing," *Journal of Economic Perspectives*, Vol. 18, No. 4, Fall 2004, pp. 93–114; and Steve Lohr, "An Elder Challenges Outsourcing's Orthodoxy," *New York Times*, September 9, 2004, p. C1.

YOUR TURN: Test your understanding by doing related problem 3.7 on page 22 at the end of this chapter.

Normative and Positive Analysis

Positive analysis Analysis concerned with what is.

Normative analysis Analysis concerned with what ought to be.

Throughout this book, as we build economic models and use them to answer questions, we need to bear in mind the distinction between *positive analysis* and *normative analysis*. **Positive analysis** is concerned with *what is*, and **normative analysis** is concerned with *what ought to be*. Economics is about positive analysis, which measures the costs and benefits of different courses of action.

We can use the federal government's minimum wage law to compare positive and normative analysis. In 2008, under this law, it was illegal for an employer to hire a worker at a wage less than $6.55 per hour (the minimum wage is scheduled to increase to $7.25 per hour in 2009). Without the minimum wage law, some firms and some workers would voluntarily agree to a lower wage. Because of the minimum wage law, some workers have difficulty finding jobs, and some firms end up paying more for labor than they otherwise would have. A positive analysis of the federal minimum wage law uses an economic model to estimate how many workers have lost their jobs because of the law, its impact on the costs and profits of businesses, and the gains to workers receiving the minimum wage. After economists complete this positive analysis, the decision as to whether the minimum wage law is a good idea or a bad idea is a normative one and depends on how people evaluate the trade-off involved. Supporters of the law believe that the losses to employers and to workers who are unemployed as a result of the law are more than offset by the gains to workers who receive higher wages than they would without the law. Opponents of the law believe the losses are greater than the gains. The assessment by any individual would depend, in part, on that person's values and political views. The positive analysis provided by an economist would play a role in the decision but can't by itself decide the issue one way or the other.

In each chapter, you will see a *Don't Let This Happen to You!* box like the one below. These boxes alert you to common pitfalls in thinking about economic ideas. After reading the box, test your understanding by working the related problem that appears at the end of the chapter.

Economics as a Social Science

Because economics is based on studying the actions of individuals, it is a social science. Economics is therefore similar to other social science disciplines, such as psychology, political science, and sociology. As a social science, economics considers human behavior—particularly decision-making behavior—in every context, not just in the context of business. Economists have studied such issues as how families decide the number of children

---

Don't Let This Happen to **YOU!**

Don't Confuse Positive Analysis with Normative Analysis

"Economic analysis has shown that the minimum wage law is a bad idea because it causes unemployment." Is this statement accurate? As of 2008, the federal minimum wage law prevents employers from hiring workers at a wage of less than $6.55 per hour. This wage is higher than some employers are willing to pay some workers. If there were no minimum wage law, some workers who currently cannot find any firm willing to hire them at $6.55 per hour would be able to find employment at a lower wage. Therefore, positive economic analysis indicates that the minimum wage law causes unemployment (although economists disagree about how much unemployment is caused by the minimum wage). *But,*

those workers who still have jobs benefit from the minimum wage because they are paid a higher wage than they otherwise would be. In other words, the minimum wage law creates both losers (the workers who become unemployed and the firms that have to pay higher wages) and winners (the workers who receive higher wages).

Should we value the gains to the winners more than we value the losses to the losers? The answer to that question involves normative analysis. Positive economic analysis can only show the consequences of a particular policy; it cannot tell us whether the policy is "good" or "bad." So, the statement at the beginning of this box is inaccurate.

YOUR TURN: Test your understanding by doing related problem 3.9 on page 23 at the end of this chapter.

to have, why people have difficulty losing weight or attaining other desirable goals, and why people often ignore relevant information when making decisions. Economics also has much to contribute to questions of government policy. As we will see throughout this book, economists have played an important role in formulating government policies in areas such as the environment, health care, and poverty.

1.4 | Distinguish between microeconomics and macroeconomics.

Microeconomics and Macroeconomics

Economic models can be used to analyze decision making in many areas. We group some of these areas together as *microeconomics* and others as *macroeconomics*. **Microeconomics** is the study of how households and firms make choices, how they interact in markets, and how the government attempts to influence their choices. Microeconomic issues include explaining how consumers react to changes in product prices and how firms decide what prices to charge. Microeconomics also involves policy issues, such as analyzing the most efficient way to reduce teenage smoking, analyzing the costs and benefits of approving the sale of a new prescription drug, and analyzing the most efficient way to reduce air pollution.

Macroeconomics is the study of the economy as a whole, including topics such as inflation, unemployment, and economic growth. Macroeconomic issues include explaining why economies experience periods of recession and increasing unemployment and why over the long run, some economies have grown much faster than others. Macroeconomics also involves policy issues, such as whether government intervention can reduce the severity of recessions.

The division between microeconomics and macroeconomics is not hard and fast. Many economic situations have *both* a microeconomic and a macroeconomic aspect. For example, the level of total investment by firms in new machinery and equipment helps to determine how rapidly the economy grows—which is a macroeconomic issue. But to understand how much new machinery and equipment firms decide to purchase, we have to analyze the incentives individual firms face—which is a microeconomic issue.

Microeconomics The study of how households and firms make choices, how they interact in markets, and how the government attempts to influence their choices.

Macroeconomics The study of the economy as a whole, including topics such as inflation, unemployment, and economic growth.

1.5 | Become familiar with important economic terms.

A Preview of Important Economic Terms

In the following chapters, you will encounter certain important terms again and again. Becoming familiar with these terms is a necessary step in learning economics. Here we provide a brief introduction to some of these terms. We will discuss them all in greater depth in later chapters:

- *Entrepreneur.* An entrepreneur is someone who operates a business. In a market system, entrepreneurs decide what goods and services to produce and how to produce them. An entrepreneur starting a new business puts his or her own funds at risk. If an entrepreneur is wrong about what consumers want or about the best way to produce goods and services, the entrepreneur's funds can be lost. This is not an unusual occurrence: In the United States, about half of new businesses close within four years. Without entrepreneurs willing to assume the risk of starting and operating businesses, economic progress would be impossible in a market system.

- *Innovation.* There is a distinction between an *invention* and *innovation*. An invention is the development of a new good or a new process for making a good. An innovation is the practical application of an invention. (*Innovation* may also be used more broadly to refer to any significant improvement in a good or in the

2.6 Centrally planned economies have been less efficient than market economies.

  a. Has this happened by chance, or is there some underlying reason?

  b. If market economies are more economically efficient than centrally planned economies, would there ever be a reason to prefer having a centrally planned economy rather than a market economy?

2.7 Thomas Sowell, an economist at the Hoover Institution at Stanford University, has written, "All economic systems not only provide people with goods and services, but also restrict or prevent them from getting as much of these goods and services as they wish." Why is it necessary for all economic systems to do this? How does a market system prevent people from getting as many goods and services as they wish?

Source: Thomas Sowell, *Applied Economics: Thinking Beyond Stage One*, New York: Basic Books, 2004, p. 16.

2.8 Suppose that your local police department recovers 100 tickets to a big NASCAR race in a drug raid. It decides to distribute these to residents and announces that tickets will be given away at 10 A.M. Monday at City Hall.

  a. What groups of people will be most likely to try to get the tickets? Think of specific examples and then generalize.

  b. What is the opportunity cost of distributing the tickets this way?

  c. Productive efficiency occurs when a good or service (such as the distribution of tickets) is produced at the lowest possible cost. Is this an efficient way to distribute the tickets? If possible, think of a more efficient method of distributing the tickets.

  d. Is this an equitable way to distribute the tickets? Explain.

>> **End Learning Objective 1.2**

1.3 LEARNING OBJECTIVE   1.3 | Understand the role of models in economic analysis, **pages 11–15.**

Economic Models

Summary

Economists rely on economic models when they apply economic ideas to real-world problems. **Economic models** are simplified versions of reality used to analyze real-world economic situations. Economists accept and use an economic model if it leads to hypotheses that are confirmed by statistical analysis. In many cases, the acceptance is tentative, however, pending the gathering of new data or further statistical analysis. Economics is a **social science** because it applies the scientific method to the study of the interactions among individuals. Economics is concerned with positive analysis rather than normative analysis. **Positive analysis** is concerned with what is. **Normative analysis** is concerned with what ought to be. Because economics is based on studying the actions of individuals, it is a social science. As a social science, economics considers human behavior in every context of decision making, not just in business.

myeconlab Visit www.myeconlab.com to complete these exercises
Get Ahead of the Curve online and get instant feedback.

Review Questions

3.1 Why do economists use models? How are economic data used to test models?

3.2 Describe the five steps by which economists arrive at a useful economic model.

3.3 What is the difference between normative analysis and positive analysis? Is economics concerned mainly with

normative analysis or mainly with positive analysis? Briefly explain.

Problems and Applications

3.4 Do you agree or disagree with the following assertion: "The problem with economics is that it assumes consumers and firms always make the correct decision. But we know everyone's human, and we all make mistakes."

3.5 Suppose an economist develops an economic model and finds that "it works great in theory, but it fails in practice." What should the economist do next?

3.6 Dr. Strangelove's theory is that the price of mushrooms is determined by the activity of subatomic particles that exist in another universe parallel to ours. When the subatomic particles are emitted in profusion, the price of mushrooms is high. When subatomic particle emissions are low, the price of mushrooms also is low. How would you go about testing Dr. Strangelove's theory? Discuss whether this theory is useful.

3.7 (Related to the *Making the Connection* on page 13) The *Making the Connection* that discusses the debate between Paul Samuelson and Jahdish Bhagwati over outsourcing mentions that the two economists disagree over how to interpret the relevant economic statistics. What economic statistics would be most useful in evaluating the positions these economists hold? Assuming these statistics are available or could be gathered, are they likely to finally resolve the debate?

3.8 (Related to the *Chapter Opener* on page 2) Many large firms have begun outsourcing work to China.

a. Why have large firms done this?

b. Is outsourcing work to low-wage Chinese workers a risk-free proposition for large firms?

3.9 (Related to the *Don't Let This Happen to You!* on page 14) Explain which of the following statements represent positive analysis and which represent normative analysis.

a. A 50-cent-per-pack tax on cigarettes will reduce smoking by teenagers by 12 percent.

b. The federal government should spend more on AIDS research.

c. Rising paper prices will increase textbook prices.

d. The price of coffee at Starbucks is too high.

3.10 The American Bar Association has proposed a law that would prohibit anyone except lawyers from giving legal advice. Under the proposal, income tax preparers, real estate agents, hospitals, labor unions, and anyone else who offered legal advice would be penalized. One critic of the proposal argued that the proposal would protect attorneys more than it would protect consumers.

a. How might the proposal protect consumers?

b. Why did the critic of the proposal argue that it would protect attorneys more than it would protect consumers?

c. Briefly discuss whether you consider the proposed law to be a good idea.

Source: Adam Liptak, "U.S. Opposes Proposal to Limit Who May Give Legal Advice," *The New York Times*, February 3, 2003.

>> **End Learning Objective 1.3**

1.4 LEARNING OBJECTIVE   1.4 | Distinguish between microeconomics and macroeconomics, **page 15.**

Microeconomics and Macroeconomics

Summary

Microeconomics is the study of how households and firms make choices, how they interact in markets, and how the government attempts to influence their choices. **Macroeconomics** is the study of the economy as a whole, including topics such as inflation, unemployment, and economic growth.

myeconlab Visit www.myeconlab.com to complete these exercises
Get Ahead of the Curve online and get instant feedback.

Review Question

4.1 Briefly discuss the difference between microeconomics and macroeconomics.

Problems and Applications

4.2 Briefly explain whether each of the following is primarily a microeconomic issue or a macroeconomic issue.

a. The effect of higher cigarette taxes on the quantity of cigarettes sold.

b. The effect of higher income taxes on the total amount of consumer spending.

c. The reasons for the economies of East Asian countries growing faster than the economies of sub-Saharan African countries.

d. The reasons for low rates of profit in the airline industry.

4.3 Briefly explain whether you agree with the following assertion: "Microeconomics is concerned with things that happen in one particular place, such as the unemployment rate in one city. In contrast, macroeconomics is concerned with things that affect the country as a whole, such as how the rate of teenage smoking in the United States would be affected by an increase in the tax on cigarettes."

>> **End Learning Objective 1.4**

1.5 LEARNING OBJECTIVE   1.5 | Become familiar with important economic terms, **pages 15–16.**

A Preview of Important Economic Terms

Summary

Becoming familiar with important terms is a necessary step in learning economics. These important economic terms include *capital, entrepreneur, factors of production, firm, goods, household, human capital, innovation, profit, revenue,* and *technology*.

Appendix

Using Graphs and Formulas

Review the use of **graphs** and **formulas**.

Graphs are used to illustrate key economics ideas. Graphs appear not just in economics textbooks but also on Web sites and in newspaper and magazine articles that discuss events in business and economics. Why the heavy use of graphs? Because they serve two useful purposes: (1) They simplify economic ideas, and (2) they make the ideas more concrete so they can be applied to real-world problems. Economic and business issues can be complicated, but a graph can help cut through complications and highlight the key relationships needed to understand the issue. In that sense, a graph can be like a street map.

For example, suppose you take a bus to New York City to see the Empire State Building. After arriving at the Port Authority Bus Terminal, you will probably use a map similar to the one shown below to find your way to the Empire State Building.

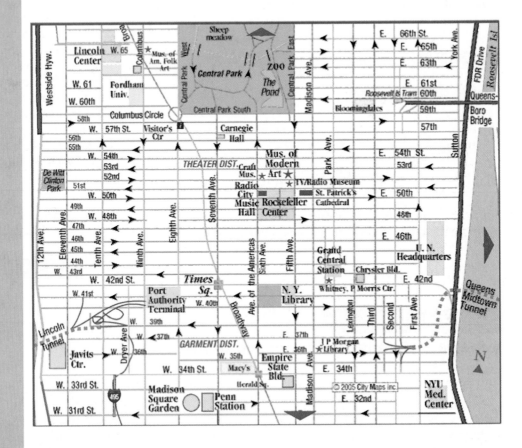

Maps are very familiar to just about everyone, so we don't usually think of them as being simplified versions of reality, but they are. This map does not show much more than the streets in this part of New York City and some of the most important buildings. The names, addresses, and telephone numbers of the people who live and work in the area aren't given. Almost none of the stores and buildings those people work and live in are shown either. The map doesn't tell which streets allow curbside parking and which don't. In fact, the map tells almost nothing about the messy reality of life in this section of New York City, except how the streets are laid out, which is the essential information you need to get from the Port Authority to the Empire State Building.

Think about someone who says, "I know how to get around in the city, but I just can't figure out how to read a map." It certainly is possible to find your destination in a city without a map, but it's a lot easier with one. The same is true of using graphs in economics. It is possible to arrive at a solution to a real-world problem in economics and business without using graphs, but it is usually a lot easier if you do use them.

Often, the difficulty students have with graphs and formulas is a lack of familiarity. With practice, all the graphs and formulas in this text will become familiar to you. Once you are familiar with them, you will be able to use them to analyze problems that would otherwise seem very difficult. What follows is a brief review of how graphs and formulas are used.

Graphs of One Variable

Figure 1A-1 displays values for *market shares* in the U.S. automobile market, using two common types of graphs. Market shares show the percentage of industry sales accounted for by different firms. In this case, the information is for groups of firms: the "Big Three"—Ford, General Motors, and DaimlerChrysler—as well as Japanese firms, European firms, and Korean firms. Panel (a) displays the information on market shares as a *bar graph*, where the market share of each group of firms is represented by the

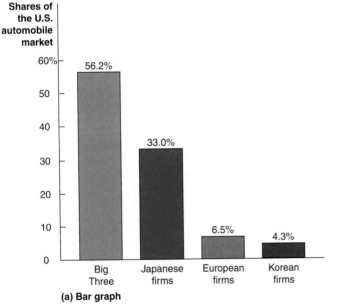
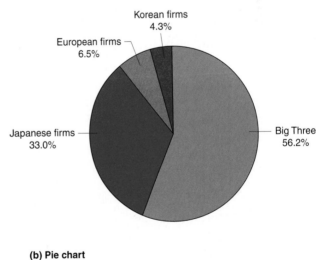

(a) Bar graph

(b) Pie chart

Figure 1A-1 | Bar Graphs and Pie Charts

Values for an economic variable are often displayed as a bar graph or as a pie chart. In this case, panel (a) shows market share data for the U.S. automobile industry as a bar graph, where the market share of each group of firms is represented by the height of its bar. Panel (b) displays the same information as a pie chart, with the market share of each group of firms represented by the size of its slice of the pie.

Source: "Auto Sales," *Wall Street Journal*, March 1, 2007.

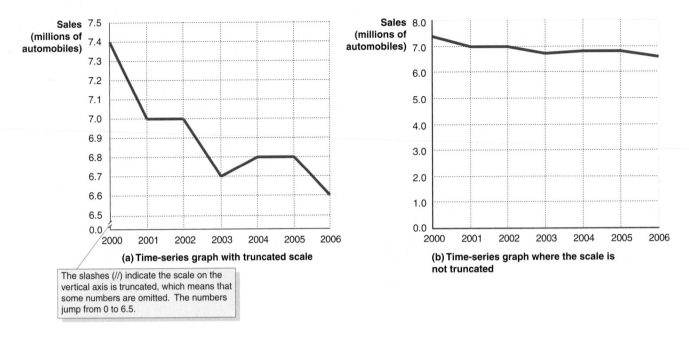

(a) Time-series graph with truncated scale

The slashes (//) indicate the scale on the vertical axis is truncated, which means that some numbers are omitted. The numbers jump from 0 to 6.5.

(b) Time-series graph where the scale is not truncated

Figure 1A-2 │ Time-Series Graphs

Both panels present time-series graphs of Ford Motor Company's worldwide sales during each year from 2000–2006. Panel (a) has a truncated scale on the vertical axis, and panel (b) does not. As a result, the fluctuations in Ford's sales appear smaller in panel (b) than in panel (a).
Source: Ford Motor Company, *Annual Report*, various years.

height of its bar. Panel (b) displays the same information as a *pie chart*, with the market share of each group of firms represented by the size of its slice of the pie.

Information on economic variables is also often displayed in *time-series graphs*. Time-series graphs are displayed on a coordinate grid. In a coordinate grid, we can measure the value of one variable along the vertical axis (or *y*-axis), and the value of another variable along the horizontal axis (or *x*-axis). The point where the vertical axis intersects the horizontal axis is called the *origin*. At the origin, the value of both variables is zero. The points on a coordinate grid represent values of the two variables. In Figure 1A-2, we measure the number of automobiles and trucks sold worldwide by the Ford Motor Company on the vertical axis, and we measure time on the horizontal axis. In time-series graphs, the height of the line at each date shows the value of the variable measured on the vertical axis. Both panels of Figure 1A-2 show Ford's worldwide sales during each year from 2000 to 2006. The difference between panel (a) and panel (b) illustrates the importance of the scale used in a time-series graph. In panel (a), the scale on the vertical axis is truncated, which means that it does not start with zero. The slashes (//) near the bottom of the axis indicate that the scale is truncated. In panel (b), the scale is not truncated. In panel (b), the decline in Ford's sales since 2000 appears smaller than in panel (a). (Technically, the horizontal axis is also truncated because we start with the year 2000, not the year 0.)

Graphs of Two Variables

We often use graphs to show the relationship between two variables. For example, suppose you are interested in the relationship between the price of a pepperoni pizza and the quantity of pizzas sold per week in the small town of Bryan, Texas. A graph showing the relationship between the price of a good and the quantity of the good demanded at each price is called a *demand curve*. (As we will discuss later, in drawing a demand curve for a good, we have to hold constant any variables other than price that might affect the

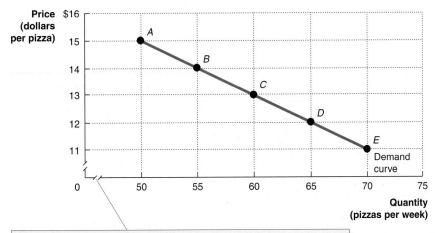

Price (dollars per pizza)	Quantity (pizzas per week)	Points
$15	50	A
14	55	B
13	60	C
12	65	D
11	70	E

As you learned in Figure 1A-2, the slashes (//) indicate the scales on the axes are truncated, which means that numbers are omitted: On the horizontal axis numbers jump from 0 to 50, and on the vertical axis numbers jump from 0 to 11.

Figure 1A-3

Plotting Price and Quantity Points in a Graph

The figure shows a two-dimensional grid on which we measure the price of pizza along the vertical axis (or *y*-axis) and the quantity of pizza sold per week along the horizontal axis (or *x*-axis). Each point on the grid represents one of the price and quantity combinations listed in the table. By connecting the points with a line, we can better illustrate the relationship between the two variables.

willingness of consumers to buy the good.) Figure 1A-3 shows the data you have collected on price and quantity. The figure shows a two-dimensional grid on which we measure the price of pizza along the *y*-axis and the quantity of pizza sold per week along the *x*-axis. Each point on the grid represents one of the price and quantity combinations listed in the table. We can connect the points to form the demand curve for pizza in Bryan, Texas. Notice that the scales on both axes in the graph are truncated. In this case, truncating the axes allows the graph to illustrate more clearly the relationship between price and quantity by excluding low prices and quantities.

Slopes of Lines

Once you have plotted the data in Figure 1A-3, you may be interested in how much the quantity of pizza sold increases as the price decreases. The *slope* of a line tells us how much the variable we are measuring on the *y*-axis changes as the variable we are measuring on the *x*-axis changes. We can use the Greek letter delta (Δ) to stand for the change in a variable. The slope is sometimes referred to as the rise over the run. So, we have several ways of expressing slope:

$$\text{Slope} = \frac{\text{Change in value on the vertical axis}}{\text{Change in value on the horizontal axis}} = \frac{\Delta y}{\Delta x} = \frac{\text{Rise}}{\text{Run}}.$$

Figure 1A-4 reproduces the graph from Figure 1A-3. Because the slope of a straight line is the same at any point, we can use any two points in the figure to calculate the slope of the line. For example, when the price of pizza decreases from $14 to $12, the quantity of pizza sold increases from 55 per week to 65 per week. Therefore, the slope is:

$$\text{Slope} = \frac{\Delta \text{Price of pizza}}{\Delta \text{Quantity of pizza}} = \frac{(\$12 - \$14)}{(65 - 55)} = \frac{-2}{10} = -0.2.$$

Figure 1A-4

Calculating the Slope of a Line

We can calculate the slope of a line as the change in the value of the variable on the *y*-axis divided by the change in the value of the variable on the *x*-axis. Because the slope of a straight line is constant, we can use any two points in the figure to calculate the slope of the line. For example, when the price of pizza decreases from $14 to $12, the quantity of pizza demanded increases from 55 per week to 65 per week. So, the slope of this line equals −2 divided by 10, or −0.2.

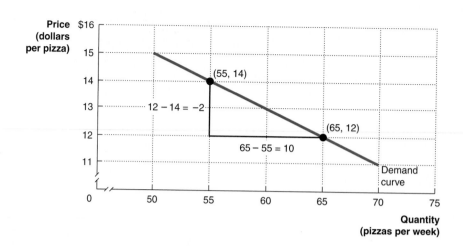

The slope of this line gives us some insight into how responsive consumers in Bryan, Texas, are to changes in the price of pizza. The larger the value of the slope (ignoring the negative sign), the steeper the line will be, which indicates that not many additional pizzas are sold when the price falls. The smaller the value of the slope, the flatter the line will be, which indicates a greater increase in pizzas sold when the price falls.

Taking into Account More Than Two Variables on a Graph

The demand curve graph in Figure 1A-4 shows the relationship between the price of pizza and the quantity of pizza sold, but we know that the quantity of any good sold depends on more than just the price of the good. For example, the quantity of pizza sold in a given week in Bryan, Texas, can be affected by such other variables as the price of hamburgers, whether an advertising campaign by local pizza parlors has begun that week, and so on. Allowing the values of any other variables to change will cause the position of the demand curve in the graph to change.

Suppose, for example, that the demand curve in Figure 1A-4 was drawn holding the price of hamburgers constant at $1.50. If the price of hamburgers rises to $2.00, then some consumers will switch from buying hamburgers to buying pizza, and more pizzas will be sold at every price. The result on the graph will be to shift the line representing the demand curve to the right. Similarly, if the price of hamburgers falls from $1.50 to $1.00, some consumers will switch from buying pizza to buying hamburgers, and fewer pizzas will be sold at every price. The result on the graph will be to shift the line representing the demand curve to the left.

The table in Figure 1A-5 shows the effect of a change in the price of hamburgers on the quantity of pizza demanded. For example, suppose at first we are on the line labeled *Demand curve₁*. If the price of pizza is $14 (point *A*), an increase in the price of hamburgers from $1.50 to $2.00 increases the quantity of pizzas demanded from 55 to 60 per week (point *B*) and shifts us to *Demand curve₂*. Or, if we start on *Demand curve₁* and the price of pizza is $12 (point *C*), a decrease in the price of hamburgers from $1.50 to $1.00 decreases the quantity of pizzas demanded from 65 to 60 per week (point *D*) and shifts us to *Demand curve₃*. By shifting the demand curve, we have taken into account the effect of changes in the value of a third variable—the price of hamburgers. We will use this technique of shifting curves to allow for the effects of additional variables many times in this book.

Positive and Negative Relationships

We can use graphs to show the relationships between any two variables. Sometimes the relationship between the variables is *negative*, meaning that as one variable increases in value, the other variable decreases in value. This was the case with the

	Quantity (pizzas per week)		
Price (dollars per pizza)	When the Price of Hamburgers = $1.00	When the Price of Hamburgers = $1.50	When the Price of Hamburgers = $2.00
$15	45	50	55
14	50	55	60
13	55	60	65
12	60	65	70
11	65	70	75

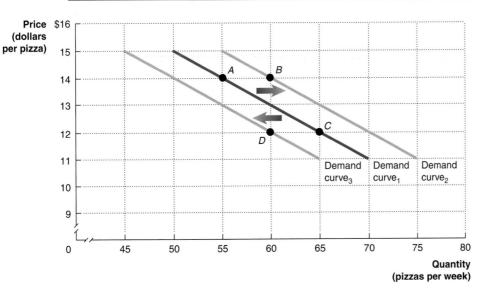

Figure 1A-5

Showing Three Variables on a Graph

The demand curve for pizza shows the relationship between the price of pizzas and the quantity of pizzas demanded, *holding constant other factors that might affect the willingness of consumers to buy pizza.* If the price of pizza is $14 (point *A*), an increase in the price of hamburgers from $1.50 to $2.00 increases the quantity of pizzas demanded from 55 to 60 per week (point *B*) and shifts us to Demand curve$_2$. Or, if we start on *Demand curve$_1$* and the price of pizza is $12 (point *C*), a decrease in the price of hamburgers from $1.50 to $1.00 decreases the quantity of pizza demanded from 65 to 60 per week (point *D*) and shifts us to *Demand curve$_3$*.

price of pizza and the quantity of pizzas demanded. The relationship between two variables can also be *positive*, meaning that the values of both variables increase or decrease together. For example, when the level of total income—or *disposable personal income*—received by households in the United States increases, the level of total *consumption spending*, which is spending by households on goods and services, also increases. The table in Figure 1A-6 shows the values for income and consumption spending for the years 2003–2006 (the values are in billions of dollars). The graph

Year	Disposable Personal Income (billions of dollars)	Consumption Spending (billions of dollars)
2003	$8,163	$7,704
2004	8,682	8,212
2005	9,036	8,742
2006	9,523	9,269

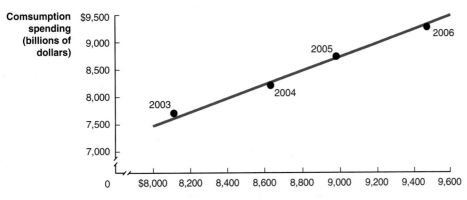

Figure 1A-6

Graphing the Positive Relationship between Income and Consumption

In a positive relationship between two economic variables, as one variable increases, the other variable also increases. This figure shows the positive relationship between disposable personal income and consumption spending. As disposable personal income in the United States has increased, so has consumption spending.
Source: U.S. Department of Commerce, Bureau of Economic Analysis.

plots the data from the table, with national income measured along the horizontal axis and consumption spending measured along the vertical axis. Notice that the four points do not all fall exactly on the line. This is often the case with real-world data. To examine the relationship between two variables, economists often use the straight line that best fits the data.

Determining Cause and Effect

When we graph the relationship between two variables, we often want to draw conclusions about whether changes in one variable are causing changes in the other variable. Doing so, however, can lead to incorrect conclusions. For example, suppose you graph the number of homes in a neighborhood that have a fire burning in the fireplace and the number of leaves on trees in the neighborhood. You would get a relationship like that shown in panel (a) of Figure 1A-7: The more fires burning in the neighborhood, the fewer leaves the trees have. Can we draw the conclusion from this graph that using a fireplace causes trees to lose their leaves? We know, of course, that such a conclusion would be incorrect. In spring and summer, there are relatively few fireplaces being used, and the trees are full of leaves. In the fall, as trees begin to lose their leaves, fireplaces are used more frequently. And in winter, many fireplaces are being used and many trees have lost all their leaves. The reason that the graph in Figure 1A-7 is misleading about cause and effect is that there is obviously an *omitted variable* in the analysis—the season of the year. An omitted variable is one that affects other variables, and its omission can lead to false conclusions about cause and effect.

Although in our example the omitted variable is obvious, there are many debates about cause and effect where the existence of an omitted variable has not been clear. For instance, it has been known for many years that people who smoke cigarettes suffer from higher rates of lung cancer than do nonsmokers. For some time, tobacco companies and some scientists argued that there was an omitted variable—perhaps psychological temperament—that made some people more likely to smoke and more likely to develop lung cancer. If this omitted variable existed, then the finding that smokers were

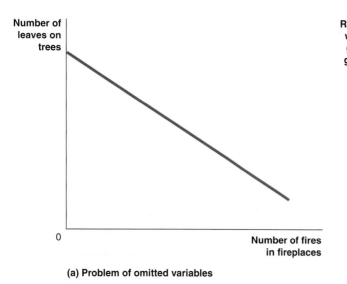

(a) Problem of omitted variables

(b) Problem of reverse causation

Figure 1A-7 | Determining Cause and Effect

Using graphs to draw conclusions about cause and effect can be hazardous. In panel (a), we see that there are fewer leaves on the trees in a neighborhood when many homes have fires burning in their fireplaces. We cannot draw the conclusion that the fires cause the leaves to fall because we have an *omitted variable*—the season of the year. In panel (b), we see that more lawn mowers are used in a neighborhood during times when the grass grows rapidly and fewer lawn mowers are used when the grass grows slowly. Concluding that using lawn mowers *causes* the grass to grow faster would be making the error of *reverse causality*.

more likely to develop lung cancer would not have been evidence that smoking *caused* lung cancer. In this case, however, nearly all scientists eventually concluded that the omitted variable did not exist and that, in fact, smoking does cause lung cancer.

A related problem in determining cause and effect is known as *reverse causality*. The error of reverse causality occurs when we conclude that changes in variable *X* cause changes in variable *Y* when, in fact, it is actually changes in variable *Y* that cause changes in variable *X*. For example, panel (b) of Figure 1A-7 plots the number of lawn mowers being used in a neighborhood against the rate at which grass on lawns in the neighborhood is growing. We could conclude from this graph that using lawn mowers *causes* the grass to grow faster. We know, however, that in reality, the causality is in the other direction: Rapidly growing grass during the spring and summer causes the increased use of lawn mowers. Slowly growing grass in the fall or winter or during periods of low rainfall causes decreased use of lawn mowers.

Once again, in our example, the potential error of reverse causality is obvious. In many economic debates, however, cause and effect can be more difficult to determine. For example, changes in the money supply, or the total amount of money in the economy, tend to occur at the same time as changes in the total amount of income people in the economy earn. A famous debate in economics was about whether the changes in the money supply caused the changes in total income or whether the changes in total income caused the changes in the money supply. Each side in the debate accused the other side of committing the error of reverse causality.

Are Graphs of Economic Relationships Always Straight Lines?

The graphs of relationships between two economic variables that we have drawn so far have been straight lines. The relationship between two variables is *linear* when it can be represented by a straight line. Few economic relationships are actually linear. For example, if we carefully plot data on the price of a product and the quantity demanded at each price, holding constant other variables that affect the quantity demanded, we will usually find a curved—or *nonlinear*—relationship rather than a linear relationship. In practice, however, it is often useful to approximate a nonlinear relationship with a linear relationship. If the relationship is reasonably close to being linear, the analysis is not significantly affected. In addition, it is easier to calculate the slope of a straight line, and it also is easier to calculate the area under a straight line. So, in this textbook, we often assume that the relationship between two economic variables is linear even when we know that this assumption is not precisely correct.

Slopes of Nonlinear Curves

In some situations, we need to take into account the nonlinear nature of an economic relationship. For example, panel (a) of Figure 1A-8 shows the hypothetical relationship between Apple's total cost of producing iPods and the quantity of iPods produced. The relationship is curved, rather than linear. In this case, the cost of production is increasing at an increasing rate, which often happens in manufacturing. Put a different way, as we move up the curve, its slope becomes larger. (Remember that with a straight line, the slope is always constant.) To see this effect, first remember that we calculate the slope of a curve by dividing the change in the variable on the *y*-axis by the change in the variable on the *x*-axis. As we move from point *A* to point *B*, the quantity produced increases by 1 million iPods, while the total cost of production increases by $50 million. Farther up the curve, as we move from point *C* to point *D*, the change in quantity is the same—1 million iPods—but the change in the total cost of production is now much larger: $250 million. Because the change in the *y* variable has increased, while the change in the *x* variable has remained the same, we know that the slope has increased.

To measure the slope of a nonlinear curve at a particular point, we must measure the slope of the *tangent line* to the curve at that point. A tangent line will only touch the curve at that point. We can measure the slope of the tangent line just as we would

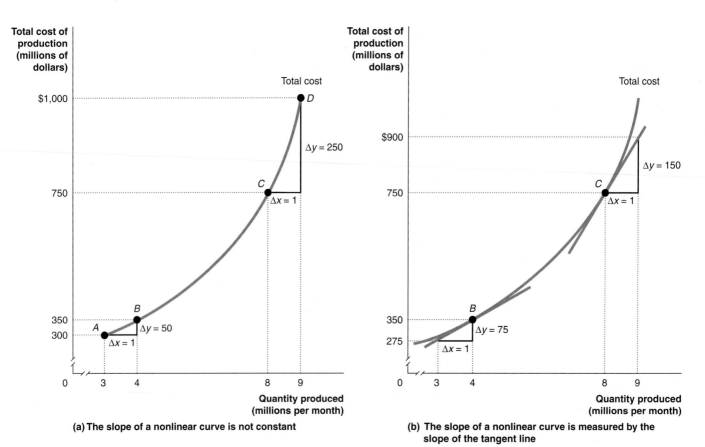

Figure 1A-8 | The Slope of a Nonlinear Curve

The relationship between the quantity of iPods produced and the total cost of production is curved, rather than liner. In panel (a), in moving from point *A* to point *B*, the quantity produced increases by 1 million iPods, while the total cost of production increases by $50 million. Farther up the cure, as we move from point *C* to point *D*, the change in quantity is the same—1 million iPods—but the change in the total cost of production is now much larger: $250 million.

Because the change in the *y* variable has increased, while the change in the *x* variable has remained the same, we know that the slope has increased. In panel (b), we measure the slope of the curve at a particular point by the slope of the tangent line. The slope of the tangent line at point *B* is 75, and the slope of the tangent line at point *C* is 150.

the slope of any straight line. In panel (b), the tangent line at point *B* has a slope equal to:

$$\frac{\Delta \text{Cost}}{\Delta \text{Quantity}} = \frac{75}{1} = 75.$$

The tangent line at point *C* has a slope equal to:

$$\frac{\Delta \text{Cost}}{\Delta \text{Quantity}} = \frac{150}{1} = 150.$$

Once again, we see that the slope of the curve is larger at point *C* than at point *B*.

Formulas

We have just seen that graphs are an important economic tool. In this section, we will review several useful formulas and show how to use them to summarize data and to calculate important relationships.

Formula for a Percentage Change

One important formula is the percentage change. The *percentage change* is the change in some economic variable, usually from one period to the next, expressed as a percentage. An important macroeconomic measure is the real gross domestic product (GDP). *GDP* is the value of all the final goods and services produced in a country during a year. "Real" GDP is corrected for the effects of inflation. When economists say that the U.S. economy grew 3.3 percent during 2006, they mean that real GDP was 3.3 percent higher in 2006 than it was in 2005. The formula for making this calculation is:

$$\left(\frac{GDP_{2006} - GDP_{2005}}{GDP_{2005}} \right) \times 100$$

or, more generally, for any two periods:

$$\text{Percentage change} = \frac{\text{Value in the second period} - \text{Value in the first period}}{\text{Value in the first period}} \times 100.$$

In this case, real GDP was $11,049 billion in 2005 and $11,415 billion in 2006. So, the growth rate of the U.S. economy during 2006 was:

$$\left(\frac{\$11,415 - \$11,049}{\$11,049} \right) \times 100 = 3.3\%.$$

Notice that it didn't matter that in using the formula, we ignored the fact that GDP is measured in billions of dollars. In fact, when calculating percentage changes, *the units don't matter.* The percentage increase from $11,049 billion to $11,415 billion is exactly the same as the percentage increase from $11,049 to $11,415.

Formulas for the Areas of a Rectangle and a Triangle

Areas that form rectangles and triangles on graphs can have important economic meaning. For example, Figure 1A-9 shows the demand curve for Pepsi. Suppose that the price is currently $2.00 and that 125,000 bottles of Pepsi are sold at that price. A firm's *total revenue* is equal to the amount it receives from selling its product, or the quantity sold multiplied by the price. In this case, total revenue will equal 125,000 bottles times $2.00 per bottle, or $250,000.

The formula for the area of a rectangle is:

$$\text{Area of a rectangle} = \text{Base} \times \text{Height}$$

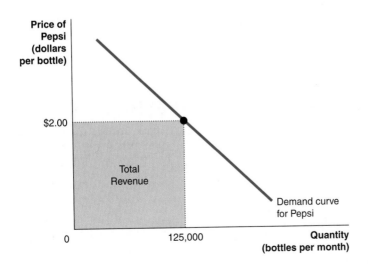

Figure 1A-9

Showing a Firm's Total Revenue on a Graph

The area of a rectangle is equal to its base multiplied by its height. Total revenue is equal to quantity multiplied by price. Here, total revenue is equal to the quantity of 125,000 bottles times the price of $2.00 per bottle, or $250,000. The area of the green-shaded rectangle shows the firm's total revenue.

Figure 1A-10

The Area of a Triangle

The area of a triangle is equal to ½ multiplied by its base multiplied by its height. The area of the blue-shaded triangle has a base equal to 150,000 − 125,000, or 25,000, and a height equal to $2.00 − $1.50, or $0.50. Therefore, its area equals ½ × 25,000 × $0.50, or $6,250.

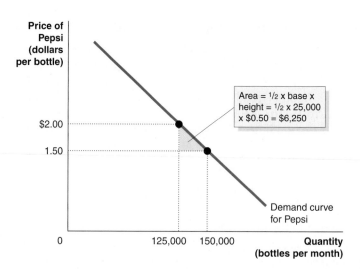

In Figure 1A-9, the green-shaded rectangle also represents the firm's total revenue because its area is given by the base of 125,000 bottles multiplied by the price of $2.00 per bottle.

We will see in later chapters that areas that are triangles can also have economic significance. The formula for the area of a triangle is:

$$\text{Area of a triangle} = \frac{1}{2} \times \text{Base} \times \text{Height}.$$

The blue-shaded area in Figure 1A-10 is a triangle. The base equals 150,000 − 125,000, or 25,000. Its height equals $2.00 − $1.50, or $0.50. Therefore, its area equals ½ × 25,000 × $0.50, or $6,250. Notice that the blue area is a triangle only if the demand curve is a straight line, or linear. Not all demand curves are linear. However, the formula for the area of a triangle will usually still give a good approximation, even if the demand curve is not linear.

Summary of Using Formulas

You will encounter several other formulas in this book. Whenever you must use a formula, you should follow these steps:

1 Make sure you understand the economic concept that the formula represents.

2 Make sure you are using the correct formula for the problem you are solving.

3 Make sure that the number you calculate using the formula is economically reasonable. For example, if you are using a formula to calculate a firm's revenue and your answer is a negative number, you know you made a mistake somewhere.

LEARNING OBJECTIVE   Review the use of graphs and formulas, **pages 24–34.**

myeconlab   Visit www.myeconlab.com to complete these exercises
Get Ahead of the Curve online and get instant feedback.

Problems and Applications

1A.1 The following table gives the relationship between the price of custard pies and the number of pies Jacob buys per week.

PRICE	QUANTITY OF PIES	WEEK
$3.00	6	July 2
2.00	7	July 9
5.00	4	July 16
6.00	3	July 23
1.00	8	July 30
4.00	5	August 6

a. Is the relationship between the price of pies and the number of pies Jacob buys a positive relationship or a negative relationship?

b. Plot the data from the table on a graph similar to Figure 1A-3. Draw a straight line that best fits the points.

c. Calculate the slope of the line.

1A.2 The following table gives information on the quantity of glasses of lemonade demanded on sunny and overcast days. Plot the data from the table on a graph similar to Figure 1A-5. Draw two straight lines representing the two demand curves—one for sunny days and one for overcast days.

PRICE (DOLLARS PER GLASS)	QUANTITY (GLASSES OF LEMONADE PER DAY)	WEATHER
$0.80	30	Sunny
0.80	10	Overcast
0.70	40	Sunny
0.70	20	Overcast
0.60	50	Sunny
0.60	30	Overcast
0.50	60	Sunny
0.50	40	Overcast

1A.3 Using the information in Figure 1A-2, calculate the percentage change in auto sales from one year to the next. Between which years did sales fall at the fastest rate?

1A.4 Real GDP in 1981 was $5,292 billion. Real GDP in 1982 was $5,189 billion. What was the percentage change in real GDP from 1981 to 1982? What do economists call the percentage change in real GDP from one year to the next?

1A.5 Assume that the demand curve for Pepsi passes through the following two points:

PRICE PER BOTTLE OF PEPSI	NUMBER OF BOTTLES OF PEPSI SOLD
$2.50	100,000
1.25	200,000

a. Draw a graph with a linear demand curve that passes through these two points.

b. Show on the graph the areas representing total revenue at each price. Give the value for total revenue at each price.

1A.6 What is the area of the blue triangle shown in the following figure?

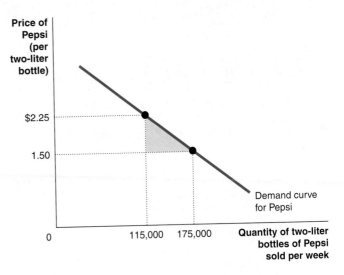

1A.7 Calculate the slope of the total cost curve at point *A* and at point *B* in the following figure.

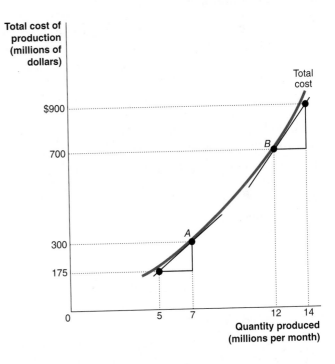

» End Appendix Learning Objective

Chapter 2

Trade-offs, Comparative Advantage, and the Market System

Managers Making Choices at BMW

When you think of cars that combine fine engineering, high performance, and cutting-edge styling, you are likely to think of BMW. The Bayerische Motoren Werke, or Bavarian Motor Works, was founded in Germany in 1916. Today, BMW employs more than 100,000 workers in 23 factories in 15 countries to produce eight car models. In 2006, it had worldwide sales of nearly 1.4 million cars.

To compete in the automobile market, the managers of BMW must make many strategic decisions, such as whether to introduce a new car model. In 2006, for example, BMW announced that it would introduce a hydrogen-powered version of the 7-Series sedan and was also working on fuel-cell powered cars. Another strategic decision BMW's managers face is where to focus their advertising. In the late 1990s, for example, some of BMW's managers opposed advertising in China because they were skeptical about the country's sales potential.

Other managers, however, argued that rising incomes were rapidly increasing the size of the Chinese market. BMW decided to advertise in China, and it has become the company's eighth-largest market, with sales increasing by 50 percent in 2006 alone.

Over the years, BMW's managers have also faced the strategic decision of whether to concentrate production in factories in Germany or to build new factories in its overseas markets. Keeping production in Germany makes it easier for BMW's managers to supervise production and to employ German workers, who generally have high levels of technical training. Building factories in other countries, however, has two benefits. First, the lower wages paid to workers in other countries reduce the cost of manufacturing vehicles. Second, BMW can reduce political friction by producing vehicles in the same country in which it sells them. In 2003, BMW opened a plant at Shenyang, in northeast China, to build its 3-Series and 5-Series cars. Previously, in 1994, BMW opened a U.S. factory in Spartanburg, South Carolina, which currently produces the Z4 roadster and X5 sports utility vehicle (SUV) for sale both in the United States and worldwide.

Managers also face smaller-scale—or tactical—business decisions. For instance, for many years, BMW used two workers to attach the gearbox to the engine in each car. In 2002, an alternative method of attaching the gearbox using a robot, rather than workers, was developed. In choosing which method to use, managers at BMW faced a trade-off because the robot method had a higher cost, but installed the gearbox in exactly the correct position, which reduces engine noise when the car is driven. Ultimately, the managers decided to adopt the robot method. A similar tactical business decision must be made in scheduling production at BMW's Spartanburg, South Carolina, plant. The plant produces both the Z4 and the X5 models, and each month managers must decide the quantity of each model that should be produced.

AN INSIDE LOOK on **page 58** discusses how BMW managers in the Spartanburg plant prepared to manufacture a new sports-activity coupe.

LEARNING Objectives

After studying this chapter, you should be able to:

2.1 Use a **production possibilities frontier** to analyze opportunity costs and trade-offs, page 38.

2.2 Understand **comparative advantage** and explain how it is the basis for **trade**, page 44.

2.3 Explain the basic idea of how a **market system** works, page 50.

Economics in YOUR Life!

The Trade-offs When You Buy a Car

When you buy a car, you probably consider factors such as safety and gas mileage. To increase gas mileage, automobile manufacturers make cars small and light. Large cars absorb more of the impact of an accident than do small cars. As a result, people are usually safer driving large cars than small cars. What can we conclude from these facts about the relationship between safety and gas mileage? Under what circumstances would it be possible for car manufacturers to make cars safer and more fuel efficient? As you read the chapter, see if you can answer these questions. You can check your answer against those provided at the end of the chapter. **>> Continued on page 56**

Scarcity The situation in which unlimited wants exceed the limited resources available to fulfill those wants.

In a market system, managers at most firms must make decisions like those made by BMW's managers. The decisions managers face reflect a key fact of economic life: *Scarcity requires trade-offs.* **Scarcity** exists because we have unlimited wants but only limited resources available to fulfill those wants. Goods and services are scarce. So, too, are the economic resources, or *factors of production*—workers, capital, natural resources, and entrepreneurial ability—used to make goods and services. Your time is scarce, which means you face trade-offs: If you spend an hour studying for an economics exam, you have one less hour to spend studying for a psychology exam or going to the movies. If your university decides to use some of its scarce budget funds to buy new computers for the computer labs, those funds will not be available to buy new books for the library or to resurface the student parking lot. If BMW decides to devote some of the scarce workers and machinery in its Spartanburg assembly plant to producing more Z4 roadsters, those resources will not be available to produce more X5 SUVs.

Many of the decisions of households and firms are made in markets. One key activity that takes place in markets is trade. Trade involves the decisions of millions of households and firms spread around the world. By engaging in trade, people can raise their standard of living. In this chapter, we provide an overview of how the market system coordinates the independent decisions of these millions of households and firms. We begin our analysis of the economic consequences of scarcity and the working of the market system by introducing an important economic model: the *production possibilities frontier*.

2.1 LEARNING OBJECTIVE

2.1 | Use a production possibilities frontier to analyze opportunity costs and trade-offs.

Production Possibilities Frontiers and Opportunity Costs

As we saw in the opening to this chapter, BMW operates an automobile factory in Spartanburg, South Carolina, where it assembles Z4 roadsters and X5 SUVs. Because the firm's resources—workers, machinery, materials, and entrepreneurial skills—are limited, BMW faces a trade-off: Resources devoted to producing Z4s are not available for producing X5s and vice versa. Chapter 1 explained that economic models can be useful in analyzing many questions. We can use a simple model called the *production possibilities frontier* to analyze the trade-offs BMW faces in its Spartanburg plant. A **production possibilities frontier** (**PPF**) is a curve showing the maximum attainable combinations of two products that may be produced with available resources and current technology. In BMW's case, the two products are Z4 roadsters and X5 SUVs, and the resources are BMW's workers, materials, robots, and other machinery.

Production possibilities frontier (**PPF**) A curve showing the maximum attainable combinations of two products that may be produced with available resources and current technology.

Graphing the Production Possibilities Frontier

Figure 2-1 uses a production possibilities frontier to illustrate the trade-offs that BMW faces. The numbers from the table are plotted in the graph. The line in the graph is BMW's production possibilities frontier. If BMW uses all its resources to produce roadsters, it can produce 800 per day—point *A* at one end of the production possibilities frontier. If BMW uses all its resources to produce SUVs, it can produce 800 per day—point *E* at the other end of the production possibilities frontier. If BMW devotes resources to producing both vehicles, it could be at a point like *B*, where it produces 600 roadsters and 200 SUVs.

All the combinations either on the frontier—like *A*, *B*, *C*, *D*, and *E*—or inside the frontier—like point *F*—are *attainable* with the resources available. Combinations on

BMW's Production Choices at Its Spartanburg Plant		
Choice	Quantity of Roadsters Produced	Quantity of SUVs Produced
A	800	0
B	600	200
C	400	400
D	200	600
E	0	800

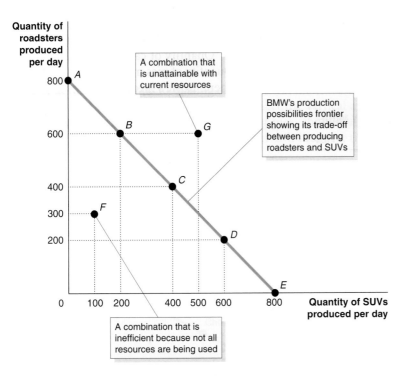

Figure 2-1

BMW's Production Possibilities Frontier

BMW faces a trade-off: To build one more roadster, it must build one less SUV. The production possibilities frontier illustrates the trade-off BMW faces. Combinations on the production possibilities frontier—like points *A, B, C, D,* and *E*—are *technically efficient* because the maximum output is being obtained from the available resources. Combinations inside the frontier—like point *F*—are *inefficient* because some resources are not being used. Combinations outside the frontier—like point *G*—are *unattainable* with current resources.

the frontier are *efficient* because all available resources are being fully utilized, and the fewest possible resources are being used to produce a given amount of output. Combinations inside the frontier—like point *F*—are *inefficient* because maximum output is not being obtained from the available resources—perhaps because the assembly line is not operating at capacity. BMW might like to be beyond the frontier—at a point like *G*, where it would be producing 600 roadsters and 500 SUVs—but points beyond the production possibilities frontier are *unattainable*, given the firm's current resources. To produce the combination at *G*, BMW would need more machines or more workers.

Notice that if BMW is producing efficiently and is on the production possibilities frontier, the only way to produce more of one vehicle is to produce less of the other vehicle. Recall from Chapter 1 that the **opportunity cost** of any activity is the highest valued alternative that must be given up to engage in that activity. For BMW, the opportunity cost of producing one more SUV is the number of roadsters the company will not be able to produce because it has shifted those resources to producing SUVs. For example, in moving from point *B* to point *C*, the opportunity cost of producing 200 more SUVs per day is the 200 fewer roadsters that can be produced.

What point on the production possibilities frontier is best? We can't tell without further information. If consumer demand for SUVs is greater than demand for roadsters, the company is likely to choose a point closer to *E*. If demand for roadsters is greater than demand for SUVs, the company is likely to choose a point closer to *A*.

Opportunity cost The highest-valued alternative that must be given up to engage in an activity.

had a similar experience: "What they've told us is there are so many important causes that they are aware of that they want to support. The choices are greater than what they've been faced with before."

Unfortunately, the trade-off of an increase in charitable giving to one cause resulting in a decrease in charitable giving to other causes is common following a disaster. In December 2004, an earthquake caused a tidal wave—or tsunami—to flood coastal areas of Indonesia, Thailand, Sri Lanka, and other countries bordering the Indian Ocean. More than 280,000 people died, and billions of dollars worth of property was destroyed. Governments and individuals around the world moved quickly to donate to relief efforts. The U.S. government donated $950 million, and individual U.S. citizens donated an additional $500 million. Both governments and individuals face limited budgets, however, and funds used for one purpose are unavailable to be used for another purpose. Although governments and individuals did increase their total charitable giving following the tsunami disaster, much of the funds spent on tsunami relief appear to have been diverted from other uses. A difficult trade-off resulted: Giving funds to victims of the tsunami meant fewer funds were available to aid other good causes.

For example, some of the funds provided by the U.S. government for reconstruction in the tsunami-devastated areas came from existing aid programs. As a result, spending on other aid projects in the region declined. Similarly, nonprofit organizations in New York City reported sharp declines in donations to the homeless and the poor, as donors gave funds for tsunami relief instead. According to a report in the newspaper *Crain's New York Business*, "Some groups such as Bailey House, which helps homeless people who have AIDS, have even started receiving letters from longtime donors warning that this year's gifts are being redirected to the tsunami relief effort." As one commentator observed, "The milk of human kindness is probably flowing at the usual rate in the United States. It's just getting channeled in different directions."

Source: Steve Levin, "Disaster Aid Is Extra Giving," *Pittsburgh Post Gazette*, April 22, 2006; Jacqueline L. Salmon, "Katrina Compassion Drives Disaster Donations to a Record," *Washington Post*, June 19, 2006, p. A05; and Daniel Gross, "Zero-Sum Charity," *Slate*, January 20, 2005.

YOUR TURN: Test your understanding by doing related problem 1.10 on page 61 at the end of this chapter.

Increasing Marginal Opportunity Costs

We can use the production possibilities frontier to explore issues related to the economy as a whole. For example, suppose we divide all the goods and services produced in the economy into just two types: military goods and civilian goods. In Figure 2-2, we let tanks represent military goods and automobiles represent civilian goods. If all the coun-

Figure 2-2

Increasing Marginal Opportunity Cost

As the economy moves down the production possibilities frontier, it experiences *increasing marginal opportunity costs* because increasing automobile production by a given quantity requires larger and larger decreases in tank production. For example, to increase automobile production from 0 to 200—moving from point *A* to point *B*—the economy has to give up only 50 tanks. But to increase automobile production by another 200 vehicles—moving from point *B* to point *C*—the economy has to give up 150 tanks.

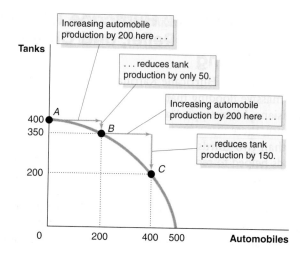

try's resources are devoted to producing military goods, 400 tanks can be produced in one year. If all resources are devoted to producing civilian goods, 500 automobiles can be produced in one year. Devoting resources to producing both goods results in the economy being at other points along the production possibilities frontier.

Notice that this production possibilities frontier is bowed outward rather than being a straight line. Because the curve is bowed out, the opportunity cost of automobiles in terms of tanks depends on where the economy currently is on the production possibilities frontier. For example, to increase automobile production from 0 to 200—moving from point *A* to point *B*—the economy has to give up only 50 tanks. But to increase automobile production by another 200 vehicles—moving from point *B* to point *C*—the economy has to give up 150 tanks.

As the economy moves down the production possibilities frontier, it experiences *increasing marginal opportunity costs* because increasing automobile production by a given quantity requires larger and larger decreases in tank production. Increasing marginal opportunity costs occurs because some workers, machines, and other resources are better suited to one use than to another. At point *A*, some resources that are well suited to producing automobiles are forced to produce tanks. Shifting these resources into producing automobiles by moving from point *A* to point *B* allows a substantial increase in automobile production, without much loss of tank production. But as the economy moves down the production possibilities frontier, more and more resources that are better suited to tank production are switched into automobile production. As a result, the increases in automobile production become increasingly smaller, while the decreases in tank production become increasingly larger. We would expect in most situations that production possibilities frontiers will be bowed outward rather than linear, as in the BMW example discussed earlier.

The idea of increasing marginal opportunity costs illustrates an important economic concept: *The more resources already devoted to any activity, the smaller the payoff to devoting additional resources to that activity.* For example, the more hours you have already spent studying economics, the smaller the increase in your test grade from each additional hour you spend—and the greater the opportunity cost of using the hour in that way. The more funds a firm has devoted to research and development during a given year, the smaller the amount of useful knowledge it receives from each additional dollar—and the greater the opportunity cost of using the funds in that way. The more funds the federal government spends cleaning up the environment during a given year, the smaller the reduction in pollution from each additional dollar—and, once again, the greater the opportunity cost of using the funds in that way.

Economic Growth

At any given time, the total resources available to any economy are fixed. Therefore, if the United States produces more automobiles, it must produce less of something else—tanks in our example. Over time, though, the resources available to an economy may increase. For example, both the labor force and the capital stock—the amount of physical capital available in the country—may increase. The increase in the available labor force and the capital stock shifts the production possibilities frontier outward for the U.S. economy and makes it possible to produce both more automobiles and more tanks. Panel (a) of Figure 2-3 shows that the economy can move from point *A* to point *B*, producing more tanks and more automobiles.

Similarly, technological advance makes it possible to produce more goods with the same amount of workers and machinery, which also shifts the production possibilities frontier outward. Technological advance need not affect all sectors equally. Panel (b) of Figure 2-3 shows the results of technological advance in the automobile industry that increases the quantity of automobile workers can produce per year while leaving unchanged the quantity of tanks that can be produced.

Shifts in the production possibilities frontier represent **economic growth** because they allow the economy to increase the production of goods and services, which ultimately raises the standard of living. In the United States and other high-income countries, the

Economic growth The ability of the economy to produce increasing quantities of goods and services.

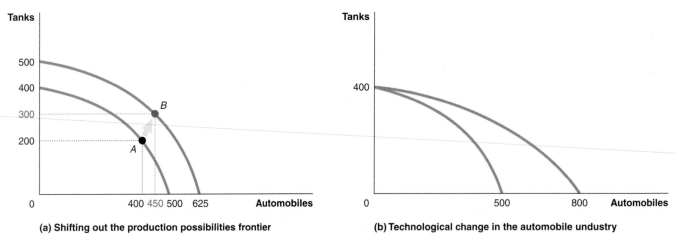

(a) Shifting out the production possibilities frontier

(b) Technological change in the automobile undustry

Figure 2-3 | Economic Growth

Panel (a) shows that as more economic resources become available and technological change occurs, the economy can move from point *A* to point *B*, producing more tanks and more automobiles. Panel (b) shows the results of technological advance in the automobile industry that increases the quantity of vehicles workers can produce per year while leaving the maximum quantity of tanks that can be produced unchanged. Shifts in the production possibilities frontier represent *economic growth*.

market system has aided the process of economic growth, which over the past 200 years has greatly increased the well-being of the average person.

2.2 LEARNING OBJECTIVE

2.2 | Understand comparative advantage and explain how it is the basis for trade.

Comparative Advantage and Trade

We can use the ideas of production possibilities frontiers and opportunity costs to understand the basic economic activity of *trade*. Markets are fundamentally about **trade**, which is the act of buying and selling. Sometimes we trade directly, as when children trade one baseball card for another baseball card. But often we trade indirectly: We sell our labor services as, say, an accountant, a salesperson, or a nurse for money, and then we use the money to buy goods and services. Although in these cases, trade takes place indirectly, ultimately the accountant, salesperson, or nurse is trading his or her services for food, clothing, and other goods and services. One of the great benefits to trade is that it makes it possible for people to become better off by increasing both their production and their consumption.

Trade The act of buying or selling.

Specialization and Gains from Trade

Consider the following situation: You and your neighbor both have fruit trees on your property. Initially, suppose you have only apple trees and your neighbor has only cherry trees. In this situation, if you both like apples and cherries, there is an obvious opportunity for both of you to gain from trade: You trade some of your apples for some of your neighbor's cherries, making you both better off. But what if there are apple and cherry trees growing on both of your properties? In that case, there can still be gains from trade. For example, your neighbor might be very good at picking apples, and you might be very good at picking cherries. It would make sense for your neighbor to concentrate on picking apples and for you to concentrate on picking cherries. You can then trade some of the cherries you pick for some of the apples your neighbor picks. But what if your neighbor is actually better at picking both apples and cherries than you are?

We can use production possibilities frontiers (*PPF*s) to show how your neighbor can benefit from trading with you even though she is better than you are at picking both apples and cherries. (For simplicity, and because it will not have any effect on the conclusions we draw, we will assume that the *PPFs* in this example are straight lines.) The table in Figure 2-4 shows how many apples and how many cherries you and your neighbor can pick in one week. The graph in the figure uses the data from the table to construct *PPFs*. Panel (a) shows your *PPF*. If you devote all your time to picking apples, you can pick 20 pounds of apples per week. If you devote all your time to picking cherries, you can pick 20 pounds per week. Panel (b) shows that if your neighbor devotes all her time to picking apples, she can pick 30 pounds. If she devotes all her time to picking cherries, she can pick 60 pounds.

The production possibilities frontiers in Figure 2-4 show how many apples and cherries you and your neighbor can consume, *without trade.* Suppose that when you don't trade with your neighbor, you pick and consume 8 pounds of apples and 12 pounds of cherries per week. This combination of apples and cherries is represented by point *A* in panel (a) of Figure 2-5, on page 46. When your neighbor doesn't trade with you, she picks and consumes 9 pounds of apples and 42 pounds of cherries per week. This combination of apples and cherries is represented by point *B* in panel (b) of Figure 2-5.

After years of picking and consuming your own apples and cherries, suppose your neighbor comes to you one day with the following proposal: She offers to trade you 15 pounds of her cherries for 10 pounds of your apples next week. Should you accept this offer? You should accept because you will end up with more apples and more cherries to consume. To take advantage of her proposal, you should specialize in picking only apples rather than splitting your time between picking apples and picking cherries. We know this will allow you to pick 20 pounds of apples. You can trade 10 pounds of apples to your neighbor for 15 pounds of her cherries. The result is that you will be able to consume 10 pounds of apples and 15 pounds of cherries (point *A'* in panel (a) of Figure 2-5). You are clearly better off as a result of trading with your neighbor: You now can consume 2 more pounds of apples and 3 more pounds of cherries than you were consuming without trading. You have moved beyond your *PPF*!

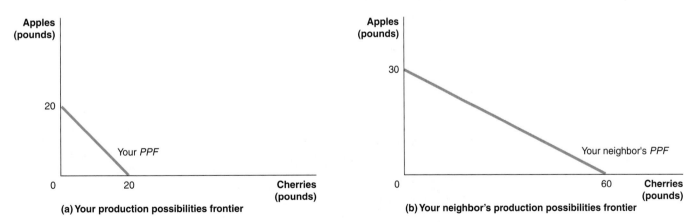

	You		**Your Neighbor**	
	Apples	Cherries	Apples	Cherries
Devote all time to picking apples	20 pounds	0 pounds	30 pounds	0 pounds
Devote all time to picking cherries	0 pounds	20 pounds	0 pounds	60 pounds

(a) Your production possibilities frontier

(b) Your neighbor's production possibilities frontier

Figure 2-4 | Production Possibilities for You and Your Neighbor, without Trade

The table in this figure shows how many pounds of apples and how many pounds of cherries you and your neighbor can each pick in one week. The graphs in the figure use the data from the table to construct production possibilities frontiers (*PPFs*) for you and your neighbor. Panel (a) shows your *PPF*. If you devote all your time to picking apples and none of your time to picking cherries, you can pick 20 pounds. If you devote all your time to picking cherries, you can pick 20 pounds. Panel (b) shows that if your neighbor devotes all her time to picking apples, she can pick 30 pounds. If she devotes all her time to picking cherries, she can pick 60 pounds.

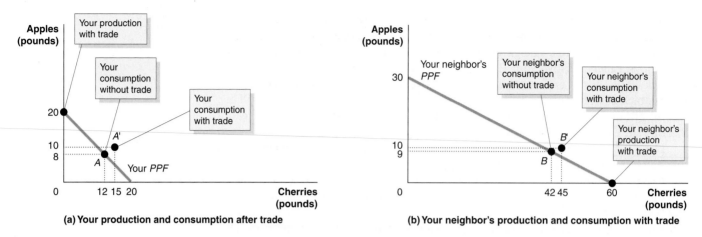

Figure 2-5 | Gains from Trade

When you don't trade with your neighbor, you pick and consume 8 pounds of apples and 12 pounds of cherries per week—point A in panel (a). When your neighbor doesn't trade with you, she picks and consumes 9 pounds of apples and 42 pounds of cherries per week—point B in panel (b). If you specialize in picking apples, you can pick 20 pounds. If your neighbor specializes in picking cherries, she can pick 60 pounds. If you trade 10 pounds of your apples for 15 pounds of your neighbor's cherries, you will be able to consume 10 pounds of apples and 15 pounds of cherries—point A' in panel (a). Your neighbor can now consume 10 pounds of apples and 45 pounds of cherries—point B' in panel (b). You and your neighbor are both better off as a result of trade.

Your neighbor has also benefited from the trade. By specializing in picking only cherries, she can pick 60 pounds. She trades 15 pounds of cherries to you for 10 pounds of apples. The result is that she can consume 10 pounds of apples and 45 pounds of cherries (point B' in panel (b) of Figure 2-5). This is 1 more pound of apples and 3 more pounds of cherries than she was consuming before trading with you. She also has moved beyond her *PPF*. Table 2-1 summarizes the changes in production and consumption that result from your trade with your neighbor. (In this example, we chose one specific rate of trading cherries for apples—15 pounds of cherries for 10 pounds of apples. There are, however, many other rates of trading cherries for apples that would also make you and your neighbor better off.)

Absolute Advantage versus Comparative Advantage

Perhaps the most remarkable aspect of the preceding example is that your neighbor benefits from trading with you even though she is better than you at picking both apples and cherries. **Absolute advantage** is the ability of an individual, a firm, or a country to

Absolute advantage The ability of an individual, a firm, or a country to produce more of a good or service than competitors, using the same amount of resources.

TABLE 2-1

A Summary of the Gains from Trade

	YOU		YOUR NEIGHBOR	
	APPLES (IN POUNDS)	CHERRIES (IN POUNDS)	APPLES (IN POUNDS)	CHERRIES (IN POUNDS)
Production *and* consumption *without* trade	8	12	9	42
Production *with* trade	20	0	0	60
Consumption *with* trade	10	15	10	45
Gains from trade (increased consumption)	2	3	1	3

produce more of a good or service than competitors, using the same amount of resources. Your neighbor has an absolute advantage over you in producing both apples and cherries because she can pick more of each fruit than you can in the same amount of time. Although it seems that your neighbor should pick her own apples *and* her own cherries, we have just seen that she is better off specializing in cherry picking and leaving the apple picking to you.

We can consider further why both you and your neighbor benefit from specializing in picking only one fruit. First, think about the opportunity cost to each of you of picking the two fruits. We saw from the *PPF* in Figure 2-4 that if you devoted all your time to picking apples, you would be able to pick 20 pounds of apples per week. As you move down your *PPF* and shift time away from picking apples to picking cherries, you have to give up 1 pound of apples for each pound of cherries you pick (the slope of your *PPF* is −1). (For a review of calculating slopes, see the appendix to Chapter 1.) Therefore, your opportunity cost of picking 1 pound of cherries is 1 pound of apples. By the same reasoning, your opportunity cost of picking 1 pound of apples is 1 pound of cherries. Your neighbor's *PPF* has a different slope, so she faces a different trade-off: As she shifts time from picking apples to picking cherries, she has to give up 0.5 pound of apples for every 1 pound of cherries she picks (the slope of your neighbor's *PPF* is −0.5). As she shifts time from picking cherries to picking apples, she gives up 2 pounds of cherries for every 1 pound of apples she picks. Therefore, her opportunity cost of picking 1 pound of apples is 2 pounds of cherries, and her opportunity cost of picking 1 pound of cherries is 0.5 pound of apples.

Table 2-2 summarizes the opportunity costs for you and your neighbor of picking apples and cherries. Note that even though your neighbor can pick more apples in a week than you can, the *opportunity cost* of picking apples is higher for her than for you because when she picks apples, she gives up more cherries than you do. So, even though she has an absolute advantage over you in picking apples, it is more costly for her to pick apples than it is for you. The table also shows that her opportunity cost of picking cherries is lower than your opportunity cost of picking cherries. **Comparative advantage** is the ability of an individual, a firm, or a country to produce a good or service at a lower opportunity cost than competitors. In apple picking, your neighbor has an *absolute advantage* over you, but you have a *comparative advantage* over her. Your neighbor has both an absolute and a comparative advantage over you in picking cherries. As we have seen, you are better off specializing in picking apples, and your neighbor is better off specializing in picking cherries.

Comparative advantage The ability of an individual, a firm, or a country to produce a good or service at a lower opportunity cost than competitors.

Comparative Advantage and the Gains from Trade

We have just derived an important economic principle: *The basis for trade is comparative advantage, not absolute advantage.* The fastest apple pickers do not necessarily do much apple picking. If the fastest apple pickers have a comparative advantage in some other activity—picking cherries, playing major league baseball, or being industrial engineers—they are better off specializing in that other activity. Individuals, firms, and countries are better off if they specialize in producing goods and services for which they have a comparative advantage and obtain the other goods and services they need by trading. We will return to the important concept of comparative advantage in Chapter 8, which is devoted to the subject of international trade.

	OPPORTUNITY COST OF PICKING 1 POUND OF APPLES	OPPORTUNITY COST OF PICKING 1 POUND OF CHERRIES
YOU	1 pound of cherries	1 pound of apples
YOUR NEIGHBOR	2 pounds of cherries	0.5 pound of apples

TABLE 2-2

Opportunity Costs of Picking Apples and Cherries

Don't Let This Happen to **YOU!**

Don't Confuse Absolute Advantage and Comparative Advantage

First, make sure you know the definitions:

- **Absolute advantage.** The ability of an individual, a firm, or a country to produce more of a good or service than competitors, using the same amount of resources. In our example, your neighbor has an absolute advantage over you in both picking apples and picking cherries.

- **Comparative advantage.** The ability of an individual, a firm, or a country to produce a good or service at a lower opportunity cost than competitors. In our example, your neighbor has a comparative advantage in picking cherries, but you have a comparative advantage in picking apples.

Keep these two key points in mind:

1. It is possible to have an absolute advantage in producing a good or service without having a comparative advantage. This is the case with your neighbor picking apples.

2. It is possible to have a comparative advantage in producing a good or service without having an absolute advantage. This is the case with you picking apples.

YOUR TURN: Test your understanding by doing related problem 2.7 on page 63 at the end of this chapter.

Solved Problem │ **2-2**

Comparative Advantage and the Gains from Trade

Suppose that Canada and the United States both produce maple syrup and honey. These are the combinations of the two goods that each country can produce in one day:

CANADA		UNITED STATES	
HONEY (IN TONS)	MAPLE SYRUP (IN TONS)	HONEY (IN TONS)	MAPLE SYRUP (IN TONS)
0	60	0	50
10	45	10	40
20	30	20	30
30	15	30	20
40	0	40	10
		50	0

a. Who has a comparative advantage in producing maple syrup? Who has a comparative advantage in producing honey?

b. Suppose that Canada is currently producing 30 tons of honey and 15 tons of maple syrup and the United States is currently producing 10 tons of honey and 40 tons of maple syrup. Demonstrate that Canada and the United States can both be better off if they specialize in producing only one good and engage in trade.

c. Illustrate your answer to question (b) by drawing a *PPF* for the United States and a *PPF* for Canada. Show on your *PPF*s the combinations of honey and maple syrup produced and consumed in each country before and after trade.

SOLVING THE PROBLEM:

Step 1: **Review the chapter material.** This problem concerns comparative advantage, so you may want to review the section "Absolute Advantage versus Comparative Advantage," which begins on page 46.

Step 2: **Answer question (a) by calculating who has a comparative advantage in each activity.** Remember that a country has a comparative advantage in producing a good if it can produce the good at the lowest opportunity cost. When

Canada produces 1 more ton of honey, it produces 1.5 fewer tons of maple syrup. On the one hand, when the United States produces 1 more ton of honey, it produces 1 less ton of maple syrup. Therefore, the United States's opportunity cost of producing honey—1 ton of maple syrup—is lower than Canada's—1.5 tons of maple syrup. On the other hand, when Canada produces 1 more ton of maple syrup, it produces 0.67 ton less of honey. When the United States produces 1 more ton of maple syrup, it produces 1 less ton of honey. Therefore, Canada's opportunity cost of producing maple syrup—0.67 ton of honey—is lower than that of the United States—1 ton of honey. We can conclude that the United States has a comparative advantage in the production of honey and Canada has a comparative advantage in the production of maple syrup.

Step 3: **Answer question (b) by showing that specialization makes Canada and the United States better off.** We know that Canada should specialize where it has a comparative advantage and the United States should specialize where it has a comparative advantage. If both countries specialize, Canada will produce 60 tons of maple syrup and 0 tons of honey, and the United States will produce 0 tons of maple syrup and 50 tons of honey. After both countries specialize, the United States could then trade 30 tons of honey to Canada in exchange for 40 tons of maple syrup. (Other mutually beneficial trades are possible as well.) We can summarize the results in a table:

	BEFORE TRADE		**AFTER TRADE**	
	HONEY (IN TONS)	**MAPLE SYRUP (IN TONS)**	**HONEY (IN TONS)**	**MAPLE SYRUP (IN TONS)**
CANADA	30	15	30	20
UNITED STATES	10	40	20	40

The United States is better off after trade because it can consume the same amount of maple syrup and 10 more tons of honey. Canada is better off after trade because it can consume the same amount of honey and 5 more tons of maple syrup.

Step 4: **Answer question (c) by drawing the *PPF*s.**

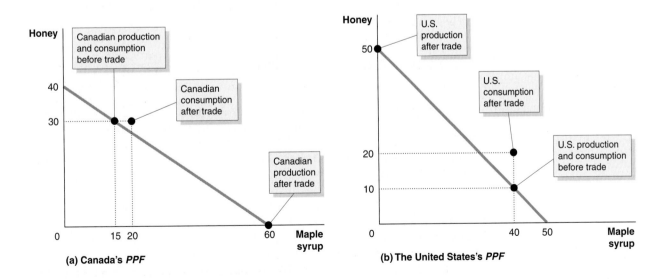

(a) Canada's *PPF*

(b) The United States's *PPF*

YOUR TURN: For more practice, do related problems 2.5 and 2.6 on pages 62 and 63 at the end of this chapter.

>> End Solved Problem 2-2

The Market System

We have seen that households, firms, and the government face trade-offs and incur opportunity costs because of the scarcity of resources. We have also seen that trade allows people to specialize according to their comparative advantage. By engaging in trade, people can raise their standard of living. Of course, trade in the modern world is much more complex than the examples we have considered so far. Trade today involves the decisions of millions of people spread around the world. But how does an economy make trade possible, and how are the decisions of these millions of people coordinated? In the United States and most other countries, trade is carried out in markets. Markets also determine the answers to the three fundamental questions discussed in Chapter 1: *What* goods and services will be produced? *How* will the goods and services be produced? and *Who* will receive the goods and services?

Market A group of buyers and sellers of a good or service and the institution or arrangement by which they come together to trade.

Recall that the definition of **market** is a group of buyers and sellers of a good or service and the institution or arrangement by which they come together to trade. Markets take many forms: They can be physical places, like a local pizza parlor or the New York Stock Exchange, or virtual places, like eBay. In a market, the buyers are demanders of goods or services, and the sellers are suppliers of goods or services. Households and firms interact in two types of markets: *product markets* and *factor markets*. **Product markets** are markets for goods—such as computers—and services—such as medical treatment. In product markets, households are demanders, and firms are suppliers. **Factor markets** are markets for the *factors of production*. **Factors of production** are the inputs used to make goods and services. Factors of production are divided into four broad categories:

Product markets Markets for goods—such as computers—and services—such as medical treatment.

Factor markets Markets for the factors of production, such as labor, capital, natural resources, and entrepreneurial ability.

Factors of production The inputs used to make goods and services.

- *Labor* includes all types of work, from the part-time labor of teenagers working at McDonald's to the work of top managers in large corporations.

- *Capital* refers to physical capital, such as computers and machine tools, that is used to produce other goods.

- *Natural resources* include land, water, oil, iron ore, and other raw materials (or "gifts of nature") that are used in producing goods.

- An *entrepreneur* is someone who operates a business. *Entrepreneurial ability* is the ability to bring together the other factors of production to successfully produce and sell goods and services.

The Circular Flow of Income

Two key groups participate in markets:

- A *household* consists of all the individuals in a home. Households are suppliers of factors of production—particularly labor—used by firms to make goods and services. Households use the income they receive from selling the factors of production to purchase the goods and services supplied by firms. We are used to thinking of households as suppliers of labor because most people earn most of their income by going to work, which means they are selling their labor services to firms in the labor market. But households own the other factors of production, as well, either directly or indirectly, by owning the firms that have these resources. All firms are owned by households. Small firms, like a neighborhood restaurant, might be owned by one person. Large firms, like Microsoft or BMW, are owned by millions of households who own shares of stock in them. (We discuss the stock market in Chapter 7.) When firms pay profits to the people who own them, the firms are paying for using the capital and natural resources that are supplied to them by those owners. So, we can generalize by saying that in factor markets, households are suppliers, and firms are demanders.

- *Firms* are suppliers of goods and services. Firms use the funds they receive from selling goods and services to buy the factors of production needed to make the goods and services.

We can use a simple economic model called the **circular-flow diagram** to see how participants in markets are linked. Figure 2-6 shows that in factor markets, households supply labor and other factors of production in exchange for wages and other payments from firms. In product markets, households use the payments they earn in factor markets to purchase the goods and services supplied by firms. Firms produce these goods and services using the factors of production supplied by households. In the figure, the blue arrows show the flow of factors of production from households through factor markets to firms. The red arrows show the flow of goods and services from firms through product markets to households. The green arrows show the flow of funds from firms through factor markets to households and the flow of spending from households through product markets to firms.

Like all economic models, the circular-flow diagram is a simplified version of reality. For example, Figure 2-6 leaves out the important role of government in buying goods from firms and in making payments, such as Social Security or unemployment insurance payments, to households. The figure also leaves out the roles played by banks, the stock and bond markets, and other parts of the *financial system* in aiding the flow of funds from lenders to borrowers. Finally, the figure does not show that some goods and services purchased by domestic households are produced in foreign countries and some goods and services produced by domestic firms are sold to foreign households. The government, the financial system, and the international sector are explored further in later chapters. Despite these simplifications, the circular-flow diagram in Figure 2-6 is useful for seeing how product markets, factor markets, and their participants are linked

Circular-flow diagram A model that illustrates how participants in markets are linked.

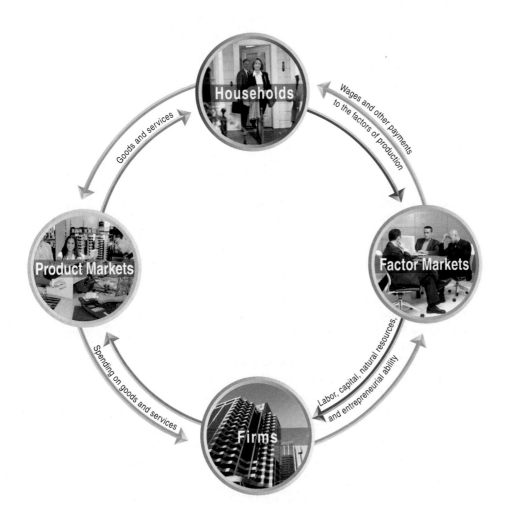

Figure 2-6

The Circular-Flow Diagram

Households and firms are linked together in a circular flow of production, income, and spending. The blue arrows show the flow of the factors of production. In factor markets, households supply labor, entrepreneurial ability, and other factors of production to firms. Firms use these factors of production to make goods and services that they supply to households in product markets. The red arrows show the flow of goods and services from firms to households. The green arrows show the flow of funds. In factor markets, households receive wages and other payments from firms in exchange for supplying the factors of production. Households use these wages and other payments to purchase goods and services from firms in product markets. Firms sell goods and services to households in product markets, and they use the funds to purchase the factors of production from households in factor markets.

together. One of the great mysteries of the market system is that it manages to success-fully coordinate the independent activities of so many households and firms.

The Gains from Free Markets

Free market A market with few government restrictions on how a good or service can be produced or sold or on how a factor of production can be employed.

A **free market** exists when the government places few restrictions on how a good or a service can be produced or sold or on how a factor of production can be employed. Governments in all modern economies intervene more than is consistent with a fully free market. In that sense, we can think of the free market as being a benchmark against which we can judge actual economies. There are relatively few government restrictions on economic activity in the United States, Canada, the countries of Western Europe, Hong Kong, Singapore, and Estonia. So these countries come close to the free market benchmark. In countries such as Cuba and North Korea, the free market system has been rejected in favor of centrally planned economies with extensive government control over product and factor markets. Countries that come closest to the free-market benchmark have been more successful than countries with centrally planned economies in providing their people with rising living standards.

The Scottish philosopher Adam Smith is considered the father of modern economics because his book *An Inquiry into the Nature and Causes of the Wealth of Nations*, published in 1776, was an early and very influential argument for the free market system. Smith was writing at a time when extensive government restrictions on markets were still very common. In many parts of Europe, the *guild system* still prevailed. Under this system, governments would give guilds, or organizations of producers, the authority to control the production of a good. For example, the shoemakers' guild controlled who was allowed to produce shoes, how many shoes they could produce, and what price they could charge. In France, the cloth makers' guild even dictated the number of threads in the weave of the cloth.

Smith argued that such restrictions reduced the income, or wealth, of a country and its people by restricting the quantity of goods produced. Some people at the time supported the restrictions of the guild system because it was in their financial interest to do so. If you were a member of a guild, the restrictions served to reduce the competition you faced. But other people sincerely believed that the alternative to the guild system was economic chaos. Smith argued that these people were wrong and that a country could enjoy a smoothly functioning economic system if firms were freed from guild restrictions.

The Market Mechanism

In Smith's day, defenders of the guild system worried that if, for instance, the shoemakers' guild did not control shoe production, either too many or too few shoes would be produced. Smith argued that prices would do a better job of coordinating the activities of buyers and sellers than the guilds could. A key to understanding Smith's argument is the assumption that *individuals usually act in a rational, self-interested way*. In particular, individuals take those actions most likely to make themselves better off financially. This assumption of rational, self-interested behavior underlies nearly all economic analysis. In fact, economics can be distinguished from other fields that study human behavior—such as sociology and psychology—by its emphasis on the assumption of self-interested behavior. Adam Smith understood—as economists today understand—that people's motives can be complex. But in analyzing people in the act of buying and selling, the motivation of financial reward usually provides the best explanation for the actions people take.

For example, suppose that a significant number of consumers switch from buying regular gasoline-powered cars to buying gasoline/electric-powered hybrid cars, such as the Toyota Prius, as in fact happened in the United States during the 2000s. Firms will find that they can charge relatively higher prices for hybrid cars than they can for regular cars. The self-interest of these firms will lead them to respond to consumers' wishes by producing more hybrids and fewer regular cars. Or suppose that consumers decide that they want to eat less bread, pasta, and other foods high in carbohydrates, as many did following the increase in popularity of the Atkins and South Beach diets. Then the prices firms can charge for bread and pasta will fall. The self-interest of firms will lead them to produce less bread and pasta, which in fact is what happened.

In the case where consumers want more of a product, and in the case where they want less of a product, the market system responds without a guild or the government giving orders about how much to produce or what price to charge. In a famous phrase, Smith said that firms would be led by the "invisible hand" of the market to provide consumers with what they wanted. Firms would respond to changes in prices by making decisions that ended up satisfying the wants of consumers.

Making the Connection | A Story of the Market System in Action: How Do You Make an iPod?

The iPod is a product of Apple, which has its headquarters in Cupertino, California. It seems reasonable to assume that iPods are also manufactured in California. In fact, Apple produces none of the components of the iPod, nor does it assemble the components into a finished product. Far from being produced entirely by one company in one place, the iPod requires the coordinated activities of thousands of workers and dozens of firms, spread around the world.

The market coordinates the activities of the many people spread around the world who contribute to the making of an iPod.

Several Asian firms, including Asustek, Inventec Appliances, and Foxconn, assemble the iPod, which is then shipped to Apple for sale in the United States. But the firms doing final assembly don't make any of the components. For example, the iPod's hard drive is manufactured by the Japanese firm, Toshiba, although Toshiba actually assembles the hard drive in factories in China and the Philippines. Apple purchases the controller chip that manages the iPod's functions from PortalPlayer, which is based in Santa Clara, California. But PortalPlayer actually has the chip manufactured for it by Taiwan Semiconductor Manufacturing Corporation, and the chip's processor core was designed by ARM, a British company. Taiwan Semiconductor Manufacturing Corporation's factories are for the most part not in Taiwan, but in mainland China and Eastern Europe.

All told, the iPod contains 451 parts, designed and manufactured by firms around the world. Many of these firms are not even aware of which other firms are also producing components for the iPod. Few of the managers of these firms have met managers of the other firms or shared knowledge of how their particular components are produced. In fact, no one person from Steve Jobs, the head of Apple, on down possesses the knowledge of how to produce all of the components that are assembled into an iPod. Instead, the invisible hand of the market has led these firms to contribute their knowledge to the process that ultimately results in an iPod available for sale in a store in the United States. Apple has so efficiently organized the process of producing the iPod that you can order a custom iPod with a personal engraving and have it delivered from an assembly plant in China to your doorstep in the United States in as little as three days.

Hal Varian, an economist at the University of California, Berkeley, has summarized the iPod story: "Those clever folks at Apple figured out how to combine 451 mostly generic parts into a valuable product. They may not make the iPod, but they created it."

Sources: Hal Varian, "An iPod Has Global Value. Ask the (Many) Countries That Make It," *New York Times*, June 28, 2007; and Greg Linden, Kenneth L. Kraemer, Jaon Dedrick, "Who Captures Value in a Global Innovation System? The Case of Apple's iPod," Personal Computing Industry Center, June 2007.

YOUR TURN: Test your understanding by doing related problem 3.8 on page 64 at the end of this chapter.

The Role of the Entrepreneur

Entrepreneurs are central to the working of the market system. An **entrepreneur** is someone who operates a business. Entrepreneurs must first determine what goods and services they believe consumers want, and then they must decide how to produce those goods and services most profitably. Entrepreneurs bring together the factors of production—labor, capital, and natural resources—to produce goods and services. They put their own funds

Entrepreneur Someone who operates a business, bringing together the factors of production—labor, capital, and natural resources—to produce goods and services.

at risk when they start businesses. If they are wrong about what consumers want or about the best way to produce goods and services, they can lose those funds. In fact, it is not unusual for entrepreneurs who eventually achieve great success to fail at first. For instance, early in their careers, both Henry Ford and Sakichi Toyoda, who eventually founded the Toyota Motor Corporation, started companies that quickly failed.

The Legal Basis of a Successful Market System

In a free market, government does not restrict how firms produce and sell goods and services or how they employ factors of production, but the absence of government intervention is not enough for a market system to work well. Government has to provide secure rights to private property for a market system to work at all. In addition, government can aid the working of the market by enforcing contracts between private individuals through an independent court system. Many economists would also say the government has a role in facilitating the development of an efficient financial system as well as systems of education, transportation, and communication. The protection of private property and the existence of an independent court system to impartially enforce the law provide a *legal environment* that will allow a market system to succeed.

Protection of Private Property For a market system to work well, individuals must be willing to take risks. Someone with $250,000 can be cautious and keep it safely in a bank—or even in cash, if the person doesn't trust the banking system. But the market system won't work unless a significant number of people are willing to risk their funds by investing them in businesses. Investing in businesses is risky in any country. Many businesses fail every year in the United States and other high-income countries. But in the high-income countries, someone who starts a new business or invests in an existing business doesn't have to worry that the government, the military, or criminal gangs might decide to seize the business or demand payments for not destroying the business. Unfortunately, in many poor countries, owners of businesses are not well protected from having their businesses seized by the government or from having their profits taken by criminals. Where these problems exist, opening a business can be extremely risky. Cash can be concealed easily, but a business is difficult to conceal and difficult to move.

Property rights The rights individuals or firms have to the exclusive use of their property, including the right to buy or sell it.

Property rights are the rights individuals or firms have to the exclusive use of their property, including the right to buy or sell it. Property can be tangible, physical property, such as a store or factory. Property can also be intangible, such as the right to an idea.

Two amendments to the U.S. Constitution guarantee property rights: The 5th Amendment states that the federal government shall not deprive any person "of life, liberty, or property, without due process of law." The 14th Amendment extends this guarantee to the actions of state governments: "No state . . . shall deprive any person of life, liberty, or property, without due process of law." Similar guarantees exist in every high-income country. Unfortunately, in many developing countries, such guarantees do not exist or are poorly enforced.

In any modern economy, *intellectual property rights* are very important. Intellectual property includes books, films, software, and ideas for new products or new ways of producing products. To protect intellectual property, the federal government grants a *patent* that gives an inventor—which is often a firm—the exclusive right to produce and sell a new product for a period of 20 years from the date the product was invented. For instance, because Microsoft has a patent on the Windows operating system, other firms cannot sell their own versions of Windows. The government grants patents to encourage firms to spend money on the research and development necessary to create new products. If other companies could freely copy Windows, Microsoft would not have spent the funds necessary to develop it. Just as a new product or a new method of making a product receives patent protection, books, films, and software receive *copyright* protection. Under U.S. law, the creator of a book, film, or piece of music has the exclusive right to use the creation during the creator's lifetime. The creator's heirs retain this exclusive right for 50 years after the death of the creator.

Making the Connection

Property Rights in Cyberspace: YouTube and MySpace

The development of the Internet has led to new problems in protecting intellectual property rights. People can copy and e-mail songs, newspaper and magazine articles, and even entire motion pictures and television programs or post them on Web sites. Controlling unauthorized copying is more difficult today than it was when "copying" meant making a physical copy of a book, CD, or DVD. The popularity of YouTube and MySpace highlights the problem of unauthorized copying of videos and music. YouTube, founded in 2005, quickly became an enormous success because it provided an easy way to upload videos, which could then be viewed by anyone with an Internet connection. By 2007, thousands of new videos were being uploaded each day, and the site was receiving more than 20 million visitors per month. YouTube earned substantial profits from selling online advertising. Unfortunately, many of the videos on the site contained copyrighted material.

At first, YouTube's policy was to remove any video containing unauthorized material if the holder of the copyright complained. Then YouTube began to negotiate with the copyright holders to pay a fee in return for allowing the copyrighted material to remain on the site. For music videos, YouTube was usually able to obtain the needed permission directly from the

Some recording artists worry that the copyrights for their songs are not being protected on the Internet.

recording company. Things were more complicated when videos on YouTube used copyrighted songs as background music. In those cases, YouTube needed to obtain permissions from the songwriters as well as the record company, which could be a time-consuming process. Obtaining permission to use videos that contained material from television shows or movies was even more complicated because sometimes dozens of people—including the actors, directors, and composers of music—held rights to the television show or movie. YouTube's vice president for business development was quoted as saying, "It's almost like technology has pushed far beyond the business practices and the law, and now everything needs to kind of catch up." In November 2006, YouTube agreed to be purchased by Google for $1.65 billion, which made the young entrepreneurs who started the company very wealthy. The willingness of YouTube's owners to sell their company to Google was motivated at least partly by the expectation that Google had the resources to help them resolve their copyright problems.

MySpace had similar problems because many Web pages on the site contained copyrighted music or videos. Universal Music sued MySpace after music from rapper Jay-Z's latest album started appearing on the site even before the album was released. In its lawsuit, Universal claimed that the illegal use of its copyrighted music had "created hundreds of millions of dollars of value for the owners of MySpace."

Music, television, and movie companies believe that the failure to give the full protection of property rights to the online use of their material reduces their ability to sell CDs and DVDs.

Sources: Kevin J. Delaney, Ethan Smith, and Brooks Barnes, "YouTube Finds Signing Rights Deals Complex, Frustrating," *Wall Street Journal*, November 3, 2006, p. B1; and Ethan Smith and Julia Angwin, "Universal Music Sues MySpace Claiming Copyright Infringement," *Wall Street Journal*, November 18, 2006, p. A3.

YOUR TURN: Test your understanding by doing related problem 3.14 on page 64 at the end of this chapter.

Enforcement of Contracts and Property Rights Much business activity involves someone agreeing to carry out some action in the future. For example, you may borrow $20,000 to buy a car and promise the bank—by signing a loan contract—that you will pay back the money over the next five years. Or Microsoft may sign a licensing agreement with a small technology company, agreeing to use that company's technology for a period of several years in return for a fee. Usually these agreements take the form of legal contracts. For a market system to work, businesses and individuals have to rely on these contracts being carried out. If one party to a legal contract does not fulfill its obligations—perhaps the small company had promised Microsoft exclusive use of its technology but then began licensing it to other companies—the other party could go to court to have the agreement enforced. Similarly, if property owners in the United States believe that the federal or state government has violated their rights under the 5th or 14th Amendments, they can go to court to have their rights enforced.

But going to court to enforce a contract or private property rights will be successful only if the court system is independent and judges are able to make impartial decisions on the basis of the law. In the United States and other high-income countries, the court systems have enough independence from other parts of the government and enough protection from intimidation by outside forces—such as criminal gangs—that they are able to make their decisions based on the law. In many developing countries, the court systems lack this independence and will not provide a remedy if the government violates private property rights or if a person with powerful political connections decides to violate a business contract.

If property rights are not well enforced, fewer goods and services will be produced. This reduces economic efficiency, leaving the economy inside its production possibilities frontier.

>> Continued from page 37

Economics in YOUR Life!

At the beginning of the chapter, we asked you to think about two questions: When buying a new car, what is the relationship between safety and gas mileage? and Under what circumstances would it be possible for car manufacturers to make cars safer and more fuel efficient? To answer the first question, you have to recognize that there is a trade-off between safety and gas mileage. With the technology available at any particular time, an automobile manufacturer can increase gas mileage by making a car smaller and lighter. But driving a lighter car increases your chances of being injured if you have an accident. The trade-off between safety and gas mileage would look much like the relationship in Figure 2-1. To get more of both safety and gas mileage, automobile makers would have to discover new technologies that allow them to make the car lighter and safer at the same time. Such new technologies would make points like *G* in Figure 2-1 attainable.

Conclusion

We have seen that by trading in markets, people are able to specialize and pursue their comparative advantage. Trading on the basis of comparative advantage makes all participants in trade better off. The key role of markets is to facilitate trade. In fact, the market system is a very effective means of coordinating the decisions of millions of consumers, workers, and firms. At the center of the market system is the consumer. To be successful, firms must respond to the desires of consumers. These desires are communicated to firms through prices. To explore how markets work, we must study the behavior of consumers and firms. We continue this exploration of markets in Chapter 3, when we develop the model of demand and supply.

Before moving on to Chapter 3, read *An Inside Look* on the next page to learn how BMW managers reallocate scarce resources in the firm's South Carolina plant to prepare to manufacture a new sports-activity coupe.

KNIGHT RIDDER TRIBUNE BUSINESS NEWS, JANUARY 25, 2007

Redesigned X5 to lead increase; new coupe to debut in 2008

BMW expects production to rise 58 percent this year, nearly reaching its record production of 2002 and ending the string of production declines since then. The plant's 4,500 workers [based in Spartanburg, South Carolina] are expected to make 165,000 vehicles this year, up from 104,632 in 2006, spokesman Bob Nitto said Wednesday. The redesigned X5 sport utility vehicle is expected to drive the increase, with its production nearly doubling to about 130,000 vehicles. Production of the Z4 and related coupes is expected to decline slightly to 35,000 cars, down from 38,756 last year.

And in 2008, the plant is expected to add a new coupe to the production line, one that BMW now refers to as a sports-activity coupe. The term is a variation of the moniker BMW adopted in 1999 for the X5—a sports-activity vehicle. The automotive press is referring to the new car as the BMW X6, the crossover vehicle company officials have said previously would be built at Greer.

But even with a third vehicle, plant employment is not likely to increase substantially, plant spokeswoman Bunny Richardson said. Production workers at the plant earn about $25 to $26 per hour.

Richardson and Nitto spoke with about a dozen area journalists allowed to see the plant for the first time since November 2005. That winter, the facility was shut down for two months as its separate assembly lines for the X5 and Z4 were merged into a single line.

One reason for the change was the increasing imbalance in production. The Z4s are smaller cars with fewer parts than the large, complex X5s. Also, Z4 sales have flattened, while X5 sales have risen. As a result, X5s are expected to account for 80 percent of the cars made at the plant this year.

The plant continues to become more dense. When it opened in 1994, aisles were wide and heavy equipment thin. Now many parts move overhead, and robots have become more numerous.

The appearance has changed as the plant's production has climbed:

- At the end of 1995, the first full year of production, the plant had 1,556 workers and made 13,943 cars, or about nine cars per worker.

- At the end of 2000—the first full year of production of the original X5—the plant had 4,058 workers and made 83,672 vehicles, about 21 vehicles per worker.

- Production peaked in 2003, when the plant's work force swelled to 4,700, making 166,090 vehicles, or about 35 per worker.

- This year, the plant is expected to exceed 2003 in productivity, with production of 37 cars per worker.

This will be all the more challenging because of the size and complexity of the new X5, which first reached U.S. dealers in November, and is being rolled out to the European market this year. The X5 is filled with gizmos designed to allow it to shift from trips to the grocery store to fording creeks. Even the tires are complex: Run-flat tires now are standard equipment. Those supplied by Michelin are made at its Lexington plant, Richardson said.

Journalists were allowed to test the cars driving on a test track and off-road trail near the plant. Some versions carried an option that BMW calls Active Steering, a form of power steering that varies response depending on speed.

In a parking lot, only a slight motion is needed to steer into a space, while at higher speeds, sharp turns require more turning.

"You don't want to sneeze and change lanes," said Larry Parmele, a 55-year-old former race car driver and instructor at BMW's Performance Center test tracks in Greer.

Source: Jim Duplessis, "BMW Expects Turnaround," Knight Ridder Tribune Business News, January 25, 2007, p.1. Reprinted by permission of the Permissions Group.

Key Points in the Article

The article discusses the trade-offs that BMW managers face when making production decisions, given the size of the manufacturing plant and the technology used at the plant. The article also points out that these production decisions depend on the characteristics of the cars being produced, the number of workers at the plant, the technology of production, and the sales of the different car models.

Analyzing the News

a BMW plans to produce about 60,000 more automobiles at the Spartanburg, South Carolina plant during 2007. Even though the total number of automobiles produced is going to increase, BMW is going to cut back on the production of the Z4 and other coupes. Figure 1 shows the increase in total production as a movement toward the production possibilities frontier. Notice that even though BMW is producing more automobiles, it is choosing to produce fewer coupes, so total production of coupes is declining as the production at the plant is moving toward the frontier.

b Production at plants frequently responds to changes in the marketplace. If sales of one model decline, then automobile companies often reduce production of that model and expand production of the models that are selling. At this plant, production of the Z4 model is declining, while production of the X5 model is expanding. These changes in production decisions are a direct response to changes in the sales of these models. In addition, managers sometimes have to stop production so that they can retool the plant. In this case, managers closed the plant for two months during 2005, so that they could introduce a new assembly line that produced both the X5 and Z4 models. This allowed the managers to expand production at the plant and make it easier to introduce a new "sports-activity coupe" model that will begin production in 2008. The managers may have to close the plant again to prepare for production of the new sports-activity couple. In effect, the managers would be giving up production of existing models in 2007 while the plant is closed so that they can increase production of the new model in the future. Sometimes the trade-offs that managers face are trade-offs between the present and the future.

c As the demand for BMW models has increased, the automobile factory has changed. Managers introduced more machinery and workers and changed the layout of the factory. Moving the X5 and Z4 to the same assembly line so the plant can produce the new sports-activity coupe model is just the latest in a long line of changes that the managers have made. These changes provide the plant with more resources for producing BMW cars. We show this by shifting out the production possibilities frontier in Figure 2. You should also notice that as output at the plant expanded, BMW increased employment and the number of robots. As output at a firm or a plant expands, BMW tends to use more of all types of inputs, including labor.

Thinking Critically

1. Launching the new sports-activity coupe may require that the BMW managers shut down the Spartanburg plant for some period. Besides the direct costs of installing a new assembly line and new machinery, what would be the costs to BMW of shutting down the plant for a period of months? If shutting down the plant is costly, why would BMW do it?

2. Some BMWs are made in Germany, some in South Carolina, and some in other places. Should the United States government encourage the domestic production of BMWs by banning imports of BMWs?

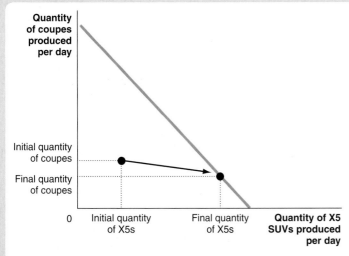

Figure 1. The increase in production at the plant in 2008.

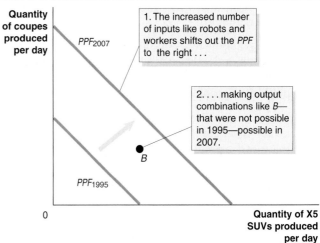

Figure 2. The effect of increasing inputs on output at the plant.

Key Terms

2.1 LEARNING OBJECTIVE   2.1 | Use a production possibilities frontier to analyze opportunity costs and trade-offs, pages 38–44.

Production Possibilities Frontiers and Opportunity Costs

Summary

The **production possibilities frontier** (*PPF*) is a curve that shows the maximum attainable combinations of two products that may be produced with available resources. The *PPF* is used to illustrate the trade-offs that arise from **scarcity**. Points on the frontier are technically efficient. Points inside the frontier are inefficient, and points outside the frontier are unattainable. The **opportunity cost** of any activity is the highest valued alternative that must be given up to engage in that activity. Because of increasing marginal opportunity costs, production possibilities frontiers are usually bowed out rather than straight lines. This illustrates the important economic concept that the more resources that are already devoted to any activity, the smaller the payoff to devoting additional resources to that activity is likely to be. **Economic growth** is illustrated by shifting a production possibilities frontier outward.

myeconlab   Visit www.myeconlab.com to complete these exercises
Get Ahead of the Curve online and get instant feedback.

Review Questions

1.1 What do economists mean by scarcity? Can you think of anything that is not scarce according to the economic definition?

1.2 What is a production possibilities frontier? How can we show economic efficiency on a production possibilities frontier? How can we show inefficiency? What causes a production possibilities frontier to shift outward?

1.3 What does increasing marginal opportunity costs mean? What are the implications of this idea for the shape of the production possibilities frontier?

Problems and Applications

1.4 Draw a production possibilities frontier that shows the trade-off between the production of cotton and the production of soybeans.
  a. Show the effect that a prolonged drought would have on the initial production possibilities frontier.

  b. Suppose genetic modification makes soybeans resistant to insects, allowing yields to double. Show the effect of this technological change on the initial production possibilities frontier.

1.5 (Related to the *Chapter Opener* on page 36) One of the trade-offs BMW faces is between safety and gas mileage. For example, adding steel to a car makes it safer but also heavier, which results in lower gas mileage. Draw a hypothetical production possibilities frontier that BMW engineers face that shows this trade-off.

1.6 Suppose you win free tickets to a movie plus all you can eat at the snack bar for free. Would there be a cost to you to attend this movie? Explain.

1.7 Suppose we can divide all the goods produced by an economy into two types: consumption goods and capital goods. Capital goods, such as machinery, equipment, and computers, are goods used to produce other goods.
  a. Use a production possibilities frontier graph to illustrate the trade-off to an economy between producing consumption goods and producing capital goods. Is it likely that the production possibilities frontier in this situation would be a straight line (as in Figure 2-1 on page 39) or bowed out (as in Figure 2-2 on page 42)? Briefly explain.

  b. Suppose a technological advance occurs that affects the production of capital goods but not consumption goods. Show the effect on the production possibilities frontier.

  c. Suppose that country A and country B currently have identical production possibilities frontiers but that country A devotes only 5 percent of its resources to producing capital goods over each of the next 10 years, whereas country B devotes 30 percent. Which country is likely to experience more rapid economic growth in the future? Illustrate using a production possibilities frontier graph. Your graph should include production possibilities frontiers for country A today and in 10 years and production possibilities frontiers for country B today and in 10 years.

1.8 Use the production possibilities frontier for a country to answer the following questions.

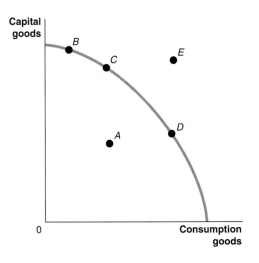

a. Which point(s) are unattainable? Briefly explain why.
b. Which point(s) are efficient? Briefly explain why.
c. Which point(s) are inefficient? Briefly explain why.
d. At which point is the country's future growth rate likely to be the highest? Briefly explain why.

1.9 (Related to *Solved Problem 2-1* on page 40) You have exams in economics and chemistry coming up and five hours available for studying. The following table shows the trade-offs you face in allocating the time you will spend in studying each subject.

	HOURS SPENT STUDYING		MIDTERM SCORE	
CHOICE	ECONOMICS	CHEMISTRY	ECONOMICS	CHEMISTRY
A	5	0	95	70
B	4	1	93	78
C	3	2	90	84
D	2	3	86	88
E	1	4	81	90
F	0	5	75	91

a. Use the data in the table to draw a production possibilities frontier graph. Label the vertical axis "Score on economics exam" and label the horizontal axis "Score on chemistry exam." Make sure to label the values where your production possibilities frontier intersects the vertical and horizontal axes.
b. Label the points representing choice *C* and choice *D*. If you are at choice *C*, what is your opportunity cost of increasing your chemistry score?
c. Under what circumstances would *A* be a sensible choice?

1.10 (Related to the *Making the Connection* on page 41) Suppose the president is attempting to decide whether the federal government should spend more on research to find a cure for heart disease. He asks you, one of his economic advisors, to prepare a report discussing the relevant factors he should consider. Discuss the main issues you would deal with in your report.

1.11 Lawrence Summers served as secretary of the treasury in the Clinton administration and later as the president of Harvard University. He has been quoted as giving the following moral defense of the economic approach:

> There is nothing morally unattractive about saying: We need to analyze which way of spending money on health care will produce more benefit and which less, and using our money as efficiently as we can. I don't think there is anything immoral about seeking to achieve environmental benefits at the lowest possible costs.

Would it be more moral to reduce pollution without worrying about the cost or by taking the cost into account? Briefly explain.

Source: David Wessel, "Precepts from Professor Summers," *Wall Street Journal*, October 17, 2002.

1.12 In *The Wonderful Wizard of Oz* and his other books about the Land of Oz, L. Frank Baum observed that if people's wants were modest enough, most goods would not be scarce. According to Baum, this was the case in Oz:

> There were no poor people in the Land of Oz, because there was no such thing as money. . . . Each person was given freely by his neighbors whatever he required for his use, which is as much as anyone may reasonably desire. Some tilled the lands and raised great crops of grain, which was divided equally among the whole population, so that all had enough. There were many tailors and dressmakers and shoemakers and the like, who made things that any who desired them might wear. Likewise there were jewelers who made ornaments for the person, which pleased and beautified the people, and these ornaments also were free to those who asked for them. Each man and woman, no matter what he or she produced for the good of the community, was supplied by the neighbors with food and clothing and a house and furniture and ornaments and games. If by chance the supply ever ran short, more was taken from the great storehouses of the Ruler, which were afterward filled up again when there was more of any article than people needed. . . .

You will know, by what I have told you here, that the Land of Oz was a remarkable country. I do not suppose such an arrangement would be practical with us.

Do you agree with Baum that the economic system in Oz wouldn't work in the contemporary United States? Briefly explain why or why not.

Source: L. Frank Baum, *The Emerald City of Oz*, pp. 30–31. First edition published in 1910.

>> End Learning Objective 2.1

2.2 LEARNING OBJECTIVE   2.2 | Understand comparative advantage and explain how it is the basis for trade, pages 44–49.

Comparative Advantage and Trade

Summary

Fundamentally, markets are about **trade**, which is the act of buying or selling. People trade on the basis of comparative advantage. An individual, a firm, or a country has a **comparative advantage** in producing a good or service if it can produce the good or service at the lowest opportunity cost. People are usually better off specializing in the activity for which they have a comparative advantage and trading for the other goods and services they need. It is important not to confuse comparative advantage with absolute advantage. An individual, a firm, or a country has an **absolute advantage** in producing a good or service if it can produce more of that good or service from the same amount of resources. It is possible to have an absolute advantage in producing a good or service without having a comparative advantage.

myeconlab Visit www.myeconlab.com to complete these exercises
Get Ahead of the Curve online and get instant feedback.

Review Questions

2.1 What is absolute advantage? What is comparative advantage? Is it possible for a country to have a comparative advantage in producing a good without also having an absolute advantage? Briefly explain.

2.2 What is the basis for trade? What advantages are there to specialization?

Problems and Applications

2.3 Look again at the information in Figure 2-4 on page 45. Choose a rate of trading cherries for apples different than the rate used in the text (15 pounds of cherries for 10 pounds of apples) that will allow you and your neighbor to benefit from trading apples and cherries. Prepare a table like Table 2-1 on page 46 to illustrate your answer.

2.4 Using the same amount of resources, the United States and Canada can both produce lumberjack shirts and lumberjack boots, as shown in the following production possibilities frontiers.

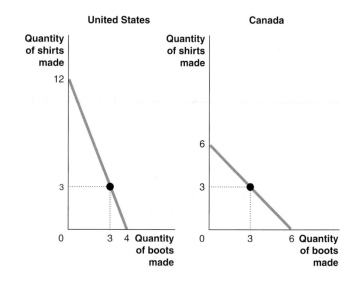

a. Who has a comparative advantage in producing lumberjack boots? Who has a comparative advantage in producing lumberjack shirts? Explain your reasoning.

b. Does either country have an absolute advantage in producing both goods? Explain.

c. Suppose that both countries are currently producing three pairs of boots and three shirts. Show that both can be better off if they specialize in producing one good and then engage in trade.

2.5 (Related to *Solved Problem 2-2* on page 48) Suppose Iran and Iraq both produce oil and olive oil. The following table shows combinations of both goods that each country can produce in a day, measured in thousands of barrels.

IRAQ		IRAN	
OIL	OLIVE OIL	OIL	OLIVE OIL
0	8	0	4
2	6	1	3
4	4	2	2
6	2	3	1
8	0	4	0

a. Who has the comparative advantage in producing oil? Explain.

b. Can these two countries gain from trading oil and olive oil? Explain.

2.6 (Related to *Solved Problem 2-2* on page 48) Suppose that France and Germany both produce schnitzel and wine. The following table shows combinations of the goods that each country can produce in a day.

FRANCE		GERMANY	
WINE (BOTTLES)	SCHNITZEL (POUNDS)	WINE (BOTTLES)	SCHNITZEL (POUNDS)
0	8	0	15
1	6	1	12
2	4	2	9
3	2	3	6
4	0	4	3
		5	0

a. Who has a comparative advantage in producing wine? Who has a comparative advantage in producing schnitzel?

b. Suppose that France is currently producing 1 bottle of wine and 6 pounds of schnitzel, and Germany is currently producing 3 bottles of wine and 6 pounds of schnitzel. Demonstrate that France and Germany can both be better off if they specialize in producing only one good and then engage in trade.

2.7 (Related to *Don't Let This Happen to You!* on page 48) In the 1950s, the economist Bela Balassa compared 28 manufacturing industries in the United States and Britain. In every one of the 28 industries, Balassa found that the United States had an absolute advantage. In these circumstances, would there have been any gain to the United States from importing any of these products from Britain? Explain.

2.8 In colonial America, the population was spread thinly over a large area, and transportation costs were very high because it was difficult to ship products by road for more than short distances. As a result, most of the free population lived on small farms where they not only grew their own food but also usually made their own clothes and very rarely bought or sold anything for money. Explain why the incomes of these farmers were likely to rise as transportation costs fell. Use the concept of comparative advantage in your answer.

2.9 During the 1928 presidential election campaign, Herbert Hoover, the Republican candidate, argued that the United States should only import those products that could not be produced here. Do you believe that this would be a good policy? Explain.

>> **End Learning Objective 2.2**

2.3 LEARNING OBJECTIVE 2.3 | Explain the basic idea of how a market system works, **pages 50–56.**

The Market System

Summary

A **market** is a group of buyers and sellers of a good or service and the institution or arrangement by which they come together to trade. **Product markets** are markets for goods and services, such as computers and medical treatment. **Factor markets** are markets for the **factors of production**, such as labor, capital, natural resources, and entrepreneurial ability. A **circular-flow diagram** shows how participants in product markets and factor markets are linked. Adam Smith argued in his 1776 book *The Wealth of Nations* that in a **free market** where the government does not control the production of goods and services, changes in prices lead firms to produce the goods and services most desired by consumers. If consumers demand more of a good, its price will rise. Firms respond to rising prices by increasing production. If consumers demand less of a good, its price will fall. Firms respond to falling prices by producing less of a good. An **entrepreneur** is someone who operates a business. In a market system, entrepreneurs are responsible for organizing the production of goods and services. A market system will work well only if there is protection for **property rights**, which are the rights of individuals and firms to use their property.

myeconlab Visit www.myeconlab.com to complete these exercises Get Ahead of the Curve online and get instant feedback.

Review Questions

3.1 What is the circular-flow diagram, and what does it demonstrate?

3.2 What are the two main categories of participants in markets? Which participants are of greatest importance in determining what goods and services are produced?

3.3 What is a free market? In what ways does a free market economy differ from a centrally planned economy?

3.4 What is an entrepreneur? Why do entrepreneurs play a key role in a market system?

3.5 Under what circumstances are firms likely to produce more of a good or service? Under what circumstances are firms likely to produce less of a good or service?

3.6 What are private property rights? What role do they play in the working of a market system? Why are independent courts important for a well-functioning economy?

Problems and Applications

3.7 Identify whether each of the following transactions will take place in the factor market or in the product market and whether households or firms are supplying the good or service or demanding the good or service:
  a. George buys a BMW X5 SUV.
  b. BMW increases employment at its Spartanburg plant.
  c. George works 20 hours per week at McDonald's.
  d. George sells land he owns to McDonald's so it can build a new restaurant.

3.8 **(Related to the *Making the Connection* on page 53)** In *The Wealth of Nations*, Adam Smith wrote the following (Book I, Chapter II): "It is not from the benevolence of the butcher, the brewer, or the baker, that we expect our dinner, but from their regard to their own interest." Briefly discuss what he meant by this.

3.9 In a commencement address to economics graduates at the University of Texas, Robert McTeer, Jr., who was then the president of the Federal Reserve Bank of Dallas, argued, "For my money, Adam Smith's invisible hand is the most important thing you've learned by studying economics." What's so important about the idea of the invisible hand?

Source: Robert D. McTeer, Jr., "The Dismal Science? Hardly!" *Wall Street Journal*, June 4, 2003.

3.10 Evaluate the following argument: "Adam Smith's analysis is based on a fundamental flaw: He assumes that people are motivated by self-interest. But this isn't true. I'm not selfish, and most people I know aren't selfish."

3.11 Writing in the *New York Times*, Michael Lewis argued that "a market economy is premised on a system of incentives designed to encourage an ignoble human trait: self-interest." Do you agree that self-interest is an "ignoble human trait"? What incentives does a market system provide to encourage self-interest?

Source: Michael Lewis, "In Defense of the Boom," *New York Times*, October 27, 2002.

3.12 An editorial in *BusinessWeek* magazine offered this opinion: "Economies should be judged on a simple measure: their ability to generate a rising standard of living for all members of society, including people at the bottom." Briefly discuss whether you agree.

Source: "Poverty: The Bigger Picture," *BusinessWeek*, October 7, 2002.

3.13 An estimated 400 million to 600 million people worldwide are squatters who live on land to which they have no legal title, usually on the outskirts of cities in developing countries. Economist Hernando de Soto persuaded Peru's government to undertake a program to make it cheap and easy for such squatters to obtain a title to the land they had been occupying. How would this creation of property rights be likely to affect the economic opportunities available to these squatters?

Source: Alan B. Krueger, "A Study Looks at Squatters and Land Title in Peru," *New York Times*, January 9, 2003.

3.14 **(Related to the *Making the Connection* on page 55)** A columnist for the *Wall Street Journal* argued that most copyright holders are not damaged by having their material shown on YouTube:

> It's [laughable] to suggest that content owners are hurt by videos of teenagers lip-synching to hip-hop songs, that the market for sports DVDs is destroyed by fans being allowed to relive a team's great moment, or that artists reusing footage of famous televised events destroys interest in documentaries.

Do you agree with the argument that the copyright owners of the material mentioned should not be paid a fee if their material is on YouTube? Are there other types of material not mentioned by this columnist with which the copyright holders might suffer significant financial damages by having their material available on YouTube?

Source: Jason Fry, "The Revolution May Be Briefly Televised," *Wall Street Journal*, November 13, 2006.

>> End Learning Objective 2.3

Where Prices Come From: The Interaction of Demand and Supply

Apple and the Demand for iPods

During the last three months of 2006, Apple sold $3.43 billion worth of iPods. iPods seemed to be everywhere, but during 2007 it became clear that the market for digital music players was becoming much more competitive.

Steve Jobs and Steve Wozniak started Apple in 1976. Working out of Jobs's parents' garage, the two friends created the Apple I computer. By 1980, although Jobs was still only in his mid-twenties, Apple had become the first firm in history to join the Fortune 500 list of largest U.S. firms in less than five years. Apple's success in the computer business has been up and down, but when the company introduced the iPod digital music player in 2001, it had a runaway success on its hands. The most obvious reasons for the iPod's success are its ease of use and sleek design. But also important has been iTunes, Apple's online music store. Apple decided to offer individual songs, as well as whole albums, for download at a price of just $0.99 per song. After paying a royalty to the record company, Apple makes very little profit from the songs it sells on iTunes. Apple was willing to accept a small profit on the sale of each song to make the purchase of the iPod more attractive to consumers.

At a price of several hundred dollars, the iPod might be relatively expensive, but purchasing the music is very inexpensive. In addition, the songs on iTunes are playable only on iPods, and iPods can only play songs downloaded from iTunes (although with enough technical skill, it's possible to get around both restrictions). So, owners of other digital music players do not have easy access to iTunes, and iPod owners have little incentive to download music from other online sites. In addition, because Apple makes the iPod and owns iTunes, the two systems work smoothly together, which is not the case for many of Apple's competitors. Microsoft's Vice President Bryan Lee says, "That's something that Apple has played up very well. One brand, one device, one service."

By early 2007, more than 100 million iPods had been sold and more than 2 billion songs had been downloaded from iTunes. Clearly, the strategy of selling an expensive digital music player and selling the music cheaply has been very successful for Apple. But how long will the iPod's dominance last? By 2007, competitors were flooding into the market. New digital music players, such as Microsoft's Zune, Toshiba's Gigabeat, and iRiver's H10, among many others, were rapidly gaining customers. In addition, firms were introducing new "music phones" that combined the features of a cell phone with the features of a digital music player. Although this wave of competition might be bad news for Apple, it could be good news for consumers by increasing the choices available and lowering prices. **AN INSIDE LOOK** on **page 90** discusses how Apple responded to competition by teaming with AT&T to create its own music phone, the iPhone.

Sources: Nick Wingfield and Robert Guth, "iPod, TheyPod: Rivals Imitate Apple's Success," *Wall Street Journal*, September 18, 2006, p. B1; and Nick Wingfield, "iPod Demand Lifts Apple's Results," *Wall Street Journal*, January 18, 2007, p. A2.

LEARNING Objectives

After studying this chapter, you should be able to:

3.1 Discuss the variables that influence **demand** page 68.

3.2 Discuss the variables that influence **supply**, page 75.

3.3 Use a graph to illustrate **market equilibrium** page 79.

3.4 Use **demand and supply graphs** to predict changes in prices and quantities, page 83.

Economics in YOUR Life!

Will you buy an iPod or a Zune?

Suppose you are about to buy a new digital music player and that you are choosing between Apple's iPod and Microsoft's Zune. As the industry leader, the iPod has many advantages over a new entrant like Zune. One strategy Microsoft can use to overcome those advantages is to compete based on price. Would you choose a Zune if it had a lower price than a comparable iPod? Would you choose a Zune if the songs sold on Zune Marketplace were cheaper than the songs sold on iTunes? As you read the chapter, see if you can answer these questions. You can check your answers against those we provide at the end of the chapter. ▶▶ **Continued on page 89**

I n Chapter 1, we explored how economists use models to predict human behavior. In Chapter 2, we used the model of production possibilities frontiers to analyze scarcity and trade-offs. In this chapter and the next, we explore the model of demand and supply, which is the most powerful tool in economics, and use it to explain how prices are determined.

Recall from Chapter 1 that economic models rely on assumptions and that these assumptions are simplifications of reality. In some cases, the assumptions of the model may not seem to describe exactly the economic situation being analyzed. For example, the model of demand and supply assumes that we are analyzing a *perfectly competitive market*. In a **perfectly competitive market**, there are many buyers and sellers, all the products sold are identical, and there are no barriers to new firms entering the market. These assumptions are very restrictive and apply exactly to only a few markets, such as the markets for wheat and other agricultural products. Experience has shown, however, that the model of demand and supply can be very useful in analyzing markets where competition among sellers is intense, even if there are relatively few sellers and the products being sold are not identical. In fact, in recent studies the model of demand and supply has been successful in analyzing markets with as few as four buyers and four sellers. In the end, the usefulness of a model depends on how well it can predict outcomes in a market. As we will see in this chapter, the model of demand and supply is often very useful in predicting changes in quantities and prices in many markets.

We begin considering the model of demand and supply by discussing consumers and the demand side of the market, then we turn to firms and the supply side. As you will see, we will apply this model throughout this book to understand business, the economy, and economic policy.

Perfectly competitive market
A market that meets the conditions of (1) many buyers and sellers, (2) all firms selling identical products, and (3) no barriers to new firms entering the market.

3.1 LEARNING OBJECTIVE

3.1 | Discuss the variables that influence demand.

The Demand Side of the Market

Chapter 2 explained that in a market system, consumers ultimately determine which goods and services will be produced. The most successful businesses are the ones that respond best to consumer demand. But what determines consumer demand for a product? Certainly, many factors influence the willingness of consumers to buy a particular product. For example, consumers who are considering buying a digital music player, such as Apple's iPod or Microsoft's Zune, will make their decisions based on, among other factors, the income they have available to spend and the effectiveness of the advertising campaigns of the companies that sell digital music players. The main factor in consumer decisions, though, will be the price of the digital music player. So, it makes sense to begin with price when analyzing the decisions of consumers to buy a product. It is important to note that when we discuss demand, we are considering not what a consumer *wants* to buy but what the consumer is both willing and *able* to buy.

Demand Schedules and Demand Curves

Tables that show the relationship between the price of a product and the quantity of the product demanded are called **demand schedules**. The table in Figure 3-1 shows the number of players consumers would be willing to buy over the course of a month at five different prices. The amount of a good or a service that a consumer is willing and able to purchase at a given price is referred to as the **quantity demanded**. The graph in Figure 3-1 plots the numbers from the table as a **demand curve**, a curve that shows the relationship between the price of a product and the quantity of the product demanded. (Note that for convenience, we made the demand curve in Figure 3-1 a straight line, or linear. There is no reason that all demand curves need to be straight lines.) The demand curve in Figure 3-1 shows the **market demand**, or the demand by all the consumers of a

Demand schedule A table showing the relationship between the price of a product and the quantity of the product demanded.

Quantity demanded The amount of a good or service that a consumer is willing and able to purchase at a given price.

Demand curve A curve that shows the relationship between the price of a product and the quantity of the product demanded.

Market demand The demand by all the consumers of a given good or service.

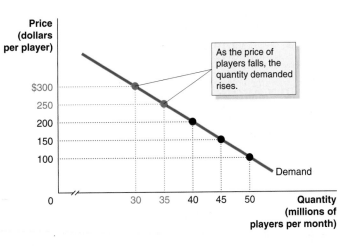

Demand Schedule	
Price (dollars per player)	Quantity (millions of players per month)
$300	30
250	35
200	40
150	45
100	50

As the price of players falls, the quantity demanded rises.

Demand

Figure 3-1

A Demand Schedule and Demand Curve

As the price changes, consumers change the quantity of digital music players they are willing to buy. We can show this as a *demand schedule* in a table or as a *demand curve* on a graph. The table and graph both show that as the price of players falls, the quantity demanded rises. When the price of a player is $300, consumers buy 30 million. When the price drops to $250, consumers buy 35 million. Therefore, the demand curve for digital music players is downward sloping.

given good or service. The market for a product, such as restaurant meals, that is purchased locally would include all the consumers in a city or a relatively small area. The market for a product that is sold internationally, such as digital music players, would include all the consumers in the world.

The demand curve in Figure 3-1 slopes downward because consumers will buy more players as the price falls. When the price of players is $300, consumers buy 30 million players per month. If the price of players falls to $250, consumers buy 35 million players. Buyers demand a larger quantity of a product as the price falls because the product becomes less expensive relative to other products and because they can afford to buy more at a lower price.

The Law of Demand

The inverse relationship between the price of a product and the quantity of the product demanded is known as the **law of demand**: Holding everything else constant, when the price of a product falls, the quantity demanded of the product will increase, and when the price of a product rises, the quantity demanded of the product will decrease. The law of demand holds for any market demand curve. Economists have never found an exception to it. In fact, Nobel Prize–winning economist George Stigler once remarked that the surest way for an economist to become famous would be to discover a market demand curve that sloped upward rather than downward.

Law of demand The rule that, holding everything else constant, when the price of a product falls, the quantity demanded of the product will increase, and when the price of a product rises, the quantity demanded of the product will decrease.

What Explains the Law of Demand?

It makes sense that consumers will buy more of a good when the price falls and less of a good when the price rises, but let's look more closely at why this is true. When the price of digital music players falls, consumers buy a larger quantity because of the *substitution effect* and the *income effect*.

Substitution Effect The **substitution effect** refers to the change in the quantity demanded of a good that results from a change in price, making the good more or less expensive *relative* to other goods that are *substitutes*. When the price of digital music players falls, consumers will substitute buying music players for buying other goods, such as radios or compact stereos.

Substitution effect The change in the quantity demanded of a good that results from a change in price, making the good more or less expensive relative to other goods that are substitutes.

The Income Effect The **income effect** of a price change refers to the change in the quantity demanded of a good that results from the effect of a change in the good's price on consumers' purchasing power. Purchasing power is the quantity of goods a consumer can buy with a fixed amount of income. When the price of a good falls, the increased purchasing power of consumers' incomes will usually lead them to purchase a larger quantity of the good. When the price of a good rises, the decreased purchasing power of consumers' incomes will usually lead them to purchase a smaller quantity of the good.

Note that although we can analyze them separately, the substitution effect and the income effect happen simultaneously whenever a price changes. Thus, a fall in the price

Income effect The change in the quantity demanded of a good that results from the effect of a change in the good's price on consumers' purchasing power.

of digital music players leads consumers to buy more players, both because the players are now cheaper relative to substitute products and because the purchasing power of the consumers' incomes has increased.

Holding Everything Else Constant: The *Ceteris Paribus* Condition

Notice that the definition of the law of demand contains the phrase *holding everything else constant.* In constructing the market demand curve for digital music players, we focused only on the effect that changes in the price of players would have on the quantity of players consumers would be willing and able to buy. We were holding constant other variables that might affect the willingness of consumers to buy players. Economists refer to the necessity of holding all variables other than price constant in constructing a demand curve as the **ceteris paribus** condition; *ceteris paribus* is Latin for "all else equal."

What would happen if we allowed a change in a variable—other than price—that might affect the willingness of consumers to buy music players? Consumers would then change the quantity they demand at each price. We can illustrate this effect by shifting the market demand curve. A shift of a demand curve is *an increase or a decrease in demand.* A movement along a demand curve is *an increase or a decrease in the quantity demanded.* As Figure 3-2 shows, we shift the demand curve to the right if consumers decide to buy more of the good at each price, and we shift the demand curve to the left if consumers decide to buy less at each price.

Variables That Shift Market Demand

Many variables other than price can influence market demand. These five are the most important:

- Income
- Prices of related goods
- Tastes
- Population and demographics
- Expected future prices

We next discuss how changes in each of these variables affect the market demand curve for digital music players.

Ceteris paribus ("all else equal") The requirement that when analyzing the relationship between two variables—such as price and quantity demanded—other variables must be held constant.

Figure 3-2

Shifting the Demand Curve

When consumers increase the quantity of a product they wish to buy at a given price, the market demand curve shifts to the right, from D_1 to D_2. When consumers decrease the quantity of a product they wish to buy at any given price, the demand curve shifts to the left, from D_1 to D_3.

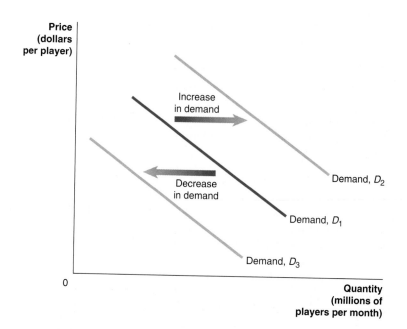

Income The income that consumers have available to spend affects their willingness and ability to buy a good. Suppose that the market demand curve in Figure 3-1 represents the willingness of consumers to buy digital music players when average household income is $43,000. If household income rises to $45,000, the demand for players will increase, which we show by shifting the demand curve to the right. A good is a **normal good** when demand increases following a rise in income and decreases following a fall in income. Most goods are normal goods, but the demand for some goods falls when income rises and rises when income falls. For instance, as your income rises, you might buy less canned tuna fish or fewer hot dogs and buy more shrimp or prime rib. A good is an **inferior good** when demand decreases following a rise in income and increases following a fall in income. So, for you hot dogs and tuna fish would be examples of inferior goods—not because they are of low quality but because you buy less of them as your income increases.

Normal good A good for which the demand increases as income rises and decreases as income falls.

Inferior good A good for which the demand increases as income falls and decreases as income rises.

Prices of Related Goods The prices of other goods can also affect consumers' demand for a product. Suppose that the market demand curve in Figure 3-1 represents the willingness and ability of consumers to buy digital music players during a year when the average price of compact stereos, such as the Bose Wave music system, is $500. If the average price of these stereo systems falls to $400, how will the market demand for digital music players change? Fewer players will be demanded at every price. We show this by shifting the demand curve for players to the left.

Goods and services that can be used for the same purpose—such as digital music players and compact stereos—are **substitutes**. When two goods are substitutes, the more you buy of one, the less you will buy of the other. A decrease in the price of a substitute causes the demand curve for a good to shift to the left. An increase in the price of a substitute causes the demand curve for a good to shift to the right.

Substitutes Goods and services that can be used for the same purpose.

Many consumers play songs downloaded from a Web site, such as iTunes or Zune Marketplace, on their digital music players. Suppose the market demand curve in Figure 3-1 represents the willingness of consumers to buy players at a time when the average price to download a song is $0.99. If the price to download a song falls to $0.49, consumers will buy more song downloads *and* more digital music players: The demand curve for music players will shift to the right.

Products that are used together—such as digital music players and song downloads—are **complements**. When two goods are complements, the more consumers buy of one, the more they will buy of the other. A decrease in the price of a complement causes the demand curve for a good to shift to the right. An increase in the price of a complement causes the demand curve for a good to shift to the left.

Complements Goods and services that are used together.

Making the Connection | Why Supermarkets Need to Understand Substitutes and Complements

Supermarkets sell what sometimes seems like a bewildering variety of goods. The first row of the following table shows the varieties of eight products stocked by five Chicago supermarkets.

	COFFEE	FROZEN PIZZA	HOT DOGS	ICE CREAM	POTATO CHIPS	REGULAR CEREAL	SPAGHETTI SAUCE	YOGURT
Varieties in five Chicago supermarkets	391	337	128	421	285	242	194	288
Varieties introduced in a 2-year period	113	109	47	129	93	114	70	107
Varieties removed in a 2-year period	135	86	32	118	77	75	36	51

Source: Juin-Kuan Chong, Teck-Hua Ho, and Christopher S. Tang, "A Modeling Framework for Category Assortment Planning," *Manufacturing & Service Operations Management*, 2001, Vol. 3, No. 3, pp. 191–210.

TABLE 3-1

Variables That Shift Market Demand Curves

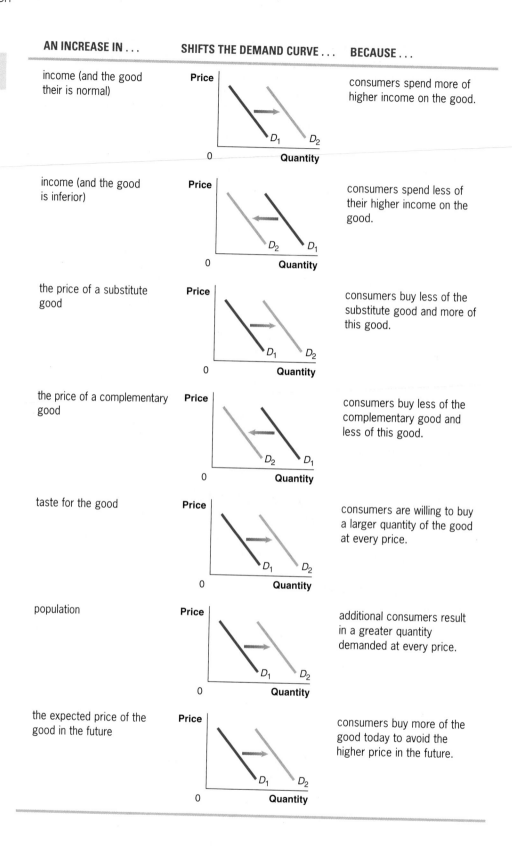

AN INCREASE IN . . .	SHIFTS THE DEMAND CURVE . . .	BECAUSE . . .
income (and the good their is normal)		consumers spend more of higher income on the good.
income (and the good is inferior)		consumers spend less of their higher income on the good.
the price of a substitute good		consumers buy less of the substitute good and more of this good.
the price of a complementary good		consumers buy less of the complementary good and less of this good.
taste for the good		consumers are willing to buy a larger quantity of the good at every price.
population		additional consumers result in a greater quantity demanded at every price.
the expected price of the good in the future		consumers buy more of the good today to avoid the higher price in the future.

point A to point B—an increase in quantity demanded from 30 million to 35 million. If consumers' incomes increase, or if another factor changes that makes consumers want more of the product at every price, the demand curve will shift to the right—an increase in demand. In this case, the increase in demand from D_1 to D_2 causes the quantity of digital music players demanded at a price of $300 to increase from 30 million at point A to 40 million at point C.

Making the Connection

Apple Forecasts the Demand for iPhones and other Consumer Electronics

Will Apple's iPhone match the success of its iPod?

One of the most important decisions that the managers of any large firm have to make is which new products to develop. A firm must devote people, time, and money to designing the product, negotiating with suppliers, formulating a marketing campaign, and many other tasks. But any firm has only limited resources and so faces a trade-off: Resources used to develop one product will not be available to develop another product. Ultimately, the products a firm chooses to develop will be those which it believes will be the most profitable. So, to decide which products to develop, firms need to forecast the demand for those products.

David Sobotta, who worked at Apple for 20 years, eventually becoming its national sales manager, has described the strategy Apple has used to decide which consumer electronics products will have the greatest demand. Sobotta describes discussions at Apple during 2002 about whether to develop a tablet personal computer. A tablet PC is a laptop with a special screen that allows the computer to be controlled with a stylus or pen and that has the capability of converting handwritten input into text. The previous year, Bill Gates, chairman of Microsoft, had predicted that "within five years . . . [tablet PCs] will be the most popular form of PC sold in America." Representatives of the federal government's National Institutes of Health also urged Apple to develop a tablet PC, arguing that it would be particularly useful to doctors, nurses, and hospitals. Apple's managers decided not to develop a tablet PC, however, because they believed the technology was too complex for the average computer user and did not believe that the demand from doctors and nurses would be very large. This forecast turned out to be correct. Despite Bill Gates's prediction, in 2006, tablets made up only 1 percent of the computer market, and they were forecast to increase to only 5 percent by 2009.

According to Sobotta, "Apple executives had a theory that the route to success will not be through selling thousands of relatively expensive things, but millions of very inexpensive things like iPods." In fact, although many business analysts were skeptical that the iPod would succeed, demand grew faster than even Apple's most optimistic forecasts. By the beginning of 2007, 100 million iPods had been sold. So, it was not very surprising when in early 2007, Apple Chief Executive Officer Steve Jobs announced that the company would be combining the iPod with a cell phone to create the iPhone. With more than 900 million cell phones sold each year, Apple expects the demand for the iPhone to be very large. As Sobotta noted, "And there's an 'Apple gap': mobile phone users often find their interfaces confusing. . . . Apple's unique ability to simplify while innovating looks like a good fit there."

Apple forecast that it would sell 10 million iPhones during the product's first year on the market, with much larger sales expected in future years. Time will tell whether Apple's forecast of a large demand for the iPhone will turn out to be correct.

Source: David Sobotta, "Technology: What Jobs Told Me on the iPhone," *The Guardian* (London), January 4, 2007, p. 1; and Connie Guglielmo, "Apple First-Quarter Profit Rises on iPod, Mac Sales," Bloomberg.com, January 17, 2007.

YOUR TURN: For more practice, do problem 1.10 on page 93 at the end of this chapter.

3.2 | Discuss the variables that influence supply.

The Supply Side of the Market

Just as many variables influence the willingness and ability of consumers to buy a particular good or service, many variables also influence the willingness and ability of firms to sell a good or service. The most important of these variables is price. The amount of a good or service that a firm is willing and able to supply at a given price is the **quantity supplied**. Holding other variables constant, when the price of a good rises, producing

Quantity supplied The amount of a good or service that a firm is willing and able to supply at a given price.

letters" and the other "Demand for Booth's letters." Make sure that the Lincoln demand curve is much farther to the right than the Booth demand curve.

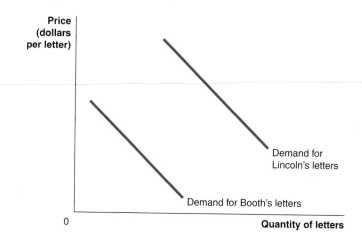

Step 3:   **Draw supply curves that illustrate the equilibrium price of Booth's letters being higher than the equilibrium price of Lincoln's letters.** Based on the demand curves you have just drawn, think about how it might be possible for the market price of Lincoln's letters to be lower than the market price of Booth's letters. The only way this can be true is if the supply of Lincoln's letters is much greater than the supply of Booth's letters. Draw on your graph a supply curve for Lincoln's letters and a supply curve for Booth's letters that will result in an equilibrium price of Booth's letters of $31,050 and an equilibrium price of Lincoln's letters of $21,850. You have now solved the problem.

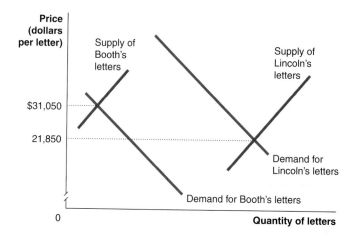

EXTRA CREDIT: The explanation for this puzzle is that both demand and supply count when determining market price. The demand for Lincoln's letters is much greater than the demand for Booth's letters, but the supply of Booth's letters is very small. Historians believe that only eight letters written by Booth exist today. (Note that the supply curves for letters written by Booth and by Lincoln slope up even though only a fixed number of each of these types of letters is available and, obviously, no more can be produced. The upward slope of the supply curves occurs because the higher the price, the larger the quantity of letters that will be offered for sale by people who currently own them.)

>> End Solved Problem 3-3

YOUR TURN: For more practice, do related problem 3.4 on page 94 at the end of this chapter.

3.4 LEARNING OBJECTIVE

The Effect of Demand and Supply Shifts on Equilibrium

We have seen that the interaction of demand and supply in markets determines the quantity of a good that is produced and the price at which it sells. We have also seen that several variables cause demand curves to shift, and other variables cause supply curves to shift. As a result, demand and supply curves in most markets are constantly shifting, and the prices and quantities that represent equilibrium are constantly changing. In this section, we see how shifts in demand and supply curves affect equilibrium price and quantity.

The Effect of Shifts in Supply on Equilibrium

When Microsoft decided to start selling the Zune music player, the market supply curve for music players shifted to the right. Figure 3-9 shows the supply curve shifting from S_1 to S_2. When the supply curve shifts to the right, there will be a surplus at the original equilibrium price, P_1. The surplus is eliminated as the equilibrium price falls to P_2, and the equilibrium quantity rises from Q_1 to Q_2. If existing firms exit the market, the supply curve will shift to the left, causing the equilibrium price to rise and the equilibrium quantity to fall.

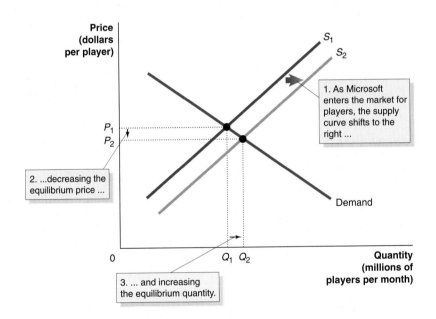

Figure 3-9

The Effect of an Increase in Supply on Equilibrium

If a firm enters a market, as Microsoft entered the market for digital music players when it launched the Zune, the equilibrium price will fall, and the equilibrium quantity will rise.

1. As Microsoft enters the market for digital music players, a larger quantity of players will be supplied at every price, so the market supply curve shifts to the right, from S_1 to S_2, which causes a surplus of players at the original price, P_1.
2. The equilibrium price falls from P_1 to P_2.
3. The equilibrium quantity rises from Q_1 to Q_2.

Making
the
Connection

The Falling Price of LCD Televisions

Research on flat-screen televisions using liquid crystal displays (LCDs) began in the 1960s. However, it was surprisingly difficult to use this research to produce a television priced low enough for many consumers to purchase. One researcher noted, "In the 1960s, we used to say 'In ten years, we're going to have the TV on the wall.' We said the same thing in the seventies and then in the eighties." A key technical problem in manufacturing LCD televisions was making glass sheets large enough, thin enough, and clean enough to be used as LCD screens. Finally, in 1999, Corning, Inc., developed a process to manufacture glass that was less than 1 millimeter thick and very clean because it was produced without being touched by machinery.

Corning's breakthrough led to what the *Wall Street Journal* described as a "race to build new, better factories." The firms producing the flat screens are all located in Taiwan, South Korea, and Japan. The leading firms are Korea's Samsung Electronics and LG Phillips LCD, Taiwan's AU Optronics, and Japan's Sharp Corporation. In 2004, AU Optronics opened a new factory with 2.4 million square feet of clean room in which the LCD screens are manufactured. This factory is nearly five times as large as the largest factory in which Intel makes computer chips. In all, 10 new factories manufacturing LCD screens came into operation between late 2004 and late 2005. The figure shows that this increase in supply drove the price of a typical large LCD television from $4,000 in the fall of 2004 to $1,600 at the end of 2006, increasing the quantity demanded worldwide from 8 million to 46 million.

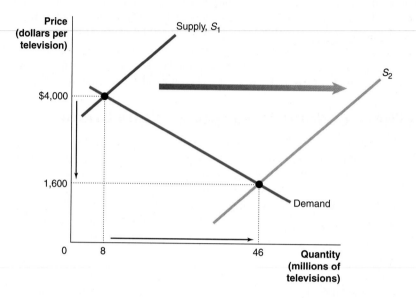

Sources: David Richards, "Sony and Panasonic Flat Screen Kings," Smarthouse.com, February 13, 2007; Evan Ramstad, "Big Display: Once a Footnote, Flat Screens Grow into Huge Industry," *Wall Street Journal*, August 30, 2004, p. A1; and Michael Schuman, "Flat Chance: Prices on Cool TVs Are Dropping as New Factories Come on Line," *Time*, October 18, 2004, pp. 64–66.

YOUR TURN: For more practice, do problem 4.7 on page 95 at the end of this chapter.

The Effect of Shifts in Demand on Equilibrium

When population growth and income growth occur, the market demand for music players shifts to the right. Figure 3-10 shows the effect of a demand curve shifting to the right, from D_1 to D_2. This shift causes a shortage at the original equilibrium price, P_1. To eliminate the shortage, the equilibrium price rises to P_2, and the equilibrium quantity

Figure 3-10

The Effect of an Increase in Demand on Equilibrium

Increases in income and population will cause the equilibrium price and quantity to rise:

1. As population and income grow, the quantity demanded increases at every price, and the market demand curve shifts to the right, from D_1 to D_2, which causes a shortage of digital music players at the original price, P_1.
2. The equilibrium price rises from P_1 to P_2.
3. The equilibrium quantity rises from Q_1 to Q_2.

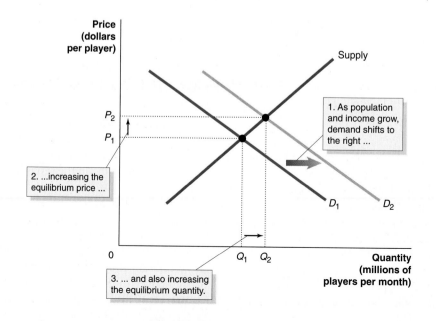

rises from Q_1 to Q_2. By contrast, if the price of a complementary good, such as downloads from music Web sites, were to rise, the demand for music players would decrease. This change would cause the demand curve for players to shift to the left, and the equilibrium price and quantity would both decrease.

The Effect of Shifts in Demand and Supply over Time

Whenever only demand or only supply shifts, we can easily predict the effect on equilibrium price and quantity. But what happens if *both* curves shift? For instance, in many markets, the demand curve shifts to the right over time, as population and income grow. The supply curve also often shifts to the right as new firms enter the market and positive technological change occurs. Whether the equilibrium price in a market rises or falls over time depends on whether demand shifts to the right more than does supply. Panel (a) of Figure 3-11 shows that when demand shifts to the right more than supply, the equilibrium price rises. But, as panel (b) shows, when supply shifts to the right more than demand, the equilibrium price falls.

Table 3-3 on page 86 summarizes all possible combinations of shifts in demand and supply over time and the effects of the shifts on equilibrium price (P) and quantity (Q). For example, the entry in red in the table shows that if the demand curve shifts to the right and the supply curve also shifts to the right, then the equilibrium quantity will increase, while the equilibrium price may increase, decrease, or remain unchanged. To make sure you understand each entry in the table, draw demand and supply graphs to check whether you can reproduce the predicted changes in equilibrium price and quantity. If the entry in the table says the predicted change in equilibrium price or quantity can be either an increase or a decrease, draw two graphs similar to panels (a) and (b) of Figure 3-11, one showing the equilibrium price or quantity increasing and the other showing it decreasing. Note also that in the ambiguous cases where either price or quantity might increase or decrease, it is also possible that price or quantity might remain unchanged. Be sure you understand why this is true.

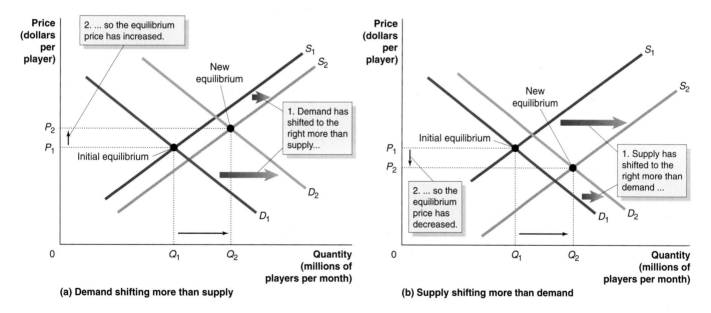

(a) Demand shifting more than supply

(b) Supply shifting more than demand

Figure 3-11 | Shifts in Demand and Supply over Time

Whether the price of a product rises or falls over time depends on whether demand shifts to the right more than supply.

In panel (a), demand shifts to the right more than supply, and the equilibrium price rises.
1. Demand shifts to the right more than supply.
2. Equilibrium price rises from P_1 to P_2.

In panel (b), supply shifts to the right more than demand, and the equilibrium price falls.
1. Supply shifts to the right more than demand.
2. Equilibrium price falls from P_1 to P_2.

TABLE 3-3

		SUPPLY CURVE UNCHANGED	SUPPLY CURVE SHIFTS TO THE RIGHT	SUPPLY CURVE SHIFTS TO THE LEFT
	DEMAND CURVE UNCHANGED	Q unchanged P unchanged	Q increases P decreases	Q decreases P increases
	DEMAND CURVE SHIFTS TO THE RIGHT	Q increases P increases	Q increases P increases or decreases	Q increases or decreases P increases
	DEMAND CURVE SHIFTS TO THE LEFT	Q decreases P decreases	Q increases or decreases P decreases	Q decreases P decreases or decreases

TABLE 3-3

How Shifts in Demand and Supply Affect Equilibrium Price (*P*) and Quantity (*Q*)

Solved Problem | **3-4**

High Demand and Low Prices in the Lobster Market?

During the spring, when demand for lobster is relatively low, Maine lobstermen are able to sell their lobster catches for about $4.50 per pound. During the summer, when demand for lobster is much higher, Maine lobstermen are able to sell their lobster catches for only about $3.00 per pound. It may seem strange that the market price is higher when demand is low than when demand is high. Can you resolve this paradox with the help of a demand and supply graph?

SOLVING THE PROBLEM:

Step 1: **Review the chapter material.** This problem is about how shifts in demand and supply curves affect the equilibrium price, so you may want to review the section "The Effect of Shifts in Demand and Supply over Time," which begins on page 85.

Step 2: **Draw the demand and supply graph.** Draw a demand and supply graph, showing the market equilibrium in the spring. Label the equilibrium price $4.50. Label both the demand and supply curves "spring."

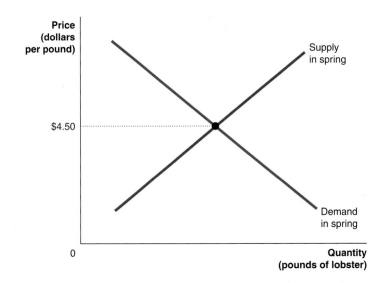

Step 3: Add to your graph a demand curve for summer.

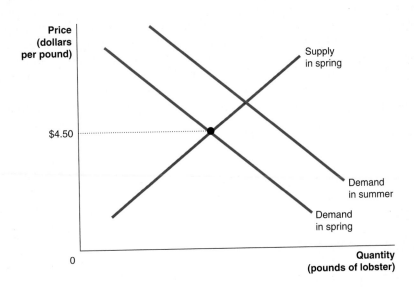

Step 4: **Explain the graph.** After studying the graph, it is possible to see how the equilibrium price can fall from $4.50 to $3.00, despite the increase in demand: The supply curve must have shifted to the right by enough to cause the equilibrium price to fall to $3.00. Draw the new supply curve, label it "summer," and label the new equilibrium price $3.00. The demand for lobster does increase in summer compared with the spring. But the increase in the supply of lobster between spring and summer is even greater. So, the equilibrium price falls.

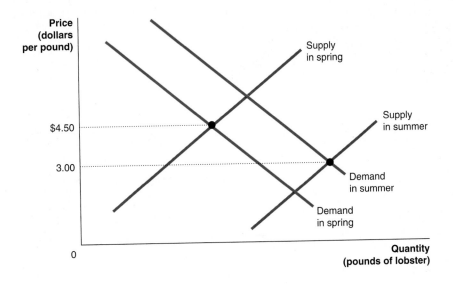

Source: Carey Goldberg, "Down East, the Lobster Hauls Are Up Big," *New York Times*, May 31, 2001.

YOUR TURN: For more practice, do related problem 4.5 on page 95 at the end of this chapter.

>> End Solved Problem 3-4

Shifts in a Curve versus Movements along a Curve

When analyzing markets using demand and supply curves, it is important to remember that *when a shift in a demand or supply curve causes a change in equilibrium price, the change in price does not cause a further shift in demand or supply.* For instance, suppose an increase in supply causes the price of a good to fall, while everything else that affects the willingness of consumers to buy the good is constant. The result will be an increase in the quantity demanded but not an increase in demand. For demand to increase, the whole curve must shift. The point is the same for supply: If the price of the good falls but everything else that affects the willingness of sellers to supply the good is constant, the quantity supplied decreases, but the supply does not. For supply to decrease, the whole curve must shift.

Don't Let This Happen to **YOU!**

Remember: A Change in a Good's Price Does *Not* Cause the Demand or Supply Curve to Shift

Suppose a student is asked to draw a demand and supply graph to illustrate how an increase in the price of oranges would affect the market for apples, other variables being constant. He draws the graph on the left below and explains it as follows: "Because apples and oranges are substitutes, an increase in the price of oranges will cause an initial shift to the right in the demand curve for apples, from D_1 to D_2. However, because this initial shift in the demand curve for apples results in a higher price for apples, P_2, consumers will find apples less desirable, and the demand curve will shift to the left, from D_2 to D_3, resulting in a final equilibrium price of P_3." Do you agree or disagree with the student's analysis?

You should disagree. The student has correctly understood that an increase in the price of oranges will cause the demand curve for apples to shift to the right. But the sec-

ond demand curve shift the student describes, from D_2 to D_3, will not take place. Changes in the price of a product do not result in shifts in the product's demand curve. Changes in the price of a product result only in movements along a demand curve.

The graph on the right below shows the correct analysis. The increase in the price of oranges causes the demand curve for apples to increase from D_1 to D_2. At the original price, P_1, the increase in demand initially results in a shortage of apples equal to $Q_3 - Q_1$. But, as we have seen, a shortage causes the price to increase until the shortage is eliminated. In this case, the price will rise to P_2, where the quantity demanded and the quantity supplied are both equal to Q_2. Notice that the increase in price causes a decrease in the *quantity demanded* from Q_3 to Q_2, but does *not* cause a decrease in demand.

YOUR TURN: Test your understanding by doing related problems 4.13 and 4.14 on page 96 at the end of this chapter.

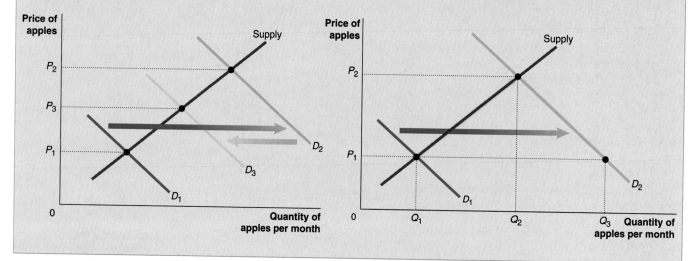

>> Continued from page 67

Economics in YOUR Life!

At the beginning of the chapter, we asked you to consider two questions: Would you choose to buy a Zune if it had a lower price than a comparable iPod? and Would you choose a Zune if the songs sold on Zune Marketplace were cheaper than the songs sold on iTunes? To determine the answers, you have to recognize that iPods and Zunes are substitutes, while Zunes and songs sold on Zune Marketplace are complements. If a Zune had a lower price than an iPod, this would cause consumers to purchase the Zune rather than the iPod, provided that the two players have the same features. If consumers believe that the Zune and the iPod are very close substitutes, a fall in the price of Zunes would cause the demand for iPods to decline, as the quantity of Zunes demanded increased. If Microsoft reduced the price of a song sold on Zune Marketplace so that it was lower than the price of the same song on iTunes, even if iPods and Zunes had the same price, the demand for Zunes would increase, and the demand for iPods would decrease.

Conclusion

The interaction of demand and supply determines market equilibrium. The model of demand and supply provides us with a powerful tool for predicting how changes in the actions of consumers and firms will cause changes in equilibrium prices and quantities. As we have seen in this chapter, the model can often be used to analyze markets that do not meet all the requirements for being perfectly competitive. As long as there is intense competition among sellers, the model of demand and supply can often successfully predict changes in prices and quantities. We will use the model in the next chapter to analyze economic efficiency and the results of government-imposed price floors and price ceilings. Before moving on, read *An Inside Look* on the next page to learn how Apple and AT&T benefit from collaborating on the iPhone.

How Does the iPhone Help Apple and AT&T?

WALL STREET JOURNAL, FEBRUARY 17, 2007

Apple Coup: How Steve Jobs Played Hardball in iPhone Birth

During a visit to Las Vegas last December for a rodeo event, Cingular Wireless chief executive Stan Sigman received a welcome guest: Steve Jobs. The Apple Inc. chief stopped by Mr. Sigman's Four Seasons hotel suite to show off the iPhone, a sleek cellphone designed to surf the Web and double as an iPod music player.

The phone had been in development by Apple and Cingular [now AT&T] for two years and was weeks away from being revealed to the world. And yet this was the first time Mr. Sigman got to see it. For three hours, Mr. Jobs played with the device, with its touch-screen that allows users to view contacts, dial numbers and flip through photos with the swipe of a finger. Mr. Sigman looked on in awe, according to a person familiar with the meeting . . .

Mr. Jobs is famous for making a splash with new products that upend industry models. Several years ago, he personally lobbied music industry executives and obtained licenses for songs that gave Apple the flexibility to build its successful iTunes store.

Apple eyed the cellphone market as both an opportunity to expand its iPod business and, if ignored, a potential threat to the company, people familiar with its strategy say. Cellphones are gradually offering more sophisticated capabilities and features, including increased storage capacity and entertainment functions. That stands to make them more competitive with iPods over time. Already, music phones like Samsung Electronics Co.'s BlackJack, Sony Ericsson's Walkman models and LG Electronic Inc.'s Chocolate are edging onto Apple's turf . . .

In early 2005, Mr. Jobs called Mr. Sigman to pitch the initial concept of the iPhone. The two executives later met in New York, and agreed to pursue the idea. Mr. Sigman is a Texan who wears cowboy boots and business suits, while Mr. Jobs is a former hippie who sports black turtlenecks and jeans. Despite their vastly different styles, the two executives found common ground. Over the next year and a half, the two sides negotiated to reach an agreement that would make sense for both of them . . .

While Mr. Jobs considered Cingular a logical choice as a partner to carry the device—its GSM technology is the prevailing standard in much of the world—Apple continued to shop its ideas to other carriers. Mr. Jobs reached out to Verizon Wireless chief executive Denny Strigl in the middle of 2005 and proposed a partnership with the carrier, a joint venture of Verizon Communications Inc. and Vodafone Group PLC. The companies held a few discussions over the next year, but the talks eventually soured.

There were a few sticking points. Verizon balked at the notion of cutting out its big retail partners, like Circuit City, who would not be allowed to sell the phone. And the company's chief marketing officer, John Stratton, was firm that Verizon wouldn't give up its ability to sell content like music and videos through its proprietary V Cast service, people familiar with the discussions say. . . .

In January, Mr. Jobs finally unveiled the phone at Macworld, the conference he has used to launch such key products as the iPod Mini. Since then, the two companies have continued to test the iPhone at an undisclosed facility, a person familiar with the matter said. The handful of Cingular people who have access to the sample phones at the company's headquarters were required to sign confidentiality agreements, a person familiar with the matter says. Meanwhile, competitors already are responding. Samsung and LG both have announced phones in recent weeks with designs that look similar to the iPhone. Apple has said it intends to sell 10 million of the devices by 2008, with price tags for two different versions set steeply at $499 and $599.

Cingular, which has more than 60 million customers, hopes the iPhone will give it a lift when it hits stores in June, at a time when attracting new subscribers is getting more difficult for all operators.

Source: Amol Sharma, Nick Wingfield, and Li Yuan, "Apple Coup: How Steve Jobs Played Hardball in iPhone Birth," Wall Street Journal, February 17, 2007, p. A1. Copyright © 2007 Dow Jones. Reprinted by permission of Dow Jones.

Key Points in the Article

The article discusses Apple's new iPhone, which combines features of the iPod and a cell phone. Apple has teamed up with Cingular, now AT&T, to provide cell phone service for the iPhone. The phone will also function as an iPod that plays music in Apple's proprietary format. The iPhone helps both companies. Apple gains because it now has a digital music player that doubles as a cell phone and competes with the other music phones on the market. AT&T gains a potentially large customer base for its cell phone services.

Analyzing the News

a Apple has viewed the evolution of the cell phone as a threat to the iPod because over time, cell phone manufacturers have added features that are similar to those of the iPod. For example, manufacturers have increased the storage capacity of cell phones so that people can store their music, pictures, and videos. Cell phones can also function as cameras and video recorders. These cell phones are a threat to the iPod because they are substitute goods that offer many of the same features.

If people are forced to choose just one product, then they might choose a cell phone that can play music over an iPod that cannot function as a phone. The figure shows the result. The demand curve for iPods shifts to the left, which reduces the price and quantity sold of iPods. Because the iPod is a critical product for Apple, this would significantly harm the entire company. Introducing the iPhone is a strategy to protect a very lucrative market for Apple.

b Apple could have worked with a number of different cell phone service providers. Ultimately, Apple chose to partner with Cingular for a couple of reasons. First, Cingular uses technology that is the industry standard. Second, Cingular was willing to make concessions that other cell phone service providers were not willing to make. The chapter opener pointed out that one of the key factors in the iPod's success was that Apple both made the iPod and sold music through iTunes. This means that the two products were developed by the same company and worked seamlessly together. One reason that Apple did not end up partnering with Verizon is that Verizon insisted on the right to continue to sell downloads of music and videos. This raised the possibility of compatibility problems with downloads available through iTunes.

c AT&T also benefits from the introduction of the iPhone. The iPhone will work only with AT&T's cellular phone service, so if you want to purchase an iPhone, you have to purchase AT&T's service. That means the iPhone and AT&T's services are complementary goods—and as sales of iPhones increase, the demand for AT&T's services should also increase.

Thinking Critically

1. What effect will the introduction of the iPhone have on sales of the iPod? Are there any reasons why someone might want to own both an iPhone and an iPod? Would it be better to think of the iPhone and the iPod as substitutes or complements? Briefly explain.

2. Apple plans to sell two versions of the iPhone: one for $499 and one for $599, which are significantly higher than the price of the most expensive iPod and much higher than the prices of cell phones. Are most customers likely to see the iPhone as a closer substitute for other cell phones or for other digital music players? Is the high price of the iPhone relevant to your answer? Briefly explain.

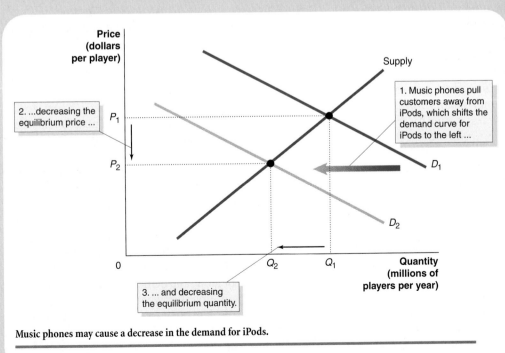

Music phones may cause a decrease in the demand for iPods.

Key Terms

Ceteris paribus ("all else equal"), p. 70	Demographics, p. 72	Market equilibrium, p. 80	Substitutes, p. 71
Competitive market equilibrium, p. 80	Income effect, p. 69	Normal good, p. 71	Substitution effect, p. 69
	Inferior good, p. 71	Perfectly competitive market, p. 68	Supply curve, p. 76
Complements, p. 71	Law of demand, p. 69		Supply schedule, p. 76
Demand curve, p. 68	Law of supply, p. 76	Quantity demanded, p. 68	Surplus, p. 80
Demand schedule, p. 68	Market demand, p. 68	Quantity supplied, p. 75	Technological change, p. 77
		Shortage, p. 80	

3.1 LEARNING OBJECTIVE   3.1 | Discuss the variables that influence demand, **pages 68–75.**

The Demand Side of the Market

Summary

The model of demand and supply is the most powerful in economics. The model applies exactly only to **perfectly competitive markets**, where there are many buyers and sellers, all the products sold are identical, and there are no barriers to new sellers entering the market. But the model can also be useful in analyzing markets that don't meet all of these requirements. The **quantity demanded** is the amount of a good or service that a consumer is willing and able to purchase at a given price. A **demand schedule** is a table that shows the relationship between the price of a product and the quantity of the product demanded. A **demand curve** is a graph that shows the relationship between the price of a good and the quantity of the good consumers are willing and able to buy over a period of time. **Market demand** is the demand by all consumers of a given good or service. The **law of demand** states that *ceteris paribus*—holding everything else constant—the quantity of a product demanded increases when the price falls and decreases when the price rises. Demand curves slope downward because of the **substitution effect**, which is the change in quantity demanded that results from a price change making one good more or less expensive relative to another good, and the **income effect**, which is the change in quantity demanded of a good that results from the effect of a change in the good's price on consumer purchasing power. Changes in income, the prices of related goods, tastes, population and demographics, and expected future prices all cause the demand curve to shift. **Substitutes** are goods that can be used for the same purpose. **Complements** are goods that are used together. A **normal good** is a good for which demand increases as income increases. An **inferior good** is a good for which demand decreases as income increases. **Demographics** are the characteristics of a population with respect to age, race, and gender. A change in demand refers to a shift of the demand curve. A change in quantity demanded refers to a movement along the demand curve as a result of a change in the product's price.

 Visit www.myeconlab.com to complete these exercises online and get instant feedback.

Review Questions

1.1 What is a demand schedule? What is a demand curve?

1.2 What do economists mean when they use the Latin expression *ceteris paribus*?

1.3 What is the difference between a change in demand and a change in quantity demanded?

1.4 What is the law of demand? What are the main variables that will cause the demand curve to shift? Give an example of each.

Problems and Applications

1.5 (Related to the *Making the Connection* on page 71) For each of the following pairs of products, state which are complements, which are substitutes, and which are unrelated.
   a. Pepsi and Coke
   b. Oscar Mayer hot dogs and Wonder hot dog buns
   c. Jif peanut butter and Smucker's strawberry jam
   d. iPods and Texas Instruments financial calculators

1.6 (Related to the *Chapter Opener* on page 66) Suppose Apple discovers that it is selling relatively few downloads of television programs on iTunes. Are downloads of television programs substitutes or complements for downloads of music? For downloads of movies? How might the answers to these questions affect Apple's decision about whether to continue offering downloads of television programs on iTunes?

1.7 State whether each of the following events will result in a movement along the demand curve for McDonald's Big Mac hamburgers or whether it will cause the curve to shift. If the demand curve shifts, indicate whether it will shift to the left or to the right and draw a graph to illustrate the shift.
   a. The price of Burger King's Whopper hamburger declines.

b. McDonald's distributes coupons for $1.00 off on a purchase of a Big Mac.

c. Because of a shortage of potatoes, the price of French fries increases.

d. Kentucky Fried Chicken raises the price of a bucket of fried chicken.

1.8 (Related to the *Making the Connection* on page 72) Name three products whose demand is likely to increase rapidly if the following demographic groups increase at a faster rate than the population as a whole:

a. Teenagers

b. Children under five

c. People over age 65

1.9 Suppose the data in the following table present the price of a base model Ford Explorer sport-utility vehicle (SUV) and the quantity of Explorers sold. Do these data indicate that the demand curve for Explorers is upward sloping? Explain.

YEAR	PRICE	QUANTITY
2006	$27,865	325,265
2007	28,325	330,648
2008	28,765	352,666

1.10 (Related to the *Making the Connection* on page 75) In early 2007, Apple forecast that it would sell 10 million iPhones during the product's first year on the market. What factors could affect the accuracy of this forecast? Is the forecast likely to be more or less accurate than Apple's forecast of how many iPods they would sell during the same time period? Briefly explain.

>> **End Learning Objective 3.1**

3.2 LEARNING OBJECTIVE 3.2 | Discuss the variables that influence supply, **pages 75-79.**

The Supply Side of the Market

Summary

The **quantity supplied** is the amount of a good that a firm is willing and able to supply at a given price. A **supply schedule** is a table that shows the relationship between the price of a product and the quantity of the product supplied. A **supply curve** shows on a graph the relationship between the price of a product and the quantity of the product supplied. When the price of a product rises, producing the product is more profitable, and a greater amount will be supplied. The **law of supply** states that, holding everything else constant, the quantity of a product supplied increases when the price rises and decreases when the price falls. Changes in the prices of inputs, technology, the prices of substitutes in production, expected future prices, and the number of firms in a market all cause the supply curve to shift. **Technological change** is a positive or negative change in the ability of a firm to produce a given level of output with a given quantity of inputs. A change in supply refers to a shift of the supply curve. A change in quantity supplied refers to a movement along the supply curve as a result of a change in the product's price.

myeconlab Visit www.myeconlab.com to complete these exercises
Get Ahead of the Curve online and get instant feedback.

Review Questions

2.1 What is a supply schedule? What is a supply curve?

2.2 What is the law of supply? What are the main variables that will cause a supply curve to shift? Give an example of each.

Problems and Applications

2.3 Briefly explain whether each of the following statements describes a change in supply or a change in the quantity supplied.

a. To take advantage of high prices for snow shovels during a very snowy winter, Alexander Shovels, Inc., decides to increase output.

b. The success of Apple's iPod leads more firms to begin producing digital music players.

c. In the six months following Hurricane Katrina, production of oil in the Gulf of Mexico declined by 25 percent.

2.4 Will each firm in a given industry always supply the same quantity as every other firm at each price? What factors might cause the quantity of digital music players supplied by each firm at each price to be different?

2.5 If the price of a good increases, is the increase in the quantity of the good supplied likely to be smaller or larger, the longer the time period being considered? Briefly explain.

>> **End Learning Objective 3.2**

3.3 LEARNING OBJECTIVE   3.3 | Use a graph to illustrate market equilibrium, **pages 79-82.**

Market Equilibrium: Putting Demand and Supply Together

Summary

Market equilibrium occurs where the demand curve intersects the supply curve. A **competitive market equilibrium** has a market equilibrium with many buyers and many sellers. Only at this point is the quantity demanded equal to the quantity supplied. Prices above equilibrium result in **surpluses,** with the quantity supplied being greater than the quantity demanded. Surpluses cause the market price to fall. Prices below equilibrium result in **shortages,** with the quantity demanded being greater than the quantity supplied. Shortages cause the market price to rise.

 Visit www.myeconlab.com to complete these exercises *Get Ahead of the Curve* online and get instant feedback.

Review Questions

3.1 What do economists mean by market equilibrium?

3.2 What happens in a market if the current price is above the equilibrium price? What happens if the current price is below the equilibrium price?

Problems and Applications

3.3 Briefly explain whether you agree with the following statement: "When there is a shortage of a good, con-

sumers eventually give up trying to buy it, so the demand for the good declines, and the price falls until the market is finally in equilibrium."

3.4 (Related to *Solved Problem 3-3* on page 81) In *The Wealth of Nations,* Adam Smith discussed what has come to be known as the "diamond and water paradox":

> Nothing is more useful than water: but it will purchase scarce anything; scarce anything can be had in exchange for it. A diamond, on the contrary, has scarce any value in use; but a very great quantity of other goods may frequently be had in exchange for it.

Graph the market for diamonds and the market for water. Show how it is possible for the price of water to be much lower than the price of diamonds, even though the demand for water is much greater than the demand for diamonds.

3.5 Briefly explain under what conditions zero would be the equilibrium quantity.

3.6 If a market is in equilibrium, is it necessarily true that all buyers and all sellers are satisfied with the market price? Briefly explain.

>> **End Learning Objective 3.3**

3.4 LEARNING OBJECTIVE   3.4 | Use demand and supply graphs to predict changes in prices and quantities, **pages 83-89.**

The Effect of Demand and Supply Shifts on Equilibrium

Summary

In most markets, demand and supply curves shift frequently, causing changes in equilibrium prices and quantities. Over time, if demand increases more than supply, equilibrium price will rise. If supply increases more than demand, equilibrium price will fall.

 Visit www.myeconlab.com to complete these exercises *Get Ahead of the Curve* online and get instant feedback.

Review Questions

4.1 Draw a demand and supply curve to show the effect on the equilibrium price in a market in the following two situations:
  a. The demand curve shifts to the right.
  b. The supply curve shifts to the left.

4.2 If, over time, the demand curve for a product shifts to the right more than the supply curve does, what will happen to the equilibrium price? What will happen to the equilibrium price if the supply curve shifts to the right more than the demand curve? For each case, draw a demand and supply graph to illustrate your answer.

Problems and Applications

4.3 As oil prices rose during 2006, the demand for alternative fuels increased. Ethanol, one alternative fuel, is made from corn. According to an article in the *Wall Street Journal,* the price of tortillas, which are made from corn, also rose during 2006: "The price spike [in tortillas] is part of a ripple effect from the ethanol boom."

a. Draw a demand and supply graph for the corn market and use it to show the effect on this market of an increase in the demand for ethanol. Be sure to indicate the equilibrium price and quantity before and after the increase in the demand for ethanol.

b. Draw a demand and supply graph for the tortilla market and use it to show the effect on this market of an increase in the price of corn. Once again, be sure to indicate the equilibrium price and quantity before and after the increase in the demand for ethanol.

Source: Mark Gongloff, "Tortilla Soup," *Wall Street Journal*, January 25, 2007.

4.4 A recent study indicated that "stricter college alcohol policies, such as raising the price of alcohol, or banning alcohol on campus, decrease the number of students who use marijuana."

a. On the basis of this information, are alcohol and marijuana substitutes or complements?

b. Suppose that campus authorities reduce the supply of alcohol on campus. Use demand and supply graphs to illustrate the impact on the campus alcohol and marijuana markets.

Source: Jenny Williams, Rosalie Pacula, Frank Chaloupka, and Henry Wechsler, "Alcohol and Marijuana Use Among College Students: Economic Complements or Substitutes?" *Health Economics*, Volume 13, Issue 9, September 2005, pp. 825–843.

4.5 (Related to *Solved Problem 3-4* on page 86) The demand for watermelons is highest during summer and lowest during winter. Yet watermelon prices are normally lower in summer than in winter. Use a demand and supply graph to demonstrate how this is possible. Be sure to carefully label the curves in your graph and to clearly indicate the equilibrium summer price and the equilibrium winter price.

4.6 According to an article in the *Wall Street Journal*:

As occupancy rates at luxury hotels have grown 13% over the last five years, prices have risen by 19%, according to Smith Travel Research. (That comes despite an 18.5% increase in the number of rooms over the same period.)

Use a demand and supply graph to explain how these three things could be true: an increase in the equilibrium quantity of hotel rooms occupied, an increase in the equilibrium price of hotel rooms, and an increase in the number of hotel rooms available.

Source: Nancy Keates, "Cracking Down on Chair Hogs," *Wall Street Journal*, February 23, 2007, p. W1.

4.7 (Related to the *Making the Connection* on page 83) The average price of a high-definition plasma or LCD television fell between 2001 and 2006, from more than $8,000 to about $1,500. During that period, Sharp, Matsushita Electric Industrial, and Samsung all began producing plasma or LCD televisions. Use a demand and supply graph to explain what happened to the quantity of plasma and LCD televisions sold during this period.

4.8 According to an article in the *Wall Street Journal*, during 2006, the demand for full-size pickup trucks declined as a result of rising gas prices and a decline in housing construction (construction firms are an important part of the market for full-size pickup trucks). At the same time, Toyota began production of trucks at a new truck factory in Texas.

a. Draw a demand and supply graph illustrating these developments in the market for full-size pickup trucks. Be sure to indicate changes in the equilibrium price and equilibrium quantity.

b. Briefly discuss whether this problem provides enough information to determine whether the equilibrium quantity of trucks increased or decreased.

Source: Neal E. Boudette and Jeffrey C. McCracken, "Detroit's Cash Cow Stumbles," *Wall Street Journal*, August 1, 2006, p. B1.

4.9 Beginning in the late 1990s, many consumers were having their vision problems corrected with laser surgery. An article in the *Wall Street Journal* noted two developments in the market for laser eye surgery. The first involved increasing concerns related to side effects from the surgery, including blurred vision and, occasionally, blindness. The second development was that the companies renting eye-surgery machinery to doctors had reduced their charges. One large company had cut its charge from $250 per patient to $100. Use a demand and supply graph to illustrate the effects of these two developments on the market for laser eye surgery.

Source: Laura Johannes and James Bandler, "Slowing Economy, Safety Concerns Zap Growth in Laser Eye Surgery," *Wall Street Journal*, January 8, 2001, p. B1.

4.10 The market for autographs, including letters or other documents signed by famous people, is subject to frequent large price changes, as are markets for most collectibles. The following table is adapted from one that originally appeared in an article in the *Wall Street Journal*. It gives the 1997 price for an autograph, the 2001 price, and a brief comment by the *Wall Street Journal* reporter. Use the information contained in the Comment column of the table to draw a demand and supply graph for each of the three autographs listed that can account for the change in its market price from 1997 to 2001.

AUTOGRAPH	1997 PRICE	2001 PRICE	COMMENT
The Beatles	$2,500	$7,475	"As boomers get rich, so do prices for pieces . . . signed by the Fab Four."
Princess Diana	14,000	2,000	"Demand rose after her death in 1997, but now the market's full of items like her signed Christmas cards."
Robert E. Lee	200,000	100,000	"The Civil War's out."

Source: Brooks Barnes, "Signature Market: Hard to Read," *Wall Street Journal*, July 13, 2001.

4.11 Historically, the production of many perishable foods, such as dairy products, was highly seasonal. Thus, as the supply of those products fluctuated, prices tended to fluctuate tremendously—typically by 25 to 50 percent or more—over the course of the year. One impact of mechanical refrigeration, which was commercialized on a large scale in the last decade of the nineteenth century, was that suppliers could store perishables from one season to the next. Economists have estimated that as a result of refrigerated storage, wholesale prices rose by roughly 10 percent during peak supply periods, while they fell by almost the same amount during the off season. Use a demand and supply graph for each season to illustrate how refrigeration affected the market for perishable food.

Source: Lee A. Craig, Barry Goodwin, and Thomas Grennes, "The Effect of Mechanical Refrigeration on Nutrition in the U.S.," *Social Science History*, Vol. 28, No. 2 (Summer 2004), pp. 327–328.

4.12 Briefly explain whether each of the following statements is true or false.

a. If the demand and supply for a product both increase, the equilibrium quantity of the product must also increase.

b. If the demand and supply for a product both increase, the equilibrium price of the product must also increase.

c. If the demand for a product decreases and the supply of the product increases, the equilibrium price of the product may increase or decrease, depending on whether supply or demand has shifted more.

4.13 (Related to the *Don't Let This Happen to You!* on page 88) A student writes the following: "Increased production leads to a lower price, which in turn increases demand." Do you agree with his reasoning? Briefly explain.

4.14 (Related to the *Don't Let This Happen To You!* on page 88) A student was asked to draw a demand and supply graph to illustrate the effect on the laptop computer market of a fall in the price of computer hard drives, *ceteris paribus*. She drew the graph at the top of the next column and explained it as follows:

> Hard drives are an input to laptop computers, so a fall in the price of hard drives will cause the supply curve for personal computers to shift to the right (from S_1 to S_2). Because this shift in the supply curve results in a lower price (P_2), consumers will want to buy more laptops, and the demand curve will shift to the right (from D_1 to D_2). We know that more laptops will be sold, but we can't be sure whether the price of laptops will rise or fall. That depends on whether the supply curve or the demand curve has shifted farther to the right. I assume that the effect on supply is greater than the effect on demand, so

I show the final equilibrium price (P_3) as being lower than the initial equilibrium price (P_1).

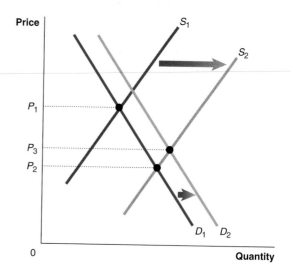

Explain whether you agree or disagree with the student's analysis. Be careful to explain exactly what—if anything—you find wrong with her analysis.

4.15 Following are four graphs and four market scenarios, each of which would cause either a movement along the supply curve for Pepsi or a shift of the supply curve. Match each scenario with the appropriate graph.

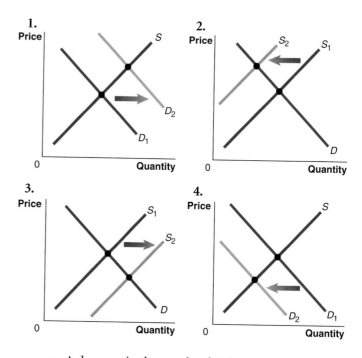

a. A decrease in the supply of Coke

b. A drop in the average household income in the United States from $42,000 to $41,000

c. An improvement in soft-drink bottling technology

d. An increase in the price of sugar

4.16 David Surdam, an economist at Loyola University of Chicago, makes the following observation of the world cotton market at the beginning of the Civil War:

> As the supply of American-grown raw cotton decreased and the price of raw cotton increased, there would be a *movement along* the supply curve of non-American raw cotton suppliers, and the quantity supplied by these producers would increase.

Illustrate this observation with one demand and supply graph for the market for American-grown cotton and another demand and supply graph for the market for non-American cotton. Make sure your graphs clearly show (1) the initial equilibrium before the decrease in the supply of American-grown cotton and (2) the final equilibrium. Also clearly show any shifts in the demand and supply curves for each market.

Source: David G. Surdam, "King Cotton: Monarch or Pretender? The State of the Market for Raw Cotton on the Eve of the American Civil War," *The Economic History Review*, Vol. 51, No. 1 (February 1998), p. 116.

4.17 Proposals have been made to increase government regulation of firms providing childcare services by, for instance, setting education requirements for childcare workers. Suppose that these regulations increase the quality of childcare and cause the demand for childcare services to increase. At the same time, assume that complying with the new government regulations increases the costs of firms providing childcare services. Draw a demand and supply graph to illustrate the effects of these changes in the market for childcare services. Briefly explain whether the total quantity of childcare services purchased will increase or decrease as a result of regulation.

4.18 Below are the supply and demand functions for two markets. One of the markets is for BMW automobiles, and the other is for a cancer-fighting drug, without which lung cancer patients will die. Briefly explain which diagram most likely represents which market.

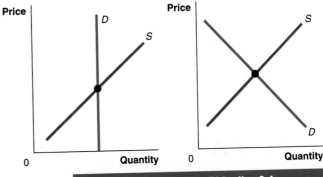

>> **End Learning Objective 3.4**

Economic Efficiency, Government Price Setting, and Taxes

Should the Government Control Apartment Rents?

Robert F. Moss owns an apartment building in New York City. Unlike most other business owners, he is not free to charge the prices he would like for the service he offers. In New York, San Francisco, Los Angeles, and nearly 200 smaller cities, apartments are subject to rent control by the local government. Rent control puts a legal limit on the rent that landlords can charge for an apartment.

New York City has two million apartments, about one million of which are subject to rent control. The other one million apartments have their rents determined in the market by the demand and supply for apartments. Mr. Moss's building includes apartments that are rent controlled and apartments that are not. The market-determined rents are usually far above the controlled rents. The government regulations that determine what Mr. Moss can charge for a rent-controlled apartment are very complex. The following is Mr. Moss's description:

When [an apartment] is vacated, state rent laws entitle landlords to raise rents in three primary ways: a vacancy increase of 20 percent for a new tenant's two-year lease (a bit less for a one-year lease); one-fortieth per month of the cost of any improvements, and a "longevity bonus" for longtime residents (calculated at six-tenths of 1 percent times the tenant's last legal rent multiplied by the number of years of residency beyond eight). . . . Apartments renting for $2,000 a month are automatically deregulated if they are vacant. Occupied apartments whose rent reaches that figure can be deregulated if the income of the tenants has been $175,000 or more for two years.

As this description shows, someone earning a living by renting out apartments in New York City has to deal with much more complex government regulation of prices than someone who owns, for instance, a McDonald's restaurant.

Larger companies also struggle with the complexity of rent-control regulations. This was the case for several companies that built multiple apartment buildings in New York dur-

ing the 1970s. In exchange for renting apartments to moderate- and low-income tenants at controlled rents, the companies were allowed to charge market rents after 20 years. Unfortunately for the companies, when the 20 years were over, attempts to start charging market rents were often met with lawsuits from unhappy tenants. New York Mayor Michael Bloomberg proposed that the law be changed to keep many of these apartment buildings under rent control.

Tenants in rent-controlled apartments in New York are very reluctant to see rent control end because rents for rent-controlled apartments are much lower than rents for apartments that aren't rent controlled. As we will see in this chapter, however rent control can also cause significant problems for renters. **AN INSIDE LOOK AT POLICY** on **page 122** explores the debate over rent control laws in Los Angeles.

Source: Robert F. Moss, "A Landlord's Lot is Sometimes Not an Easy One," New York Times, August 3, 2003, Section 11, p. 1.

LEARNING Objectives

After studying this chapter, you should be able to:

4.1 Distinguish between the concepts of **consumer surplus** and **producer surplus**, page 100.

4.2 Understand the concept of **economic efficiency**, page 105.

4.3 Explain the economic effect of government-imposed **price ceilings** and **price floors**, page 107.

4.4 Analyze the economic impact of **taxes**, page 115.

APPENDIX Use **quantitative** demand and supply **analysis**, page 131.

Economics in YOUR Life!

Does Rent Control Make It Easier to Find an Affordable Apartment?

Suppose you have job offers in two cities. One factor in deciding which job to accept is whether you can find an affordable apartment. If one city has rent control, are you more likely to find an affordable apartment in that city, or would you be better off looking for an apartment in a city without rent control? As you read the chapter, see if you can answer this question. You can check your answer against the one we provide at the end of the chapter. **>> Continued on page 120**

W
e saw in Chapter 3 that, in a competitive market, the price adjusts to ensure that the quantity demanded equals the quantity supplied. Stated another way, in equilibrium, every consumer willing to pay the market price is able to buy as much of the product as the consumer wants, and every firm willing to accept the market price can sell as much as it wants. Even so, consumers would naturally prefer to pay a lower price, and sellers would prefer to receive a higher price. Normally, consumers and firms have no choice but to accept the equilibrium price if they wish to participate in the market. Occasionally, however, consumers succeed in having the government impose a **price ceiling**, which is a legally determined maximum price that sellers may charge. Rent control is an example of a price ceiling. Firms also sometimes succeed in having the government impose a **price floor**, which is a legally determined minimum price that sellers may receive. In markets for farm products such as milk, the government has been setting price floors that are above the equilibrium market price since the 1930s.

> **Price ceiling** A legally determined maximum price that sellers may charge.

> **Price floor** A legally determined minimum price that sellers may receive.

Another way in which the government intervenes in markets is by imposing taxes. The government relies on the revenue raised from taxes to finance its operations. As we will see, though, imposing taxes alters the equilibrium in a market.

Unfortunately, whenever the government imposes a price ceiling, a price floor, or a tax, there are predictable negative economic consequences. It is important for government policymakers and voters to understand these negative consequences when evaluating the effects of these policies. Economists have developed the concepts of *consumer surplus, producer surplus,* and *economic surplus,* which we discuss in the next section. In the sections that follow, we use these concepts to analyze the economic effects of price ceilings, price floors, and taxes. (As we will see in later chapters, these concepts are also useful in many other contexts.)

4.1 LEARNING OBJECTIVE

4.1 | Distinguish between the concepts of consumer surplus and producer surplus.

Consumer Surplus and Producer Surplus

Consumer surplus measures the dollar benefit consumers receive from buying goods or services in a particular market. Producer surplus measures the dollar benefit firms receive from selling goods or services in a particular market. Economic surplus in a market is the sum of consumer surplus plus producer surplus. As we will see, *when the government imposes a price ceiling or a price floor, the amount of economic surplus in a market is reduced*—in other words, price ceilings and price floors reduce the total benefit to consumers and firms from buying and selling in a market. To understand why this is true, we need to understand how consumer surplus and producer surplus are determined.

Consumer Surplus

Consumer surplus measures the difference between the highest price a consumer is willing to pay and the price the consumer actually pays. For example, suppose you are in Wal-Mart and you see a DVD of *Spider-Man 3* on the rack. No price is indicated on the package, so you bring it over to the register to check the price. As you walk to the register, you think to yourself that $20 is the highest price you would be willing to pay. At the register, you find out that the price is actually $12, so you buy the DVD. Your consumer surplus in this example is $8: the difference between the $20 you were willing to pay and the $8 you actually paid.

> **Consumer surplus** The difference between the highest price a consumer is willing to pay and the price the consumer actually pays.

We can use the demand curve to measure the total consumer surplus in a market. Demand curves show the willingness of consumers to purchase a product at different prices. Consumers are willing to purchase a product up to the point where the marginal benefit of consuming a product is equal to its price. The **marginal benefit** is the addi-

> **Marginal benefit** The additional benefit to a consumer from consuming one more unit of a good or service.

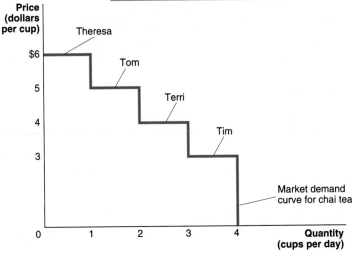

Consumer	Highest Price Willing to Pay
Theresa	$6
Tom	5
Terri	4
Tim	3

Figure 4-1

Deriving the Demand Curve for Chai Tea

With four consumers in the market for chai tea, the demand curve is determined by the highest price each consumer is willing to pay. For prices above $6, no tea is sold because $6 is the highest price any consumer is willing to pay. For prices of $3 and below, all four consumers are willing to buy a cup of tea.

tional benefit to a consumer from consuming one more unit of a good or service. As a simple example, suppose there are only four consumers in the market for chai tea: Theresa, Tom, Terri, and Tim. Because these four consumers have different tastes for tea and different incomes, the marginal benefit each of them receives from consuming a cup of tea will be different. Therefore, the highest price each is willing to pay for a cup of tea is also different. In Figure 4-1, the information from the table is used to construct a demand curve for chai tea. For prices above $6 per cup, no tea is sold because $6 is the highest price any of the consumers is willing to pay. At a price of $5, both Theresa and Tom are willing to buy, so two cups are sold. At prices of $3 and below, all four consumers are willing to buy, and four cups are sold.

Suppose the market price of tea is $3.50 per cup. As Figure 4-2 on page 102 shows, the demand curve allows us to calculate the total consumer surplus in this market. In panel (a), we can see that the highest price Theresa is willing to pay is $6, but because she pays only $3.50, her consumer surplus is $2.50 (shown by the area of rectangle A). Similarly, Tom's consumer surplus is $1.50 (rectangle B), and Terri's consumer surplus is $0.50 (rectangle C). Tim is unwilling to buy a cup of tea at a price of $3.50, so he doesn't participate in this market and receives no consumer surplus. In this simple example, the total consumer surplus is equal to $2.50 + $1.50 + $0.50 = $4.50 (or the sum of the areas of rectangles A, B, and C). Panel (b) shows that a lower price will increase consumer surplus. If the price of tea drops from $3.50 per cup to $3.00, Theresa, Tom, and Terri each receive $0.50 more in consumer surplus (shown by the shaded areas), so total consumer surplus in the market rises to $6.00. Tim now buys a cup of tea but doesn't receive any consumer surplus because the price is equal to the highest price he is willing to pay. In fact, Tim is indifferent between buying the cup or not—his well-being is the same either way.

The market demand curves shown in Figures 4-1 and 4-2 do not look like the smooth curves we saw in Chapter 3. This is because this example uses a small number of consumers, each consuming a single cup of tea. With many consumers, the market demand curve for chai tea will have the normal smooth shape shown in Figure 4-3. In this figure, the quantity demanded at a price of $2.00 is 15,000 cups per day. We can calculate total consumer surplus in Figure 4-3 the same way we did in Figures 4-1 and

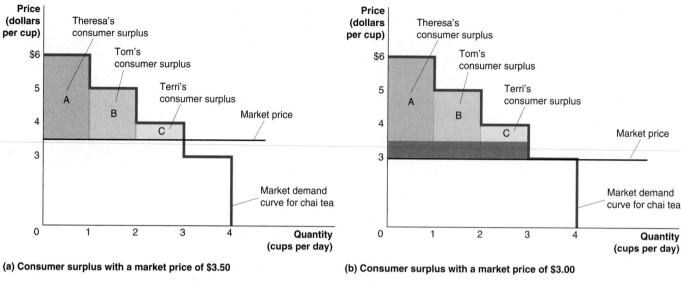

(a) Consumer surplus with a market price of $3.50

(b) Consumer surplus with a market price of $3.00

Figure 4-2 | Measuring Consumer Surplus

Panel (a) shows the consumer surplus for Theresa, Tom, and Terri when the price of tea is $3.50 per cup. Theresa's consumer surplus is equal to the area of rectangle A and is the difference between the highest price she would pay—$6—and the market price of $3.50. Tom's consumer surplus is equal to the area of rectangle B, and Terri's con-

sumer surplus is equal to the area of rectangle C. Total consumer surplus in this market is equal to the sum of the areas of rectangles A, B, and C, or the total area below the demand curve and above the market price. In panel (b), consumer surplus increases by the shaded area as the market price declines from $3.50 to $3.00.

4-2: by adding up the consumer surplus received on each unit purchased. Once again, we can draw an important conclusion: *The total amount of consumer surplus in a market is equal to the area below the demand curve and above the market price.* Consumer surplus is shown as the blue area in Figure 4-3 and represents the benefit to consumers in excess of the price they paid to purchase the product—in this case, chai tea.

Figure 4-3

Total Consumer Surplus in the Market for Chai Tea

The demand curve tells us that most buyers of chai tea would have been willing to pay more than the market price of $2.00. For each buyer, consumer surplus is equal to the difference between the highest price he or she is willing to pay and the market price actually paid. Therefore, the total amount of consumer surplus in the market for chai tea is equal to the area below the demand curve and above the market price. Consumer surplus represents the benefit to consumers in excess of the price they paid to purchase the product.

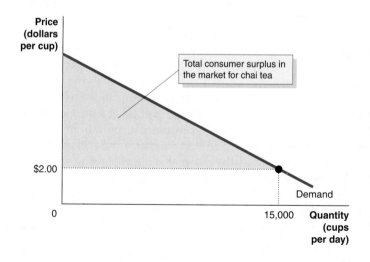

Making the Connection | **The Consumer Surplus from Satellite Television**

Consumer surplus allows us to measure the benefit consumers receive in excess of the price they paid to purchase a product. Recently, Austan Goolsbee and Amil Petrin, economists at the Graduate

School of Business at the University of Chicago, estimated the consumer surplus that households receive from subscribing to satellite television. To do this, they estimated the demand curve for satellite television and then computed the shaded area shown in the graph.

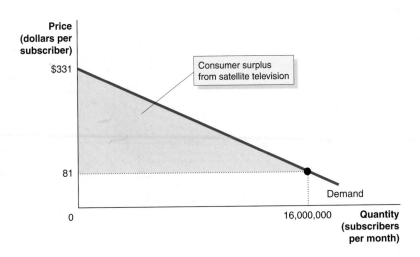

In 2001, the year for which the study was conducted, 16 million consumers paid an average price of $81 per month to subscribe to DIRECTV or DISH Network, the two main providers of satellite television. The demand curve shows that many consumers would have been willing to pay more than $81 rather than do without satellite television. Goolsbee and Petrin calculated that the consumer surplus for households subscribing to satellite television averaged $127 per month, which is the difference between the price they would have paid and the $81 they did pay. The shaded area on the graph represents the total consumer surplus in the market for satellite television. Goolsbee and Petrin estimate that the value of this area is $2 billion. This is one year's benefit to the consumers who subscribe to satellite television.

Source: Austan Goolsbee and Amil Petrin, "The Consumer Gains from Direct Broadcast Satellites and the Competition with Cable TV," *Econometrica*, Vol. 72, No. 2, March 2004, pp. 351–381.

YOUR TURN: Test your understanding by doing related problem 1.8 on page 124 at the end of this chapter.

Producer Surplus

Just as demand curves show the willingness of consumers to buy a product at different prices, supply curves show the willingness of firms to supply a product at different prices. The willingness to supply a product depends on the cost of producing it. Firms will supply an additional unit of a product only if they receive a price equal to the additional cost of producing that unit. **Marginal cost** is the additional cost to a firm of producing one more unit of a good or service. Consider the marginal cost to the firm Heavenly Tea of producing one more cup: In this case, the marginal cost includes the ingredients to make the tea and the wages paid to the worker preparing the tea. Often, the marginal cost of producing a good increases as more of the good is produced during a given period of time. This is the key reason—as we saw in Chapter 3—that supply curves are upward sloping.

Panel (a) of Figure 4-4 shows Heavenly Tea's producer surplus. For simplicity, we show Heavenly producing only a small quantity of tea. The figure shows that Heavenly's marginal cost of producing the first cup of tea is $1.00. Its marginal cost of producing

Marginal cost The additional cost to a firm of producing one more unit of a good or service.

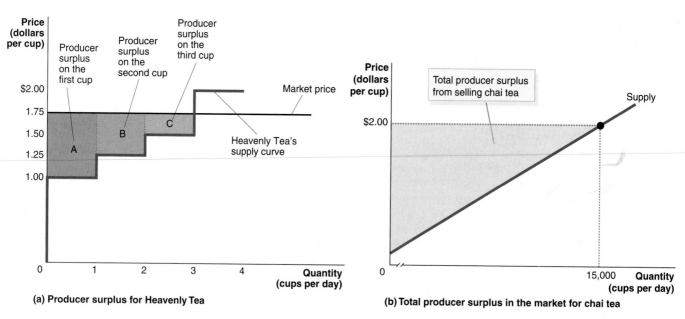

Figure 4-4 | Calculating Producer Surplus

Panel (a) shows Heavenly Tea's producer surplus. Producer surplus is the difference between the lowest price a firm would be willing to accept and the price it actually receives. The lowest price Heavenly Tea is willing to accept to supply a cup of tea is equal to its marginal cost of producing that cup. When the market price of tea is $1.75, Heavenly receives producer surplus of $0.75 on the first cup (the area of rectangle *A*), $0.50 on the second cup (rectangle *B*), and $0.25 on the third cup (rectangle *C*). In panel (b), the total amount of producer surplus tea sellers receive from selling chai tea can be calculated by adding up for the entire market the producer surplus received on each cup sold. In the figure, total producer surplus is equal to the area above the supply curve and below the market price, shown in red.

Producer surplus The difference between the lowest price a firm would be willing to accept and the price it actually receives.

the second cup is $1.25, and so on. The marginal cost of each cup of tea is the lowest price Heavenly is willing to accept to supply that cup. The supply curve, then, is also a marginal cost curve. Suppose the market price of tea is $1.75 per cup. On the first cup of tea, the price is $0.75 higher than the lowest price Heavenly is willing to accept. **Producer surplus** is the difference between the lowest price a firm would be willing to accept and the price it actually receives. Therefore, Heavenly's producer surplus on the first cup is $0.75 (shown by the area of rectangle *A*). Its producer surplus on the second cup is $0.50 (rectangle *B*). Its producer surplus on the third cup is $0.25 (rectangle *C*). Heavenly will not be willing to supply the fourth cup because the marginal cost of producing it is less than the market price. Heavenly Tea's total producer surplus is equal to $0.75 + $0.50 + $0.25 = $1.50 (or the sum of rectangles *A, B,* and *C*). A higher price will increase producer surplus. For example, if the market price of chai tea rises from $1.75 to $2.00, Heavenly Tea's producer surplus will increase from $1.50 to $2.25. (Make sure you understand how the new level of producer surplus was calculated.)

The supply curve shown in panel (a) of Figure 4-4 does not look like the smooth curves we saw in Chapter 3 because this example uses a single firm producing only a small quantity of tea. With many firms, the market supply curve for chai tea will have the normal smooth shape shown in panel (b) of Figure 4-4. In panel (b), the quantity supplied at a price of $2.00 is 15,000 cups per day. We can calculate total producer surplus in panel (b) the same way we did in panel (a): by adding up the producer surplus received on each cup sold. Therefore, *the total amount of producer surplus in a market is equal to the area above the market supply curve and below the market price.* The total producer surplus tea sellers receive from selling chai tea is shown as the red area in panel (b) of Figure 4-4.

What Consumer Surplus and Producer Surplus Measure

We have seen that consumer surplus measures the benefit to consumers from participating in a market, and producer surplus measures the benefit to producers from participating in a market. It is important, however, to be clear what we mean by this. In a sense, consumer surplus measures the *net* benefit to consumers from participating in a market rather than the *total* benefit. That is, if the price of a product were zero, the consumer surplus in a market would be all of the area under the demand curve. When the price is not zero, consumer surplus is the area below the demand curve and above the market price. So, consumer surplus in a market is equal to the total benefit received by consumers minus the total amount they must pay to buy the good.

Similarly, producer surplus measures the *net* benefit received by producers from participating in a market. If producers could supply a good at zero cost, the producer surplus in a market would be all of the area below the market price. When cost is not zero, producer surplus is the area below the market price and above the supply curve. So, producer surplus in a market is equal to the total amount firms receive from consumers minus the cost of producing the good.

4.2 | Understand the concept of economic efficiency.

4.2 LEARNING OBJECTIVE

The Efficiency of Competitive Markets

In Chapter 3, we defined a *competitive market* as a market with many buyers and many sellers. An important advantage of the market system is that it results in efficient economic outcomes. But what do we mean by *economic efficiency*? The concepts we have developed so far in this chapter give us two ways to think about the economic efficiency of competitive markets. We can think in terms of marginal benefit and marginal cost. We can also think in terms of consumer surplus and producer surplus. As we will see, these two approaches lead to the same outcome, but using both can increase our understanding of economic efficiency.

Marginal Benefit Equals Marginal Cost in Competitive Equilibrium

Figure 4-5 again shows the market for chai tea. Recall from our discussion that the demand curve shows the marginal benefit received by consumers, and the supply curve shows the marginal cost of production. To achieve economic efficiency in this market, the marginal

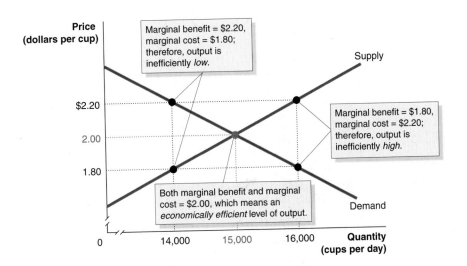

Figure 4-5

Marginal Benefit Equals Marginal Cost Only at Competitive Equilibrium

In a competitive market, equilibrium occurs at a quantity of 15,000 cups and price of $2.00 per cup, where marginal benefit equals marginal cost. This is the economically efficient level of output because every cup has been produced where the marginal benefit to buyers is greater than or equal to the marginal cost to producers.

benefit from the last unit sold should equal the marginal cost of production. The figure shows that this equality occurs at competitive equilibrium where 15,000 cups per day are produced, and marginal benefit and marginal cost are both equal to $2.00. Why is this outcome economically efficient? Because every cup of chai tea has been produced where the marginal benefit to buyers is greater than or equal to the marginal cost to producers.

Another way to see why the level of output at competitive equilibrium is efficient is to consider what would be true if output were at a different level. For instance, suppose that output of chai tea were 14,000 cups per day. Figure 4-5 shows that at this level of output, the marginal benefit from the last cup sold is $2.20, whereas the marginal cost is only $1.80. This level of output is not efficient because 1,000 more cups could be produced for which the additional benefit to consumers would be greater than the additional cost of production. Consumers would willingly purchase those cups, and tea sellers would willingly supply them, making both consumers and sellers better off. Similarly, if the output of chai tea were 16,000 cups per day, the marginal cost of the 16,000th cup is $2.20, whereas the marginal benefit is only $1.80. Tea sellers would only be willing to supply this cup at a price of $2.20, which is $0.40 higher than consumers would be willing to pay. In fact, consumers would not be willing to pay the price tea sellers would need to receive for any cup beyond the 15,000th.

To summarize, we can say this: *Equilibrium in a competitive market results in the economically efficient level of output, where marginal benefit equals marginal cost.*

Economic Surplus

Economic surplus The sum of consumer surplus and producer surplus.

Economic surplus in a market is the sum of consumer surplus and producer surplus. In a competitive market, with many buyers and sellers and no government restrictions, economic surplus is at a maximum when the market is in equilibrium. To see this, let's look one more time at the market for chai tea shown in Figure 4-6. The consumer surplus in this market is the blue area below the demand curve and above the line indicating the equilibrium price of $2.00. The producer surplus is the red area above the supply curve and below the price line.

Deadweight Loss

To show that economic surplus is maximized at equilibrium, consider the situation in which the price of chai tea is *above* the equilibrium price, as shown in Figure 4-7. At a price of $2.20 per cup, the number of cups consumers are willing to buy per day drops from 15,000 to 14,000. At competitive equilibrium, consumer surplus is equal to the sum of areas *A, B,* and *C.* At a price of $2.20, fewer cups are sold at a higher price, so consumer surplus declines to just the area of *A.* At competitive equilibrium, producer surplus is equal to the sum of areas *D* and *E.* At the higher price of $2.20, producer surplus changes to be equal to the sum of areas *B* and *D.* The sum of consumer and producer surplus—economic surplus—has been reduced to the sum of areas *A, B,* and *D.* Notice that this is less than the original economic surplus by an amount equal to areas *C* and *E.*

Figure 4-6

Economic Surplus Equals the Sum of Consumer Surplus and Producer Surplus

The economic surplus in a market is the sum of the blue area representing consumer surplus and the red area representing producer surplus.

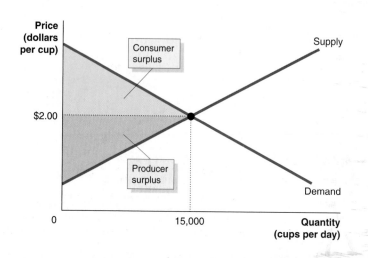

Figure 4-7

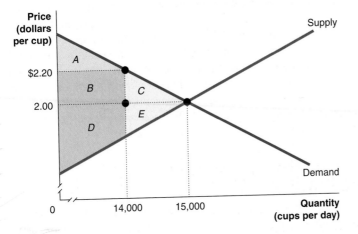

	At Competitive Equilibrium	At a Price of $2.20
Consumer Surplus	A + B + C	A
Producer Surplus	D + E	B + D
Deadweight Loss	None	C + E

When a Market Is Not in Equilibrium, There Is a Deadweight Loss

Economic surplus is maximized when a market is in competitive equilibrium. When a market is not in equilibrium, there is a deadweight loss. When the price of chai tea is $2.20, instead of $2.00, consumer surplus declines from an amount equal to the sum of areas *A*, *B*, and *C* to just area *A*. Producer surplus increases from the sum of areas *D* and *E* to the sum of areas *B* and *D*. At competitive equilibrium, there is no deadweight loss. At a price of $2.20, there is a deadweight loss equal to the sum of areas *C* and *E*.

Economic surplus has declined because at a price of $2.20, all the cups between the 14,000th and the 15,000th, which would have been produced in competitive equilibrium, are not being produced. These "missing" cups are not providing any consumer or producer surplus, so economic surplus has declined. The reduction in economic surplus resulting from a market not being in competitive equilibrium is called the **deadweight loss**. In the figure, it is equal to the sum of areas *C* and *E*.

Deadweight loss The reduction in economic surplus resulting from a market not being in competitive equilibrium.

Economic Surplus and Economic Efficiency

Consumer surplus measures the benefit to consumers from buying a particular product, such as chai tea. Producer surplus measures the benefit to firms from selling a particular product. Therefore, economic surplus—which is the sum of the benefit to firms plus the benefit to consumers—is the best measure we have of the benefit to society from the production of a particular good or service. This gives us a second way of characterizing the economic efficiency of a competitive market: *Equilibrium in a competitive market results in the greatest amount of economic surplus, or total net benefit to society, from the production of a good or service.* Anything that causes the market for a good or service not to be in competitive equilibrium reduces the total benefit to society from the production of that good or service.

Now we can give a more general definition of *economic efficiency* in terms of our two approaches: **Economic efficiency** is a market outcome in which the marginal benefit to consumers of the last unit produced is equal to its marginal cost of production and in which the sum of consumer surplus and producer surplus is at a maximum.

Economic efficiency A market outcome in which the marginal benefit to consumers of the last unit produced is equal to its marginal cost of production and in which the sum of consumer surplus and producer surplus is at a maximum.

4.3 | Explain the economic effect of government-imposed price ceilings and price floors.

Government Intervention in the Market: Price Floors and Price Ceilings

Notice that we have *not* concluded that every *individual* is better off if a market is at competitive equilibrium. We have only concluded that economic surplus, or the *total* net benefit to society, is greatest at competitive equilibrium. Any individual producer would rather charge a higher price, and any individual consumer would rather pay a lower price, but usually producers can sell and consumers can buy only at the competitive equilibrium price.

Producers or consumers who are dissatisfied with the competitive equilibrium price can lobby the government to legally require that a different price be charged. The U.S. government only occasionally overrides the market outcome by setting prices. When the government does intervene, it can either attempt to aid sellers by requiring that a price be above equilibrium—a *price floor*—or aid buyers by requiring that a price be below equilibrium—a *price ceiling*. To affect the market outcome, a price floor must be set above the equilibrium price and a price ceiling must be set below the equilibrium price. Otherwise, the price ceiling or price floor will not be *binding* on buyers and sellers. The preceding section demonstrates that moving away from competitive equilibrium will reduce economic efficiency. We can use the concepts of consumer surplus, producer surplus, and deadweight loss to see more clearly the economic inefficiency of binding price floors and price ceilings.

Price Floors: Government Policy in Agricultural Markets

The Great Depression of the 1930s was the greatest economic disaster in U.S. history, affecting every sector of the U.S. economy. Many farmers were unable to sell their products or could sell them only at very low prices. Farmers were able to convince the federal government to intervene to raise prices by setting price floors for many agricultural products. Government intervention in agriculture—often referred to as the "farm program"—has continued ever since. To see how a price floor in an agricultural market works, suppose that the equilibrium price in the wheat market is $3.00 per bushel but the government decides to set a price floor of $3.50 per bushel. As Figure 4-8 shows, the price of wheat rises from $3.00 to $3.50, and the quantity of wheat sold falls from 2.0 billion bushels per year to 1.8 billion. Initially, suppose that production of wheat also falls to 1.8 billion bushels.

Just as we saw in the earlier example of the market for chai tea (refer to Figure 4-7), the producer surplus received by wheat farmers increases by an amount equal to the area of the red rectangle *A* and falls by an amount equal to the area of the yellow triangle *C*. The area of the red rectangle *A* represents a transfer from consumer surplus to producer surplus. The total fall in consumer surplus is equal to the area of the red rectangle *A* plus the area of the yellow triangle *B*. Wheat farmers benefit from this program, but consumers lose. There is also a deadweight loss equal to the areas of the yellow triangles *B* and *C*, which represents the decline in economic efficiency due to the price floor. There

Figure 4-8

The Economic Effect of a Price Floor in the Wheat Market

If wheat farmers convince the government to impose a price floor of $3.50 per bushel, the amount of wheat sold will fall from 2.0 billion bushels per year to 1.8 billion. If we assume that farmers produce 1.8 billion bushels, producer surplus then increases by the red rectangle *A*—which is transferred from consumer surplus—and falls by the yellow triangle *C*. Consumer surplus declines by the red rectangle *A* plus the yellow triangle *B*. There is a deadweight loss equal to the yellow triangles *B* and *C*, representing the decline in economic efficiency due to the price floor. In reality, a price floor of $3.50 per bushel will cause farmers to expand their production from 2.0 billion to 2.2 billion bushels, resulting in a surplus of wheat.

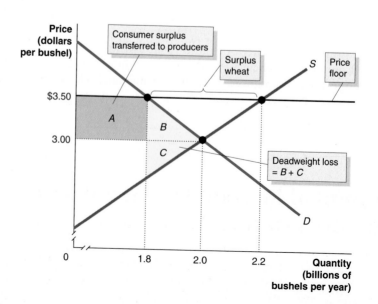

is a deadweight loss because the price floor has reduced the amount of economic surplus in the market for wheat. Or, looked at another way, the price floor has caused the marginal benefit of the last bushel of wheat to be greater than the marginal cost of producing it. We can conclude that a price floor reduces economic efficiency.

The actual federal government farm programs have been more complicated than just legally requiring farmers not to sell their output below a minimum price. We assumed initially that farmers reduce their production of wheat to the amount consumers are willing to buy. In fact, as Figure 4-8 shows, a price floor will cause the quantity of wheat that farmers want to supply to increase from 2.0 billion to 2.2 billion bushels. Because the higher price also reduces the amount of wheat consumers wish to buy, the result is a surplus of 0.4 billion bushels of wheat (the 2.2 billion bushels supplied minus the 1.8 billion demanded).

The federal government's farm programs have often resulted in large surpluses of wheat and other agricultural products. The government has usually either bought the surplus food or paid farmers to restrict supply by taking some land out of cultivation. Because both of these options are expensive, Congress passed the Freedom to Farm Act of 1996. The intent of the act was to phase out price floors and government purchases of surpluses and return to a free market in agriculture. To allow farmers time to adjust, the federal government began paying farmers *subsidies*, or cash payments based on the number of acres planted. Although the subsidies were originally scheduled to be phased out, Congress has continued to pay them.

Making the Connection | Price Floors in Labor Markets: The Debate over Minimum Wage Policy

The minimum wage may be the most controversial "price floor." Supporters see the minimum wage as a way of raising the incomes of low-skilled workers. Opponents argue that it results in fewer jobs and imposes large costs on small businesses.

In summer 2008, the national minimum wage as set by Congress is $6.55 per hour for most occupations. (The minimum wage is scheduled to increase to $7.25 per hour in 2009.) It is illegal for an employer to pay less than this wage in those occupations. For most workers, the minimum wage is irrelevant because it is well below the wage employers are voluntarily willing to pay them. But for low-skilled workers—such as workers in fast-food restaurants—the minimum wage is above the wage they would otherwise receive. The following figure shows the effect of the minimum wage on employment in the market for low-skilled labor.

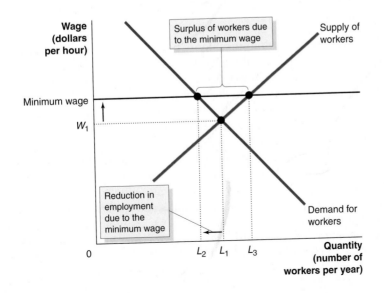

Without a minimum wage, the equilibrium wage would be W_1, and the number of workers hired would be L_1. With a minimum wage set above the equilibrium wage, the quantity of workers demanded by employers declines from L_1 to L_2, and the quantity of labor supplied increases to L_3, leading to a surplus of workers unable to find jobs equal to $L_3 - L_2$. The quantity of labor supplied increases because the higher wage attracts more people to work. For instance, some teenagers may decide that working after school is worthwhile at the minimum wage of $6.55 per hour but would not be worthwhile at a lower wage.

This analysis is very similar to our analysis of the wheat market in Figure 4-8. Just as a price floor in the wheat market leads to less wheat consumed, a price floor in the labor market should lead to fewer workers hired. Views differ sharply among economists, however, concerning how large a reduction in employment the minimum wage causes. For instance, David Card of the University of California, Berkeley, and Alan Krueger of Princeton University conducted a study of fast-food restaurants in New Jersey and Pennsylvania that indicates that the effect of minimum wage increases on employment is very small. Card and Krueger's study has been very controversial, however. Other economists have examined similar data and have come to the different conclusion that the minimum wage leads to a significant decrease in employment.

Whatever the extent of employment losses from the minimum wage, because it is a price floor, it will cause a deadweight loss, just as a price floor in the wheat market does. Therefore, many economists favor alternative policies for attaining the goal of raising the incomes of low-skilled workers. One policy many economists support is the *earned income tax credit*. The earned income tax credit reduces the amount of tax that low-income wage earners would otherwise pay to the federal government. Workers with very low incomes who do not owe any tax receive a payment from the government. Compared with the minimum wage, the earned income tax credit can increase the incomes of low-skilled workers without reducing employment. The earned income tax credit also places a lesser burden on the small businesses that employ many low-skilled workers, and it might cause a smaller loss of economic efficiency.

Sources: David Card and Alan B. Krueger, *Myth and Measurement: The New Economics of the Minimum Wage*, Princeton, NJ: Princeton University Press, 1995; David Neumark and William Wascher, "Minimum Wages and Employment: A Case Study of the Fast-Food Industry in New Jersey and Pennsylvania: Comment," *American Economic Review*, Vol. 90, No. 5, December 2000, pp. 1362–1396; and David Card and Alan B. Krueger, "Minimum Wages and Employment: A Case Study of the Fast-Food Industry in New Jersey and Pennsylvania: Reply," *American Economic Review*, Vol. 90, No. 5, December 2000, pp. 1397–1420.

YOUR TURN: Test your understanding by doing related problem 3.12 on page 127 at the end of this chapter.

▬▬▬▬▬

Price Ceilings: Government Rent Control Policy in Housing Markets

Support for governments setting price floors typically comes from sellers, and support for governments setting price ceilings typically comes from consumers. For example, when there is a sharp increase in gasoline prices, there are often proposals for the government to impose a price ceiling on the market for gasoline. As we saw in the opener to this chapter, New York is one of the cities that imposes rent controls, which put a ceiling on the maximum rent that landlords can charge for an apartment. Figure 4-9 shows the market for apartments in a city that has rent controls.

Without rent control, the equilibrium rent would be $1,500 per month, and 2,000,000 apartments would be rented. With a maximum legal rent of $1,000 per month, landlords reduce the quantity of apartments supplied to 1,900,000. The fall in the quantity of apartments supplied is the result of some apartments being converted to offices or sold off as condominiums, some small apartment buildings being converted to single-family homes, and, over time, some apartment buildings being abandoned. In New York City, rent control has resulted in whole city blocks being abandoned by land-

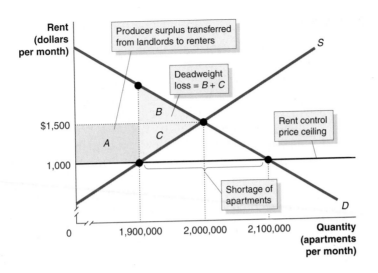

Figure 4-9

The Economic Effect of a Rent Ceiling

Without rent control, the equilibrium rent is $1,500 per month. At that price, 2,000,000 apartments would be rented. If the government imposes a rent ceiling of $1,000, the quantity of apartments supplied falls to 1,900,000, and the quantity of apartments demanded increases to 2,100,000, resulting in a shortage of 200,000 apartments. Producer surplus equal to the area of the blue rectangle *A* is transferred from landlords to renters, and there is a deadweight loss equal to the areas of yellow triangles *B* and *C*.

lords who were unable to cover their costs with the rents they were allowed to charge. In London, when rent controls were applied to rooms and apartments located in a landlord's own home, the quantity of these apartments supplied dropped by 75 percent.

In Figure 4-9, with the rent ceiling of $1,000, the quantity of apartments demanded rises to 2,100,000. There is a shortage of 200,000 apartments. Consumer surplus increases by rectangle *A* and falls by triangle *B*. Rectangle *A* would have been part of producer surplus if rent control were not in place. With rent control, it is part of consumer surplus. Rent control causes the producer surplus received by landlords to fall by rectangle *A* plus triangle *C*. Triangles *B* and *C* represent the deadweight loss. There is a deadweight loss because rent control has reduced the amount of economic surplus in the market for apartments. Rent control has caused the marginal benefit of the last apartment rented to be greater than the marginal cost of supplying it. We can conclude that a price ceiling, such as rent control, reduces economic efficiency. The appendix to this chapter shows how we can make quantitative estimates of the deadweight loss, and it shows the changes in consumer surplus and producer surplus that result from rent control.

Renters as a group benefit from rent controls—total consumer surplus is larger—but landlords lose. Because of the deadweight loss, the total loss to landlords is greater than the gain to renters. Notice also that although renters as a group benefit, the number of renters is reduced, so some renters are made worse off by rent controls because they are unable to find an apartment at the legal rent.

Don't Let This Happen to **YOU!**

Don't Confuse "Scarcity" with a "Shortage"

At first glance, the following statement seems correct: "There is a shortage of every good that is scarce." In everyday conversation, we describe a good as "scarce" if we have trouble finding it. For instance, if you are looking for a present for a child, you might call the latest hot toy "scarce" if you are willing to buy it at its listed price but can't find it online or in any store. But recall from Chapter 2 that economists have a broad definition of *scarce.* In the economic sense, almost everything—except undesirable things like garbage—is scarce. A shortage of a good occurs only if the quantity demanded is greater than the quantity supplied at the current price. Therefore, the preceding statement— "There is a shortage of every good that is scarce"—is incorrect. In fact, there is no shortage of most scarce goods.

YOUR TURN: Test your understanding by doing related problem 3.16 on page 128 at the end of this chapter.

Black Markets

To this point, our analysis of rent controls is incomplete. In practice, renters may be worse off and landlords may be better off than Figure 4-9 makes it seem. We have assumed that renters and landlords actually abide by the price ceiling, but sometimes they don't. Because rent control leads to a shortage of apartments, renters who would otherwise not be able to find apartments have an incentive to offer landlords rents above the legal maximum. When governments try to control prices by setting price ceilings or price floors, buyers and sellers often find a way around the controls. The result is a **black market** where buying and selling take place at prices that violate government price regulations.

Black market A market in which buying and selling take place at prices that violate government price regulations.

In a housing market with rent controls, the total amount of consumer surplus received by renters may be reduced and the total amount of producer surplus received by landlords may be increased if apartments are being rented at prices above the legal price ceiling.

Solved Problem | 4-3

What's the Economic Effect of a "Black Market" for Apartments?

In many cities with rent controls, the actual rents paid can be much higher than the legal maximum. Because rent controls cause a shortage of apartments, desperate tenants are often willing to pay landlords rents that are higher than the law allows, perhaps by writing a check for the legally allowed rent and paying an additional amount in cash. Look again at Figure 4-9 on page 111. Suppose that competition among tenants results in the black market rent rising to $2,000 per month. At this rent, tenants demand 1,900,000 apartments. Use a graph showing the market for apartments to compare this situation with the one shown in Figure 4-9. Be sure to note any differences in consumer surplus, producer surplus, and deadweight loss.

SOLVING THE PROBLEM:

Step 1: **Review the chapter material.** This problem is about price controls in the market for apartments, so you may want to review the section "Price Ceilings: Government Rent Control Policy in Housing Markets," which begins on page 110.

Step 2: **Draw a graph similar to Figure 4-9, with the addition of the black market price.**

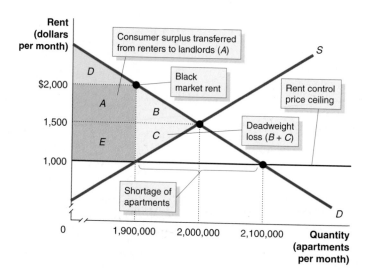

Step 3: **Analyze the changes from Figure 4-9.** Because the black market rent is now $2,000—even higher than the original competitive equilibrium rent of $1,500—compared with Figure 4-9, consumer surplus declines by an amount equal to the red rectangle *A* plus the red rectangle *E*. The remaining consumer surplus is the blue triangle *D*. Note that the rectangle *A*, which would have been part of consumer surplus without rent control, represents a transfer from renters to landlords. Compared with the situation shown in Figure 4-9, producer surplus has increased by an amount equal to rectangles *A* and *E*, and consumer surplus has declined by the same amount. Deadweight loss is equal to triangles *B* and *C*, the same as in Figure 4-9.

EXTRA CREDIT: This analysis leads to a surprising result: With an active black market in apartments, rent control may leave renters as a group worse off—with less consumer surplus—than if there were no rent control. There is one more possibility to consider, however. If enough landlords become convinced that they can get away with charging rents above the legal ceiling, the quantity of apartments supplied will increase. Eventually, the market could even end up at the competitive equilibrium, with an equilibrium rent of $1,500 and equilibrium quantity of 2,000,000 apartments. In that case the rent control price ceiling becomes nonbinding, not because it was set below the equilibrium price but because it was not legally enforced.

YOUR TURN: For more practice, do related problems 3.14 on page 127 and 3.23 on page 129 at the end of this chapter.

>> **End Solved Problem 4-3**

Rent controls can also lead to an increase in racial and other types of discrimination. With rent controls, more renters are looking for apartments than there are apartments to rent. Landlords can afford to indulge their prejudices by refusing to rent to people they don't like. In cities without rent controls, landlords face more competition, which makes it more difficult to turn down tenants on the basis of irrelevant characteristics, such as race.

Making the Connection | Does Holiday Gift Giving Have a Deadweight Loss?

The deadweight loss that results from rent control occurs, in part, because consumers rent fewer apartments than they would in a competitive equilibrium. Their choices are *constrained* by government. When you receive a gift, you are also constrained because the person who gave the gift has already chosen the product. In many cases, you would have chosen a different gift for yourself. Economist Joel Waldfogel of the University of Pennsylvania points out that gift giving results in a deadweight loss. The amount of the deadweight loss is equal to the difference between the gift's price and the dollar value the recipient places on the gift. Waldfogel surveyed his students, asking them to list every gift they had received for Christmas, to estimate the retail price of each gift, and to state how much they would have been willing to pay for each gift. Waldfogel's students estimated that their families and friends had paid $438 on average for the students' gifts. The students themselves, however, would have been willing to pay only $313 to buy the presents. If the deadweight losses experienced by Waldfogel's students were extrapolated to the whole population, the deadweight loss of Christmas gift giving could be as much as $13 billion.

Gift giving may lead to deadweight loss.

If the gifts had been cash, the people receiving the gifts would not have been constrained by the gift givers' choices, and there would have been no deadweight loss. If your sister had given you cash instead of that sweater you didn't like, you could have bought whatever you wanted. Why then do people continue giving presents rather than cash? One answer is that most people receive more satisfaction from giving or receiving a present than from giving or receiving cash. If we take this satisfaction into account, the deadweight loss from gift giving will be lower than in Waldfogel's calculations. In fact, a later study by economists John List of the University of Maryland and Jason Shogren of the University of Wyoming showed that as much as half the value of a gift to a recipient was its sentimental value. As Professor Shogren concluded, "People get a whole heck of a lot of value out of doing something for others and other people doing something for them. Aunt Helga gave you that ugly scarf, but hey, it's Aunt Helga."

Sources: Mark Whitehouse, "How Christmas Brings Out the Grinch in Economists," *Wall Street Journal*, December 23, 2006, p. A1; Joel Waldfogel, "The Deadweight Loss of Christmas," *American Economic Review*, Vol. 83, No. 4, December 1993, pp. 328–336; and John A. List and Jason F. Shogren, "The Deadweight Loss of Christmas: Comment," *American Economic Review*, Vol. 88, No, 5, 1998, pp. 1350–1355.

YOUR TURN: Test your understanding by doing related problem 3.15 on page 128 at the end of this chapter.

The Results of Government Price Controls: Winners, Losers, and Inefficiency

When the government imposes price floors or price ceilings, three important results occur:

- Some people win.

- Some people lose.

- There is a loss of economic efficiency.

The winners with rent control are the people who are paying less for rent because they live in rent-controlled apartments. Landlords may also gain if they break the law by charging rents above the legal maximum for their rent-controlled apartments, provided that those illegal rents are higher than the competitive equilibrium rents would be. The losers from rent control are the landlords of rent-controlled apartments who abide by the law and renters who are unable to find apartments to rent at the controlled price. Rent control reduces economic efficiency because fewer apartments are rented than would be rented in a competitive market (refer again to Figure 4-9). The resulting deadweight loss measures the decrease in economic efficiency.

Positive and Normative Analysis of Price Ceilings and Price Floors

Are rent controls, government farm programs, and other price ceilings and price floors bad? As we saw in Chapter 1, questions of this type have no right or wrong answers. Economists are generally skeptical of government attempts to interfere with competitive market equilibrium. Economists know the role competitive markets have played in raising the average person's standard of living. They also know that too much government intervention has the potential to reduce the ability of the market system to produce similar increases in living standards in the future.

But recall from Chapter 1 the difference between positive and normative analysis. Positive analysis is concerned with *what is*, and normative analysis is concerned with *what should be*. Our analysis of rent control and of the federal farm programs in this chapter is positive analysis. We discussed the economic results of these programs. Whether these programs are desirable or undesirable is a normative question. Whether the gains to the winners more than make up for the losses to the losers and for the decline in economic efficiency is a matter of judgment and not strictly an economic question. Price ceilings and price floors continue to exist partly because people who understand their downside still believe they are good policies and therefore support them. The policies also persist because many people who support them do not understand the economic analysis in this chapter and so do not understand the drawbacks to these policies.

4.4 LEARNING OBJECTIVE

4.4 | Analyze the economic impact of taxes.

The Economic Impact of Taxes

Supreme Court Justice Oliver Wendell Holmes once remarked, "Taxes are what we pay for a civilized society." When the government taxes a good, however, it affects the market equilibrium for that good. Just as with a price ceiling or price floor, one result of a tax is a decline in economic efficiency. Analyzing taxes is an important part of the field of economics known as *public finance*. In this section, we will use the model of demand and supply and the concepts of consumer surplus, producer surplus, and deadweight loss to analyze the economic impact of taxes.

The Effect of Taxes on Economic Efficiency

Whenever a government taxes a good or service, less of that good or service will be produced and consumed. For example, a tax on cigarettes will raise the cost of smoking and reduce the amount of smoking that takes place. We can use a demand and supply graph to illustrate this point. Figure 4-10 shows the market for cigarettes.

Without the tax, the equilibrium price of cigarettes would be $4.00 per pack, and 4 billion packs of cigarettes would be sold per year (point A). If the federal government requires sellers of cigarettes to pay a $1.00-per-pack tax, then their cost of selling cigarettes will increase by $1.00 per pack. This causes the supply curve for cigarettes to

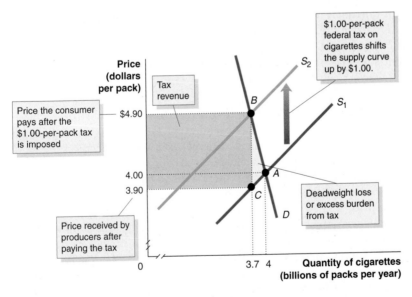

Figure 4-10 | The Effect of a Tax on the Market for Cigarettes

Without the tax, market equilibrium occurs at point A. The equilibrium price of cigarettes is $4.00 per pack, and 4 billion packs of cigarettes are sold per year. A $1.00-per-pack tax on cigarettes will cause the supply curve for cigarettes to shift up by $1.00, from S_1 to S_2. The new equilibrium occurs at point B. The price of cigarettes will increase by $0.90, to $4.90 per pack, and the quantity sold will fall to 3.7 billion packs. The tax on cigarettes has increased the price paid by consumers from $4.00 to $4.90 per pack. Producers receive a price of $4.90 per pack (point B), but after paying the $1.00 tax, they are left with $3.90 (point C). The government will receive tax revenue equal to the green shaded box. Some consumer surplus and some producer surplus will become tax revenue for the government and some will become deadweight loss, shown by the yellow-shaded area.

shift up by $1.00 because sellers will now require a price that is $1.00 greater to supply the same quantity of cigarettes. In Figure 4-10, for example, without the tax, sellers would be willing to supply a quantity of 3.7 billion packs of cigarettes at a price of $3.90 per pack (point *C*). With the tax, they will supply only 3.7 billion packs of cigarettes if the price is $4.90 per pack (point *B*). The shift in the supply curve will result in a new equilibrium price of $4.90 and a new equilibrium quantity of 3.7 billion packs (point *B*).

The federal government will collect tax revenue equal to the tax per pack multiplied by the number of packs sold, or $3.7 billion. The area shaded in green in Figure 4-10 represents the government's tax revenue. Consumers will pay a higher price of $4.90 per pack. Although sellers appear to be receiving a higher price per pack, after they have paid the tax, the price they receive falls from $4.00 per pack to $3.90 per pack. There is a loss of consumer surplus because consumers are paying a higher price. The price producers receive falls, so there is also a loss of producer surplus. Therefore, the tax on cigarettes has reduced *both* consumer surplus and producer surplus. Some of the reduction in consumer and producer surplus becomes tax revenue for the government. The rest of the reduction in consumer and producer surplus is equal to the deadweight loss from the tax, shown by the yellow-shaded triangle in the figure.

We can conclude that the true burden of a tax is not just the amount paid to government by consumers and producers but also includes the deadweight loss. The deadweight loss from a tax is referred to as the *excess burden* of the tax. *A tax is efficient if it imposes a small excess burden relative to the tax revenue it raises.* One contribution economists make to government tax policy is to provide advice to policymakers on which taxes are most efficient.

Tax Incidence: Who Actually Pays a Tax?

The answer to the question "Who pays a tax?" seems obvious: Whoever is legally required to send a tax payment to the government pays the tax. But there can be an important difference between who is legally required to pay the tax and who actually *bears the burden* of the tax. The actual division of the burden of a tax is referred to as **tax incidence**. The federal government currently levies an excise tax of 18.4 cents per gallon of gasoline sold. Gas station owners collect this tax and forward it to the federal government, but who actually bears the burden of the tax?

Tax incidence The actual division of the burden of a tax between buyers and sellers in a market.

Determining Tax Incidence on a Demand and Supply Graph Suppose that the retail price of gasoline—including the federal excise tax—is $3.08 per gallon, 140 billion gallons of gasoline are sold in the United States per year, and the federal excise tax is 10 cents per gallon. Figure 4-11 allows us to analyze the incidence of the tax.

Consider the market for gasoline if there were no federal excise tax on gasoline. This equilibrium occurs at the intersection of the demand curve and supply curve, S_1. The equilibrium price is $3.00 per gallon, and the equilibrium quantity is 144 billion gallons. If the federal government imposes a 10-cents-per-gallon tax, the supply curve for gasoline will shift up by 10 cents per gallon. At the new equilibrium, where the demand curve intersects the supply curve, S_2, the price has risen by 8 cents per gallon, from $3.00 to $3.08. Notice that only in the extremely unlikely case that demand is a vertical line will the market price rise by the full amount of the tax. Consumers are paying 8 cents more per gallon. Sellers of gasoline receive a new higher price of $3.08 per gallon, but after paying the 10-cents-per-gallon tax, they are left with $2.98 per gallon, or 2 cents less than they had been receiving in the old equilibrium.

Although the sellers of gasoline are responsible for collecting the tax and sending the tax receipts to the government, they do not bear most of the burden of the tax. In this case, consumers pay 8 cents of the tax because the market price has risen by 8 cents, and sellers pay 2 cents of the tax because after sending the tax to the government, they are receiving 2 cents less per gallon of gasoline sold. Expressed in percentage terms, consumers pay 80 percent of the tax, and sellers pay 20 percent of the tax.

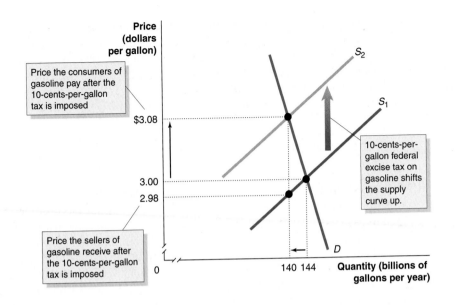

Price the consumers of gasoline pay after the 10-cents-per-gallon tax is imposed

Price the sellers of gasoline receive after the 10-cents-per-gallon tax is imposed

10-cents-per-gallon federal excise tax on gasoline shifts the supply curve up.

Figure 4-11

The Incidence of a Tax on Gasoline

With no tax on gasoline, the price would be $3.00 per gallon, and 144 billion gallons of gasoline would be sold each year. A 10-cents-per-gallon excise tax shifts up the supply curve from S_1 to S_2, raises the price consumers pay from $3.00 to $3.08, and lowers the price producers receive from $3.00 to $2.98. Therefore, consumers pay 8 cents of the 10-cents-per-gallon tax on gasoline, and producers pay 2 cents.

Solved Problem | 4-4

When Do Consumers Pay All of a Sales Tax Increase?

Briefly explain whether you agree with the following statement: "If the federal government raises the sales tax on gasoline by $0.25, then the price of gasoline will rise by $0.25. Consumers can't get by without gasoline, so they have to pay the whole amount of any increase in the sales tax." Illustrate your answer with a graph.

SOLVING THE PROBLEM:

Step 1: **Review the chapter material.** This problem is about tax incidence, so you may want to review the section "Tax Incidence: Who Actually Pays a Tax?" which begins on page 116.

Step 2: **Draw a graph like Figure 4-11 to illustrate the circumstances when consumers will pay all of an increase in a sales tax.**

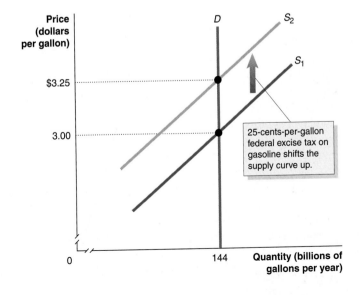

25-cents-per-gallon federal excise tax on gasoline shifts the supply curve up.

Step 3: **Use the graph to evaluate the statement.** The graph shows that consumers will pay all of an increase in a sales tax only if the demand curve is a vertical line. It is very unlikely that the demand for gasoline looks like this because we expect that for every good, an increase in price will cause a decrease in the quantity demanded. Because the demand curve for gasoline is not a vertical line, the statement is incorrect.

>> **End Solved Problem 4-4**

YOUR TURN: For more practice, do related problem 4.5 on page 130 at the end of the chapter.

Does It Matter Whether the Tax Is on Buyers or Sellers? We have already seen the important distinction between the true burden of a tax and whether buyers or sellers are legally required to pay a tax. We can reinforce this point by noting explicitly that the incidence of a tax does *not* depend on whether a tax is collected from the buyers of a good or from the sellers. Figure 4-12 illustrates this point by showing the effect on equilibrium in the market for gasoline if a 10-cents-per-gallon tax is imposed on buyers rather than on sellers. That is, we are now assuming that instead of sellers having to collect the 10-cents-per-gallon tax at the pump, buyers are responsible for keeping track of how many gallons of gasoline they purchase and sending the tax to the government. (Of course, it would be very difficult for buyers to keep track of their purchases or for the government to check whether they were paying all of the tax they owed. That is why the government collects the tax on gasoline from sellers.)

Figure 4-12 is similar to Figure 4-11 except that it shows the gasoline tax being imposed on buyers rather than sellers. In Figure 4-12, the supply curve does not shift because nothing has happened to change the willingness of sellers to change the quantity of gasoline they supply. The demand curve has shifted, however, because consumers now have to pay a 10-cent tax on every gallon of gasoline they buy. Therefore, at every quantity, they are willing to pay a price 10 cents less than they would have without the tax. We indicate this in the figure by shifting the demand curve down by 10 cents, from D_1 to D_2. Once the tax has been imposed and the demand curve has shifted down, the new equilibrium quantity of gasoline is 140 billion gallons, which is exactly the same as in Figure 4-11.

The new equilibrium price after the tax is imposed appears to be different in Figure 4-12 than in Figure 4-11, but if we include the tax, buyers will pay and sellers will receive the same price in both figures. To see this, notice that in Figure 4-11, buyers paid sellers a price of $3.08 per gallon. In Figure 4-12, they pay sellers only $2.98, but they must also pay the government a tax of 10 cents per gallon. So, the total price buyers pay remains

Figure 4-12

The Incidence of a Tax on Gasoline Paid by Buyers

With no tax on gasoline, the demand curve is D_1. If a 10-cents-per-gallon tax is imposed that consumers are responsible for paying, the demand curve shifts down by the amount of the tax, from D_1 to D_2. In the new equilibrium, consumers pay a price of $3.08 per gallon, including the tax. Producers receive $2.98 per gallon. This is the same result we saw when producers were responsible for paying the tax.

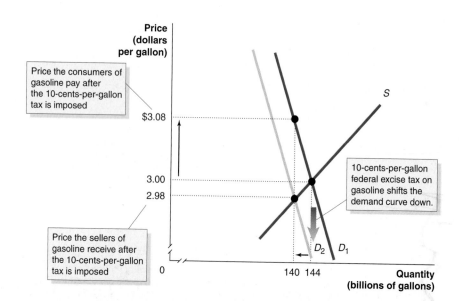

Price the consumers of gasoline pay after the 10-cents-per-gallon tax is imposed

10-cents-per-gallon federal excise tax on gasoline shifts the demand curve down.

Price the sellers of gasoline receive after the 10-cents-per-gallon tax is imposed

$3.08 per gallon. In Figure 4-11, sellers receive $3.08 per gallon from buyers, but after they pay the tax of 10 cents per gallon, they are left with $2.98, which is the same amount they receive in Figure 4-12.

Making the Connection | Is the Burden of the Social Security Tax Really Shared Equally between Workers and Firms?

Everyone who receives a paycheck has several different taxes withheld from it by their employers, who forward these taxes directly to the government. In fact, many people are shocked after getting their first job, when they discover the gap between their gross pay and their net pay after taxes have been deducted. The largest tax many people of low or moderate income pay is the FICA, which stands for the Federal Insurance Contributions Act. The FICA funds the Social Security and Medicare programs, which provide income and health care to the elderly and disabled. The FICA is sometimes referred to as the *payroll tax*. When Congress passed the FICA, it wanted employers and workers to equally share the burden of the tax. Currently, the FICA is 15.3 percent of wages, with 7.65 percent paid by workers by being withheld from their paychecks and the other 7.65 percent paid by employers.

But does requiring workers and employers to each pay half the tax mean that the burden of the tax is also shared equally? Our discussion in this chapter shows us that the answer is no. In the

How much FICA do you think this employee pays?

labor market, employers are buyers, and workers are sellers. As we saw in the example of federal taxes on gasoline, whether the tax is collected from buyers or from sellers does not affect the incidence of the tax. Most economists believe, in fact, that the burden of the FICA falls almost entirely on workers. The following figure, which shows the market for labor, illustrates why.

(a) The Social Security tax paid by employers

(b) The Social Security tax paid by workers

In the market for labor, the demand curve reflects the quantity of labor demanded by employers at various wages, and the supply curve reflects the quantity of labor supplied by workers at various wages. The intersection of the demand curve and the supply curve determines the equilibrium wage. In both panels, the equilibrium wage without a Social Security payroll tax is $10 per hour. For simplicity, let's assume that the payroll tax equals $1 per hour of work. In panel (a), we assume that employers must pay the tax. The tax causes the demand for labor curve to shift down by $1 at every quantity of labor because firms now must pay a $1 tax for every hour of labor they hire. We have drawn the supply curve for labor as being very steep because most economists believe the quantity of labor supplied by workers does not change much as the wage rate changes. Workers pay $0.95 of the tax because their wages fall from $10 before the tax to $9.05 after the tax. Firms pay only $0.05 of the tax because the amount they pay for an hour of labor increases from $10 before the tax to $10.05 after the tax. In panel (a), after the tax is imposed, the equilibrium wage declines from $10 per hour to $9.05 per hour. Firms are now paying a total of $10.05 for every hour of work they hire: $9.05 in wages to workers and $1 in tax to the government. In other words, workers have paid $0.95 of the $1 tax, and firms have paid only $0.05.

Panel (b) shows that this result is exactly the same if the tax is imposed on workers rather than on firms. In this case, the tax causes the supply curve for labor to shift up by $1 at every quantity of labor because workers must now pay a tax of $1 for every hour they work. After the tax is imposed, the equilibrium wage increases to $10.05 per hour. But workers receive only $9.05 after they have paid the $1.00 tax. Once again, workers have paid $0.95 of the $1 tax, and firms have paid only $0.05.

Although the figure presents a simplified analysis, it reflects the conclusion of most economists who have studied the incidence of the FICA: Even though Congress requires half the tax to be paid by employers and the other half to be paid by workers, in fact, the burden of the tax falls almost entirely on workers. This conclusion would not be changed even if Congress revised the law to require either employers or workers to pay all of the tax. The forces of demand and supply working in the labor market, and not Congress, determine the incidence of the tax.

YOUR TURN: Test your understanding by doing related problem 4.6 on page 130 at the end of this chapter.

Economics in YOUR Life!

▶▶ **Continued from page 99**

At the beginning of the chapter, we posed the following question: If you have two job offers in different cities, one with rent control and one without, will you be more likely to find an affordable apartment in the city with rent control? In answering the question, this chapter has shown that although rent control can keep rents lower than they might otherwise be, it can also lead to a permanent shortage of apartments. You may have to search for a long time to find a suitable apartment, and landlords may even ask you to give them payments "under the table," which would make your actual rent higher than the controlled rent. Finding an apartment in a city without rent control should be much easier, although the rent may be higher.

Conclusion

The model of demand and supply introduced in Chapter 3 showed that markets free from government intervention eliminate surpluses and shortages and do a good job of responding to the wants of consumers. We have seen in this chapter that both consumers and firms sometimes try to use the government to change market outcomes in their favor. The concepts of consumer and producer surplus and deadweight loss allow us to measure the benefits consumers and producers receive from competitive market equilibrium. They also allow us to measure the effects of government price floors and price ceilings and the economic impact of taxes.

Read *An Inside Look at Policy* on page 122 for a discussion of the debate over rent control in Los Angeles.

LOS ANGELES TIMES, JANUARY 14, 2007

The Landlords: Two Sides of a Coin

With apologies to David Letterman, the Top Five reasons why landlords hate rent control are:

No. 1. As private citizens, they believe they shouldn't be forced to do the government's job of providing low-cost housing.

No. 2. In few sectors of private enterprise does a city tell a business how much it may charge.

No. 3. Rent-control buildings sell for less, even in high-rolling realty days.

No. 4. Capping what they may collect in rents translates to capping what they can spend on maintenance and repair—and then they get dinged for lousy upkeep.

No. 5: It's virtually impossible to evict undesirable tenants from a rent-controlled building; owners of buildings not under rent control can boot them out for nearly any reason. . . .

Some Westside owners [in Los Angeles], in particular, complain that longtime renters get a lifetime break, even when they easily can afford market rates. Rent-control laws do not require financial-means testing, so professionals, for example, could still be living in rent-controlled units they secured when they were struggling students. Also, some renters secretly sublet their cheap units for market rate, flouting the terms of their contracts, landlords say. . . .

In an identical unit in the building, a recent tenant was paying about $900 a month while charging $1,000 for one of the bedrooms she rented out on the side, Lambert [a Santa Monica landlord of a rent-controlled building] said.

Selling rent-controlled buildings is no cakewalk, either, said Bruce Bernard, who has bought and sold scores of such buildings in Los Angeles. He recently got his asking price of $6.5 million for a 42-unit building in Hollywood that was not under rent control. One mile away, he also recently sold a 20-unit rent-controlled building with similar amenities for $2.3 million, which was $1.1 million less than his listing price.

More dramatically, Lambert got zero offers on his 15-unit rent-controlled building listed for $890,000 just before the 1994 Northridge earthquake. The temblor shoved the building off the foundation, resulting in all of the tenants vacating the red-tagged structure. Despite $500,000 in needed repairs and not a penny of rent coming in, Lambert quickly sold the building after it was legally rent decontrolled—for $950,000. "It was worth more with all that damage and no rent control than the day before the quake, when it had paying tenants. What does that tell you?"

Hard as it is to sell rent-controlled units for a market-rate profit, owners of those buildings face more urgent daily concerns: covering rising insurance, taxes, upkeep, water, plumbing, landscaping and other costs with 3% or 4% annual rent increases. The result often is that repairs are not made in a timely fashion. . . .

The Rent Stabilization Ordinance allows owners to "pass through" half of the costs of capital improvements to tenants. For example, when an owner replaces a roof for $20,000, he or she may divide half of that cost by the number of units in the building and charge the tenants of each unit up to $55 per month—spread out over multiple years—to cover the cost of the repair.

Even so, Stephens [a landlord near the Hollywood Bowl] said, "sometimes you get killed" economically. Landlords complain that some renters, hip to the strict Rent Escrow Account Program—which allows them to pay the city up to 50% of their rent and landlords nothing while units with health or safety violations are being brought up to code—deliberately ruin buildings to avoid paying full rent.

Attorney Harold Greenberg, who owns buildings and represents landlords, recalled a tenant who took a sledgehammer to the walls of his apartment, then reported the damage to the city, getting a rent discount while repairs were underway.

Bennett said he fixed a broken pole in the parking lot of one of his buildings and tenants subsequently rammed their cars into it five more times. Bennett finally closed the lot.

"We pay for repairs and pay for the inspections," said Jim Clarke, manager of government relations for the Apartment Assn. of Greater Los Angeles. "We've become the housing department's cash cow." . . .

Source: Diane Wedner, "The Landlords: Two Sides of a Coin," Los Angeles Times, January 14, 2007, p. K1. Copyright © 2007 Los Angeles Times. Reprinted with permission.

Key Points in the Article

The article discusses the effects of rent-control laws in the Los Angeles market. Los Angeles, like New York City, which we discussed in the chapter opener, places limits on the rents that landlords can charge some tenants. The purpose of rent-control laws is to ensure that low-income people can find affordable housing. As the article and the chapter explain, rent controls impose substantial costs on landlords, which, in turn, may also harm renters.

Analyzing the News

(a) The law in Los Angeles does not require that tenants in rent-controlled apartments prove they have low incomes, so some rent-controlled apartments are rented to people with high incomes. In other words, there is nothing in the law to guarantee that rent-controlled apartments go to the intended beneficiaries of the law. A rent-control law may actually increase the rent some tenants pay. The figure in Solved Problem 4-3 on page 112 shows that the rent-control laws create a shortage of apartments and that the resulting black market rent is often higher than the rent without rent-control laws. That is why the Santa Monica tenant in the article was able to charge $1,000 to rent a single room of her rent-controlled apartment when she paid just $900 to rent the entire apartment.

(b) Not surprisingly, rent-control laws reduce the price for which a landlord can sell a rent-controlled apartment complex. Clearly, this hurts the landlord, but it can also harm renters. The lower selling price for rent-controlled apartment complexes makes building those complexes less profitable. If developers can't make a profit building rent-controlled apartment complexes, then they won't build them. Over time, the number of rent-controlled complexes should decrease as old complexes become run down and developers lack the incentive to build new ones. The supply of rent-controlled apartments should decrease, making the apartment shortage worse. The figure below shows the effect of the decrease in rent-controlled apartment complexes as a shift of the supply curve to the left, from S_1 to S_2. This shift causes the shortage of apartments to increase from $(Q_1 - Q_2)$ to $(Q_1 - Q_3)$. In addition, the black market rent also increases from Black Market$_1$ to Black Market$_2$.

(c) Rent-control laws also limit the ability of landlords to raise rents to pay for repairs. Indeed, as the article indicates, some of the laws are written in a way that actually gives tenants an incentive to purposely damage the apartment complex. Both the limit on recovering repair costs and the incentives for tenants to damage the property increase the costs of running rent-controlled apartment complexes. These costs can cause the supply curve in this market to shift even further to the left and make the effects we described in part b even larger.

Thinking Critically About Policy

1. The article describes the significant costs associated with rent-control laws. Despite these costs, rent-control laws are very popular with tenants and local politicians. Why would some tenants support rent-control laws? Do all tenants in the market gain from rent-control laws?

2. Economists are critical of rent-control laws for several reasons. One reason is that the laws create a deadweight loss. The magnitude of this deadweight loss depends on the slopes of the demand and supply curves. Look at the figure for Solved Problem 4-3 on page 112. The deadweight loss equals $B + C$, which is the yellow area. What causes the deadweight loss? What would the supply curve have to look like for the deadweight loss to equal zero?

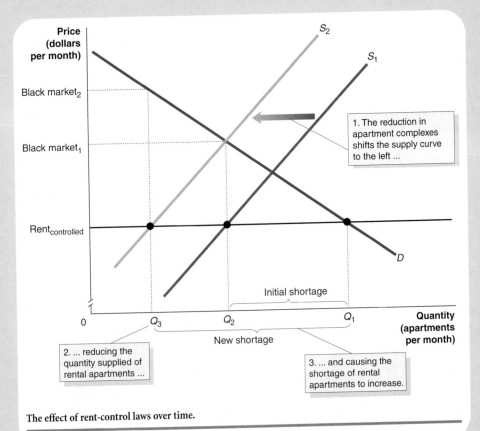

The effect of rent-control laws over time.

123

Key Terms

Black market, p. 112

Consumer surplus, p. 100

Deadweight loss, p. 107

Economic efficiency, p. 107

Economic surplus, p. 106

Marginal benefit, p. 100

Marginal cost, p. 103

Price ceiling, p. 100

Price floor, p. 100

Producer surplus, p. 104

Tax incidence, p. 116

4.1 LEARNING OBJECTIVE
pages 100–105.

4.1 | Distinguish between the concepts of consumer surplus and producer surplus.

Consumer Surplus and Producer Surplus

Summary

Although most prices are determined by demand and supply in markets, the government sometimes imposes *price ceilings* and *price floors*. A **price ceiling** is a legally determined maximum price that sellers may charge. A **price floor** is a legally determined minimum price that sellers may receive. Economists analyze the effects of price ceilings and price floors using *consumer surplus* and *producer surplus*. **Marginal benefit** is the additional benefit to a consumer from consuming one more unit of a good or service. The demand curve is also a marginal benefit curve. **Consumer surplus** is the difference between the highest price a consumer is willing to pay for a product and the price the consumer actually pays. The total amount of consumer surplus in a market is equal to the area below the demand curve and above the market price. **Marginal cost** is the additional cost to a firm of producing one more unit of a good or service. The supply curve is also a marginal cost curve. **Producer surplus** is the difference between the lowest price a firm is willing to accept and the price it actually receives. The total amount of producer surplus in a market is equal to the area above the supply curve and below the market price.

myeconlab Visit www.myeconlab.com to complete these exercises *Get Ahead of the Curve* online and get instant feedback.

Review Questions

1.1 What is marginal benefit? Why is the demand curve referred to as a marginal benefit curve?

1.2 What is marginal cost? Why is the supply curve referred to as a marginal cost curve?

1.3 What is consumer surplus? How does consumer surplus change as the equilibrium price of a good rises or falls?

1.4 What is producer surplus? How does producer surplus change as the equilibrium price of a good rises or falls?

Problems and Applications

1.5 Suppose that a frost in Florida reduces the size of the orange crop, which causes the supply curve for oranges to shift to the left. Briefly explain whether each of the following will increase or decrease. Use demand and supply to illustrate your answers.
   a. Consumer surplus
   b. Producer surplus

1.6 A student makes the following argument: "When a market is in equilibrium, there is no consumer surplus. We know this because in equilibrium, the market price is equal to the price consumers are willing to pay for the good." Briefly explain whether you agree with the student's argument.

1.7 The following graph illustrates the market for a breast cancer–fighting drug, without which breast cancer patients cannot survive. What is the consumer surplus in this market? How does it differ from the consumer surplus in the markets you have studied up to this point?

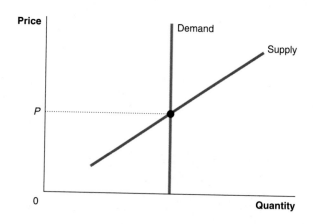

1.8 (Related to the *Making the Connection* on page 102) The *Making the Connection* states that the value of the area representing consumer surplus from satellite television is $2 billion. Use the information from the graph in the *Making the Connection* to show how this value was calculated. (For a review of how to calculate the area of a triangle, see the appendix to Chapter 1.)

1.9 The graph in the next column shows the market for tickets to a concert that will be held in a local arena that seats 15,000 people. What is the producer surplus in this market? How does it differ from the producer surplus in the markets you have studied up to this point?

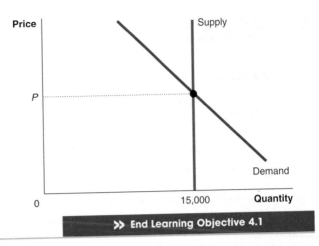

>> End Learning Objective 4.1

4.2 LEARNING OBJECTIVE

4.2 | Understand the concept of economic efficiency, **pages 105–107.**

The Efficiency of Competitive Markets

Summary

Equilibrium in a competitive market is **economically efficient. Economic surplus** is the sum of consumer surplus and producer surplus. Economic efficiency is a market outcome in which the marginal benefit to consumers from the last unit produced is equal to the marginal cost of production and where the sum of consumer surplus and producer surplus is at a maximum. When the market price is above or below the equilibrium price, there is a reduction in economic surplus. The reduction in economic surplus resulting from a market not being in competitive equilibrium is called the **deadweight loss.**

myeconlab Visit www.myeconlab.com to complete these exercises *Get Ahead of the Curve* online and get instant feedback.

Review Questions

2.1 Define economic surplus and deadweight loss?

2.2 What is economic efficiency? Why do economists define efficiency in this way?

Problems and Applications

2.3 Suppose you were assigned the task of coming up with a single number that would allow someone to compare the economic activity in one country to that in another country. How might such a number be related to economic efficiency and consumer and producer surplus?

2.4 Briefly explain whether you agree with the following statement: "If at the current quantity marginal benefit is greater than marginal cost, there will be a deadweight loss in the market. However, there is no deadweight loss when marginal cost is greater than marginal benefit."

2.5 Briefly explain whether you agree with the following statement: "If consumer surplus in a market increases, producer surplus must decrease."

2.6 Does an increase in economic surplus in a market always mean that economic efficiency in the market has increased? Briefly explain.

2.7 Using the graph below, explain why economic surplus would be smaller if Q_1 or Q_3 were the quantity produced than if Q_2 is the quantity produced.

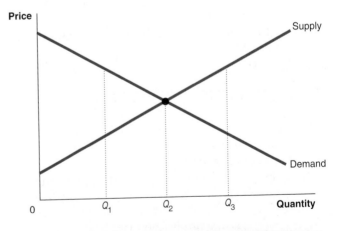

>> End Learning Objective 4.2

4.3 LEARNING OBJECTIVE   4.3 | Explain the economic effect of government-imposed price ceilings and price floors, **pages 107–115.**

Government Intervention in the Market: Price Floors and Price Ceilings

Summary

Producers or consumers who are dissatisfied with the market outcome can attempt to convince the government to impose price floors or price ceilings. Price floors usually increase producer surplus, decrease consumer surplus, and cause a deadweight loss. Price ceilings usually increase consumer surplus, reduce producer surplus, and cause a deadweight loss. The results of the government imposing price ceilings and price floors are that some people win, some people lose, and a loss of economic efficiency occurs. Price ceilings and price floors can lead to a **black market**, where buying and selling takes place at prices that violate government price regulations. Positive analysis is concerned with what is, and normative analysis is concerned with what should be. Positive analysis shows that price ceilings and price floors cause deadweight losses. Whether these policies are desirable or undesirable, though, is a normative question.

myeconlab Visit www.myeconlab.com to complete these exercises *Get Ahead of the Curve* online and get instant feedback.

Review Questions

3.1 Why do some consumers tend to favor price controls while others tend to oppose them?

3.2 Do producers tend to favor price floors or price ceilings? Why?

3.3 What is a black market? Under what circumstances do black markets arise?

3.4 Can economic analysis provide a final answer to the question of whether the government should intervene in markets by imposing price ceilings and price floors? Why or why not?

Problems and Applications

3.5 The graph in the next column shows the market for apples. Assume the government has imposed a price floor of $10 per crate.
   a. How many crates of apples will be sold after the price floor has been imposed?
   b. Will there be a shortage or a surplus? If there is a shortage or a surplus, how large will it be?
   c. Will apple producers benefit from the price floor? If so, explain how they will benefit.

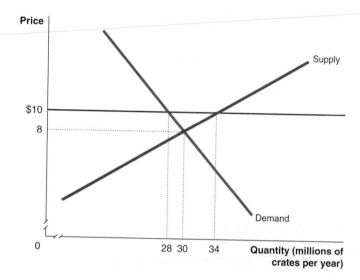

3.6 Use the information on the kumquat market in the table to answer the following questions.

PRICE (PER CRATE)	QUANTITY DEMANDED (MILLIONS OF CRATES PER YEAR)	QUANTITY SUPPLIED (MILLIONS OF CRATES PER YEAR)
$10	120	20
15	110	60
20	100	100
25	90	140
30	80	180
35	70	220

   a. What are the equilibrium price and quantity? How much revenue do kumquat producers receive when the market is in equilibrium? Draw a graph showing the market equilibrium and the area representing the revenue received by kumquat producers.
   b. Suppose the federal government decides to impose a price floor of $30 per crate. Now how many crates of kumquats will consumers purchase? How much revenue will kumquat producers receive? Assume that the government does not purchase any surplus kumquats. On your graph from question (a), show the price floor, the change in the quantity of kumquats purchased, and the revenue received by kumquat producers after the price floor is imposed.
   c. Suppose the government imposes a price floor of $30 per crate and purchases any surplus kumquats from producers. Now how much revenue will kumquat producers receive? How much will the

government spend purchasing surplus kumquats? On your graph from question (a), show the area representing the amount the government spends to purchase the surplus kumquats.

3.7 Suppose that the government sets a price floor for milk that is above the competitive equilibrium price.
   a. Draw a graph showing this situation. Be sure your graph shows the competitive equilibrium price, the price floor, the quantity that would be sold in competitive equilibrium, and the quantity that is sold with the price floor.
   b. Compare the economic surplus in this market when there is a price floor and when there is no price floor.

3.8 During 2007, the Venezuelan government allowed consumers to buy only a limited quantity of sugar. The government also imposed a ceiling on the price of sugar. As a result, both the quantity of sugar consumed and the market price of sugar were below the competitive equilibrium price and quantity. Draw a graph to illustrate this situation. On your graph, be sure to indicate the areas representing consumer surplus, producer surplus, and deadweight loss.

3.9 Refer again to question 3.8. An article in the *New York Times* contained the following (Hugo Chávez is the president of Venezuela):

> José Vielma Mora, the chief of Seniat, the government's tax agency, oversaw a raid this month on a warehouse here where officials seized about 165 tons of sugar. Mr. Vielma said the raid exposed hoarding by vendors who were unwilling to sell the sugar at official prices. He and other officials in Mr. Chávez's government have repeatedly blamed the shortages on producers, intermediaries and grocers.

Do you agree that the shortages in the Venezuelan sugar market are the fault of "producers, intermediaries and grocers"? Briefly explain.

Source: Simon Romero, "Chavez Threatens to Jail Price Control Violators," *New York Times*, February 17, 2007.

3.10 To drive a taxi legally in New York City, you must have a medallion issued by the city government. City officials have issued only 12,187 medallions. Let's assume this puts an absolute limit on the number of taxi rides that can be supplied in New York City on any day because no one breaks the law by driving a taxi without a medallion. Let's also assume that each taxi can provide 6 trips per day. In that case, the supply of taxi rides is fixed at 73,122 (or 6 rides per taxi × 12,187 taxis). We show this in the following graph, with a vertical line at this quantity. *Assume that there are no government controls on the prices that drivers can charge for rides.* Use the graph to answer the following questions.

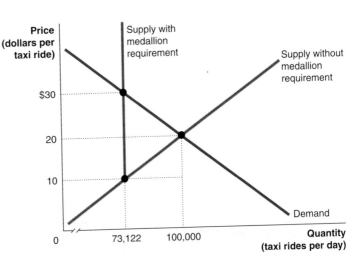

a. What would the equilibrium price and quantity be in this market if there were no medallion requirement?
b. What are the price and quantity with the medallion requirement?
c. Indicate on the graph the areas representing consumer surplus and producer surplus if there were no medallion requirement.
d. Indicate on the graph the areas representing consumer surplus, producer surplus, and deadweight loss with the medallion requirement.

3.11 If the goal of the federal government's farm program is to raise the incomes of poor family farmers, is the current system of price floors and subsidy payments based on the number of acres farmed a good way to reach the goal? Briefly explain. What other ways might the federal government attempt to reach its goals?

3.12 (Related to the *Making the Connection* on page 109) Some economists studying the effects of the minimum wage law have found that it tends to reduce the employment of black teenagers relative to white teenagers. Does the graph in the *Making the Connection* on page 109 help you understand why black teenagers may have been disproportionately affected by the minimum wage? Briefly explain.

3.13 (Related to the *Chapter Opener* on page 98) Suppose the competitive equilibrium rent for a standard two-bedroom apartment in Lawrence is $600. Now suppose the city council passes a rent-control law imposing a price ceiling of $500. Use a demand and supply graph to illustrate the impact of the rent-control law. Suppose that shortly after the law is passed, a large employer in the area announces that it will close a plant in Lawrence and lay off 5,000 workers. Show on your graph how this will affect the market for rental property in Lawrence.

3.14 (Related to *Solved Problem 4-3* on page 112) Use the information on the market for apartments in Bay City in the table on the next page to answer the following questions.

Compared with its value in competitive equilibrium, producer surplus has been reduced by a value equal to the area of the yellow triangle C plus a value equal to the area of the blue rectangle. The area of the yellow triangle C is:

$$\tfrac{1}{2} \times 1,500,000 - 850,000) \times (1,500 - 1,000) = \$162,500,000.$$

We have already calculated the area of the blue rectangle A as \$425,000,000. The value of producer surplus in competitive equilibrium was \$865,500,000. As a result of the rent ceiling, it will be reduced to:

$$\$865,500,000 - \$162,500,000 - \$425,000,000 = \$278,000,000.$$

The loss of economic efficiency, as measured by the deadweight loss, is equal to the value represented by the areas of the yellow triangles B and C, or:

$$\$211,250,000 + \$162,500,000 = \$373,750,000.$$

The following table summarizes the results of the analysis (the values are in millions of dollars).

CONSUMER SURPLUS		PRODUCER SURPLUS		DEADWEIGHT LOSS	
COMPETITIVE EQUILIBRIUM	RENT CONTROL	COMPETITIVE EQUILIBRIUM	RENT CONTROL	COMPETITIVE EQUILIBRIUM	RENT CONTROL
$1,125	$1,338.75	$865.50	$278	$0	$373.75

Qualitatively, we know that imposing rent controls will make consumers better off, make landlords worse off, and decrease economic efficiency. The advantage of the analysis we have just gone through is that it puts dollar values on the qualitative results. We can now see how much consumers have gained, how much landlords have lost, and how great the decline in economic efficiency has been. Sometimes the quantitative results can be surprising. Notice, for instance, that after the imposition of rent control, the deadweight loss is actually greater than the remaining producer surplus.

Economists often study issues where the qualitative results of actions are apparent, even to non-economists. You don't have to be an economist to understand who wins and loses from rent control or that if a company cuts the price of its product, its sales will increase. Business managers, policymakers, and the general public do, however, need economists to measure quantitatively the effects of different actions—including policies such as rent control—so that they can better assess the results of these actions.

LEARNING OBJECTIVE   Use Quantitative Demand and Supply Analysis, **pages 131-134.**

myeconlab   Visit www.myeconlab.com to complete these exercises
Get Ahead of the Curve online and get instant feedback.

Review Questions

4A.1 In a linear demand equation, what economic information is conveyed by the intercept on the price axis?

4A.2 Suppose you were assigned the task of choosing a price that maximized economic surplus in a market. What price would you choose? Why?

4A.3 Consumer surplus is used as a measure of a consumer's net benefit from purchasing a good or service. Explain why consumer surplus is a measure of net benefit.

4A.4 Why would economists use the term *deadweight loss* to describe the impact on consumer and producer surplus from a price control?

Problems and Applications

4A.5 Suppose that you have been hired to analyze the impact on employment from the imposition of a minimum wage in the labor market. Further suppose that you estimate the supply and demand functions for labor, where L stands for the quantity of labor (measured in thousands of workers) and W stands for the wage rate (measured in dollars per hour):

Demand: $L^D = 100 - 4W$
Supply: $L^S = 6W$

First, calculate the free-market equilibrium wage and quantity of labor. Now suppose the proposed minimum wage is \$12. How large will the surplus of labor in this market be?

4A.6 The following graphs illustrate the markets for two different types of labor. Suppose an identical minimum wage is imposed in both markets. In which market will the minimum wage have the largest impact on employment? Why?

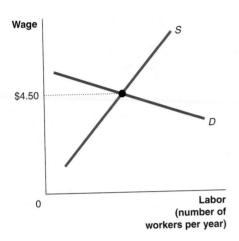

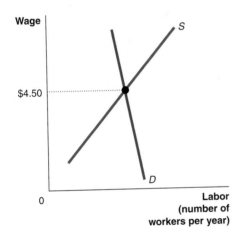

4A.7 Suppose that you are the vice president of operations of a manufacturing firm that sells an industrial lubricant in a competitive market. Further suppose that your economist gives you the following supply and demand functions:

Demand: $Q^D = 45 - 2P$
Supply: $Q^S = -15 + P$

What is the consumer surplus in this market? What is the producer surplus?

4A.8 The following graph shows a market in which a price floor of $3.00 per unit has been imposed. Calculate the values of each of the following.
  a. The deadweight loss
  b. The transfer of producer surplus to consumers or the transfer of consumer surplus to producers
  c. Producer surplus after the price floor is imposed
  d. Consumer surplus after the price floor is imposed

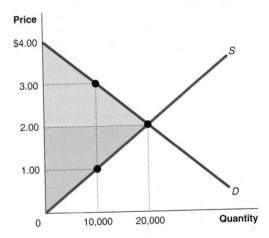

4A.9 Construct a table like the one in this appendix on page 134, but assume that the rent ceiling is $1,200 rather than $1,000.

>> **End Appendix Learning Objective**

Chapter 5

Externalities, Environmental Policy, and Public Goods

Economic Policy and the Environment

Pollution is a part of economic life. Consumers create air pollution by burning gasoline to power their cars and natural gas to heat their homes. Firms create air pollution when they produce electricity, pesticides, or plastics, among other products. Utilities produce sulfur dioxide when they burn coal to generate electricity. Sulfur dioxide contributes to acid rain, which can damage trees, crops, and buildings. The burning of fossil fuels generates carbon dioxide and other greenhouse gases that can increase global warming.

How should government policy deal with the problem of pollution? Can economic analysis help in formulating more efficient pollution policies? In the past, Congress frequently employed policies that ordered firms to use particular methods to reduce pollution. But many economists are critical of this approach—known as *command and control*—because some companies are able to reduce their emissions much more inexpensively if they are allowed to choose the method. To deal with reducing sulfur dioxide emissions in the most efficient way, economists recommended, and Congress adopted, a *market-based approach* called *tradable emissions allowances*.

Under this system, which went into operation in 1995, the federal government gives utility companies allowances to produce a target amount of sulfur dioxide emissions. Utilities are free to buy and sell allowances, although they must end up with allowances equal to the amount of sulfur dioxide they wish to emit: one allowance for every ton of sulfur dioxide emitted. Utilities that initially lack sufficient allowances either must reduce the amount of sulfur dioxide they emit or buy allowances from other utilities that are polluting less.

For example, Duke Energy generates electricity using coal-burning plants, which emit sulfur dioxide. Because Duke Energy already burns low-sulfur coal, reducing emissions of sulfur dioxide even further would be expensive. Many electric utilities in the Midwest, however, burn high-sulfur coal, and their emissions can be reduced greatly by installing anti-pollution devices known as "scrubbers." As a result, these utilities can drastically reduce their emissions and still have allowances left that they can sell to utilities like Duke Energy. According to the manager in charge of environmental compliance at the company, reducing emissions of sulfur dioxide would cost Duke Energy about $300 per ton. A Midwestern utility could reduce emissions for only about $100 per ton. These utilities were willing to sell allowances to Duke Energy for $200 each. As the manager put it, "They would make $100, and Duke would save $100." Not only would the utilities gain, but sulfur dioxide emissions would be reduced at a lower total cost to the economy.

Some economists have advocated a similar program of tradable permits to reduce emissions of carbon dioxide from burning fossil fuels. Other economists have endorsed a carbon tax, which is a tax on energy sources that emit carbon dioxide. With a government carbon tax, the generation of power by burning gasoline, natural gas, coal, or other carbon-based fuels would be taxed. As we will see in this chapter, economic analysis can play a significant role in shaping environmental policies.

AN INSIDE LOOK AT POLICY on **page 164** discusses how tradable emissions permits are also being used to reduce emissions of carbon dioxide, one of the gases suspected of contributing to global warming.

Sources: Jeffrey Ball, "New Consensus: In Climate Controversy, Industry Cedes Ground," *Wall Street Journal*, January 23, 2007, p. A1; and Daniel Altman, "Just How Far Can Trading of Emissions Be Extended?" *New York Times*, May 31, 2002.

LEARNING Objectives

After studying this chapter, you should be able to:

5.1 Identify examples of positive and negative **externalities** and use graphs to show how externalities affect **economic efficiency**, page 138.

5.2 Discuss the **Coase theorem** and explain how private bargaining can lead to economic efficiency in a market with an externality, page 141.

5.3 Analyze **government policies** to achieve economic efficiency in a market with an externality, page 147.

5.4 Explain how goods can be categorized on the basis of whether they are **rival or excludable**, and use graphs to illustrate the efficient quantities of **public goods** and **common resources**, page 152.

Economics in YOUR Life!

What's the "Best" Level of Pollution?

Carbon taxes and carbon trading are alternative approaches for achieving the goal of reducing carbon dioxide emissions. But how do we know the "best" level of carbon emissions? If carbon dioxide emissions hurt the environment, should the government take action to eliminate them completely? As you read the chapter, see if you can answer these questions. You can check your answers against those we provide at the end of the chapter. **>> Continued on page 162**

Externality A benefit or cost that affects someone who is not directly involved in the production or consumption of a good or service.

P ollution is just one example of an *externality*. An **externality** is a benefit or cost that affects someone who is not directly involved in the production or consumption of a good or service. In the case of air pollution, there is a *negative externality* because, for example, people with asthma may bear a cost even though they were not involved in the buying or selling of the electricity that caused the pollution. *Positive externalities* are also possible. For instance, medical research can provide a positive externality because people who are not directly involved in producing it or paying for it can benefit. A competitive market usually does a good job of producing the economically efficient amount of a good or service. This may not be true, though, if there is an externality in the market. When there is a negative externality, the market may produce a quantity of the good that is greater than the efficient amount. When there is a positive externality, the market may produce a quantity that is less than the efficient amount. In Chapter 4, we saw that government interventions in the economy—such as price floors on agricultural products or price ceilings on rents—can reduce economic efficiency. But when there are externalities, government intervention may actually increase economic efficiency and enhance the well-being of society. The way in which government intervenes is important, however. As the example of the program to reduce acid rain by reducing sulfur dioxide emissions shows, economists can help policymakers ensure that government programs are as efficient as possible.

In this chapter, we explore how best to deal with the problem of pollution and other externalities. We also look at *public goods*, which are goods that may not be produced at all unless the government produces them.

5.1 LEARNING OBJECTIVE

5.1 | Identify examples of positive and negative externalities and use graphs to show how externalities affect economic efficiency.

Externalities and Economic Efficiency

When you consume a Big Mac, only you benefit, but when you consume a college education, other people also benefit. College-educated people are less likely to commit crimes and, by being better-informed voters, more likely to contribute to better government policies. So, although you capture most of the benefits of your college education, you do not capture all of them.

When you buy a Big Mac, the price you pay covers all McDonald's costs of producing the Big Mac. When you buy electricity from a utility that burns coal and generates acid rain, the price you pay for the electricity does not cover the cost of the damage caused by the acid rain.

So, there is a *positive externality* in the production of college educations because people who do not pay for college educations will nonetheless benefit from them. There is a *negative externality* in the generation of electricity because, for example, people with homes on a lake from which fish and wildlife have disappeared because of acid rain have incurred a cost, even though they might not have bought their electricity from the polluting utility.

The Effect of Externalities

Private cost The cost borne by the producer of a good or service.

Social cost The total cost of producing a good or service, including both the private cost and any external cost.

Externalities interfere with the *economic efficiency* of a market equilibrium. We saw in Chapter 4 that a competitive market achieves economic efficiency by maximizing the sum of consumer surplus and producer surplus. *But that result holds only if there are no externalities in production or consumption.* An externality causes a difference between the *private cost* of production and the *social cost*, or the *private benefit* from consumption and the *social benefit*. The **private cost** is the cost borne by the producer of a good or service. The **social cost** is the private cost plus any external cost resulting from production,

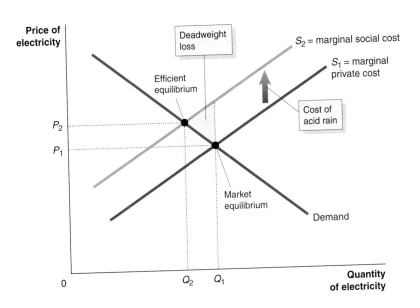

Figure 5-1

The Effect of Pollution on Economic Efficiency

Because utilities do not bear the cost of acid rain, they produce electricity beyond the economically efficient level. Supply curve S_1 represents just the marginal private cost that the utility has to pay. Supply curve S_2 represents the marginal social cost, which includes the costs to those affected by acid rain. The figure shows that if the supply curve were S_2, rather than S_1, market equilibrium would occur at a price of P_2 and a quantity of Q_2, the economically efficient level of output. But when the supply curve is S_1, the market equilibrium occurs at a price of P_1 and a quantity of Q_1 where there is a deadweight loss equal to the area of the yellow triangle. Because of the deadweight loss, this equilibrium is not efficient.

such as the cost of pollution. Unless there is an externality, the private cost and the social cost are equal. The **private benefit** is the benefit received by the consumer of a good or service. The **social benefit** is the private benefit plus any external benefit, such as the benefit to others resulting from your college education. Unless there is an externality, the private benefit and the social benefit are equal.

How a Negative Externality in Production Reduces Economic Efficiency

Consider first how a negative externality in production affects economic efficiency. In Chapters 3 and 4, we assumed that the producer of a good or service must bear all the costs of production. We now know that this observation is not always true. In producing electricity, some private costs are borne by the utility, but some external costs of acid rain are borne by farmers, fishermen, and the general public. The social cost of producing electricity is the sum of the private cost plus the external cost. Figure 5-1 shows the effect on the market for electricity of a negative externality in production.

S_1 is the market supply curve and represents only the private costs that utilities have to bear in generating electricity. As we saw in Chapter 4, firms will supply an additional unit of a good or service only if they receive a price equal to the additional cost of producing that unit, so a supply curve represents the *marginal cost* of producing a good or service. If utilities also had to bear the cost of acid rain, the supply curve would be S_2, which represents the true marginal social cost of generating electricity. The equilibrium with a price P_2 and quantity Q_2 is efficient. The equilibrium with a price P_1 and quantity Q_1 is not efficient. To see why, remember from Chapter 4 that an equilibrium is economically efficient if economic surplus—which is the sum of consumer surplus plus producer surplus—is at a maximum. When economic surplus is at a maximum, the net benefit to society from the production of the good or service is at a maximum. With an equilibrium quantity of Q_2, economic surplus is at a maximum, so this equilibrium is efficient. But with an equilibrium quantity of Q_1, economic surplus is reduced by the deadweight loss, shown in Figure 5-1 by the yellow triangle, and the equilibrium is not efficient. The deadweight loss occurs because the supply curve is above the demand curve for the production of the units of electricity between Q_2 and Q_1. That is, the additional cost—including the external cost—of producing these units is greater than the marginal benefit to consumers, as represented by the demand curve. In other words, because of the cost of the acid rain, economic efficiency would be improved if less electricity were produced.

We can conclude the following: *When there is a negative externality in producing a good or service, too much of the good or service will be produced at market equilibrium.*

Private benefit The benefit received by the consumer of a good or service.

Social benefit The total benefit from consuming a good or service, including both the private benefit and any external benefit.

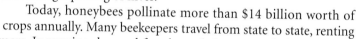

Making the Connection

The Fable of the Bees

Apple trees must be pollinated by bees to bear fruit. Bees need the nectar from apple trees (or other plants) to produce honey. In a famous article published in the early 1950s, the British economist James Meade, winner of the 1977 Nobel Prize in Economics, argued that there were positive externalities in both apple growing and beekeeping. The more apple trees growers planted, the more honey would be produced in the hives of local beekeepers. And the more hives beekeepers kept, the larger the apple crops in neighboring apple orchards. Meade assumed that beekeepers were not being compensated by apple growers for the pollination services they were providing to apple growers and that apple growers were not being compensated by beekeepers for the use of their nectar in honey making. Therefore, he concluded that unless the government intervened, the market would not supply enough apple trees and beehives.

Some apple growers and beekeepers make private arrangements to arrive at an economically efficient outcome.

Steven Cheung of the University of Washington showed, however, that government intervention was not necessary because beekeepers and apple growers had long since arrived at private agreements. In fact, in Washington State, farmers with fruit orchards had been renting beehives to pollinate their trees since at least World War I. According to Cheung, "Pollination contracts usually include stipulations regarding the number and strength of the [bee] colonies, the rental fee per hive, the time of delivery and removal of hives, the protection of bees from pesticide sprays, and the strategic placing of hives."

Today, honeybees pollinate more than $14 billion worth of crops annually. Many beekeepers travel from state to state, renting out their bees to farmers. Increasing demand for almonds has expanded the crop in California until it now stretches for 300 miles across 580,000 acres. Currently, more than one million beehives are required to pollinate the California almond crop. Beehives are shipped into the state in February and March to pollinate the almond trees, and then they are shipped to Oregon and Washington to pollinate the cherry, pear, and apple orchards in those states during April and May.

Sources: J. E. Meade, "External Economies and Diseconomies in a Competitive Situation," *Economic Journal*, Vol. 62, March 1952, pp. 54–67; Steven N. S. Cheung, "The Fable of the Bees: An Economic Investigation," *Journal of Law and Economics*, Vol. 16, 1973, pp. 11–33; and Alexei Barrionuevo, "Honey Bees Vanish, Leaving Keepers in Peril," *New York Times*, February 27, 2007.

YOUR TURN: Test your understanding by doing related problem 2.9 on page 168 at the end of this chapter.

Do Property Rights Matter?

In discussing the bargaining between the electric utilities and the people suffering the effects of the utlities' pollution, we assumed that the electric utilities were not legally liable for the damage they were causing. In other words, the victims of pollution could not legally enforce the right of their property not to be damaged, so they would have to pay the utilities to reduce the pollution. But would it make any difference if the utilities were legally liable for the damages? Surprisingly, as Coase was the first to point out, it does not matter for the amount of pollution reduction. The only difference would be that now the electric utilities would have to pay the victims of pollution for the right to pollute rather than the victims having to pay the utilities. Because the marginal benefits and marginal costs of pollution reduction would not change, the bargaining would still result in the efficient level of pollution reduction—in this case, 8.5 million tons.

In the absence of the utilities being legally liable, the victims of pollution have an incentive to pay the utilities to reduce pollution up to the point where the marginal benefit of the last ton of reduction is equal to the marginal cost. If the utilities are legally liable, they have an incentive to pay the victims of pollution to allow them to pollute up to the same point.

The Problem of Transactions Costs

Unfortunately, there are frequently practical difficulties in the way of a private solution to the problem of externalities. In cases of pollution, for example, there are often both many polluters and many people suffering from the negative effects of pollution. Bringing together all those suffering from pollution with all those causing the pollution and negotiating an agreement often fails due to *transactions costs*. **Transactions costs** are the costs in time and other resources that parties incur in the process of agreeing to and carrying out an exchange of goods or services. In this case, the transactions costs would include the time and other costs of negotiating an agreement, drawing up a binding contract, purchasing insurance, and monitoring the agreement. Unfortunately, when many people are involved, the transactions costs are often higher than the net benefits from reducing the externality. Thus, the cost of transacting ends up exceeding the gain from the transaction. In such cases, a private solution to an externality problem is not feasible.

Transactions costs The costs in time and other resources that parties incur in the process of agreeing to and carrying out an exchange of goods or services.

The Coase Theorem

Coase's argument that private solutions to the problem of externalities are possible is summed up in the **Coase theorem**: If transactions costs are low, private bargaining will result in an efficient solution to the problem of externalities. We have seen the basis for the Coase theorem in the preceding example of pollution by electric utilities: Because the benefits from reducing an externality are often greater than the costs, private bargaining can arrive at an efficient outcome. But we have also seen that this outcome will occur only if transactions costs are low, and in the case of pollution, they usually are not. In general, private bargaining is most likely to reach an efficient outcome if the number of parties bargaining is small.

Coase theorem The argument of economist Ronald Coase that if transactions costs are low, private bargaining will result in an efficient solution to the problem of externalities.

In practice, we must add a couple of other qualifications to the Coase theorem. In addition to low transactions costs, private solutions to the problem of externalities will occur only if all parties to the agreement have full information about the costs and benefits associated with the externality, and all parties must be willing to accept a reasonable agreement. For example, if those suffering from the effects of pollution do not have information on the costs of reducing pollution, it is unlikely that the parties can reach an agreement. Unreasonable demands can also hinder an agreement. For instance, in the example of pollution by electric utilities, we saw that the total benefit of reducing sulfur dioxide emissions was $375 million. Even if transactions costs are very low, if the utilities insist on being paid more than $375 million to reduce emissions, no agreement will be reached because the amount paid exceeds the value of the reduction to those suffering from the emissions.

5.3 | Analyze government policies to achieve economic efficiency in a market with an externality.

Government Policies to Deal with Externalities

When private solutions to externalities are not feasible, how should the government intervene? The first economist to analyze market failure systematically was A. C. Pigou, a British economist at Cambridge University. Pigou argued that to deal with a negative externality in production, the government should impose a tax equal to the cost of the externality. The effect of such a tax is shown in Figure 5-5, which reproduces the negative externality from acid rain shown in Figure 5-1.

By imposing a tax equal to the cost of acid rain on the production of electricity, the government will cause electric utilities to *internalize* the externality. As a consequence, the cost of the acid rain will become a private cost borne by the utilities, and

Figure 5-5

When There Is a Negative Externality, a Tax Can Bring about the Efficient Level of Output

Because utilities do not bear the cost of acid rain, they produce electricity beyond the economically efficient level. If the government imposes a tax equal to the cost of acid rain, the utilities will internalize the externality. As a consequence, the supply curve will shift up from S_1 to S_2. The market equilibrium quantity changes from Q_1, where an inefficiently high level of electricity is produced, to Q_2, the economically efficient equilibrium quantity. The price of electricity will rise from P_1—which does not include the cost of acid rain—to P_2—which does include the cost.

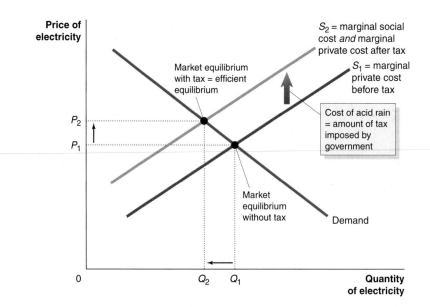

the supply curve for electricity will shift from S_1 to S_2. The result will be a decrease in the equilibrium output of electricity from Q_1 to the efficient level, Q_2. The price of electricity will rise from P_1—which does not include the cost of acid rain—to P_2—which does include the cost.

Solved Problem | **5-3**

Using a Tax to Deal with a Negative Externality

Companies that produce toilet paper bleach the paper to make it white. Some paper plants discharge the bleach into rivers and lakes, causing substantial environmental damage. Suppose the following graph illustrates the situation in the toilet paper market.

Explain how the federal government can use a tax on toilet paper to bring about the efficient level of production. What should the value of the tax be?

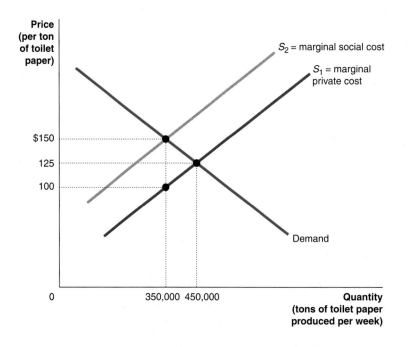

SOLVING THE PROBLEM:

Step 1: **Review the chapter material.** This problem is about the government using a tax to deal with a negative externality in production, so you may want to review the section "Government Policies to Deal with Externalities," which begins on page 147.

Step 2: **Use the information from the graph to determine the necessary tax.** The efficient level of toilet paper production will occur where the marginal social benefit from consuming toilet paper, as represented by the demand curve, is equal to the marginal social cost of production. The graph shows that this will occur at a price of $150 per ton and production of 350,000 tons. In the absence of government intervention, the price will be $125 per ton, and production will be 450,000 tons. It is tempting—but incorrect!—to think that the government could bring about the efficient level of production by imposing a per-ton tax equal to the difference between the price when production is at its optimal level and the current market price. But this would be a tax of only $25. The graph shows that at the optimal level of production, the difference between the marginal private cost and the marginal social cost is $50. Therefore, a tax of $50 per ton is required to shift the supply curve up from S_1 to S_2.

YOUR TURN: For more practice, do related problem 3.8 on page 169 at the end of this chapter.

≫ End Solved Problem 5-3

Pigou also argued that the government can deal with a positive externality in consumption by giving consumers a subsidy, or payment, equal to the value of the externality. The effect of the subsidy is shown in Figure 5-6, which reproduces the positive externality from college education shown in Figure 5-2.

By paying college students a subsidy equal to the external benefit from a college education, the government will cause students to *internalize* the externality. That is, the external benefit from a college education will become a private benefit received by college students, and the demand curve for college educations will shift from D_1 to D_2. The equilibrium number of college educations supplied will increase from Q_1 to the efficient level, Q_2. In fact, the government does heavily subsidize college educations. All states have government-operated universities that charge tuitions well below the cost of providing the education. The state and federal governments also provide students with grants and low-interest loans that subsidize college educations. The economic justification for these programs is that college educations provide an external benefit to society.

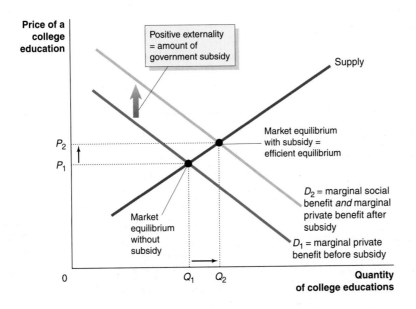

Figure 5-6

When There Is a Positive Externality, a Subsidy Can Bring about the Efficient Level of Output

People who do not consume college educations can benefit from them. As a result, the social benefit from a college education is greater than the private benefit seen by college students. If the government pays a subsidy equal to the external benefit, students will internalize the externality. The subsidy will cause the demand curve to shift up, from D_1 to D_2. The result will be that market equilibrium quantity shifts from Q_1, where an inefficiently low level of college educations is supplied, to Q_2, the economically efficient equilibrium quantity.

Pigovian taxes and subsidies
Government taxes and subsidies
intended to bring about an efficient
level of output in the presence of
externalities.

Because A. C. Pigou was the first economist to propose using government taxes and subsidies to deal with externalities, they are sometimes referred to as **Pigovian taxes and subsidies**. Note that a Pigovian tax eliminates deadweight loss and improves economic efficiency. This situation is the opposite of the one we saw in Chapter 4, in which we discussed how most taxes reduce consumer surplus and producer surplus and create a deadweight loss. In fact, one reason that economists support Pigovian taxes as a way to deal with negative externalities is that the government can use the revenues raised by Pigovian taxes to lower other taxes that reduce economic efficiency.

Command and Control versus Tradable Emissions Allowances

Command and control approach An approach that involves the government imposing quantitative limits on the amount of pollution firms are allowed to emit or requiring firms to install specific pollution control devices.

Although the federal government has sometimes used taxes and subsidies to deal with externalities, in dealing with pollution, it has traditionally used a *command and control approach* with firms that pollute. A **command and control approach** to reducing pollution involves the government imposing quantitative limits on the amount of pollution firms are allowed to generate or requiring firms to install specific pollution control devices. For example, in 1983, the federal government required auto manufacturers such as Ford and General Motors to install catalytic converters to reduce auto emissions on all new automobiles.

Congress could have used direct pollution controls to deal with the problem of acid rain. To achieve its objective of a reduction of 8.5 million tons per year in sulfur dioxide emissions by 2010, it could have required every utility to reduce sulfur dioxide emissions by the same specified amount. However, this approach would not have been an economically efficient solution to the problem. As we saw at the beginning of this chapter, utilities can have very different costs of reducing sulfur dioxide emissions. Some utilities, like Duke Energy, that already use low-sulfur coal can reduce emissions further only at a high cost. Other utilities, particularly those in the Midwest, are able to reduce emissions at a lower cost.

Congress decided to use a market-based approach to reducing sulfur dioxide emissions by setting up a system of tradable emissions allowances. The federal government gave utilities allowances equal to the total amount of allowable sulfur dioxide emissions. The utilities were then free to buy and sell the allowances. An active market where the allowances can be bought and sold is conducted on the Chicago Mercantile Exchange. Utilities that could reduce emissions at low cost did so and sold their allowances. Utilities that could only reduce emissions at high cost bought allowances. Using tradable emissions allowances to reduce acid rain has been a great success and has made it possible for utilities to meet Congress's emissions goal at a much lower cost than expected. As Figure 5-7 shows, just before Congress enacted the allowances program in 1990, the Edison Electrical Institute estimated that the cost to utilities of complying with the program would be $7.4 billion by 2010. By 1994, the federal government's General Accounting Office estimated that the cost would be less than $2 billion. In practice, the cost appears likely to be almost 90 percent less than the initial estimate, or only about $870 *million*.

Are Tradable Emissions Allowances Licenses to Pollute?

Some environmentalists have criticized tradable emissions allowances, labeling them "licenses to pollute." They argue that just as the government does not issue licenses to rob banks or to drive drunk, it should not issue licenses to pollute. But this criticism ignores one of the central lessons of economics: Resources are scarce, and trade-offs exist. Resources that are spent reducing one type of pollution are not available to reduce other types of pollution or for any other use. Because reducing acid rain using tradable emissions allowances cost utilities $870 million, rather than $7.4 billion, as originally estimated, society saved more than $6.5 billion.

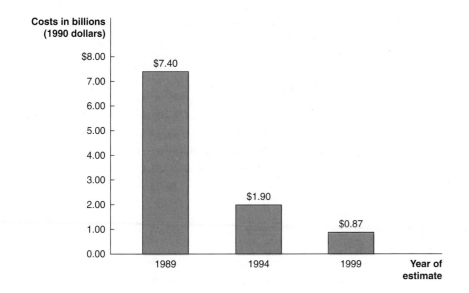

Figure 5-7

Estimated Cost of the Acid Rain Program in 2010

The Edison Electric Institute estimated in 1989 that the program to reduce acid rain pollution would cost utilities a total of $7.4 billion by 2010. The system of tradable emissions allowances used in the program resulted in the bulk of the reduction in pollution being carried out by the utilities that could do it at the lowest cost. As a result, the program is likely to cost $870 million, which is almost 90 percent less than the original estimate. (*Note:* To correct for the effect of inflation, the costs are measured in dollars of 1990 purchasing power.)

Source: Environmental Protection Agency, *Progress Report on the EPA Acid Rain Program,* November 1999, Figure 2.

Making the Connection

Can Tradable Permits Reduce Global Warming?

In the past 25 years, the global surface temperature has increased about three-quarters of 1 degree Fahrenheit (or four-tenths of 1 degree Centigrade) compared with the average for the previous 30 years. The following graph shows changes in temperature over the years since 1880.

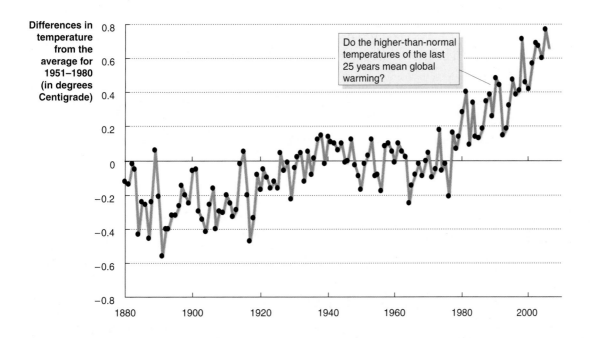

Global temperatures have gone through many periods of warming and cooling. In fact, the below-normal temperatures that prevailed before 1970 led some scientists to predict the eventual arrival of a new ice age. Nevertheless, many scientists are convinced that the recent warming is not part of the natural fluctuations in temperature but is instead due to the burning of fossil fuels, such as coal, natural gas, and petroleum. Burning these fuels releases CO_2 (carbon dioxide), which accumulates in the atmosphere as a "greenhouse gas." Greenhouse gases cause some of the heat released from the earth to be reflected back, increasing temperatures.

If greenhouse gases continue to accumulate in the atmosphere, according to some estimates, global temperatures could increase by 3 degrees Fahrenheit or more during the next 100 years. Such increases in temperature could lead to significant changes in climate, which might result in more storms and flooding as well as other problems. By 1995, a number of nations had concluded that the threat of global warming was significant enough to take steps toward reducing emissions of CO_2 and other greenhouse gases. The result was the 1997 Kyoto Treaty, which, if accepted, would have required the high-income countries to reduce their CO_2 emissions by more than 5 percent compared with their 1990 levels. However, President George W. Bush was not willing to commit the United States to the treaty. He argued that the costs to the United States of complying with the treaty were too high, particularly because some scientists were still skeptical that CO_2 emissions actually were causing the increase in temperature. Even scientists who believed that CO_2 emissions contribute to rising temperatures were skeptical that the Kyoto Treaty would have much effect on global warming. President Bush also argued that developing countries should be included in any agreement. Some developing countries, such as China and India, are experiencing rapid economic growth, which in turn has led to rapid increases in CO_2 emissions. European countries that ratified the Kyoto Treaty have had difficulty fulfilling their commitments to reduce CO_2 emissions to the levels indicated by the treaty. Of the larger European countries, only Great Britain, where emissions have declined by more than 15 percent since 1990, seems likely to succeed in fulfilling its commitments by 2012.

The mechanism by which reductions in CO_2 emissions would occur has also been in dispute. The United States has favored a global system of tradable emission permits for CO_2 that would be similar to the system for sulfur dioxide discussed earlier in this chapter. As we have seen, this type of system has the potential to reduce CO_2 emissions at a lower cost. Most European countries, however, have been reluctant to fully accept such a system, preferring instead to require that each country reduce emissions by a specified amount. In recent years, though, support has grown in Europe for using tradable allowances, and an active market in these allowances has developed under the European Union Greenhouse Gas Emission Trading Scheme, which began operation in 2005. It seems unlikely that the debate over the costs and benefits of reducing CO_2 emissions will be resolved any time soon.

Sources: Juliet Eilperin and Steven Mufson, "Tax on Carbon Emissions Gains Support," *Washington Post*, April 1, 2007, p. A05; United Nations Framework Convention on Climate Change, *National Greenhouse Gas Inventory Data for the Period 1990–2004*, October 19, 2006; and (for data in the graph) NASA, Goddard Institute for Space Studies, http://data.giss.nasa.gov/gistemp/graphs/.

YOUR TURN: Test your understanding by doing related problem 3.11 on page 169 at the end of this chapter.

5.4 LEARNING OBJECTIVE

5.4 | Explain how goods can be categorized on the basis of whether they are rival or excludable, and use graphs to illustrate the efficient quantities of public goods and common resources.

Four Categories of Goods

We can explore further the question of when the market is likely to succeed in supplying the efficient quantity of a good by noting that goods differ on the basis of whether their consumption is *rival* and *excludable*. **Rivalry** occurs when one person's consuming a unit of a good means no one else can consume it. If you consume a Big Mac, for example, no one else can consume it. **Excludability** means that anyone who does not pay for a good cannot consume it. If you don't pay for a Big Mac, for example, MacDonald's can exclude you from consuming it. The consumption of a Big Mac is rival and excludable. The consumption of some goods, however, can be either *nonrival or nonexcludable*. Nonrival means that one person's consumption does not interfere with another person's consumption. Nonexcludable means that it is impossible to exclude others from con-

Rivalry The situation that occurs when one person's consuming a unit of a good means no one else can consume it.

Excludability The situation in which anyone who does not pay for a good cannot consume it.

	Excludable	Nonexcludable
Rival	**Private Goods** *Examples:* *Big Macs* *Running shoes*	**Common Resources** *Examples:* *Tuna in the ocean* *Public pasture land*
Nonrival	**Quasi-Public Goods** *Examples:* *Cable TV* *Toll road*	**Public Goods** *Examples:* *National defense* *Court system*

Figure 5-8

Four Categories of Goods

Goods and services can be divided into four categories on the basis of whether people can be excluded from consuming them and whether they are rival in consumption. A good or service is rival in consumption if it can be consumed by only one person at the same time.

suming the good, whether they have paid for it or not. Figure 5-8 shows four possible categories into which goods can fall.

We next consider each of the four categories:

1 *Private goods.* A good that is both rival and excludable is a **private good**. Food, clothing, haircuts, and many other goods and services fall into this category. One person's consuming a unit of these goods precludes other people from consuming that unit, and anyone who does not buy these goods can't consume them. Although we didn't state it explicitly, when we analyzed the demand and supply for goods and services in Chapter 3, we assumed that the goods and services were all private goods.

Private good A good that is both rival and excludable.

2 *Public goods.* A **public good** is both nonrivalrous and nonexcludable. Public goods are often, although not always, supplied by a government rather than by private firms. The classic example of a public good is national defense. Your consuming national defense does not interfere with your neighbor's consuming it, so consumption is nonrivalrous. You also cannot be excluded from consuming it, whether you pay for it or not. No private firm would be willing to supply national defense because everyone can consume national defense without paying for it. The behavior of consumers in this situation is referred to as *free riding*. **Free riding** involves individuals benefiting from a good—in this case, the provision of national defense—without paying for it.

Public good A good that is both nonrivalrous and nonexcludable.

Free riding Benefiting from a good without paying for it.

3 *Quasi-public goods.* Some goods are excludable but not rival. An example is cable television. People who do not pay for cable television do not receive it, but one person's watching it doesn't affect other people's watching it. The same is true of a toll road. Anyone who doesn't pay the toll doesn't get on the road, but one person using the road doesn't interfere with someone else using the road (unless so many people are using the road that it becomes congested). Goods that fall into this category are called *quasi-public goods*.

4 *Common resources.* If a good is rival but not excludable, it is a **common resource**. Forest land in many poor countries is a common resource. If one person cuts down a tree, no one else can use the tree. But if no one has a property right to the forest, no one can be excluded from using it. As we will discuss in more detail later, people often overuse common resources.

Common resource A good that is rival but not excludable.

Making the Connection | Should the Government Run the Health Care System?

In many countries, such as Canada, Japan, the United Kingdom, and France, the government either supplies health care directly by operating hospitals and employing doctors and nurses, or pays for most health care expenses even if hospitals are not government owned and doctors are not government employees. In the United States, the federal government supplies health care to veterans of the armed forces through the Veterans Administration (VA) system and pays for the health care of people over age 65 under the Medicare program. The federal government also contributes to the Medicaid program under which state governments pay for health care for some poor people. Most medium and large-size firms provide health insurance as a fringe benefit to their employees. About 88 percent of individuals who have private health insurance receive it as part of a benefits package from their employers. Those individuals not covered by health insurance plans and not eligible for government aid must pay for their own health care bills out of pocket, just as they pay their other bills, or receive charity care. The chart shows that in 2006, government spending on Medicare, Medicaid, and other government health care programs was about 47 percent of total health care spending.

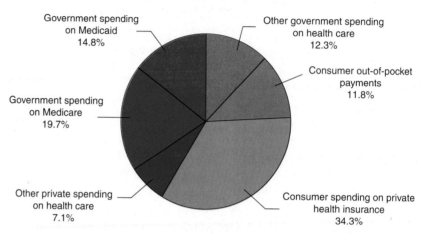

Source: John A. Poisal, et al., *Health Spending Projections through 2016*, Washington, DC: National Health Statistics Group, Centers for Medicare & Medicaid Services, U.S. Department of Health and Human Services.

What should be the government's role in health care? Is health care a public good that government should supply—or, at least, pay for? Is it a private good, like food, clothing, or television sets, that private firms should supply and consumers should pay for without government aid? Should private firms supply most health care, subject to some government regulation? Economists differ in their answers to these questions because the delivery of health care involves a number of complex issues. But we can consider briefly some of the most important points. We have seen that a public good is both nonrivalrous and nonexcludable. In this sense, health care does not qualify as a public good. More than one person cannot simultaneously consume the same surgical operation, for example. And someone who will not pay for an operation can be excluded from consuming it. (Most states require hospitals to treat patients who are too poor to pay for treatment, and many doctors will treat poor people at a reduced price. But because there is nothing in the nature of health care that keeps people who do not pay for it from being excluded from consuming it, health care does not fit the definition of a public good.)

There are aspects of the delivery of health care that have convinced some economists that government intervention is justified, however. For example, consuming certain types of health care generates positive externalities. In particular, being vaccinated against a communicable disease, such as influenza or chicken pox, not only reduces the chance that the person vaccinated will catch the disease but also reduces the probability that an epidemic of the disease will occur. Therefore, the market may supply an inefficiently small quantity of vaccinations unless vaccinations receive a government subsidy. Information problems can also be important in the market for private health insurance. Consumers as buyers of health insurance often know much more about the state of their health than do the companies selling health insurance. This information problem may raise costs to insurance companies when the pool of people being insured is small, making insurance companies less willing to offer health insurance to consumers the companies suspect may file too many claims. Economists debate how important information problems are in health care markets and whether government intervention is required to reduce them. We will consider this question further in Chapter 17, when we discuss the economics of information.

Many economists believe that market-based solutions are the best approach to improving the health care system. Currently, the U.S. health care system is a world leader in innovation in medical technology and prescription drugs. The market-oriented approach to reforming health care starts with the goal of preserving incentives for U.S. firms to continue with innovations in medical screening equipment, surgical procedures, and prescription drugs. Presently, markets are delivering inaccurate signals to consumers because when buying health care, unlike when buying most other goods and services, consumers pay a price well *below* the true cost of providing the service. Consumers usually pay less than the true cost of medical treatment because a third party—typically, an insurance company—often pays most of the bill. For example, consumers who have health insurance provided by their employers usually pay only a small amount—perhaps $20—for a visit to a doctor's office, when the true cost of the visit might be $80 or $90. The result is that consumers demand a larger quantity of health care services than they would if they paid a price that better represented the cost of providing the services. Doctors and other health care providers also have a reduced incentive to control costs because they know that an insurance company will pick up most of the bill.

Under current tax laws, individuals do not pay taxes on health insurance benefits they receive from their employers, and this encourages them to want very generous coverage that reduces incentives to control costs. But individuals get no tax break for buying insurance on their own or for out-of-pocket medical spending. Some economists have proposed making the tax treatment of health insurance and health spending more uniform, a change that could, potentially, significantly reduce spending on health care without reducing the effectiveness of the health care received. Such tax law changes would make it more likely that company-provided health insurance would focus on large medical bills—such as those resulting from hospitalizations—while consumers would pay prices closer to the costs of providing routine medical care.

Because health care is so important to consumers and because health care spending looms so large in the U.S. economy, the role of the government in the health care system is likely to be the subject of intense debate for some time to come.

Source: To read more on the role of the government in the market for health care, see Sherman Folland, Allen C. Goodman, and Miron Stano, *The Economics of Health and Health Care*, 5th ed., Upper Saddle River, NJ: Prentice Hall, 2007, Chapter 19; and John F. Coogan, R. Glenn Hubbard, and Daniel P. Kessler, *Healthy, Wealthy, and Wise: Five Steps to a Better Health Care System*, Washington, DC: The AEI Press, 2005.

YOUR TURN: Test your understanding by doing related problem 4.9 on page 171 at the end of this chapter.

We discussed the demand and supply for private goods in Chapter 3. For the remainder of this chapter, we focus on the categories of public goods and common resources. To determine the optimal quantity of a public good, we have to modify the demand and supply analysis of Chapter 3 to take into account that a public good is both nonrivalrous and nonexcludable.

The Demand for a Public Good

We can determine the market demand curve for a good or service by adding up the quantity of the good demanded by each consumer at each price. To keep things simple, let's take the case of a market with only two consumers. Figure 5-9 shows that the market demand curve for hamburgers depends on the individual demand curves of Jill and Joe.

At a price of $4.00, Jill demands 2 hamburgers per week and Joe demands 4. Adding horizontally, the combination of a price of $4.00 per hamburger and a quantity demanded of 6 hamburgers will be a point on the market demand curve for hamburgers. Similarly, adding horizontally at a price of $1.50, we have a price of $1.50 and a quantity demanded of 11 as another point on the market demand curve. A consumer's demand curve for a good represents the marginal benefit the consumer receives from the good, so when we add together the consumers' demand curves, we not only have the

Figure 5-11

The Optimal Quantity of a Public Good

The optimal quantity of a public good is produced where the sum of consumer surplus and producer surplus is maximized, which occurs where the demand curve intersects the supply curve. In this case, the optimal quantity of security guard services is 15 hours at a price of $9 per hour.

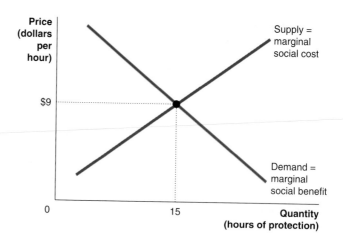

bargaining will result in an efficient quantity of the public good. This outcome is not likely for a public good—such as national defense—that is supplied by the government to millions of consumers.

Governments sometimes use *cost–benefit analysis* to determine what quantity of a public good should be supplied. For example, before building a dam on a river, the federal government will attempt to weigh the costs against the benefits. The costs include the opportunity cost of other projects the government cannot carry out if it builds the dam. The benefits include improved flood control or new recreational opportunities on the lake formed by the dam. However, for many public goods, including national defense, the government does not use a formal cost–benefit analysis. Instead, the quantity of national defense supplied is determined by a political process involving Congress and the president. Even here, of course, Congress and the president realize that trade-offs are involved: The more resources used for national defense, the fewer resources available for other public goods or for private goods.

Solved Problem | 5-5

Determining the Optimal Level of Public Goods

Suppose, once again, that Jill and Joe run isolated businesses that are next door to each other and in need of the services of a security guard. Their demand schedules for security guard services are as follows:

JOE	
PRICE (DOLLARS PER HOUR)	QUANTITY (HOURS OF PROTECTION)
$20	0
18	1
16	2
14	3
12	4
10	5
8	6
6	7
4	8
2	9

JILL	
PRICE (DOLLARS PER HOUR)	QUANTITY (HOURS OF PROTECTION)
$20	1
18	2
16	3
14	4
12	5
10	6
8	7
6	8
4	9
2	10

The supply schedule for security guard services is as follows:

PRICE (DOLLARS PER HOUR)	QUANTITY (HOURS OF PROTECTION)
$8	1
10	2
12	3
14	4
16	5
18	6
20	7
22	8
24	9

a. Draw a graph that shows the optimal level of security guard services. Be sure to label the curves on the graph.

b. Briefly explain why 8 hours of security guard protection is not an optimal quantity.

SOLVING THE PROBLEM:

Step 1: **Review the chapter material.** This problem is about the determination of the optimal level of public goods, so you may want to review the section "The Optimal Quantity of a Public Good," which begins on page 156.

Step 2: **Begin by deriving the demand curve or marginal social benefit curve for security guard services.** To calculate the marginal social benefit of guard services, we need to add the prices that Jill and Joe are willing to pay at each quantity:

DEMAND OR MARGINAL SOCIAL BENEFIT	
PRICE (DOLLARS PER HOUR)	QUANTITY (HOURS OF PROTECTION)
$38	1
34	2
30	3
26	4
22	5
18	6
14	7
10	8
6	9

Step 3: **Answer question (a) by plotting the demand (marginal social benefit) and supply (marginal social cost) curves.** The graph shows that the optimal level of security guard services is 6 hours.

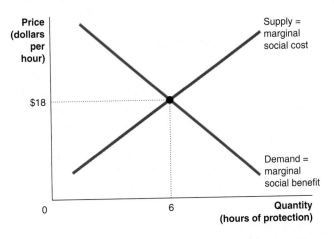

Step 4: **Answer question (b) by explaining why 8 hours of security guard protection is not an optimal quantity.** For each hour beyond 6, the supply curve is above the demand curve. Therefore, the marginal social benefit received will be less than the marginal social cost of supplying these hours. This results in a dead-weight loss and a reduction in economic surplus.

>> **End Solved Problem 5-5**

YOUR TURN: For more practice, do related problem 4.4 on page 170 at the end of this chapter.

Common Resources

In England during the Middle Ages, each village had an area of pasture, known as a *commons*, on which any family in the village was allowed to graze its cows or sheep without charge. Of course, the grass one family's cow ate was not available for another family's cow, so consumption was rival. But every family in the village had the right to use the commons, so it was nonexcludable. Without some type of restraint on usage, the commons would end up overgrazed. To see why, consider the economic incentives facing a family that was thinking of buying another cow and grazing it on the commons. The family would gain the benefits from increased milk production, but adding another cow to the commons would create a negative externality by reducing the amount of grass available for the cows of other families. Because this family—and the other families in the village—did not take this negative externality into account when deciding whether to add another cow to the commons, too many cows would be added. The grass on the commons would eventually be depleted, and no family's cow would get enough to eat.

Tragedy of the commons The tendency for a common resource to be overused.

The Tragedy of the Commons The tendency for a common resource to be overused is called the **tragedy of the commons**. A modern example is the forests in many poor countries. When a family chops down a tree in a public forest, it takes into account the benefits of gaining firewood or wood for building, but it does not take into account the costs of deforestation. Haiti, for example, was once heavily forested. Today, 80 percent of the country's forests have been cut down, primarily to be burned to create charcoal, which is used for heating and cooking. Because the mountains no longer have tree roots to hold the soil, heavy rains lead to devastating floods. The following is from a newspaper account of tree cutting in Haiti:

> "No Tree Cutting" signs hang over the park entrance, but without money and manpower, there is no way to enforce that. Loggers make nightly journeys, hacking away at trees until they fall. The next day, they're on a truck out. Days later, they've been chopped up, burned and packaged in white bags offered for sale by soot-covered women. "This is the only way I can feed my four kids," said Vena Verone, one of the vendors. "I've heard about the floods and deforestation that caused them, but there's nothing I can do about that."

Figure 5-12 shows that with a common resource such as wood from a forest, the efficient level of use, Q_2, is determined by the intersection of the demand curve—which represents the marginal social benefit received by consumers—and S_2, which represents the marginal social cost of cutting the wood. As in our discussion of negative externalities, the social cost is equal to the private cost of cutting the wood plus the external cost. In this case, the external cost represents the fact that the more wood each person cuts, the less wood there is available for others, and the greater the deforestation, which increases the chances of floods. Because each individual tree cutter ignores the external cost, the equilibrium quantity of wood cut is Q_1, which is greater than the efficient quantity. At the equilibrium level of output, there is a deadweight loss, as shown in Figure 5-12 by the yellow triangle.

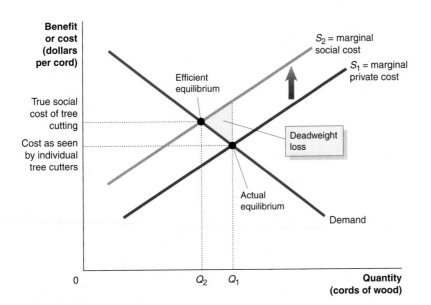

Figure 5-12

For a common resource such as wood from a forest, the efficient level of use, Q_2, is determined by the intersection of the demand curve—which represents the marginal benefit received by consumers—and S_2, which represents the marginal social cost of cutting the wood. Because each individual tree cutter ignores the external cost, the equilibrium quantity of wood cut is Q_1, which is greater than the efficient quantity. At the equilibrium level of output, there is a deadweight loss, as shown by the yellow triangle.

Is There a Way Out of the Tragedy of the Commons? Notice that our discussion of the tragedy of the commons is very similar to our earlier discussion of negative externalities. The source of the tragedy of the commons is the same as the source of negative externalities: lack of clearly defined and enforced property rights. For instance, suppose that instead of being held as a collective resource, a piece of pastureland is owned by one person. That person will take into account the effect of adding another cow on the food available to cows already using the pasture. As a result, the optimal number of cows will be placed on the pasture. Over the years, most of the commons lands in England were converted to private property. Most of the forest land in Haiti and other developing countries is actually the property of the government. The failure of the government to protect the forests against trespassers or convert them to private property is the key to their overuse.

Should these fishermen have unlimited access to the ocean?

In some situations, though, enforcing property rights is not feasible. An example is the oceans. Because no country owns the oceans beyond its own coastal waters, the fish and other resources of the ocean will remain a common resource. In situations in which enforcing property rights is not feasible, two types of solutions to the tragedy of the commons are possible. If the geographic area involved is limited and the number of people involved is small, access to the commons can be restricted through community norms and laws. If the geographic area or the number of people involved is large, legal restrictions on access to the commons are required. As an example of the first type of solution, the tragedy of the commons was avoided in the Middle Ages by traditional limits on the number of animals each family was allowed to put on the common pasture. Although these traditions were not formal laws, they were usually enforced adequately by social pressure.

With the second type of solution, the government imposes restrictions on access to the common resources. These restrictions can take several different forms, of which taxes, quotas, and tradable permits are the most common. By setting a tax equal to the external cost, governments can ensure that the efficient quantity of a resource is used. Quotas, or legal limits, on the quantity of the resource that can be taken during a given time period have been used in the United States to limit access to pools of oil when the pool is beneath property owned by many different persons. The governments of Canada, New Zealand, and Iceland have used a system of tradable permits to restrict access to ocean fisheries. Under this system, a total allowable catch (TAC) limits the number of fish that fishermen can catch during a season. The fishmen are then assigned permits called Individual Transferable Quotas (ITQs) that are equal to the total allowable catch. This system operates like the tradable emissions allowances described earlier in this chapter. The fishermen are free to use the ITQs or to sell them, which ensures that the fishermen with the lowest costs use the ITQs. The use of ITQs has sometimes proven controversial, which has limited their use in managing fisheries along the coastal United States. Critics argue that allowing trading of ITQs can result in their concentration in the hands of a relatively few large commercial fishing firms. Such a concentration may, though, be economically efficient if these firms have lower costs than smaller, family-based firms.

▷▷ **Continued from page 137**

Economics in YOUR Life!

At the beginning of the chapter, we asked you to think about what the "best" level of carbon emissions is. Conceptually, this is a straightforward question to answer: The correct level of carbon emissions is the level for which the marginal benefit of reducing carbon emissions exactly equals the marginal cost of reducing carbon emissions. In practice, however, this is a very difficult question to answer. Scientists disagree about how much carbon emissions are contributing to the damage from climate change. In addition, the cost of reducing carbon emissions depends on the method of reduction used. As a result, neither the marginal cost curve nor the marginal benefit curve for reducing carbon emissions is known with certainty. This uncertainty makes it difficult for policymakers to determine the correct level of carbon emissions and is the source of much of the current debate. In any case, economists agree that the total cost of *completely* eliminating carbon emissions are much greater than the total benefits.

Conclusion

In Chapter 4, we saw that government intervention in the economy can reduce economic efficiency. In this chapter, however, we have seen that the government has an indispensable role to play in the economy when the absence of well-defined and enforceable property rights keeps the market from operating efficiently. Because no one has a property right for clean air, in the absence of government intervention, firms will produce too great a quantity of products that generate air pollution. We have also seen that public goods are nonrivalrous and nonexcludable and are, therefore, often supplied directly by the government.

Read *An Inside Look at Policy*, which begins on the following page, to learn about problems with carbon trading.

Key Terms

5.1 LEARNING OBJECTIVE   5.1 | Identify examples of positive and negative externalities and use graphs to show how externalities affect economic efficiency. **pages 138-141.**

Externalities and Economic Efficiency

Summary

An **externality** is a benefit or cost to parties who are not involved in a transaction. Pollution and other externalities in production cause a difference between the **private cost** borne by the producer of a good or services and the **social cost**, which includes any external cost, such as the cost of pollution. An externality in consumption causes a difference between the **private benefit** received by the consumer and the **social benefit**, which includes any external benefit. If externalities exist in production or consumption, the market will not produce the optimal level of a good or service. This outcome is referred to as **market failure**. Externalities arise when property rights do not exist or cannot be legally enforced. **Property rights** are the rights individuals or businesses have to the exclusive use of their property, including the right to buy or sell it.

 Visit www.myeconlab.com to complete these exercises online and get instant feedback.

Review Questions

1.1 What is an externality? Give an example of a positive externality and give an example of a negative externality.

1.2 When will the private cost of producing a good differ from the social cost? Give an example. When will the private benefit from consuming a good differ from the social benefit? Give an example.

1.3 What is economic efficiency? How do externalities affect the economic efficiency of a market equilibrium?

1.4 What is market failure? When is market failure likely to arise?

1.5 Briefly discuss the relationship between property rights and the existence of externalities.

Problems and Applications

1.6 The chapter states that your consuming a Big Mac does not create an externality. But suppose you arrive at your favorite McDonald's at lunchtime and get in a long line to be served. By the time you reach the counter, there are 10 people in line behind you. Because you decided to have a Big Mac for lunch—instead of, say, a pizza—each of those 10 people must wait in line an additional 2 minutes. Or suppose that after a lifetime of consuming Big Macs, you develop heart disease. Because you are now over age 65, the government must pay most of your medical bills through the Medicare system. Is it still correct to say that your consuming a Big Mac created no externalities? Might there be a justification here for the government to intervene in the market for Big Macs? Explain.

1.7 The chapter discusses the cases of consumption generating a positive externality and production generating a negative externality. Is it possible for consumption to generate a negative externality? If so, give an example. Is it possible for production to generate a positive externality? If so, give an example.

1.8 In a recent study at a large state university, students were randomly assigned roommates. Researchers found that, on average, males assigned to roommates who reported drinking alcohol in the year before entering college had GPAs one-quarter point lower than those assigned to non-drinking roommates. For males who drank frequently before college, being assigned to a roommate who also drank frequently before college reduced their GPAs by two-thirds of a point. Draw a graph showing the price of alcohol and the quantity of alcohol consumption on college campuses. Include in the graph the private and social cost of drinking. Label any deadweight loss that arises in this market.

Source: Michael Kremer and Dan M. Levy, "Peer Effects and Alcohol Use Among College Students," National Bureau of Economic Research working paper 9876, July 2003.

1.9 Tom and Jacob are college students. Each of them will probably get married later and have two or three children. Each knows that if he studies more in college, he'll get a better job and earn more than if he doesn't study. Earning more means the ability to spend more on their future families—things like orthodontia, nice clothes, admission to an expensive college, and travel. Tom thinks about the potential benefits to his potential children when he decides how much studying to do. Jacob doesn't.
   a. What type of externality arises from studying?
   b. Draw a graph showing this externality, contrasting the responses of Tom and Jacob. Who studies more? Who acts more efficiently? Why?

1.10 For several years, *The Sopranos* television series was available only on the HBO cable network. The series was a hit and attracted more viewers than many programs available on the broadcast networks NBC, CBS, ABC, and Fox. But Chris Albrecht, the chair of HBO, found that he was unable to use the popularity of *The Sopranos* to increase the number of subscribers to HBO. To receive HBO, cable viewers usually had to pay for a "premium package" that included not just HBO but other services, like Showtime, that were owned by other companies. As Albrecht put it, "That means we're just part of everything else. First the consumer is asked to pay $60 for the basic cable service and then it's another $40 for the platinum package, and they're selling Showtime and Starz in with us." Is there an externality involved here? If so, is it an externality in production or consumption, and is it positive or negative? If there is an externality, discuss possible solutions.

Source: Excerpt from Bill Carter, "Cable Conquered, What's Next for 'The Sopranos'?" *New York Times*, October 7, 2002. Copyright © 2002 by The New York Times Co. Reprinted with permission.

1.11 A columnist for the *Wall Street Journal* observes: "No one collects money from those who benefit from the flood control a wetland provides, or the nutrient recycling a forest does. . . . In a nutshell, market failures help drive habitat loss." What does the columnist mean by *market failures*? What does she mean by *habitat loss*? Explain why she believes one is causing the other. Illustrate your argument with a graph showing the market for land to be used for development.

Source: Sharon Begley, "Furry Math? Market Has Failed to Capture True Value of Nature," *Wall Street Journal*, August 9, 2002, p. B1.

>> **End Learning Objective 5.1**

5.2 LEARNING OBJECTIVE | 5.2 | Discuss the Coase theorem and explain how private bargaining can lead to economic efficiency in a market with an externality, **pages 141–147.**

Private Solutions to Externalities: The Coase Theorem

Summary

Externalities and market failures result from incomplete property rights or from the difficulty of enforcing property rights in certain situations. When an externality exists, and the efficient quantity of a good is not being produced, the total cost of reducing the externality is usually less than the total benefit. According to the **Coase theorem**, if **transactions costs** are low, private bargaining will result in an efficient solution to the problem of externalities.

myeconlab Visit www.myeconlab.com to complete these exercises *Get Ahead of the Curve* online and get instant feedback.

Review Questions

2.1 What do economists mean by "an economically efficient level of pollution"?

2.2 What is the Coase theorem? What are transactions costs? When are we likely to see private solutions to the problem of externalities?

Problems and Applications

2.3 Is it ever possible for an *increase* in pollution to make society better off? Briefly explain using a graph like Figure 5-3 on page 144.

2.4 If the marginal cost of reducing a certain type of pollution is zero, should all of that pollution be eliminated? Briefly explain.

2.5 Discuss the factors that determine the marginal cost of reducing crime. Discuss the factors that determine the marginal benefit of reducing crime. Would it be economically efficient to reduce the amount of crime to zero? Briefly explain.

2.6 (Related to the *Don't Let This Happen to You!* on page 144) Briefly explain whether you agree or disagree with the following statement: "Sulfur dioxide emissions cause acid rain and breathing difficulties for people with respiratory problems. The total benefit to society is greatest if we completely eliminate sulfur dioxide emissions. Therefore, the economically efficient level of emissions is zero."

2.7 In discussing cleaning up oil spills, Gary Shigenka of the National Oceanographic and Atmospheric Agency observed, "The first 90% of any cleanup comes easy. But the tradeoffs for the remaining bits are brutal." He estimates that the last 1 percent of oil removed can cost seven times as much as the first 99 percent. Why should it be any more costly to clean up the last 1 percent of an oil spill than to clean up the first 1 percent? What trade-offs do you think Shigenka was referring to?

Source: Keith Johnson and Gautam Naik, "For Spain, Exxon Valdez Offers Some Surprising Lessons," *Wall Street Journal,* November 22, 2002.

2.8 **(Related to the *Making the Connection* on page 142)** In the first years following the passage of the Clean Air Act in 1970, air pollution declined sharply and there were important health benefits, including a decline in infant mortality. Should the government take action to reduce air pollution further? How should government go about deciding this question?

2.9 **(Related to the *Making the Connection* on page 146)** We know that owners of apple orchards and owners of beehives are able to negotiate private agreements. Is it likely that as a result of these private agreements the market supplies the efficient quantities of apple trees and beehives? Are there any real-world difficulties that might stand in the way of achieving this efficient outcome?

>> **End Learning Objective 5.2**

5.3 LEARNING OBJECTIVE   5.3 | Analyze government policies to achieve economic efficiency in a market with an externality, **pages 147–152.**

Government Policies to Deal with Externalities

Summary

When private solutions to externalities are unworkable, the government sometimes intervenes. One way to deal with a negative externality in production is to impose a tax equal to the cost of the externality. The tax causes the producer of the good to internalize the externality. The government can deal with a positive externality in consumption by giving consumers a subsidy, or payment, equal to the value of the externality. Government taxes and subsidies intended to bring about an efficient level of output in the presence of externalities are called **Pigovian taxes and subsidies**. Although the federal government has sometimes used subsidies and taxes to deal with externalities, in dealing with pollution, it has more often used a command and control approach. A **command and control approach** involves the government imposing quantitative limits on the amount of pollution allowed or requiring firms to install specific pollution control devices. Direct pollution controls of this type are not economically efficient, however. As a result, Congress decided to use a system of tradable emissions allowances to reduce sulfur dioxide emissions.

myeconlab   Visit www.myeconlab.com to complete these exercises
Get Ahead of the Curve online and get instant feedback.

Review Questions

3.1 What is a Pigovian tax? At what level must a Pigovian tax be set to achieve efficiency?

3.2 Why do most economists prefer tradable emissions allowances rather than the command and control approach to pollution?

Problems and Applications

3.3 Why does the government subsidize the purchase of college educations but not the purchase of hamburgers?

3.4 Writing in the *New York Times*, Michael Lewis argues: "Good new technologies are a bit like good new roads: Their social benefits far exceed what any one person or company can get paid for creating them." Does this observation justify the government subsidizing the production of new technologies? If so, how might the government do this?

Source: Michael Lewis, "In Defense of the Boom," *New York Times,* October 27, 2002.

3.5 In 2007, Governor Deval Patrick of Massachusetts proposed that criminals would have to pay a "safety fee" to the government. The size of the fee would be based on the seriousness of the crime (that is, the fee would be larger for more serious crimes).
a. Is there an economically efficient amount of crime? Briefly explain.
b. Briefly explain whether the "safety fee" is a Pigovian tax of the type discussed in this chapter.

Source: Michael Levenson, "Patrick Proposes New Fee on Criminals," *Boston Globe,* January 14, 2007.

3.6 We saw in this chapter that market failure occurs when firms ignore the costs generated by pollution in deciding how much to produce. Government intervention is usually necessary to bring about a more efficient level of production. Before 1989, the Communist governments of Eastern Europe directly controlled the production of most goods and were free to choose how much of each good would be produced and what production process would be used. When these Communist governments collapsed, it was revealed that the countries of Eastern Europe suffered from very high levels of pollution, much higher than had existed in the United States and other high-income countries even before there was government anti-pollution legislation. Discuss reasons why the nonmarket Communist system generated more pollution than market economies.

3.7 Bjorn Lomborg, director of the Environmental Assessment Institute in Denmark, argued in a column in the *New York Times*: "Traditionally, the developed nations of the West have shown a greater concern for environmental sustainability, while the third world countries have a stronger desire for economic development." Recall the definition of *normal good* given in Chapter 3. Is environmental protection a normal good? If so, is there any connection between this fact and Lomborg's observation? Briefly explain. How do the marginal cost and marginal benefit of environmental protection change with economic development?

Source: Bjorn Lomborg, "The Environmentalists Are Wrong," *New York Times*, August 26, 2002.

3.8 (Related to *Solved Problem 5-3* on page 148) The fumes from dry cleaners can contribute to air pollution. Suppose the following graph illustrates the situation in the dry cleaning market.

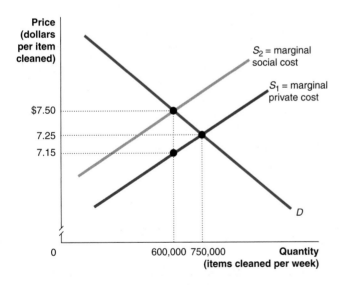

a. Explain how a government can use a tax on dry cleaning to bring about the efficient level of production. What should the value of the tax be?
b. How large is the deadweight loss (in dollars) from excessive dry cleaning, according to the figure?

3.9 The graph in the next column illustrates the situation in the dry cleaning market. In contrast to problem 3.8, the marginal social cost of the pollution rises as the quantity of items cleaned per week increases. In addi-

tion, there are two demand curves, one for a smaller city, D_S, the other for a larger city, D_L.
a. Explain why the marginal social cost curve has a different slope than the marginal private cost curve.
b. What tax per item cleaned will achieve economic efficiency in the smaller city? In the larger city? Explain why the efficient tax is different in the two cities.

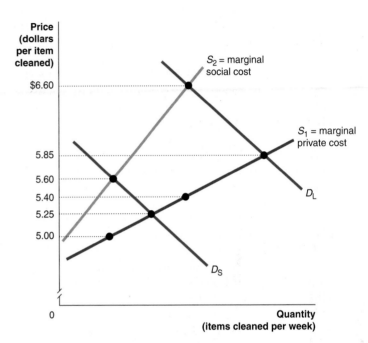

3.10 (Related to the *Chapter Opener* on page 136) Anyone can purchase sulfur dioxide emissions allowances on the Chicago Mercantile Exchange. Several environmental groups have raised money to buy allowances. As part of their fundraising, these groups have urged contributors to buy the allowances as gifts. As one newspaper story put it, "For the environmentalist in your life, here's a gift that is sold by the ton, fits in an envelope and will last forever." What would be the impact of environmental groups buying emission allowances on the total amount of sulfur dioxide pollution in the United States? What would be the impact on the price of the emission allowances?

Source: Randall Edwards, "Dear Santa: Please Bring Me Sulfur Dioxide for Christmas," *Columbus (Ohio) Dispatch*, December 19, 1999.

3.11 (Related to the *Making the Connection* on page 151) As discussed in the chapter, a system of tradable permits was very successful in efficiently reducing emissions of sulfur dioxide in the United States. Why have some economists proposed a similar system of tradable permits to reduce carbon dioxide emissions? Briefly discuss similarities and differences between the problem of reducing sulfur dioxide emissions and the problem of reducing carbon dioxide emissions.

>> End Learning Objective 5.3

5.4 LEARNING OBJECTIVE 5.4 | Explain how goods can be categorized on the basis of whether they are rival or excludable and use graphs to illustrate the efficient quantities of public goods and common resources, **pages 152–163.**

Four Categories of Goods

Summary

There are four categories of goods: private goods, public goods, quasi-public goods, and common resources. **Private goods** are both rival and excludable. **Rivalry** means that when one person consumes a unit of a good, no one else can consume that unit. **Excludability** means that anyone who does not pay for a good cannot consume it. **Public goods** are both nonrivalrous and nonexcludable. Private firms are usually not willing to supply public goods because of free riding. **Free riding** involves benefiting from a good without paying for it. **Quasi-public goods** are excludable but not rival. **Common resources** are rival but not excludable. The **tragedy of the commons** refers to the tendency for a common resource to be overused. The tragedy of the commons results from a lack of clearly defined and enforced property rights. We find the market demand curve for a private good by adding the quantity of the good demanded by each consumer at each price. We find the demand curve for a public good by adding vertically the price each consumer would be willing to pay for each quantity of the good. The optimal quantity of a public good occurs where the demand curve intersects the curve representing the marginal cost of supplying the good.

 Visit www.myeconlab.com to complete these exercises *Get Ahead of the Curve* online and get instant feedback.

Review Questions

4.1 Define rivalry and excludability and use these terms to discuss the four categories of goods.

4.2 What is a public good? What is free riding? How is free riding related to the tendency of a public good to create market failure?

4.3 What is the tragedy of the commons? How can it be avoided?

Problems and Applications

4.4 **(Related to *Solved Problem 5-5* on page 158)** Suppose that Jill and Joe are the only two people in the small town of Andover. Andover has land available to build a park of no more than 9 acres. Jill and Joe's demand schedules for the park are as follows:

JOE	
PRICE PER ACRE	NUMBER OF ACRES
$10	0
9	1
8	2
7	3
6	4
5	5
4	6
3	7
2	8
1	9

JILL	
PRICE PER ACRE	NUMBER OF ACRES
$15	0
14	1
13	2
12	3
11	4
10	5
9	6
8	7
7	8
6	9

The supply curve is as follows:

PRICE	NUMBER OF ACRES
$11	1
13	2
15	3
17	4
19	5
21	6
23	7
25	8
27	9

a. Draw a graph showing the optimal size of the park. Be sure to label the curves on the graph.

b. Briefly explain why a park of 2 acres is not optimal.

4.5 Commercial whaling has been described as a modern example of the tragedy of the commons. Briefly explain whether you agree or disagree.

4.6 According to an article in the *Wall Street Journal*, economist Paul Romer of Stanford University has argued: "The market mechanism and property rights are excellent at conserving scarce resources and putting them to the most profitable use. . . . They aren't so good at encouraging the production and distribution of new ideas, which are critical to progress." What characteristics of the production and distribution of new ideas might make it difficult for the market to produce the optimal amount?

Source: David Wessel, "Precepts from Professor Summers," *Wall Street Journal*, October 17, 2002.

4.7 The more frequently bacteria are exposed to antibiotics, the more quickly the bacteria will develop resistance to the antibiotics. A columnist for the *Wall Street Journal* observes:

> Each parent will press a pediatrician for a drug if there's any chance it will cure a child. Yet if every parent and pediatrician does the same, they will speed the evolution of drug-resistant microbes. And what drug company will enlist its marketers to prod doctors to prescribe its antibiotics less?

Briefly discuss in what sense antibiotics can be considered a common resource.

Source: David Wessel, "Losing the Race with Bugs: Bacteria Beats New Drugs," *Wall Street Journal*, April 25, 2002.

4.8 Put each of these goods or services into one of the boxes in Figure 5-8 on page 153. That is, categorize them as private goods, public goods, quasi-public goods, or common resources.
a. A television broadcast of the World Series
b. Home mail delivery
c. Education in a public school
d. Education in a private school
e. Hiking in a park surrounded by a fence
f. Hiking in a park not surrounded by a fence
g. An apple

4.9 (Related to the *Making the Connection* on page 153) Explain whether you agree or disagree with the following statement: "Providing health care is obviously a public good. If one person becomes ill and doesn't receive treatment, that person may infect many other people. If many people become ill, then the output of the economy will be negatively affected. Therefore, providing health care is a public good that should be supplied by the government."

>> **End Learning Objective 5.4**

Chapter 6

Elasticity: The Responsiveness of Demand and Supply

Do People Care about the Prices of Books?

Some observers have been predicting for years that the printed book will be replaced with the electronic book. The printed book is still holding its own, however. In 2006, U.S. consumers spent almost $54 billion to buy 3.2 billion copies of new printed books. By contrast, although thousands of books were available in electronic format, total sales amounted to only a few million dollars.

While the printed book lives on, book publishers face a problem unique to the industry: Unlike most retailers, bookstores have the right to return unsold books. For example, when a local supermarket orders shampoo, apple juice, or dog food, it knows that if it has overestimated consumer demand, it will be stuck with the unsold items. By contrast, to give bookstores an incentive to order more books, publishers have given the stores the right to return unsold copies. On average, bookstores return 35 percent of books to publishers.

The high return rate of books means that publishers have to be very careful when deciding how many copies of a book to print and ship to bookstores. In 2007, Scholastic, the largest publisher of children's books in the world, published the final installment of the hugely popular Harry Potter series. Barnes & Noble bookstores have a special membership program that gives customers a 20 percent discount on most hardcover books. But on *Harry Potter and the Deathly Hallows*, Barnes & Noble offered a 40 percent discount. The company was willing to accept a small profit on each book in hopes of selling a very large quantity. Scholastic could not simply print all the books ordered by bookstores like Barnes & Noble because it feared that the bookstores might overestimate the quantity of books actually demanded by consumers. Executives at Scholastic knew that the number of copies of the book demanded by consumers would depend in part on the price of the book. But how responsive are consumers to changes in book prices? Will a lower price significantly increase sales? Publishers debate this point.

For example, Stephen Rubin, president and publisher of Doubleday, has made the following argument about book prices: "I am just convinced that there is no difference between $22 and $23. Let's face it. If you want a book in translation from a Czech writer, you are going to buy the book—price is not a factor if it is a book that you really want." On the other hand, Barnes & Noble's program of discounting books for members will be effective only if consumers are sufficiently responsive to lower prices for books. As Bill Armstrong, an industry analyst, put it: "[Barnes & Noble's discount program] will only be a success if these lower prices produce greater unit volume enough to offset the lower price per book." **AN INSIDE LOOK** on **page 198** discusses the effectiveness of Borders bookstores' Borders Rewards program.

Sources: Henry Sanderson, "Barnes & Noble Disappoints Investors with Outlook," Wall Street Journal, March 5, 2007; and data on book sales from U.S. Census Bureau, The 2007 Statistical Abstract.

LEARNING Objectives

After studying this chapter, you should be able to:

6.1 Define the **price elasticity of demand** and understand how to measure it, page 174.

6.2 Understand the **determinants** of the **price elasticity** of **demand**, page 180.

6.3 Understand the relationship between the **price elasticity of demand** and **total revenue**, page 182.

6.4 Define the **cross-price elasticity** of demand and the **income elasticity** of demand, and understand their determinants and how they are measured, page 186.

6.5 Use **price elasticity** and **income elasticity** to analyze economic issues, page 189.

6.6 Define the **price elasticity** of **supply** and understand its main determinants and how it is measured, page 191.

Economics in YOUR Life!

How Much Do Book Prices Matter to You?

We have just seen that there is a debate in the publishing industry about how responsive consumers are to changes in book prices. Barnes & Noble was willing to reduce the price of *Harry Potter and the Deathly Hallows* because it believed doing so would significantly increase sales. Some book executives, like Stephen Rubin of Doubleday, seem to think that prices do not matter. What factors would make you more or less sensitive to price when purchasing a book? Is Barnes & Noble's strategy likely to succeed? As you read the chapter, see if can answer these questions. You can check your answers against those we provide at the end of the chapter. **▶▶ Continued on page 196**

Whether you are managing a publishing company, bookstore, or coffee shop, you need to know how an increase or decrease in the price of your products will affect the quantity consumers are willing to buy. We saw in Chapter 3 that cutting the price of a good increases the quantity demanded and that raising the price reduces the quantity demanded. But the critical question is this: *How much* will the quantity demanded change as a result of a price increase or decrease? Economists use the concept of **elasticity** to measure how one economic variable—such as the quantity demanded—responds to changes in another economic variable—such as the price. For example, the responsiveness of the quantity demanded of a good to changes in its price is called the *price elasticity of demand*. Knowing the price elasticity of demand allows you to compute the effect of a price change on the quantity demanded.

> **Elasticity** A measure of how much one economic variable responds to changes in another economic variable.

We also saw in Chapter 3 that the quantity of a good that consumers demand depends not just on the price of the good but also on consumer income and on the prices of related goods. As a manager, you would also be interested in measuring the responsiveness of demand to these other factors. As we will see, we can use the concept of elasticity here as well. We also are interested in the responsiveness of the quantity supplied of a good to changes in its price, which is called the *price elasticity of supply*.

Elasticity is an important concept not just for business managers but for policymakers as well. If the government wants to discourage teenage smoking, it can raise the price of cigarettes by increasing the tax on them. If we know the price elasticity of demand for cigarettes, we can calculate how many fewer cigarettes will be demanded at a higher price. In this chapter, we will also see how policymakers use the concept of elasticity.

6.1 LEARNING OBJECTIVE

6.1 | Define the price elasticity of demand and understand how to measure it.

The Price Elasticity of Demand and Its Measurement

We know from the law of demand that when the price of a product falls, the quantity demanded of the product increases. But the law of demand tells firms only that the demand curves for their products slope downward. More useful is a measure of the responsiveness of the quantity demanded to a change in price. This measure is called the **price elasticity of demand**.

> **Price elasticity of demand** The responsiveness of the quantity demanded to a change in price, measured by dividing the percentage change in the quantity demanded of a product by the percentage change in the product's price.

Measuring the Price Elasticity of Demand

We might measure the price elasticity of demand by using the slope of the demand curve because the slope of the demand curve tells us how much quantity changes as price changes. Using the slope of the demand curve to measure price elasticity has a drawback, however: The measurement of slope is sensitive to the units chosen for quantity and price. For example, suppose a $1 decrease in the price of *Harry Potter and the Deathly Hallows* leads to an increase in the quantity demanded from 10.1 million books to 10.2 million books. The change in quantity is 0.1 million books, and the change in price is −$1, so the slope is 0.1/−1 = −0.1. But if we measure price in cents, rather than dollars, the slope is 0.1/−100 = −0.001. If we measure price in dollars and books in thousands, instead of millions, the slope is 100/−1 = −100. Clearly, the value we compute for the slope can change dramatically, depending on the units we use for quantity and price.

To avoid this confusion over units, economists use *percentage changes* when measuring the price elasticity of demand. Percentage changes are not dependent on units. (For a review of calculating percentage changes, see the appendix to Chapter 1.) No matter what units we use to measure the quantity of wheat, 10 percent more wheat is 10 percent more wheat. Therefore, the price elasticity of demand is measured by dividing the percentage change in the quantity demanded by the percentage change in the price. Or:

$$\text{Price elasticity of demand} = \frac{\text{Percentage change in quantity demanded}}{\text{Percentage change in price}}.$$

It's important to remember that *the price elasticity of demand is not the same as the slope of the demand curve.*

If we calculate the price elasticity of demand for a price cut, the percentage change in price will be negative, and the percentage change in quantity demanded will be positive. Similarly, if we calculate the price elasticity of demand for a price increase, the percentage change in price will be positive, and the percentage change in quantity will be negative. Therefore, the price elasticity of demand is always negative. In comparing elasticities, though, we are usually interested in their relative size. So, we often drop the minus sign and compare their *absolute values*. In other words, although −3 is actually a smaller number than −2, a price elasticity of −3 is larger than a price elasticity of −2.

Elastic Demand and Inelastic Demand

If the quantity demanded is responsive to changes in price, the percentage change in quantity demanded will be *greater* than the percentage change in price, and the price elasticity of demand will be greater than 1 in absolute value. In this case, demand is **elastic**. For example, if a 10 percent fall in the price of bagels results in a 20 percent increase in the quantity of bagels demanded, then:

$$\text{Price elasticity of demand} = \frac{20\%}{-10\%} = -2,$$

and we can conclude that the price of bagels is **elastic**.

When the quantity demanded is not very responsive to price, however, the percentage change in quantity demanded will be *less* than the percentage change in price, and the price elasticity of demand will be less than 1 in absolute value. In this case, demand is **inelastic**. For example, if a 10 percent fall in the price of wheat results in a 5 percent increase in the quantity of wheat demanded, then:

$$\text{Price elasticity of demand} = \frac{5\%}{-10\%} = -0.5,$$

and we can conclude that the demand for wheat is **inelastic**.

In the special case in which the percentage change in the quantity demanded is equal to the percentage change in price, the price elasticity of demand equals −1 (or 1 in absolute value). In this case, demand is **unit-elastic**.

Elastic demand Demand is elastic when the percentage change in quantity demanded is *greater* than the percentage change in price, so the price elasticity is *greater* than 1 in absolute value.

Inelastic demand Demand is inelastic when the percentage change in quantity demanded is *less* than the percentage change in price, so the price elasticity is *less* than 1 in absolute value.

Unit-elastic demand Demand is unit-elastic when the percentage change in quantity demanded is *equal to* the percentage change in price, so the price elasticity is equal to 1 in absolute value.

An Example of Computing Price Elasticities

Suppose you own a small bookstore and you are trying to decide whether to cut the price you are charging for a new John Grisham mystery novel. You are currently at point *A* in Figure 6-1: selling 16 copies of the novel per day at a price of $30 per copy. How many more copies you will sell by cutting the price to $20 depends on the price elasticity of demand for this novel. Let's consider two possibilities: If D_1 is the demand curve for this novel in your store, your sales will increase to 28 copies per day, point *B*. But if D_2 is your demand curve, your sales will increase only to 20 copies per day, point *C*. We might expect—correctly, as we will see—that between these points, demand curve D_1 is *elastic*, and demand curve D_2 is *inelastic*.

To confirm that D_1 is elastic between these points and that D_2 is inelastic, we need to calculate the price elasticity of demand for each curve. In calculating price elasticity between two points on a demand curve, though, we run into a problem because we get

Figure 6-1

Elastic and Inelastic Demand Curves

Along D_1, cutting the price from $30 to $20 increases the number of copies sold from 16 per day to 28 per day, so demand is elastic between point A and point B. Along D_2, cutting the price from $30 to $20 increases the number of copies sold from 16 per day to only 20 per day, so demand is inelastic between point A and point C.

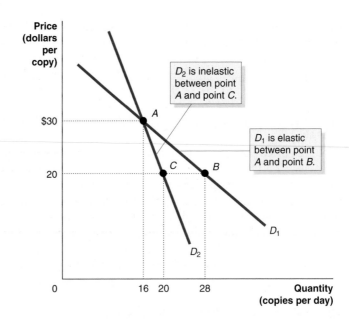

a different value for price increases than for price decreases. For example, suppose we calculate the price elasticity for D_2 as the price is cut from $30 to $20. This reduction is a 33 percent price cut that increases the quantity demanded from 16 books to 20 books, or by 25 percent. Therefore, the price elasticity of demand between points A and C is 25/−33 = −0.8. Now let's calculate the price elasticity for D_2 as the price is *increased* from $20 to $30. This is a 50 percent price increase that decreases the quantity demanded from 20 books to 16 books, or by 20 percent. So, now our measure of the price elasticity of demand between points A and C is −20/50 = −0.4. It can be confusing to have different values for the price elasticity of demand between the same two points on the same demand curve.

The Midpoint Formula

We can use the *midpoint formula* to ensure that we have only one value of the price elasticity of demand between the same two points on a demand curve. The midpoint formula uses the *average* of the initial and final quantities and the initial and final prices. If Q_1 and P_1 are the initial quantity and price and Q_2 and P_2 are the final quantity and price, the midpoint formula is:

$$\text{Price elasticity of demand} = \frac{(Q_2 - Q_1)}{\left(\dfrac{Q_1 + Q_2}{2}\right)} \div \frac{(P_2 - P_1)}{\left(\dfrac{P_1 + P_2}{2}\right)}.$$

The midpoint formula may seem challenging at first, but the numerator is just the change in quantity divided by the average of the initial and final quantities, and the denominator is just the change in price divided by the average of the initial and final prices.

Let's apply the formula to calculating the price elasticity of D_2 in Figure 6-1. Between point A and point C on D_2, the change in quantity is 4, and the average of the two quantities is 18. Therefore, there is a 22.2 percent change in quantity. The change in price is −$10, and the average of the two prices is $25. Therefore, there is a −40 percent change in price. So, the price elasticity of demand is 22.2/−40.0 = −0.6. Notice these three results from calculating the price elasticity of demand using the midpoint formula: First, as we suspected from examining Figure 6-1, demand curve D_2 is inelastic between points A and C. Second, our value for the price elasticity calculated using the midpoint formula is between the two values we calculated earlier. Third, the midpoint formula will give us the same value whether we are moving from the higher price to the lower price or from the lower price to the higher price.

We can also use the midpoint formula to calculate the elasticity of demand between point A and point B on D_1. In this case, there is a 54.5 percent change in quantity and a −40 percent change in price. So, the elasticity of demand is 54.5/−40.0 = −1.4. Once again, as we suspected, demand curve D_1 is price elastic between points A and B.

Solved Problem | 6-1

Calculating the Price Elasticity of Demand

Scholastic Corporation's suggested retail price for *Harry Potter and the Deathly Hallows* is $35. Suppose you own a small bookstore, and you believe that if you keep the price of the book at $35, you will be able to sell 40 copies per day. You are considering cutting the price to $25. The graph below shows two possible increases in the quantity sold as a result of your price cut. Use the information in the graph to calculate the price elasticity between these two prices on each of the demand curves. Use the midpoint formula in your calculations. State whether each demand curve is elastic or inelastic between these two prices.

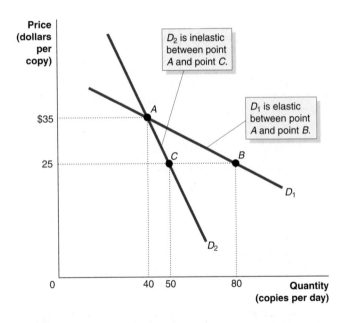

SOLVING THE PROBLEM:

Step 1: **Review the chapter material.** This problem requires calculating the price elasticity of demand, so you may want to review the material in the section "The Midpoint Formula," which begins on page 176.

Step 2: **As the first step in using the midpoint formula, calculate the average quantity and the average price for demand curve D_1.**

$$\text{Average quantity} = \frac{40 + 80}{2} = 60$$

$$\text{Average price} = \frac{\$35 + \$25}{2} = \$30$$

Step 3: **Now calculate the percentage change in the quantity demanded and the percentage change in price for demand curve D_1.**

$$\text{Percentage change in quantity demanded} = \frac{80 - 40}{60} \times 100 = 66.7\%$$

$$\text{Percentage change in price} = \frac{\$25 - \$35}{\$30} \times 100 = -33.3\%$$

Step 4:   **Divide the percentage change in the quantity demanded by the percentage change in price to arrive at the price elasticity for demand curve D_1.**

$$\text{Price elasticity of demand} = \frac{66.7\%}{-33.3\%} = -2$$

Because the elasticity is greater than 1 in absolute value, D_1 is price *elastic* between these two prices.

Step 5:   **Calculate the price elasticity of demand curve D_2 between these two prices.**

$$\text{Percentage change in quantity demanded} = \frac{50 - 40}{45} \times 100 = 22.2\%$$

$$\text{Percentage change in price} = \frac{\$25 - \$35}{\$30} \times 100 = -33.3\%$$

$$\text{Price elasticity of demand} = \frac{22.2\%}{-33.3\%} = -0.7$$

Because the elasticity is less than 1 in absolute value, D_2 is price *inelastic* between these two prices.

>> **End Solved Problem 6-1**   **YOUR TURN:** For more practice, do related problem 1.6 on page 200 at the end of this chapter.

When Demand Curves Intersect, the Flatter Curve Is More Elastic

Remember that elasticity is not the same thing as slope. While slope is calculated using changes in quantity and price, elasticity is calculated using percentage changes. But it *is* true that if two demand curves intersect, the one with the smaller slope (in absolute value)—the flatter demand curve—is more elastic, and the one with the larger slope (in absolute value)—the steeper demand curve—is less elastic. In Figure 6-1, demand curve D_1 is more elastic than demand curve D_2.

Polar Cases of Perfectly Elastic and Perfectly Inelastic Demand

Perfectly inelastic demand The case where the quantity demanded is completely unresponsive to price, and the price elasticity of demand equals zero.

Although they do not occur frequently, you should be aware of the extreme, or polar, cases of price elasticity. If a demand curve is a vertical line, it is **perfectly inelastic** . In this case, the quantity demanded is completely unresponsive to price, and the price elasticity of demand equals zero. However much price may increase or decrease, the quantity remains the same. For only a very few products will the quantity demanded be completely unresponsive to the price, making the demand curve a vertical line. The drug insulin is an example. Diabetics must take a certain amount of insulin each day. If the price of insulin declines, it will not affect the required dose and thus will not increase the quantity demanded. Similarly, a price increase will not affect the required dose or decrease the quantity demanded. (Of course, some diabetics will not be able to afford insulin at a higher price. If so, even in this case, the demand curve may not be completely vertical and, therefore, not perfectly inelastic.)

Perfectly elastic demand The case where the quantity demanded is infinitely responsive to price, and the price elasticity of demand equals infinity.

If a demand curve is a horizontal line, it is **perfectly elastic**. In this case, the quantity demanded would be infinitely responsive to price, and the price elasticity of demand equals infinity. If a demand curve is perfectly elastic, an increase in price causes the quantity demanded to fall to zero. Once again, perfectly elastic demand curves are rare, and it is important not to confuse *elastic* with *perfectly elastic*. Table 6-1 summarizes the different price elasticities of demand.

IF DEMAND IS...	THEN THE ABSOLUTE VALUE OF PRICE ELASTICITY IS
elastic	greater than 1
inelastic	less than 1
unit-elastic	equal to 1
perfectly elastic	equal to infinity
perfectly inelastic	equal to 0

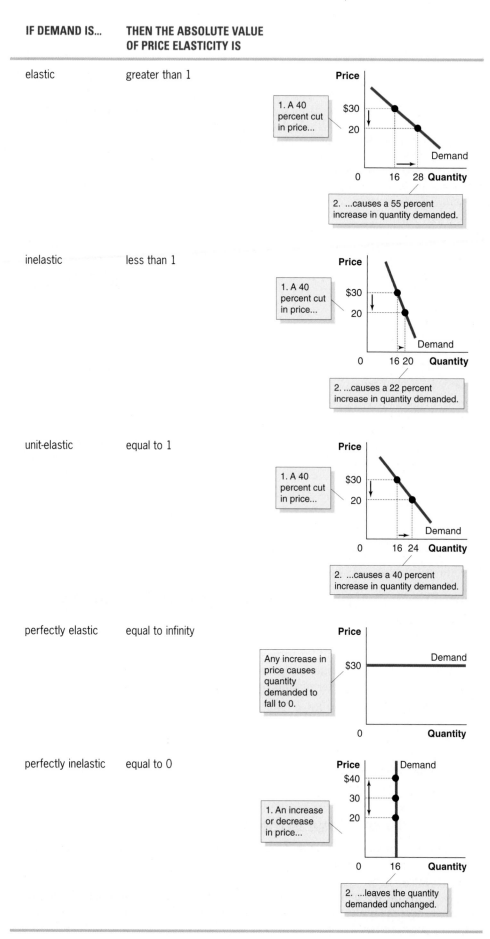

TABLE 6-1

Summary of the Price Elasticities of Demand

(Note that the percentage increases shown in the boxes in the graphs were calculated using the midpoint formula on page 176.)

Don't Let This Happen to YOU!

Don't Confuse Inelastic with *Perfectly* Inelastic

You may be tempted to simplify the concept of elasticity by assuming that any demand curve described as being inelastic is *perfectly* inelastic. You should never assume this because perfectly inelastic demand curves are rare. For example, consider the following problem: "Use a demand and supply graph to show how a decrease in supply affects the equilibrium quantity of gasoline. Assume that the demand for gasoline is inelastic." The following graph would be an *incorrect* answer to this problem.

The demand for gasoline is inelastic, but it is not *perfectly* inelastic. When the price of gasoline rises, the quantity demanded falls. So, the graph that would be the correct answer to this problem would show a normal downward-sloping demand curve rather than a vertical demand curve.

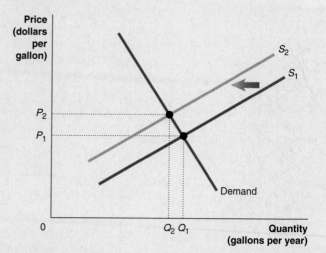

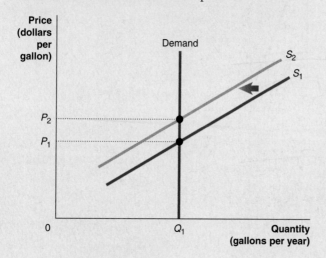

YOUR TURN: Test your understanding by doing related problem 1.11 on page 201 at the end of this chapter.

6.2 LEARNING OBJECTIVE

6.2 | Understand the determinants of the price elasticity of demand.

The Determinants of the Price Elasticity of Demand

We have seen that the demand for some products may be elastic, while the demand for other products may be inelastic. In this section, we examine why price elasticities differ among products. The key determinants of the price elasticity of demand are as follows:

*   Availability of close substitutes
*   Passage of time
*   Necessities versus luxuries
*   Definition of the market
*   Share of the good in the consumer's budget

Availability of Close Substitutes

The availability of substitutes is the most important determinant of price elasticity of demand because how consumers react to a change in the price of a product depends on what alternatives they have. When the price of gasoline rises, consumers have few alternatives, so the quantity demanded falls only a little. But if Domino's raises the price of pizza, consumers have many alternatives, so the quantity demanded is likely to fall quite a lot. In fact, a key constraint on a firm's pricing policies is how many close substitutes exist for its product. In general, *if a product has more substitutes available, it will have more elastic demand. If a product has fewer substitutes available, it will have less elastic demand.*

Passage of Time

It usually takes consumers some time to adjust their buying habits when prices change. If the price of chicken falls, for example, it takes a while before consumers decide to change from eating chicken for dinner once per week to eating it twice per week. If the price of gasoline increases, it also takes a while for consumers to decide to shift toward buying more fuel-efficient cars to reduce the quantity of gasoline they buy. *The more time that passes, the more elastic the demand for a product becomes.*

Luxuries versus Necessities

Goods that are luxuries usually have more elastic demand curves than goods that are necessities. For example, the demand for milk is inelastic because milk is a necessity, and the quantity that people buy is not very dependent on its price. Tickets to a concert are a luxury, so the demand for concert tickets is much more elastic than the demand for milk. *The demand curve for a luxury is more elastic than the demand curve for a necessity.*

Definition of the Market

In a narrowly defined market, consumers have more substitutes available. If the price of Kellogg's Raisin Bran rises, many consumers will start buying another brand of raisin bran. If the prices of all brands of raisin bran rise, the responsiveness of consumers will be lower. If the prices of all breakfast cereals rise, the responsiveness of consumers will be even lower. *The more narrowly we define a market, the more elastic demand will be.*

Making the Connection | The Price Elasticity of Demand for Breakfast Cereal

MIT economist Jerry Hausman has estimated the price elasticity of demand for breakfast cereal. He divided breakfast cereals into three categories: children's cereals, such as Trix and Froot Loops; adult cereals, such as Special K and Grape-Nuts; and family cereals, such as Corn Flakes and Raisin Bran. Some of the results of his estimates are given in the following table.

CEREAL	PRICE ELASTICITY OF DEMAND
Post Raisin Bran	−2.5
All family breakfast cereals	−1.8
All types of breakfast cereals	−0.9

Source: Jerry A. Hausman, "The Price Elasticity of Demand for Breakfast Cereal," in Timothy F. Bresnahan and Robert J. Gordon, eds., *The Economics of New Goods*, Chicago: University of Chicago Press, 1997. Used with permission of The University of Chicago Press.

What happens when the price of raisin bran increases?

Just as we would expect, the price elasticity for a particular brand of raisin bran was larger in absolute value than the elasticity for all family cereals, and the elasticity for all family cereals was larger than the elasticity for all types of breakfast cereals. If Post increases the price of its Raisin Bran by 10 percent, sales will decline by 25 percent, as many consumers switch to another brand of raisin bran. If the prices of all family breakfast cereals rise by 10 percent, sales will decline by 18 percent, as consumers switch to child or adult cereals. In both of these cases, demand is elastic. But if the prices of all types of breakfast cereals rise by 10 percent, sales will decline by only 9 percent. Demand for all breakfast cereals is inelastic.

Source: Jerry A. Hausman, "Valuation of New Goods under Perfect and Imperfect Competition," in Timothy F. Bresnahan and Robert J. Gordon, eds., *The Economics of New Goods*, Chicago: University of Chicago Press, 1997.

YOUR TURN: Test your understanding by doing related problem 2.4 on page 202 at the end of this chapter.

Share of a Good in a Consumer's Budget

Goods that take only a small fraction of a consumer's budget tend to have less elastic demand than goods that take a large fraction. For example, most people buy salt infrequently and in relatively small quantities. The share of the average consumer's budget that is spent on salt is very low. As a result, even a doubling of the price of salt is likely to result in only a small decline in the quantity of salt demanded. "Big-ticket items," such as houses, cars, and furniture, take up a larger share in the average consumer's budget. Increases in the prices of these goods are likely to result in significant declines in quantity demanded. In general, *the demand for a good will be more elastic the larger the share of the good in the average consumer's budget.*

Is the Demand for Books Perfectly Inelastic?

At the beginning of the chapter we quoted Stephen Rubin, publisher of Doubleday, as saying, "I am just convinced that there is no difference between $22 and $23. . . . Price is not a factor if it is a book that you really want." Taken literally, Rubin seems to be arguing that the demand for books is perfectly inelastic because only when demand is perfectly inelastic is price "not a factor." It's unlikely that this is what he means because if demand were really perfectly inelastic, he could charge $200 or $2,000 instead of charging $23 and still sell the same number of books. It is more likely he is arguing that demand is inelastic, so that even though he will sell fewer books at a price of $23 than at a price of $22, the decline in sales will be small.

Notice also that the book he mentions is a "translation from a Czech writer." Specialized books of this type will have relatively few substitutes (although a consumer can buy a used copy or borrow a copy from the library). A cut in price is unlikely to attract many new customers, and an increase in price is unlikely to cause many existing customers to not buy. This lack of substitutes is the main factor that makes demand inelastic. The situation may be different for light fiction written by popular novelists, like John Grisham, Stephen King, or Dean Koontz. Many consumers see books written by these authors as close substitutes. Someone looking for a "good read" on an airplane trip or at the beach may switch from Stephen King to Dean Koontz if the price of the Stephen King book is significantly higher.

6.3 LEARNING OBJECTIVE

6.3 | Understand the relationship between the price elasticity of demand and total revenue.

The Relationship between Price Elasticity of Demand and Total Revenue

Total revenue The total amount of funds received by a seller of a good or service, calculated by multiplying price per unit by the number of units sold.

A firm is interested in price elasticity because it allows the firm to calculate how changes in price will affect its **total revenue**, which is the total amount of funds it receives from selling a good or service. Total revenue is calculated by multiplying price per unit by the number of units sold. When demand is inelastic, price and total revenue move in the same direction: An increase in price raises total revenue, and a decrease in price reduces total revenue. When demand is elastic, price and total revenue move inversely: An increase in price reduces total revenue, and a decrease in price raises total revenue.

To understand the relationship between price elasticity and total revenue, consider Figure 6-2. Panel (a) shows a demand curve for a John Grisham novel (as in Figure 6-1 on page 176). This demand curve is inelastic between point *A* and point *B*. The total revenue received by a bookseller at point *A* equals the price of $30 multiplied by the 16 copies sold, or $480. This amount equals the areas of the rectangles *C* and *D* in the figure because together the rectangles have a height of $30 and a base of 16 copies. Because this demand curve is inelastic between point *A* and point *B* (it was demand curve D_2 in Figure 6-1), cutting the price to $20 (point *B*) reduces total revenue. The new total revenue is shown by the areas of rectangles *D* and *E*, and it is equal to $20 multiplied by 20 copies, or $400. Total revenue falls because the increase in the quantity demanded is not large enough to make up for the

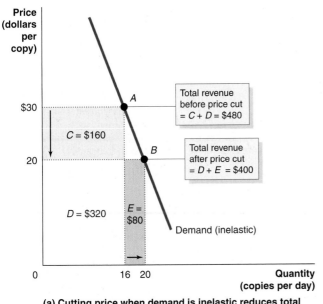

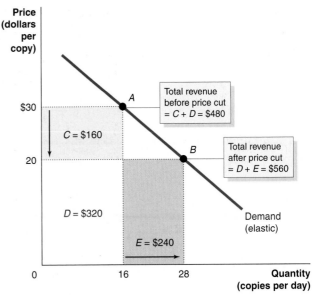

(a) Cutting price when demand is inelastic reduces total revenue.

(b) Cutting price when demand is elastic increases total revenue.

Figure 6-2 | The Relationship between Price Elasticity and Total Revenue

When demand is inelastic, a cut in price will decrease total revenue. In panel (a), at point A, the price is $30, 16 copies are sold, and total revenue received by the bookseller equals $30 × 16 copies, or $480. At point B, cutting price to $20 increases the quantity demanded to 20 copies, but the fall in price more than offsets the increase in quantity. As a result, revenue falls to $20 × 20 copies, or $400. When demand is elastic, a cut in price will increase total revenue. In panel (b), at point A, the area of rectangles C and D is still equal to $480. But at point B, the area of rectangles D and E is equal to $20 × 28 copies, or $560. In this case, the increase in the quantity demanded is large enough to offset the fall in price, so total revenue increases.

decrease in price. As a result, the $80 increase in revenue gained as a result of the price cut—dark-green rectangle E—is less than the $160 in revenue lost—light-green rectangle C.

Panel (b) of Figure 6-2 shows a demand curve that is elastic between point A and point B (it was demand curve D_1 in Figure 6-1). In this case, cutting the price increases total revenue. At point A, the areas of rectangles C and D are still equal to $480, but at point B, the areas of rectangles D and E are equal to $20 multiplied by 28 copies, or $560. Here, total revenue rises because the increase in the quantity demanded is large enough to offset the lower price. As a result, the $240 increase in revenue gained as a result of the price cut—dark-green rectangle E—is greater than the $160 in revenue lost—light-green rectangle C.

The third, less common, possibility is that demand is unit elastic. In that case, a change in price is exactly offset by a proportional change in quantity demanded, leaving revenue unaffected. Therefore, when demand is unit elastic, neither a decrease in price nor an increase in price affects revenue. Table 6-2 summarizes the relationship between price elasticity and revenue.

Elasticity and Revenue with a Linear Demand Curve

Along most demand curves, elasticity is not constant at every point. For example, a straight-line, or linear, demand curve for DVDs is shown in panel (a) of Figure 6-3. The numbers from the table are plotted in the graphs. The demand curve shows that when the price falls by $1, consumers always respond by buying 2 more DVDs per month. When the price is high and the quantity demanded is low, demand is elastic. This is true because a $1 fall in price is a smaller percentage change when the price is high, and an increase of 2 DVDs is a larger percentage change when the quantity of DVDs is small. By similar reasoning, we can see why demand is inelastic when the price is low and the quantity demanded is high. Panel (a) in Figure 6-3 shows that when price is between $8 and $4 and quantity is between 0 and 6, demand is elastic. Panel (b) shows that over this same range, total revenue will increase as price falls. For example, in panel (a), as price falls from $7 to $6,

TABLE 6-2

The Relationship between Price Elasticity and Revenue

IF DEMAND IS ...	THEN ...	BECAUSE ...
elastic	an increase in price reduces revenue	the decrease in quantity demanded is proportionally *greater* than the increase in price.
elastic	a decrease in price increases revenue	the increase in quantity demanded is proportionally *greater* than the decrease in price.
inelastic	an increase in price increases revenue	the decrease in quantity demanded is proportionally *smaller* than the increase in price.
inelastic	a decrease in price reduces revenue	the increase in quantity demanded is proportionally *smaller* than the decrease in price.
unit elastic	an increase in price does not affect revenue	the decrease in quantity demanded is proportionally *the same as* the increase in price.
unit elastic	a decrease in price does not affect revenue	the increase in quantity demanded is proportionally *the same as* the decrease in price.

quantity demand increases from 2 to 4, and in panel (b), total revenue increases from $14 to $24. Similarly, when price is between $4 and zero and quantity is between 8 and 16, demand is inelastic. Over this same range, total revenue will decrease as price falls. For example, as price falls from $3 to $2 and quantity increases from 10 to 12, total revenue decreases from $30 to $24.

Solved Problem | 6-3

Price and Revenue Don't Always Move in the Same Direction

Briefly explain whether you agree or disagree with the following statement: "The only way to increase the revenue from selling a product is to increase the product's price."

SOLVING THE PROBLEM:

Step 1: **Review the chapter material.** This problem deals with the effect of a price change on a firm's revenue, so you may want to review the section "The Relationship between Price Elasticity and Total Revenue," which begins on page 182.

Step 2: **Analyze the statement.** We have seen that a price increase will increase revenue only if demand is inelastic. In Figure 6-3, for example, increasing the rental price of DVDs from $1 to $2 *increases* revenue from $14 to $24 because demand is inelastic along this portion of the demand curve. But increasing the price from $5 to $6 *decreases* revenue from $30 to $24 because demand is elastic along this portion of the demand curve. If the price is currently $5, increasing revenue would require a price *cut*, not a price increase. As this example shows, the statement is incorrect and you should disagree with it.

» End Solved Problem 6-3

YOUR TURN: For more practice, do related problem 3.6 on page 203 at the end of this chapter.

Price	Quantity Demanded	Total Revenue
$8	0	$0
7	2	14
6	4	24
5	6	30
4	8	32
3	10	30
2	12	24
1	14	14
0	16	0

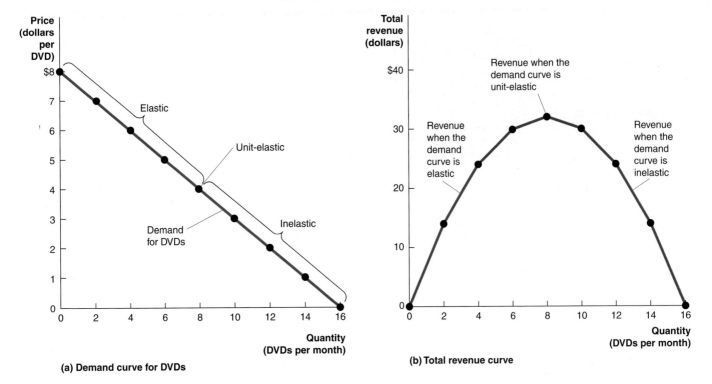

(a) Demand curve for DVDs

(b) Total revenue curve

Figure 6-3 | Elasticity Is Not Constant Along a Linear Demand Curve

The data from the table are plotted in the graphs. Panel (a) shows that as we move down the demand curve for DVDs, the price elasticity of demand declines. In other words, at higher prices, demand is elastic, and at lower prices, demand is inelastic. Panel (b) shows that as the quantity of DVDs sold increases from zero, revenue will increase until it reaches a maximum of $32 when 8 DVDs are sold. As sales increase beyond 8 DVDs, revenue falls because demand is inelastic on this portion of the demand curve.

Estimating Price Elasticity of Demand

To estimate the price elasticity of demand, economists need to know the demand curve for a product. To calculate the price elasticity of demand for new products, firms often rely on market experiments. With market experiments, firms try different prices and observe the change in quantity demanded that results.

Making
the
Connection

Determining the Price Elasticity of Demand for DVDs by Market Experiment

DVDs were a relatively new product in 2001. The movie studios producing them were unsure of the price elasticity of the demand curves they were facing, so they experimented with different prices to help determine the price elasticity.

Following are four films and the prices for DVDs and VHS tapes that the studios suggested stores such as Blockbuster Video charge for them:

FILM	DVD PRICE	VHS PRICE
Rugrats in Paris	$22.46	$22.99
The Mummy Returns	26.98	22.98
Miss Congeniality	16.69	22.98
The Perfect Storm	24.98	22.99

When DVDs were first introduced, the movie studios were uncertain about their price elasticity of demand.

VHS tapes had been on the market for many years, and the studios had determined their pricing strategies, given their estimates of the price elasticity of demand. As a result, the prices of VHS tapes were usually very similar; for these four films, the prices were almost identical. The prices of DVDs were much less standardized because the studios were unsure of their price elasticities. Tom Adams, the head of Adams Market Research, a company that does research on the home video market, summed up the situation: "The studios have different views of the market, so they are setting different suggested retail prices, and the stores are discounting those prices to different degrees."

After several years of market experiments, the move studios had more accurate estimates of the price elasticity of DVDs, and the prices of most DVDs became similar. For instance, in 2007, nearly all newly released DVDs had a list price of about $29, which was often discounted to about $17 when they were sold online or in discount department stores, such as Wal-Mart. When HD-DVDs were introduced, the studios apparently felt confident that they understood their price elasticity, because in 2007 most had list prices of $39.95, discounted to $27.95 in many online stores.

Sources: Geraldine Fabrikant, "Sale of DVDs Are Challenging Movie Rental Business," *New York Times*, April 16, 2001; prices from Amazon.com.

YOUR TURN: Test your understanding by doing related problem 3.12 on page 204 at the end of this chapter.

6.4 LEARNING OBJECTIVE

6.4 | Define the cross-price elasticity of demand and the income elasticity of demand, and understand their determinants and how they are measured.

Other Demand Elasticities

Elasticity is an important concept in economics because it allows us to quantify the responsiveness of one economic variable to changes in another economic variable. In addition to price elasticity, two other demand elasticities are important: *cross-price elasticity of demand* and *income elasticity of demand*.

Cross-Price Elasticity of Demand

Cross-price elasticity of demand
The percentage change in quantity demanded of one good divided by the percentage change in the price of another good.

Suppose you work at Apple and you need to predict the effect of an increase in the price of Microsoft's Zune on the quantity of iPods demanded, holding other factors constant. You can do this by calculating the **cross-price elasticity of demand**, which is the percentage change in the quantity of iPods demanded divided by the percentage change in the price of Zunes—or, in general:

$$\text{Cross-price elasticity of demand} = \frac{\text{Percentage change in quantity demanded of one good}}{\text{Percentage change in price of another good}}.$$

TABLE 6-3

Summary of Cross-Price Elasticity of Demand

IF THE PRODUCTS ARE . . .	THEN THE CROSS-PRICE ELASTICITY OF DEMAND WILL BE . . .	EXAMPLE
substitutes	positive	Two brands of digital music players
complements	negative	Digital music players and song downloads from online music stores
unrelated	zero	Digital music players and peanut butter

The cross-price elasticity of demand is positive or negative, depending on whether the two products are substitutes or complements. Recall that substitutes are products that can be used for the same purpose, such as two brands of digital music players. Complements are products that are used together, such as digital music players and song downloads from online music sites. An increase in the price of a substitute will lead to an increase in quantity demanded, so the cross-price elasticity of demand will be positive. An increase in the price of a complement will lead to a decrease in the quantity demanded, so the cross-price elasticity of demand will be negative. Of course, if the two products are unrelated—such as digital music players and peanut butter—the cross-price elasticity of demand will be zero. Table 6-3 summarizes the key points concerning the cross-price elasticity of demand.

Cross-price elasticity of demand is important to firm managers because it allows them to measure whether products sold by other firms are close substitutes for their products. For example, Amazon.com and Barnesandnoble.com are the leading online booksellers. We might predict that if Amazon raises the price of a new John Grisham novel, many consumers will buy it from Barnesandnoble.com instead. But Jeff Bezos, Amazon's chief executive officer, has argued that because of Amazon's reputation for good customer service and because more customers are familiar with the site, ordering a book from Barnesandnoble.com is not a good substitute for ordering a book from Amazon. In effect, Bezos is arguing that the cross-price elasticity between Amazon's books and Barnesandnoble.com's books is low. Economists Judith Chevalier of Yale University and Austan Goolsbee of the University of Chicago used data on prices and quantities of books sold on these Web sites to estimate the cross-price elasticity. They found that the cross-price elasticity of demand between books at Amazon and books at Barnesandnoble.com was 3.5. This estimate means that if Amazon raises its prices by 10 percent, the quantity of books demanded on Barnesandnoble.com will increase by 35 percent. This result indicates that, contrary to Jeff Bezos's argument, consumers do consider books sold on the two Web sites to be close substitutes.

Income Elasticity of Demand

The **income elasticity of demand** measures the responsiveness of quantity demanded to changes in income. It is calculated as follows:

$$\text{Income elasticity of demand} = \frac{\text{Percentage change in quantity demanded}}{\text{Percentage change in income}}.$$

Income elasticity of demand
A measure of the responsiveness of quantity demanded to changes in income, measured by the percentage change in quantity demanded divided by the percentage change in income.

As we saw in Chapter 3, if the quantity demanded of a good increases as income increases, then the good is a *normal good*. Normal goods are often further subdivided into *luxury goods* and *necessity goods*. A good is a luxury if the quantity demanded is very responsive to changes in income, so that a 10 percent increase in income results in more than a 10 percent increase in quantity demanded. Expensive jewelry and vacation homes are examples of luxuries. A good is a necessity if the quantity demanded is not very responsive to changes in income, so that a 10 percent increase in income results in less than a 10 percent increase in quantity demanded. Food and clothing are examples of

A large shift in supply, a small shift in demand, and an inelastic demand curve combined to drive down the price of wheat from $15.81 per bushel in 1950 to $3.40 per bushel in 2006. (The 1950 price is measured in terms of prices in 2006, to adjust for the general increase in prices since 1950.) With low prices, only the most efficiently run farms have been able to remain profitable. Smaller, family-run farms have found it difficult to survive, and many of these farms have disappeared. The markets for most food products are similar to the market for wheat. They are characterized by rapid output growth and low income and price elasticities. The result is the paradox of American farming: ever more abundant and cheaper food, supplied by fewer and fewer farms. American consumers have benefited, but most family farmers have not.

Solved Problem | 6-5

Using Price Elasticity to Analyze Policy toward Illegal Drugs

An ongoing policy debate concerns whether to legalize the use of drugs such as marijuana and cocaine. Some researchers estimate that legalizing cocaine would cause its price to fall by as much as 95 percent. Proponents of legalization argue that legalizing drug use would lower crime rates by eliminating the main reason for the murderous gang wars that plague many big cities and by reducing the incentive for drug addicts to commit robberies and burglaries. Opponents of legalization argue that lower drug prices would lead more people to use drugs.

a. Suppose the price elasticity of demand for cocaine is −2. If legalization causes the price of cocaine to fall by 95 percent, what will be the percentage increase in the quantity of cocaine demanded?

b. If the price elasticity is −0.02, what will be the percentage increase in the quantity demanded?

c. Discuss how the size of the price elasticity of demand for cocaine is relevant to the debate over its legalization.

SOLVING THE PROBLEM:

Step 1: **Review the chapter material.** This problem deals with applications of the price elasticity of demand formula, so you may want to review the section "Measuring the Price Elasticity of Demand," which begins on page 174.

Step 2: **Answer question (a) using the formula for the price elasticity of demand.**

$$\text{Price elasticity of demand} = \frac{\text{Percentage change in quantity demanded}}{\text{Percentage change in price}}.$$

We can plug into this formula the values we are given for the price elasticity and the percentage change in price:

$$-2 = \frac{\text{Percentage change in quantity demanded}}{-95\%}.$$

Or, rearranging:

$$\text{Percentage change in quantity demanded} = -2 \times -95\% = 190\%$$

Step 3: **Use the same method to answer question (b).** We only need to substitute −0.02 for −2 as the price elasticity of demand:

$$\text{Percentage change in quantity demanded} = -0.02 \times -95\% = 1.9\%$$

Step 4: **Answer question (c) by discussing how the size of the price elasticity of demand for cocaine helps us to understand the effects of legalization.** Clearly, the higher the absolute value of the price elasticity of demand for cocaine, the greater the increase in cocaine use that would result from legalization. If the price elasticity is as high as in question (a), legalization will lead to a large increase in use. If, however, the price elasticity is as low as in question (b), legalization will lead to only a small increase in use.

EXTRA CREDIT: One estimate puts the price elasticity at −0.28, which suggests that even a large fall in the price of cocaine might lead to only a moderate increase in cocaine use. However, even a moderate increase in cocaine use would have costs. Some studies have shown that cocaine users are more likely to commit crimes, to abuse their children, to have higher medical expenses, and to be less productive workers. Moreover, many people object to the use of cocaine and other narcotics on moral grounds and would oppose legalization even if it led to no increase in use. Ultimately, whether the use of cocaine and other drugs should be legalized is a normative issue. Economics can contribute to the discussion but cannot decide the issue.

Source for estimate of price elasticity of cocaine: Henry Saffer and Frank Chaloupka, "The Demand for Illicit Drugs," *Economic Inquiry*, Vol. 37, No. 3, July 1999, pp. 401–411.

YOUR TURN: For more practice, do related problems 5.2 and 5.3 on page 206 at the end of this chapter.

≫ End Solved Problem 6-5

6.6 LEARNING OBJECTIVE

6.6 | Define the price elasticity of supply and understand its main determinants and how it is measured.

The Price Elasticity of Supply and Its Measurement

We can use the concept of elasticity to measure the responsiveness of firms to a change in price just as we used it to measure the responsiveness of consumers. We know from the law of supply that when the price of a product increases, the quantity supplied increases. To measure how much quantity supplied increases when price increases, we use the *price elasticity of supply*.

Measuring the Price Elasticity of Supply

Just as with the price elasticity of demand, we calculate the **price elasticity of supply** using percentage changes:

$$\text{Price elasticity of supply} = \frac{\text{Percentage change in quantity supplied}}{\text{Percentage change in price}}.$$

Notice that because supply curves are upward sloping, the price elasticity of supply will be a positive number. We categorize the price elasticity of supply the same way we categorized the price elasticity of demand: If the price elasticity of supply is less than 1, then supply is *inelastic*. For example, the price elasticity of supply of gasoline from U.S. oil refineries is about 0.20, and so it is inelastic. A 10 percent increase in the price of gasoline will result in only a 2 percent increase in the quantity supplied. If the price elasticity of supply is greater than 1, then supply is *elastic*. If the price elasticity of supply is equal to 1, then supply is *unit elastic*. As with other elasticity calculations, when we calculate the price elasticity of supply, we hold the values of other factors constant.

Price elasticity of supply
The responsiveness of the quantity supplied to a change in price, measured by dividing the percentage change in the quantity supplied of a product by the percentage change in the product's price.

If a supply curve is a horizontal line, it is *perfectly elastic*. In this case, the quantity supplied is infinitely responsive to price, and the price elasticity of supply equals infinity. If a supply curve is perfectly elastic, a very small increase in price causes a very large increase in quantity supplied. Just as with demand curves, it is important not to confuse a supply curve being elastic with its being perfectly elastic and not to confuse a supply curve being inelastic with its being perfectly inelastic. Table 6-5 summarizes the different price elasticities of supply.

Using Price Elasticity of Supply to Predict Changes in Price

Figure 6-5 illustrates the important point that, when demand increases, the amount that price increases depends on the price elasticity of supply. The figure shows the demand and supply for parking spaces at a beach resort. In panel (a), on a typical summer weekend, equilibrium occurs at point A, where Demand (typical) intersects a supply curve that is inelastic. The increase in demand for parking spaces on the Fourth of July shifts the demand curve to the right, moving the equilibrium to point B. Because the supply curve is inelastic, the increase in demand results in a large increase in price—from $2.00 per hour to $4.00—but only a small increase in the quantity of spaces supplied—from 1,200 to 1,400.

In panel (b), supply is elastic, perhaps because the resort has vacant land that can be used for parking during periods of high demand. As a result, the shift in equilibrium from point A to point B results in a smaller increase in price and a larger increase in the quantity supplied. An increase in price from $2.00 per hour to $2.50 is sufficient to increase the quantity of parking supplied from 1,200 to 2,100. Knowing the price elasticity of supply makes it possible to predict more accurately how much price will change following an increase or a decrease in demand.

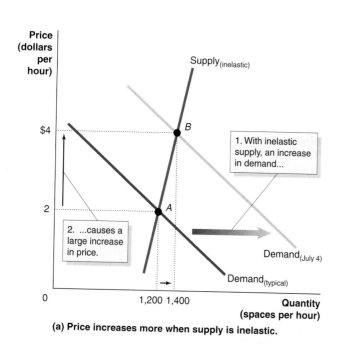

(a) Price increases more when supply is inelastic.

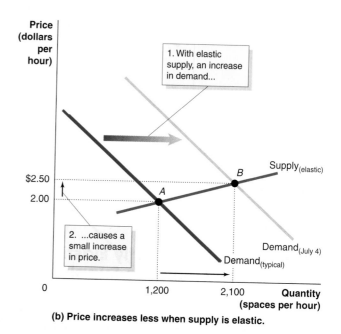

(b) Price increases less when supply is elastic.

Figure 6-5 | Changes in Price Depend on the Price Elasticity of Supply

In panel (a), Demand (typical) represents the typical demand for parking spaces on a summer weekend at a beach resort. Demand (July 4) represents demand on the Fourth of July. Because supply is inelastic, the shift in equilibrium from point A to point B results in a large increase in price—from $2.00 per hour to $4.00—but only a small increase in the quantity of spaces supplied—from 1,200 to 1,400. In panel (b), supply is elastic. As a result, the shift in equilibrium from point A to point B results in a smaller increase in price and a larger increase in the quantity supplied. An increase in price from $2.00 per hour to $2.50 is sufficient to increase the quantity of parking supplied from 1,200 to 2,100.

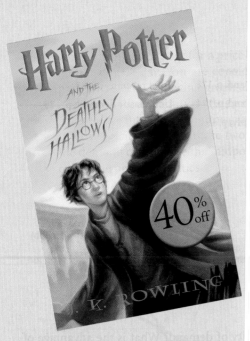

Key Points in the Article

Many retailers have programs that provide repeat buyers with price discounts. From a firm's point of view, whether a discount program is a good idea depends on how customers respond—that is, it depends on the price elasticity of demand. The Borders Rewards program reduces the price of books, but if the lower prices cause enough additional books to be sold, then total revenue will rise. This is why firms offer discount programs: They believe the programs raise total profits. However, not all discount programs increase total profits, and Borders recently changed its discount program for this reason.

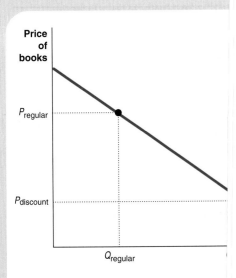

Figure 1. The discount program increases sales.

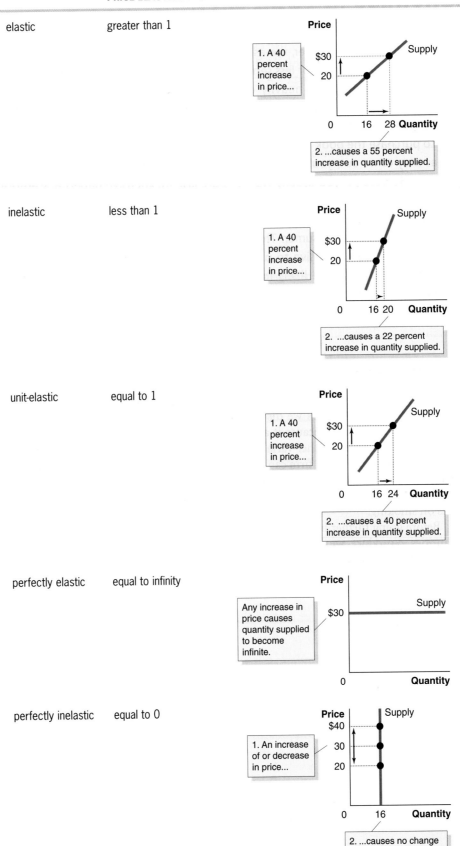

TABLE 6-5

Summary of the Price Elasticities of Supply

(Note that the percentage increases shown in the boxes in the graphs were calculated using the midpoint formula on page 176.)

Chapter 7

Firms, the **Stock Market,** and **Corporate Governance**

Borders Slashes Buyer Rewards, Cuts Discounts

The nation's second-largest book retailer, Borders Group Inc., ha... decided there can be too much of a good thing when it comes to its free membership-rewards program.

Less than a week after it reported disappointing fourth-quarter and annual results, Borders said that it is phasing out its popular Holiday Savings Rewards and Personal Shopping Days benefits and replacing them with a simpler, less-generous promotion called Borders Bucks.

The move will dramatically alter a program that has been a tremendous hit with consumers. Since the launch of the Borders Rewards membership club in February 2006, nearly 17 million people have signed up, and Borders continues to add an estimated 150,000 new customers each week. Borders' announcement comes at a time when many reward programs—including those from credit-card companies and airlines' frequent-flier plans—are tightening eligibility rules or becoming stingier with benefits.

Under the new Borders plan, each time customers reach $150 in purchases at Borders superstores or Waldenbooks stores, they will receive $5 in Borders Bucks at the beginning of the following month. They can then use that $5 until the end of that month, at which point the offer expires. Users will be contacted by e-mail and urged to print

Google: From Dorm Room to Wall Street

There could be no question that Google was cool. The world's most widely used Internet search engine, Google had become the essence of cool as a way to research information stored on Web sites. Founded in 1998 by Larry Page and Sergey Brin, Google grew quickly. By 2006, Google employed 10,000 people and earned $10.6 billion in revenue. Google's founders had transformed the Internet search engine and brought value to users through a combination of intellect, technology, and the talents of many employees. Google's key advantage over competitors such as A9 and Ask Jeeves was its search algorithms that allowed users to easily find the Web sites most relevant to a subject. Google had other advantages as well, such as its automatic foreign-language translation. Google had become so dominant that other major Web sites, such as AOL and Yahoo, were using it as their search engine. Google has also succeeded in expanding into foreign markets. In China, Google has been successful even though it remains in a struggle for market share with the local Chinese firm Baidu.com.

And Google was hot. In 2004, Google sold part of the firm to outside investors by offering stock—and partial ownership—to the public. This stock offering vaulted Larry Page and Sergey Brin to the ranks of the super-rich. Google's stock offering also gained significant press attention, as the firm bypassed conventional financial practice and used an automated online auction to help set the share price and determine who should receive stock. The offering's size grabbed attention, too: It was the most anticipated stock sale since the 1995 launch of Netscape, a deal that sparked the late-1990s Internet gold rush on Wall Street.

As Google grew larger, it was less the informal organization put together by the founders and more a complex organization with greater need for management and funds to grow. Indeed, Google's offering of stock to outside investors provided the firm with a major inflow of funds for growth.

Once a firm grows very large, its owners often do not continue to manage it. Large corporations are owned by millions of individual investors who have purchased the firms' stock. With ownership so dispersed, the top managers who actually run a firm have the opportunity to make decisions that are in the managers' best interests but that may not be in the best interests of the stockholders who own the firm.

Against this backdrop, Google faced significant costs associated with selling stock to the public. High-profile corporate accounting scandals in 2001 and 2002 at major U.S. firms, such as Enron, WorldCom, and Tyco, led to the passage of stronger—and more costly—securities regulation under the Sarbanes-Oxley Act, enacted by Congress in 2002. Google's growth prospects and the health of the financial system were intertwined. **AN INSIDE LOOK** on **page 226** discusses the compensation Google pays its top executives.

LEARNING Objectives

After studying this chapter, you should be able to:

7.1 Categorize the major **types of firms** in the United States, page 210.

7.2 Describe the typical **management structure** of corporations and understand the concepts of **separation of ownership from control** and the **principal-agent problem**, page 212.

7.3 Explain how firms obtain the **funds** they need to **operate** and **expand**, page 214.

7.4 Understand the information provided in corporations' **financial statements**, page 219.

7.5 Understand the role of government in **corporate governance**, page 221.

APPENDIX Understand the concept of **present value** and the information contained on a firm's **income statement** and **balance sheet**, page 233.

Economics in YOUR Life!

Is It Risky to Own Stock?

Although stockholders legally own corporations, managers often have a great deal of freedom in deciding how corporations are run. As a result, managers can make decisions, such as spending money on large corporate headquarters or decorating their offices with expensive paintings, that are in their interests but not in the interests of the shareholders. If managers make decisions that waste money and lower the profits of a firm, the price of the firm's stock will fall, which hurts the investors who own the stock. Suppose you own stock in a corporation, such as Google. Why is it difficult to get the managers to act in your interest rather than in their own? Given this problem, should you ever take on the risk of buying stock? As you read the chapter, see if you can answer these questions. You can check your answers against those we provide at the end of the chapter.

>> Continued on page 225

In this chapter, we look at the firm: how it is organized, how it raises funds, and the information it provides to investors. As we have already discussed, firms in a market system are responsible for organizing the factors of production to produce goods and services. Firms are the vehicles entrepreneurs use to earn profits. To succeed, entrepreneurs must meet consumer wants by producing new or better goods and services or by finding ways of producing existing goods and services at a lower cost so they can be sold at a lower price. Entrepreneurs also need access to sufficient funds, and they must be able to efficiently organize production. As the typical firm in many industries has become larger during the past 100 years, the task of efficiently organizing production has become more difficult. Toward the end of this chapter, we look at why a series of corporate scandals occurred beginning in 2002 and at the steps firms and the government have taken to avoid similar problems in the future.

7.1 LEARNING OBJECTIVE

7.1 | Categorize the major types of firms in the United States.

Types of Firms

Sole proprietorship A firm owned by a single individual and not organized as a corporation.

Partnership A firm owned jointly by two or more persons and not organized as a corporation.

Corporation A legal form of business that provides the owners with limited liability.

In studying a market economy, it is important to understand the basics of how firms operate. In the United States, there are three legal categories of firms: *sole proprietorships*, *partnerships*, and *corporations*. A **sole proprietorship** is a firm owned by a single individual. Although most sole proprietorships are small, some are quite large in terms of sales, number of persons employed, and profits earned. **Partnerships** are firms owned jointly by two or more—sometimes many—persons. Most law and accounting firms are partnerships. The famous Lloyd's of London insurance company is a partnership. Although some partnerships, such as Lloyd's, can be quite large, most large firms are organized as *corporations*. A **corporation** is a legal form of business that provides the owners with limited liability.

Who Is Liable? Limited and Unlimited Liability

Asset Anything of value owned by a person or a firm.

A key distinction among the three types of firms is that the owners of sole proprietorships and partnerships have unlimited liability. Unlimited liability means there is no legal distinction between the personal assets of the owners of the firm and the assets of the firm. An **asset** is anything of value owned by a person or a firm. If a sole proprietorship or a partnership owes a lot of money to the firm's suppliers or employees, the suppliers and employees have a legal right to sue the firm for payment, even if this requires the firm's owners to sell some of their personal assets, such as stocks or bonds. In other words, with sole proprietorships and partnerships, the owners are not legally distinct from the firms they own.

It may seem only fair that the owners of a firm be responsible for a firm's debts. But early in the nineteenth century, it became clear to many state legislatures in the United States that unlimited liability was a significant problem for any firm that was attempting to raise funds from large numbers of investors. An investor might be interested in making a relatively small investment in a firm but be unwilling to become a partner in the firm for fear of placing at risk all of his or her personal assets if the firm were to fail. To get around this problem, state legislatures began to pass *general incorporation laws*, which allowed firms to be organized as corporations. Under the corporate form of business, the owners of a firm have **limited liability**, which means that if the firm fails, the owners can never lose more than the amount they had invested in the firm. The personal assets of the owners of the firm are not affected by the failure of the firm. In fact, in the eyes of the law, a corporation is a legal "person" separate from its owners. Limited

Limited liability The legal provision that shields owners of a corporation from losing more than they have invested in the firm.

	SOLE PROPRIETORSHIP	PARTNERSHIP	CORPORATION
ADVANTAGES	• Control by owner • No layers of management	• Ability to share work • Ability to share risks	• Limited personal liability • Greater ability to raise funds
DISADVANTAGES	• Unlimited personal liability • Limited ability to raise funds	• Unlimited personal liability • Limited ability to raise funds	• Costly to organize • Possible double taxation of income

TABLE 7-1

Differences among Business Organizations

liability has made it possible for corporations to raise funds by issuing shares of stock to large numbers of investors. For example, if you buy a share of Google stock, you are a part owner of the firm, but even if Google were to go bankrupt, you would not be personally responsible for any of Google's debts. Therefore, you could not lose more than the amount you paid for the stock.

Corporate organizations also have some disadvantages. In the United States, corporate profits are taxed twice—once at the corporate level and again when investors receive a share of corporate profits. Corporations generally are larger than sole proprietorships and partnerships and therefore more difficult to organize and run. Table 7-1 reviews the advantages and disadvantages of different forms of business organization.

Making the Connection | What's in a "Name"? Lloyd's of London Learns about Unlimited Liability the Hard Way

Investors in Lloyd's of London lost billions of dollars during the 1980s and 1990s.

The world-famous insurance company Lloyd's of London got its start in Edward Lloyd's coffeehouse in London in the late 1600s. Ship owners would come to the coffeehouse looking for someone to insure (or "underwrite") their ships and cargos in exchange for a flat fee (or "premium"). The customers of the coffeehouse, themselves merchants or ship owners, who agreed to insure ships or cargos would have to make payment from their personal funds if an insured ship was lost at sea. By the late 1700s, the system had become more formal: Each underwriter would recruit investors, known as "Names," and use the funds raised to back insurance policies sold to a wide variety of clients. In the twentieth century, Lloyd's became famous for some of its unusual insurance policies. It issued a policy insuring the legs of Betty Grable, a 1940s movie star. One man bought an insurance policy against seeing a ghost.

By the late 1980s, 34,000 persons around the world had invested in Lloyd's as Names. A series of disasters in the late 1980s and early 1990s—including the *Exxon Valdez* oil spill in Alaska, Hurricane Hugo in South Carolina, and an earthquake in San Francisco—resulted in huge payments on insurance policies written by Lloyd's. In 1989, Lloyd's lost $3.85 billion. In 1990, it lost an additional $4.4 billion. It then became clear to many of the Names that Lloyd's was not a corporation and that the Names did not have the limited liability enjoyed by corporate shareholders. On the contrary, the Names were personally responsible for paying the losses on the insurance policies. Many Names lost far more than they had invested. Some investors, such as Charles Schwab, the discount stockbroker, were wealthy enough to sustain their losses, but others were less fortunate. One California investor ended up living in poverty after having to sell his $1 million house to pay his share of the losses. Another Name, Sir Richard Fitch, a British admiral, committed suicide after most of his wealth was wiped out. As many as 30 Names may have committed suicide as a result of their losses.

By 2007, only 1,100 Names—undoubtedly sadder but wiser—remained as investors in Lloyd's. New rules have allowed insurance companies to underwrite

Lloyd's policies for the first time. Today, Names provide only about 20 percent of Lloyd's funds.

Sources: "The Rip van Winkle of Risk," *Economist*, January 4, 2007; Charles Fleming, "The Master of Disaster Is Trying to Avoid One," *Wall Street Journal*, November 17, 2003; and "Lloyd's of London: Insuring for the Future," *Economist*, September 16, 2004.

YOUR TURN: Test your understanding by doing related problem 1.4 and 1.5 on page 228 at the end of this chapter.

Corporations Earn the Majority of Revenue and Profits

Figure 7-1 gives basic statistics on the three types of business organizations. Panel (a) shows that almost three-quarters of all firms are sole proprietorships. Panels (b) and (c) show that although only 20 percent of all firms are corporations, corporations account for the majority of revenue and profits earned by all firms. *Profit* is the difference between revenue and the total cost to a firm of producing the goods and services it offers for sale.

There are more than 5 million corporations in the United States, but only 26,000 have annual revenues of more than $50 million. We can think of these 26,000 firms—including Microsoft, General Electric, and Google—as representing "big business." These large firms earn almost 85 percent of the total profits of all corporations in the United States.

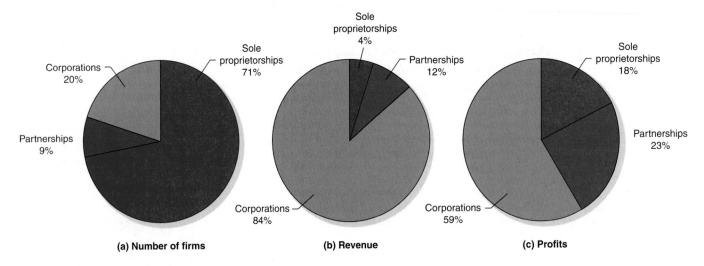

(a) Number of firms   **(b) Revenue**   **(c) Profits**

Figure 7-1 | Business Organizations: Sole Proprietorships, Partnerships, and Corporations

The three types of firms in the United States are sole proprietorships, partnerships, and corporations. Panel (a) shows that only 20 percent of all firms are corporations.

Yet, as panels (b) and (c) show, corporations account for a majority of the total revenue and profits earned by all firms.
Source: U.S. Census Bureau, *The 2007 Statistical Abstract of the United States.*

7.2 LEARNING OBJECTIVE

7.2 | Describe the typical management structure of corporations and understand the concepts of separation of ownership from control and the principal–agent problem.

The Structure of Corporations and the Principal-Agent Problem

Corporate governance The way in which a corporation is structured and the effect a corporation's structure has on the firm's behavior.

Because large corporations account for most sales and profits in the economy, it is important to know how they are managed. Most large corporations have a similar management structure. The way in which a corporation is structured and the effect a corporation's structure has on the firm's behavior is referred to as **corporate governance**.

Corporate Structure and Corporate Governance

Corporations are legally owned by their *shareholders*, the owners of the corporation's stock. Unlike family businesses, a corporation's shareholders, although they are the firm's owners, do not manage the firm directly. Instead, they elect a *board of directors* to represent their interests. The board of directors appoints a *chief executive officer* (CEO) to run the day-to-day operations of the corporation. Sometimes the board of directors also appoints other members of *top management*, such as the *chief financial officer* (CFO). At other times, the CEO appoints other members of top management. Members of top management, including the CEO and CFO, often serve on the board of directors. Members of management serving on the board of directors are referred to as *inside directors*. Members of the board of directors who do not have a direct management role in the firm are referred to as *outside directors*. The outside directors are intended to act as checks on the decisions of top managers, but the distinction between an outside director and an inside director is not always clear. For example, the CEO of a firm that sells a good or service to a large corporation may sit on the board of directors of that corporation. Although an outside director, this person may be reluctant to displease the top managers because the top managers have the power to stop purchasing from his firm. In some instances, top managers have effectively controlled their firms' boards of directors.

Unlike founder-dominated businesses, the top management of large corporations does not generally own a large share of the firm's stock, so large corporations have a **separation of ownership from control**. Although the shareholders actually own the firm, top management controls the day-to-day operations of the firm. Because top managers do not own the entire firm, they may have an incentive to decrease the firm's profits by spending money to purchase private jets or schedule management meetings at luxurious resorts. Economists refer to the conflict between the interests of shareholders and the interests of top management as a **principal–agent problem**. This problem occurs when agents—in this case, a firm's top management—pursue their own interests rather than the interests of the principal who hired them—in this case, the shareholders of the corporation. To reduce the impact of the principal–agent problem, many boards of directors in the 1990s began to tie the salaries of top managers to the profits of the firm or to the price of the firm's stock. They hoped this would give top managers an incentive to make the firm as profitable as possible, thereby benefiting its shareholders.

> **Separation of ownership from control** A situation in a corporation in which the top management, rather than the shareholders, control day-to-day operations.
>
> **Principal–agent problem** A problem caused by an agent pursuing his own interests rather than the interests of the principal who hired him.

Solved Problem | 7-2

Does the Principal–Agent Problem Apply to the Relationship between Managers and Workers?

Briefly explain whether you agree or disagree with the following argument:

> The principal–agent problem applies not just to the relationship between shareholders and top managers. It also applies to the relationship between managers and workers. Just as shareholders have trouble monitoring whether top managers are earning as much profit as possible, managers have trouble monitoring whether workers are working as hard as possible.

SOLVING THE PROBLEM:

Step 1: Review the chapter material. This problem concerns the principal–agent problem, so you may want to review the section "Corporate Structure and Corporate Governance," which is on this page.

Step 2: **Evaluate the argument.** You should agree with the argument. A corporation's shareholders have difficulty monitoring the activities of top managers. In practice, they attempt to do so indirectly through the corporation's board of directors. But the firm's top managers may influence—or even control—the firm's board of directors. Even if top managers do not control a board of directors, it may be difficult for the board to know whether actions managers take—say, opening a branch office in Paris—will increase the profitability of the firm or just increase the enjoyment of the top managers.

To answer the problem, we must extend this analysis to the relationship between managers and workers: Managers would like workers to work as hard as possible. Workers would often rather not work hard, particularly if they do not see a direct financial reward for doing so. Managers can have trouble monitoring whether workers are working hard or goofing off. Is that worker in his cubicle diligently staring at a computer screen because he is hard at work on a report or because he is surfing the Web for sports scores or writing a long e-mail to his girlfriend? So, the principal–agent problem does apply to the relationship between managers and workers.

EXTRA CREDIT: Boards of directors try to reduce the principal–agent problem by designing compensation policies for top managers that give them financial incentives to increase profits. Similarly, managers try to reduce the principal–agent problem by designing compensation policies that give workers an incentive to work harder. For example, some manufacturers pay factory workers on the basis of how much they produce rather than on the basis of how many hours they work.

YOUR TURN: For more practice, do related problems 2.4 and 2.5 on page 229 at the end of this chapter.

>> **End Solved Problem 7-2**

7.3 LEARNING OBJECTIVE

7.3 | Explain how firms obtain the funds they need to operate and expand.

How Firms Raise Funds

Owners and managers of firms try to earn a profit. To earn a profit, a firm must raise funds to pay for its operations, including paying its employees and buying machines. Indeed, a central challenge for anyone running a firm, whether that person is a sole proprietor or a top manager of a large corporation, is raising the funds needed to operate and expand the business. Suppose you decide to open an online trading service using $100,000 you have saved in a bank. You use the $100,000 to rent a building for your firm, to buy computers, and to pay other start-up expenses. Your firm is a great success, and you decide to expand by moving to a larger building and buying more computers. As the owner of a small business, you can obtain the funds for this expansion in three ways:

1   If you are making a profit, you could reinvest the profits back into your firm. Profits that are reinvested in a firm rather than taken out of a firm and paid to the firm's owners are *retained earnings*.

2   You could obtain funds by taking on one or more partners who invest in the firm. This arrangement would increase the firm's *financial capital*.

3   Finally, you could borrow the funds from relatives, friends, or a bank.

The managers of a large firm have some additional ways to raise funds, as we will see in the next section.

Sources of External Funds

Unless firms rely on retained earnings, they have to obtain the *external funds* they need from others who have funds available to invest. It is the role of an economy's *financial system* to transfer funds from savers to borrowers—directly through financial markets or indirectly through financial intermediaries such as banks.

Firms can raise external funds in two ways. The first relies on financial intermediaries such as banks and is called **indirect finance**. If you put $1,000 in a checking account or a savings account, or if you buy a $1,000 certificate of deposit (CD), the bank will loan most of those funds to borrowers. The bank will combine your funds with those of other depositors and, for example, make a $100,000 loan to a local business. Small businesses rely heavily on bank loans as their primary source of external funds.

The second way for firms to acquire external funds is through *financial markets*. Raising funds in these markets, such as the New York Stock Exchange on Wall Street in New York, is called **direct finance**. Direct finance usually takes the form of the borrower selling the lender a *financial security*. A financial security is a document—sometimes in electronic form—that states the terms under which the funds have passed from the buyer of the security—who is lending funds—to the borrower. *Bonds* and *stocks* are the two main types of financial securities. Typically, only large corporations are able to sell bonds and stocks on financial markets. Investors are generally unwilling to buy securities issued by small and medium-sized firms because the investors lack sufficient information on the financial health of smaller firms.

Bonds Bonds are financial securities that represent promises to repay a fixed amount of funds. When General Electric (GE) sells a bond to raise funds, it promises to pay the purchaser of the bond an interest payment each year for the term of the bond, as well as a final payment of the amount of the loan, or the *principal*, at the end of the term. GE may need to raise many millions of dollars to build a factory, but each individual bond has a principal, or *face value*, of $1,000, which is the amount each bond purchaser is lending GE. So, GE must sell many bonds to raise all the funds it needs. Suppose GE promises it will pay interest of $60 per year to anyone who will buy one of its bonds. The interest payments on a bond are referred to as **coupon payments**. The **interest rate** is the cost of borrowing funds, usually expressed as a percentage of the amount borrowed. If we express the coupon as a percentage of the face value of the bond, we find the interest rate on the bond, called the *coupon rate*. In this case, the interest rate is:

$$\frac{\$60}{\$1,000} = 0.06, \text{ or } 6\%.$$

Many bonds that corporations issue have terms, or *maturities*, of 30 years. For example, if you bought a bond from GE, GE would pay you $60 per year for 30 years, and at the end of the thirtieth year, GE would pay you back the $1,000 principal.

Stocks When you buy a newly issued bond from a firm, you are lending funds to that firm. When you buy **stock** issued by a firm, you are actually buying part ownership of the firm. When a corporation sells stock, it is doing the same thing the owner of a small business does when she takes on a partner: The firm is increasing its financial capital by bringing additional owners into the firm. Any individual shareholder usually owns only a small fraction of the total shares of stock issued by a corporation.

A shareholder is entitled to a share of the corporation's profits, if there are any. Corporations generally keep some of their profits—known as retained earnings—to finance future expansion. The remaining profits are paid to shareholders as **dividends**. If investors expect the firm to earn economic profits on its retained earnings, the firm's share price will rise, providing a *capital gain* for investors. If a corporation is unable to

Indirect finance A flow of funds from savers to borrowers through financial intermediaries such as banks. Intermediaries raise funds from savers to lend to firms (and other borrowers).

Direct finance A flow of funds from savers to firms through financial markets, such as the New York Stock Exchange.

Bond A financial security that represents a promise to repay a fixed amount of funds.

Coupon payment An interest payment on a bond.

Interest rate The cost of borrowing funds, usually expressed as a percentage of the amount borrowed.

Stock A financial security that represents partial ownership of a firm.

Dividends Payments by a corporation to its shareholders.

make a profit, it usually does not pay a dividend. Under the law, corporations must make payments on any debt they have before making payments to their owners. That is, a corporation must make promised payments to bondholders before it may make any dividend payments to shareholders. In addition, when firms sell stock, they acquire from investors an open-ended commitment of funds to the firm. Therefore, unlike bonds, stocks do not have a maturity date, so the firm is not obliged to return the investor's funds at any particular date.

Stock and Bond Markets Provide Capital—and Information

The original purchasers of stocks and bonds may resell them to other investors. In fact, most of the buying and selling of stocks and bonds that takes place each day is investors reselling existing stocks and bonds to each other rather than corporations selling new stocks and bonds to investors. The buyers and sellers of stocks and bonds together make up the *stock and bond markets*. There is no single place where stocks and bonds are bought and sold. Some trading of stocks and bonds takes place in buildings known as *exchanges*, such as the New York Stock Exchange or Tokyo Stock Exchange. In the United States, the stocks and bonds of the largest corporations are traded on the New York Stock Exchange. The development of computer technology has spread the trading of stocks and bonds outside exchanges to *securities dealers* linked by computers. These dealers comprise the *over-the-counter market*. The stocks of many computer and other high-technology firms—including Apple, Google, and Microsoft—are traded in the most important of the over-the-counter markets, the *National Association of Securities Dealers Automated Quotation* system, which is referred to by its acronym, Nasdaq.

Don't Let This Happen to **YOU!**

When Google Shares Change Hands, Google Doesn't Get the Money

Google is a popular investment, with investors buying and selling shares often as their views about the firm's valuation shift. That's great for Google, right? Think of all that money flowing into Google's coffers as shares change hands and the stock price goes up. *Wrong*. Google raises funds in a primary market, but shares change hands in a secondary market. Those trades don't put money into Google's hands, but they do give important information to the firm's managers. Let's see why.

Primary markets are those in which newly issued claims are sold to initial buyers by the issuer. Businesses can raise funds in a primary financial market in two ways—by borrowing (selling bonds) or by selling shares of stock—which result in different types of claims on the borrowing firm's future income. Although you hear about the stock market fluctuations each night on the evening news, bonds actually account for more of the funds raised by borrowers. In mid-2007, the value of bonds in the United States was about $27 trillion compared to $15 trillion for stocks, or equities.

In *secondary markets*, stocks and bonds that have already been issued are sold by one investor to another. If Google sells shares to the public, it is turning to a primary market for new funds. Once Google shares are issued, investors trade the shares in the secondary market. The founders of Google do not receive any new funds when Google shares are traded on secondary markets. The initial seller of a stock or bond raises funds from a lender only in the primary market. Secondary markets convey information to firms' managers and to investors by determining the price of financial instruments. For example, a major increase in Google's stock price conveys the market's good feelings about the firm, and the firm may decide to raise funds to expand. Hence, secondary markets are valuable sources of information for corporations that are considering raising funds.

Primary and secondary markets are both important, but they play different roles. As an investor, you principally trade stocks and bonds in a secondary market. As a corporate manager, you may help decide how to raise new funds to expand the firm where you work.

YOUR TURN: Test your understanding by doing related problem 3.10 on page 230 at the end of this chapter.

Shares of stock represent claims on the profits of the firms that issue them. Therefore, as the fortunes of the firms change and they earn more or less profit, the prices of the stock the firms have issued should also change. Similarly, bonds represent claims to receive coupon payments and one final payment of principal. Therefore, a particular bond that was issued in the past may have its price go up or down, depending on whether the coupon payments being offered on newly issued bonds are higher or lower than on existing bonds. If you hold a bond with a coupon of $80 per year, and newly issued bonds have coupons of $100 per year, the price of your bond will fall because it is less attractive to investors. The price of a bond will be affected by changes in investors' perceptions of the issuing firm's ability to make the coupon payments. For example, if investors begin to believe that a firm may soon go out of business and stop making coupon payments to its bondholders, the price of the firm's bonds will fall to very low levels.

Changes in the value of a firm's stocks and bonds offer important information for a firm's managers, as well as for investors. An increase in the stock price means that investors are more optimistic about the firm's profit prospects, and the firm's managers may wish to expand the firm's operations as a result. By contrast, a decrease in the firm's stock price indicates that investors are less optimistic about the firms' profit prospects, so management may want to shrink the firm's operations. Likewise, changes in the value of the firm's bonds imply changes in the cost of external funds to finance the firm's investment in research and development or in new factories. A higher bond price indicates a lower cost of new external funds, while a lower bond price indicates a higher cost of new external funds.

Making the Connection | Following Abercrombie & Fitch's Stock Price in the Financial Pages

If you read the stock listings in your local paper or the *Wall Street Journal*, you will notice that newspapers manage to pack into a small space a lot of information about what happened to stocks during the previous day's trading. The figure on the next page reproduces a small portion of the listings from the *Wall Street Journal* from March 6, 2007, for stocks listed on the New York Stock Exchange. The listings provide information on the buying and selling of the stock of five firms during the previous day. Let's focus on the highlighted listing for Abercrombie & Fitch, the clothing store, and examine the information in each column:

- The first column gives the name of the company.

- The second column gives the firm's "ticker" symbol (ANF), which you may have seen scrolling along the bottom of the screen on cable financial news channels.

- The third column (Open) gives the price (in dollars) of the stock at the time that trading began, which is 9:30 A.M. on the New York Stock Exchange. Abercrombie & Fitch had opened for trading the previous day at a price of $74.54.

- The fourth column (High) and the fifth column (Low) give the highest price and the lowest price the stock sold for during the previous day.

- The sixth column (Close) gives the price the stock sold for the last time it was traded before the close of trading on the previous day (4:30 P.M.), which in this case was $73.42.

- The seventh column (Net Chg) gives the amount by which the closing price changed from the closing price the day before. In this case, the price of Abercrombie

& Fitch's stock had fallen by $1.52 per share from its closing price the day before. Changes in Abercrombie & Fitch's stock price give the firm's managers a signal that they may want to expand or contract the firm's operations.

- The eighth column (% Chg) gives the change in the price in percentage terms rather than in dollar terms.

- The ninth column (Vol) gives the number of shares of stock traded on the previous day.

- The tenth column (52 Week High) and the eleventh column (52 Week Low) give the highest price the stock has sold for and the lowest price the stock has sold for during the previous year. These numbers tell how *volatile* the stock price is—that is, how much it fluctuates over the course of the year.

- The twelfth column (Div) gives the dividend expressed in dollars. In this case, .70 means that Abercrombie paid a dividend of $0.70 per share.

- The thirteenth column (Yield) gives the *dividend yield*, which is calculated by dividing the dividend by the *closing price* of the stock—that is, the price at which Abercrombie's stock last sold before the close of trading on the previous day.

- The fourteenth column (PE) gives the *P-E ratio* (or *price-earnings ratio*), which is calculated by dividing the price of the firm's stock by its earnings per share. (Remember that because firms retain some earnings, earnings per share is not necessarily the same as dividends per share.) Abercrombie's P-E ratio was 16, meaning that its price per share was 16 times its earnings per share. You would have to pay $16 to buy $1 of Abercrombie & Fitch's earnings.

- The final column (Year-To-Date % Chg) gives the percentage change in the price of the stock from the beginning of the year to the previous day. In this case, the price of Abercrombie's stock had increased by 5.4 percent since the beginning of 2007.

	Symbol	Open	High	Low	Close	Net Chg	%Chg	Vol	52 Week High	52 Week Low	Div	Yield	PE	Year-To-Date %Chg
ABB LTD ADS	ABB	15.95	16.21	15.94	15.96	-0.56	-3.39	4,478,028	19.3	10.1	0.1	0.6	25	-11.2
ABBOTT LABORATORIES	ABT	52.80	53.59	52.72	52.75	-0.26	-0.49	6,910,610	55.1	40.6	1.30	2.5	48	8.3
ABERCROMBIE & FITCH CO.	ANF	74.54	75.07	73.37	73.42	-1.52	-2.03	1,580,908	83.8	50	0.7	1.0	16	5.4
ABITIBI-CONSOLIDATED INC.	ABY	2.72	2.74	2.70	2.70	-0.03	-1.1	965,400	4.53	2.23	...	...	...	5.5
ACADIA REALTY TRUST SBI	AKR	26.65	26.77	26.30	26.36	-0.49	-1.82	429,604	28.1	19.5	.80	3.0	22	5.4

Source: Wall Street Journal Eastern Edition [Staff produced copy only] by *Wall Street Journal*. Copyright 2007 by Dow Jones & Co Inc. Reproduced with permission of Dow Jones & Co. Inc. in the format Textbook via Copyright Clearance Center.

YOUR TURN: Test your understanding by doing related problem 3.11 on page 230 at the end of this chapter.

Using Financial Statements to Evaluate a Corporation

To raise funds, a firm's managers must persuade financial intermediaries or buyers of its bonds or stock that it will be profitable. Before a firm can sell new issues of stock or bonds, it must first provide investors and financial regulators with information about its finances. To borrow from a bank or another financial intermediary, the firm must disclose financial information to the lender as well.

In most high-income countries, government agencies require firms that want to sell securities in financial markets to disclose specific financial information to the public. In the United States, the Securities and Exchange Commission requires publicly owned firms to report their performance in financial statements prepared using standard accounting methods, often referred to as *generally accepted accounting principles*. Such disclosure reduces information costs, but it doesn't eliminate them—for two reasons. First, some firms may be too young to have much information for potential investors to evaluate. Second, managers may try to present the required information in the best possible light so that investors will overvalue their securities.

Private firms also collect information on business borrowers and sell the information to lenders and investors. As long as the information-gathering firm does a good job, lenders and investors purchasing the information will be better able to judge the quality of borrowing firms. Firms specializing in information—including Moody's Investors Service, Standard & Poor's Corporation, Value Line, and Dun & Bradstreet—collect information from businesses and sell it to subscribers. Buyers include individual investors, libraries, and financial intermediaries. You can find some of these publications in your college library or through online information services.

Making the Connection

A Bull in China's Financial Shop

Prospects for Sichuan Changhong Electric Co., manufacturer of plasma televisions and liquid crystal displays, looked excellent in 2007, with rapidly growing output, employment, and profits earned from trade in the world economy. And Changhong was not alone. In the 2000s, the Chinese economy was sizzling. China's output grew by 10.7 percent during 2006, dominated by an astonishing 24 percent growth in investment in plant and equipment. The Chinese economic juggernaut caught the attention of the global business community—and charged onto the U.S. political stage, as China's growth fueled concerns about job losses in the United States.

Yet at the same time, many economists and financial commentators worried that the Chinese expansion—which was fueling rising living standards in a rapidly developing economy with 1.3 billion people—would come to an end. Indeed, the debate seemed to be over whether China's boom would have a "soft landing" (with gradually declining growth) or a "hard landing" (possibly leading to an economic financial crisis).

Why the debate? Although China's saving rate was estimated to be a very high 40 percent of gross domestic product (GDP)—double or triple the rate in most other countries—the financial system was doing a poor job of allocating capital. Excessive expansion in office construction and factories was fueled less by careful

Will China's weak financial system derail economic growth?

financial analysis than by the directions of national and local government officials trying to encourage growth. With nonperforming loans—where the borrower cannot make promised payments to lenders—at unheard-of levels, China's banks were in financial trouble. Worse still, they continued to lend to weak, politically connected borrowers.

China's prospects for long-term economic growth depend importantly on a better-developed financial system to generate information for borrowers and lenders. Many economists have urged Chinese officials to improve accounting transparency and information disclosure so that stock and bond markets can flourish. In the absence of well-functioning financial markets, banks are crucial allocators of capital. There, too, information disclosure and less government direction of lending will help oil the Chinese growth machine in the long run.

Chinese firms, like Changhong, may well play a major role on the world's economic stage. But China's creaky financial system needs repair if Chinese firms are to grow rapidly enough to raise the standard of living for Chinese workers over the long run.

YOUR TURN: Test your understanding by doing related problem 4.7 on page 231 at the end of this chapter.

What kind of information do investors and firm managers need? A firm must answer three basic questions: What to produce? How to produce it? and What price to charge? To answer these questions, a firm's managers need two pieces of information: The first is the firm's revenues and costs, and the second is the value of the property and other assets the firm owns and the firm's debts, or other **liabilities**, that it owes to other persons and firms. Potential investors in the firm also need this information to decide whether to buy the firm's stocks or bonds. Managers and investors find this information in the firm's *financial statements*, principally its income statement and balance sheet, which we discuss next.

Liability Anything owed by a person or a firm.

The Income Statement

A firm's **income statement** sums up its revenues, costs, and profit over a period of time. Corporations issue annual income statements, although the 12-month *fiscal year* covered may be different from the calendar year to represent the seasonal pattern of the business better. We explore income statements in greater detail in the appendix to this chapter.

Income statement A financial statement that sums up a firm's revenues, costs, and profit over a period of time.

Getting to Accounting Profit An income statement shows a firm's revenue, costs, and profit for the firm's fiscal year. To determine profitability, the income statement starts with the firm's revenue and subtracts its operating expenses and taxes paid. The remainder, *net income*, is the **accounting profit** of the firm.

Accounting profit A firm's net income measured by revenue minus operating expenses and taxes paid.

... And Economic Profit Accounting profit provides information on a firm's current net income measured according to accepted accounting standards. Accounting profit is not, however, the ideal measure of a firm's profits because it neglects some of the firm's costs. By taking into account all costs, *economic profit* provides a better indication than accounting profit of how successful a firm is. Firms making an economic profit will remain in business and may even expand. Firms making an *economic loss* are unlikely to remain in business in the long run. To understand how economic profit is calculated, remember that economists always measure cost as *opportunity cost*. The **opportunity cost** of any activity is the highest-valued alternative that must be given up to engage in that activity. Costs are either *explicit* or *implicit*. When a firm spends money, an **explicit cost** results. If a firm incurs an opportunity cost but does not spend money, an **implicit cost** results. For example, firms incur an explicit

Opportunity cost The highest-valued alternative that must be given up to engage in an activity.

Explicit cost A cost that involves spending money.

Implicit cost A nonmonetary opportunity cost.

labor cost when they pay wages to employees. Firms have many other explicit costs as well, such as the cost of the electricity used to light their buildings or the costs of advertising or insurance.

Some costs are implicit, however. The most important of these is the opportunity cost to investors of the funds they have invested in the firm. Economists refer to the minimum amount that investors must earn on the funds they invest in a firm, expressed as a percentage of the amount invested, as a *normal rate of return*. If a firm fails to provide investors with at least a normal rate of return, it will not be able to remain in business over the long run because investors will not continue to invest their funds in the firm. For example, Bethlehem Steel was once the second-leading producer of steel in the United States and a very profitable firm with stock that sold for more than $50 per share. By 2002, investors became convinced that the firm's uncompetitive labor costs in world markets meant that the firm would never be able to provide investors with a normal rate of return. Many investors expected that the firm would eventually have to declare bankruptcy, and as a result, the price of Bethlehem Steel's stock plummeted to $1 per share. Shortly thereafter, the firm declared bankruptcy, and its remaining assets were sold off to a competing steel firm. The return (in dollars) that investors require to continue investing in a firm is a true cost to the firm and should be subtracted from the firm's revenues to calculate its profits.

The necessary rate of return that investors must receive to continue investing in a firm varies from firm to firm. If the investment is risky—as would be the case with a biotechnology start-up—investors may require a high rate of return to compensate them for the risk. Investors in firms in more established industries, such as electric utilities, may require lower rates of return. The exact rate of return investors require to invest in any particular firm is difficult to calculate, which also makes it difficult for an accountant to include the return as a cost on an income statement. Firms have other implicit costs besides the return investors require that can also be difficult to calculate. As a result, the rules of accounting generally require that accounts include only explicit costs in the firm's financial records. *Economic costs* include both explicit costs *and* implicit costs. **Economic profit** is equal to a firm's revenues minus all of its costs, implicit and explicit. Because accounting profit excludes some implicit costs, it is larger than economic profit.

Economic profit A firm's revenues minus all of its implicit and explicit costs.

The Balance Sheet

A firm's **balance sheet** sums up its financial position on a particular day, usually the end of a quarter or year. Recall that an asset is anything of value that a firm owns, and a liability is a debt or obligation owed by a firm. Subtracting the value of a firm's liabilities from the value of its assets leaves its *net worth*. We can think of the net worth as what the firm's owners would be left with if the firm were closed, its assets were sold, and its liabilities were paid off. Investors can determine a firm's net worth by inspecting its balance sheet. We analyze a balance sheet in detail in the appendix to this chapter, which begins on page 233.

Balance sheet A financial statement that sums up a firm's financial position on a particular day, usually the end of a quarter or year.

7.5 | Understand the role of government in corporate governance.

Corporate Governance Policy

A firm's financial statements provide important information on the firm's ability to add value for investors and the economy. Accurate and easy-to-understand financial statements are inputs for decisions by the firm's managers and investors. Indeed, the information in accounting statements helps guide resource allocation in the economy.

Firms disclose financial statements in periodic filings to the federal government and in *annual reports* to shareholders. An investor is more likely to buy a firm's stock if the firm's income statement shows a large after-tax profit and if its balance sheet shows a large net worth. The top management of a firm has at least two reasons to attract investors and keep the firm's stock price high. First, a higher stock price increases the funds the firm can raise when it sells a given amount of stock. Second, to reduce the principal–agent problem, boards of directors often tie the salaries of top managers to the firm's stock price or to the profitability of the firm.

Top managers clearly have an incentive to maximize the profits reported on the income statement and the net worth reported on the balance sheet. If top managers make good decisions, the firm's profits will be high, and the firm's assets will be large relative to its liabilities. The business scandals that came to light in 2002 revealed, however, that some top managers have inflated profits and hidden liabilities that should have been listed on their balance sheets.

At Enron, an energy trading firm, CFO Andrew Fastow was accused of creating partnerships that were supposedly independent of Enron but in fact were owned by the firm. He was accused of transferring large amounts of Enron's debts to these partnerships, which reduced the liabilities on Enron's balance sheet, thereby increasing the firm's net worth. Fastow's deception made Enron more attractive to investors, increasing its stock price—and Fastow's compensation. In 2001, however, Enron was forced into bankruptcy. The firm's shareholders lost billions of dollars, and many employees lost their jobs. In 2004, Fastow pleaded guilty to conspiracy and was sentenced to 10 years in federal prison. Enron's CEO, Kenneth Lay, was found guilty of securities fraud in 2006 but died prior to being sentenced.

At WorldCom, a telecommunications firm, David Myers, the firm's controller, pleaded guilty to falsifying "WorldCom's books, to reduce WorldCom's reported actual costs and therefore increase WorldCom's reported earnings." Myers's actions caused WorldCom's income statement to overstate the firm's profits by more than $10 billion. WorldCom CEO Bernard Ebbers is serving a 25-year prison sentence for fraud. The scandals at Enron and WorldCom were the largest cases of corporate fraud in U.S. history.

How was it possible for corporations such as Enron and WorldCom to falsify their financial statements? The federal government regulates how financial statements are prepared, but this regulation cannot by itself guarantee the accuracy of the statements. All firms that issue stock to the public have certified public accountants *audit* their financial statements. The accountants are employees of accounting firms, *not* of the firms being audited. The audits are intended to provide investors with an independent opinion as to whether a firm's financial statements fairly represent the true financial condition of the firm. Unfortunately, as the Enron and WorldCom scandals revealed, top managers who are determined to deceive investors about the true financial condition of their firms can also deceive outside auditors.

The private sector's response to the corporate scandals was almost immediate. In addition to the reexamination of corporate governance practices at many corporations, the New York Stock Exchange and the Nasdaq put forth initiatives to ensure the accuracy and accessibility of information.

To guard against future scandals, new federal legislation was enacted in 2002. The landmark *Sarbanes-Oxley Act of 2002* requires that corporate directors have a certain level of expertise with financial information and mandates that CEOs personally certify the accuracy of financial statements. The Sarbanes-Oxley Act also requires that financial analysts and auditors disclose whether any conflicts of interest might exist that would limit their independence in evaluating a firm's financial condition. The purpose of this provision is to ensure that analysts and auditors are acting in the best interests of shareholders. The act promotes management accountability by specifying the responsibilities of corporate officers and by increasing penalties, including long jail sentences, for managers who do not meet their responsibilities.

Perhaps the most noticeable corporate governance reform under the Sarbanes-Oxley Act is the creation of the Public Company Accounting Oversight Board, a national board that oversees the auditing of public companies' financial reports. The board's mission is to promote the independence of auditors to ensure that they disclose accurate information. On balance, most observers acknowledge that the Sarbanes-Oxley Act brought back confidence in the U.S. corporate governance system, though questions remain for the future about whether the act may chill legitimate business risk-taking by diverting management attention from the core business toward regulatory compliance. And the high accounting costs of implementing Sarbanes-Oxley are borne by all shareholders.

By 2007, it had become clear that Sarbanes-Oxley had raised the costs to firms of issuing stocks and bonds in the United States. Section 404 of Sarbanes-Oxley is intended to reassure investors that accounting "errors"—whether from fraud, mistakes, or omissions—will be minimized by requiring firms to maintain effective controls over financial reporting. Many economists believe, though, that the rules for implementing Section 404 set forth by the Securities and Exchange Commission and the Public Company Accounting Oversight Board have turned out to be much more costly to firms than anticipated and that these costs may exceed the benefits of the regulations. As a result, the share of new issues of stocks and bonds being listed on the New York Stock Exchange or Nasdaq has declined relative to listings on foreign stock markets, such as the London Stock Exchange. Some economists, though, are skeptical that the decline in the share of new listings on the New York Stock Exchange and Nasdaq is due to the effects of Sarbanes-Oxley. These economists argue that as other global exchanges become more mature, they are naturally able to attract new listings from local firms. Therefore, in this view, the declining fraction of foreign firms willing to list new issues on the New York Stock Exchange or Nasdaq is not an indication that the burden of U.S. regulations is too heavy.

Outside the United States, the European Commission and Japan have also tightened corporate governance rules. The challenge of ensuring the accurate reporting of firms' economic profits without excessively raising firms' costs is a global one.

Solved Problem | 7-5

What Makes a Good Board of Directors?

Western Digital Corporation makes computer hard drives. *BusinessWeek* magazine published the following analysis by Standard & Poor's Equity Research Services of Western Digital's corporate governance:

> Overall, we view Western Digital's corporate-governance policies favorably and believe the company compares well in this regard relative to peers. We see the following factors as positives: the board is controlled by a supermajority (greater than 67%) of independent outsiders; the nominating and compensation committees are comprised solely of independent outside directors; all directors with more than one year of service own stock. . . .

a. What is an "independent outsider" on a board of directors?

b. Why is it good for a firm to have a large majority of independent outsiders on the board of directors?

c. Why would it be good for a firm to have the auditing and compensation committees composed of outsiders?

d. Why would it be good for a firm if its directors own the firm's stock?

Source: Jawahar Hingorani, "Western Digital: A Drive Buy," *BusinessWeek*, January 9, 2007.

SOLVING THE PROBLEM:

Step 1: **Review the chapter material.** The context of this problem is the business scandals of 2002 and the underlying principal–agent problem that arises because of the separation of ownership from control in large corporations, so you may want to review the section "Corporate Governance Policy," which begins on page 221.

Step 2: **Answer question (a) by defining "independent outsiders."** *Insiders* are members of top management who also serve on the board of directors. *Outsiders* are members of the board of directors who are not otherwise employed by the firm. *Independent outsiders* are outsiders who have no business connections with the firm.

Step 3: **Answer question (b) by explaining why it is good for a firm to have a large majority of independent outsiders on the board of directors.** Having members of top management on the board of directors provides the board with information about the firm that only top managers possess. Having too many insiders on a board, however, means that top managers may end up controlling the board rather than the other way around. A corporation's board of directors is supposed to provide the monitoring and control of top managers that shareholders cannot provide directly. This is most likely to happen when a larger majority of the board of directors consists of independent outsiders.

Step 4: **Answer question (c) by explaining why it may be good for a firm to have the auditing and compensation committees composed of outsiders.** The auditing committee is responsible for ensuring that the firm's financial statements are accurate, and the compensation committee is responsible for setting the pay of top management. It is of vital importance to a firm that these activities be carried out in an honest and impartial way. Having these two important committees composed exclusively of independent outside members increases the chances that the committees will act in the best interests of the shareholders rather than in the best interests of top management.

Step 5: **Answer question (d) by explaining why it may be good for a firm to have directors owning the firm's stock.** When directors own the firm's stock, they will then share with other stockholders the desire to see the firm maximize profits. The directors will be more likely to insist that top managers take actions to increase profits rather than to pursue other objectives that may be in the interests of the managers but not the stockholders. Of course, when directors own the firm's stock the directors may be tempted not to object if top managers take steps to improperly inflate the firm's profits, as happened during the business scandals of 2002. On balance, though, most economists believe that it improves corporate governance when a firm's directors own the firm's stock.

YOUR TURN: For more practice, do related problems 5.3 and 5.4 on page 232 at the end of this chapter.

>> End Solved Problem 7-5

Economics in YOUR Life!

>> Continued from page 209

At the beginning of the chapter, we asked you to consider two questions: Why is it difficult to get the managers of a firm to act in your interest rather than in their own? and Given this problem, should you ever take on the risk of buying stock? The reason managers may not act in shareholders' interest is that in large corporations, there is separation of ownership from control: The shareholders own the firm, but the top managers actually control it. This results in the principal–agent problem discussed in the chapter. The principal–agent problem clearly adds to the risk you would face by buying stock rather than doing something safe with your money, such as putting it in the bank. But the rewards to owning stock can also be substantial, potentially earning you far more over the long run than a bank account will. Buying the stock of well-known firms, such as Google, that are closely followed by Wall Street investment analysts helps to reduce the principal–agent problem. It is less likely that the managers of these firms will take actions that are clearly not in the best interests of shareholders because the managers' actions are difficult to conceal. Buying the stock of large, well-known firms certainly does not completely eliminate the risk from principal–agent problems, however. Enron, WorldCom, and some of the other firms that were involved in the scandals discussed in this chapter were all well known and closely followed by Wall Street analysts, but the misbehavior of their managers went undetected, at least for awhile.

Conclusion

In a market system, firms make independent decisions about which goods and services to produce, how to produce them, and what prices to charge. In modern high-income countries, such as the United States, large corporations account for a majority of the sales and profits earned by firms. Generally, the managers of these corporations do a good job of representing the interests of stockholders, while providing the goods and services demanded by consumers. As the business scandals of 2002 showed, however, some top managers enriched themselves at the expense of stockholders and consumers by manipulating financial statements. Passage of the Sarbanes-Oxley Act of 2002 and other new government regulations have helped restore investor and management confidence in firms' financial statements. However, economists debate whether the benefits from these regulations are greater than their costs.

An Inside Look on the next page discusses the compensation Google pays its top executives.

Executive Compensation at Google

ASSOCIATED PRESS, APRIL 4, 2007

Google CEO, Co-Founders Get $1 Salary

The trio of billionaires who run Google Inc. collected less than $600,000 in combined compensation last year while they raked in big jackpots by selling some of their holdings in the online search leader.

The total amount that Google paid its chief executive, Eric Schmidt, and co-founders Larry Page and Sergey Brin during 2006 would have been less than $5,200 if not for personal security and transportation costs, according to documents filed Wednesday with the Securities and Exchange Commission.

Schmidt's package totaled $557,466, including $532,755 for personal security. Page's pay totaled $38,519, with most of the money covering personal transportation, logistics and security. Brin's 2006 pay consisted solely of a $1 salary and $1,723 bonus. Google paid the same salary and holiday bonus to Schmidt and Page.

The Associated Press bases its executive pay totals on salary, bonus, incentives, perks, above-market returns on deferred compensation and the estimated value of stock options and awards granted during the year.

Schmidt, Page and Brin have refused to take anything more than a token paycheck for the past three years to promote the egalitarian spirit championed by the Mountain View-based company.

It's a sacrifice that the three executives can afford to make because Google's high-flying stock has elevated them into the ranks of the world's richest people. Meanwhile, hundreds of Google's early employees have become millionaires.

As of March 1, Page, 34, owned 29.2 million Google shares currently worth $13.8 billion while Brin, 33, held 28.6 million shares worth about $13.5 billion. Schmidt, 51, owns 10.7 million shares currently worth $5 billion. The three men have been converting some of their holdings into cash by regularly selling some of their stockholdings since the company went public in August 2004.

Last year, Brin, Page and Schmidt made more than $2 billion combined from their Google stock sales, according to data compiled from SEC filings by Thomson Financial. Brin sold 1.99 million shares for a total windfall of $788 million last year while Page pocketed $666 million by selling 1.72 million shares. Schmidt cashed out 1.39 million shares during 2006 for a total $580 million.

Google's stock price rose by 11 percent last year, a gain that lagged the Standard & Poor's 500 index—a blue-chip bellwether that the company joined during 2006. The S&P 500 rose by 13.6 percent last year.

Since its IPO, Google shares have surged to a more than fivefold increase, a meteoric performance that has created more than $120 billion in shareholder wealth. Google shares fell $1.58 Wednesday to close at $471.02 the Nasdaq Stock Market.

The rapid run-up in Google's stock has been driven by its search engine, which has become synonymous with looking things up on the Internet. The search engine also propels a lucrative online advertising network that enabled Google to turn a 2006 profit of $3.1 billion, more than doubling its earnings from the previous year. The robust growth has enabled Google to add more than 8,000 workers during the past three years. At the end of 2006, Google had 10,674 employees—all of whom were eligible for the same holiday bonus paid to Schmidt, Page and Brin.

Google's brain trust has already agreed to settle for a $1 salary again this year, rejecting an opportunity for a raise, according to the SEC filing.

Source: Michael Liedtke, "Google CEO, Co-Founders Get $1 Salary," Associated Press, April 4, 2007. Reprinted by permission of Associated Press via Reprint Management Services.

Key Points in the Article

The article discusses how Google CEO Eric Schmidt and the firm's co-founders Sergey Brin and Larry Page are compensated. Google is different from most large corporations in that most of the compensation for the CEO comes in the form of stock. The figure tracks the performance of Google's stock. Prior to August 2004, when Google had its initial public offering (IPO), Eric Schmidt and the co-founders agreed to cut their salaries to $1 a year plus some fringe benefits and stock in the company. Essentially, they bet that the price of the stock would rise. This turned out to be a good bet. Google's IPO was in August 2004. The price opened at $100 per share and closed at $104.06 that day. Google's stock has performed very well since the initial offering, and on April 4, 2007 (the date of the article) the price closed at $471.02 per share. As a result, the CEO and co-founders of Google have become billionaires.

The chapter discusses the principal–agent problem facing modern corporations. In large corporations, the executives of a firm are not usually the owners of the firm. In this situation, executives (especially the CEO) can take actions that are in their own interests rather than the interests of the shareholders. For example, the executives could use their influence to obtain large base salaries that are not sensitive to the firm's stock price. This reduces the executives' incentive to perform well. After all, the executives have large salaries, regardless of whether the firm does well.

Analyzing the News

a At Google, the CEO actually has a low base salary. Eric Schmidt earns a salary of $1 per year. He receives other compensation in the form of bonuses and compensation for security. Schmidt's combined compensation package was only $557,466, which is much less than those of most executives at similar firms.

b Instead of having a large base salary, most of Eric Schmidt's income comes from the sale of Google stock that he owned at the time Google went public or has received since then. He owns 10.7 million shares of Google stocks, making him a major shareholder in the firm. For each $1 increase in the stock price, Schmidt's wealth increases by $10.7 million. This is a strong incentive for him to take actions that will increase the stock price. This is good news to other Google shareholders, because Schmidt's income is tied to increases in the value of Google's stock. It seems Google has significantly reduced the principal–agent problem.

Thinking Critically

1. Compensating executives with stock, or equity, is a way to solve the principal–agent problem, but the practice is not without flaws. Critics of equity compensation point out that it can create incentives for executives to take actions not in the best interests of other shareholders and may have contributed to the corporate scandals discussed in the chapter. How could equity compensation contribute to these scandals?

2. An executive at Google who knew that Google was about to announce a larger than expected profit could have earned a bundle quickly by buying Google stock at $470 per share and then selling it at a higher price a day or so later. Such insider trading is illegal, however. Do you think that insider trading should be illegal? Are there benefits to other investors or to the economy as a whole associated with such trading? Are there problems associated with such trading?

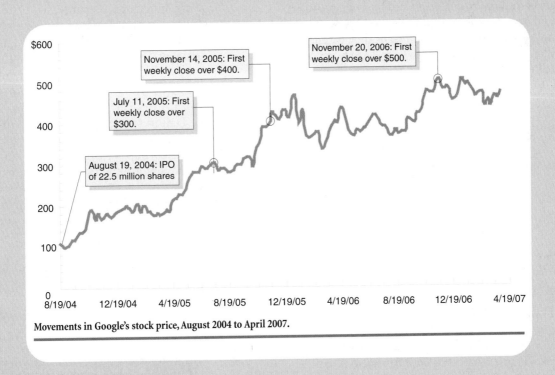

Movements in Google's stock price, August 2004 to April 2007.

Key Terms

7.1 LEARNING OBJECTIVE   7.1 | Categorize the major types of firms in the United States, **pages 210–212.**

Types of Firms

Summary

There are three types of firms: A **sole proprietorship** is a firm owned by a single individual and not organized as a corporation. A **partnership** is a firm owned jointly by two or more persons and not organized as a corporation. A **Corporation** is a legal form of business that provides the owners with limited liability. An **asset** is anything of value owned by a person or a firm. The owners of sole proprietorships and partners have unlimited liability, which means there is no legal distinction between the personal assets of the owners of the business and the assets of the business. The owners of corporations have **limited liability**, which means they can never lose more than their investment in the firm. Although only 20 percent of firms are corporations, they account for the majority of revenue and profit earned by all firms.

 Visit www.myeconlab.com to complete these exercises online and get instant feedback.

Review Questions

1.1 What are the three major types of firms in the United States? Briefly discuss the most important characteristics of each type.

1.2 What is limited liability? Why does the government grant limited liability to the owners of corporations?

Problems and Applications

1.3 Suppose that shortly after graduating from college, you decide to start your own business. Will you be likely to organize the business as a sole proprietorship, a partnership, or a corporation? Explain your reasoning.

1.4 (Related to the *Making the Connection* on page 211) Evaluate the following argument:

> I would like to invest in the stock market, but I think that buying shares of stock in a corporation is too risky. Suppose I buy $10,000 of General Motors stock, and the company ends up going bankrupt. Because as a stockholder, I'm part owner of the company, I might be responsible for paying hundreds of thousands of dollars of the company's debts.

1.5 (Related to the *Making the Connection* on page 211) In an article in the *New York Times*, sociologist Dalton Conley proposed the *elimination* of limited liability for corporate shareholders. Do you think that corporations should be granted limited liability? What are the benefits of limited liability? What is its downside? Would you be more willing to buy bonds from a corporation with limited liability? Would you be more willing to buy the stock of a corporation with limited liability?

Source: Dalton Conley, "Reward but No Risk," *New York Times*, May 10, 2003.

>> End Learning Objective 7.1

The Structure of Corporations and the Principal–Agent Problem

Summary

Corporate governance refers to the way in which a corporation is structured and the impact a corporation's structure has on the firm's behavior. Most corporations have a similar management structure: The shareholders elect a board of directors that appoints the corporation's top managers, such as the chief executive officer (CEO). Because the top management often does not own a large fraction of the stock in the corporation, large corporations have a **separation of ownership from control**. Because top managers have less incentive to increase the corporation's profits than to increase their own salaries and their own enjoyment, corporations can suffer from a **principal–agent problem**. A principal–agent problem exists when the principals—in this case, the shareholders of the corporation—have difficulty in getting the agent—the corporation's top management—to carry out their wishes.

myeconlab Visit www.myeconlab.com to complete these exercises
Get Ahead of the Curve online and get instant feedback.

Review Questions

2.1 What do we mean by the separation of ownership from control in large corporations?

2.2 How is the separation of ownership from control related to the principal–agent problem?

Problems and Applications

2.3 The principal–agent problem arises almost everywhere in the business world—but it also crops up even closer to home. Discuss the principal–agent problem that exists in the college classroom. Who is the principal? Who is the agent? What is the problem between this principal and this agent?

2.4 (Related to *Solved Problem 7-2* on page 213) Briefly explain whether you agree or disagree with the following argument: "The separation of ownership from control in large corporations and the principal–agent problem means that top managers can work short days, take long vacations, and otherwise slack off."

2.5 (Related to *Solved Problem 7-2* on page 213) An economic consultant gives the board of directors of a firm the following advice:

> You can increase the profitability of the firm if you change your method of compensating top management. Instead of paying your top management a straight salary, you should pay them a salary plus give them the right to buy the firm's stock in the future at a price above the stock's current market price.

Explain the consultant's reasoning. To what difficulties might this compensation scheme lead?

2.6 The following is from an article in the *New York Times*: "In theory, boards [of directors] design pay packages to attract and inspire good chief executives and to align their interests with those of shareholders. . . . But what kind of pay packages are appropriate at companies still run by the founding family?" The article quotes one expert as arguing: "There is little or no justification for treating an owner-manager in exactly the same way as a standard CEO." What does the article mean by saying that pay packages should "align [chief executives'] interests with those of shareholders"? What kind of pay packages would achieve this objective? Do you agree that an "owner-manager" should have a pay package different from that of a CEO who is not a member of the family that started the firm? Briefly explain.

Source: Diana B. Henriques, "What's Fair Pay for Running the Family Store?" *New York Times*, January 12, 2003.

>> End Learning Objective 7.2

How Firms Raise Funds

Summary

Firms rely on retained earnings—which are profits retained by the firm and not paid out to the firm's owners—or on using the savings of households for the funds they need to operate and expand. With **direct finance**, the savings of households flow directly to businesses when investors buy **stocks** and **bonds** in financial markets. With **indirect finance**, savings flow indirectly to businesses when households deposit money in saving and checking accounts in banks and the banks lend these funds to businesses. Federal, state, and local governments also sell bonds in financial markets and households also borrow funds from banks. When a firm sells a bond, it is borrowing money from the buyer of the bond. The firm makes a **coupon payment** to the buyer of the bond. The **interest rate** is the cost of borrowing funds, usually expressed as a percentage of the amount borrowed. When a firm sells stock, it is selling part ownership of the firm to the buyer of the stock. **Dividends** are payments by a corporation to its shareholders. The original purchasers of stocks and bonds may resell them in stock and bond markets, such as the New York Stock Exchange.

 Visit www.myeconlab.com to complete these exercises *Get Ahead of the Curve* online and get instant feedback.

Review Questions

3.1 What is the difference between direct finance and indirect finance? If you borrow money from a bank to buy a new car, are you using direct finance or indirect finance?

3.2 Why is a bond considered to be a loan but a share of stock is not? Why do corporations issue both bonds and shares of stock?

3.3 How do the stock and bond markets provide information to businesses? Why do stock and bond prices change over time?

Problems and Applications

3.4 Suppose that a firm in which you have invested is losing money. Would you rather own the firm's stock or the firm's bonds? Explain.

3.5 Suppose you originally invested in a firm when it was small and unprofitable. Now the firm has grown considerably and is large and profitable. Would you be better off if you had bought the firm's stock or the firm's bonds? Explain.

3.6 If you deposit $20,000 in a savings account at a bank, you might earn 3 percent interest per year. Someone who borrows $20,000 from a bank to buy a new car might have to pay an interest rate of 8 percent per year on the loan. Knowing this, why don't you just lend your money directly to the car buyer, cutting out the bank?

3.7 (Related to the *Chapter Opener* on page 208) When Google's owners wanted to raise funds for expansion in 2004, they decided to sell stock in their company rather than borrow the money. Why do some companies fund their expansion by borrowing, while others fund expansion by issuing new stock?

3.8 (Related to the *Chapter Opener* on page 208) What impact would the following events be likely to have on the price of Google's stock?
   a. A competitor launches a search engine that's just as good as Google's.
   b. The corporate income tax is abolished.
   c. Google's board of directors becomes dominated by close friends and relatives of its top management.
   d. The price of wireless Internet connections unexpectedly drops, so more and more people use the Internet.
   e. Google announces a huge profit of $1 billion, but everybody anticipated that Google would earn a huge profit of $1 billion.

3.9 In 2005, the French government began issuing bonds with 50-year maturities. Would this bond be purchased only by very young investors who expect to still be alive when the bond matures? Briefly explain.

3.10 (Related to the *Don't Let This Happen to You!* on page 216) Briefly explain whether you agree or disagree with the following statement: "The total value of the shares of Microsoft stock traded on the Nasdaq last week was $250 million, so the firm actually received more revenue from stock sales than from selling software."

3.11 (Related to the *Making the Connection* on page 217) Loans from banks are the most important external source of funds to businesses because most businesses are too small to borrow in financial markets by issuing stocks or bonds. Most investors are reluctant to buy the stocks or bonds of small businesses because of the difficulty of gathering accurate information on the financial strength and profitability of the businesses. Nevertheless, news about the stock market is included in nearly every network news program and is often the lead story in the business section of most newspapers. Is there a contradiction here? Why is the average viewer of TV news or the average reader of a newspaper interested in the fluctuations in prices in the stock market?

>> End Learning Objective 7.3

Using Financial Statements to Evaluate a Corporation

Summary

A firm's **income statement** sums up its revenues, costs, and profit over a period of time. A firm's **balance sheet** sums up its financial position on a particular day, usually the end of a quarter or year. A balance sheet records a firms assets and liabilities. A **liability** is anything owed by a person or a firm. Firms report their **accounting profit** on their income statements. Accounting profit does not always include all of a firm's **opportunity cost**. **Explicit cost** is a cost that involves spending money. **Implicit cost** is a nonmonetary opportunity cost. Because accounting profit excludes some implicit costs, it is larger than **economic profit**.

myeconlab   Visit www.myeconlab.com to complete these exercises
Get Ahead of the Curve online and get instant feedback.

Review Questions

4.1 What is the difference between a firm's assets and its liabilities? Give an example of an asset and an example of a liability.

4.2 What is the difference between a firm's balance sheet and a firm's income statement?

Problems and Applications

4.3 Paolo currently has $100,000 invested in bonds that earn him 10 percent interest per year. He wants to open a pizza restaurant and is considering either selling the bonds and using the $100,000 to start his restaurant or borrowing the $100,000 from a bank, which would charge him an annual interest rate of 7 percent. He finally decides to sell the bonds and not take out the bank loan. He reasons, "Because I already have the $100,000 invested in the bonds, I don't have

to pay anything to use the money. If I take out the bank loan, I have to pay interest, so my costs of producing pizza will be higher if I take out the loan than if I sell the bonds." What do you think of Paolo's reasoning?

4.4 Paolo and Alfredo are twins who both want to open pizza restaurants. Because their parents always liked Alfredo best, they buy two pizza ovens and give both to him. Unfortunately, Paolo must buy his own pizza ovens. Does Alfredo have lower cost of producing pizza than Paolo does because Alfredo received his pizza ovens as a gift while Paolo had to pay for his? Briefly explain.

4.5 Dane decides to give up a job earning $100,000 per year as a corporate lawyer and converts the duplex that he owns into a UFO museum. (He had been renting out the duplex for $20,000 a year.) His direct expenses include $50,000 per year paid to his assistants and $10,000 per year for utilities. Fans flock to the museum to see his collection of extraterrestrial paraphernalia, which he could easily sell on eBay for $1,000,000. Over the course of the year, the museum brings in revenues of $100,000.
   a. How much is Dane's accounting profit for the year?
   b. Is Dane earning an economic profit? Explain.

4.6 The Securities and Exchange Commission requires that every firm that wishes to issue stock and bonds to the public make available its balance sheet and income statement. Briefly explain how information useful to investors can be found in these financial statements.

4.7 (Related to the *Making the Connection* on page 219) The Making the Connection on China argues that "In the absence of well-functioning financial markets, banks are crucial allocators of capital." What is the difference between a financial market and a bank? What is an "allocator of capital"? How do banks allocate capital?

>> End Learning Objective 7.4

Corporate Governance Policy

Summary

Because their compensation often rises with the profitability of the corporation, top managers have an incentive to overstate the profits reported on their firm's income statements. During 2002, it became clear that the

top managers of several large corporations had done this, even though intentionally falsifying financial statements is illegal. The *Sarbanes-Oxley Act* of 2002 and greater scrutiny of financial statements have helped to restore investor and management confidence in firms' financial statements.

Visit www.myeconlab.com to complete these exercises online and get instant feedback.

Review Questions

5.1 What is the Sarbanes-Oxley Act? Why was it passed?

5.2 Why are some policymakers and business owners concerned about the Sarbanes-Oxley Act?

Problems and Applications

5.3 (Related to *Solved Problem 7-5* on page 223) When Buford Yates, director of accounting at WorldCom, pleaded guilty to fraud, he stated in federal court that top managers at WorldCom ordered him to make certain adjustments to the firm's financial statements:

> I came to believe that the adjustments I was being directed to make in World-Com's financial statements had no justification and contravened generally accepted accounting principles. I concluded that the purpose of these adjustments was to incorrectly inflate World-Com's reported earnings.

What are "generally accepted accounting principles"? How would the "adjustments" Yates was ordered to make benefit top managers at WorldCom? Would these adjustments also benefit WorldCom's stockholders? Briefly explain.

Source: Devlin Barrett, "Ex-WorldCom Exec Pleads Guilty," Associated Press, October 8, 2002.

5.4 (Related to *Solved Problem 7-5* on page 223) In 2002, *BusinessWeek* listed Apple Computer as having one of the worst boards of directors:

> Founder Steve Jobs owns just two shares in the company. . . . The CEO of Micro Warehouse, which accounted for nearly 2.9% of Apple's net sales in 2001, sits on the compensation committee. . . . There is an interlocking directorship—with Gap CEO Mickey Drexler and Jobs sitting on each other's boards.

Why might investors be concerned that a top manager like Steve Jobs owns only two shares in the firm? Why might investors be concerned if a member of the board of directors also has a business relationship with the firm? What is an "interlocking directorship"? Why is it a bad thing?

Source: "The Best Boards and the Worst Boards," *BusinessWeek*, October 7, 2002, p. 107.

5.5 The following is from a *BusinessWeek* editorial:

> Welcome to the revolution. After years of paying lip service to reform, Enron Corp. and the ensuing wave of business scandal has finally produced a dramatic change in corporate governance. . . . Investors are rewarding companies with good governance and punishing those without it.

How are investors able to reward or punish firms? What impact will these rewards and punishments have on boards of directors and top managers?

Source: "Boardrooms Are Starting to Wake Up," *BusinessWeek*, October 7, 2002, p. 107.

5.6 An article in *BusinessWeek* stated that the Allstate Corporation, a large insurance company, would now require a simple majority vote, rather than a two-thirds majority vote, to elect members to its board of directors and to remove directors in between annual meetings when elections are held. The article also stated that the price of Allstate's stock rose following the announcement. Briefly discuss whether there may have been a possible connection between these changes in Allstate's corporate governance and the increase in the firm's stock price.

Source: "Allstate Announces Changes to Governance," *BusinessWeek*, February 20, 2007.

5.7 According to a survey in 2007, 78 percent of corporate executives responding believed that the costs of complying with the Sarbanes-Oxley Act outweighed the benefits. The total costs of compliance were about $2.92 million dollars per company. Is it possible to put a dollar value on the benefits to complying with Sarbanes-Oxley? Which groups are likely to receive the most benefits from Sarbanes-Oxley: investors, corporations, or some other group?

Source: Kara Scannell, "Costs to Comply with Sarbanes-Oxley Decline Again," *Wall Street Journal*, May 16, 2007, p. C7.

>> **End Learning Objective 7.5**

Appendix

Tools to Analyze Firms' Financial Information

Understand the concept of present value and the information contained on a firm's income statement and balance sheet.

LEARNING OBJECTIVE

As we saw in the chapter, modern business organizations are not just "black boxes" transforming inputs into output. Most business revenues and profits are earned by large corporations. Unlike founder-dominated firms, the typical large corporation is run by managers who generally do not own a controlling interest in the firm. Large firms raise funds from outside investors, and outside investors seek information on firms and the assurance that the managers of firms will act in the interests of the investors.

This chapter showed how corporations raise funds by issuing stocks and bonds. This appendix provides more detail to support that discussion. We begin by analyzing *present value* as a key concept in determining the prices of financial securities. We then provide greater information on *financial statements* issued by corporations, using Google as an example.

Using Present Value to Make Investment Decisions

Firms raise funds by selling equity (stock) and debt (bonds and loans) to investors and lenders. If you own shares of stock or a bond, you will receive payments in the form of dividends or coupons over a number of years. Most people value funds they already have more highly than funds they will not receive until some time in the future. For example, you would probably not trade $1,000 you already have for $1,000 you will not receive for one year. The longer you have to wait to receive a payment, the less value it will have for you. One thousand dollars you will not receive for two years is worth less to you than $1,000 you will receive after one year. The value you give today to money you will receive in the future is called the future payment's **present value**. The present value of $1,000 you will receive in one year will be less than $1,000.

Why is this true? Why is the $1,000 you will not receive for one year less valuable to you than the $1,000 you already have? The most important reason is that if you have $1,000 today, you can use that $1,000 today. You can buy goods and services with the money and receive enjoyment from them. The $1,000 you receive in one year does not have direct use to you now.

Also, prices will likely rise during the year you are waiting to receive your $1,000. So, when you finally do receive the $1,000 in one year, you will not be able to buy as much with it as you could with $1,000 today. Finally, there is some risk that you will not receive the $1,000 in one year. The risk may be very great if an unreliable friend borrows $1,000 from you and vaguely promises to pay you back in one year. The risk may be very small if you lend money to the federal government by buying a United States Treasury bond. In either case, though, there is at least some risk that you will not receive the funds promised.

When someone lends money, the lender expects to be paid back both the amount of the loan and some additional interest. Say that you decide that you are willing to lend your $1,000 today if you are paid back $1,100 one year from now. In this case, you are charging $100/$1,000 = 0.10, or 10 percent interest on the funds you have loaned. Economists would say that you value $1,000 today as equivalent to the $1,100 to be received one year in the future.

Present value The value in today's dollars of funds to be paid or received in the future.

Notice that $1,100 can be written as $1,000 $(1 + 0.10)$. That is, the value of money received in the future is equal to the value of money in the present multiplied by 1 plus the interest rate, with the interest rate expressed as a decimal. Or:

$$\$1,100 = 1,000 \ (1 + 0.10).$$

Notice, also, that if we divide both sides by $(1 + 0.10)$, we can rewrite this formula as:

$$\$1,000 = \frac{\$1,100}{(1 + 0.10)}.$$

The rewritten formula states that the present value is equal to the future value to be received in one year divided by one plus the interest rate. This formula is important because you can use it to convert any amount to be received in one year into its present value. Writing the formula generally, we have:

$$\text{Present Value} = \frac{\text{Future Value}_1}{(1 + i)}.$$

The present value of funds to be received in one year—Future Value$_1$—can be calculated by dividing the amount of those funds to be received by 1 plus the interest rate. With an interest rate of 10 percent, the present value of $1,000,000 to be received one year from now is:

$$\frac{\$1,000,000}{(1 + 0.10)} = \$909,090.91.$$

This method is a very useful way of calculating the value today of funds that won't be received for one year. But financial securities such as stocks and bonds involve promises to pay funds over many years. Therefore, it would be even more useful if we could expand this formula to calculate the present value of funds to be received more than one year in the future.

This expansion is easy to do. Go back to the original example where we assumed you were willing to loan out your $1,000 for one year, provided that you received 10 percent interest. Suppose you are asked to lend the funds for two years and that you are promised 10 percent interest per year for each year of the loan. That is, you are lending $1,000, which at 10 percent interest will grow to $1,100 after one year, and you are agreeing to loan that $1,100 out for a second year at 10 percent interest. So, after two years, you will be paid back $1,100 $(1 + 0.10)$, or $1,210. Or:

$$\$1,210 = \$1,000 \ (1 + 0.10)(1 + 0.10),$$

or:

$$\$1,210 = \$1,000 \ (1 + 0.10)^2.$$

This formula can also be rewritten as:

$$\$1,000 = \frac{\$1,210}{(1 + 0.10)^2}.$$

To put this formula in words, the $1,210 you receive two years from now has a present value equal to $1,210 divided by the quantity 1 plus the interest rate squared. If you were to agree to lend out your $1,000 for three years at 10 percent interest, you would receive:

$$\$1,331 = \$1,000 \ (1 + 0.10)^3.$$

Notice, again, that:

$$\$1,000 = \frac{\$1,331}{(1 + 0.10)^3}.$$

You can probably see a pattern here. We can generalize the concept to say that the present value of funds to be received n years in the future—whether n is 1, 20, or 85 does not matter—equals the amount of the funds to be received divided by the quantity 1 plus the interest rate raised to the nth power. For instance, with an interest rate of 10 percent, the value of $1,000,000 to be received 25 years in the future is:

$$\text{Present Value} = \frac{\$1,000,000}{(1+0.10)^{25}} = \$92,296.$$

Or, more generally:

$$\text{Present Value} = \frac{\text{Future Value}_n}{(1+i)^n},$$

where Future Value$_n$ represents funds that will be received in n years.

Solved Problem | 7A-1

How to Receive Your Contest Winnings

Suppose you win a contest and are given the choice of the following prizes:

Prize 1: $50,000 to be received right away, with four additional payments of $50,000 to be received each year for the next four years

Prize 2: $175,000 to be received right away

Explain which prize you would choose and the basis for your decision.

SOLVING THE PROBLEM:

Step 1: **Review the material.** This problem involves applying the concept of present value, so you may want to review the section "Using Present Value to Make Investment Decisions," which begins on page 233.

Step 2: **Explain the basis for choosing the prize.** Unless you need immediate cash, you should choose the prize with the highest present value.

Step 3: **Calculate the present value of each prize.** Prize 2 consists of one payment of $175,000 received right away, so its present value is $175,000. Prize 1 consists of five payments spread out over time. To find the present value of the prize, we must find the present value of each of these payments and add them together. To calculate present value, we must use an interest rate. Let's assume an interest rate of 10 percent. In that case, the present value of Prize 1 is:

$$\$50,000 + \frac{\$50,000}{(1+0.10)} + \frac{\$50,000}{(1+0.10)^2} + \frac{\$50,000}{(1+0.10)^3} + \frac{\$50,000}{(1+0.10)^4} =$$

$$\$50,000 + \$45,454.55 + \$41,322.31 + \$37,565.74 + \$34,150.67 = \$208,493.$$

Step 4: **State your conclusion.** Prize 1 has the greater present value, so you should choose it rather than Prize 2.

YOUR TURN: For more practice, do related problems 7A.6, 7A.8, 7A.9, and 7A.10 and on pages 240–241 at the end of this appendix.

>> **End Solved Problem 7A-1**

Using Present Value to Calculate Bond Prices

Anyone who buys a financial asset, such as shares of stock or a bond, is really buying a promise to receive certain payments—dividends in the case of shares of stock or coupons in the case of a bond. The price investors are willing to pay for a financial asset should be equal to the value of the payments they will receive as a result of owning the asset. Because most of the coupon or dividend payments will be received in the future, it is their present value that matters. Put another way, we have the following important idea: *The price of a financial asset should be equal to the present value of the payments to be received from owning that asset.*

Let's consider an example. Suppose that in 1980, General Electric issued a bond with an $80 coupon that will mature in 2010. It is now 2008, and that bond has been bought and sold by investors many times. You are considering buying it. If you buy the bond, you will receive two years of coupon payments plus a final payment of the bond's principal or face value of $1,000. Suppose, once again, that you need an interest rate of 10 percent to invest your funds. If the bond has a coupon of $80, the present value of the payments you receive from owning the bond—and, therefore, the present value of the bond—will be:

$$\text{Present Value} = \frac{\$80}{(1+0.10)} + \frac{\$80}{(1+0.10)^2} + \frac{\$1,000}{(1+0.10)^2} = \$965.29.$$

That is, the present value of the bond will equal the present value of the three payments you will receive during the two years you own the bond. You should, therefore, be willing to pay $965.29 to own this bond and have the right to receive these payments from GE. This process of calculating present values of future payments is used to determine bond prices, with one qualification. The relevant interest rate used by investors in the bond market to calculate the present value and, therefore, the price of an existing bond is usually the coupon rate on comparable newly issued bonds. Therefore, the general formula for the price of a bond is:

$$\text{Bond Price} = \frac{\text{Coupon}_1}{(1+i)} + \frac{\text{Coupon}_2}{(1+i)^2} + \cdots + \frac{\text{Coupon}_n}{(1+i)^n} + \frac{\text{Face Value}}{(1+i)^n},$$

where Coupon_1 is the coupon payment to be received after one year, Coupon_2 is the coupon payment to be received after two years, up to Coupon_n, which is the coupon payment received in the year the bond matures. The ellipsis takes the place of the coupon payments—if any—received between the second year and the year the bond matures. Face Value is the face value of the bond, to be received when the bond matures. The interest rate on comparable newly issued bonds is i.

Using Present Value to Calculate Stock Prices

When you own a firm's stock, you are legally entitled to your share of the firm's profits. Remember that the profits a firm pays out to its shareholders are referred to as dividends. The price of a share of stock should be equal to the present value of the dividends investors expect to receive as a result of owning that stock. Therefore, the general formula for the price of a stock is:

$$\text{Stock Price} = \frac{\text{Dividend}_1}{(1+i)} + \frac{\text{Dividend}_2}{(1+i)^2} + \cdots$$

Notice that this formula looks very similar to the one we used to calculate the price of a bond, with a couple of important differences. First, unlike a bond, stock has no maturity date, so we have to calculate the present value of an infinite number of dividend payments. At first, it may seem that the stock's price must be infinite as well, but remember that dollars you don't receive for many years are worth very little today. For instance, a dividend payment of $10 that will be received 40 years in the future is worth only a little more than $0.20 today at a 10 percent interest rate. The second difference between the stock price formula and the bond price formula is that whereas the coupon payments you receive from owning the bond are known with certainty—they are written on the bond and cannot be changed—you don't know for sure what the dividend payments from owning a stock will be. How large a dividend payment you will receive depends on how profitable the company will be in the future.

Although it is possible to forecast the future profitability of a company, this cannot be done with perfect accuracy. To emphasize this point, some economists rewrite the basic stock price formula by adding a superscript e to each Dividend term to emphasize that these are *expected* dividend payments. Because the future profitability of companies is often very difficult to forecast, it is not surprising that differences of opinion exist over what the price of a particular stock should be. Some investors will be very optimistic about the future profitability of a company and will, therefore, believe that the company's stock should have a high price. Other investors might be very pessimistic and believe that the company's stock should have a low price.

A Simple Formula for Calculating Stock Prices

It is possible to simplify the formula for determining the price of a stock, if we assume that dividends will grow at a constant rate:

$$\text{Stock Price} = \frac{\text{Dividend}}{(i - \text{Growth Rate})}.$$

In this equation, Dividend is the dividend expected to be received one year from now, and Growth Rate is the rate at which those dividends are expected to grow. If a company pays a dividend of $1 per share to be received one year from now and Growth Rate is 10 percent, the company is expected to pay a dividend of $1.10 the following year, $1.21 the year after that, and so on.

Now suppose that IBM pays a dividend of $5 per share, the consensus of investors is that these dividends will increase at a rate of 5 percent per year for the indefinite future, and the interest rate is 10 percent. Then the price of IBM's stock should be:

$$\text{Stock Price} = \frac{\$5.00}{(0.10 - 0.05)} = \$100.00.$$

Particularly during the years 1999 and 2000, there was much discussion of whether the high prices of many Internet stocks—such as the stock of Amazon.com—were justified, given that many of these companies had not made any profit yet and so had not paid any dividends. Is there any way that a rational investor would pay a high price for the stock of a company currently not earning profits? The formula for determining stock prices shows that it is possible, provided that the investor's assumptions are optimistic enough! For example, during 1999, one stock analyst predicted that Amazon.com would soon be earning $10 per share of stock. That is, Amazon.com's total earnings divided by the number of shares of its stock outstanding would be $10. Suppose Amazon.com pays out that $10 in dividends and that the $10 will grow rapidly over the years, by, say, 7 percent per year. Then our formula indicates that the price of Amazon.com stock should be:

$$\text{Stock Price} = \frac{\$10.00}{(\$0.10 - 0.07)} = \$333.33.$$

If you are sufficiently optimistic about the future prospects of a company, a high stock price can be justified even if the company is not currently earning a profit. But investors in growth stocks must be careful. Suppose investors believe that growth prospects for Amazon are only 4 percent per year instead of 7 percent because the firm turns out not to be as profitable as initially believed. Then our formula indicates that the price of Amazon.com stock should be:

$$\text{Stock Price} = \frac{\$10.00}{(\$0.10 - 0.04)} = \$166.67,$$

This price is only half the price assuming a more optimistic growth rate. Hence investors use information about a firm's profitability and growth prospects to determine what the firm is worth.

Going Deeper into Financial Statements

Corporations disclose substantial information about their business operations and financial position to actual and potential investors. Some of this information meets the demands of participants in financial markets and of information-collection agencies, such as Moody's Investors Service, which develops credit ratings that help investors judge how risky corporate bonds are. Other information meets the requirements of the U.S. Securities and Exchange Commission.

Key sources of information about a corporation's profitability and financial position are its principal financial statements—the *income statement* and the *balance sheet.* These important information sources were first introduced in the chapter. Here we go into more detail, using recent data for Google as an example.

Analyzing Income Statements

As discussed in the chapter, a firm's income statement summarizes its revenues, costs, and profit over a period of time. Figure 7A-1 shows Google's income statement for 2006.

Google's income statement presents the results of the company's operations during the year. Listed first are the revenues it earned, largely from selling advertising on its Web site, from January 1, 2006, to December 31, 2006: $10,605 million. Listed next are Google's operating expenses, the most important of which is its *cost of revenue*—which is commonly known as *cost of sales* or *cost of goods sold*: $4,225 million. Cost of revenue is the direct cost of producing the products sold, including in this case the salaries of the computer programmers Google hires to write the software for its Web site. Google also has substantial costs for researching and developing its products ($1,229 million) and for advertising and marketing them ($850 million). General and administrative expenses ($850 million) include costs such as the salaries of top managers.

The difference between a firm's revenue and its costs is its profit. "Profit" shows up in several forms on an income statement. A firm's *operating income* is the difference between its revenue and its operating expenses. Most corporations, including Google, also have investments, such as government and corporate bonds, that normally generate some income for them. In this case, Google earned $461 million on its investments, which increased its *income before taxes* to $4,011 million. The federal government taxes the profits of corporations. During 2006, Google paid $934 million—or about 23 percent

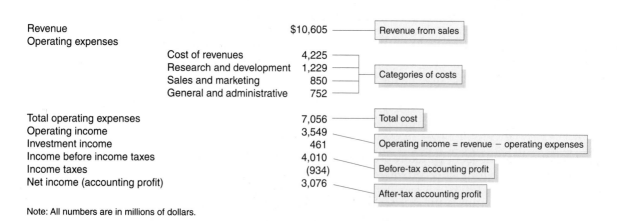

Revenue	$10,605	Revenue from sales
Operating expenses		
Cost of revenues	4,225	
Research and development	1,229	Categories of costs
Sales and marketing	850	
General and administrative	752	
Total operating expenses	7,056	Total cost
Operating income	3,549	
Investment income	461	Operating income = revenue − operating expenses
Income before income taxes	4,010	
Income taxes	(934)	Before-tax accounting profit
Net income (accounting profit)	3,076	After-tax accounting profit

Note: All numbers are in millions of dollars.

Figure 7A-1 | Google's Income Statement for 2006

Google's income statement shows the company's revenue, costs, and profit for 2006. The difference between its revenue ($10,605 million) and its operating expenses ($7,055 million) is its operating income ($3,550 million). Most corporations also have investments, such as government or corporate bonds, that generate some income for them. In this case, Google earned $461 million, giving the firm an income before taxes

of $4,011 million. After paying taxes of $934 million, Google was left with a net income, or accounting profit, of $3,076 million for the year.

Source: Google's Income Statement for 2006. Google Inc., "Consolidated Statements of Income," February 1, 2007. Used with permission of Google, Inc.

of its profits—in taxes. *Net income* after taxes was $3,077 million. The net income that firms report on their income statements is referred to as their after-tax *accounting profit.*

Analyzing Balance Sheets

As discussed in the chapter, whereas a firm's income statement reports a firm's activities for a period of time, a firm's balance sheet summarizes its financial position on a particular day, usually the end of a quarter or year. To understand how a balance sheet is organized, first recall that an asset is anything of value that the firm owns, and a liability is a debt or an obligation that the firm owes. Subtracting the value of a firm's liabilities from the value of its assets leaves its *net worth.* Because a corporation's stockholders are its owners, net worth is often listed as **stockholders' equity** on a balance sheet. Using these definitions, we can state the balance sheet equation (also called the basic accounting equation) as follows:

Stockholders' equity The difference between the value of a corporation's assets and the value of its liabilities; also known as net worth.

$$\text{Assets} - \text{Liabilities} = \text{Stockholders' Equity,}$$

or:

$$\text{Assets} = \text{Liabilities} + \text{Stockholders' Equity.}$$

This formula tells us that the value of a firm's assets must equal the value of its liabilities plus the value of stockholders' equity. An important accounting rule dating back to the beginning of modern bookkeeping in fifteenth-century Italy holds that balance sheets should list assets on the left side and liabilities and net worth, or stockholders' equity, on the right side. Notice that this means that *the value of the left side of the balance sheet must always equal the value of the right side.* Figure 7A-2 shows Google's balance sheet as of December 31, 2006.

A couple of the entries on the asset side of the balance sheet may be unfamiliar: *Current assets* are assets that the firm could convert into cash quickly, such as the balance in its checking account or its accounts receivable, which is money currently owed to the firm for products that have been delivered but not yet paid for. *Goodwill* represents the difference between the purchase price of a company and the market value of its assets. It represents the ability of a business to earn an economic profit from its assets. For example, if you buy a restaurant that is located on a busy intersection and you employ a chef with a reputation for preparing delicious food, you may pay more than the market value of the tables, chairs, ovens, and other assets. This additional amount you pay will be entered on the asset side of your balance sheet as goodwill.

Current liabilities are short-term debts such as accounts payable, which is money owed to suppliers for goods received but not yet paid for, or bank loans that will be paid back in less than one year. Long-term bank loans and the value of outstanding corporate bonds are *long-term liabilities.*

ASSETS		LIABILITIES AND STOCKHOLDERS' EQUITY	
Current Assets	$13,040	Current Liabilities	$1,305
Property and Equipment	2,395	Long-term liabilities	129
Investments	1,032	Total Liabilities	1,434
Goodwill	1,545	Stockholders' Equity	17,040
Other long-term assets	461		
Total Assets	18,473	Total liabilites and stockholders' equity	18,473

Figure 7A-2 | Google's Balance Sheet as of December 31, 2006

Corporations list their assets on the left of their balance sheets and their liabilities on the right. The difference between the value of the firm's assets and the value of its liabilities equals the net worth of the firm, or stockholders' equity. Stockholders' equity is listed on the right side of the balance sheet. Therefore, the value of the left side of the balance sheet must always equal the value of the right side.
Note: All numbers are in millions of dollars.
Source: Google's Balance Sheet as of December 31, 2006, Google, Inc., "Consolidated Balance Sheets," February 1, 2007. Used with permission of Google, Inc.

Key Terms

Present value, p. 233   Stockholders' equity, p. 239

LEARNING OBJECTIVE   Understand the concept of present value and the information contained on a firm's income statement and balance sheet, **pages 233–239.**

 Visit www.myeconlab.com to complete these exercises *Get Ahead of the Curve* online and get instant feedback.

Review Questions

7A.1 Why is money you receive at some future date worth less than money you receive today? If the interest rate rises, what effect does this have on the present value of payments you receive in the future?

7A.2 Give the formula for calculating the present value of a bond that will pay a coupon of $100 per year for 10 years and that has a face value of $1,000.

7A.3 Compare the formula for calculating the present value of the payments you will receive from owning a bond to the formula for calculating the present value of the payments you will receive from owning a stock. What are the key similarities? What are the key differences?

7A.4 How is operating income calculated? How does operating income differ from net income? How does net income differ from accounting profit?

7A.5 What's the key difference between a firm's income statement and its balance sheet? What is listed on the left side of a balance sheet? What is listed on the right side?

Problems and Applications

7A.6 (Related to *Solved Problem 7A-1* on page 235) If the interest rate is 10 percent, what is the present value of a bond that matures in two years, pays $85 one year from now, and pays $1,085 two years from now?

7A.7 The following is from an Associated Press story on the contract of baseball star Carlos Beltran:

> Beltran's contract calls for his $11 million signing bonus to be paid in four installments: $5 million upon approval and $2 million each this June 15, 2005, and on Jan. 15, 2006, and Jan. 15, 2007. He gets a $10 million salary this year, $12 million in each of the following two seasons and

$18.5 million in each of the final four seasons, with $8.5 million deferred annually from 2008–11. The players' association calculated the present day value of the contract at $115,726,946, using a 6 percent discount rate (the prime rate [which is the interest rate banks charge on loans to their best customers] plus 1 percent, rounded to the nearest whole number). For purposes of baseball's luxury tax, which currently uses a 3.62 percent discount rate, the contract is valued at $116,695,898.

Briefly explain why the present value of Beltran's contract is lower if a higher interest is used to make the calculation than if a lower interest rate is used.

Source: "Like Pedro, Beltran Gets Suite on Road," Associated Press, January 18, 2005.

7A.8 (Related to *Solved Problem 7A-1* on page 235) Before the 2007 season, the Seattle Mariners baseball team signed catcher Kenji Johjima to a contract that would pay him the following amounts: an immediate $1 million signing bonus, $5.1 million for the 2007 season, $5.2 million for the 2008 season, and $5.2 million for the 2009 season. Assume that he receives each of his three seasonal salaries as a lump sum payment at the end of the season and that he receives his 2007 salary one year after he signed the contract.

a. Some newspaper reports described Johjima as having signed a "$16.5 million contract" with the Mariners. Do you agree that $16.5 million was the value of this contract? Briefly explain.

b. What was the present value of Johjima's contract at the time he signed it (assuming an interest rate of 10 percent)?

c. If you use an interest rate of 5 percent, what was the present value of Johjima's contract?

7A.9 (Related to *Solved Problem 7A-1* on page 235) A winner of the Pennsylvania Lottery was given the choice of receiving $18 million at once or $1,440,000 per year for 25 years.

a. If the winner had opted for the 25 annual payments, how much in total would she have received?

b. At an interest rate of 10 percent, what would be the present value of the 25 payments?

c. At an interest rate of 5 percent, what would be the present value of the 25 payments?

d. What interest rate would make the present value of the 25 payments equal to the one payment of $18 million? (This question is difficult and requires the use of a financial calculator or a spreadsheet. *Hint:* If you are familiar with the Excel spreadsheet program, use the RATE function. Questions (b) and (c) can be answered by using the Excel NPV—Net Present Value—function.)

7A.10 (Related to *Solved Problem 7A-1* on page 235) Before the start of the 2000 baseball season, the New York Mets decided they didn't want Bobby Bonilla playing for them any longer. But Bonilla had a contract with the Mets for the 2000 season that would have obliged the Mets to pay him $5.9 million. When the Mets released Bonilla, he agreed to take the following payments in lieu of the $5.9 million the Mets would have paid him in the year 2000: He will receive 25 equal payments of $1,193,248.20 each July 1 from 2011 to 2035. If you were Bobby Bonilla, which would you rather have had, the lump sum $5.9 million or the 25 payments beginning in 2011? Explain the basis for your decision.

7A.11 Suppose that eLake, an online auction site, is paying a dividend of $2 per share. You expect this dividend to grow 2 percent per year, and the interest rate is 10 percent. What is the most you would be willing to pay for a share of stock in eLake? If the interest rate is 5 percent, what is the most you would be willing to pay? When interest rates in the economy decline, would you expect stock prices in general to rise or fall? Explain.

7A.12 Suppose you buy the bond of a large corporation at a time when the inflation rate is very low. If the inflation rate increases during the time you hold the bond, what is likely to happen to the price of the bond?

7A.13 Use the information in the following table for calendar year 2006 to prepare the McDonald's Corporation's income statement. Be sure to include entries for operating income and net income.

Revenue from company restaurants	$16,083 million
Revenue from franchised restaurants	5,503 million
Cost of operating company-owned restaurants	13,542 million
Income taxes	1,293 million
Interest expense	402 million
General and administrative cost	2,338 million
Cost of restaurant leases	1,060 million
Other operating costs	67 million

Source: McDonald's Corporation, *Annual Report, 2006*, February 26, 2007.

7A.14 Use the information in the following table on the financial situation of Starbucks Corporation as of December 31, 2006, to prepare the firm's balance sheet. Be sure to include an entry for stockholders' equity.

Current assets	$1,530 million
Current liabilities	1,936 million
Property and equipment	2,288 million
Long-term liabilities	50 million
Goodwill	161 million
Other assets	187 million

Source: Starbucks Corporation, *Annual Report*, 2006.

7A.15 The *current ratio* is equal to a firm's current assets divided by its current liabilities. Use the information in Figure 7A-2 on page 239 to calculate Google's current ratio on December 31, 2006. Investors generally prefer that a firm's current ratio be greater than 1.5. What problems might a firm encounter if the value of its current assets is low relative to the value of its current liabilities?

>> End Appendix Learning Objective

Chapter 8

Comparative Advantage and the **Gains** from International Trade

Is Using Trade Policy to Help U.S. Industries a Good Idea?

Trade is, simply, the act of buying or selling. Is there a difference between trade that takes place within a country and international trade? Within the United States, domestic trade makes it possible for consumers in Ohio to eat salmon caught in Alaska or for consumers in Montana to drive cars built in Michigan or Kentucky. Similarly, international trade makes it possible for consumers in the United States to drink wine from France or use HD-DVD players from Japan. But one significant difference between domestic trade and international trade is that international trade is more controversial. At one time, nearly all the televisions, shoes, clothing, and toys consumed in the United States were also produced in the United States. Today, these goods are produced mainly by firms in other countries. This shift has benefited U.S. consumers because foreign-made goods have lower prices than the U.S.-made goods they have replaced. But at the same time, many U.S. firms that produced these goods have gone out of business, and their workers have had to find other jobs. Not surprisingly, opinion polls show that many Americans favor reducing international trade because they believe doing so would preserve jobs in the United States.

But do restrictions on trade actually preserve jobs? In fact, restrictions on trade may preserve jobs in particular industries, but only at the cost of reducing jobs in other industries. Consider, for example, U.S. policy on imports of sugar and imports of sugar-based ethanol. Ethanol is made from corn or sugar and can be used as a substitute for gasoline as a fuel in automobiles. Sugar is a better base for ethanol than corn because it ferments more quickly and is therefore cheaper to produce. In Brazil, ethanol is made from sugar, but in the United States, ethanol is made from corn. As a result, Brazilian ethanol costs just 80 cents a gallon, about half the cost of ethanol produced in the United States using corn. The Brazilian makers of ethanol would like to ship this cheap fuel to the United States, but the U.S. government has imposed a 54-cent-per-gallon tariff on imported ethanol. The tariff, combined with the cost of transporting the ethanol to the United States, effectively prices Brazilian ethanol out of the market.

The tariff helps U.S. firms that produce corn-based ethanol and U.S. farmers who grown corn, but it effectively increases fuel costs for many U.S. firms. The higher fuel costs make the products these firms produce more expensive, reducing sales and employment in the industries affected.

In addition to the tariff on sugar-based ethanol, Congress has also enacted a sugar quota, which limits the quantity of raw sugar allowed into the United States. Several countries around the world can produce sugar at lower costs than can U.S. sugar producers. As a result, the *world price* of sugar, which is the price at which sugar can be bought on the world market, is too low for U.S. sugar companies to cover their costs. The sugar quota allows U.S. companies to sell sugar domestically for a price that is about three times as high as the world price. Without the sugar quota, competition from foreign sugar producers would drive many U.S. producers out of business. But the United States also has a large candy industry, which uses many tons of sugar. The high price of sugar has led many U.S. candy firms to relocate their operations to other countries where the price of sugar is much lower. Life Savers, Star Brite mints, and Cherry Balls are a few of the candies no longer manufactured in the United States.

Should the United States have a tariff on imports of sugar-based ethanol and a quota on imports of raw sugar? The tariff and the quota create winners—U.S. producers of corn-based ethanol, U.S. sugar companies, and U.S. corn farmers—and losers—U.S. companies that use sugar, their employees, and U.S. consumers who must pay higher prices for goods that contain sugar and who are not able to buy low-priced sugar-based ethanol as an alternative to gasoline. In this chapter, we will explore who wins and who loses from international trade and review the political debate over whether international trade should be restricted. **AN INSIDE LOOK AT POLICY** on **page 268** discusses a recent trade agreement between the United States and South Korea.

Economics in YOUR Life!

Why Haven't You Heard of the Sugar Quota?

Politicians often support restrictions on trade to convince people to vote for them. The workers in the industries protected by tariffs and quotas are likely to vote for these politicians because the workers think trade restrictions will protect their jobs. But most people are not workers in industries protected from foreign competition by trade restrictions. We have seen that the sugar quota protects U.S. sugar companies and the people who work for them, but this amounts to only a few thousand people. Millions of consumers, though, have to pay higher prices for soft drinks, bakery goods, and candy because of the sugar quota. How, then, have sugar companies convinced Congress to enact the sugar quota and why have very few people even heard of the quota? As you read the chapter, see if can answer this question. You can check your answers against those we provide at the end of the chapter. >> Continued on page 267

M arkets for internationally traded goods and services can be analyzed using the tools of demand and supply that we developed in Chapter 3. We saw in Chapter 2 that trade in general—whether within a country or between countries—is based on the principle of comparative advantage. In this chapter, we look more closely at the role of comparative advantage in international trade. We also use the concepts of consumer surplus, producer surplus, and deadweight loss from Chapter 4 to analyze government policies, such as the sugar quota, that interfere with trade. With this background, we can return to the political debate over whether the United States benefits from international trade. We begin by looking at how large a role international trade plays in the U.S. economy.

8.1 LEARNING OBJECTIVE

8.1 | Discuss the role of international trade in the U.S. economy.

The United States in the International Economy

International trade has grown tremendously over the past 50 years. The increase in trade is the result of the falling costs of shipping products around the world, the spread of inexpensive and reliable communications, and changes in government policies. Firms can use large container ships to send their products across the oceans at low cost. Businesspeople today can travel to Europe or Asia using fast, inexpensive, and reliable air transportation. The Internet allows managers to communicate instantaneously and at a very low cost with customers and suppliers around the world. These and other improvements in transportation and communication have created a global marketplace that earlier generations of businesspeople could only dream of.

In addition, over the past 50 years, many governments have changed policies to facilitate international trade. For example, tariff rates have fallen. A **tariff** is a tax imposed by a government on *imports* of a good into a country. **Imports** are goods and services bought domestically but produced in other countries. In the 1930s, the United States charged an average tariff rate above 50 percent. Today, the rate is less than 2 percent. In North America, most tariffs between Canada, Mexico, and the United States were eliminated following the passage of the North American Free Trade Agreement (NAFTA) in 1994. Twenty-seven countries in Europe have formed the European Union, which has eliminated all tariffs among member countries, greatly increasing both imports and **exports**, which are goods and services produced domestically but sold to other countries.

The Importance of Trade to the U.S. Economy

U.S. consumers buy increasing quantities of goods and services produced in other countries. At the same time, U.S. businesses sell increasing quantities of goods and services to consumers in other countries. Figure 8-1 shows that since 1950, both exports and imports have been steadily increasing as a fraction of U.S. gross domestic product (GDP). Recall that GDP is the value of all the goods and services produced in a country during a year. In 1950, exports and imports were both about 4 percent of GDP. In 2006, exports were about 11 percent of GDP, and imports were about 17 percent.

Not all sectors of the U.S. economy are affected equally by international trade. For example, although it's difficult to import or export some services, such as haircuts or appendectomies, a large percentage of U.S. agricultural production is exported. Each year, the United States exports about 50 percent of the wheat crop, 40 percent of the rice crop, and 20 percent of the corn crop.

Many U.S. manufacturing industries also depend on trade. About 20 percent of U.S. manufacturing jobs depend directly or indirectly on exports. In some industries, such as computers, the products these workers make are directly exported. In other industries, such as steel, the products are used to make other products, such as bulldozers or

Tariff A tax imposed by a government on imports.

Imports Goods and services bought domestically but produced in other countries.

Exports Goods and services produced domestically but sold to other countries.

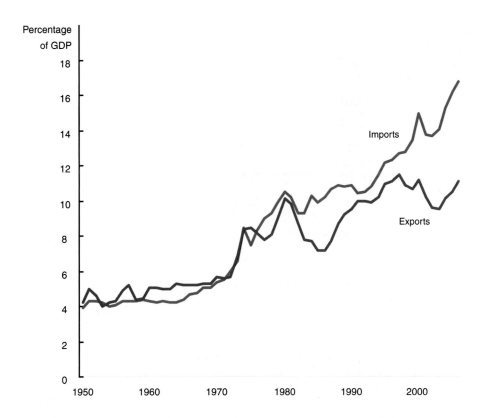

Figure 8-1

International Trade Is of Increasing Importance to the United States

Exports and imports of goods and services as a percentage of total production—measured by GDP—show the importance of international trade to an economy. Since 1950, both imports and exports have been steadily rising as a fraction of the U.S. GDP.
Source: U.S. Department of Commerce, Bureau of Economic Analysis.

machine tools, that are then exported. In all, about two-thirds of U.S. manufacturing industries depend on exports for at least 10 percent of jobs.

U.S. International Trade in a World Context

The United States is the largest exporter in the world, as Figure 8-2 illustrates. Six of the other seven leading exporting countries are also large, high-income countries. Although China is still a relatively low-income country, the rapid growth of the Chinese economy over the past 20 years has resulted in its becoming the third largest exporter.

International trade remains less important to the United States than it is to most other countries. Figure 8-3 shows that imports and exports remain smaller fractions of GDP in the United States than in other countries. In some smaller countries, like Belgium, imports and exports make up more than half of GDP. Japan is the only high-income country that is less dependent on international trade than is the United States.

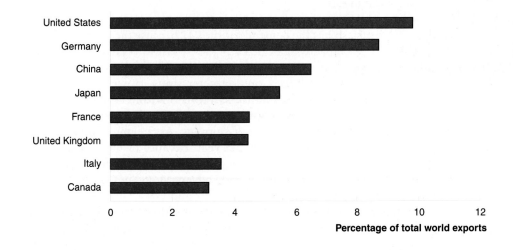

Figure 8-2

The Eight Leading Exporting Countries

The United States is the leading exporting country, accounting for about 10 percent of total world exports. The values are the shares of total world exports of merchandise and commercial services.
Source: World Trade Organization, *International Trade Statistics*, 2006. Reprinted by permission of WTO.

Figure 8-3

International Trade as a
Percentage of GDP

International trade is still less important to the
United States than to most other countries,
with the exception of Japan.
Source: International Monetary Fund, *International Financial Statistics Yearbook*, 2006.

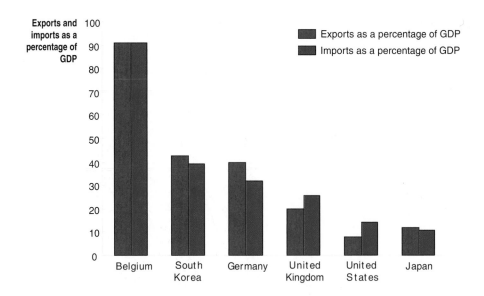

Exports and
imports as a
percentage of
GDP

Legend:
- Exports as a percentage of GDP
- Imports as a percentage of GDP

(Countries: Belgium, South Korea, Germany, United Kingdom, United States, Japan)

Making
the
Connection

How Expanding International Trade Has Helped Boeing

The Boeing 747 jumbo jet was a wonder of modern technology when it was introduced in 1970. With a much wider body than existing passenger planes, the 747 had two aisles, with as many as 10 seats per row, and could carry more than 500 passengers. Many early models had a second level with a passenger lounge, complete with a piano. Its range of more than 5,000 miles made it a truly intercontinental plane.

By the late 1990s, however, Boeing, which is based in Chicago and assembles the 747 outside of Seattle, Washington, was experiencing declining sales for the plane. Planes with newer technology were being introduced, and rising prices for jet fuel led some airlines to conclude that jumbo jets were too costly to operate. The decline in passenger travel after September 11, 2001, appeared to be the last nail in the 747's coffin. An executive for Airbus, a European firm that is Boeing's main competitor, boasted, "The 747 is on its last legs. It doesn't have any legs to stand on. Boeing is trying to breathe life into a 1960s-era design. There is only so much you can do with a plane." But in the past few years, the 747 has gone through an unexpected revival, spurred largely by recent growth in international trade. In the 1960s, Boeing's managers made the important decision that the 747 be designed to serve as both a cargo plane and a passenger plane. For example, the nose cone was designed to open to make loading cargo easier.

As international trade has grown rapidly in the past few years, so has the demand for the 747 because the plane has larger cargo capacity than other planes. Most low-value goods being shipped long distances—for instance, from China to Europe—are still sent by sea on container ships. However, high-value goods—such as computers, televisions, and some food products—are increasingly likely to be sent by plane, which is a much faster and safer method of shipping. Air freight shipments have been growing at the rapid rate of 6 percent per year. Because of its large carrying capacity, currently about 60 percent of all air freight worldwide is carried on 747s. The latest model, the 747-400, has new, technologically advanced engines and redesigned wings. It has a maximum speed of 675 miles per hour and has a range of more than 7,500 miles—enough to fly nonstop from Los Angeles to Melbourne, Australia. The increased fuel efficiency of the new engines has reduced operating costs. In 2006,

Rapid growth of international trade has spurred demand for the 747 because it has larger cargo capacity than other planes.

Boeing received orders for 67 airplanes worth $16.75 billion. That's good news for Boeing's 120,000 employees in the United States.

Sources: Leslie Wayne, "Boeing Not Afraid to Say 'Sold Out,'" *New York Times*, November 28, 2006; Leslie Wayne, "Far from Extinct," *New York Times*, December 7, 2006; and Leslie Wayne, "Still Flying High," *New York Times*, December 25, 2006.

YOUR TURN: Test your understanding by doing related problem 1.4 on page 270 at the end of this chapter.

8.2 | Understand the difference between comparative advantage and absolute advantage in international trade.

Comparative Advantage in International Trade

Why have businesses around the world increasingly looked for markets in other countries? Why have consumers increasingly purchased goods and services made in other countries? People trade for one reason: Trade makes them better off. Whenever a buyer and seller agree to a sale, they must both believe they are better off; otherwise, there would be no sale. This outcome must hold whether the buyer and seller live in the same city or in different countries. As we will see, governments are more likely to interfere with international trade than they are with domestic trade, but the reasons for the interference are more political than economic.

A Brief Review of Comparative Advantage

In Chapter 2, we discussed the key economic concept of *comparative advantage*. **Comparative advantage** is the ability of an individual, a firm, or a country to produce a good or service at a lower opportunity cost than competitors. Recall that **opportunity cost** is the highest-valued alternative that must be given up to engage in an activity. People, firms, and countries specialize in economic activities in which they have a comparative advantage. In trading, we benefit from the comparative advantage of other people (or firms or countries), and others benefit from our comparative advantage.

A good way to think of comparative advantage is to recall the example in Chapter 2 of you and your neighbor picking fruit. Your neighbor is better at picking both apples and cherries than you are. Why, then, doesn't your neighbor pick both types of fruit? Because the opportunity cost to your neighbor of picking her own apples is very high: She is a particularly skilled cherry picker, and every hour spent picking apples is an hour taken away from picking cherries. You can pick apples at a much lower opportunity cost than your neighbor, so you have a comparative advantage in picking apples. Your neighbor can pick cherries at a much lower opportunity cost than you can, so she has a comparative advantage in picking cherries. Your neighbor is better off specializing in picking cherries, and you are better off specializing in picking apples. You can then trade some of your apples for some of your neighbor's cherries, and both of you will end up with more of each fruit.

Comparative advantage The ability of an individual, a firm, or a country to produce a good or service at a lower opportunity cost than competitors.

Opportunity Cost The highest-valued alternative that must be given up to engage in an activity.

Comparative Advantage in International Trade

The principle of comparative advantage can explain why people pursue different occupations. It can also explain why countries produce different goods and services. International trade involves many countries importing and exporting many different goods and services. Countries are better off if they specialize in producing the goods for which they have a comparative advantage. They can then trade for the goods for which other countries have a comparative advantage.

We can illustrate why specializing on the basis of comparative advantage makes countries better off with a simple example involving just two countries and two products.

TABLE 8-1

An Example of Japanese Workers Being More Productive Than American Workers

	OUTPUT PER HOUR OF WORK	
	CELL PHONES	DIGITAL MUSIC PLAYERS
JAPAN	12	6
UNITED STATES	2	4

Suppose the United States and Japan produce only cell phones and digital music players, like Apple's iPod. Assume that each country uses only labor to produce each good, and that Japanese and U.S. cell phones and digital music players are exactly the same. Table 8-1 shows how much each country can produce of each good with one hour of labor.

Notice that Japanese workers are more productive than U.S. workers in making both goods. In one hour of work, Japanese workers can make six times as many cell phones and one and one-half times as many digital music players as U.S. workers. Japan has an *absolute advantage* over the United States in producing both goods. **Absolute advantage** is the ability to produce more of a good or service than competitors when using the same amount of resources. In this case, Japan can produce more of both goods using the same amount of labor as the United States.

It might seem at first that Japan has nothing to gain from trading with the United States because it has an absolute advantage in producing both goods. However, Japan should specialize and produce only cell phones and obtain the digital music players it needs by exporting cell phones to the United States in exchange for digital music players. The reason that Japan benefits from trade is that although it has an *absolute advantage* in the production of both goods, it has a *comparative advantage* only in the production of cell phones. The United States has a comparative advantage in the production of digital music players.

If it seems contrary to common sense that Japan should import digital music players from the United States even though Japan can produce more players per hour of work, think about the opportunity cost to each country of producing each good. If Japan wants to produce more digital music players, it has to switch labor away from cell phone production. Every hour of labor switched from producing cell phones to producing digital music players increases digital music player production by 6 and reduces cell phone production by 12. Japan has to give up 12 cell phones for every 6 digital music players it produces. Therefore, the opportunity cost to Japan of producing one more digital music player is 12/6, or 2 cell phones.

If the United States switches one hour of labor from cell phones to digital music players, production of cell phones falls by 2, and production of digital music players rises by 4. Therefore, the opportunity cost to the United States of producing one more digital music player is 2/4, or 0.5 cell phone. The United States has a lower opportunity cost of producing digital music players and, therefore, has a comparative advantage in making this product. By similar reasoning, we can see that Japan has a comparative advantage in producing cell phones. Table 8-2 summarizes the opportunity each country faces in producing these goods.

Absolute advantage The ability to produce more of a good or service than competitors when using the same amount of resources.

TABLE 8-2 | The Opportunity Costs of Producing Cell Phones and Digital Music Players

The table shows the opportunity cost each country faces in producing cell phones and digital music players. For example, the entry in the first row and second column shows that Japan must give up 2 cell phones for every digital music player it produces.

	OPPORTUNITY COSTS	
	CELL PHONES	DIGITAL MUSIC PLAYERS
JAPAN	0.5 digital music player	2 cell phones
UNITED STATES	2 digital music players	0.5 cell phone

How Countries Gain from International Trade

Can Japan really gain from producing only cell phones and trading with the United States for digital music players? To see that it can, assume at first that Japan and the United States do not trade with each other. A situation in which a country does not trade with other countries is called **autarky**. Assume that in autarky each country has 1,000 hours of labor available to produce the two goods, and each country produces the quantities of the two goods shown in Table 8-3. Because there is no trade, these quantities also represent consumption of the two goods in each country.

Autarky A situation in which a country does not trade with other countries.

Increasing Consumption through Trade

Suppose now that Japan and the United States begin to trade with each other. The **terms of trade** is the ratio at which a country can trade its exports for imports from other countries. For simplicity, let's assume that the terms of trade end up with Japan and the United States being willing to trade one cell phone for one digital music player.

Once trade has begun, the United States and Japan can exchange digital music players for cell phones or cell phones for digital music players. For example, if Japan specializes by using all 1,000 available hours of labor to produce cell phones, it will be able to produce 12,000. It then could export 1,500 cell phones to the United States in exchange for 1,500 digital music players. (Remember: We are assuming that the terms of trade are one cell phone for one digital music player.) Japan ends up with 10,500 cell phones and 1,500 digital music players. Compared with the situation before trade, Japan has the same number of digital music players but 1,500 more cell phones. If the United States specializes in producing digital music players, it will be able to produce 4,000. It could then export 1,500 digital music players to Japan in exchange for 1,500 cell phones. The United States ends up with 2,500 digital music players and 1,500 cell phones. Compared with the situation before trade, the United States has the same number of cell phones but 1,500 more digital music players. Trade has allowed both countries to increase the quantities of goods consumed. Table 8-4 summarizes the gains from trade for the United States and Japan.

By trading, Japan and the United States are able to consume more than they could without trade. This outcome is possible because world production of both goods increases after trade. (Remember that, in this example, our "world" consists of just the United States and Japan.)

Why does total production of cell phones and digital music players increase when the United States specializes in producing digital music players and Japan specializes in producing cell phones? A domestic analogy helps to answer this question: If a company shifts production from an old factory to a more efficient modern factory, its output will increase. In effect, the same thing happens in our example. Producing digital music players in Japan and cell phones in the United States is inefficient. Shifting production to the more efficient country—the one with the comparative advantage—increases total production. The key point is this: *Countries gain from specializing in producing goods in which they have a comparative advantage and trading for goods in which other countries have a comparative advantage.*

Terms of trade The ratio at which a country can trade its exports for imports from other countries.

	PRODUCTION AND CONSUMPTION	
	CELL PHONES	DIGITAL MUSIC PLAYERS
JAPAN	9,000	1,500
UNITED STATES	1,500	1,000

TABLE 8-3

Production without Trade

TABLE 8-4

The Gains from Trade for Japan and the United States

WITHOUT TRADE

Production and Consumption

	CELL PHONES	MP3 PLAYERS
Japan	9,000	1,500
United States	1,500	1,000

WITH TRADE

	Production with Trade		Trade		Consumption with Trade	
	CELL PHONES	MP3 PLAYERS	CELL PHONES	MP3 PLAYERS	CELL PHONES	MP3 PLAYERS
Japan	12,000	0	Export 1,500	Import 1,500	10,500	1,500
United States	0	4,000	Import 1,500	Export 1,500	1,500	2,500

With trade, the United States and Japan specialize in the good they have a comparative advantage in producing . . .

. . . and export some of that good in exchange for the good the other country has a comparative advantage in producing.

GAINS FROM TRADE

Increased Consumption

Japan	1,500 Cell Phones
United States	1,500 MP3 Players

The increased consumption made possible by trade represents the gains from trade.

Solved Problem │ 8-3

The Gains from Trade

The first discussion of comparative advantage appears in *On the Principles of Political Economy and Taxation*, a book written by David Ricardo in 1817. Ricardo provided a famous example of the gains from trade, using wine and cloth production in Portugal and England. The following table is adapted from Ricardo's example, with cloth measured in sheets and wine measured in kegs.

OUTPUT PER YEAR OF LABOR

	CLOTH	WINE
PORTUGAL	100	150
ENGLAND	90	60

a. Explain which country has an absolute advantage in the production of each good.

b. Explain which country has a comparative advantage in the production of each good.

c. Suppose that Portugal and England currently do not trade with each other. Each country has 1,000 workers, so each has 1,000 years of labor time to use producing cloth and wine, and the countries are currently producing the amounts of each good shown in the table:

	CLOTH	WINE
PORTUGAL	18,000	123,000
ENGLAND	63,000	18,000

Show that Portugal and England can both gain from trade. Assume that the terms of trade are that one sheet of cloth can be traded for one keg of wine.

SOLVING THE PROBLEM:

Step 1: **Review the chapter material.** This problem is about absolute and comparative advantage and the gains from trade, so you may want to review the section "Comparative Advantage in International Trade," which begins on page 247, and the section "How Countries Gain from International Trade," which begins on page 249.

Step 2: **Answer question (a) by determining which country has an absolute advantage.** Remember that a country has an absolute advantage over another country when it can produce more of a good using the same resources. The first table in the problem shows that Portugal can produce more cloth *and* more wine with one year's worth of labor than can England. Thus, Portugal has an absolute advantage in the production of both goods and, therefore, England does not have an absolute advantage in the production of either good.

Step 3: **Answer question (b) by determining which country has a comparative advantage.** A country has a comparative advantage when it can produce a good at a lower opportunity cost. To produce 100 sheets of cloth, Portugal must give up 150 kegs of wine. Therefore, the opportunity cost to Portugal of producing one sheet of cloth is 150/100, or 1.5 kegs of wine. England has to give up 60 kegs of wine to produce 90 sheets of cloth, so its opportunity cost of producing one sheet of cloth is 60/90, or 0.67 keg of wine. The opportunity costs of producing wine can be calculated in the same way. The following table shows the opportunity cost to Portugal and England of producing each good.

OPPORTUNITY COSTS

	CLOTH	WINE
PORTUGAL	1.5 kegs of wine	0.67 sheets of cloth
ENGLAND	0.67 keg of wine	1.5 sheets of cloth

Portugal has a comparative advantage in wine because its opportunity cost is lower. England has a comparative advantage in cloth because its opportunity cost is lower.

Step 4: **Answer question (c) by showing that both countries can benefit from trade.** By now it should be clear that both countries will be better off if they specialize where they have a comparative advantage and trade for the other product. The following table is very similar to Table 8-4 and shows one example of trade making both countries better off. (To test your understanding, construct another example.)

WITHOUT TRADE

	PRODUCTION AND CONSUMPTION	
	CLOTH	WINE
PORTUGAL	18,000	123,000
ENGLAND	63,000	18,000

WITH TRADE

	PRODUCTION WITH TRADE		TRADE		CONSUMPTION WITH TRADE	
	CLOTH	WINE	CLOTH	WINE	CLOTH	WINE
PORTUGAL	0	150,000	Import 18,000	Export 18,000	18,000	132,000
ENGLAND	90,000	0	Export 18,000	Import 18,000	72,000	18,000

GAINS FROM TRADE

	INCREASED CONSUMPTION
PORTUGAL	9,000 wine
ENGLAND	9,000 cloth

YOUR TURN: For more practice, do related problems 3.4 and 3.5 on page 272 at the end of this chapter.

>> End Solved Problem 8-3

Why Don't We See Complete Specialization?

In our example of two countries producing only two products, each country specializes in producing one of the goods. In the real world, many goods and services are produced in more than one country. For example, the United States and Japan both produce automobiles. We do not see complete specialization in the real world for three main reasons:

- *Not all goods and services are traded internationally.* Even if, for example, Japan had a comparative advantage in the production of medical services, it would be difficult for Japan to specialize in producing medical services and then export them. There is no easy way for U.S. patients who need appendectomies to receive them from surgeons in Japan.

- *Production of most goods involves increasing opportunity costs.* Recall from Chapter 2 that production of most goods involves increasing opportunity costs. As a result, when the United States devotes more workers to producing digital music players, the opportunity cost of producing more digital music players will increase. At some point, the opportunity cost of producing digital music players in the United States may rise to the level of the opportunity cost of producing digital music players in Japan. When that happens, international trade will no longer push the United States further toward complete specialization. The same will be true of Japan: Increasing opportunity cost will cause Japan to stop short of complete specialization in producing cell phones.

- *Tastes for products differ.* Most products are *differentiated*. Cell phones, digital music players, cars, and televisions—to name just a few products—come with a wide variety of features. When buying automobiles, some people look for reliability and good gasoline mileage, others look for room to carry seven passengers, and still others want styling and high performance. So, some car buyers prefer Toyota Prius hybrids, some prefer Chevy Suburbans, and others prefer BMWs. As a result, Japan, the United States, and Germany may each have a comparative advantage in producing different types of automobiles.

Does Anyone Lose as a Result of International Trade?

In our cell phone and digital music player example, consumption increases in both the United States and Japan as a result of trade. Everyone gains, and no one loses. Or do they? In our example, we referred repeatedly to "Japan" or the "United States" producing cell phones or digital music players. But countries do not produce goods—firms do. In a

Don't Let This Happen to **YOU!**

Remember That Trade Creates Both Winners and Losers

The following statement is from a Federal Reserve publication: "Trade is a win–win situation for all countries that participate." Statements like this are sometimes taken to mean that there are no losers from international trade. But notice that the statement refers to *countries*, not individuals. When countries participate in trade, they make their consumers better off by increasing the quantity of goods and services available to them. As we have seen, however, expanding trade eliminates the jobs of workers employed at companies that are less efficient than foreign companies. Trade also creates new jobs at companies that export to foreign markets. It may be difficult, though, for workers who

lose their jobs because of trade to easily find others. That is why in the United States, the federal government uses the Trade Adjustment Assistance program to provide funds for workers who have lost their jobs due to international trade. These funds can be used for retraining, for searching for new jobs, or for relocating to areas where new jobs are available. This program—and similar programs in other countries—recognizes that there are losers from international trade as well as winners.

Source: Quote from Federal Reserve Bank of Dallas Web site, *International Trade and the Economy*, www.dallasfed.org/educate/everyday/ev7.html.

YOUR TURN: Test your understanding by doing related problem 3.12 on page 272 at the end of this chapter.

world without trade, there would be cell phone and digital music player firms in both Japan and the United States. In a world with trade, there would only be Japanese cell phone firms and U.S. digital music player firms. Japanese digital music player firms and U.S. cell phone firms would close. Overall, total employment will not change and production will increase as a result of trade. Nevertheless, the owners of Japanese digital music player firms, the owners of U.S. cell phone firms, and the people who work for them are worse off as a result of trade. The losers from trade are likely to do their best to convince the Japanese and U.S. governments to interfere with trade by barring imports of the competing products from the other country or by imposing high tariffs on them.

Where Does Comparative Advantage Come From?

Among the main sources of comparative advantage are the following:

- *Climate and natural resources.* This source of comparative advantage is the most obvious. Because of geology, Saudi Arabia has a comparative advantage in the production of oil. Because of climate and soil conditions, Costa Rica has a comparative advantage in the production of bananas, and the United States has a comparative advantage in the production of wheat.

- *Relative abundance of labor and capital.* Some countries, such as the United States, have many highly skilled workers and a great deal of machinery. Other countries, such as China, have many unskilled workers and relatively little machinery. As a result, the United States has a comparative advantage in the production of goods that require highly skilled workers or sophisticated machinery to manufacture, such as aircraft, semiconductors, and computer software. China has a comparative advantage in the production of goods that require unskilled workers and small amounts of simple machinery, such as children's toys.

- *Technology.* Broadly defined, *technology* is the process firms use to turn inputs into goods and services. At any given time, firms in different countries do not all have access to the same technologies. In part, this difference is the result of past investments countries have made in supporting higher education or in providing support for research and development. Some countries are strong in *product technologies*, which involve the ability to develop new products. For example, firms in the United States have pioneered the development of such products as televisions, digital computers, airliners, and many prescription drugs. Other countries are strong in *process technologies*, which involve the ability to improve the processes used to make existing products. For example, firms in Japan, such as Toyota and Nissan, have succeeded by greatly improving the processes for designing and manufacturing automobiles.

- *External economies.* It is difficult to explain the location of some industries on the basis of climate, natural resources, the relative abundance of labor and capital, or technology. For example, why does Southern California have a comparative advantage in making movies or Switzerland in making watches or New York in providing financial services? The answer is that once an industry becomes established in an area, firms that locate in that area gain advantages over firms located elsewhere. The advantages include the availability of skilled workers, the opportunity to interact with other firms in the same industry, and being close to suppliers. These advantages result in lower costs to firms located in the area. Because these lower costs result from increases in the size of the industry in an area, economists refer to them as **external economies**.

External economies Reductions in a firm's costs that result from an increase in the size of an industry.

Making the Connection | Why Is Dalton, Georgia, the Carpet-Making Capital of the World?

Factories within a 65-mile radius of Dalton, Georgia account for 80 percent of U.S. carpet production and more than half of world carpet production. Carpet production is highly automated and relies primarily on synthetic fibers. Dalton, a small city located in rural northwest Georgia, would not seem to have any advantages in carpet production. In fact, the location of the carpet industry in Dalton was a historical accident.

In the early 1900s, Catherine Evans Whitener started making bedspreads using a method called "tufting," in which she sewed cotton yarn through the fabric and then cut the ends of the yarn so it would fluff up. These bedspreads became very popular. By the 1930s, the process was mechanized and was then applied to carpets. In the early years, the industry used cotton grown in Georgia, but today synthetic fibers, such as nylon and olefin, have largely replaced cotton and wool in carpet manufacturing.

More than 170 carpet factories are now located in the Dalton area. Supporting the carpet industry are local yarn manufacturers, machinery suppliers, and maintenance firms. Dye plants have opened solely to supply the carpet industry. Printing shops have opened, solely to print tags and labels for carpets. Box factories have opened to produce cartons designed specifically for shipping carpets. The local workforce has developed highly specialized skills for running and maintaining the carpet-making machinery.

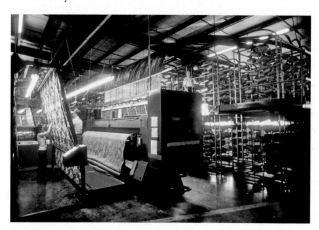

Because Catherine Evans Whitener started making bedspreads by hand in Dalton, Georgia, 100 years ago, a multibillion-dollar carpet industry is now located there.

A company establishing a carpet factory outside the Dalton area is unable to use the suppliers or the skilled workers available to factories in Dalton. As a result, carpet factories located outside Dalton may have higher costs than factories located in Dalton. Although there is no particular reason why the carpet industry should have originally located in Dalton, external economies gave the area a comparative advantage in carpet making once it began to grow there.

YOUR TURN: Test your understanding by doing related problem 3.13 on page 272 at the end of this chapter.

Comparative Advantage Over Time: The Rise and Fall—and Rise—of the U.S. Consumer Electronics Industry

A country may develop a comparative advantage in the production of a good, and then, as time passes and circumstances change, the country may lose its comparative advantage in producing that good and develop a comparative advantage in producing other goods. For several decades, the United States had a comparative advantage in the production of consumer electronic goods, such as televisions, radios, and stereos. The comparative advantage of the United States in these products was based on having developed most of the underlying technology, having the most modern factories, and having a skilled and experienced workforce. Gradually, however, other countries, particularly Japan, gained access to the technology, built modern factories, and developed skilled workforces. As mentioned earlier, Japanese firms have excelled in process technologies, which involve the ability to improve the processes used to make existing products. By the 1970s and 1980s, Japanese firms were able to produce many consumer electronic goods more cheaply and with higher quality than could U.S. firms. Japanese firms Sony, Panasonic, and Pioneer replaced U.S. firms Magnavox, Zenith, and RCA as world leaders in consumer electronics.

By 2007, however, as the technology underlying consumer electronics evolved, comparative advantage had shifted again, and several U.S. firms surged ahead of their Japanese competitors. For example, Apple Computer had developed the iPod and iPhone; Linksys, a division of Cisco Systems, took the lead in home wireless networking technology; and Kodak developed digital cameras with EasyShare software that made it easy to organize, enhance, and share digital pictures. As pictures and music converted to digital data, process technologies became less important than the ability to design and develop new products. These new consumer electronics products required skills similar to those in computer design and software writing, where the United States had long maintained a comparative advantage.

Once a country has lost its comparative advantage in producing a good, its income will be higher and its economy will be more efficient if it switches from producing the good to importing it, as the United States did when it switched from producing televisions to importing them. As we will see in the next section, however, there is often political pressure on governments to attempt to preserve industries that have lost their comparative advantage.

8.4 | Analyze the economic effects of government policies that restrict international trade.

8.4 LEARNING OBJECTIVE

Government Policies That Restrict International Trade

Free trade, or trade between countries that is without government restrictions, makes consumers better off. We can expand on this idea by using the concepts of consumer surplus and producer surplus from Chapter 4. Figure 8-4 shows the market for the biofuel ethanol in the United States, assuming autarky, where the United States does not trade with other countries. The equilibrium price of ethanol is $2.00 per gallon, and the equilibrium quantity is 6.0 billion gallons per year. The blue area represents consumer surplus, and the red area represents producer surplus.

Now suppose that the United States begins importing ethanol from Brazil and other countries that produce lower-priced sugar-based ethanol and that ethanol is selling in those countries for $1.00 per gallon. Because the world market for ethanol is large, we will assume that the United States can buy as much ethanol as it wants without causing

Free trade Trade between countries that is without government restrictions.

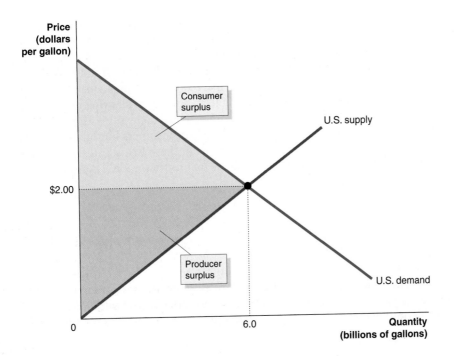

Figure 8-4

The U.S. Market for Ethanol under Autarky

This figure shows the market for ethanol in the United States, assuming autarky, where the United States does not trade with other countries. The equilibrium price of ethanol is $2.00 per gallon, and the equilibrium quantity is 6.0 billion gallons per year. The blue area represents consumer surplus, and the red area represents producer surplus.

Figure 8-5

The Effect of Imports on the U.S. Ethanol Market

When imports are allowed into the United States, the price of ethanol falls from $2.00 to $1.00. U.S. consumers increase their purchases from 6.0 billion gallons to 9.0 billion gallons. Equilibrium moves from point F to point G. U.S. producers reduce the quantity of ethanol they supply from 6.0 billion gallons to 3.0 billion gallons. Imports equal 6.0 billion gallons, which is the difference between U.S. consumption and U.S. production. Consumer surplus equals the areas A, B, C, and D. Producer surplus equals the area E.

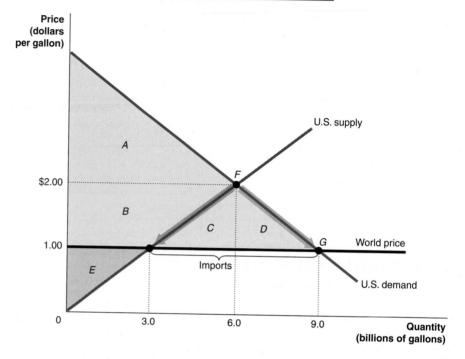

	Under Autarky	With Imports
Consumer Surplus	A	$A + B + C + D$
Producer Surplus	$B + E$	E
Economic Surplus	$A + B + E$	$A + B + C + D + E$

the *world price* of $1.00 per gallon to rise. Therefore, once imports of ethanol are permitted into the United States, U.S. firms will not be able to sell ethanol at prices higher than the world price of $1.00, and the U.S. price will become equal to the world price.

Figure 8-5 shows the result of allowing imports of ethanol into the United States. With the price lowered from $2.00 to $1.00, U.S. consumers increase their purchases from 6.0 billion gallons to 9.0 billion gallons. Equilibrium moves from point F to point G. In the new equilibrium, U.S. producers have reduced the quantity of ethanol they supply from 6.0 billion gallons to 3.0 billion gallons. Imports will equal 6.0 billion gallons, which is the difference between U.S. consumption and U.S. production.

Under autarky, consumer surplus would be area A in Figure 8-5. With imports, the reduction in price increases consumer surplus, so it is now equal to the sum of areas A, B, C, and D. Although the lower price increases consumer surplus, it reduces producer surplus. Under autarky, producer surplus was equal to the sum of the areas B and E. With imports, producer surplus is equal to only area E. Recall that economic surplus equals the sum of consumer surplus and producer surplus. Moving from autarky to allowing imports increases economic surplus in the United States by an amount equal to the sum of areas C and D.

We can conclude that international trade helps consumers but hurts firms that are less efficient than foreign competitors. As a result, these firms and their workers are often strong supporters of government policies that restrict trade. These policies usually take one of two forms:

- Tariffs

- Quotas and voluntary export restraints

Tariffs

The most common interferences with trade are *tariffs*, which are taxes imposed by a government on goods imported into a country. Like any other tax, a tariff increases the cost of selling a good. Figure 8-6 shows the impact of a tariff of $0.50 per gallon on ethanol

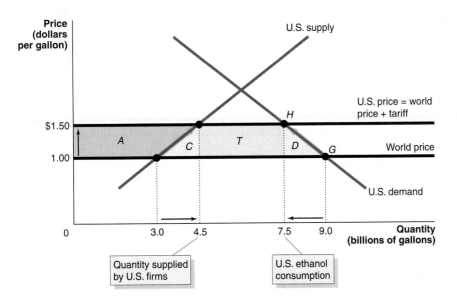

Loss of Consumer Surplus	=	Increase in Producer Surplus	+	Government Tariff Revenue	+	Deadweight Loss
A + C + T + D		A		T		C + D

Figure 8-6

The Effects of a Tariff on Ethanol

Without a tariff on ethanol, U.S. producers will sell 3.0 billion gallons of ethanol, U.S. consumers will purchase 9.0 billion gallons, and imports will be 6.0 billion gallons. The U.S. price will equal the world price of $1.00 per gallon. The $0.50-per-gallon tariff raises the price of ethanol in the United States to $1.50 per gallon, and U.S. producers increase the quantity they supply to 4.5 billion gallons. U.S. consumers reduce their purchases to 7.5 billion gallons. Equilibrium moves from point *G* to point *H*. The ethanol tariff causes a loss of consumer surplus equal to the area *A* + *C* + *T* + *D*. The area *A* is the increase in producer surplus due to the higher price. The area *T* is the government's tariff revenue. The areas *C* and *D* represent deadweight loss.

imports into the United States. The $0.50 tariff raises the price of ethanol in the United States from the world price of $1.00 per gallon to $1.50 per gallon. At this higher price, U.S. ethanol producers increase the quantity they supply from 3.0 billion gallons to 4.5 billion gallons. U.S. consumers, though, cut back their purchases of ethanol from 9.0 billion gallons to 7.5 billion gallons. Imports decline from 6.0 billion gallons (9 billion − 6 billion) to 3.0 billion (7.5 billion − 4.5 billion). Equilibrium moves from point *G* to point *H*.

By raising the price of ethanol from $1.00 to $1.50, the tariff reduces consumer surplus by the sum of areas *A*, *T*, *C*, and *D*. Area *A* is the increase in producer surplus from the higher price. The government collects tariff revenue equal to the tariff of $0.50 per gallon multiplied by the 3.0 billion gallons imported. Area *T* represents the government's tariff revenue. Areas *C* and *D* represent losses to U.S. consumers that are not captured by anyone. They are deadweight loss and represent the decline in economic efficiency resulting from the ethanol tariff. Area *C* shows the effect on U.S. consumers of being forced to buy from U.S. producers who are less efficient than foreign producers, and area *D* shows the effect of U.S. consumers buying less ethanol than they would have at the world price. As a result of the tariff, economic surplus has been reduced by the sum of areas *C* and *D*. Recall from Chapter 4 that deadweight loss represents a loss of economic efficiency.

We can conclude that the tariff succeeds in helping U.S. ethanol producers but hurts U.S. consumers and the efficiency of the U.S. economy.

Quotas and Voluntary Export Restraints

A **quota** is a numeric limit on the quantity of a good that can be imported, and it has an effect similar to a tariff. A quota is imposed by the government of the importing country. A **voluntary export restraint (VER)** is an agreement negotiated between two countries that places a numeric limit on the quantity of a good that can be imported by one country from the other country. In the early 1980s, the United States and Japan negotiated a VER that limited the quantity of automobiles the United States would import from Japan. The Japanese government agreed to the VER primarily because it was afraid

Quota A numeric limit imposed by a government on the quantity of a good that can be imported into the country.

Voluntary export restraint (VER) An agreement negotiated between two countries that places a numeric limit on the quantity of a good that can be imported by one country from the other country.

that if it did not, the United States would impose a tariff or quota on imports of Japanese automobiles. Quotas and VERs have similar economic effects.

The main purpose of most tariffs and quotas is to reduce the foreign competition that domestic firms face. We saw an example of this at the beginning of this chapter when we discussed the sugar quota, which Congress imposed to protect U.S. sugar producers. Figure 8-7 shows the actual statistics for the U.S. sugar market in 2006. The effect of a quota is very similar to the effect of a tariff. By limiting imports, a quota forces the domestic price of a good above the world price. In this case, the sugar quota limits sugar imports to 3.5 billion pounds (shown by the bracket in Figure 8-7), forcing the U.S. price of sugar up to $0.22 per pound, or $0.10 higher than the world price. The U.S. price is above the world price because the quota keeps foreign sugar producers from selling the additional sugar in the United States that would drive the price down to the world price. At a price of $0.22 cents per pound, U.S. producers increased the quantity of sugar they supply from 5.9 billion pounds to 18.0 billion pounds, and U.S. consumers cut back their purchases of sugar from 23.1 billion pounds to 21.5 billion pounds. Equilibrium moves from point E to point F.

Measuring the Economic Effect of the Sugar Quota

Once again, we can use the concepts of consumer surplus, producer surplus, and deadweight loss to measure the economic impact of the sugar quota. Without a sugar quota, the world price of $0.12 per pound would also be the U.S. price. In Figure 8-7, consumer surplus equals the area above the $0.12 price line and below the demand curve. The sugar quota causes the U.S. price to rise to $0.22 cents and reduces consumer surplus by the area $A + B + C + D$. Without a sugar quota, producer surplus received by U.S. sugar producers would be equal to the area below the $0.12 price line and above the supply

Figure 8-7

The Economic Effect of the U.S. Sugar Quota

Without a sugar quota, U.S. sugar producers would have sold 5.9 billion pounds of sugar, U.S. consumers would have purchased 23.1 billion pounds of sugar, and imports would have been 17.2 billion pounds. The U.S. price would have equaled the world price of $0.12 per pound. Because the sugar quota limits imports to 3.5 billion pounds (the bracket in the graph), the price of sugar in the United States rises to $0.22 per pound, and U.S. producers increase the quantity of sugar they supply to 18.0 billion pounds. U.S. consumers reduce their sugar purchases to 21.5 billion pounds. Equilibrium moves from point E to point F. The sugar quota causes a loss of consumer surplus equal to the area $A + B + C + D$. The area A is the gain to U.S. sugar producers. The area B is the gain to foreign sugar producers. The areas C and D represent deadweight loss. The total loss to U.S. consumers in 2006 was $2.24 billion.

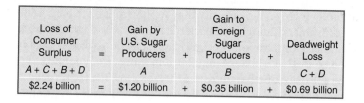

Loss of Consumer Surplus	=	Gain by U.S. Sugar Producers	+	Gain to Foreign Sugar Producers	+	Deadweight Loss
$A + C + B + D$		A		B		$C + D$
$2.24 billion	=	$1.20 billion	+	$0.35 billion	+	$0.69 billion

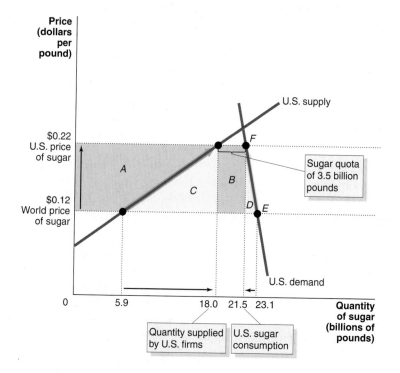

curve. The higher U.S. price resulting from the sugar quota increases the producer surplus of U.S. sugar producers by an amount equal to area *A*.

A foreign producer must have a license from the U.S. government to import sugar under the quota system. Therefore, a foreign sugar producer that is lucky enough to have an import license also benefits from the quota because it is able to sell sugar on the U.S. market at $0.22 per pound instead of $0.12 per pound. The gain to foreign sugar producers is area *B*. Areas *A* and *B* represent transfers from U.S. consumers of sugar to U.S. and foreign producers of sugar. Areas *C* and *D* represent losses to U.S. consumers that are not captured by anyone. They are deadweight losses and represent the decline in economic efficiency resulting from the sugar quota. Area *C* shows the effect of U.S. consumers being forced to buy from U.S. producers that are less efficient than foreign producers, and area *D* shows the effect of U.S. consumers buying less sugar than they would have at the world price.

Figure 8-7 provides enough information to calculate the dollar value of each of the four areas. The results of these calculations are shown in the table in the figure. The total loss to consumers from the sugar quota was $2.24 billion in 2006. About 53 percent of the loss to consumers, or $1.20 billion, was gained by U.S. sugar producers as increased producer surplus. About 16 percent, or $0.35 billion, was gained by foreign sugar producers as increased producer surplus, and about 31 percent, or $0.69 billion, was a deadweight loss to the U.S. economy. The U.S. International Trade Commission estimates that eliminating the sugar quota would result in the loss of about 3,000 jobs in the U.S. sugar industry. The cost to U.S. consumers of saving these jobs is equal to $2.24 billion/3,000, or about $750,000 per job. In fact, this cost is an underestimate because eliminating the sugar quota would result in new jobs being created, particularly in the candy industry. As we saw at the beginning of this chapter, U.S. candy companies have been moving factories to other countries to escape the impact of the sugar quota.

Solved Problem | 8-4

Measuring the Economic Effect of a Quota

Suppose that the United States currently both produces and imports apples. The U.S. government then decides to restrict international trade in apples by imposing a quota that allows imports of only 4 million boxes of apples into the United States each year. The figure shows the results of imposing the quota.

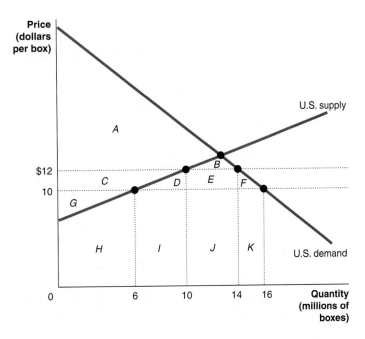

Fill in the following table, using the prices, quantities, and letters in the figure:

	WITHOUT QUOTA	WITH QUOTA
World price of apples	_____	_____
U.S. price of apples	_____	_____
Quantity supplied by U.S. firms	_____	_____
Quantity demanded by U.S. consumers	_____	_____
Quantity imported	_____	_____
Area of consumer surplus	_____	_____
Area of producer surplus	_____	_____
Area of deadweight loss	_____	_____

SOLVING THE PROBLEM:

Step 1: **Review the chapter material.** This problem is about measuring the economic effects of a quota, so you may want to review the section "Quotas and Voluntary Export Restraints," which begins on page 257, and "Measuring the Economic Effect of the Sugar Quota," which begins on page 258.

Step 2: **Fill in the table.** After studying Figure 8-7, you should be able to fill in the table. Remember that consumer surplus is the area below the demand curve and above the market price.

	WITHOUT QUOTA	WITH QUOTA
World price of apples	$10	$10
U.S. price of apples	$10	$12
Quantity supplied by U.S. firms	6 million boxes	10 million boxes
Quantity demanded by U.S. consumers	16 million boxes	14 million boxes
Quantity imported	10 millions boxes	4 million boxes
Area of consumer surplus	$A + B + C + D + E + F$	$A + B$
Area of domestic producer surplus	G	$G + C$
Area of deadweight loss	No deadweight loss	$D + F$

>> End Solved Problem 8-4

YOUR TURN: For more practice, do related problem 4.14 on page 274 at the end of this chapter.

The High Cost of Preserving Jobs with Tariffs and Quotas

The sugar quota is not alone in imposing a high cost on U.S. consumers to save jobs at U.S. firms. Table 8-5 shows, for several industries, the cost tariffs and quotas impose on U.S. consumers per year for each job saved.

Many countries besides the United States also use tariffs and quotas to try to protect jobs. Table 8-6 shows the cost to Japanese consumers per year for each job saved as a result of tariffs and quotas in the listed industries. Note the staggering cost of $51 million for each job saved that is imposed on Japanese consumers by the Japanese government's restrictions on imports of rice.

Just as the sugar quota costs jobs in the candy industry, other tariffs and quotas cost jobs outside the industries immediately affected. For example, in 1991, the United States imposed tariffs on flat-panel displays used in laptop computers. This was good news for U.S. producers of these displays but bad news for companies producing laptop computers. Toshiba, Sharp, and Apple all closed their U.S. laptop production facilities and moved production overseas. In fact, whenever one industry receives tariff or quota protection, jobs are lost in other domestic industries.

PRODUCT	NUMBER OF JOBS SAVED	COST TO CONSUMERS PER YEAR FOR EACH JOB SAVED
Benzenoid chemicals	216	$1,376,435
Luggage	226	1,285,078
Softwood lumber	605	1,044,271
Dairy products	2,378	685,323
Frozen orange juice	609	635,103
Ball bearings	146	603,368
Machine tools	1,556	479,452
Women's handbags	773	263,535
Canned tuna	390	257,640

TABLE 8-5

Preserving U.S. Jobs with Tariffs and Quotas Is Expensive

Source: Federal Reserve Bank of Dallas, *2002 Annual Report*, Exhibit 11.

Gains from Unilateral Elimination of Tariffs and Quotas

Some politicians argue that eliminating U.S. tariffs and quotas would help the U.S. economy only if other countries eliminated their tariffs and quotas in exchange. It is easier to gain political support for reducing or eliminating tariffs or quotas if it is done as part of an agreement with other countries that involves their eliminating some of their tariffs or quotas. But as the example of the sugar quota shows, *the U.S. economy would gain from the elimination of tariffs and quotas even if other countries do not reduce their tariffs and quotas.*

Other Barriers to Trade

In addition to tariffs and quotas, governments sometimes erect other barriers to trade. For example, all governments require that imports meet certain health and safety requirements. Sometimes, however, governments use these requirements to shield domestic firms from foreign competition. This can be true when a government imposes stricter health and safety requirements on imported goods than on goods produced by domestic firms.

PRODUCT	COST TO CONSUMERS PER YEAR FOR EACH JOB SAVED
Rice	$51,233,000
Natural gas	27,987,000
Gasoline	6,329,000
Paper	3,813,000
Beef, pork, and poultry	1,933,000
Cosmetics	1,778,000
Radio and television sets	915,000

TABLE 8-6

Preserving Japanese Jobs with Tariffs and Quotas Is Also Expensive

Source: Yoko Sazabami, Shujiro Urata, and Hiroki Kawai, *Measuring the Cost of Protection in Japan*, Washington, DC: Institute for International Economics, 1995. Used with permission.

Many governments also restrict imports of certain products on national security grounds. The argument is that in time of war, a country should not be dependent on imports of critical war materials. Once again, these restrictions are sometimes used more to protect domestic companies from competition than to protect national security. For example, for years, the U.S. government would buy military uniforms only from U.S. manufacturers, even though uniforms are not a critical war material.

8.5 LEARNING OBJECTIVE

8.5 | Evaluate the arguments over trade policy and globalization.

The Argument over Trade Policies and Globalization

The argument over whether the U.S. government should regulate international trade dates back to the early days of the country. One particularly controversial attempt to restrict trade took place during the Great Depression of the 1930s. At that time, the United States and other countries attempted to help domestic firms by raising tariffs on foreign imports. The United States started the process by passing the Smoot-Hawley Tariff in 1930, which raised average tariff rates to more than 50 percent. As other countries retaliated by raising their tariffs, international trade collapsed.

By the end of World War II in 1945, government officials in the United States and Europe were looking for a way to reduce tariffs and revive international trade. To help achieve this goal, they set up the General Agreement on Tariffs and Trade (GATT) in 1948. Countries that joined GATT agreed not to impose new tariffs or import quotas. In addition, a series of *multilateral negotiations*, called *trade rounds*, took place, in which countries agreed to reduce tariffs from the very high levels of the 1930s.

In the 1940s, most international trade was in goods, and the GATT agreement covered only goods. In the following decades, trade in services and in products incorporating *intellectual property*, such as software programs and movies, grew in importance. Many GATT members pressed for a new agreement that would cover services and intellectual property, as well as goods. A new agreement was negotiated, and in January 1995, GATT was replaced by the **World Trade Organization (WTO)**, headquartered in Geneva, Switzerland. More than 130 countries are currently members of the WTO.

World Trade Organization (WTO) An international organization that oversees international trade agreements.

Why Do Some People Oppose the World Trade Organization?

During the years immediately after World War II, many low-income, or developing, countries erected high tariffs and restricted investment by foreign companies. When these policies failed to produce much economic growth, many of these countries decided during the 1980s to become more open to foreign trade and investment. This process became known as **globalization**. Most developing countries joined the WTO and began to follow its policies.

Globalization The process of countries becoming more open to foreign trade and investment.

During the 1990s, opposition to globalization began to increase. In 1999, this opposition took a violent turn at a meeting of the WTO in Seattle, Washington. The purpose of the meeting was to plan a new round of negotiations aimed at further reductions in trade barriers. A large number of protestors assembled in Seattle to meet the WTO delegates. Protests started peacefully but quickly became violent. Protesters looted stores and burned cars, and many delegates were unable to leave their hotel rooms.

Why would attempts to reduce trade barriers with the objective of increasing income around the world cause such a furious reaction? The opposition to the WTO comes from three sources. First, some opponents are specifically against the globalization process that began in the 1980s and became widespread in the 1990s. Second, other opponents have the same motivation as the supporters of tariffs in the 1930s—to erect trade barriers to protect domestic firms from foreign competition. Third, some critics of the WTO support globalization in principle but believe that the WTO favors the interests of the high-income countries at the expense of the low-income countries. Let's look more closely at the sources of opposition to the WTO.

Anti-Globalization Many of the protestors in Seattle distrust globalization. Some believe that free trade and foreign investment destroy the distinctive cultures of many countries. As developing countries began to open their economies to imports from the United States and other high-income countries, these imports of food, clothing, movies, and other goods began to replace the equivalent local products. So, a teenager in Thailand might be sitting in a McDonald's restaurant, wearing Levi's jeans and a Ralph Lauren shirt, listening to a recording by U2 on his iPod, before going to the local movie theater to watch *Spider-Man 3*. Globalization has increased the variety of products available to consumers in developing countries, but some people argue that this is too high a price to pay for what they see as damage to local cultures.

Globalization has also allowed multinational corporations to relocate factories from high-income countries to low-income countries. These new factories in Indonesia, Malaysia, Pakistan, and other countries pay much lower wages than are paid in the United States, Europe, and Japan and often do not meet the environmental or safety regulations that are imposed in high-income countries. Some factories use child labor, which is illegal in high-income countries. Some people have argued that firms with factories in developing countries should pay workers wages as high as those paid in the high-income countries. They also believe these firms should follow the health, safety, and environmental regulations that exist in the high-income countries.

The governments of most developing countries have resisted these proposals. They argue that when the currently rich countries were poor, they also lacked environmental or safety standards, and their workers were paid low wages. They argue that it is easier for rich countries to afford high wages and environmental and safety regulations than it is for poor countries. They also point out that many jobs that seem very poorly paid by high-income country standards are often better than the alternatives available to workers in low-income countries.

Making *the* Connection	# The Unintended Consequences of Banning Goods Made with Child Labor

In many developing countries, such as Indonesia, Thailand, and Peru, children as young as seven or eight work 10 or more hours a day. Reports of very young workers laboring long hours, producing goods for export, have upset many people in high-income countries. In the United States, boycotts have been organized against stores that stock goods made in developing countries with child labor. Many people assume that if child workers in developing countries weren't working in factories making clothing, toys, and other products, they would be in school, as are children in high-income countries.

In fact, children in developing countries usually have few good alternatives to work. Schooling is frequently available for only a few months each year, and even children who attend school rarely do so for more than a few years. Poor families are often unable to afford even the small costs of sending their children to school. Families may even rely on the earnings of very young children

Would eliminating child labor in developing countries be a good thing?

to survive, as poor families once did in the United States, Europe, and Japan. There is substantial evidence that as incomes begin to rise in poor countries, families rely less on child labor. The United States eventually outlawed child labor, but not until 1938. In developing countries where child labor is common today, jobs producing export goods are usually better paying and less hazardous than the alternatives.

As preparations began in France for the 1998 World Cup, there were protests that Baden Sports—the main supplier of soccer balls—was purchasing the balls from suppliers in Pakistan that used child workers. France decided to ban all use of soccer balls made by child workers. Bowing to this pressure, Baden Sports moved production from Pakistan, where the balls were hand-stitched by child workers, to China, where the balls were machine-stitched by adult workers in factories. There was some criticism of the boycott of hand-stitched soccer balls at the time. In a broad study of child labor, three economists argued:

> Of the array of possible employment in which impoverished children might engage, soccer ball stitching is probably one of the most benign. . . . [In Pakistan] children generally work alongside other family members in the home or in small workshops. . . . Nor are the children exposed to toxic chemicals, hazardous tools or brutal working conditions. Rather, the only serious criticism concerns the length of the typical child stitcher's work-day and the impact on formal education.

In fact, the alternatives to soccer ball stitching for child workers in Pakistan turned out to be extremely grim. According to Keith Maskus, an economist at the University of Colorado and the World Bank, a "large proportion" of the children who lost their jobs stitching soccer balls ended up begging or in prostitution.

Sources: Drusilla K. Brown, Alan V. Deardorff, and Robert M. Stern, "U.S. Trade and Other Policy Options to Deter Foreign Exploitation of Child Labor," in Magnus Blomstrom and Linda S. Goldberg, eds., *Topics in Empirical International Economics: A Festschrift in Honor of Bob Lipsey*, Chicago: University of Chicago Press, 2001; Tomas Larsson, *The Race to the Top: The Real Story of Globalization*, Washington, DC: Cato Institute, 2001, p. 48; and Eric V. Edmonds and Nina Pavcnik, "Child Labor in the Global Economy," *Journal of Economic Perspectives*, Vol. 19, No. 1, Winter 2005, pp. 199–220.

YOUR TURN: Test your understanding by doing related problem 5.5 on page 275 at the end of this chapter.

"Old-Fashioned" Protectionism The anti-globalization argument against free trade and the WTO is relatively new. Another argument against free trade, called *protectionism*, has been around for centuries. **Protectionism** is the use of trade barriers to shield domestic firms from foreign competition. For as long as international trade has existed, governments have attempted to restrict it to protect domestic firms. As we saw with the analysis of the sugar quota, protectionism causes losses to consumers and eliminates jobs in the domestic industries that use the protected product. In addition, by reducing the ability of countries to produce according to comparative advantage, protectionism reduces incomes.

Protectionism The use of trade barriers to shield domestic firms from foreign competition.

Why, then, does protectionism attract support? Protectionism is usually justified on the basis of one of the following arguments:

- ***Saving jobs.*** Supporters of protectionism argue that free trade reduces employment by driving domestic firms out of business. It is true that when more-efficient foreign firms drive less-efficient domestic firms out of business, jobs are lost, but jobs are also lost when more-efficient domestic firms drive less-efficient domestic firms out of business. These job losses are rarely permanent. In the U.S. economy, jobs are lost and new jobs are created continually. No economic study has ever found a long-term connection between the total number of jobs available and the level of tariff protection for domestic industries. In addition, trade restrictions destroy jobs in some industries at the same time that they preserve jobs in others. The U.S. sugar quota may have saved jobs in the U.S. sugar industry, but, as we saw at the beginning of this chapter, it also has destroyed jobs in the U.S. candy industry.

- ***Protecting high wages.*** Some people worry that firms in high-income countries will have to start paying much lower wages to compete with firms in developing countries.

This fear is misplaced, however, because free trade actually raises living standards by increasing economic efficiency. When a country practices protectionism and produces goods and services it could obtain more inexpensively from other countries, it reduces its standard of living. The United States could ban imports of coffee and begin growing it domestically. But this would entail a very high opportunity cost because coffee could only be grown in the continental United States in greenhouses and would require large amounts of labor and equipment. The coffee would have to sell for a very high price to cover these costs. Suppose the United States did ban coffee imports: Eliminating the ban at some future time would eliminate the jobs of U.S. coffee workers, but the standard of living in the United States would rise as coffee prices declined and labor, machinery, and other resources moved out of coffee production and into production of goods and services for which the United States has a comparative advantage.

- **Protecting infant industries.** It is possible that firms in a country may have a comparative advantage in producing a good, but because the country begins production of the good later than other countries, its firms initially have higher costs. In producing some goods and services, substantial "learning by doing" occurs. As workers and firms produce more of the good or service, they gain experience and become more productive. Over time, costs and prices will fall. As the firms in the "infant industry" gain experience, their costs will fall, and they will be able to compete successfully with foreign producers. Under free trade, however, they may not get the chance. The established foreign producers can sell the product at a lower price and drive domestic producers out of business before they gain enough experience to compete. To economists, this is the most persuasive of the protectionist arguments. It has a significant drawback, however. Tariffs used to protect an infant industry eliminate the need for the firms in the industry to become productive enough to compete with foreign firms. After World War II, the governments of many developing countries used the "infant industry" argument to justify high tariff rates. Unfortunately, most of their infant industries never grew up, and they continued for years as inefficient drains on their economies.

- **Protecting national security.** As already discussed, a country should not rely on other countries for goods that are critical to its military defense. For example, the United States would probably not want to import all its jet fighter engines from China. The definition of which goods are critical to military defense is a slippery one, however. In fact, it is rare for an industry to ask for protection without raising the issue of national security, even if its products have mainly nonmilitary uses.

Making the Connection | Has NAFTA Helped or Hurt the U.S. Economy?

The North American Free Trade Agreement (NAFTA) was very controversial when it was being negotiated in the early 1990s. During the 1992 presidential campaign, independent candidate Ross Perot claimed to hear a "giant sucking sound" as jobs were pulled out of the United States and into Mexico. NAFTA, which went into effect in 1994, eliminated most tariffs on products shipped between the United States, Canada, and Mexico. This policy change made it possible for each of these countries to better pursue its comparative advantage. For example, before NAFTA, the Mexican government had used tariffs to protect its domestic automobile industry, but that industry was much less efficient than the U.S. automobile industry. When tariffs were removed, Mexican consumers could take advantage of the efficiency of the U.S. industry, and U.S. exports of motor vehicles to Mexico soared. Similarly, Canadian consumers could take advantage of lower-priced U.S. beef, and U.S. consumers could take advantage of lower-priced Canadian lumber. As we would expect, expanding trade increased consumption in all three countries. In the United States, consumption increased about $400 per year for a family of four as a result of NAFTA.

Contrary to Ross Perot's prediction, NAFTA did not lead to a loss of jobs in the United States. Between 1994, when NAFTA went into effect, and 2007, the number of

Despite resistance to NAFTA, time proved that the U.S. economy gained jobs.

jobs in the United States increased by more than 21 million. Some commentators argued that jobs in the United States could be preserved with NAFTA, but only if wages for U.S. workers declined to the much lower levels being paid Mexican workers. In fact, a study by Gordon Hanson of the University of California, San Diego, showed that the opposite occurred: Wages for both U.S. and Mexican workers increased following NAFTA. In addition, the gap between U.S. wages and Mexican wages did not close.

There were, of course, people in all three countries who were made worse off by NAFTA. Some firms in each country were no longer competitive after tariffs were lowered. In the United States, government assistance helped workers who lost their jobs to retrain or relocate. Overall, most economists have concluded that NAFTA helped the U.S. economy become more efficient, thereby expanding the consumption of U.S. households.

Source: Gordon H. Hanson, "What Has Happened to Wages in Mexico Since NAFTA? Implications for Hemispheric Free Trade," in Toni Estevadeordal, Dani Rodrick, Alan Taylor, and Andres Velasco, eds., *FTAA and Beyond: Prospects for Integration in the Americas*, Cambridge, MA: Harvard University Press, 2004.

YOUR TURN: Test your understanding by doing related problem 5.7 on page 276 at the end of this chapter.

Dumping

Dumping Selling a product for a price below its cost of production.

In recent years, the United States has extended protection to some domestic industries by using a provision in the WTO agreement that allows governments to impose tariffs in the case of *dumping*. **Dumping** is selling a product for a price below its cost of production. Although allowable under the WTO agreement, using tariffs to offset the effects of dumping is very controversial.

In practice, it is difficult to determine whether foreign companies are dumping goods because the true production costs of a good are not easy for foreign governments to calculate. As a result, the WTO allows countries to determine that dumping has occurred if a product is exported for a lower price than it sells for on the home market. There is a problem with this approach, however. Often there are good business reasons for a firm to sell a product for different prices to different consumers. For example, the airlines charge business travelers higher ticket prices than leisure travelers. Firms also use "loss leaders"—products that are sold below cost, or even given away free—when introducing a new product or, in the case of retailing, to attract customers who will also buy full-price products. For example, when Sun Microsystems attempted to establish StarOffice as a competitor to Microsoft Office, Sun gave the software away free on its Web site. During the Christmas season, Wal-Mart sometimes offers toys at prices below what they pay to buy them from manufacturers. It's unclear why these normal business practices should be unacceptable when used in international trade.

Positive versus Normative Analysis (Once Again)

Economists emphasize the burden on the economy imposed by tariffs, quotas, and other government restrictions on free trade. Does it follow that these interferences are bad? Remember from Chapter 1 the distinction between *positive analysis* and *normative analysis*. Positive analysis concerns what *is*. Normative analysis concerns what *ought to be*. Measuring the impact of the sugar quota on the U.S. economy is an example of positive analysis. Asserting that the sugar quota is bad public policy and should be eliminated is normative analysis. The sugar quota—like all other interferences with trade—makes some people better off and some people worse off, and it reduces total income and consumption. Whether increasing the profits of U.S. sugar companies and the number of workers they employ justifies the costs imposed on consumers and the reduction in economic efficiency is a normative question.

Most economists do not support interferences with trade, such as the sugar quota. Few people become economists if they don't believe that markets should usually be as free as possible. But the opposite view is certainly intellectually respectable. It is possible for someone to understand the costs of tariffs and quotas but still believe that tariffs and quotas are a good idea, perhaps because they believe unrestricted free trade would cause too much disruption to the economy.

The success of industries in getting the government to erect barriers to foreign competition depends partly on some members of the public knowing full well the costs of trade barriers but supporting them anyway. However, two other factors are also at work:

1 The costs tariffs and quotas impose on consumers are large in total but relatively small per person. For example, the sugar quota imposes a total burden of about $2.24 billion per year on consumers. Spread across 300 million Americans, the burden is only about $7.50 per person: too little for most people to worry about, even if they know the burden exists.

2 The jobs lost to foreign competition are easy to identify, but the jobs created by foreign trade are less easy to identify.

In other words, the industries that benefit from tariffs and quotas benefit a lot—the sugar quota increases the profits of U.S. sugar producers by more than $1 billion—whereas each consumer loses relatively little. This concentration of benefits and widely spread burdens makes it easy to understand why members of Congress receive strong pressure from some industries to enact tariffs and quotas and relatively little pressure from the general public to reduce them.

Economics in YOUR Life!

>> Continued from page 243

At the beginning of the chapter, we asked you to consider how sugar companies have convinced Congress to enact the sugar quota and why relatively few people have heard of this quota. In the chapter, we saw that the sugar quota costs U.S. consumers more than $2 billion per year as a result of higher sugar prices and has led several U.S. candy makers to eliminate domestic jobs and move their facilities to other countries. This might seem to increase the mystery of why Congress has enacted the sugar quota, especially because it saves relatively few jobs in the U.S. sugar industry. We have also seen, though, that *per person*, the burden of the sugar quota is small—only about $7.50 per person per year. Not many people will take the trouble of writing a letter to their member of Congress or otherwise make their views known in the hope of saving $7.50 per year. In fact, few people will even spend the time to become aware that the quota exists. So, if before you read this chapter you had never heard of the sugar quota, you are certainly not alone.

Conclusion

There are few issues economists agree upon more than the economic benefits of free trade. However, there are few political issues as controversial as government policy toward trade. Many people who would be reluctant to see the government interfere with domestic trade are quite willing to see it interfere with international trade. The damage high tariffs inflicted on the world economy during the 1930s shows what can happen when governments around the world abandon free trade. Whether future episodes of that type can be avoided is by no means certain.

Read *An Inside Look at Policy* on the next page for a discussion of how eliminating tariffs on cars and other goods benefits the United States and South Korea.

The United States and South Korea Reach a Trade Deal

NEW YORK TIMES, APRIL 3, 2007

U.S. and South Korea Agree to Sweeping Trade Deal

United States and South Korean negotiators struck the world's largest bilateral free trade agreement on Monday, giving the United States a badly needed lift to its trade policy at home and South Korea a chance to reinvigorate its export economy. . . .

If ratified, the trade deal would eliminate tariffs on more than 90 percent of the product categories traded between the countries. South Korea agreed to lift trade barriers to important American products like cars and beef, while the United States agreed to allow Seoul to continue to subsidize South Korean rice. . . .

As South Korean workers and farmers protested in the streets—on Sunday, one man even set himself on fire—negotiators haggled to the end early Monday.

The breakthrough came when both sides compromised on the most delicate deal-breaking issues. Washington dropped its demand that the South Korean government stop protecting its politically powerful rice farmers, and Seoul agreed to resume imports of American beef, halted three years ago over fears of mad cow disease, if, as expected, the World Organization on Animal Health declares United States meat safe in a ruling next month.

South Korea also agreed to phase out the 40 percent tariff on American beef over 15 years. It will remove an 8 percent duty on cars and revise a domestic vehicle tax system that United States officials say discriminates against American cars with bigger engines.

The United States will eliminate the 2.5 percent tariff on South Korean cars with engines smaller than 3,000 cubic centimeters; phase out the 25 percent duty on trucks over the course of 10 years; and remove tariffs, which average 8.9 percent, on 61 percent of South Korean textiles. . . .

The deal is the biggest of its kind for the United States since the North American Free Trade Agreement in 1994 with Canada and Mexico. It is Washington's first bilateral trade pact with a major Asian economy.

Studies have estimated that the accord would add $20 billion to bilateral trade, estimated last year at $78 billion. Potential gains to the United States economy range from $17 billion to $43 billion, according to Usha C. H. Haley, director of the Global Business Center at the University of New Haven. South Korea's exports to the United States are expected to rise in the first year by 12 percent.

Analysts doubt that the deal will provide an immediate lift to American car manufacturers. Only 5,000 American cars were sold here last year, while South Korean automakers sold 800,000 vehicles in the United States. The gap accounted for 80 percent of the $13 billion United States trade deficit with South Korea last year.

American officials hope that the deal will placate American cattle farmers, who are struggling to recapture global market share after an outbreak of mad cow disease in late 2003. Before the import ban, South Korea was the world's third-largest consumer of American beef, importing $800 million a year.

Consumers in both countries are the deal's biggest winners. Hyundai cars and Samsung flat-panel TV sets, as well as Korean-made clothing, will become significantly cheaper in the United States.

American beef and oranges, as well as Ford cars and Toyota vehicles built in the United States, will be more affordable in South Korea. South Korean TV networks will be able to broadcast more American movies and TV series like "CSI," which already command a huge following here, after Seoul eases a cap on foreign content to 80 percent of total airtime from 75 percent.

The deal entails heavy political costs for South Korea, which can expect the loss of tens of thousands of farming jobs. Up to 2 trillion won ($2.2 billion) in agricultural revenue will be lost as cheap American corn, soybeans and processed foods come in, according to studies by South Korean economists. . . .

Source: Choe Sang-Hun, "U.S. and South Korea Agree to Sweeping Trade Deal," New York Times, April 3, 2007, p. C1. Copyright © 2007 The New York Times Co. Reprinted by permission.

Key Points in the Article

The article discusses a recent trade agreement negotiated between the United States and South Korea that will reduce restrictions on trade between the two countries. Agreements such as this one to expand trade between two countries are known as *bilateral agreements*. The trade agreements worked out by the World Trade Organization are *multilateral agreements*. Neither Congress nor the South Korean National Assembly has yet ratified the agreement. However, if the legislatures do ratify the agreement, a free-trade zone covering the world's largest and eleventh-largest economies would be created.

Analyzing
the News

(a) In this chapter, we have seen that expanding trade raises living standards by increasing consumption and economic efficiency. Reducing tariffs on trade between South Korea and the United States will aid consumers in both countries. The figure shows the U.S. market following the elimination of the tariff on South Korean cars. (For simplicity, we assume that there are no remaining U.S. tariffs on cars.) The price of cars in the United States falls from P_1 to P_2, and equilibrium in the U.S. car market moves from point E to point F. U.S. consumption of cars increases from Q_3 to Q_4, the quantity of cars supplied by U.S. car makers declines from Q_2 to Q_1, and imports increase from $Q_3 - Q_2$ to $Q_4 - Q_1$. Consumer surplus increases by the sum of areas A, B, C, and D. Area A represents a transfer from producer surplus under the tariff to consumer surplus. Areas C and D represent the conversion of deadweight loss to consumer surplus. Area B represents a conversion of government tariff revenue to consumer surplus. Eliminating the tariff reduces the cost to South Korean car producers of selling their product in the United States. U.S. consumers purchase a larger quantity of South Korean cars at a lower price.

(b) The figure shows that eliminating the tariff on cars also eliminates the revenue the U.S. government had been collecting from this tariff. In high-income countries, such as the United States, governments receive most of their revenue from taxes on personal and corporate income. For example, tariff revenue in the United States for 2006 amounted to only about 1 percent of all revenue received by the federal government, but governments in low-income countries often have difficulty collecting income taxes, so they rely heavily on tariffs for revenue. In these countries, the government's need for revenue can pose a serious barrier to expanding international trade by reducing tariffs because governments have difficulty replacing the revenues lost from tariff reductions. This was also true in the United States early in its history. In 1800, tariffs brought in 90 percent of all federal government revenue. As late as the 1950s, tariffs accounted for 14 percent of federal revenues.

(c) Trade benefits the entire economy but can create losses for certain groups in the economy. While South Korean consumers will gain from less expensive food, agricultural interests in South Korea will be hurt. These interests are likely to lobby against ratification of the agreement.

Thinking Critically
About Policy

1. Tariffs on South Korean car and textile imports save jobs for Americans working in those industries. Do you support these tariffs? Why or why not?
2. In which goods mentioned in the article does the United States have a comparative advantage? In which does South Korea have a comparative advantage? Explain your reasoning.

Increase in Consumer Surplus	=	Decrease in Producer Surplus	+	Decrease in Government Tariff Revenue	+	Decrease in Deadweight Loss
$A + C + B + D$		A		B		$C + D$

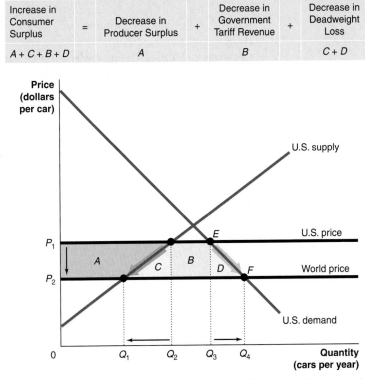

The market for cars in the United States after the tariff on South Korean cars is eliminated.

Key Terms

Absolute advantage, p. 248

Autarky, p. 249

Comparative advantage, p. 247

Dumping, p. 266

Exports, p. 244

External economies, p. 253

Free trade, p. 255

Globalization, p. 262

Imports, p. 244

Opportunity cost, p. 247

Protectionism, p. 264

Quota, p. 257

Tariff, p. 244

Terms of trade, p. 249

Voluntary export restraint (VER), p. 257

World Trade Organization (WTO), p. 262

8.1 LEARNING OBJECTIVE   8.1 | Discuss the role of international trade in the U.S. economy, **pages 244–247.**

The United States in the International Economy

Summary

International trade has been increasing in recent decades, in part because of reductions in *tariffs* and other barriers to trade. A **tariff** is a tax imposed by a government on imports. The quantity of goods and services the United States imports and exports has been continually increasing. **Imports** are goods and services bought domestically but produced in other countries. **Exports** are goods and services produced domestically but sold to other countries. Today, the United States is the leading exporting country in the world, and about 20 percent of U.S. manufacturing jobs depend on exports.

myeconlab Visit www.myeconlab.com to complete these exercises *Get Ahead of the Curve* online and get instant feedback.

Review Questions

1.1 Briefly explain whether you agree or disagree with the following statement: "International trade is more important to the U.S. economy than to most other economies."

Problems and Applications

1.2 If the United States were to stop trading goods and services with other countries, which U.S. industries would be likely to see their sales decline the most? Briefly explain.

1.3 Briefly explain whether you agree with the following statement: "Japan has always been much more heavily involved in international trade than are most other nations. In fact, today Japan exports a larger fraction of its GDP than do Germany, Great Britain, or the United States."

1.4 **(Related to the *Making the Connection* on page 246)** Some politicians in the United States believe that European governments unfairly help Airbus, Boeing's main competitor, by subsidizing, or making payments, to Airbus. Suppose that the U.S. Congress passes legislation forbidding U.S. airlines from buying planes from Airbus or any other non-U.S. aircraft firm. Would this legislation be likely to actually help Boeing? Briefly explain.

>> End Learning Objective 8.1

8.2 LEARNING OBJECTIVE   8.2 | Understand the difference between comparative advantage and absolute advantage in international trade, **pages 247–248.**

Comparative Advantage in International Trade

Summary

Comparative advantage is the ability of an individual, a business, or a country to produce a good or service at the lowest **opportunity cost**. **Absolute advantage** is the ability to produce more of a good or service than competitors when using the same amount of resources. Countries trade on the basis of comparative advantage, not on the basis of absolute advantage.

 myeconlab Visit www.myeconlab.com to complete these exercises *Get Ahead of the Curve* online and get instant feedback.

Review Questions

2.1 A World Trade Organization publication calls comparative advantage "arguably the single most powerful insight in economics." What is comparative advantage? What makes it such a powerful insight?

Source: World Trade Organization, *Trading into the Future*, April 1999.

2.2 What is the difference between absolute advantage and comparative advantage? Will a country always be an exporter of a good where it has an absolute advantage in production?

Problems and Applications

2.3 Why do the goods that countries import and export change over time? Use the concept of comparative advantage in your answer.

2.4 Briefly explain whether you agree with the following argument: "Unfortunately, Bolivia does not have a comparative advantage with respect to the United States in the production of any good or service." (*Hint:* You do not need any specific information about the economies of Bolivia or the United States to be able to answer this question.)

2.5 In 1987, an economic study showed that, on average, workers in the Japanese consumer electronics industry produced less output per hour than did U.S. workers producing the same goods. Despite this fact, Japan exported large quantities of consumer electronics to the United States. Briefly explain how this is possible.

Source: Study cited in Douglas A. Irwin, *Free Trade under Fire*, Princeton, NJ: Princeton University Press, 2002, p. 27.

2.6 Patrick J. Buchanan, a former presidential candidate, argues in his book on the global economy that there is a flaw in David Ricardo's theory of comparative advantage:

> Classical free trade theory fails the test of common sense. According to Ricardo's law of comparative advantage . . . if America makes better computers and textiles than China does, but our advantage in computers is greater than our advantage in textiles, we should (1) focus on computers, (2) let China make textiles, and (3) trade U.S. computers for Chinese textiles. . . .
>
> The doctrine begs a question. If Americans are more efficient than Chinese in making clothes . . . why surrender the more efficient American industry? Why shift to a reliance on a Chinese textile industry that will take years to catch up to where American factories are today?

Do you agree with Buchanan's argument? Briefly explain.

Source: Patrick J. Buchanan, *The Great Betrayal: How American Sovereignty and Social Justice Are Being Sacrificed to the Gods of the Global Economy*, Boston: Little, Brown, 1998, p. 66.

≫ End Learning Objective 8.2

8.3 LEARNING OBJECTIVE   8.3 | Explain how countries gain from international trade, **pages 249–255.**

How Countries Gain from International Trade

Summary

Autarky is a situation in which a country does not trade with other countries. The **terms of trade** is the ratio at which a country can trade its exports for imports from other countries. When a country specializes in producing goods where it has a comparative advantage and trades for the other goods it needs, the country will have a higher level of income and consumption. We do not see complete specialization in production for three reasons: Not all goods and services are traded internationally, production of most goods involves increasing opportunity costs, and tastes for products differ across countries. Although the population of a country as a whole benefits from trade, companies—and their workers—that are unable to compete with lower-cost foreign producers lose. Among the main sources of comparative advantage are climate and natural resources, relative abundance of labor and capital, technology, and *external economies*. **External economies** are reductions in a firm's

cost that result from an increase in the size of an industry. A country may develop a comparative advantage in the production of a good, and then as time passes and circumstances change, the country may lose its comparative advantage in producing that good and develop a comparative advantage in producing other goods.

X **myeconlab** Visit www.myeconlab.com to complete these exercises
Get Ahead of the Curve online and get instant feedback.

Review Questions

3.1 Briefly explain how international trade increases a country's consumption.

3.2 What is meant by a country specializing in the production of a good? Is it typical for countries to be completely specialized? Briefly explain.

3.3 What are the main sources of comparative advantage?

Problems and Applications

3.4 (Related to *Solved Problem 8-3* on page 250) The following table shows the hourly output per worker in two industries in Chile and Argentina.

	OUTPUT PER HOUR OF WORK	
	HATS	BEER
CHILE	8	6
ARGENTINA	1	2

a. Explain which country has an absolute advantage in the production of hats and which country has an absolute advantage in the production of beer.

b. Explain which country has a comparative advantage in the production of hats and which country has a comparative advantage in the production of beer.

c. Suppose that Chile and Argentina currently do not trade with each other. Each has 1,000 hours of labor to use producing hats and beer, and the countries are currently producing the amounts of each good shown in the following table.

	HATS	BEER
CHILE	7,200	600
ARGENTINA	600	800

Using this information, give a numeric example of how Chile and Argentina can both gain from trade. Assume that after trading begins, one hat can be exchanged for one barrel of beer.

3.5 (Related to *Solved Problem 8-3* on page 250) A political commentator makes the following statement:

> The idea that international trade should be based on the comparative advantage of each country is fine for rich countries like the United States and Japan. Rich countries have educated workers and large quantities of machinery and equipment. These advantages allow them to produce every product more efficiently than poor countries can. Poor countries like Kenya and Bolivia have nothing to gain from international trade based on comparative advantage.

Do you agree with this argument? Briefly explain.

3.6 Demonstrate how the opportunity costs of producing cell phones and digital music players in Japan and the United States were calculated in Table 8-2 on page 248.

3.7 Briefly explain whether you agree or disagree with the following statement: "Most countries exhaust their comparative advantage in producing a good or service before they reach complete specialization."

3.8 Is free trade likely to benefit a large, populous country more than a small country with fewer people? Briefly explain.

3.9 A Federal Reserve publication offers the following observation: "Too many U.S. citizens associate free trade with job losses rather than opportunities and a higher standard of living." Do you agree? Briefly explain.

Source: Surya Sen and Dan Wassmann, *The Great Trade Debate: From Rhetoric to Reality*, Federal Reserve Bank of Chicago, January 1999.

3.10 Hal Varian, an economist at the University of California, Berkeley, has made two observations about international trade:

a. Trade allows a country "to produce more with less."

b. There is little doubt who wins [from trade] in the long run: consumers.

Briefly explain whether you agree with either or both of these observations.

Source: Hal R. Varian, "The Mixed Bag of Productivity," *New York Times*, October 23, 2003.

3.11 In a recent public opinion poll, 41 percent of people responding believed that free trade hurts the U.S. economy, while only 28 percent believed that it helps the economy. (The remaining people were uncertain of the effects of free trade.) What is "free trade"? Do you believe it helps or hurts the economy? (Be sure to define what you mean by "helps" or "hurts.") Why do you think that more Americans appear to believe that free trade hurts the economy than believe that it helps the economy?

Source: Matthew Benjamin, "Americans Souring on Free Trade Amid Optimism About Economy," *Bloomberg News*, January 19, 2007.

3.12 (Related to the *Don't Let This Happen to You!* on page 252) Briefly explain whether you agree or disagree with the following statement: "I can't believe that anyone opposes expanding international trade. After all, when international trade expands, everyone wins."

3.13 (Related to the *Making the Connection* on page 253) Explain why there are advantages to a movie studio operating in southern California, rather than in, say, Florida.

>> **End Learning Objective 8.3**

Government Policies That Restrict International Trade

Summary

Free trade is trade between countries without government restrictions. Government policies that interfere with trade usually take the form of: *tariffs, quotas,* or *voluntary export restraints* (VERs). A **tariff** is a tax imposed by a government on imports. A **quota** is a numeric limit imposed by a government on the quantity of a good that can be imported into the country. A **voluntary export restraint (VER)** is an agreement negotiated between two countries that places a numeric limit on the quantity of a good that can be imported by one country from the other country. The federal government's sugar quota costs U.S. consumers $2.24 billion per year, or about $750,000 per year for each job saved in the sugar industry. Saving jobs by using tariffs and quotas is often very expensive.

myeconlab Visit www.myeconlab.com to complete these exercises
Get Ahead of the Curve online and get instant feedback.

Review Questions

4.1 What is a tariff? What is a quota? Give an example of a non-tariff barrier to trade.

4.2 Who gains and who loses when a country imposes a tariff or a quota on imports of a good?

Problems and Applications

4.3 An editorial in *BusinessWeek* argued the following:

[President] Bush needs to send a pure and clear signal that the U.S. supports free trade on its merits. . . . That means resisting any further protectionist demands by lawmakers. It could even mean unilaterally reducing tariffs or taking down trade barriers rather than erecting new ones. Such moves would benefit U.S. consumers while giving a needed boost to struggling economies overseas.

What does the editorial mean by "protectionist demands"? How would the unilateral elimination of U.S. trade barriers benefit both U.S. consumers and economies overseas?

Source: "The Threat of Protectionism," *BusinessWeek,* June 3, 2002.

4.4 Political commentator B. Bruce-Biggs once wrote the following in the *Wall Street Journal*: "This is not to say that the case for international free trade is invalid; it is just irrelevant. It is an 'if only everybody . . .' argu-

ment. . . . In the real world almost everybody sees benefits in economic nationalism." What do you think he means by "economic nationalism"? Do you agree that a country benefits from free trade only if every other country also practices free trade? Briefly explain.

Source: B. Bruce-Biggs, "The Coming Overthrow of Free Trade," *Wall Street Journal,* February 24, 1983, p. 28.

4.5 Two U.S. senators make the following argument against allowing free trade: "Fewer and fewer Americans support our government's trade policy. They see a shrinking middle class, lost jobs and exploding trade deficits. Yet supporters of free trade continue to push for more of the same—more job-killing trade agreements. . . . " Do you agree with these senators that reducing barriers to trade reduces the number of jobs available to workers in the United States? Briefly explain.

Source: Byron Dorgan and Sherrod Brown, "How Free Trade Hurts," *Washington Post,* December 23, 2006, p. A21.

4.6 The United States produces beef and also imports beef from other countries.
   a. Draw a graph showing the supply and demand for beef in the United States. Assume that the United States can import as much as it wants at the world price of beef without causing the world price of beef to increase. Be sure to indicate on the graph the quantity of beef imported.
   b. Now show on your graph the effect of the United States imposing a tariff on beef. Be sure to indicate on your graph the quantity of beef sold by U.S. producers before and after the tariff is imposed, the quantity of beef imported before and after the tariff, and the price of beef in the United States before and after the tariff.
   c. Discuss who benefits and who loses when the United States imposes a tariff on beef.

4.7 (Related to the *Chapter Opener* on page 242) Which industries are affected unfavorably by the sugar quota and by the tariff on imports of sugar-based ethanol? Are any industries (other than the sugar industry) affected favorably by the sugar quota and the tariff on imports of sugar-based ethanol? (*Hint:* Think about what sugar is used for and whether substitutes exist for these uses and what the substitutes are for sugar-based ethanol.)

4.8 When Congress was considering a bill to impose quotas on imports of textiles, shoes, and other products, Milton Friedman, a Nobel Prize–winning economist, made the following comment: "The consumer will be forced to spend several extra dollars to subsidize the producers [of these goods] by one dollar. A straight handout would be far cheaper." Why would a quota result in consumers paying much more than domestic producers receive? Where do the other dollars go? What does Friedman mean by a "straight handout"? Why would this be cheaper than a quota?

Source: Milton Friedman, "Free Trade," *Newsweek*, August 27, 1970.

4.9 The United States has about 9,000 rice farmers. In 2006, these rice farmers received $780 million in subsidy payments from the U.S. government (or nearly $87,000 per farmer). These payments result in U.S. farmers producing much more rice than they otherwise would, a substantial amount of which is exported. According to an article in the *Wall Street Journal*, Kpalagim Mome, a farmer in the African country of Ghana, can no longer find buyers in Ghana for his rice:

> "We can't sell our rice anymore. It gets worse every year," Mr. Mome says. . . . Years of economic hardship have driven three of his brothers to walk and hitchhike 2,000 miles across the Sahara to reach the Mediterranean and Europe. His sister plans to leave next year. Mr. Mome's plight is repeated throughout farm communities in Africa and elsewhere in the developing world.

Why would subsidies paid by the U.S. government to U.S. rice farmers reduce the incomes of rice farmers in Africa?

Source: Juliane von Reppert-Bismarck, "How Trade Barriers Keep Africans Adrift," *Wall Street Journal*, December 27, 2006.

4.10 An economic analysis of a proposal to impose a quota on steel imports into the United States indicated that the quota would save 3,700 jobs in the steel industry but cost about 35,000 jobs in other U.S. industries. Why would a quota on steel imports cause employment to fall in other industries? Which other industries are likely to be most affected?

Source: Study cited in Douglas A. Irwin, *Free Trade Under Fire*, Princeton, NJ: Princeton University Press, 2002, p. 82.

4.11 A student makes the following argument:

> Tariffs on imports of foreign goods into the United States will cause the foreign companies to add the amount of the tariff to the prices they charge in the United States for those goods. Instead of putting a tariff on imported goods, we should ban importing them. Banning imported goods is better than putting tariffs on them because U.S. producers benefit from the reduced competition and U.S. consumers don't have to pay the higher prices caused by tariffs.

Briefly explain whether you agree with the student's reasoning.

4.12 Suppose China decides to pay large subsidies to any Chinese company that exports goods or services to the United States. As a result, these companies are able to sell products in the United States at far below their cost of production. In addition, China decides to bar all imports from the United States. The dollars that the United States pays to import Chinese goods are left in banks in China. Will this strategy raise or lower the standard of living in China? Will it raise or lower the standard of living in the United States? Briefly explain. Be sure to provide a definition of "standard of living" in your answer.

4.13 **(Related to the *Chapter Opener* on page 242)** According to an editorial in the *New York Times*, because of the sugar quota, "Sugar growers in this country, long protected from global competition, have had a great run at the expense of just about everyone else—refineries, candy manufacturers, other food companies, individual consumers and farmers in the developing world." Briefly explain how each group mentioned in this editorial is affected by the sugar quota.

Source: "America's Sugar Daddies," *New York Times*, November 29, 2003.

4.14 **(Related to *Solved Problem 8-4* on page 259)** Suppose that the United States currently both produces kumquats and imports them. The U.S. government then decides to restrict international trade in kumquats by imposing a quota that allows imports of only six million pounds of kumquats into the United States each year. The figure shows the results of imposing the quota.

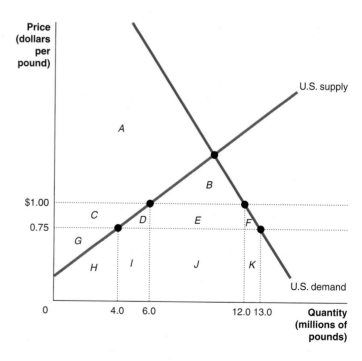

Fill in the table on the following page using the letters in the figure:

	WITHOUT QUOTA	WITH QUOTA
World price of kumquats	_____	_____
U.S. price of kumquats	_____	_____
Quantity supplied by U.S. firms	_____	_____
Quantity demanded	_____	_____
Quantity imported	_____	_____
Area of consumer surplus	_____	_____
Area of domestic producer surplus	_____	_____
Area of deadweight loss	_____	_____

>> End Learning Objective 8.4

8.5 LEARNING OBJECTIVE   8.5 | Evaluate the arguments over trade policy and globalization, **pages 262–267.**

The Argument over Trade Policies and Globalization

Summary

The **World Trade Organization (WTO)** is an international organization that enforces international trade agreements. The WTO has promoted **globalization**, the process of countries becoming more open to foreign trade and investment. Some critics of the WTO argue that globalization has damaged local cultures around the world. Other critics oppose the WTO because they believe in **protectionism**, which is the use of trade barriers to shield domestic firms from foreign competition. The WTO allows countries to use tariffs in cases of **dumping**, when an imported product is sold for a price below its cost of production. Economists can point out the burden imposed on the economy by tariffs, quotas, and other government interferences with free trade. But whether these policies should be used is a normative decision.

 Visit www.myeconlab.com to complete these exercises *Get Ahead of the Curve* online and get instant feedback.

Review Questions

5.1 What events led to the General Agreement on Tariffs and Trade? Why did the World Trade Organization eventually replace GATT?

5.2 What is globalization? Why are some people opposed to globalization?

5.3 What is protectionism? Who benefits and who loses from protectionist policies? What are the main arguments people use to justify protectionism?

5.4 What is dumping? Who benefits and who loses from dumping? What problems arise when implementing anti-dumping laws?

Problems and Applications

5.5 (Related to the *Making the Connection* on page 263) The following excerpt is from a newspaper story on President Bill Clinton's proposals for changes in the World Trade Organization. The story was published just before the 1999 World Trade Organization meeting in Seattle that ended in rioting:

> [President Clinton] suggested that a working group on labor be created within the WTO to develop core labor standards that would become "part of every trade agreement. And ultimately I would favor a system in which sanctions would come for violating any provision of a trade agreement. . . . " But the new U.S. stand is sure to meet massive resistance from developing countries, which make up more than 100 of the 135 countries in the WTO. They are not interested in adopting tougher U.S. labor standards.

What did President Clinton mean by "core labor standards"? Why would developing countries resist adopting these standards?

5.6 Steven Landsburg, an economist at the University of Rochester, wrote the following in an article in the *New York Times*:

> Free trade is not only about the right of American consumers to buy at the cheapest possible price; it's also about the right of foreign producers to earn a living. Steelworkers in West Virginia struggle hard to make ends meet. So do steelworkers in South Korea. To protect one at the expense of the other, solely because of where they happened to be born, is a moral outrage.

How does the U.S. government protect steelworkers in West Virginia at the expense of steelworkers in South Korea? Is Landsburg making a positive or a normative statement? A few days later, Tom Redburn published an article disagreeing with Landsburg:

> It is not some evil character flaw to care more about the welfare of people nearby

than about that of those far away—it's human nature. And it is morally—and economically—defensible. . . . A society that ignores the consequences of economic disruption on those among its citizens who come out at the short end of the stick is not only heartless, it also undermines its own cohesion and adaptability.

Which of the two arguments do you find most convincing?

Sources: Steven E. Landsburg, "Who Cares if the Playing Field Is Level?" *New York Times*, June 13, 2001; and Tom Redburn, "Economic View: Of Politics, Free Markets, and Tending to Society," *New York Times*, June 17, 2001.

5.7 (Related to the *Making the Connection* on page 265) An editorial in the *New York Times* contained the following observation:

> Globalization is tough to sell to average people. Economists can promote the very

real benefits of a robustly growing world: when they sell more overseas, American businesses can employ more people. But what sticks in our minds is the television image of the father of three laid off when his factory moves offshore.

Do you agree that the negative effects of international trade are more visible than the positive effects? Briefly explain.

Source: "Still Flying High," *New York Times*, December 25, 2006.

5.8 The following appeared in an article in *BusinessWeek* that argued against free trade: "The U.S. is currently in a precarious position. In addition to geopolitical threats, we face a severe economic shock. We have already lost trillions of dollars and millions of jobs to foreigners." If a country engages in free trade, is the total number of jobs in the country likely to decline? Briefly explain.

Source: Vladimir Masch, "A Radical Plan to Manage Globalization," *BusinessWeek*, February 14, 2007.

>> **End Learning Objective 8.5**

Appendix

Multinational Firms

Understand why firms operate in more than one country.

LEARNING OBJECTIVE

Most large corporations are multinational. **Multinational enterprises** are firms that conduct operations in more than one country—as opposed to simply trading with other countries. For example, the U.S. firm General Electric employs more than 300,000 people in more than 100 countries. Toyota Motor Corporation of Japan has invested more than $10 billion in factories and other facilities in the United States and assembles more than a million cars and trucks in North American factories. (Almost two-thirds of the cars and trucks Toyota sells in the United States are assembled in North American factories.) The Nestlé Company is headquartered in the small city of Vevey, Switzerland, but it produces and sells food products in practically every country in the world. It has more than 500 factories worldwide, employing about 260,000 people.

Table 8A-1 shows the top 25 multinational corporations, ranked by the value of their revenues in 2006. Large corporations based in the United States generally established multinational operations earlier than did firms based in other countries. Today, 5 of the 10 largest multinational corporations in the world are based in the United States. The table shows that large corporations in the motor vehicle, banking, insurance, and petroleum refining industries are most likely to have extensive multinational operations.

Multinational enterprise A firm that conducts operations in more than one country.

A Brief History of Multinational Enterprises

From at least 2500 B.C., companies have traded over long distances. Well-developed systems of long-distance trade existed in the eastern Mediterranean by 1500 B.C. By the Middle Ages, a number of multinational firms had been established in Europe. For example, the Medici bank was based in Florence, Italy, but had branches in France, Switzerland, and England. Some multinational companies founded during these years still exist. The Austrian freight forwarding firm Gebrueder Weiss, which had offices in several countries in the fourteenth century, continues to operate today. Before the twentieth century, multinational firms were still relatively rare, however.

In the late nineteenth and early twentieth centuries, a few large U.S. corporations began to expand their operations beyond the domestic market. Two key technological innovations made it possible for these firms to coordinate operations on several continents. The first innovation was the successful completion of the transatlantic cable in 1866, which made possible instant communication by telegraph between the United States and Europe. The second innovation was the development of more efficient steam engines, which reduced the cost and increased the speed of long ocean voyages. U.S. firms such as Standard Oil, the Singer Sewing Machine Company, and the American Tobacco Company took advantage of these innovations to establish factories and distribution networks around the world. When firms build or buy facilities in foreign countries, they are engaging in **foreign direct investment**. When individuals or firms buy stocks or bonds issued in another country, they are engaging in **foreign portfolio investment**. In the early twentieth century, most U.S. firms expanded abroad through foreign direct investment because the stock and bond markets in other countries were often too poorly developed to make foreign portfolio investment practical.

Foreign direct investment The purchase or building by a domestic firm of a facility in a foreign country.

Foreign portfolio investment The purchase by an individual or a firm of stocks or bonds issued in another country.

TABLE 8A-1

Top 25 Multinational Corporations, 2007

RANK	CORPORATION	HOME COUNTRY	INDUSTRY
1	Wal-Mart Stores	United States	Retailing
2	Exxon Mobil	United States	Petroleum refining
3	Royal Dutch Shell	The Netherlands/ United Kingdom	Petroleum refining
4	BP	Great Britain	Petroleum refining
5	General Motors	United States	Motor vehicles
6	Toyota Motor	Japan	Motor vehicles
7	Chevron	United States	Petroleum refining
8	DaimlerChrysler	Germany	Motor vehicles
9	ConocoPhillips	United States	Petroleum refining
10	Total	France	Petroleum refining
11	General Electric	United States	Diversified Financials
12	Ford Motor	United States	Motor vehicles
13	ING Group	The Netherlands	Insurance
14	Citigroup	United States	Banking
15	AXA	France	Insurance
16	Volkswagen	Germany	Motor vehicles
17	Sinopec	China	Petroleum refining
18	Crédit Agricole	France	Banking
19	Allianz	Germany	Insurance
20	Fortis	Belgium	Banking
21	Bank of America Corp.	United States	Banking
22	HSBC Holdings	Great Britain	Banking
23	American International Group	United States	Insurance
24	China National Petroleum	China	Petroleum refining
25	BNP Paribas	France	Banking

Note: Corporations are ranked by their revenue.

Source: "Fortune Global 500," *Fortune*, July 23, 2007. © 2007 Time Inc. All rights reserved. Reprinted by permission.

Strategic Factors in Moving from Domestic to Foreign Markets

Today, most large U.S. corporations have established factories and other facilities overseas. Corporations expand their operations outside the United States when they expect to increase their profitability by doing so. Firms might expect to increase their profits through overseas operations for five main reasons:

- *To avoid tariffs or the threat of tariffs.* As we saw in this chapter, tariffs are taxes imposed by countries on imports from other countries. Sometimes firms establish factories in other countries to avoid having to pay tariffs. At other times, a firm establishes a factory in a country to which it is exporting because it fears the other country's government will impose a tariff or some other restriction on its product. Governments often are less concerned about domestic production by foreign-owned companies than they are about imports. As we also saw in this chapter, government restrictions on imports frequently result from a fear that imports will cause job losses in domestic industries. For example, in the 1970s and 1980s, many Americans feared that imports of Japanese automobiles would reduce employment in the U.S. automobile industry. Members of Congress threatened to increase tariffs or impose quotas on imports of Japanese automobiles. In fact, beginning in 1981, a voluntary export restraint reduced imports of Japanese automobiles. In response to this political pressure, the Japanese automobile companies established assembly plants in the United States. Now that a majority of Japanese automobiles sold in the United States are also assembled in the United States by U.S. workers, the Japanese share of the U.S. automobile market is a less heated political issue than it was during the 1970s and 1980s.

- *To gain access to raw materials.* Some U.S. firms have expanded abroad to secure supplies of raw materials. U.S. oil firms—beginning with Standard Oil in the late nineteenth century—have had extensive overseas operations aimed at discovering, recovering, and refining crude oil. In early 2001, one of Standard Oil's successor firms, ChevronTexaco, headquartered in San Francisco, opened its largest oil field in Kazakstan, in the former Soviet Union. ChevronTexaco also constructed a 990-mile pipeline to bring the oil from this field on the Caspian Sea across Russia to a port on the Black Sea.

- *To gain access to low-cost labor.* In the past 20 years, some U.S. firms have located factories or other facilities in countries such as China, India, Malaysia, and El Salvador to take advantage of the lower wages paid to workers in those countries. Most economists believe that this *outsourcing* ultimately improves the efficiency of the economy and raises the consumption of U.S. households, but it can also disrupt the lives of U.S. workers who lose their jobs. For this reason, outsourcing has caused political controversy.

- *To minimize exchange-rate risk.* The exchange rate tells us how many units of foreign currency are received in exchange for a unit of domestic currency. Fluctuations in exchange rates can reduce the profits of a firm that exports goods to other countries. The J. M. Smucker Company, headquartered in Orrville, Ohio, ships jams, ice cream toppings, peanut butter, and other products to more than 70 other countries. Suppose Smucker's has contracted to sell 200,000 cases of jam to a British importer. The British importer will be paying for the shipment in British currency, the pound (the symbol for the pound is £). The importer will pay Smucker's £21 million in 60 days. It is currently possible to exchange $1 for £0.7, so Smucker's expects to receive $30 million (£21 million/£0.70 per dollar) in 60 days. But if the value of the pound falls against the dollar during the next 60 days, the amount Smucker's receives in dollars could be significantly reduced. For example, if the value of the pound falls to £0.80 per $1, then Smucker's will receive only $26.25 million (£21 million/£0.80 per dollar).

  Firms like Smucker's that have extensive international operations are exposed to significant risk to their profits from fluctuations in the values of international currencies. This risk is known as *exchange-rate risk*. If Smucker's began producing jam in Britain, it would reduce its exposure to exchange-rate risk.

- *To respond to industry competition.* In some instances, companies expand overseas as a competitive response to an industry rival. The worldwide competition for markets between Pepsi and Coke is an example of this kind of expansion. Coke began expanding overseas before World War II, and by the 1970s it was earning more from its foreign sales than from its sales in the United States. It became clear to Pepsi's management that the firm needed to compete with Coke in foreign as well as domestic markets. In 1972, Pepsi had a major success when it signed an agreement with the Soviet Union to become the first foreign product sold in that country. Coke and Pepsi continue to compete vigorously in many countries, with their shares of the market often fluctuating significantly.

Many U.S. jobs require technical training and pay higher wages.

Making the Connection

Have Multinational Corporations Reduced Employment and Lowered Wages in the United States?

During the 1990s, some U.S. corporations responded to the greater economic openness of many poorer countries by relocating manufacturing operations to those countries. For example, most U.S. toy firms, such as Mattel, now produce nearly all their toys in factories in China. Most U.S. clothing manufacturers now produce the bulk of their goods in factories in Central America or Asia. These firms have reduced their production costs by paying much lower wages in their overseas factories than they were paying in the United States. The workers who lost their jobs in U.S. factories have often experienced periods of unemployment and have sometimes had to accept lower wages when they find new jobs. Towns and cities where factories closed have also been hurt by losses of tax revenues to support schools and other local services.

Most economists, however, do not believe that relocating jobs abroad has reduced either total employment in the United States or the average wage paid to U.S. workers. The overall level of employment in the United States in the long run is not affected by job losses in particular industries, however painful the losses may be to those experiencing them. The U.S. economy creates more than 2 million additional new jobs during a typical year. Nearly all workers who lose jobs at one firm eventually find new ones at other firms.

Competition from low-wage foreign workers has not reduced the average wages of U.S. workers. Wages are determined by the ability of workers to produce goods and services. This ability depends in part on the workers' education and training and in part on the machinery and equipment available to them. American workers have high wages because, on average, they are well trained and because of the quantity and quality of the machinery and equipment they work with. Low-wage foreign workers are generally less well trained and work with smaller amounts of machinery and equipment than do American workers.

Beginning in the 1990s and continuing through the 2000s, the gap in the United States between the wages of skilled workers and the wages of unskilled workers increased. It has been suggested that competition from low-wage foreign workers forced unskilled U.S. workers to accept lower wages to keep their jobs. To a small extent, the increase in the wage gap in the United States may have been due to this cause. But careful economic studies have shown that most of the increase in the wage gap is due to developments within the U.S. economy—such as the increasing number of jobs that require technical training—that have resulted in higher pay to skilled workers rather than to competition from low-wage foreign workers.

YOUR TURN: Test your understanding by doing related problem 8A.12 on page 282 at the end of this appendix.

Most U.S. firms have followed similar steps in expanding their operations overseas: Newly established firms usually begin by selling only within the United States. If successful in the domestic market, they begin to export. They initially use foreign firms to market and distribute their products. If sales are good in these foreign markets, U.S. firms establish their own overseas marketing and distribution networks. Finally, firms establish their own production facilities in these foreign countries. Since World War II, many U.S. firms have switched from building their own production facilities to a strategy of acquiring local firms that were already producing the good. Some firms have first licensed production to local firms, later acquiring the firms. U.S.-based Colgate-Palmolive, for example, typically has entered a foreign market first by licensing a foreign soap manufacturer to produce its brands, while keeping control over marketing and distribution. Typically, Colgate-Palmolive has eventually acquired ownership of the foreign firm.

Challenges to U.S. Firms in Foreign Markets

It seems obvious that any successful firm will want to expand into foreign markets. After all, it is always better to have more customers than fewer customers. In fact, however, expanding into foreign markets can often be quite difficult, and the additional costs incurred may end up being greater than the additional revenue gained. One problem encountered by U.S. firms is differences in tastes between U.S. and foreign consumers. Although products like Coke seem to appeal to consumers everywhere in the world, other products run into problems because of cultural differences among countries. For example, Singapore banned Janet Jackson's album *All for You* because, according to a government spokesman, its "sexually explicit lyrics" were "not acceptable to our society." In 2002, eBay closed its online auction site in Japan. Although eBay is successful selling collectibles in the United States, many Japanese consumers do not like to buy used goods. In 2006, Wal-Mart announced it would sell its 85 stores in Germany, taking a loss of $1 billion. German consumers were not as receptive as U.S. consumers are to buying groceries, clothes, consumer electronics, and other products in one very large store.

Some U.S. companies have had difficulty adapting their employment practices to deal with the differences between U.S. and foreign labor markets. Many countries have much stronger labor unions than does the United States, and many foreign governments regulate labor markets much more than does the U.S. government. For example, government regulations in most European countries make it much more difficult than it is in the United States to lay off workers.

Competitive Advantages of U.S. Firms

Some U.S. firms have successful foreign operations because of the strength of their brand names. Many producers of soft drinks and many fast food restaurants can be found in nearly every foreign country, but Coca-Cola and McDonald's have such strong name recognition that their appeal extends around the world. Other firms have developed a significant technological edge over foreign rivals. Microsoft, the software giant, and Hewlett-Packard, the computer and printer firm, are examples. Some U.S. firms, such as Dell Computer and Boeing, have advantages over foreign manufacturers based on having developed the most efficient and low-cost way of producing a good.

A U.S. firm's global competitive advantage changes over time. This change is illustrated dramatically by the experience of U.S. semiconductor firms. The semiconductor industry originated in the United States, with the invention of the transistor at Bell Telephone Laboratories in 1947. U.S. predominance in the industry was enhanced further in 1959, with the invention of the integrated circuit, which contains multiple transistors on a single silicon chip. Through 1980, U.S. firms held between 60 and 80 percent of the global market for semiconductors. Beginning in the 1970s, the Japanese government moved to establish a strong domestic semiconductor industry by subsidizing domestic firms and by limiting imports of semiconductors from the United States. The Japanese policy was very successful with respect to DRAM—dynamic random access memory—the most basic chip. By the mid-1980s, Japanese firms dominated the global market, and nearly all U.S. chipmakers had abandoned DRAM manufacture. Many observers predicted the collapse of the U.S. semiconductor industry. Even Intel Corporation, the most successful U.S. semiconductor firm, appeared to be close to bankruptcy.

From this low point, U.S. semiconductor firms rebounded to regain global predominance by the 1990s. The key to the rebound of U.S. firms was the decreasing demand for simple memory chips and the increasing demand for two products: microprocessors—such as Intel's Pentium 4 chip used in personal computers—and ASICs—application-specific integrated circuits—which are used in many electronic products. In manufacturing microprocessors and ASICs, a firm's ability to rapidly design and develop new products is more important than using low-cost production processes. U.S. firms, such as Intel, have proven to be much better at designing and rapidly bringing to market advanced microprocessors and ASICs than have competing firms in Japan, South Korea, and elsewhere.

Key Terms

Foreign direct investment,
p. 277

Foreign portfolio investment,
p. 277

Multinational enterprise,
p. 277

LEARNING OBJECTIVE   Understand the reasons why firms operate in more than one country, **pages 277–281.**

 Visit www.myeconlab.com to complete these exercises
Get Ahead of the Curve online and get instant feedback.

Review Questions

8A.1 When did large U.S. corporations first begin to operate internationally? What key technological changes made it easier for U.S. corporations to operate overseas?

8A.2 What is the difference between foreign direct investment and foreign portfolio investment? Is the Camry assembly plant that Toyota operates in Kentucky an example of foreign direct investment or foreign portfolio investment?

8A.3 What are the five main reasons firms expand their operations overseas? Which of these reasons explains why U.S.-based oil companies have extensive overseas operations?

8A.4 What are the main reasons U.S. firms succeed overseas?

Problems and Applications

8A.5 Suppose it is 1850 and you are operating a large factory manufacturing cotton cloth. You are considering expanding your operations overseas. What technical problems are you likely to encounter in coordinating your overseas and domestic operations?

8A.6 The Ford Motor Company and the International Harvester Company were two of the first U.S. firms to establish extensive manufacturing operations overseas. Why might a producer of automobiles and a producer of farm machinery find it particularly advantageous to manufacture their products in countries in which they have substantial sales?

8A.7 Why might many U.S. firms that were expanding their operations overseas after World War II have been more likely to acquire an existing firm in the market they were entering rather than build new facilities there?

8A.8 Would a firm based in the United States ever produce a good in another country if it cost less to produce it in the United States and ship it to the other country? Explain.

8A.9 Is expanding a firm's operations internationally really any different than expanding within a nation? For example, if a firm is based in Texas, what's the difference between it expanding operations to Mexico, Canada, Singapore, or Germany rather than to North Carolina or Pennsylvania?

8A.10 Is expanding a firm's operations internationally really any different than expanding into a new product market? For example, is Whirlpool's expanding into Europe different than Whirlpool's expanding by making a new line of appliances, such as humidifiers?

8A.11 If you ran a successful U.S. firm like Wal-Mart, IBM, or Hershey's, into which countries would you first expand? Why?

8A.12 (Related to the *Making the Connection* on page 280) Suppose that the U.S. government wanted to help those textile workers who have lost their jobs as U.S. clothing manufacturers have moved to Central America and Asia. To do this, the government imposes a tariff on imported textiles. What would be the effects of this policy on employment in the U.S. textile industry? Would the policy increase total employment in the United States? What would happen to employment in U.S. industries other than the textile industry?

>> End Appendix Learning Objective

We begin this chapter by exploring how consumers make decisions. In Chapter 1, we saw that economists usually assume that people act in a rational, self-interested way. In explaining consumer behavior, this means economists believe consumers make choices that will leave them as satisfied as possible, given their *tastes*, their *incomes*, and the *prices* of the goods and services available to them. We will see how the downward-sloping demand curves we encountered in Chapters 3 through 5 result from the economic model of consumer behavior. We will also see that in certain situations, knowing the best decision to make can be difficult. In these cases, economic reasoning provides a powerful tool for consumers to improve their decision making. Finally, we will see that *experimental economics* has shown that factors such as social pressure and notions of fairness can affect consumer behavior. We will look at how businesses take these factors into account when setting prices. In the appendix to this chapter, we extend the analysis by using indifference curves and budget lines to understand consumer behavior.

9.1 LEARNING OBJECTIVE

9.1 | Define utility and explain how consumers choose goods and services to maximize their utility.

Utility and Consumer Decision Making

We saw in Chapter 3 that the model of demand and supply is a powerful tool for analyzing how prices and quantities are determined. We also saw that, according to the *law of demand*, whenever the price of a good falls, the quantity demanded increases. In this section, we will show how the economic model of consumer behavior leads to the law of demand.

The Economic Model of Consumer Behavior in a Nutshell

Imagine walking through a shopping mall, trying to decide how to spend your clothing budget. If you had an unlimited budget, your decision would be easy: Just buy as much of everything as you want. Given that you have a limited budget, what do you do? Economists assume that consumers act so as to make themselves as well off as possible. Therefore, you should choose the one combination of clothes that makes you as well off as possible from among those combinations that you can afford. Stated more generally, the economic model of consumer behavior predicts that consumers will choose to buy the combination of goods and services that makes them as well off as possible from among all the combinations that their budgets allow them to buy.

   This prediction may seem obvious and not particularly useful. But as we explore the implication of this prediction, we will see that it leads to conclusions that are both useful and not obvious.

Utility

Ultimately, how well off you are from consuming a particular combination of goods and services depends on your tastes, or preferences. There is an old saying—"There's no accounting for tastes"—and economists don't try to. If you buy Cherry Coke instead of Pepsi, even though Pepsi has a lower price, you must receive more enjoyment or satisfaction from drinking Cherry Coke. Economists refer to the enjoyment or satisfaction people receive from consuming goods and services as **utility**. So we can say that the goal of a consumer is to spend available income so as to maximize utility. But utility is a difficult concept to measure because there is no way of knowing exactly how much enjoyment or satisfaction someone receives from consuming a product. Similarly, it is not possible to compare utility across consumers. There is no way of knowing for sure whether Jill receives more or less satisfaction than Jack from drinking a bottle of Cherry Coke.

Utility The enjoyment or satisfaction people receive from consuming goods and services.

Two hundred years ago, economists hoped to measure utility in units called "utils." The util would be an objective measure in the same way that temperature is: If it is 70 degrees in New York and 70 degrees in Los Angeles, it is just as warm in both cities. These economists wanted to say that if Jack's utility from eating a hamburger is 10 utils and Jill's utility is 5 utils, then Jack receives exactly twice the satisfaction from eating a hamburger that Jill does. In fact, it is *not* possible to measure utility across people. It turns out that none of the important conclusions of the economic model of consumer behavior depend on utility being directly measurable (a point we demonstrate in the appendix to this chapter). Nevertheless, the economic model of consumer behavior is easier to understand if we assume that utility is something directly measurable, like temperature.

The Principle of Diminishing Marginal Utility

To make the model of consumer behavior more concrete, let's see how a consumer makes decisions in a case involving just two products: pepperoni pizza and Coke. To begin, consider how the utility you receive from consuming a good changes with the amount of the good you consume. For example, suppose that you have just arrived at a Super Bowl party where the hosts are serving pepperoni pizza, and you are very hungry. In this situation, you are likely to receive quite a lot of enjoyment, or utility, from consuming the first slice of pizza. Suppose this satisfaction is measurable and is equal to 20 units of utility, or *utils*. After eating the first slice, you decide to have a second slice. Because you are no longer as hungry, the satisfaction you receive from eating the second slice of pizza is less than the satisfaction you received from eating the first slice. Consuming the second slice increases your utility by only an *additional* 16 utils, which raises your *total* utility from eating the two slices to 36 utils. If you continue eating slices, each additional slice gives you less and less additional satisfaction.

The table in Figure 9-1 shows the relationship between the number of slices of pizza you consume while watching the Super Bowl and the amount of utility you receive. The second column in the table shows the total utility you receive from eating a particular number of slices. The third column shows the additional utility, or **marginal utility** (**MU**), you receive from consuming one additional slice. (Remember that in economics, "marginal" means additional.) For example, as you increase your consumption from 2 slices to 3 slices, your total utility increases from 36 to 46, so your marginal utility from consuming the third slice is 10 utils. As the table shows, by the time you eat the fifth slice of pizza that evening, your marginal utility is very low: only 2 utils. If you were to eat a sixth slice, you would become slightly nauseated, and your marginal utility would actually be a *negative* 3 utils.

> **Marginal utility (MU)** The change in total utility a person receives from consuming one additional unit of a good or service.

Figure 9-1 also plots the numbers from the table as graphs. Panel (a) shows how your total utility rises as you eat the first five slices of pizza and then falls as you eat the sixth slice. Panel (b) shows how your marginal utility declines with each additional slice you eat and finally becomes negative when you eat the sixth slice. The height of the marginal utility line at any quantity of pizza in panel (b) represents the change in utility as a result of consuming that additional slice. For example, the change in utility as a result of consuming 4 slices instead of 3 is 6 utils, so the height of the marginal utility line in panel (b) is 6 utils.

The relationship illustrated in Figure 9-1 between consuming additional units of a product during a period of time and the marginal utility received from consuming each additional unit is referred to as the **law of diminishing marginal utility**. For nearly every good or service, the more you consume during a period of time, the less you increase your total satisfaction from each additional unit you consume.

> **Law of diminishing marginal utility** The principle that consumers experience diminishing additional satisfaction as they consume more of a good or service during a given period of time.

The Rule of Equal Marginal Utility per Dollar Spent

The key challenge for consumers is to decide how to allocate their limited incomes among all the products they wish to buy. Every consumer has to make trade-offs: If you have $100 to spend on entertainment for the month, then the more DVDs you buy, the

Figure 9-1

Total and Marginal Utility from Eating Pizza on Super Bowl Sunday

The table shows that for the first 5 slices of pizza, the more you eat, the more your total satisfaction or utility increases. If you eat a sixth slice, you start to feel ill from eating too much pizza, and your total utility falls. Each additional slice increases your utility by less than the previous slice, so your marginal utility from each slice is less than the one before. Panel (a) shows your total utility rising as you eat the first 5 slices and falling with the sixth slice. Panel (b) shows your marginal utility falling with each additional slice you eat and becoming negative with the sixth slice. The height of the marginal utility line at any quantity of pizza in panel (b) represents the change in utility as a result of consuming that additional slice. For example, the change in utility as a result of consuming 4 slices instead of 3 is 6 utils, so the height of the marginal utility line in panel (b) for the fourth slice is 6 utils.

Number of Slices	Total Utility from Eating Pizza	Marginal Utility from the Last Slice Eaten
0	0	--
1	20	20
2	36	16
3	46	10
4	52	6
5	54	2
6	51	-3

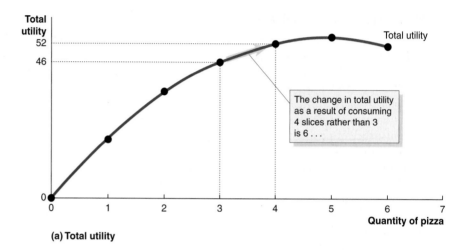

The change in total utility as a result of consuming 4 slices rather than 3 is 6 . . .

(a) Total utility

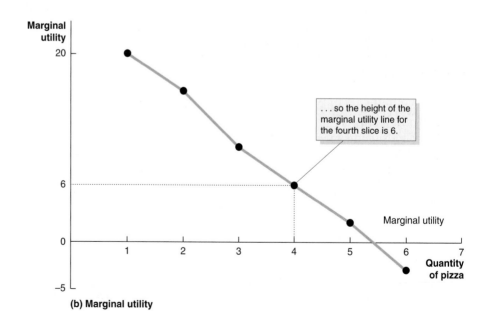

. . . so the height of the marginal utility line for the fourth slice is 6.

(b) Marginal utility

fewer movies you can see in the theater. Economists refer to the limited amount of income you have available to spend on goods and services as your **budget constraint**. The principle of diminishing marginal utility helps us understand how consumers can best spend their limited incomes on the products available to them.

> **Budget constraint** The limited amount of income available to consumers to spend on goods and services.

Suppose you attend a Super Bowl party at a restaurant, and you have $10 to spend on refreshments. Pizza is selling for $2 per slice, and Coke is selling for $1 per cup. Table 9-1 shows the relationship between the amount of pizza you eat, the amount of Coke you drink, and the amount of satisfaction, or utility, you receive. The values for pizza are repeated from the table in Figure 9-1. The values for Coke also follow the principle of diminishing marginal utility.

How many slices of pizza and how many cups of Coke do you buy if you want to maximize your utility? If you did not have a budget constraint, you would buy 5 slices of pizza and 5 cups of Coke because that would give you total utility of 107 (54 + 53), which is the maximum utility you can achieve. Eating another slice of pizza or drinking another cup of Coke during the evening would lower your utility. Unfortunately, you do have a budget constraint: You have only $10 to spend. To buy 5 slices of pizza (at $2 per slice) and 5 cups of Coke (at $1 per cup), you would need $15.

To select the best way to spend your $10, remember this key economic principle: *Optimal decisions are made at the margin.* That is, most of the time, economic decision makers—consumers, firms, and the government—are faced with decisions about whether to do a little more of one thing or a little more of an alternative. In this case, you are choosing to consume a little more pizza or a little more Coke. BMW chooses to manufacture more roadsters or more SUVs in its South Carolina factory. Congress and the president choose to spend more for research on heart disease or more for research on breast cancer. Every economic decision maker faces a budget constraint, and every economic decision maker faces trade-offs.

The key to making the best consumption decision is to maximize utility by following the *rule of equal marginal utility per dollar spent.* As you decide how to spend your income, you should buy pizza and Coke up to the point where the last slice of pizza purchased and the last cup of Coke purchased give you equal increases in utility *per dollar.* By doing this, you will have maximized your total utility.

It is important to remember that to follow this rule, you must equalize your marginal utility per dollar spent, *not* your marginal utility from each good. Buying season tickets for your favorite NFL team or for the opera or buying a BMW may give you a lot more satisfaction than drinking a cup of Coke, but the NFL tickets may well give you less

TABLE 9-1 | Total Utility and Marginal Utility from Eating Pizza and Drinking Coke

NUMBER OF SLICES OF PIZZA	TOTAL UTILITY FROM EATING PIZZA	MARGINAL UTILITY FROM THE LAST SLICE	NUMBER OF CUPS OF COKE	TOTAL UTILITY FROM DRINKING COKE	MARGINAL UTILITY FROM THE LAST CUP
0	0	—	0	0	—
1	20	20	1	20	20
2	36	16	2	35	15
3	46	10	3	45	10
4	52	6	4	50	5
5	54	2	5	53	3
6	51	−3	6	52	−1

TABLE 9-2 | Converting Marginal Utility to Marginal Utility per Dollar

(1) SLICES OF PIZZA	(2) MARGINAL UTILITY (MU_{PIZZA})	(3) MARGINAL UTILITY PER DOLLAR $\left(\dfrac{MU_{pizza}}{P_{pizza}}\right)$	(4) CUPS OF COKE	(5) MARGINAL UTILITY (MU_{COKE})	(6) MARGINAL UTILITY PER DOLLAR $\left(\dfrac{MU_{Coke}}{P_{Coke}}\right)$
1	20	10	1	20	20
2	16	8	2	15	15
3	10	5	3	10	10
4	6	3	4	5	5
5	2	1	5	3	3
6	–3	–1.5	6	–1	–1

satisfaction *per dollar* spent. To decide how many slices of pizza and how many cups of Coke to buy, you must convert the values for marginal utility in Table 9-1 into marginal utility per dollar. You can do this by dividing marginal utility by the price of each good, as shown in Table 9-2.

In column (3), we calculate marginal utility per dollar spent on pizza. Because the price of pizza is $2 per slice, the marginal utility per dollar from eating one slice of pizza equals 20 divided by $2, or 10 utils per dollar. Similarly, we show in column (6) that because the price of Coke is $1 per cup, the marginal utility per dollar from drinking 1 cup of Coke equals 20 divided by $1, or 20 utils per dollar. To maximize the total utility you receive, you must make sure that the utility per dollar of pizza for the last slice of pizza is equal to the utility per dollar of Coke for the last cup of Coke. Table 9-2 shows that there are three combinations of slices of pizza and cups of Coke where marginal utility per dollar is equalized. Table 9-3 lists the combinations, the total amount of money needed to buy each combination, and the total utility received from consuming each combination.

If you buy 4 slices of pizza, the last slice gives you 3 utils per dollar. If you buy 5 cups of Coke, the last cup also gives you 3 utils per dollar, so you have equalized your marginal utility per dollar. Unfortunately, as the third column in the table shows, to buy 4 slices and 5 cups, you would need $13, and you have only $10. You could also equalize your marginal utility per dollar by buying 1 slice and 3 cups, but that would cost just $5, leaving you with $5 to spend. Only when you buy 3 slices and 4 cups have you equalized your marginal utility per dollar and spent neither more nor less than the $10 available.

TABLE 9-3 | Equalizing Marginal Utility per Dollar Spent

COMBINATIONS OF PIZZA AND COKE WITH EQUAL MARGINAL UTILITIES PER DOLLAR	MARGINAL UTILITY PER DOLLAR (MARGINAL UTILITY/PRICE)	TOTAL SPENDING	TOTAL UTILITY
1 slice of pizza and 3 cups of Coke	10	$2 + $3 = $5	20 + 45 = 65
3 slices of pizza and 4 cups of Coke	5	$6 + $4 = $10	46 + 50 = 96
4 slices of pizza and 5 cups of Coke	3	$8 + $5 = $13	52 + 53 = 105

We can summarize the two conditions for maximizing utility:

1 $$\frac{MU_{Pizza}}{P_{Pizza}} = \frac{MU_{Coke}}{P_{Coke}}$$

2 Spending on pizza + Spending on Coke = Amount available to be spent

The first condition shows that the marginal utility per dollar spent must be the same for both goods. The second condition is the budget constraint, which states that total spending on both goods must equal the amount available to be spent. Of course, these conditions for maximizing utility apply not just to pizza and Coke but to any two pairs of goods.

Solved Problem | 9-1

Finding the Optimal Level of Consumption

The following table shows Lee's utility from consuming ice cream cones and cans of Lime Fizz soda.

NUMBER OF ICE CREAM CONES	TOTAL UTILITY FROM ICE CREAM CONES	MARGINAL UTILITY FROM LAST CONE	NUMBER OF CANS OF LIME FIZZ	TOTAL UTILITY FROM CANS OF LIME FIZZ	MARGINAL UTILITY FROM LAST CAN
0	0	—	0	0	—
1	30	30	1	40	40
2	55	25	2	75	35
3	75	20	3	101	26
4	90	15	4	119	18
5	100	10	5	134	15
6	105	5	6	141	7

a. Ed inspects this table and concludes, "Lee's optimal choice would be to consume 4 ice cream cones and 5 cans of Lime Fizz because with that combination, his marginal utility from ice cream cones is equal to his marginal utility from Lime Fizz." Do you agree with Ed's reasoning? Briefly explain.

b. Suppose that Lee has an unlimited budget to spend on ice cream cones and cans of Lime Fizz. Under these cir-cumstances, how many ice cream cones and how many cans of Lime Fizz will he consume?

c. Suppose that Lee has $7 per week to spend on ice cream cones and Lime Fizz. The price of an ice cream cone is $2, and the price of a can of Lime Fizz is $1. If Lee wants to maximize his utility, how many ice cream cones and how many cans of Lime Fizz should he buy?

SOLVING THE PROBLEM:

Step 1: **Review the chapter material.** This problem involves finding the optimal consumption of two goods, so you may want to review the section "The Rule of Equal Marginal Utility per Dollar Spent," which begins on page 287.

Step 2: **Answer question (a) by analyzing Ed's reasoning.** Ed's reasoning is incorrect. To maximize utility, Lee needs to equalize marginal utility per dollar for the two goods.

The Income Effect and Substitution Effect of a Price Change

We can use the rule of equal marginal utility per dollar to analyze how consumers adjust their buying decisions when a price changes. Suppose you are back at the restaurant for the Super Bowl party, but this time the price of pizza is $1.50 per slice, rather than $2. You still have $10 to spend on pizza and Coke.

When the price of pizza was $2 per slice and the price of Coke was $1 per cup, your optimal choice was to consume 3 slices of pizza and 4 cups of Coke. The fall in the price of pizza to $1.50 per slice has two effects on the quantity of pizza you consume: the *income effect* and the *substitution effect*. First, consider the income effect. When the price of a good falls, you have more purchasing power. In our example, 3 slices of pizza and 4 cups of Coke now cost a total of only $8.50 instead of $10.00. An increase in purchasing power is essentially the same thing as an increase in income. The change in the quantity of pizza you will demand because of this increase in purchasing power—holding all other factors constant—is the **income effect** of the price change. Recall from Chapter 3 that if a product is a *normal good*, a consumer increases the quantity demanded as the consumer's income rises, but if a product is an *inferior good*, a consumer decreases the quantity demanded as the consumer's income rises. So, if we assume that for you pizza is a normal good, the income effect of a fall in price causes you to consume more pizza. If pizza had been an inferior good for you, the income effect of a fall in the price would have caused you to consume less pizza.

The second effect of the price change is the substitution effect. When the price of pizza falls, pizza becomes cheaper *relative* to Coke, and the marginal utility per dollar for each slice of pizza you consume increases. If we hold constant the effect of the price change on your purchasing power and just focus on the effect of the price being lower relative to the price of the other good, we have isolated the **substitution effect** of the price change. The lower price of pizza relative to the price of Coke has lowered the *opportunity cost* to you of consuming pizza because now you have to give up less Coke to consume the same quantity of pizza. Therefore, the substitution effect from the fall in the price of pizza relative to the price of Coke will cause you to eat more pizza and drink less Coke. In this case, both the income effect and the substitution effect of the fall in price cause you to eat more pizza. If the price of pizza had risen, both the income effect and the substitution effect would have caused you to eat less pizza. Table 9-4 summarizes the effect of a price change on the quantity demanded.

We can use Table 9-5 to determine the effect of the fall in the price of pizza on your optimal consumption. Table 9-5 has the same information as Table 9-2, with one change: The marginal utility per dollar from eating pizza has been changed to reflect the new lower price of $1.50 per slice. Examining the table, we can see that the fall in the price of pizza will result in your eating 1 more slice of pizza, so your optimal consumption now becomes 4 slices of pizza and 4 cups of Coke. You will be spending all of your $10, and the last dollar you spend on pizza will provide you with about the same marginal utility per dollar as the last dollar you spend on Coke. You will not be receiving

Income effect The change in the quantity demanded of a good that results from the effect of a change in price on consumer purchasing power, holding all other factors constant.

Substitution effect The change in the quantity demanded of a good that results from a change in price making the good more or less expensive relative to other goods, holding constant the effect of the price change on consumer purchasing power.

TABLE 9-4

Income Effect and Substitution Effect of a Price Change

		INCOME EFFECT		SUBSTITUTION EFFECT
PRICE DECREASE	Increases the consumer's purchasing power, which . . .	. . . if a normal good, causes the quantity demanded to increase.	. . . if an inferior good, causes the quantity demanded to decrease.	Lowers the opportunity cost of consuming the good, which causes the quantity of the good demanded to increase.
PRICE INCREASE	Decreases the consumer's purchasing power, which . . .	. . . if a normal good, causes the quantity demanded to decrease.	. . . if an inferior good, causes the quantity demanded to increase.	Raises the opportunity cost of consuming the good, which causes the quantity of the good demanded to decrease.

TABLE 9-5 | Adjusting Optimal Consumption to a Lower Price of Pizza

NUMBER OF SLICES OF PIZZA	MARGINAL UTILITY FROM LAST SLICE (MU_{Pizza})	MARGINAL UTILITY PER DOLLAR $\left(\dfrac{MU_{Pizza}}{P_{Pizza}}\right)$	NUMBER OF CUPS OF COKE	MARGINAL UTILITY FROM LAST CUP (MU_{COKE})	MARGINAL UTILITY PER DOLLAR $\left(\dfrac{MU_{Coke}}{P_{Coke}}\right)$
1	20	13.33	1	20	20
2	16	10.67	2	15	15
3	10	6.67	3	10	10
4	6	4	4	5	5
5	2	1.33	5	3	3
6	−3	—	6	−1	—

exactly the same marginal utility per dollar spent on the two products. As Table 9-5 shows, the last slice of pizza gives you 4 utils per dollar, and the last cup of Coke gives you 5 utils per dollar. But this is as close as you can come to equalizing marginal utility per dollar for the two products, unless you can buy a fraction of a slice of pizza or a fraction of a cup of Coke.

9.2 | Use the concept of utility to explain the law of demand.

Where Demand Curves Come From

We saw in Chapter 3 that, according to the *law of demand*, whenever the price of a product falls, the quantity demanded increases. Now that we have covered the concepts of total utility, marginal utility, and the budget constraint, we can look more closely at why the law of demand holds.

In our example of optimal consumption of pizza and Coke at the Super Bowl party, we found the following:

Price of pizza = $2 per slice ⇒ Quantity of pizza demanded = 3 slices

Price of pizza = $1.50 per slice ⇒ Quantity of pizza demanded = 4 slices

In panel (a) of Figure 9-2, we plot the two points showing the optimal number of pizza slices you choose to consume at each price. In panel (b) of Figure 9-2, we draw a line connecting the two points. This downward-sloping line represents your demand curve for pizza. We could find more points on the line by changing the price of pizza and using the information in Table 9-2 to find the new optimal number of slices of pizza you would demand at each price.

To this point in this chapter, we have been looking at an individual demand curve. As we saw in Chapter 3, however, economists are typically interested in market demand curves. We can construct the market demand curve from the individual demand curves for all the consumers in the market. To keep things simple, let's assume that there are only three consumers in the market for pizza: you, David, and Sharon. The table in Figure 9-3 shows the individual demand schedules for the three consumers. Because consumers differ in their incomes and their preferences for products, we would not expect every consumer to demand the same quantity of a given product at each price. The final column gives the market demand, which is simply the sum of the quantities demanded by each of the three consumers at each price. For example, at a price of $1.50 per slice, your quantity demanded is 4 slices, David's quantity demanded is 6 slices, and Sharon's quantity demanded is 5 slices. So, at a price of $1.50, a quantity of 15 slices is demanded in the market. The graphs in the figure show that we can obtain the market demand curve by adding horizontally the individual demand curves.

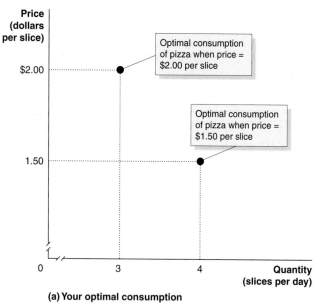

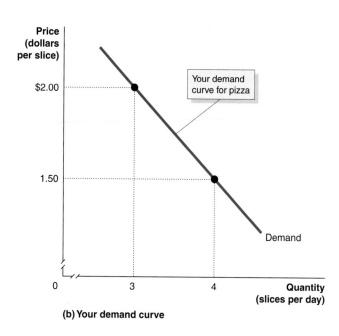

Figure 9-2 | Deriving the Demand Curve for Pizza

A consumer responds optimally to a fall in the price of a product by consuming more of that product. In panel (a), the price of pizza falls from $2 per slice to $1.50, and the optimal quantity of slices consumed rises from 3 to 4. When we graph this result in panel (b), we have the consumer's demand curve.

	Quantity (slices per day)			
Price (dollars per slice)	You	David	Sharon	Market
$2.50	2	4	1	7
2.00	3	5	3	11
1.50	4	6	5	15
1.00	5	7	7	19
0.50	6	8	9	23

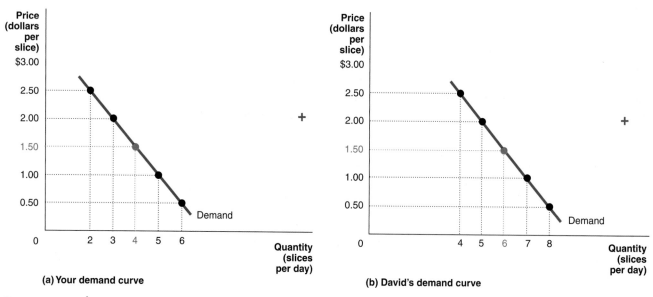

Figure 9-3 | Deriving the Market Demand Curve from Individual Demand Curves

The table shows that the total quantity demanded in a market is the sum of the quantities demanded by each buyer. We can find the market demand curve by adding horizontally the individual demand curves in parts (a), (b), and (c). For instance, at a price of $1.50, your quantity demanded is 4 slices, David's quantity demanded is 6 slices, and Sharon's quantity demanded is 5 slices. Therefore, part (d) shows a price of $1.50, and a quantity demanded of 15 is a point on the market demand curve.

Remember that according to the law of demand, market demand curves always slope downward. We now know that this is true because the income and substitution effects of a fall in price cause consumers to increase the quantity of the good they demand. There is a complicating factor, however. As we discussed earlier, only for normal goods will the income effect result in consumers increasing the quantity of the good they demand when the price falls. If the good is an inferior good, then the income effect leads consumers to *decrease* the quantity of the good they demand. The substitution effect, on the other hand, results in consumers increasing the quantity they demand of both normal and inferior goods when the price falls. So, when the price of an inferior good falls, the income and substitution effects work in opposite directions: The income effect causes consumers to decrease the quantity of the good they demand, whereas the substitution effect causes consumers to increase the quantity of the good they demand. Is it possible, then, that consumers might actually buy less of a good when the price falls? If this happened, the demand curve would be upward sloping.

For a demand curve to be upward sloping, the good would have to be an inferior good, and the income effect would have to be larger than the substitution effect. Goods that have both of these characteristics are called *Giffen goods*. Although we can conceive of there being Giffen goods, none has ever been discovered because for all actual goods, the substitution effect is larger than the income effect. Therefore, even for an inferior good, a fall in price leads to an increase in quantity demanded, and a rise in price leads to a decrease in the quantity demanded.

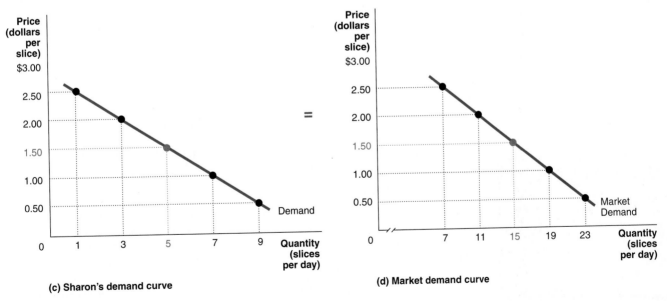

(c) Sharon's demand curve

(d) Market demand curve

Figure 9-3 | Continued

9.3 LEARNING OBJECTIVE

9.3 | Explain how social influences can affect consumption choices.

Social Influences on Decision Making

Sociologists and anthropologists have argued that social factors such as culture, customs, and religion are very important in explaining the choices consumers make. Economists have traditionally seen such factors as being relatively unimportant, if they take them into consideration at all. Recently, however, some economists have begun to study how social factors influence consumer choice.

For example, people seem to receive more utility from consuming goods they believe are popular. As the economists Gary Becker and Kevin Murphy put it:

> The utility from drugs, crime, going bowling, owning a Rolex watch, voting Democratic, dressing informally at work, or keeping a neat lawn depends on whether friends and neighbors take drugs, commit crimes, go bowling, own Rolex watches, vote Democratic, dress informally, or keep their lawns neat.

This reasoning can help to explain why one restaurant is packed, while another restaurant that serves essentially the same food and has a similar décor has many fewer customers. Consumers decide which restaurant to go to partly on the basis of food and décor but also on the basis of the restaurant's popularity. People receive utility from being seen eating at a popular restaurant because they believe it makes them appear knowledgeable and fashionable. Whenever consumption takes place publicly, many consumers base their purchasing decisions on what other consumers are buying. Examples of public consumption include eating in restaurants, attending sporting events, wearing clothes or jewelry, and driving cars. In all these cases, the decision to buy a product depends partly on the characteristics of the product and partly on how many other people are buying the product.

The Effects of Celebrity Endorsements

In many cases, it is not just the number of people who use a product that makes it desirable but the types of people who use it. If consumers believe that movie stars or professional athletes use a product, demand for the product will often increase. This may be partly because consumers believe public figures are particularly knowledgeable about products: "Tiger Woods knows more about cars than I do, so I'll buy the same car he drives." But many consumers also feel more fashionable and closer to famous people if they use the same products these people do. These considerations help to explain why companies are willing to pay millions of dollars to have celebrities endorse their products. As we saw at the beginning of this chapter, Coke has been using celebrities in its advertising for decades.

In 2006, Tiger Woods earned $12 million from playing golf and $100 million from product endorsements.

Making
the
Connection

Why Do Firms Pay Tiger Woods to Endorse Their Products?

Tiger Woods may be the best golfer who's ever lived. In his first five years as a professional, he won 27 tournaments on the Professional Golfers' Association (PGA) tour. When he won the Masters in 2001, he became the first golfer ever to win all four major professional golf championships in the same year. In late 2006 and early 2007, Tiger seemed hotter than ever when he won seven straight tournaments on the PGA tour. Even though Tiger Woods is a great golfer, should consumers care what products he uses? A number of major companies apparently believe consumers do care. The General Motors, Nike, Titleist, American Express, and Rolex companies collectively pay him more than $50 million per year to endorse their products.

There seems little doubt that consumers care what products Tiger uses, but *why* do they care? It might be that they believe Tiger has better information than they do about the products he endorses. The average weekend golfer might believe that if Tiger endorses Titleist golf clubs, maybe Titleist clubs are better than other golf clubs. But it seems more likely that people buy products associated with Tiger Woods or other celebrities because using these products makes them feel closer to the celebrity endorser or because it makes them appear to be fashionable.

YOUR TURN: Test your understanding by doing related problem 3.9 on page 315 at the end of this chapter.

▬▬▬

Network Externalities

Technology can play a role in explaining why consumers buy products that many other consumers are already buying. There is a **network externality** in the consumption of a product if the usefulness of the product increases with the number of consumers who use it. For example, if you owned the only cell phone in the world, it would not be very useful. The usefulness of cell phones increases with the number of people who own them. Similarly, your willingness to buy an iPod depends in part on the number of other people who own iPods. The more people who own iPods, the more music that will be available to download and the more useful an iPod is to you.

Some economists have suggested the possibility that network externalities may have a significant downside because they might result in consumers buying products that contain inferior technologies. This outcome could occur because network externalities can create significant *switching costs* to changing products: When a product becomes established, consumers may find it too costly to switch to a new product that contains a better technology. The selection of products may be *path dependent*. This means that because of switching costs, the technology that was first available may have advantages over better technologies that were developed later. In other words, the path along which the economy has developed in the past is important.

One example of path dependency and the use of an inferior technology is the QWERTY order of the letters along the top row of most computer keyboards. This order became widely used when manual typewriters were developed in the late nineteenth century. The metal keys on manual typewriters would stick together if a user typed too fast, and the QWERTY keyboard was designed to slow down typists and minimize the problem of the keys sticking together. With computers, the problem that QWERTY was developed to solve no longer exists, so keyboards could be changed easily to have letters in a more efficient layout. But because the overwhelming majority of people have learned to use keyboards with the QWERTY layout, there might be significant costs to them if they had to switch, even if a new layout ultimately made them faster typists.

Other products that supposedly embodied inferior technologies are VHS video recorders—supposedly inferior to Sony Betamax recorders—and the Windows computer operating system—supposedly inferior to the Macintosh operating system. Some economists have argued that because of path dependence and switching costs, network externalities can result in *market failures*. As we saw in Chapter 5, a market failure is a situation in which the market fails to produce the efficient level of output. If network externalities result in market failure, government intervention in these markets might improve economic efficiency. Many economists are skeptical, however, that network externalities really do lead to consumers being locked into products with inferior technologies. In particular, economists Stan Leibowitz of the University of Texas, Dallas, and Stephen Margolis of North Carolina State University have argued that in practice, the gains from using a superior technology are larger than the losses due to switching costs. After carefully studying the cases of the QWERTY keyboard, VHS video recorders, and the Windows computer operating system, they have concluded that there is no good evidence that the alternative technologies were actually superior. The implications of network externalities for economic efficiency remain controversial among economists.

Network externality This situation where the usefulness of a product increases with the number of consumers who use it.

In each of these cases, it appears that a firm could increase its profits by raising prices. The seller would be selling the same quantity—of seats in a theater or a football stadium or meals in a restaurant—at a higher price, so profits should increase. Economists have provided two explanations why firms sometimes do not raise prices in these situations. Gary Becker, winner of the Nobel Prize in Economics, has suggested that the products involved—theatrical plays, football games, rock concerts, or restaurant meals—are all products that buyers consume together with other buyers. In those situations, the amount consumers wish to buy may be related to how much of the product other people are consuming. People like to consume, and be seen consuming, a popular product. In this case, a popular restaurant that increased its prices enough to eliminate lines might find that it had also eliminated its popularity.

Daniel Kahneman, Jack Knetsch, and Richard Thaler have offered another explanation for why firms don't always raise prices when doing so would seem to increase their profits. In surveys of consumers, these researchers found that most people considered it fair for firms to raise their prices following an increase in costs but unfair to raise prices following an increase in demand. For example, Kahneman, Knetsch, and Thaler conducted a survey in which people were asked their opinion of the following situation: "A hardware store has been selling snow shovels for $15. The morning after a large snowstorm, the store raises the price to $20." Eighty-two percent of those surveyed responded that they considered the hardware store's actions to be unfair. Kahneman, Knetsch, and Thaler have concluded that firms may sometimes not raise their prices even when the quantity demanded of their product is greater than the quantity supplied out of fear that in the long run, they will lose customers who believe the price increases were unfair.

These explanations share the same basic idea: Sometimes firms will give up some profits in the short run to keep their customers happy and increase their profits in the long run.

Making the Connection | Professor Krueger Goes to the Super Bowl

Economist Alan Krueger of Princeton University has studied the question of why the National Football League does not charge a price for Super Bowl tickets that is high enough to make the quantity of tickets demanded equal to the quantity of tickets available. The prices may seem high—$400 for the best seats, $325 for the rest—but the quantity demanded still greatly exceeds the quantity supplied. Most Super Bowl tickets are allocated to the two teams playing in the game or to the league's corporate sponsors. To give ordinary fans a chance to attend the game, in 2001, the NFL set aside 500 pairs of tickets. They held a lottery for the opportunity to buy these tickets, and more than 36,000 people applied. Some fans were willing to pay as much as $5,000 to buy a ticket from ticket scalpers. (Scalpers buy tickets at their face value and then resell them at much higher prices, even though in Florida, where the 2001 Super Bowl was held, ticket scalping is illegal.)

Why didn't the NFL simply raise the price of tickets to clear the market? Krueger decided to survey football fans attending the game to see if their views could help explain this puzzle. Krueger's survey provides support for the Kahneman, Knetsch, and Thaler explanation of why companies do not always raise prices when the quantity demanded is greater than the quantity supplied. When asked whether it would "be fair for the NFL to raise the [price of tickets] to $1,500 if that is still less than the amount most people are willing to pay for tickets," 92 percent of the fans surveyed answered "no." Even 83 percent of the fans who had paid more than $1,500 for their tickets answered "no." Krueger concluded

Should the NFL raise the price of Super Bowl tickets?

that whatever the NFL might gain in the short run from raising ticket prices, it would more than lose in the long run by alienating football fans.

Source: Alan B. Krueger, "Supply and Demand: An Economist Goes to the Super Bowl," *Milken Institute Review*, Second Quarter 2001.

YOUR TURN: Test your understanding by doing related problems 3.11 and 3.12 on page 315 at the end of this chapter.

9.4 | Describe the behavioral economics approach to understanding decision making.

Behavioral Economics: Do People Make Their Choices Rationally?

When economists say that consumers and firms are behaving "rationally," they mean that consumers and firms are taking actions that are appropriate to reach their goals, given the information available to them. In recent years, some economists have begun studying situations in which people do not appear to be making choices that are economically rational. This new area of economics is called **behavioral economics**. Why might consumers or businesses not act rationally? The most obvious reason would be that they do not realize that their actions are inconsistent with their goals. As we discussed in Chapter 1, one of the objectives of economics is to suggest ways to make better decisions. In this section, we discuss ways in which consumers can improve their decisions by avoiding some common pitfalls.

Behavioral economics The study of situations in which people make choices that do not appear to be economically rational.

Consumers commonly commit the following three mistakes when making decisions:

- They take into account monetary costs but ignore nonmonetary opportunity costs.

- They fail to ignore sunk costs.

- They are overly optimistic about their future behavior.

Ignoring Nonmonetary Opportunity Costs

Remember from Chapter 2 that the **opportunity cost** of any activity is the highest-valued alternative that must be given up to engage in that activity. For example, if you own something you could sell, using it yourself involves an opportunity cost. It is often difficult for people to think of opportunity costs in these terms.

Opportunity cost The highest-valued alternative that must be given up to engage in an activity.

Consider the following example: Some of the fans at the 2001 Super Bowl participated in a lottery run by the National Football League that allowed the winners to purchase tickets at their face value, which was either $325 or $400, depending on where in the stadium the seats were located. Alan Krueger surveyed the lottery winners, asking them two questions:

Question 1: If you had not won the lottery, would you have been willing to pay $3,000 for your ticket?
Question 2: If after winning your ticket (and before arriving in Florida for the Super Bowl) someone had offered you $3,000 for your ticket, would you have sold it?

In answer to the first question, 94 percent said that if they had not won the lottery, they would not have paid $3,000 for a ticket. In answer to the second question, 92 percent said they would not have sold their ticket for $3,000. But these answers are contradictory! If someone offers you $3,000 for your ticket, then by using the ticket rather than selling it, you incur an opportunity cost of $3,000. There really is a $3,000 cost involved in using that ticket, even though you do not pay $3,000 in cash. The alternatives of either paying $3,000 or not receiving $3,000 amount to exactly the same thing.

Endowment effect The tendency of people to be unwilling to sell a good they already own even if they are offered a price that is greater than the price they would be willing to pay to buy the good if they didn't already own it.

If the ticket is really not worth $3,000 to you, you should sell it. If it is worth $3,000 to you, you should be willing to pay $3,000 in cash to buy it. Not being willing to sell a ticket you already own for $3,000, while at the same time not being willing to buy a ticket for $3,000 if you didn't already own one is inconsistent behavior. The inconsistency comes from a failure to take into account nonmonetary opportunity costs. Behavioral economists believe this inconsistency is caused by the **endowment effect**, which is the tendency of people to be unwilling to sell a good they already own even if they are offered a price that is greater than the price they would be willing to pay to buy the good if they didn't already own it.

The failure to take into account opportunity costs is a very common error in decision making. Suppose, for example, that a friend is in a hurry to have his room cleaned—it's the Friday before parents' weekend—and he offers you $50 to do it for him. You turn him down and spend the time cleaning your own room, even though you know somebody down the hall who would be willing to clean your room for $20. Leave aside complicating details—the guy who asked you to clean his room is a real slob, or you don't want the person who offered to clean your room for $20 to go through your stuff—and you should see the point we are making. The opportunity cost of cleaning your own room is $50—the amount your friend offered to pay you to clean his room. It is inconsistent to turn down an offer from someone else to clean your room for $20 when you are doing it for yourself at a cost of $50. The key point here is this: *Nonmonetary opportunity costs are just as real as monetary costs and should be taken into account when making decisions.*

Business Implications of Consumers Ignoring Nonmonetary Opportunity Costs

Behavioral economist Richard Thaler has studied several examples of how businesses make use of consumers' failure to take into account opportunity costs. Whenever you buy something with a credit card, the credit card company charges the merchant a fee to process the bill. Credit card companies generally do not allow stores to charge higher prices to customers who use credit cards. A bill was introduced in Congress that would have made it illegal for credit card companies to enforce this rule. The credit card industry was afraid that if this law passed, credit card usage would drop because stores might begin charging a fee to credit card users. They attempted to have the law amended so that stores would be allowed to give a cash discount to people not using credit cards but would not be allowed to charge a fee to people using credit cards. There really is no difference in terms of opportunity cost between being charged a fee and not receiving a discount. The credit card industry was relying on the fact that *not* receiving a discount is a nonmonetary opportunity cost—and, therefore, likely to be ignored by consumers—but a fee is a monetary cost that people do take into account.

Film processing companies provide another example. Many of these companies have a policy of printing every picture on a roll of film, even if the picture is very fuzzy. Customers are allowed to ask for refunds on pictures they don't like. Once again, the companies are relying on the fact that passing up a refund once you have already paid for a picture is a nonmonetary opportunity cost rather than a direct monetary cost. In fact, customers rarely ask for refunds.

Making the Connection | **Why Do Hilton Hotels and other Firms Hide Their Prices?**

Economists recently began to use ideas from behavioral economics to understand a puzzling aspect of how some businesses price their products. David Laibson of Harvard University and Xavier Gabaix of New York University note that some products consist of a "base good" and "add-ons." For instance, to use a printer, you buy the printer itself—the base good—and replacement ink cartridges—the add-on. Typically, firms compete on the price of the base good but do their best to hide the prices of the add-ons. Because consumers sometimes spend more on the add-ons than on the base good, it may seem surprising that firms are able to successfully hide the prices of add-ons. For instance, over the life of a printer, consumers spend, on average, 10 times the price of the printer in buying ink cartridges. Yet one survey indicates that only 3 percent of consumers know the true cost of using a printer, including the cost of the ink cartridges. Similarly, many consumers are unaware of the add-on charges from using a checking account, such as ATM fees, returned check charges, and minimum balance fees. Many consumers making a hotel reservation are unaware of the hotel's charges for Internet access, for food from minibars, for breakfast at the hotel restaurant, or for local phone calls.

How are firms able to hide the prices of add-ons? Why doesn't competition lead some firms to offer lower-priced add-ons and advertise that their competitors' add-ons are higher priced? Laibson and Gabaix explain this puzzle by arguing that there are two types of consumers: sophisticated consumers, who pay attention to prices of add-ons, and myopic consumers, who ignore the prices of add-ons. It turns out that using advertising to convert myopic consumers into sophisticated consumers is not a profitable strategy. Consider the following example: Suppose that Hilton Hotels charges $80 per night for a room and the typical myopic consumer also spends $20 per night on local phone calls, food from the minibar, high-priced breakfasts, and other add-ons. Could a competing hotel, such as Marriott, attract Hilton's customers by advertising that Marriott's add-ons were more fairly priced than Hilton's? Laibson and Gabaix argue that this strategy would not work because its main effect would be to turn myopic consumers into sophisticated consumers. Once Hilton's customers become sophisticated, they will avoid the add-on fees, by, for instance, using their cell phones rather than the hotel phones to make calls or by eating breakfast in nearby restaurants rather than in the hotel. According to Laibson and Gabaix, Marriott's advertising campaign, "hurts Hilton—which sells fewer add-ons—but helps Hilton's customers, who are taught to substitute away from add-ons." But these sophisticated consumers are no more likely to switch from Hilton to Marriott than they were before Marriott incurred the cost of its advertising campaign. Exposing a competitor's hidden costs, say Laibson and Gabaix, "is good for the consumer and bad for both firms. Neither firm has an incentive to do it." As a result, many consumers remain unaware of the true prices of some of the products they purchase.

Some hotels hide what they charge for room service and Internet access.

Sources: Christopher Shay, "The Hidden-Fee Economy," *New York Times*, December 10, 2006; and Xavier Gabaix and David Laibson, "Shrouded Attributes, Consumer Myopia, and Information Suppression in Competitive Markets," *Quarterly Journal of Economics*, Vol. 121, No. 2, May 2006, pp. 351–397.

YOUR TURN: Test your understanding by doing related problem 4.10 on page 316 at the end of this chapter.

Failing to Ignore Sunk Costs

A **sunk cost** is a cost that has already been paid and cannot be recovered. Once you have paid money and can't get it back, you should ignore that money in any later decisions you make. Consider the following two situations:

Situation 1: You bought a ticket to a play for $75. The ticket is nonrefundable and must be used on Tuesday night, which is the only night the play will be performed. On Monday, a friend calls and invites you to a local comedy club to see a comedian you both like who is appearing only on Tuesday night. Your friend offers to pay the cost of going to the club.

Situation 2: It's Monday night, and you are about to buy a ticket for the Tuesday night performance of the same play as in situation 1. As you are leaving to buy the ticket, your friend calls and invites you to the comedy club.

Sunk cost A cost that has already been paid and cannot be recovered.

Would your decision to go to the play or to the comedy club be different in situation 1 than in situation 2? Most people would say that in situation 1, they would go to the play, because otherwise they would lose the $75 they had paid for the ticket. In fact, though, the $75 is "lost" no matter what you do because the ticket is not refundable. The only real issue for you to decide is whether you would prefer to see the play or prefer to go with your friend to the comedy club. If you would prefer to go to the club, the fact that you have already paid $75 for the ticket to the play is irrelevant. Your decision should be the same in situation 1 and situation 2.

Psychologists Daniel Kahneman and Amos Tversky explored the tendency of consumers to not ignore sunk costs by asking two samples of people the following questions:

Question 1: One sample of people was asked the following question: "Imagine that you have decided to see a play and have paid the admission price of $10 per ticket. As you enter the theater, you discover that you have lost the ticket. The seat was not marked, and the ticket cannot be recovered. Would you pay $10 for another ticket?" Of those asked, 46 percent answered "yes," and 54 percent answered "no."

Question 2: A different sample of people was asked the following question: "Imagine that you have decided to see a play where admission is $10 per ticket. As you enter the theater, you discover that you have lost a $10 bill. Would you still pay $10 for a ticket to the play?" Of those asked, 88 percent answered "yes," and 12 percent answered "no."

The situations presented in the two questions are actually the same and should have received the same fraction of yes and no responses. Many people, though, have trouble seeing that in question 1, when deciding whether to see the play, they should ignore the $10 already paid for a ticket because it is a sunk cost.

Being Unrealistic about Future Behavior

Studies have shown that a majority of adults in the United States are overweight. Why do many people choose to eat too much? One possibility is that they receive more utility from eating too much than they would from being thin. A more likely explanation, however, is that many people eat a lot today because they expect to eat less tomorrow. But they never do eat less, and so they end up overweight. (Of course, some people also suffer from medical problems that lead to weight gain.) Similarly, some people continue smoking today because they expect to be able to give it up sometime in the future. Unfortunately, for many people that time never comes, and they suffer the health consequences of prolonged smoking. In both these cases, people are overvaluing the utility from current choices—eating chocolate cake or smoking—and undervaluing the utility to be received in the future from being thin or not getting lung cancer.

Economists who have studied this question argue that many people have preferences that are not consistent over time. In the long run, you would like to be thin or give up smoking or achieve some other goal, but each day, you make decisions (such as to eat too much or to smoke) that are not consistent with this long-run goal. If you are unrealistic about your future behavior, you underestimate the costs of choices—like overeating or smoking—that you make today. A key way of avoiding this problem is to be realistic about your future behavior.

Making
the
Connection

Why Don't Students Study More?

Government statistics show that students who do well in college earn at least $10,000 more per year than students who fail to graduate or who graduate with low grades. So, over the course of a career of 40 years or more, students who do well in college will have earned upwards of $400,000 more than students who failed to graduate or who received low grades. Most colleges advise that students study at least two hours outside of class for every hour they spend in class. Surveys show that students often ignore this advice.

If the payoff to studying is so high, why don't students study more?

If the opportunity cost of not studying is so high, why do many students choose to study relatively little? Some students have work or family commitments that limit the amount of time they can study. But many other students study less than they would if they were more realistic about their future behavior. On any given night, a student has to choose between studying and other activities—like watching television, going to the movies, or going to a party—that may seem to provide higher utility in the short run. Many students choose one of these activities over studying because they expect to study tomorrow or the next day, but tomorrow they face the same choices and make similar decisions. As a result, they do not study enough to meet their long-run goal of graduating with high grades. If they were more realistic about their future behavior, they would not make the mistake of overvaluing the utility from activities like watching television or partying because they would realize that those activities can endanger their long-run goal of graduating with honors.

YOUR TURN: Test your understanding by doing related problem 4.13 on page 316 at the end of this chapter.

Solved Problem | 9-4

How Do You Get People to Save More of Their Income?

An article in the *New York Times* states the following:

> When it comes to saving for retirement, Americans . . . know they do not put away enough. . . . But ask them to save more in their [retirement] plans and they balk. A buck in the hand is irresistibly spent. Try a different approach. Ask them to commit now to increasing their savings in the future, make the increase coincide with the next raise, and they cheerfully sign up.

Why would people refuse to increase their savings now but agree to increase their savings in the future?

Source: Louis Uchitelle, "Why It Takes Psychology to Make People Save," *New York Times*, January 13, 2002.

SOLVING THE PROBLEM:

Step 1: **Review the chapter material.** This problem is about how people are not always realistic about their future behavior, so you may want to review the section "Being Unrealistic about Future Behavior," which begins on page 306.

Step 2: **Use your understanding of consumer decision making to show that this plan may work.** We have seen that many people are unrealistic about their future behavior. They spend money today that they should be saving for retirement, partly because they expect to increase their saving in the future. A savings plan that gets people to commit today to saving in the future takes advantage of people's optimism about their future behavior. They agree to save more in the future because they expect to be doing that anyway. In fact, without being part of a plan that automatically saves their next raise, they probably would not have increased their savings.

YOUR TURN: For more practice, do related problems 4.11 and 4.12 on page 316 at the end of this chapter.

>> **End Solved Problem 9-2**

Taking into account nonmonetary opportunity costs, ignoring sunk costs, and being more realistic about future behavior are three ways in which consumers are able to improve the decisions they make.

>> Continued from page 285

Economics in YOUR Life!

At the beginning of the chapter, we asked you to consider a situation in which you had paid $75 for a concert ticket, which is the most you would be willing to pay. Just before you enter the concert hall, someone offers you $90 for the ticket. We posed two questions: Would you sell the ticket? and Would an economist think it is rational to sell the ticket? If you answered that you would sell, then your answer is rational in the sense in which economists use the term. The cost of going to see the concert is what you have to give up for the ticket. Initially, the cost was just $75—the dollar price of the ticket. This amount was also the most you were willing to pay. However, once someone offers you $90 for the ticket, the cost of seeing the concert rises to $90. The reason the cost of the concert is now $90 is that once you turn down an offer of $90 for the ticket you have incurred a nonmonetary opportunity cost of $90 if you use the ticket yourself. The endowment effect explains why some people would not sell the ticket. People seem to value things that they have more than things that they do not have. Therefore, a concert ticket you already own may be worth more to you than a concert ticket you have yet to purchase. Behavioral economists study situations like this where people make choices that do not appear to be economically rational.

Conclusion

In a market system, consumers are in the driver's seat. Goods are produced only if consumers want them to be. Therefore, how consumers make their decisions is an important area for economists to study, a fact that was highlighted when Daniel Kahneman—whose research was mentioned several times in this chapter—shared the Nobel Prize in Economics. Economists expect that consumers will spend their incomes so that the last dollar spent on each good provides them with equal additional amounts of satisfaction, or utility. In practice, there are significant social influences on consumer decision making, particularly when a good or service is consumed in public. Fairness also seems to be an important consideration for most consumers. Finally, many consumers could improve the decisions they make if they would take into account nonmonetary opportunity costs and ignore sunk costs.

In this chapter, we studied consumers' choices. In the next several chapters, we will study firms' choices. Before moving on to the next chapter, read *An Inside Look* on the next page for a discussion of whether Elizabeth Arden made a good decision in hiring Mariah Carey to endorse its products.

Can Mariah Carey Get You to Buy Elizabeth Arden Perfume?

WOMEN'S WEAR DAILY, APRIL 7, 2006

Mariah Signs Scent Deal with Arden

NEW YORK - The celebrity fragrance craze has a new player—Mariah Carey.

The Grammy Award-winning singer has signed with Elizabeth Arden to develop and market her own line of fragrance products, the first of which are to be launched in spring 2007 in what the company described as "prestige department stores."

Financial terms of the deal, announced on Thursday, were not disclosed. However, industry experts have speculated that such agreements often include an up-front payout of $1 million to $2 million, and 1 to 3 percent of fragrance sales after the scent is on the counter.

Carey, whose projects include a self-branded line sold by costume jewelry retailer Claire's, will be involved with all aspects of the fragrance's development, Arden said in a statement. "I've already been involved with the team at Elizabeth Arden in the early stages of the creative process," Carey said.

The deal further amps up the significance of celebrities in the beauty world—particularly in the fragrance arena. Coty is arguably the most entrenched, with Jennifer Lopez, Sarah Jessica Parker, Kimora Lee Simmons, David and Victoria Beckham, Mary-Kate and Ashley Olsen, Shania Twain and the "Desperate Housewives" in its stable.

Arden's deal with Britney Spears, signed in March 2004, has yielded two top-five hits: Curious Britney Spears and Fantasy Britney Spears. Arden has had teen queen Hilary Duff under contract for beauty products since September (the first fruits of that deal have not yet been released), and it signed Catherine Zeta-Jones in February 2002 to be the face of its core Elizabeth Arden brand. In addition, NASCAR star Jeff Gordon has been the face of its Halston Z-14 brand since May 2004, and the original celebrity fragrance maven, Elizabeth Taylor, is also part of the company's constellation.

"Mariah has immense popularity with a very diverse consumer base—from teenagers to grandmothers," Ron Rolleston, executive vice president of global marketing for Elizabeth Arden, said in an interview. "She is global in terms of her appeal, which spans generations and cultures, which we believe will translate well into sales when the fragrance is launched. . . . She has already met with the four major fragrance houses that we work with, and has very definite ideas." Rolleston noted that Federated Department Stores, Belk and Dillard's are stores that would be likely to carry the scent.

Part of the reason retailers applaud the category is that many of the celebrities are drawing lapsed department store consumers back into the beauty department. "In Mariah, Arden has someone who is a proven hit-maker and an undervalued asset," said Steve Stoute—managing partner of Carol's Daughter and chairman and chief creative officer, Translation—who has brokered celebrity endorsement deals. "Her music has always been bigger than her personality, and she not only appeals to a younger consumer, she has a consumer who has grown up with her. I believe that Arden has her at the right time. I just hope that they have the bandwidth to market all of these celebrity brands.

Source: Julie Naughton, "Mariah Signs Scent Deal with Arden," Women's Wear Daily, April 7, 2006, p.11. Copyright © 2006 Conde Nast Publications. All rights reserved.

Key Points in the Article

This article discusses how firms benefit from using celebrity endorsements in their advertising. Elizabeth Arden clearly believes that hiring Mariah Carey to endorse a new line of fragrances will pay off financially. The firm believes that because Carey is a popular celebrity, some of that popularity will rub off on the new fragrance products. Essentially, the firm is betting that a large number of consumers will see Carey's endorsement and purchase the fragrance because of that endorsement. Consumers may purchase the fragrance to be like Mariah Carey or just to signal that they are like Mariah Carey. However, celebrity endorsements come with risks. Mary-Kate and Ashley Olson were dropped from the "Got Milk?" campaign after Mary-Kate was reportedly hospitalized for an eating disorder. In addition, Slim-Fast dropped Whoopi Goldberg from its advertisements after she made critical and vulgar comments about President George W. Bush. Once a firm hires a celebrity, consumers associate the product with the celebrity. This association can be a good or a bad thing depending on the celebrity's actions.

Analyzing the News

(a) Elizabeth Arden is giving Mariah Carey a large up-front payment and a significant part of the revenues from the fragrance sales. The firm is willing to hire Carey because it believes doing so will increase its profits. Her endorsement could lead to higher prices or a greater quantity sold, but the firm's profits will increase only if its increase in revenue is greater than the required payments to Carey.

We saw in Chapter 3 that when consumers' taste for a product increases, the demand curve will shift to the right, and when consumers' taste for a product decreases, the demand curve for the product will shift to the left. When a firm hires a celebrity to endorse its products, it is hoping to increase consumers' taste for its product. The figure shows that if the endorsement is successful, the demand curve for Elizabeth Arden fragrances shifts from D_1 to D_2. The increase in demand allows the firm to sell more fragrance bottles at every price. For example, at a price of P_1 it could sell Q_1 bottles without the endorsement but Q_2 fragrances with the endorsement.

(b) Elizabeth Arden's experience with celebrity endorsements has been very positive. The firm has used many celebrity endorsements in the past and the collaboration with Britney Spears produced two very successful fragrances. Therefore, the firm's experience suggests that celebrity endorsements can increase sales.

Thinking Critically

1. Celebrity endorsements may be rewarding to firms, but they can also be risky. Elizabeth Arden has committed a significant amount of money to hiring Mariah Carey and developing the fragrances that she will endorse. What do you think would happen to the demand curve for these fragrances if Mariah Carey gets involved in an embarrassing scandal?

2. Celebrity endorsements are also expensive. Should a firm whose celebrity endorser was just arrested make its decision about whether or not to cancel its ad campaign based on the amount it has already spent on making the ads? Briefly explain.

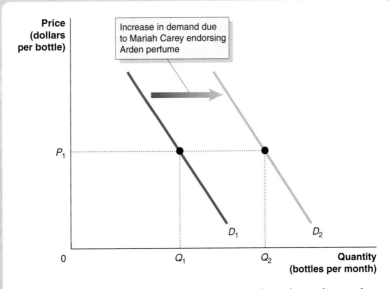

When successful, a celebrity endorsement can shift the demand curve for a product to the right, from D_1 to D_2.

I n Chapter 9, we looked behind the demand curve to better understand consumer decision making. In this chapter, we look behind the supply curve to better understand firm decision making. Earlier chapters showed that supply curves are upward sloping because marginal cost increases as firms increase the quantity of a good that they supply. In this chapter, we look more closely at why this is true. In the appendix to this chapter, we extend the analysis by using isoquants and isocost lines to understand the relationship between production and costs. Once we have a good understanding of production and cost, we can proceed in the following chapters to understand how firms decide what level of output to produce and what price to charge.

10.1 | Define technology and give examples of technological change.

Technology: An Economic Definition

The basic activity of a firm is to use *inputs*, such as workers, machines, and natural resources, to produce *outputs* of goods and services. A pizza parlor, for example, uses inputs such as pizza dough, pizza sauce, cooks, and ovens to produce pizza. A firm's **technology** is the processes it uses to turn inputs into outputs of goods and services. Notice that this economic definition of technology is broader than the everyday definition. When we use the word *technology* in everyday language, we usually refer only to the development of new products. In the economic sense, a firm's technology depends on many factors, such as the skill of its managers, the training of its workers, and the speed and efficiency of its machinery and equipment. The technology of pizza production, for example, includes not only the capacity of the pizza ovens and how quickly they bake the pizza but also how quickly the cooks can prepare the pizza for baking, how well the manager motivates the workers, and how well the manager has arranged the facilities to allow the cooks to quickly prepare the pizzas and get them in the ovens.

Whenever a firm experiences positive **technological change**, it is able to produce more output using the same inputs or the same output using fewer inputs. Positive technological change can come from many sources. The firm's managers may rearrange the factory floor or the layout of a retail store, thereby increasing production and sales. The firm's workers may go through a training program. The firm may install faster or more reliable machinery or equipment. It is also possible for a firm to experience negative technological change. If a firm hires less-skilled workers or if a hurricane damages its facilities, the quantity of output it can produce from a given quantity of inputs may decline.

Technology The processes a firm uses to turn inputs into outputs of goods and services.

Technological change A change in the ability of a firm to produce a given level of output with a given quantity of inputs.

Better inventory controls have helped reduce firms' costs.

Making the Connection | **Improving Inventory Control at Wal-Mart**

Inventories are goods that have been produced but not yet sold. For a retailer such as Wal-Mart, inventories at any point in time include the goods on the store shelves as well as goods in warehouses. Inventories are an input into Wal-Mart's output of goods sold to consumers. Having money tied up in holding inventories is costly, so firms have an incentive to hold as few inventories as possible and to *turn over* their inventories as rapidly as possible by ensuring that goods do not remain on the shelves long. Holding too few inventories, however, results in *stockouts*—that is, sales being lost because the goods consumers want to buy are not on the shelf.

Improvements in inventory control meet the economic definition of positive technological change because they allow firms to produce the same output with fewer inputs. In recent years, many firms have adopted *just-in-time* inventory systems in which firms accept shipments from suppliers as close as possible to the time they will be needed. The just-in-time system was pioneered by Toyota, which used it to reduce the inventories of parts in its automobile assembly plants. Wal-Mart has been a pioneer in using similar inventory control systems in its stores.

Wal-Mart actively manages its *supply chain*, which stretches from the manufacturers of the goods it sells to its retail stores. Entrepreneur Sam Walton, the company founder, built a series of distribution centers spread across the country to supply goods to the retail stores. As goods are sold in the stores, this *point-of-sale* information is sent electronically to the firm's distribution centers to help managers determine what products will be shipped to each store. Depending on a store's location relative to a distribution center, managers can use Wal-Mart's trucks to ship goods overnight. This distribution system allows Wal-Mart to minimize its inventory holdings without running the risk of many stockouts. Because Wal-Mart sells 15 percent to 25 percent of all the toothpaste, disposable diapers, dog food, and many other products sold in the United States, it has been able to involve many manufacturers closely in its supply chain. For example, a company such as Procter & Gamble, which is one of the world's largest manufacturers of toothpaste, laundry detergent, toilet paper, and other products, receives Wal-Mart's point-of-sale and inventory information electronically. Procter & Gamble uses that information to help determine its production schedules and the quantities it should ship to Wal-Mart's distribution centers.

Technological change has been a key to Wal-Mart's becoming one of the largest firms in the world, with 1.9 million employees and revenue of more than $348 billion in 2006.

YOUR TURN: Test your understanding by doing related problem 1.5 on page 356 at the end of this chapter.

10.2 | Distinguish between the economic short run and the economic long run.

The Short Run and the Long Run in Economics

When firms analyze the relationship between their level of production and their costs, they separate the time period involved into the short run and the long run. In the **short run**, at least one of the firm's inputs is fixed. In particular, in the short run, the firm's technology and the size of its physical plant—its factory, store, or office—are both fixed, while the number of workers the firm hires is variable. In the **long run**, the firm is able to vary all its inputs and can adopt new technology and increase or decrease the size of its physical plant. Of course, the actual length of calendar time in the short run will be different from firm to firm. A pizza parlor may be able to increase its physical plant by adding another pizza oven and some tables and chairs in just a few weeks. BMW, in contrast, may take more than a year to increase the capacity of one of its automobile assembly plants by installing new equipment.

Short run The period of time during which at least one of a firm's inputs is fixed.

Long run The period of time in which a firm can vary all its inputs, adopt new technology, and increase or decrease the size of its physical plant.

The Difference between Fixed Costs and Variable Costs

Total cost is the cost of all the inputs a firm uses in production. We have just seen that in the short run, some inputs are fixed and others are variable. The costs of the fixed inputs are *fixed costs*, and the costs of the variable inputs are *variable costs*. We can also think of **variable costs** as the costs that change as output changes. Similarly, **fixed costs** are costs that remain constant as output changes. A typical firm's variable costs include its labor costs, raw material costs, and costs of electricity and other utilities. Typical fixed costs include lease payments for factory or retail space, payments for fire insurance, and payments for newspaper and television advertising. All of a firm's costs are either fixed or variable, so we can state the following:

Total cost The cost of all the inputs a firm uses in production.

Variable costs Costs that change as output changes.

Fixed costs Costs that remain constant as output changes.

$$\text{Total Cost} = \text{Fixed Cost} + \text{Variable Cost}$$

or, using symbols:

$$TC = FC + VC.$$

Publishers consider the salaries of editors to be a fixed cost.

Making the Connection | Fixed Costs in the Publishing Industry

An editor at Cambridge University Press gives the following estimates of the annual fixed cost for a medium-size academic book publisher.

COST	AMOUNT
Salaries and benefits	$437,500
Rent	75,000
Utilities	20,000
Supplies	6,000
Postage	4,000
Travel	8,000
Subscriptions, etc.	4,000
Miscellaneous	5,000
Total	$559,500

Academic book publishers hire editors, designers, and production and marketing managers who help prepare books for publication. Because these employees work on several books simultaneously, the number of people the company hires does not go up and down with the quantity of books the company publishes during any particular year. Publishing companies therefore consider the salaries and benefits of people in these job categories as fixed costs.

In contrast, for a company that *prints* books, the quantity of workers varies with the quantity of books printed. The wages and benefits of the workers operating the printing presses, for example, would be a variable cost.

The other costs listed in the preceding table are typical of fixed costs at many firms.

Source: Beth Luey, *Handbook for Academic Authors*, 4th ed., Cambridge, UK: Cambridge University Press, 2002, p. 244.

YOUR TURN: Test your understanding by doing related problems 2.3, 2.4, and 2.5 on page 357 at the end of this chapter.

Implicit Costs versus Explicit Costs

Opportunity cost The highest-valued alternative that must be given up to engage in an activity.

Explicit cost A cost that involves spending money.

Implicit cost A nonmonetary opportunity cost.

It is important to remember that economists always measure costs as *opportunity costs*. The **opportunity cost** of any activity is the highest-valued alternative that must be given up to engage in that activity. As we saw in Chapter 7, costs are either *explicit* or *implicit*. When a firm spends money, it incurs an **explicit cost**. When a firm experiences a non-monetary opportunity cost, it incurs an **implicit cost**.

For example, suppose that Jill Johnson owns a pizza restaurant. In operating her store, Jill has explicit costs, such as the wages she pays her workers and the payments she makes for rent and electricity. But some of Jill's most important costs are implicit. Before opening her own restaurant, Jill earned a salary of $30,000 per year managing a restaurant for someone else. To start her restaurant, Jill quit her job, withdrew $50,000 from her bank account—where it earned her interest of $3,000 per year—and used the funds to equip her restaurant with tables, chairs, a cash register, and other equipment. To open her own business, Jill had to give up the $30,000 salary and the $3,000 in interest. This $33,000 is an implicit cost because it does not represent payments that Jill has to make. All the same, giving up this $33,000 per year is a real cost to Jill. In addition, during the course of the year, the $50,000 worth of tables, chairs, and other physical capital in Jill's store will lose some of its value due partly to wear and tear and partly to better furniture, cash registers, and so forth becoming available. *Economic depreciation* is the difference between what Jill paid for her capital at the beginning of the year and what she could sell the capital for at the end of the year. If Jill could sell the capital for $40,000 at the end of the year, then the $10,000 in economic depreciation represents another implicit cost.

TABLE 10-1

Jill Johnson's Costs per Year

Pizza dough, tomato sauce, and other ingredients	$20,000
Wages	48,000
Interest payments on loan to buy pizza ovens	10,000
Electricity	6,000
Lease payment for store	24,000
Foregone salary	30,000
Foregone interest	3,000
Economic depreciation	10,000
Total	$151,000

(Note that the whole $50,000 she spent on the capital is not a cost because she still has the equipment at the end of the year, although it is now worth only $40,000.)

Table 10-1 lists Jill's costs. The entries in red are explicit costs, and the entries in blue are implicit costs. As we saw in Chapter 7, the rules of accounting generally require that only explicit costs be used for purposes of keeping the company's financial records and for paying taxes. Therefore, explicit costs are sometimes called *accounting costs*. *Economic costs* include both accounting costs and implicit costs.

The Production Function

Let's look at the relationship between the level of production and costs in the short run for Jill Johnson's restaurant. To keep things simpler than in the more realistic situation in Table 10-1, let's assume that Jill uses only labor—workers—and one type of capital—pizza ovens—to produce a single good: pizzas. Many firms use more than two inputs and produce more than one good, but it is easier to understand the relationship between output and cost by focusing on the case of a firm using only two inputs and producing only one good. In the short run, Jill doesn't have time to build a larger restaurant, install additional pizza ovens, or redesign the layout of her restaurant. So, in the short run, she can increase or decrease the quantity of pizzas she produces only by increasing or decreasing the quantity of workers she employs.

The first three columns of Table 10-2 show the relationship between the quantity of workers and ovens Jill uses each week and the quantity of pizzas she can produce. The relationship between the inputs employed by a firm and the maximum output it can

TABLE 10-2 | Short-Run Production and Cost at Jill Johnson's Restaurant

QUANTITY OF WORKERS	QUANTITY OF PIZZA OVENS	QUANTITY OF PIZZAS PER WEEK	COST OF PIZZA OVENS (FIXED COST)	COST OF WORKERS (VARIABLE COST)	TOTAL COST OF PIZZAS	COST PER PIZZA (AVERAGE TOTAL COST)
0	2	0	$800	$0	$800	—
1	2	200	800	650	1,450	$7.25
2	2	450	800	1,300	2,100	4.67
3	2	550	800	1,950	2,750	5.00
4	2	600	800	2,600	3,400	5.67
5	2	625	800	3,250	4,050	6.48
6	2	640	800	3,900	4,700	7.34

Production function The relationship between the inputs employed by a firm and the maximum output it can produce with those inputs.

produce with those inputs is called the firm's **production function**. Because a firm's technology is the processes it uses to turn inputs into output, the production function represents the firm's technology. In this case, Table 10-2 shows Jill's *short-run* production function because we are assuming that the time period is too short for Jill to increase or decrease the quantity of ovens she is using.

A First Look at the Relationship between Production and Cost

Table 10-2 gives us information on Jill's costs. We can determine the total cost of producing a given quantity of pizzas if we know how many workers and ovens are required to produce that quantity of pizzas and what Jill has to pay for those workers and pizzas. Suppose Jill has taken out a bank loan to buy two pizza ovens. The cost of the loan is $800 per week. Therefore, her fixed costs are $800 per week. If Jill pays $650 per week to each worker, her variable costs depend on how many workers she hires. In the short run, Jill can increase the quantity of pizzas she produces only by hiring more workers. The table shows that if she hires 1 worker, she produces 200 pizzas during the week; if she hires 2 workers, she produces 450 pizzas; and so on. For a particular week, Jill's total cost of producing pizzas is equal to the $800 she pays on the loan for the ovens plus the amount she pays to hire workers. If Jill decides to hire 4 workers and produce 600 pizzas, her total cost is $3,400: $800 to lease the ovens and $2,600 to hire the workers. Her cost per pizza is equal to her total cost of producing pizzas divided by the quantity of pizzas produced. If she produces 600 pizzas at a total cost of $3,400, her cost per pizza, or *average total cost*, is $3,400/600 = $5.67. A firm's **average total cost** is always equal to its total cost divided by the quantity of output produced.

Average total cost Total cost divided by the quantity of output produced.

Panel (a) of Figure 10-1 uses the numbers in the next-to-last column of Table 10-2 to graph Jill's total cost. Panel (b) uses the numbers in the last column to graph her average

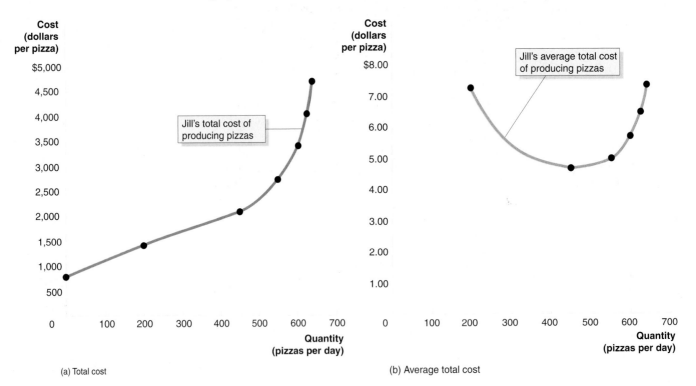

(a) Total cost

(b) Average total cost

Figure 10-1 | Graphing Total Cost and Average Total Cost at Jill Johnson's Restaurant

We can use the information from Table 10-2 to graph the relationship between the quantity of pizzas Jill produces and her total cost and average total cost. Panel (a) shows that total cost increases as the level of production increases. In panel (b), we see that the average total cost is roughly U-shaped: As production increases from low

levels, average cost falls before rising at higher levels of production. To understand why average cost has this shape, we must look more closely at the technology of producing pizzas, as shown by the production function.

total cost. Notice in panel (b) that Jill's average cost has roughly the same U shape as the average cost curve we saw Akio Morita calculate for Sony transistor radios at the beginning of this chapter. As production increases from low levels, average cost falls. Average cost then becomes fairly flat, before rising at higher levels of production. To understand why average cost has this U shape, we first need to look more closely at the technology of producing pizzas, as shown by the production function for Jill's restaurant. Then we need to look at how this technology determines the relationship between production and cost.

10.3 | Understand the relationship between the marginal product of labor and the average product of labor.

The Marginal Product of Labor and the Average Product of Labor

To better understand the choices Jill faces, given the technology available to her, think first about what happens if she hires only one worker. That one worker will have to perform several different activities, including taking orders from customers, baking the pizzas, bringing the pizzas to the customers' tables, and ringing up sales on the cash register. If Jill hires two workers, some of these activities can be divided up: One worker could take the orders and ring up the sales, and one worker could bake the pizzas. With this division of tasks, Jill will find that hiring two workers actually allows her to produce more than twice as many pizzas as she could produce with just one worker.

The additional output a firm produces as a result of hiring one more worker is called the **marginal product of labor**. We can calculate the marginal product of labor by determining how much total output increases as each additional worker is hired. We do this for Jill's restaurant in Table 10-3.

Marginal product of labor The additional output a firm produces as a result of hiring one more worker.

When Jill hires only 1 worker, she produces 200 pizzas per week. When she hires 2 workers, she produces 450 pizzas per week. Hiring the second worker increases her production by 250 pizzas per week. So, the marginal product of labor for 1 worker is 200 pizzas. For 2 workers, the marginal product of labor rises to 250 pizzas. This increase in marginal product results from the *division of labor* and from *specialization*. By dividing the tasks to be performed—the division of labor—Jill reduces the time workers lose moving from one activity to the next. She also allows them to become more specialized at their tasks. For example, a worker who concentrates on baking pizzas will become skilled at doing so quickly and efficiently.

The Law of Diminishing Returns

In the short run, the quantity of pizza ovens Jill leases is fixed, so as she hires more workers, the marginal product of labor eventually begins to decline. This happens because at some point, Jill uses up all the gains from the division of labor and from specialization

QUANTITY OF WORKERS	QUANTITY OF PIZZA OVENS	QUANTITY OF PIZZAS	MARGINAL PRODUCT OF LABOR
0	2	0	—
1	2	200	200
2	2	450	250
3	2	550	100
4	2	600	50
5	2	625	25
6	2	640	15

TABLE 10-3

The Marginal Product of Labor at Jill Johnson's Restaurant

Law of diminishing returns The principle that, at some point, adding more of a variable input, such as labor, to the same amount of a fixed input, such as capital, will cause the marginal product of the variable input to decline.

and starts to experience the effects of the **law of diminishing returns**. This law states that adding more of a variable input, such as labor, to the same amount of a fixed input, such as capital, will eventually cause the marginal product of the variable input to decline. For Jill, the marginal product of labor begins to decline when she hires the third worker. Hiring three workers raises the quantity of pizzas she produces from 450 per week to 550. But the increase in the quantity of pizzas—100—is less than the increase when she hired the second worker—250.

If Jill kept adding more and more workers to the same quantity of pizza ovens, eventually workers would begin to get in each other's way, and the marginal product of labor would actually become negative. When the marginal product is negative, the level of total output declines. No firm would actually hire so many workers as to experience a negative marginal product of labor and falling total output.

Graphing Production

Panel (a) in Figure 10-2 shows the relationship between the quantity of workers Jill hires and her total output of pizzas, using the numbers from Table 10-3. Panel (b) shows the marginal product of labor. In panel (a), output increases as more workers are hired, but the increase in output does not occur at a constant rate. Because of specialization and the division of labor, output at first increases at an increasing rate, with each additional worker hired causing production to increase by a *greater* amount than did the hiring of the previous worker. But after the second worker has been hired, hiring more workers while keeping the quantity of ovens constant results in diminishing returns. When the point of diminishing returns is reached, production increases at a decreasing rate. Each additional worker hired after the second worker causes production to increase by a *smaller* amount than did the hiring of the previous worker. In panel (b), the marginal product of labor curve rises initially because of the effects of specialization and division of labor, and then it falls due to the effects of diminishing returns.

Making the **Connection** | **Adam Smith's Famous Account of the Division of Labor in a Pin Factory**

In *The Wealth of Nations*, Adam Smith uses production in a pin factory as an example of the gains in output resulting from the division of labor. The following is an excerpt from his account of how pin making was divided into a series of tasks:

> One man draws out the wire, another straightens it, a third cuts it, a fourth points it, a fifth grinds it at the top for receiving the head; to make the head requires two or three distinct operations; to put it on is a [distinct operation], to whiten the pins is another; it is even a trade by itself to put them into the paper; and the important business of making a pin is, in this manner, divided into eighteen distinct operations.

Because the labor of pin making was divided up in this way, the average worker was able to produce about 4,800 pins per day. Smith speculated that a single worker using the pin-making machinery alone would make only about 20 pins per day. This lesson from more than 225 years ago, showing the tremendous gains from division of labor and specialization, remains relevant to most business situations today.

Source: Adam Smith, *An Inquiry into the Nature and Causes of the Wealth of Nations*, Vol. I, Oxford, UK: Oxford University Press edition, 1976, pp. 14–15.

YOUR TURN: Test your understanding by doing related problem 3.6 on page 358 at the end of this chapter.

The gains from division of labor and specialization are as important to firms today as they were in the eighteenth century, when Adam Smith first discussed them.

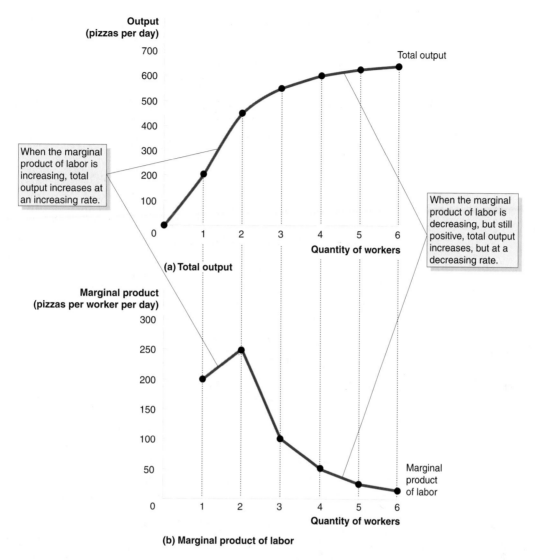

Figure 10-2 | Total Output and the Marginal Product of Labor

In panel (a), output increases as more workers are hired, but the increase in output does not occur at a constant rate. Because of specialization and the division of labor, output at first increases at an increasing rate, with each additional worker hired causing production to increase by a *greater* amount than did the hiring of the previous worker. After the third worker has been hired, hiring more workers while keeping the number of pizza ovens constant results in diminishing returns. When the point of diminishing returns is reached, production increases at a decreasing rate. Each additional worker hired after the third worker causes production to increase by a *smaller* amount than did the hiring of the previous worker. In panel (b), the *marginal product of labor* is the additional output produced as a result of hiring one more worker. The marginal product of labor rises initially because of the effects of specialization and division of labor, and then it falls due to the effects of diminishing returns.

The Relationship between Marginal and Average Product

The marginal product of labor tells us how much total output changes as the quantity of workers hired changes. We can also calculate how many pizzas workers produce on average. The **average product of labor** is the total output produced by a firm divided by the quantity of workers. For example, using the numbers in Table 10-3, if Jill hires 4 workers to produce 600 pizzas, the average product of labor is 600/4 = 150.

We can state the relationship between the marginal and average products of labor this way: *The average product of labor is the average of the marginal products of labor.* For example, the numbers from Table 10-3 show that the marginal product of the first worker Jill hires is 200, the marginal product of the second worker is 250, and the

Average product of labor The total output produced by a firm divided by the quantity of workers.

marginal product of the third worker is 100. Therefore, the average product of labor for three workers is 183.3:

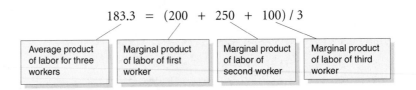

$$183.3 = (200 + 250 + 100) / 3$$

| Average product of labor for three workers | Marginal product of labor of first worker | Marginal product of labor of second worker | Marginal product of labor of third worker |

By taking the average of the marginal products of the first three workers, we have the average product of the three workers.

Whenever the marginal product of labor is greater than the average product of labor, the average product of labor must be increasing. This statement is true for the same reason that a person 6 feet, 2 inches tall entering a room where the average height is 5 feet, 9 inches raises the average height of people in the room. Whenever the marginal product of labor is less than the average product of labor, the average product of labor must be decreasing. The marginal product of labor equals the average product of labor for the quantity of workers where the average product of labor is at its maximum.

An Example of Marginal and Average Values: College Grades

The relationship between the marginal product of labor and the average product of labor is the same as the relationship between the marginal and average values of any variable. To see this more clearly, think about the familiar relationship between a student's grade point average (GPA) in one semester and his overall, or cumulative, GPA. The table in Figure 10-3 shows Paul's college grades for each semester, beginning with fall 2005. The graph in Figure 10-3 plots the grades from the table. Just as each additional worker hired adds to a firm's total production, each additional semester adds to Paul's total grade points. We can calculate what each individual worker hired adds to total production (marginal product), and we can calculate the average production of the workers hired so far (average product).

Similarly, we can calculate the GPA Paul earns in a particular semester (his "marginal GPA"), and we can calculate his cumulative GPA for all the semesters he has completed so far (his "average GPA"). As the table shows, Paul gets off to a weak start in the fall semester of his freshman year, earning only a 1.50 GPA. In each subsequent semester through the fall of his junior year, his GPA for the semester increases from the previous semester—raising his cumulative GPA. As the graph shows, however, his cumulative GPA does not increase as rapidly as his semester-by-semester GPA because his cumulative GPA is held back by the low GPAs of his first few semesters. Notice that in Paul's junior year, even though his semester GPA declines from fall to spring, his cumulative GPA rises. Only in the fall of his senior year, when his semester GPA drops below his cumulative GPA, does his cumulative GPA decline.

10.4 LEARNING OBJECTIVE

10.4 | Explain and illustrate the relationship between marginal cost and average total cost.

The Relationship between Short-Run Production and Short-Run Cost

We have seen that technology determines the values of the marginal product of labor and the average product of labor. In turn, the marginal and average products of labor affect the firm's costs. Keep in mind that the relationships we are discussing are *short-run* relationships: We are assuming that the time period is too short for the firm to change its technology or the size of its physical plant.

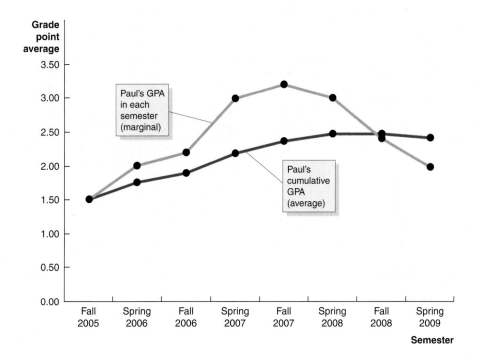

	Semester GPA (Marginal) GPA	Cumulative GPA (Average) GPA
Freshman Year		
Fall	1.50	1.50
Spring	2.00	1.75
Sophomore Year		
Fall	2.20	1.90
Spring	3.00	2.18
Junior Year		
Fall	3.20	2.38
Spring	3.00	2.48
Senior Year		
Fall	2.40	2.47
Spring	2.00	2.41

Average GPA continues to rise, although marginal GPA falls.

With the marginal GPA below the average, the average GPA falls.

Figure 10-3

Marginal and Average GPAs

The relationship between marginal and average values for a variable can be illustrated using GPAs. We can calculate the GPA Paul earns in a particular semester (his "marginal GPA"), and we can calculate his cumulative GPA for all the semesters he has completed so far (his "average GPA"). Paul's GPA is only 1.50 in the fall semester of his freshman year. In each following semester through fall of his junior year, his GPA for the semester increases—raising his cumulative GPA. In Paul's junior year, even though his semester GPA declines from fall to spring, his cumulative GPA rises. Only in the fall of his senior year, when his semester GPA drops below his cumulative GPA, does his cumulative GPA decline.

At the beginning of this chapter, we saw how Akio Morita used an average total cost curve to determine the price of radios. The average total cost curve Morita used and the average total cost curve in Figure 10-1 for Jill Johnson's restaurant both have a U shape. As we will soon see, the U shape of the average total cost curve is determined by the shape of the curve that shows the relationship between *marginal cost* and the level of production.

Marginal Cost

As we saw in Chapter 1, one of the key ideas in economics is that optimal decisions are made at the margin. Consumers, firms, and government officials usually make decisions about doing a little more or a little less. As Jill Johnson considers whether to hire additional workers to produce additional pizzas, she needs to consider how much she will add to her total cost by producing the additional pizzas. **Marginal cost** is the change in a firm's total cost from producing one more unit of a good or service. We can calculate marginal cost for a particular increase in output by dividing the change in cost by the

Marginal cost The change in a firm's total cost from producing one more unit of a good or service.

change in output. We can express this idea mathematically (remembering that the Greek letter delta, Δ, means "change in"):

$$MC = \frac{\Delta TC}{\Delta Q}.$$

In the table in Figure 10-4, we use this equation to calculate Jill's marginal cost of producing pizzas.

Why Are the Marginal and Average Cost Curves U-Shaped?

Notice in the graph in Figure 10-4 that Jill's marginal cost of producing pizzas declines at first and then increases, giving the marginal cost curve a U shape. The table in Figure 10-4 also shows the marginal product of labor. This table helps us see the important relationship between the marginal product of labor and the marginal cost of production: The marginal product of labor is *rising* for the first two workers, but the marginal cost of the pizzas produced by these workers is *falling*. The marginal product of labor is *falling* for the last four workers, but the marginal cost of pizzas produced by these workers is *rising*. To summarize this point: *When the marginal product of labor is rising, the marginal cost of output is falling. When the marginal product of labor is falling, the marginal cost of production is rising.*

Figure 10-4

Jill Johnson's Marginal Cost and Average Total Cost of Producing Pizzas

We can use the information in the table to calculate Jill's marginal cost and average total cost of producing pizzas. For the first two workers hired, the marginal product of labor is increasing. This increase causes the marginal cost of production to fall. For the last four workers hired, the marginal product of labor is falling. This causes the marginal cost of production to increase. Therefore, the marginal cost curve falls and then rises—that is, has a U shape—because the marginal product of labor rises and then falls. As long as marginal cost is below average total cost, average total cost will be falling. When marginal cost is above average total cost, average total cost will be rising. The relationship between marginal cost and average total cost explains why the average total cost curve also has a U shape.

Quantity of Workers	Quantity of Ovens	Marginal Product of Labor	Total Cost of Pizzas	Marginal Cost of Pizzas	Average Total Cost of Pizzas
0	0	—	$800	—	—
1	200	200	1,450	$3.25	$7.25
2	450	250	2,100	2.60	4.67
3	550	100	2,750	6.50	5.00
4	600	50	3,400	13.00	5.67
5	625	25	4,050	26.00	6.48
6	640	15	4,700	43.33	7.34

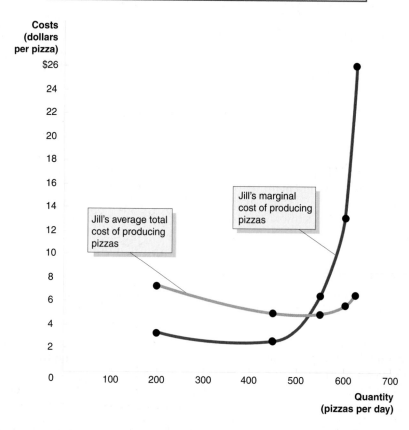

One way to understand why this point is true is first to notice that the only additional cost to Jill from producing more pizzas is the additional wages she pays to hire more workers. She pays each new worker the same $650 per week. So the marginal cost of the additional pizzas each worker makes depends on that worker's additional output, or marginal product. As long as the additional output from each new worker is rising, the marginal cost of that output is falling. When the additional output from each new worker is falling, the marginal cost of that output is rising. *We can conclude that the marginal cost of production falls and then rises—forming a U shape—because the marginal product of labor rises and then falls.*

The relationship between marginal cost and average total cost follows the usual relationship between marginal and average values. As long as marginal cost is below average total cost, average total cost falls. When marginal cost is above average total cost, average total cost rises. Marginal cost equals average total cost when average total cost is at its lowest point. Therefore, the average total cost curve has a U shape because the marginal cost curve has a U shape.

Solved Problem | 10-4

The Relationship between Marginal Cost and Average Cost

Is Jill Johnson right or wrong when she says the following? "I am currently producing 10,000 pizzas per month at a total cost of $500.00. If I produce 10,001 pizzas, my total cost will rise to $500.11. Therefore, my marginal cost of producing pizzas must be increasing." Draw a graph to illustrate your answer.

SOLVING THE PROBLEM:

Step 1: **Review the chapter material.** This problem requires understanding the relationship between marginal and average cost, so you may want to review the section "Why Are the Marginal and Average Cost Curves U-Shaped?" which begins on page 344.

Step 2: **Calculate average total cost and marginal cost.** Average total cost is total cost divided by total output. In this case, average total cost is $500.11/10,001 = $0.05. Marginal cost is the change in total cost divided by the change in output. In this case, marginal cost is $0.11/1 = $0.11.

Step 3: **Use the relationship between marginal cost and average total cost to answer the question.** When marginal cost is greater than average total cost, marginal cost must be increasing. You have shown in step 2 that marginal cost is greater than average total cost. Therefore, Jill is right: Her marginal cost of producing pizzas must be increasing.

Step 4: **Draw the graph.**

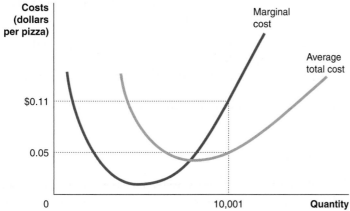

YOUR TURN: For more practice, do related problems 4.5 and 4.6 on page 359 at the end of this chapter.

>> End Solved Problem 10-4

10.5 | Graph average total cost, average variable cost, average fixed cost, and marginal cost.

Graphing Cost Curves

Average fixed cost Fixed cost divided by the quantity of output produced.

Average variable cost Variable cost divided by the quantity of output produced.

We have seen that we calculate average total cost by dividing total cost by the quantity of output produced. Similarly, we can calculate **average fixed cost** by dividing fixed cost by the quantity of output produced. And we can calculate **average variable cost** by dividing variable cost by the quantity of output produced. Or, mathematically, with Q being the level of output, we have:

$$\text{Average total cost} = ATC = \frac{TC}{Q}$$

$$\text{Average fixed cost} = AFC = \frac{FC}{Q}$$

$$\text{Average variable cost} = AVC = \frac{VC}{Q}.$$

Finally, notice that average total cost is the sum of average fixed cost plus average variable cost:

$$ATC = AFC + AVC.$$

The only fixed cost Jill incurs in operating her restaurant is the $800 per week she pays on the bank loan for her pizza ovens. Her variable costs are the wages she pays her workers. The table and graph in Figure 10-5 show Jill's costs.

We will use graphs like the one in Figure 10-5 in the next several chapters to analyze how firms decide the level of output to produce and the price to charge. Before going further, be sure you understand the following three key facts about Figure 10-5:

1 The marginal cost (*MC*), average total cost (*ATC*), and average variable cost (*AVC*) curves are all U-shaped, and the marginal cost curve intersects the average variable cost and average total cost curves at their minimum points. When marginal cost is less than either average variable cost or average total cost, it causes them to decrease. When marginal cost is above average variable cost or average total cost, it causes them to increase. Therefore, when marginal cost equals average variable cost or average total cost, they must be at their minimum points.

2 As output increases, average fixed cost gets smaller and smaller. This happens because in calculating average fixed cost, we are dividing something that gets larger and larger—output—into something that remains constant—fixed cost. Firms often refer to this process of lowering average fixed cost by selling more output as "spreading the overhead." By "overhead" they mean fixed costs.

3 As output increases, the difference between average total cost and average variable cost decreases. This happens because the difference between average total cost and average variable cost is average fixed cost, which gets smaller as output increases.

10.6 | Understand how firms use the long-run average cost curve in their planning.

Costs in the Long Run

The distinction between fixed cost and variable cost that we just discussed applies to the short run but *not* to the long run. For example, in the short run, Jill Johnson has fixed costs of $800 per week because she signed a loan agreement with a bank when she bought her pizza ovens. In the long run, the cost of purchasing more pizza ovens becomes variable because Jill can choose whether to expand her business by buying

Quantity of Workers	Quantity of Ovens	Quantity of Pizzas	Cost of Ovens (Fixed Cost)	Cost of Workers (Variable Cost)	Total Cost of Pizzas	ATC	AFC	AVC	MC
0	2	0	$800	$0	$800	–	–	–	–
1	2	200	800	650	1,450	$7.25	$4.00	$3.25	$3.25
2	2	450	800	1,300	2,100	4.67	1.78	2.89	2.60
3	2	550	800	1,950	2,750	5.00	1.45	3.55	6.50
4	2	600	800	2,600	3,400	5.67	1.33	4.33	13.00
5	2	625	800	3,250	4,050	6.48	1.28	5.2	26.00
6	2	640	800	3,900	4,700	7.34	1.25	6.09	43.33

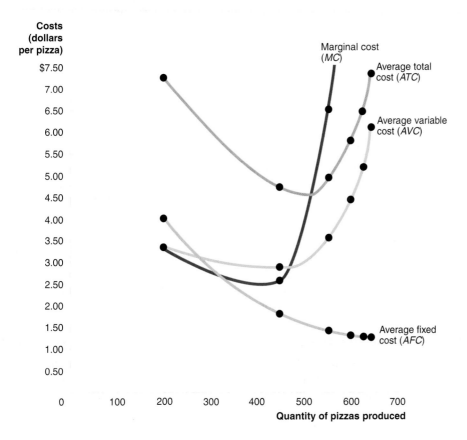

Figure 10-5

Costs at Jill Johnson's Restaurant

Jill's costs of making pizzas are shown in the table and plotted in the graph. Notice three important facts about the graph: (1) The marginal cost (*MC*), average total cost (*ATC*), and average variable cost (*AVC*) curves are all U-shaped, and the marginal cost curve intersects both the average variable cost curve and average total cost curve at their minimum points. (2) As output increases, average fixed cost (*AFC*) gets smaller and smaller. (3) As output increases, the difference between average total cost and average variable cost decreases. Make sure you can explain why each of these three facts is true. You should spend time becoming familiar with this graph because it is one of the most important graphs in microeconomics.

more ovens. The same would be true of any other fixed costs a company like Jill's might have. Once a company has purchased a fire insurance policy, the cost of the policy is fixed. But when the policy expires, the company must decide whether to renew it, and the cost becomes variable. The important point here is this: *In the long run, all costs are variable. There are no fixed costs in the long run.* In other words, in the long run, total cost equals variable cost, and average total cost equals average variable cost.

Managers of successful firms simultaneously consider how they can most profitably run their current store, factory, or office and also whether in the long run they would be more profitable if they became larger or, possibly, smaller. Jill must consider how to run her current restaurant, which has only two pizza ovens, and she must also plan what to do when her current bank loan is paid off and the lease on her store ends. Should she buy more pizza ovens? Should she lease a larger restaurant?

Economies of Scale

Short-run average cost curves represent the costs a firm faces when some input, such as the quantity of machines it uses, is fixed. The **long-run average cost curve** shows the lowest cost at which a firm is able to produce a given level of output in the long run, when no inputs are fixed. Many firms experience **economies of scale**, which means the

Long-run average cost curve A curve showing the lowest cost at which a firm is able to produce a given quantity of output in the long run, when no inputs are fixed.

Economies of scale The situation when a firm's long-run average costs fall as it increases output.

Step 3:   **Explain the curves in the graphs.** Before the proposed trade, Motorola and Siemens are producing both products at less than the minimum efficient scale, which is Q_M in both graphs. After the trade, Motorola's production of handsets will increase, moving it from Q_A to Q_B in the first graph. This increase in production will allow it to take advantage of economies of scale and reduce its average cost from Average Cost$_A$ to Average Cost$_B$. Similarly, production of wireless infrastructure by Siemens will increase from Q_A to Q_B, lowering its average cost from Average Cost$_A$ to Average Cost$_B$. As drawn, the graphs show that both firms will still be short of minimum efficient scale after the trade, although their average costs will have fallen.

EXTRA CREDIT: These were new technologies at the time Motorola and Siemens discussed the trade. As a result, companies making these products were only beginning to understand how large minimum efficient scale was. To survive in the industry, the managements of both companies wanted to lower their costs by taking advantage of economies of scale. As one industry analyst put it: "Motorola and Siemens may be driven by the conviction that they have little choice. Most observers believe consolidation in both the [wireless] networking and handset areas is inevitable."

Source for quote: Ray Hegarty, *Rumored Motorola–Siemens Business Unit Swap? A Compelling M&A Story*, www.thefeature.com.

YOUR TURN: For more practice, do related problems 6.4, 6.5, 6.6, and 6.7 on pages 361 and 362 at the end of this chapter.

>> **End Solved Problem 10-6**

Over time, most firms in an industry will build factories or stores that are at least as large as the minimum efficient scale but not so large that diseconomies of scale occur. In the bookstore industry, stores will sell between 20,000 and 40,000 books per month. However, firms often do not know the exact shape of their long-run average cost curves. As a result, they may mistakenly build factories or stores that are either too large or too small.

Making
the
Connection | **The Colossal River Rouge: Diseconomies of Scale at Ford Motor Company**

When Henry Ford started the Ford Motor Company in 1903, automobile companies produced cars in small workshops, using highly skilled workers. Ford introduced two new ideas that allowed him to take advantage of economies of scale. First, Ford used identical—or, interchangeable—parts so that unskilled workers could assemble the cars. Second, instead of having groups of workers moving from one stationary automobile to the next, he had the workers remain stationary while the automobiles moved along an assembly line. Ford built a large factory at Highland Park, outside Detroit, where he used these ideas to produce the famous Model T at an average cost well below what his competitors could match using older production methods in smaller factories.

Ford believed that he could produce automobiles at an even lower average cost by building a still larger plant along the River Rouge. Unfortunately, Ford's River Rouge plant was too large and suffered from diseconomies of scale. Ford's managers had great difficulty coordinating the production of automobiles in such a large plant. The following description of the River Rouge comes from a biography of Ford by Allan Nevins and Frank Ernest Hill:

A total of 93 separate structures stood on the [River Rouge] site. . . . Railroad trackage covered 93 miles, conveyors 27 [miles]. About 75,000 men worked in the great plant. A force of 5000 did

Is it possible for a factory to be too big?

nothing but keep it clean, wearing out 5000 mops and 3000 brooms a month, and using 86 tons of soap on the floors, walls, and 330 acres of windows. The Rouge was an industrial city, immense, concentrated, packed with power. . . . By its very massiveness and complexity, it denied men at the top contact with and understanding of those beneath, and gave those beneath a sense of being lost in inexorable immensity and power.

Beginning in 1927, Ford produced the Model A—its only car model at that time—at the River Rouge plant. Ford failed to achieve economies of scale and actually *lost money* on each of the four Model A body styles.

Ford could not raise the price of the Model A to make it profitable because at a higher price, the car could not compete with similar models produced by competitors such as General Motors and Chrysler. He eventually reduced the cost of making the Model A by constructing smaller factories spread out across the country. These smaller factories produced the Model A at a lower average cost than was possible at the River Rouge plant.

Source for quote: Allan Nevins and Frank Ernest Hill, *Ford: Expansion and Challenge, 1915–1933*, New York: Scribner, 1957, pp. 293, 295.

YOUR TURN: Test your understanding by doing related problem 6.8 on page 362 at the end of this chapter.

Don't Let This Happen to **YOU!**

DON'T CONFUSE DIMINISHING RETURNS WITH DISECONOMIES OF SCALE

The concepts of diminishing returns and diseconomies of scale may seem similar, but, in fact, they are unrelated. Diminishing returns applies only to the short run, when at least one of the firm's inputs, such as the quantity of machinery it uses, is fixed. The law of diminishing returns tells us that in the short run, hiring more workers will, at some point, result in less additional output. Diminishing returns explains why marginal cost curves eventually slope upward. Diseconomies of scale apply only in the long run, when the firm is free to vary all its inputs, can adopt new technology, and can vary the amount of machinery it uses and the size of its facility. Diseconomies of scale explain why long-run average cost curves eventually slope upward.

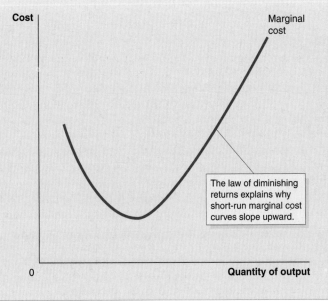

The law of diminishing returns explains why short-run marginal cost curves slope upward.

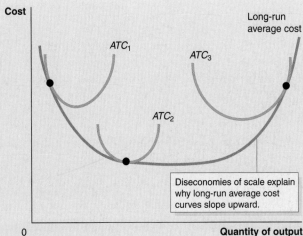

Diseconomies of scale explain why long-run average cost curves slope upward.

YOUR TURN: Test your understanding by doing related problem 6.10 on page 362 at the end of this chapter.

Economics in YOUR Life!

>> Continued from page 333

At the beginning of the chapter, we asked you to consider a situation in which you are about to open a store to sell recliners. Both you and a competing store, Bob's Big Chairs, can buy recliners from the manufacturer for $300 each. But because Bob's sells more recliners per month than you expect to be able to, his costs per recliner are lower than yours. We asked you to think about why this might be true. In this chapter, we have seen that firms often experience declining average costs as the quantity they sell increases. One significant reason Bob's average cost might be lower than yours has to do with fixed costs. Because your stores are the same size, you may be paying about the same amount to lease the store space. You may also be paying about the same amounts for utilities, insurance, and advertising. All these are fixed costs because they do not change as the quantity of recliners you sell changes. Because Bob's fixed costs are the same as yours, but he is selling more recliners, his average fixed costs are lower than yours, and, therefore, so are his average total costs. With lower average total costs, he can sell his recliners for a lower price than you do and still make a profit.

Conclusion

In this chapter, we discussed the relationship between a firm's technology, production, and costs. In the discussion, we encountered a number of definitions of costs. Because we will use these definitions in later chapters, it is useful to bring them together in Table 10-4 for you to review.

We have seen the important relationship between a firm's level of production and its costs. Just as this information was vital to Akio Morita in deciding which price to charge for his transistor radios, so it remains vital today to all firms as they attempt to decide the optimal level of production and the optimal prices to charge for their products. We will explore this point further in Chapter 11. Before moving on to that chapter, read *An Inside Look* on pages 354–355 to see how we can use long-run average cost curves to understand the effect of lower costs of production on the pricing of flat-panel TVs.

TABLE 10-4

A Summary of Definitions of Cost

TERM	DEFINITION	SYMBOLS AND EQUATIONS
Total cost	The cost of all the inputs used by a firm, or fixed cost plus variable cost	TC
Fixed cost	Costs that remain constant when a firm's level of output changes	FC
Variable cost	Costs that change when the firm's level of output changes	VC
Marginal cost	Increase in total cost resulting from producing another unit of output	$MC = \dfrac{\Delta TC}{\Delta Q}$
Average total cost	Total cost divided by the quantity of output produced	$ATC = \dfrac{TC}{Q}$
Average fixed cost	Fixed cost divided by the quantity of output produced	$AFC = \dfrac{FC}{Q}$
Average variable cost	Variable cost divided by the quantity of output produced	$AVC = \dfrac{VC}{Q}$
Implicit cost	A nonmonetary opportunity cost	—
Explicit cost	A cost that involves spending money	—

An Inside LOOK

Lower Manufacturing Costs Push Down the Price of Flat-Panel TVs

WALL STREET JOURNAL, APRIL 15, 2006

Flat-Panel TVs, Long Touted, Finally Are Becoming the Norm

After years as the Next Big Thing in consumer electronics, flat-panel TVs are finally becoming the mainstream standard. . . .

Last year, flat-screen TVs for the first time accounted for the majority of TVs bought in Japan, Hong Kong and Singapore. That crossover will happen this year or next in the U.S. and most European countries, industry watchers say, and at least one company has already stopped shipping tube TVs in the U.S. "It's happening faster than the most optimistic targets," says Ross Young, president of DisplaySearch, an Austin, Texas, market-research firm.

World-wide, sales this year of liquid-crystal display and plasma flat-panel TVs are on track to total about 44 million units, valued at as much as $54 billion, out of an overall market of 185 million TVs, according to market research firms. In the U.S., sales are expected to reach between 12 million and 14 million flat-panel TVs, or roughly half of all TVs sold. Last year, world-wide sales of flat-panel TVs totaled 25 million units.

(a) Consumers like the thin form and light weight of flat-panel TVs, but until recently, many considered them too expensive. Two years ago, a 30-inch, LCD-TV cost $3,500 to $4,000. Since then, more than a dozen factories producing critical glass and screen components have opened, which has pushed down manufacturing costs, allowing for lower prices.

Competition between LCD and plasma technologies is pushing down prices, too. Plasma models use electricity to light individual points of gas on a screen; in LCDs, a layer of liquid crystal filters a bright light. LCD beat plasma about 15 years ago as the flat-panel of choice in notebook computers. From there, plasma developers jumped to big size screens, where they have since been most cost effective, while technical challenges long limited the size of LCDs. . . .

(b) Increased production is likely to help prices continue to fall throughout the year. Seven new factories are under construction in Asia that will make LCD panels 40 inches or larger, and three new factories for plasma screens are under construction. Several are being optimized for screens that are 50 inches or larger. By late next year, prices of 40-inch models will be closing in on $1,000 as production ramps up. . . .

Japan's Matsushita Electric Industrial Co., maker of Panasonic products, has stopped shipping tube TVs altogether to the U.S., where it expects to sell about 1.5 million plasma-screen TVs this year. Just two years ago, it sold one million tube TVs and 150,000 plasma models in the U.S. Flat-panel TVs of all types have become an easier sell as popular television shows such as "CSI" and "Lost" adopt the widescreen, high-definition look of movies. The U.S. and several other countries are shifting their broadcast systems to digital signals that promise to broaden the availability of HDTV content. Higher-definition DVDs that are emerging this year may also fuel demand. . . .

(c) To meet demand, manufacturers are in a mad dash to build new factories, or change existing ones, to accommodate flat-panel TVs. In one week last month, Sony, LG Electronics Co. and China's Changhong Group announced new factories in Eastern Europe to assemble flat-panel models for the European market. Just this week, Sony and Samsung Electronics Co. said they would expand their LCD-panel joint venture by spending $2 billion on what, for the moment, will be the industry's largest factory. Hitachi Corp. a week earlier said it's considering building factories to quadruple its annual output of LCD-TVs to more than five million annually. . . .

Source: Evan Ramstad, "Flat-Panel TVs, Long Touted, Finally Are Becoming the Norm," Wall Street Journal, April 15, 2006, p. A1. Copyright © 2006 Dow Jones. Reprinted with permission of Dow Jones via Copyright Clearance Center.

Key Points in the Article

This article illustrates how several firms are racing to expand production of flat-panel televisions. The article discusses long-run decisions firms make, such as what plant size to build. It also discusses how the costs of inputs into flat-panel televisions have been declining. Lower costs of production have resulted in sharply lower prices of flat-panel televisions.

Analyzing the News

ⓐ As more factories open to produce components to make flat-panel televisions, the price of the components should fall. As a result, the marginal and average cost of producing flat-panel televisions should decline. In Figure 1, we see that more factories producing components for flat-panel TVs increases the supply of components from S_1 to S_2. The increased sup-

ply causes the price of components to fall from P_1 to P_2, while the quantity of components sold increases from Q_1 to Q_2.

Because these components are inputs in production of flat-panel TVs, as the price of components falls, the costs of producing flat-panel TVs also fall. This is seen in Figure 2, where the marginal cost curve of TVs falls from MC_1 to MC_2 and the average cost curve falls from ATC_1 to ATC_2.

Falling costs, make it possible for firms like Sony to sell TVs at lower prices and still cover their costs. You can see in Figure 2 that prior to the decrease in input prices a firm would need to receive ATC_1 dollars per TV to cover the cost of producing Q_1 TVs. After the reduction in input prices, the average cost of producing Q_1 TVs falls to ATC_2 dollars and the firm is able to cover its costs at lower prices.

ⓑ Increased production moves a firm further to the right on its cost curve. For goods like flat-panel TVs, fixed costs tend to be high relative to marginal costs, because the factories that produce the televisions are expensive to build. So, average cost will decline over large ranges of output, which makes it possible for Sony and other manufacturers to offer the televisions for sale at lower prices.

ⓒ Firms use the long-run average cost curve when choosing what size manu-

facturing plant to build. The long-run average cost curve shows the minimum cost of producing at each output level. Choosing the best point to be on the long-run average cost curve requires firms to forecast future sales. In this case, firms are expecting continuing rapid increases in demand for flat-panel televisions and are building increasingly larger plants. They are expecting that economies of scale will make the average costs of production in the larger plants lower than the average costs of production in smaller plants. But as the example of Ford's River Rouge plant discussed on pages 350–351 shows, when a new industry is rapidly expanding, it is not unusual for at least one firm to build a plant that is too large and to begin experiencing diseconomies of scale. With diseconomies of scale, the average cost of production in a larger plant is actually *higher* than in a smaller plant.

Thinking Critically

1. Suppose you are a manager at Sony and you are asked to determine what size manufacturing plants for flat-panel televisions the firm should be planning to build. What information would you need to gather in order to determine the optimal sized plant?

2. Use the concepts from this chapter to explain why the long-run supply of flat-panel TVs is more elastic than the short-run supply of flat-panel TVs.

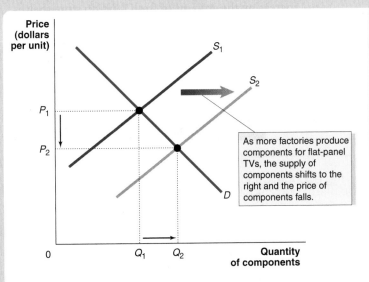

Figure 1. An increased supply of flat-panel televisions components leads to a lower price.

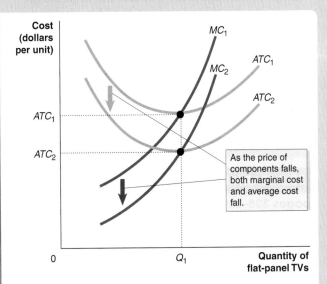

Figure 2. Lower input prices reduce the marginal and average costs of producing flat-panel televisions.

product of labor is greater than the average product of labor, the average product of labor increases. When the marginal product of labor is less than the average product of labor, the average product of labor decreases.

myeconlab Visit www.myeconlab.com to complete these exercises
Get Ahead of the Curve online and get instant feedback.

Review Questions

3.1 Draw a graph showing the usual relationship between the marginal product of labor and the average product of labor. Why do the marginal product of labor and the average product of labor have the shapes you drew?

3.2 What is the law of diminishing returns? Does it apply in the long run?

Problems and Applications

3.3 Fill in the missing values in the following table.

QUANTITY OF WORKERS	TOTAL OUTPUT	MARGINAL PRODUCT OF LABOR	AVERAGE PRODUCT OF LABOR
0	0		
1	400		
2	900		
3	1,500		
4	1,900		
5	2,200		
6	2,400		
7	2,300		

3.4 Use the numbers from problem 3.3 to draw one graph showing how total output increases with the quantity of workers hired and a second graph showing the marginal product of labor and the average product of labor.

3.5 A student looks at the data in Table 10-3 on page 339 and draws this conclusion: "The marginal product of labor is increasing for the first two workers hired, and then it declines for the next four workers. I guess each of the first two workers must have been hard workers. Then Jill must have had to settle for increasingly poor workers." Do you agree with the student's analysis? Briefly explain.

3.6 (Related to the *Making the Connection* on page 340) Briefly explain whether you agree or disagree with the following argument: Adam Smith's idea of the gains to firms from the division of labor makes a lot of sense when the good being manufactured is something complex like automobiles or computers, but it doesn't apply in the manufacturing of less complex goods or in other sectors of the economy, such as retail sales.

3.7 Sally looks at her college transcript and says to Sam, "How is this possible? My grade point average for this semester's courses is higher than my grade point average for last semester's courses, but my cumulative grade point average still went down from last semester to this semester." Explain to Sally how this is possible.

3.8 Is it possible for a firm to experience a technological change that would increase the marginal product of labor while leaving the average product of labor unchanged? Explain.

>> End Learning Objective 10.3

10.4 LEARNING OBJECTIVE 10.4 | Explain and illustrate the relationship between marginal cost and average total cost, **pages 342–345.**

The Relationship between Short-Run Production and Short-Run Cost

Summary

The **marginal cost** of production is the increase in total cost resulting from producing another unit of output. The marginal cost curve has a U shape because when the marginal product of labor is rising, the marginal cost of output is falling. When the marginal product of labor is falling, the marginal cost of output is rising. When marginal cost is less than average total cost, average total cost falls. When marginal cost is greater than average total cost, average total cost rises.

myeconlab Visit www.myeconlab.com to complete these exercises
Get Ahead of the Curve online and get instant feedback.

Review Questions

4.1 If the marginal product of labor is rising, is the marginal cost of production rising or falling? Briefly explain.

4.2 Explain why the marginal cost curve intersects the average total cost curve at the level of output where average total cost is at a minimum.

Problems and Applications

4.3 Is it possible for average total cost to be decreasing over a range of output where marginal cost is increasing? Briefly explain.

4.4 Suppose a firm has no fixed costs, so all of its costs are variable, even in the short run.
a. If the firm's marginal costs are continually increasing (that is, marginal cost is increasing from the first unit of output produced) will the firm's average total cost curve have a U shape?
b. If the firm's marginal costs are $5 at every level of output, what shape will the firm's average total cost have?

4.5 (Related to *Solved Problem 10-4* on page 345) Is Jill Johnson right or wrong when she says the following: "Currently, I am producing 20,000 pizzas per month at a total cost of $750.00. If I produce 20,001 pizzas, my total cost will rise to $750.02. Therefore, my marginal cost of producing pizzas must be increasing." Illustrate your answer with a graph.

4.6 (Related to *Solved Problem 10-4* on page 345) The following problem is somewhat advanced. Using symbols, we can write that the marginal prod-

uct of labor is equal to $\Delta Q/\Delta L$. Marginal cost is equal to $\Delta TC/\Delta Q$. Because fixed costs by definition don't change, marginal cost is also equal to $\Delta VC/\Delta Q$. If Jill Johnson's only variable cost is labor cost, then her variable cost is just the wage multiplied by the quantity of workers hired, or wL.
a. If the wage Jill pays is constant, then what is ΔVC in terms of w and L?
b. Use your answer to question (a) and the expressions given above for the marginal product of labor and the marginal cost of output to find an expression for marginal cost, $\Delta TC/\Delta Q$, in terms of the wage, w, and the marginal product of labor, $\Delta Q/\Delta L$.
c. Use your answer to question (b) to determine Jill's marginal cost of producing pizzas if the wage is $750 per week and the marginal product of labor is 150. If the wage falls to $600 per week and the marginal product of labor is unchanged, what happens to Jill's marginal cost? If the wage is unchanged at $750 per week and the marginal product rises to 250, what happens to Jill's marginal cost?

>> End Learning Objective 10.4

10.5 LEARNING OBJECTIVE 10.5 | Graph average total cost, average variable cost, average fixed cost, and marginal cost, **page 346.**

Graphing Cost Curves

Summary

Average fixed cost is equal to fixed cost divided by the level of output. **Average variable cost** is equal to variable cost divided by the level of output. Figure 10-5 on page 347 shows the relationship among marginal cost, average total cost, average variable cost, and average fixed cost. It is one of the most important graphs in microeconomics.

myeconlab Visit www.myeconlab.com to complete these exercises online and get instant feedback.

Review Questions

5.1 As the level of output increases, what happens to the value of average fixed cost?

5.2 As the level of output increases, what happens to the difference between the value of average total cost and average variable cost?

Problems and Applications

5.3 Suppose the total cost of producing 10,000 tennis balls is $30,000, and the fixed cost is $10,000.
a. What is the variable cost?
b. When output is 10,000, what are the average variable cost and the average fixed cost?
c. Assuming that the cost curves have the usual shape, is the dollar difference between the average total cost and the average variable cost greater when the output is 10,000 tennis balls or when the output is 30,000 tennis balls? Explain.

5.4 One description of the costs of operating a railroad makes the following observation: "The fixed . . . expenses which attach to the operation of railroads . . . are in the nature of a tax upon the business of the road; the smaller the [amount of] business, the larger the tax." Briefly explain why fixed costs are like a tax. In what sense is this tax smaller when the amount of business is larger?

Source for quote: Alfred D. Chandler, Jr., Thomas K. McCraw, and Richard Tedlow, *Management Past and Present*, Cincinnati: South-Western, 2000, pp. 2–27.

5.5 In the ancient world, a book could be produced either on a scroll or as a codex, which was made of folded sheets glued together, something like a modern book. One scholar has estimated the following variable costs (in Greek drachmas) of the two methods:

	SCROLL	CODEX
Cost of writing (wage of a scribe)	11.33 drachmas	11.33 drachmas
Cost of paper	16.50 drachmas	9.25 drachmas

Another scholar points out that a significant fixed cost was involved in producing a codex:

> In order to copy a codex . . . the amount of text and the layout of each page had to be carefully calculated in advance to determine the exact number of sheets . . . needed. No doubt, this is more time-consuming and calls for more experimentation than the production of a scroll would. But for the next copy, these calculations would be used again.

a. Suppose that the fixed cost of preparing a codex was 58 drachmas and that there was no similar fixed cost for a scroll. Would an ancient book publisher who intended to sell 5 copies of a book be likely to publish it as a scroll or as a codex? What if he intended to sell 10 copies? Briefly explain.

b. Although most books were published as scrolls in the first century A.D., by the third century, most were published as codices. Considering only the factors mentioned in this problem, explain why this change may have taken place.

Sources: T. C. Skeat, "The Length of the Standard Papyrus Roll and the Cost-Advantage of the Codex," *Zeitschrift fur Papyrologie und Epigraphik*, 1982, p. 175; and David Trobisch, *The First Edition of the New Testament*, New York: Oxford University Press, 2000, p. 73.

5.6 Use the information in the following graph to find the values for the following at an output level of 1,000.
a. Marginal cost
b. Total cost
c. Variable cost
d. Fixed cost

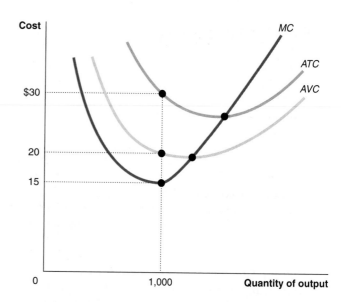

5.7 List the errors in the following graph. Carefully explain why the curves drawn this way are wrong. In other words, why can't these curves be as they are shown in the graph?

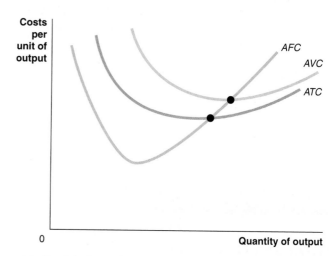

5.8 Explain how the listed events (a–d) would affect the following at Ford Motor Company:
   i. Marginal cost
   ii. Average variable cost
   iii. Average fixed cost
   iv. Average total cost

a. Ford signs a new contract with the United Automobile Workers union that requires the company to pay higher wages.
b. The federal government starts to levy a $1,500-per-vehicle tax on sport-utility vehicles.
c. Ford decides to give its senior executives a one-time $100,000 bonus.
d. Ford decides to increase the amount it spends on designing new car models.

>> End Learning Objective 10.5

10.6 LEARNING OBJECTIVE   10.6 | Understand how firms use the long-run average cost curve in their planning,

pages 346–353.

Costs in the Long Run

Summary

The **long-run average cost curve** shows the lowest cost at which a firm is able to produce a given level of output in the long run. For many firms, the long-run average cost curve falls as output expands because of **economies of scale**. **Minimum efficient scale** is the level of output at which all economies of scale have been exhausted. After economies of scale have been exhausted, firms experience **constant returns to scale**, where their long-run average cost curve is flat. At high levels of output, the long-run average cost curve turns up as the firm experiences **diseconomies of scale**.

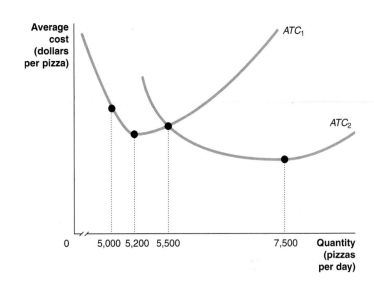

myeconlab Visit www.myeconlab.com to complete these exercises
Get Ahead of the Curve online and get instant feedback.

Review Questions

6.1 What is the difference between total cost and variable cost in the long run?

6.2 What is minimum efficient scale? What is likely to happen in the long run to firms that do not reach minimum efficient scale?

6.3 What are economies of scale? What are diseconomies of scale? What is the main reason that firms eventually encounter diseconomies of scale as they keep increasing the size of their store or factory?

Problems and Applications

6.4 (Related to *Solved Problem 10-6* on page 349) Suppose that Jill Johnson has to choose between building a smaller restaurant and a larger restaurant. In the following graph, the relationship between costs and output for the smaller restaurant is represented by the curve ATC_1, and the relationship between costs and output for the larger restaurant is represented by the curve ATC_2.
  a. If Jill expects to produce 5,100 pizzas per week, should she build a smaller restaurant or a larger restaurant? Briefly explain.
  b. If Jill expects to produce 6,000 pizzas per week, should she build a smaller restaurant or a larger restaurant? Briefly explain.
  c. A student asks, "If the average cost of producing pizzas is lower in the larger restaurant when Jill produces 7,500 pizzas per week, why isn't it also lower when Jill produces 5,200 pizzas per week?" Give a brief answer to the student's question.

6.5 (Related to *Solved Problem 10-6* on page 349) Consider the following description of U.S. manufacturing in the late nineteenth century:

> When . . . Standard Oil . . . reorganized its refinery capacity in 1883 and concentrated almost two-fifths of the nation's refinery production in three huge refineries, the unit cost dropped from 1.5 cents a gallon to 0.5 cents. A comparable concentration of two-fifths of the nation's output of textiles or shoes in three plants would have been impossible, and in any case would have brought huge diseconomies of scale and consequently higher prices.

  a. Use this information to draw a long-run average cost curve for an oil-refining firm and a long-run average cost curve for a firm manufacturing shoes.
  b. Is it likely that there were more oil refineries or more shoe factories in the United States in the late nineteenth century? Briefly explain.
  c. Why would concentrating two-fifths of total shoe output in three factories have led to higher shoe prices?

Source: Alfred D. Chandler, Jr., Thomas K. McCraw, and Richard Tedlow, *Management Past and Present,* Cincinnati: South-Western, 2000, pp. 4–53.

6.6 (Related to *Solved Problem 10-6* on page 349) The company eToys sold toys on the Internet. In 1999, the total value of the company was about $7.7 billion, but by early 2001, the company was in deep financial trouble, and it eventually closed. One of the company's key mistakes was the decision in

2000 to build a large distribution center from which it would ship toys throughout the United States. The following description of this decision appeared in an article in the *Wall Street Journal*:

> [eToys built] a giant automated distribution center in Virginia. . . . Although many analysts agreed that the costly move was a sound decision for the long run . . . [the] decision meant eToys needed to generate much higher sales to justify its costs. . . . Despite a spiffy TV ad campaign and an expanded line of goods, there weren't enough customers.

What does the author mean when she says that eToys "needed to generate much higher sales to justify its costs"? Use a graph like Figure 10-6 to illustrate your answer.

Source: Lisa Bannon, "The eToys Saga: Costs Kept Rising but Sales Slowed," *Wall Street Journal*, January 22, 2001.

6.7 **(Related to *Solved Problem 10-6* on page 349)** In 2003, Time Warner and the Walt Disney Company discussed merging their news operations. Time Warner owns the Cable News Network (CNN), and Disney owns ABC News. After analyzing the situation, the companies decided that a combined news operation would have higher average costs than either CNN or ABC News had separately. Use a long-run average cost curve graph to illustrate why the companies did not merge their news operations.

Source: Martin Peers and Joe Flint, "AOL Calls Off CNN–ABC Deal, Seeing Operating Difficulties," *Wall Street Journal*, February 14, 2003.

6.8 **(Related to the *Making the Connection* on page 350)** Suppose that Henry Ford had continued to experience increasing returns to scale, no matter how large an automobile factory he built. Discuss what the implications of this would have been for the automobile industry.

6.9 One scholar has made the following comment on the publishing industry: "If publishers were able to determine exactly what sells a book, they all would feature fewer titles and produce them in larger numbers." What must be true about the costs of publishing books for this statement to be correct? Briefly explain.

Source: David Trobisch, *The First Edition of the New Testament*, New York: Oxford University Press, 2000, p. 75.

6.10 **(Related to the *Don't Let This Happen to You!* on page 351)** Explain whether you agree or disagree with the following statement: "Henry Ford expected to be able to produce cars at a lower average cost at his River Rouge plant. Unfortunately, because of diminishing returns, his costs were actually higher."

6.11 **(Related to the *Chapter Opener* on page 332)** Review the discussion at the beginning of the chapter of Akio Morita selling transistor radios in the United States. Suppose that Morita became convinced that Sony would be able to sell more than 75,000 transistor radios each year in the United States. What steps would he have taken?

6.12 TIAA-CREF is a retirement system for people who work at colleges and universities. For some years, TIAA-CREF also sold long-term care insurance before deciding to sell that business to MetLife, a large insurance company. TIAA-CREF's chairman and chief executive officer explained the decision this way:

> In recent years, the long-term care insurance market has experienced significant consolidation. A few large insurance companies now own most of the business. MetLife has 428,000 policies, for example—nearly 10 times the number we have—and can achieve economies of scale that we can't. Over time, we would have had difficulty holding down premium rates.

Briefly explain what economies of scale have to do with the premiums (that is, the prices buyers have to pay for insurance policies) that insurance companies can charge for their policies.

Source: "Long-Term Care Sale in Best Interest of Policyholders," *Advance*, Spring 2004, p. 6.

6.13 According to one account of the problems DuPont had in entering the paint business, "the du Ponts had assumed that large volume would bring profits through lowering unit costs." In fact, according to one company report, "The more paint and varnish we sold, the more money we lost." Draw an average cost curve graph showing the relationship between paint output and average cost as DuPont expected it to be. Draw another graph that explains the result that the more paint the company sold, the more money it lost.

Source: Alfred D. Chandler, Jr., Thomas K. McCraw, and Richard Tedlow, *Management Past and Present*, Cincinnati: South-Western, 2000, pp. 3–88.

6.14 According to a study of chicken processing plants by the U.S. Department of Agriculture, the largest plants have average costs that are 20 percent lower than the smallest plants. The report concludes, "These cost differentials are consistent with the near-disappearance of small plants." Briefly explain the reasoning behind this conclusion.

Source: Michael Ollinger, James MacDonald, and Milton Madison, *Structural Change in U.S. Chicken and Turkey Slaughter*, Agricultural Economic Report No. 787, Economic Research Service, U.S. Department of Agriculture.

6.15 Michael Korda was for many years editor-in-chief at the Simon & Schuster book publishing company. He has described how during the 1980s many publishing companies merged together to form larger firms. He claims that publishers hoped to take advantage of economies of scale. But, he concludes, "sheer size did not make publishing necessarily more profitable, and most of these big publishing monoliths would continue to disappoint their corporate owners in terms of earnings." On the basis of this information, draw a long-run average cost curve for a publishing firm that reflects the economies of scale expected to result from the mergers. Draw another long-run average cost curve that reflects the actual results experienced by the new larger publishing firms.

Source: Michael Korda, *Making the List: A Cultural History of the American Bestseller, 1900–1999,* New York: Barnes & Noble Books, 2001, p. 166.

>> **End Learning Objective 10.6**

Appendix

Using Isoquants and Isocosts to Understand Production and Cost

Use isoquants and isocost lines to understand production and cost.

Isoquants

In this chapter, we studied the important relationship between a firm's level of production and its costs. In this appendix, we will look more closely at how firms choose the combination of inputs to produce a given level of output. Firms usually have a choice of how they will produce their output. For example, Jill Johnson is able to produce 5,000 pizzas per week using 10 workers and 2 ovens or using 6 workers and 3 ovens. We will see that firms search for the *cost-minimizing* combination of inputs that will allow them to produce a given level of output. The cost-minimizing combination of inputs depends on two factors: technology—which determines how much output a firm receives from employing a given quantity of inputs—and input prices—which determine the total cost of each combination of inputs.

An Isoquant Graph

We begin by graphing the levels of output that Jill can produce using different combinations of two inputs: labor—the quantity of workers she hires per week—and capital—the quantity of ovens she uses per week. In reality, of course, Jill uses more than just these two inputs to produce pizzas, but nothing important would change if we expanded the discussion to include many inputs instead of just two. Figure 10A-1 measures capital along the vertical axis and labor along the horizontal axis. The curves in the graph are **isoquants**, which show all the combinations of two inputs, in this case capital and labor, that will produce the same level of output.

The isoquant labeled $Q = 5,000$ shows all the combinations of workers and ovens that enable Jill to produce that quantity of pizzas per week. For example, at point A, she produces 5,000 pizzas using 6 workers and 3 ovens, and at point B, she produces the same output using 10 workers and 2 ovens. With more workers and ovens, she can move to a higher isoquant. For example, with 12 workers and 4 ovens, she can produce at point C on the isoquant $Q = 10,000$. With even more workers and ovens, she could move to the isoquant $Q = 13,000$. The higher the isoquant—that is, the further to the upper right on the graph—the more output the firm produces. Although we have shown only three isoquants in this graph, there are, in fact, an infinite number of isoquants—one for every level of output.

The Slope of an Isoquant

Remember that the slope of a curve is the ratio of the change in the variable on the vertical axis to the change in the variable on the horizontal axis. Along an isoquant, the slope tells us the rate at which a firm is able to substitute one input for another while

Isoquant A curve that shows all the combinations of two inputs, such as capital and labor, that will produce the same level of output.

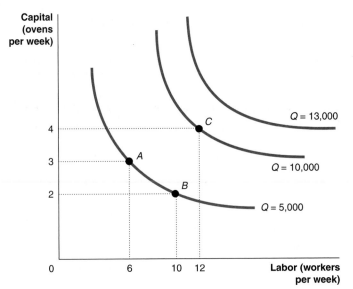

Figure 10A-1

Isoquants

Isoquants show all the combinations of two inputs, in this case capital and labor, that will produce the same level of output. For example, the isoquant labeled $Q = 5,000$ shows all the combinations of ovens and workers that enable Jill to produce that quantity of pizzas per week. At point A, she produces 5,000 pizzas using 3 ovens and 6 workers, and at point B, she produces the same output using 2 ovens and 10 workers. With more ovens and workers, she can move to a higher isoquant. For example, with 4 ovens and 12 workers, she can produce at point C on the isoquant $Q = 10,000$. With even more ovens and workers, she could move to the isoquant $Q = 13,000$.

keeping the level of output constant. The slope of an isoquant is called the **marginal rate of technical substitution** (**MRTS**).

We expect that the *MRTS* will change as we move down an isoquant. In Figure 10A-1, at a point like A on isoquant $Q = 5,000$, the isoquant is relatively steep. As we move down the curve, it becomes less steep at a point like B. This shape is the usual one for isoquants: They are bowed in, or convex. The reason isoquants have this shape is that as we move down the curve, we continue to substitute labor for capital. As the firm produces the same quantity of output using less capital, the additional labor it needs increases because of diminishing returns. Remember from the chapter that, as a consequence of diminishing returns, for a given decline in capital, increasing amounts of labor are necessary to produce the same level of output. Because the *MRTS* is equal to the change in capital divided by the change in labor, it will become smaller (in absolute value) as we move down an isoquant.

Marginal rate of technical substitution (*MRTS*) The slope of an isoquant, or the rate at which a firm is able to substitute one input for another while keeping the level of output constant.

Isocost Lines

Any firm wants to produce a given quantity of output at the lowest possible cost. We can show the relationship between the quantity of inputs used and the firm's total cost by using an *isocost* line. An **isocost line** shows all the combinations of two inputs, such as capital and labor, that have the same total cost.

Isocost line All the combinations of two inputs, such as capital and labor, that have the same total cost.

Graphing the Isocost Line

Suppose Jill has $6,000 per week to spend on capital and labor. Suppose, to simplify the analysis, that Jill can rent pizza ovens by the week. The table in Figure 10A-2 shows the combinations of capital and labor available to her if the rental price of ovens is $1,000 per week and the wage rate is $500 per week. The graph uses the data in the table to construct an isocost line. The isocost line intersects the vertical axis at the maximum number of ovens Jill can rent per week, which is shown by point A. The line intersects the horizontal axis at the maximum number of workers Jill can hire per week, which is point G. As Jill moves down the isocost line from point A, she gives up renting 1 oven for every 2 workers she hires. Any combination of inputs along the line or inside the line can be purchased with $6,000. Any combination that lies outside the line cannot be purchased because it would have a total cost to Jill of more than $6,000.

The Slope and Position of the Isocost Line

The slope of the isocost line is constant and equals the change in the quantity of ovens divided by the change in the quantity of workers. In this case, in moving from any point on the isocost line to any other point, the change in the quantity of ovens equals −1, and

Figure 10A-2

An Isocost Line

The isocost line shows the combinations of inputs with a total cost of $6,000. The rental price of ovens is $1,000 per week, so if Jill spends the whole $6,000 on ovens, she can rent 6 ovens (point A). The wage rate is $500 per week, so if Jill spends the whole $6,000 on workers, she can hire 12 workers. As she moves down the isocost line, she gives up renting 1 oven for every 2 workers she hires. Any combinations of inputs along the line or inside the line can be purchased with $6,000. Any combinations that lie outside the line cannot be purchased with $6,000.

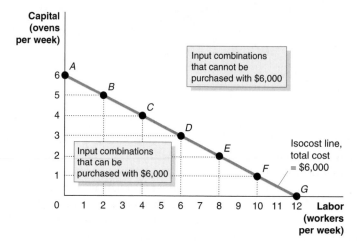

Combinations of Workers and Ovens with a Total Cost of $6,000			
Point	Ovens	Workers	Total Cost
A	6	0	(6 x $1,000) + (0 x $500) = $6,000
B	5	2	(5 x $1,000) + (2 x $500) = 6,000
C	4	4	(4 x $1,000) + (4 x $500) = 6,000
D	3	6	(3 x $1,000) + (6 x $500) = 6,000
E	2	8	(2 x $1,000) + (8 x $500) = 6,000
F	1	10	(1 x $1,000) + (10 x $500) = 6,000
G	0	12	(0 x $1,000) + (12 x $500) = 6,000

the change in the quantity of workers equals 2, so the slope equals −1/2. Notice that with a rental price of ovens of $1,000 per week and a wage rate for labor of $500 per week, the slope of the isocost line is equal to the ratio of the wage rate divided by the rental price of capital, multiplied by −1: −$500/$1,000 = −1/2. In fact, this result will always hold, whatever inputs are involved and whatever their prices may be: *The slope of the isocost line is equal to the ratio of the price of the input on the horizontal axis divided by the price of the input on the vertical axis, multiplied by −1.*

The position of the isocost line depends on the level of total cost. Higher levels of total cost shift the isocost line outward, and lower levels of total cost shift the isocost line inward. This can be seen in Figure 10A-3, which shows isocost lines for total

Figure 10A-3

The Position of the Isocost Line

The position of the isocost line depends on the level of total cost. As total cost increases from $3,000 to $6,000 to $9,000 per week, the isocost line shifts outward. For each isocost line shown, the rental price of ovens is $1,000 per week, and the wage rate is $500 per week.

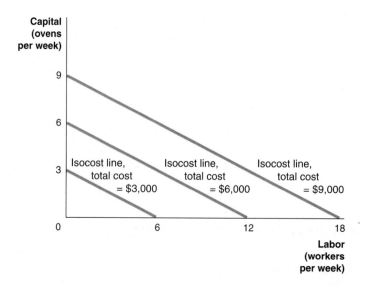

costs of $3,000, $6,000, and $9,000. We have shown only three isocost lines in the graph, but there are, in fact, an infinite number of isocost lines—one for every level of total cost.

Choosing the Cost-Minimizing Combination of Capital and Labor

Suppose Jill wants to produce 5,000 pizzas per week. Figure 10A-1 shows that there are many combinations of ovens and workers that will allow Jill to produce this level of output. There is only one combination of ovens and workers, however, that will allow her to produce 5,000 pizzas *at the lowest total cost.* Figure 10A-4 shows the isoquant $Q = 5,000$ along with three isocost lines. Point B is the lowest-cost combination of inputs shown in the graph, but this combination of 1 oven and 4 workers will produce fewer than the 5,000 pizzas needed. Points C and D are combinations of ovens and workers that will produce 5,000 pizzas, but their total cost is $9,000. The combination of 3 ovens and 6 workers at point A produces 5,000 pizzas at the lowest total cost of $6,000.

The graph shows that moving to an isocost line with a total cost of less than $6,000 would mean producing fewer than 5,000 pizzas. Being at any point along the isoquant $Q = 5,000$ other than point A would increase total cost above $6,000. In fact, the combination of inputs at point A is the only one on isoquant $Q = 5,000$ that has a total cost of $6,000. All other input combinations on this isoquant have higher total costs. Notice also that at point A, the isoquant and the isocost lines are tangent, so the slope of the isoquant is equal to the slope of the isocost line at that point.

Different Input Price Ratios Lead to Different Input Choices

Jill's cost-minimizing choice of 3 ovens and 6 workers is determined jointly by the technology available to her—as represented by her firm's isoquants—and by input prices—as represented by her firm's isocost lines. If the technology of making pizzas changes, perhaps because new ovens are developed, her isoquants will be affected, and her choice of inputs may change. If her isoquants remain unchanged but input

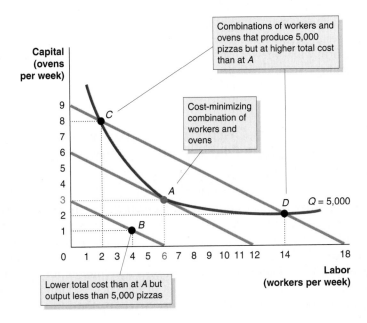

Figure 10A-4

Choosing Capital and Labor to Minimize Total Cost

Jill wants to produce 5,000 pizzas per week at the lowest total cost. Point B is the lowest-cost combination of inputs shown in the graph, but this combination of 1 oven and 4 workers will produce fewer than the 5,000 pizzas needed. Points C and D are combinations of ovens and workers that will produce 5,000 pizzas, but their total cost is $9,000. The combination of 3 ovens and 6 workers at point A produces 5,000 pizzas at the lowest total cost of $6,000.

Figure 10A-5

Changing Input Prices Affects the Cost-Minimizing Input Choice

As the graph shows, the input combination at point *A*, which was optimal for Jill, is not optimal for a businessperson in China. Using the input combination at point *A* would cost businesspeople in China more than $6,000. Instead, the Chinese isocost line is tangent to the isoquant at point *B*, where the input combination is 2 ovens and 10 workers. Because ovens cost more in China but workers cost less, a Chinese firm will use fewer ovens and more workers than a U.S. firm, even if it has the same technology as the U.S. firm.

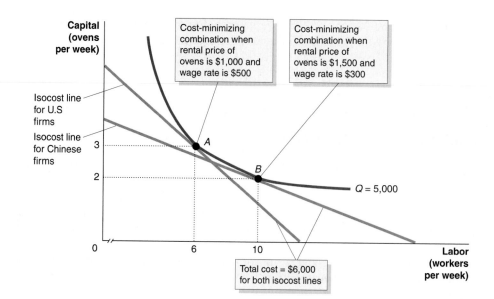

prices change, then her choice of inputs may also change. This fact can explain why firms in different countries that face different input prices may produce the same good using different combinations of capital and labor, even though they have the same technology available.

For example, suppose that in China, pizza ovens are higher priced and labor is lower priced than in the United States. In our example, Jill Johnson pays $1,000 per week to rent pizza ovens and $500 per week to hire workers. Suppose a businessperson in China must pay a price of $1,500 per week to rent the identical pizza ovens but can hire Chinese workers who are as productive as U.S. workers at a wage of $300 per week. Figure 10A-5 shows how the cost-minimizing input combination for the businessperson in China differs from Jill's.

Remember that the slope of the isocost line equals the wage rate divided by the rental price of capital, multiplied by −1. The slope of the isocost line that Jill and other U.S. firms face is −$500/$1,000, or −1/2. Firms in China, however, face an isocost line with a slope of −$300/$1,500, or −1/5. As the graph shows, the input combination at point *A*, which was optimal for Jill, is not optimal for a firm in China. Using the input combination at point *A* would cost a firm in China more than $6,000. Instead, the Chinese isocost line is tangent to the isoquant at point *B*, where the input combination is 2 ovens and 10 workers. This result makes sense: Because ovens cost more in China, but workers cost less, a Chinese firm will use fewer ovens and more workers than a U.S. firm, even if it has the same technology as the U.S. firm.

Making the Connection | The Changing Input Mix in Walt Disney Film Animation

The inputs used to make feature-length animated films have changed dramatically in the past 15 years. Prior to the early 1990s, the Walt Disney Company dominated the market for animated films. Disney's films were produced using hundreds of animators drawing most of the film by hand. Each film would contain as many as 170,000 individual drawings. Then, two developments dramatically affected how animated films are produced. First, in 1994, Disney had a huge hit with *The Lion King*, which cost only $50 million but earned the company more than $1 billion in profit. As a result of this success, Disney and other film studios began to produce more animated films, increasing the demand for animators and more than doubling their salaries. The second development came in 1995, when Pixar Animation Studios released the film *Toy Story*. This was the first successful feature-length film produced using computers, with no hand-drawn animation. In the following years, technological advance continued to reduce the cost of the computers and software necessary to produce an animated film.

As a result of these two developments, the price of capital—computers and software—fell relative to the price of labor—animators. As the figure shows, the change in the price of computers relative to animators changed the slope of the isocost line and resulted in film studios now producing animated films using many more computers and many fewer animators than in the early 1990s.

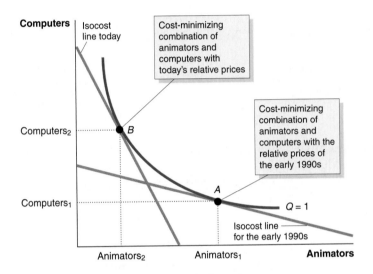

Source: Bruce Orwall, "Disney Delivers 'Lilo and Stitch' on Competition-Driven Budget," *Wall Street Journal*, June 18, 2002, p. A1.

YOUR TURN: Test your understanding by doing related problem 10A.8 on page 374 at the end of this chapter.

Another Look at Cost Minimization

In Chapter 9, we saw that consumers maximize utility when they consume each good up to the point where the marginal utility per dollar spent is the same for every good. We can derive a very similar cost-minimization rule for firms. Remember that at the point of cost minimization, the isoquant and the isocost line are tangent, so they have the same slope. Therefore, *at the point of cost minimization, the marginal rate of technical substitution* (MRTS) *is equal to the wage rate divided by the rental price of capital.*

The slope of the isoquant tells us the rate at which a firm is able to substitute labor for capital, *given existing technology*. The slope of the isocost line tells us the rate at which a firm is able to substitute labor for capital, *given current input prices*. Only at the point of cost minimization are these two rates the same.

When we move from one point on an isoquant to another, we end up using more of one input and less of the other input, but the level of output remains the same. For example, as Jill moves down an isoquant, she uses fewer ovens and more workers but produces the same quantity of pizzas. In this chapter, we defined the *marginal product of labor* (MP_L) as the additional output produced by a firm as a result of hiring one more worker. Similarly, we can define the *marginal product of capital* (MP_K) as the additional output produced by a firm as a result of using one more machine. So, when Jill uses fewer ovens by moving down an isoquant, she loses output equal to:

$$-\text{Change in the quantity of ovens} \times MP_K.$$

But she uses more workers, so she gains output equal to:

$$\text{Change in the quantity of workers} \times MP_L.$$

We know that the gain in output from the additional workers is equal to the loss from the smaller quantity of ovens because total output remains the same along an isoquant. Therefore, we can write:

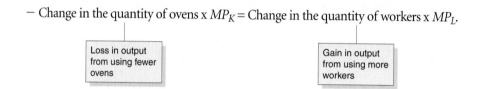

$$-\text{Change in the quantity of ovens} \times MP_K = \text{Change in the quantity of workers} \times MP_L.$$

| Loss in output from using fewer ovens | Gain in output from using more workers |

If we rearrange terms, we have the following:

$$\frac{-\text{Change in the quantity of ovens}}{\text{Change in the quantity of workers}} = \frac{MP_L}{MP_K}.$$

Because the

$$\frac{-\text{Change in the quantity of ovens}}{\text{Change in the quantity of workers}}$$

is the slope of the isoquant, or the marginal rate of technical substitution (MRTS), we can write:

$$\frac{-\text{Change in the quantity of ovens}}{\text{Change in the quantity of workers}} = MRTS = \frac{MP_L}{MP_K}.$$

The slope of the isocost line equals the wage rate (w) divided by the rental price of capital (r). At the point of cost minimization, the slope of the isoquant is equal to the slope of the isocost line. Therefore:

$$\frac{MP_L}{MP_K} = \frac{w}{r}.$$

We can rewrite this to show that at the point of cost minimization:

$$\frac{MP_L}{w} = \frac{MP_K}{r}.$$

This last expression tells us that to minimize cost, a firm should hire inputs up to the point where the last dollar spent on each input results in the same increase in output. If this equality did not hold, a firm could lower its costs by using more of one input and less of the other. For example, if the left-hand side of the equation were greater than the right-hand side, a firm could rent fewer ovens, hire more workers, and produce the same output at lower cost.

Solved Problem | 10A-1

Determining the Optimal Combination of Inputs

Consider the information in the following table for Jill Johnson's restaurant:

Marginal product of capital	3,000 pizzas
Marginal product of labor	1,200 pizzas
Wage rate	$300 per week
Rental price of ovens	$600 per week

Briefly explain whether Jill is minimizing costs. If she is not minimizing costs, explain whether she should rent more ovens and hire fewer workers or rent fewer ovens and hire more workers.

SOLVING THE PROBLEM:

Step 1: Review the chapter material. This problem is about determining the optimal choice of inputs by comparing the ratios of the marginal products of inputs to their prices, so you may want to review the section "Another Look at Cost Minimization," which begins on page 369.

Step 2: Compute the ratios of marginal product to input price to determine whether Jill is minimizing costs. If Jill is minimizing costs, the following relationship should hold:

$$\frac{MP_L}{w} = \frac{MP_K}{r}.$$

In this case, we have:

$$MP_L = 1,200$$
$$MP_K = 3,000$$
$$w = \$300$$
$$r = \$600.$$

So:

$$\frac{MP_L}{w} = \frac{1,200}{\$300} = 4 \text{ pizzas per dollar, and } \frac{MP_K}{r} = \frac{3,000}{\$600} = 5 \text{ pizzas per dollar.}$$

Because the two ratios are not equal, Jill is not minimizing cost.

Step 3: Determine how Jill should change the mix of inputs she uses. Jill produces more pizzas per dollar from the last oven than from the last worker. This indicates that she has too many workers and too few ovens. Therefore, to minimize cost, Jill should use more ovens and hire fewer workers.

YOUR TURN: For more practice, do related problem 10A.7 on page 374 at the end of this appendix.

>> **End Solved Problem 10A-1**

Making
the
Connection

Do National Football League Teams Behave Efficiently?

In the National Football League (NFL), the "salary cap" is the maximum amount each team can spend each year on salaries for football players. Each year's salary cap results from negotiations between the league and the union representing the players. To achieve efficiency, an NFL team should distribute salaries among players so as to maximize the level of output—in this case, winning football games—given the constant level of cost represented by the salary cap. (Notice that maximizing the level of output for a given level of cost is equivalent to minimizing cost for a given level of output. To see why, think about the situation where an isocost line is tangent to an isoquant. At the point of tangency, the firm has simultaneously minimized the cost of producing the level of output represented by the isoquant and maximized the output produced at the level of cost represented by the isocost line.) In distributing salaries, teams should equalize the marginal productivity of players as represented by their contribution to winning games to the salaries paid. Just as a firm may not use a machine that has a very high marginal product if its rental price is very high, a football team may not want to hire a superstar player if the salary the team would need to pay is too high.

Are the Detroit Lions paying too much to Calvin Johnson?

Economists Cade Massey, of Duke University, and Richard Thaler, of the University of Chicago, have analyzed whether NFL teams distribute their salaries efficiently. NFL teams obtain their players either by signing free agents—who are players whose contracts with other teams have expired—or by signing players chosen in the annual draft of eligible college players. The college draft consists of seven rounds, with the teams with the worst records the previous year choosing first. Massey and Thaler find that, in fact, NFL teams do not allocate salaries efficiently. In particular, the players chosen with the first few picks of the first round of the draft tend to be paid salaries that are much higher relative to their marginal products than is true for players taken later in the first round. A typical team with a high draft pick would increase its ability to win football games at the constant cost represented by the salary cap if it traded for lower draft picks. Why do NFL teams apparently make the error of not efficiently distributing salaries? Massey and Thaler argue that managers of NFL teams tend to be overconfident in their ability to forecast how well a college player is likely to perform in the NFL.

Managers of NFL teams are not alone in suffering from overconfidence. Studies have shown that, in general, people tend to overestimate their ability to forecast an uncertain outcome. Because NFL teams tend to overestimate the future marginal productivity of high draft picks, they pay them salaries that are inefficiently high when compared to salaries other draft picks receive.

This example shows that the concepts developed in this chapter provide powerful tools for analyzing whether firms are operating efficiently.

Source: Cade Massey and Richard Thaler, "Overconfidence versus Market Efficiency in the National Football League," Working Paper 11270, Cambridge, MA: National Bureau of Economic Research, April 2005.

YOUR TURN: Test your understanding by doing related problem 10A.14 on page 375 at the end of this chapter.

The Expansion Path

We can use isoquants and isocost lines to examine what happens as a firm expands its level of output. Figure 10A-6 shows three isoquants for a firm that produces bookcases. The isocost lines are drawn, assuming that the machines used in producing bookcases can be rented for $100 per day and the wage rate is $25 per day. The point where each isoquant is tangent to an isocost line determines the cost-minimizing combination of capital and labor for producing that level of output. For example, 10 machines and 40 work-

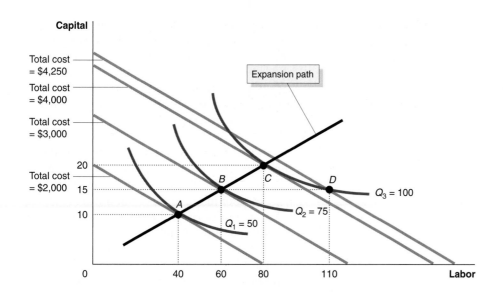

Figure 10A-6

The Expansion Path

The tangency points *A*, *B*, and *C* lie along the firm's expansion path, which is a curve that shows the cost-minimizing combination of inputs for every level of output. In the short run, when the quantity of machines is fixed, the firm can expand output from 75 bookcases per day to 100 bookcases per day at the lowest cost only by moving from point *B* to point *D* and increasing the number of workers from 80 to 110. In the long run, when it can increase the quantity of machines it uses, the firm can move from point *D* to point *C*, thereby reducing its total costs of producing 100 bookcases per day from $4,250 to $4,000.

ers is the cost-minimizing combination of inputs for producing 50 bookcases per day. The cost-minimizing points *A*, *B*, and *C* lie along the firm's **expansion path**, which is a curve that shows the cost-minimizing combination of inputs for every level of output.

An important point to note is that the expansion path represents the least-cost combination of inputs to produce a given level of output *in the long run*, when the firm is able to vary the levels of all of its inputs. We know, though, that in the short run, at least one input is fixed. We can use Figure 10A-6 to show that as the firm expands in the short run, its costs will be higher than in the long run. For example, suppose that the firm is currently at point *B*, using 15 machines and 60 workers to produce 75 bookcases per day. The firm wants to expand its output to 100 bookcases per day, but in the short run, it is unable to increase the quantity of machines it uses. Therefore, to expand output, it must hire more workers. The figure shows that in the short run, to produce 100 bookcases per day using 15 machines, the lowest costs it can attain are at point *D*, where it employs 110 workers. With a rental price of machines of $100 per day and a wage rate of $25 per day, in the short run, the firm will have total costs of $4,250 to produce 100 bookcases per day. In the long run, though, the firm can increase the number of machines it uses from 15 to 20 and reduce the number of workers from 110 to 80. This change allows it to move from point *D* to point *C* on its expansion path and to lower its total costs of producing 100 bookcases per day from $4,250 to $4,000. The firm's minimum total costs of production are lower in the long run than in the short run.

Expansion path A curve that shows a firm's cost-minimizing combination of inputs for every level of output.

Key Terms

Expansion path, p. 373

Isocost line, p. 365

Isoquant, p. 364

Marginal rate of technical substitution (*MRTS*), p. 365

LEARNING OBJECTIVE   Use isoquants and isocost lines to understand production and cost, **pages 364–373.**

myeconlab Visit www.myeconlab.com to complete these exercises *Get Ahead of the Curve* online and get instant feedback.

Review Questions

10A.1 What is an isoquant? What is the slope of an isoquant?

10A.2 What is an isocost line? What is the slope of an isocost line?

10A.3 How do firms choose the optimal combination of inputs?

Problems and Applications

10A.4 Draw an isoquant–isocost line graph to illustrate the following situation: Jill Johnson can rent pizza ovens for $400 per week and hire workers for $200 per week. She is currently using 5 ovens and 10 workers to produce 20,000 pizzas per week and has total costs of $4,000. Make sure to label your graph showing the cost-minimizing input combination and the maximum quantity of labor and capital she can use with total costs of $4,000.

10A.5 Use the following graph to answer the questions.

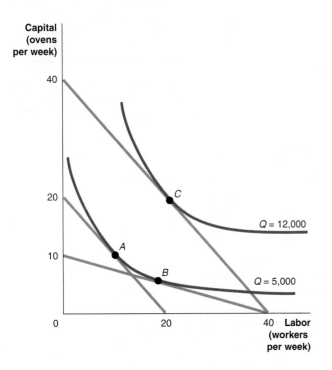

a. If the wage rate and the rental price of machines are both $100 and total cost is $2,000, is the cost-minimizing point *A*, *B*, or *C*? Briefly explain.

b. If the wage rate is $25, the rental price of machines is $100, and total cost is $1,000, is the cost-minimizing point *A*, *B*, or *C*? Briefly explain.

c. If the wage rate and the rental price of machines are both $100 and total cost is $4,000, is the cost-minimizing point *A*, *B*, or *C*? Briefly explain.

10A.6 (Related to *Solved Problem 10A-1* on page 371) Consider the information in the following table for Jill Johnson's restaurant.

Marginal product of capital	4,000
Marginal product of labor	100
Wage rate	$10
Rental price of pizza ovens	$500

Briefly explain whether Jill is minimizing costs. If she is not minimizing costs, explain whether she should rent more ovens and hire fewer workers or rent fewer ovens and hire more workers.

10A.7 (Related to *Solved Problem 10A-1* on page 371) Draw an isoquant–isocost line graph to illustrate the following situation: Jill Johnson can

rent pizza ovens for $200 per week and hire workers for $100 per week. Currently, she is using 5 ovens and 10 workers to produce 20,000 pizzas per week and has total costs of $2,000. Jill's marginal rate of technical substitution (*MRTS*) equals −1. Explain why this means that she's not minimizing costs and what she could do to minimize costs.

10A.8 (Related to the *Making the Connection* on page 368) During the eighteenth century, the American colonies had much more land per farmer than did Europe, with the result that the price of labor in the colonies was much higher relative to the price of land than was true in Europe. Assume that Europe and the colonies had access to the same technology for producing food. Use an isoquant-isocost line graph to illustrate why the combination of land and labor used in producing food in the colonies would have been different than the combination used to produce food in Europe.

10A.9 Draw an isoquant–isocost line graph to illustrate the following situation and the change that occurs: Jill Johnson can rent pizza ovens for $2,000 per week and hire workers for $1,000 per week. Currently, she is using 5 ovens and 10 workers to produce 20,000 pizzas per week and has total costs of $20,000. Then Jill reorganizes the way things are done in her business and achieves positive technological change.

10A.10 Use the following graph to answer the following questions about Jill Johnson's isoquant curve.

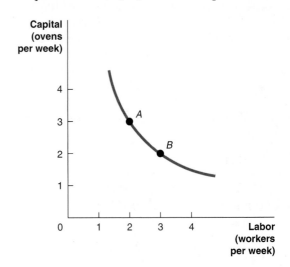

a. Which combination of inputs yields more output: combination *A* (3 ovens and 2 workers) or combination *B* (2 ovens and 3 workers)?

b. What will determine whether Jill selects *A*, *B*, or some other point along this isoquant curve?

c. Is the marginal rate of technical substitution (*MRTS*) greater at point *A* or point *B*?

10A.11 Draw an isoquant–isocost line graph to illustrate the following situation: Jill Johnson can rent pizza ovens for $2,000 per week and hire workers for $1,000 per week. She can minimize the cost of producing 20,000 pizzas per week by using 5 ovens and 10 workers, at a total cost of $20,000. She can minimize the cost of producing 45,000 pizzas per week by using 10 ovens and 20 workers, at a total cost of $40,000. And she can minimize the cost of producing 60,000 pizzas per week by using 15 ovens and 30 workers, at a total cost of $60,000. Now draw Jill's long-run average cost curve and discuss its economies and diseconomies of scale.

10A.12 In Brazil, a grove of oranges is picked using 20 workers, ladders, and baskets. In Florida, a grove of oranges is picked using 1 worker and a machine that shakes the oranges off the trees and scoops up the fallen oranges. Using an isoquant–isocost line graph, illustrate why these two different methods are used to pick the same number of oranges per day in these two locations.

10A.13 Jill Johnson is minimizing the costs of producing pizzas. The rental price of one of her ovens is $2,000 per week, and the wage rate is $600 per week. The marginal product of capital in her business is 12,000 pizzas. What must be the marginal product of her workers?

10A.14 (Related to the *Making the Connection on page 372*) If Massey and Thaler are correct, then should the team that has the first pick in the draft keep the pick or trade it to another team for a lower pick? Explain.

>> **End Appendix Learning Objective**

Chapter 11

Firms in **Perfectly Competitive Markets**

Perfect Competition in the Market for Organic Apples

The market for organically grown food has expanded rapidly in the United States. As recently as 15 years ago, organic food was sold primarily in small health food stores. By the 2000s, sales of organic foods were growing at a rate of more than 20 percent per year, and organic foods were available in nearly every supermarket. In 2002, the U.S. Department of Agriculture (USDA) established standards for organic food labeling. The standards were intended to protect consumers from false and misleading claims and to make it easier for U.S. farmers to export to foreign countries whose governments also require organic food labeling. According to the USDA, a firm can label and advertise food as "organic" only if that food is "produced without using most conventional pesticides; fertilizers made with synthetic ingredients or sewage sludge; bioengineering; or ionizing radiation."

Organically grown apples became popular with consumers during the late 1990s. Farmers growing apples organically use only organic fertilizers and control insects with sprays made from soil compounds. These growing methods add about 15 percent to the cost of growing apples. The Yakima Valley of Washington State is particularly suited to growing apples organically because of the absence of certain insects. In 1997, Yakima Valley apple farmers were able to sell organically grown apples for a price 50 percent higher than the price of regular apples, more than offsetting the higher costs of organic growing methods. This price difference made organically grown apples considerably more profitable than apples grown using traditional methods.

Between 1997 and 2001, many apple farmers switched from traditional to organic growing methods, increasing production of organically grown apples from 1.2 million boxes per year to more than 3 million boxes. The additional supply of organically grown apples forced down prices and made them no more profitable than apples grown using traditional methods. As one farmer in the Yakima Valley put it, "It's like anything else in agriculture. If people see an economic opportunity, usually it only lasts for a few years." **AN INSIDE LOOK** on **page 402** discusses how an organic farmer in South Dakota responds to large firms like Wal-Mart entering the market for organic foods.

What the organic apple farmers in the Yakima Valley experienced is not unique to agriculture. Throughout the economy, entrepreneurs are continually introducing new products, which—when successful—enable them to earn economic profits in the short run. But in the long run, competition among firms force prices to the level where they just cover the costs of production. This process of competition is at the heart of the market system and is the focus of this chapter.

Sources: Lydia Oberholtzer, Carolyn Dimitri, and Catherine Greene, "Price Premiums Hold on as U.S. Organic Produce Market Expands," Agricultural Economic Report No. VGS-308-01, Economic Research Service, U.S. Department of Agriculture, May 2005; Emily Green, "Study Gives Nod to Organic Apples, but It's Crunch Time for All State Growers," Seattle Times, April 19, 2001; quote from farmer from All Things Considered, National Public Radio, www.npr.org, April 18, 2001.

LEARNING Objectives

After studying this chapter, you should be able to:

11.1 Define a **perfectly competitive market** and explain why a perfect competitor faces a **horizontal demand curve**, page 379.

11.2 Explain how a **firm maximizes profits** in a perfectly competitive market, page 381.

11.3 Use **graphs** to show a firm's **profit or loss**, page 385.

11.4 Explain why firms may **shut down** temporarily, page 390.

11.5 Explain how **entry** and **exit** ensure that perfectly competitive firms earn **zero economic profit** in the long run, page 393.

11.6 Explain how **perfect competition** leads to **economic efficiency**, page 398.

Economics in YOUR Life!

Are You an Entrepreneur?

Were you an entrepreneur during your high school years? Perhaps you didn't have your own store, but you may have worked as a babysitter, or perhaps you mowed lawns for families in your neighborhood. While you may not think of these jobs as being small businesses, that is exactly what they are. How did you decide what price to charge for your services? You may have wanted to charge $25 per hour to babysit or mow lawns, but you probably charged much less. As you read the chapter, think about the competitive situation you faced as a teenaged entrepreneur and try to determine why the prices received by most people who babysit and mow lawns are so low. You can check your answers against those we provide at the end of the chapter. >> Continued on page 401

Organic apple growing is an example of a *perfectly competitive* industry. Firms in perfectly competitive industries are unable to control the prices of the products they sell and are unable to earn an economic profit in the long run. There are two main reasons for this result: Firms in these industries sell identical products, and it is easy for new firms to enter these industries. Studying how perfectly competitive industries operate is the best way to understand how markets answer the fundamental economic questions discussed in Chapter 1:

- What goods and services will be produced?

- How will the goods and services be produced?

- Who will receive the goods and services produced?

In fact, though, most industries are not perfectly competitive. In most industries, firms do *not* produce identical products, and in some industries, it may be difficult for new firms to enter. There are thousands of industries in the United States. Although in some ways each industry is unique, industries share enough similarities that economists group them into four market structures. In particular, any industry has three key characteristics:

- The number of firms in the industry

- The similarity of the good or service produced by the firms in the industry

- The ease with which new firms can enter the industry

Economists use these characteristics to classify industries into the four market structures listed in Table 11-1.

Many industries, including restaurants, hardware stores, and other retailers, have a large number of firms selling products that are differentiated, rather than identical, and fall into the category of *monopolistic competition*. Some industries, such as computers and automobiles, have only a few firms and are *oligopolies*. Finally, a few industries, such as the delivery of first-class mail by the U.S. Postal Service, have only one firm and are *monopolies*. After discussing perfect competition in this chapter, we will devote a chapter to each of these other market structures.

TABLE 11-1 | The Four Market Structures

	MARKET STRUCTURE			
CHARACTERISTIC	PERFECT COMPETITION	MONOPOLISTIC COMPETITION	OLIGOPOLY	MONOPOLY
Number of firms	Many	Many	Few	One
Type of product	Identical	Differentiated	Identical or differentiated	Unique
Ease of entry	High	High	Low	Entry blocked
Examples of industries	• Wheat • Apples	• Selling DVDs • Restaurants	• Manufacturing computers • Manufacturing automobiles	• First-class mail delivery • Tap water

11.1 | Define a perfectly competitive market and explain why a perfect competitor faces a horizontal demand curve.

Perfectly Competitive Markets

Why are firms in a **perfectly competitive market** unable to control the prices of the goods they sell, and why are the owners of these firms unable to earn economic profits in the long run? We can begin our analysis by listing the three conditions that make a market perfectly competitive:

1 There must be many buyers and many firms, all of whom are small relative to the market.

2 The products sold by all firms in the market must be identical.

3 There must be no barriers to new firms entering the market.

Perfectly competitive market
A market that meets the conditions of (1) many buyers and sellers, (2) all firms selling identical products, and (3) no barriers to new firms entering the market.

All three of these conditions hold in the market for organic apples. No single consumer or producer of organic apples buys or sells more than a tiny fraction of the total apple crop. The apples sold by each apple grower are identical, and there are no barriers to a new firm entering the organic apple market by purchasing land and planting apple trees. As we will see, it is the existence of many firms, all selling the same good, that keeps any single organic apple farmer from affecting the price of organic apples.

Although the market for organic apples meets the conditions for perfect competition, the markets for most goods and services do not. In particular, the second and third conditions are very restrictive. In most markets that have many buyers and sellers, firms do not sell identical products. For example, not all restaurant meals are the same, nor is all women's clothing the same. In Chapter 12, we will explore the common situation of monopolistic competition where many firms are selling similar but not identical products. In Chapters 13 and 14, we will analyze industries that are oligopolies or monopolies, where it is difficult for new firms to enter. In this chapter, we concentrate on perfectly competitive markets so we can use as a benchmark the situation in which firms are facing the maximum possible competition.

A Perfectly Competitive Firm Cannot Affect the Market Price

Prices in perfectly competitive markets are determined by the interaction of demand and supply. The actions of any single consumer or any single firm have no effect on the market price. Consumers and firms have to accept the market price if they want to buy and sell in a perfectly competitive market.

Because a firm in a perfectly competitive market is very small relative to the market and because it is selling exactly the same product as every other firm, it can sell as much as it wants without having to lower its price. But if a perfectly competitive firm tries to raise its price, it won't sell anything at all because consumers will switch to buying from the firm's competitors. Therefore, the firm will be a **price taker** and will have to charge the same price as every other firm in the market. Although we don't usually think of firms as being too small to affect the market price, consumers are often in the position of being price takers. For instance, suppose your local supermarket is selling bread for $1.50 per loaf. You can load up your shopping cart with 10 loaves of bread, and the supermarket will gladly sell them all to you for $1.50 per loaf. But if you go to the cashier and offer to buy the bread for $1.49 per loaf, he or she will not sell it to you. As a buyer, you are too small relative to the bread market to have any effect on the equilibrium price. Whether you leave the supermarket and buy no bread or you buy 10 loaves, you are unable to change the market price of bread by even 1 cent.

Price taker A buyer or seller that is unable to affect the market price.

The situation you face as a bread buyer is the same one a wheat farmer faces as a wheat seller. More than 225,000 farmers grow wheat in the United States. The market price of wheat is determined not by any individual wheat farmer but by the interaction

Figure 11-1

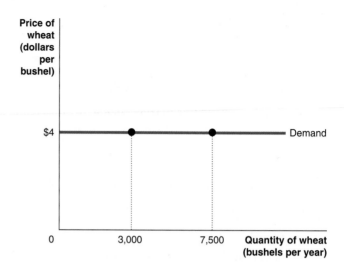

A Perfectly Competitive Firm Faces a Horizontal Demand Curve

A firm in a perfectly competitive market is selling exactly the same product as many other firms. Therefore, it can sell as much as it wants at the current market price, but it cannot sell anything at all if it raises the price by even 1 cent. As a result, the demand curve for a perfectly competitive firm's output is a horizontal line. In the figure, whether the wheat farmer sells 3,000 bushels per year or 7,500 bushels has no effect on the market price of $4.

in the wheat market of all the buyers and all the sellers. If any one wheat farmer has the best crop the farmer has ever had, or if any one wheat farmer stops growing wheat altogether, the market price of wheat will not be affected *because the market supply curve for wheat will not shift by enough to change the equilibrium price by even 1 cent.*

The Demand Curve for the Output of a Perfectly Competitive Firm

Suppose Bill Parker grows wheat on a 250-acre farm in Washington State. Farmer Parker is selling wheat in a perfectly competitive market, so he is a price taker. Because he can sell as much wheat as he chooses at the market price—but can't sell any wheat at all at a higher price—the demand curve for his wheat has an unusual shape: It is horizontal, as shown in Figure 11-1. With a horizontal demand curve, Farmer Parker must accept the market price, which in this case is $4. Whether Farmer Parker sells 3,000 bushels per year or 7,500 has no effect on the market price.

The demand curve for Farmer Parker's wheat is very different from the market demand curve for wheat. Panel (a) of Figure 11-2 shows the market for wheat. The

---

Don't Let This Happen to **YOU!**

Don't Confuse the Demand Curve for Farmer Parker's Wheat with the Market Demand Curve for Wheat

The demand curve for wheat has the normal downward-sloping shape. If the price of wheat goes up, the quantity of wheat demanded goes down, and if the price of wheat goes down, the quantity of wheat demanded goes up. But the demand curve for the output of a single wheat farmer is *not* downward sloping: It is a horizontal line. If an individual wheat farmer tries to increase the price he charges for his wheat, the quantity demanded falls to zero because buyers will purchase from one of the other 225,000 wheat farmers. But any one farmer can sell as much wheat as the farmer can produce without needing to cut the price. Both of these

things are true because each wheat farmer is very small relative to the overall market for wheat.

When we draw graphs of the wheat market, we usually show the market equilibrium quantity in millions or billions of bushels. When we draw graphs of the demand for wheat produced by one farmer, we usually show the quantity produced in smaller units, such as thousands of bushels. It is important to remember this difference in scale when interpreting these graphs.

Finally, it is not just wheat farmers who have horizontal demand curves for their products; any firm in a perfectly competitive market faces a horizontal demand curve.

YOUR TURN: Test your understanding by doing related problem 1.6 on page 404 at the end of this chapter.

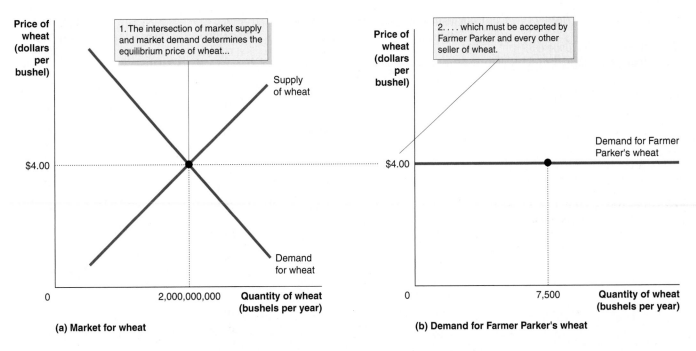

(a) Market for wheat

(b) Demand for Farmer Parker's wheat

Figure 11-2 | The Market Demand for Wheat versus the Demand for One Farmer's Wheat

In a perfectly competitive market, price is determined by the intersection of market demand and market supply. In panel (a), the demand and supply curves for wheat intersect at a price of $4 per bushel. An individual wheat farmer like Farmer Parker has no ability to affect the market price for wheat. Therefore, as panel (b) shows, the demand curve for Farmer Parker's wheat is a horizontal line. To understand this figure, it is important to notice that the scales on the horizontal axes in the two panels are very different. In panel (a), the equilibrium quantity of wheat is 2 *billion* bushels, and in panel (b), Farmer Parker is producing only 7,500 bushels of wheat.

demand curve in panel (a) is the *market demand curve for wheat* and has the normal downward slope we are familiar with from the market demand curves in Chapter 3. Panel (b) of Figure 11-2 shows the demand curve for Farmer Parker's wheat, which is a horizontal line. By viewing these graphs side by side, you can see that the price Farmer Parker receives for his wheat in panel (b) is determined by the interaction of all sellers and all buyers of wheat in the wheat market in panel (a). Keep in mind, however, that the scales on the horizontal axes in the two panels are very different. In panel (a), the equilibrium quantity of wheat is 2 *billion* bushels. In panel (b), Farmer Parker is producing only 7,500 bushels, or less than 0.0004 percent of market output. We need to use different scales in the two panels so we can display both of them on one page. Keep in mind the key point: Farmer Parker's output of wheat is very small relative to the total market output.

11.2 LEARNING OBJECTIVE

11.2 | Explain how a firm maximizes profits in a perfectly competitive market.

How a Firm Maximizes Profit in a Perfectly Competitive Market

We have seen that Farmer Parker cannot control the price of his wheat. In this situation, how does he decide how much wheat to produce? We assume that Farmer Parker's objective is to maximize profits. This is a reasonable assumption for most firms, most of the time. Remember that **profit** is the difference between total revenue (*TR*) and total cost (*TC*):

Profit Total revenue minus total cost.

$$\text{Profit} = TR - TC.$$

To maximize his profit, Farmer Parker should produce the quantity of wheat where the difference between the total revenue he receives and his total cost is as large as possible.

TABLE 11-2

Farmer Parker's Revenue from Wheat Farming

NUMBER OF BUSHELS (Q)	MARKET PRICE (PER BUSHEL) (P)	TOTAL REVENUE (TR)	AVERAGE REVENUE (AR)	MARGINAL REVENUE (MR)
0	$4	$0	—	—
1	4	4	$4	$4
2	4	8	4	4
3	4	12	4	4
4	4	16	4	4
5	4	20	4	4
6	4	24	4	4
7	4	28	4	4
8	4	32	4	4
9	4	36	4	4
10	4	40	4	4

Revenue for a Firm in a Perfectly Competitive Market

To understand how Farmer Parker maximizes profits, let's first consider his revenue. To keep the numbers simple, we will assume that he owns a very small farm and produces at most 10 bushels of wheat per year. Table 11-2 shows the revenue Farmer Parker will earn from selling various quantities of wheat if the market price for wheat is $4.

The third column in Table 11-2 shows that Farmer Parker's *total revenue* rises by $4 for every additional bushel he sells because he can sell as many bushels as he wants at the market price of $4 per bushel. The fourth and fifth columns in the table show Farmer Parker's *average revenue* and *marginal revenue* from selling wheat. His **average revenue** (**AR**) is his total revenue divided by the quantity of bushels he sells. For example, if he sells 5 bushels for a total of $20, his average revenue is $20/5 = $4. Notice that his average revenue is also equal to the market price of $4. In fact, for any level of output, a firm's average revenue is always equal to the market price. One way to see this is to note that total revenue equals price times quantity ($TR = P \times Q$), and average revenue equals total revenue divided by quantity ($AR = TR/Q$). So, $AR = TR/Q = (P \times Q)/Q = P$.

Farmer Parker's **marginal revenue** (**MR**) is the change in his total revenue from selling one more bushel:

$$\text{Marginal Revenue} = \frac{\text{Change in total revenue}}{\text{Change in quantity}}, \text{ or } MR = \frac{\Delta TR}{\Delta Q}.$$

Because for each additional bushel sold he always adds $4 to his total revenue, his marginal revenue is $4. Farmer Parker's marginal revenue is $4 per bushel because he is selling wheat in a perfectly competitive market and can sell as much as he wants at the market price. In fact, Farmer Parker's marginal revenue and average revenue are both equal to the market price. This is an important point: *For a firm in a perfectly competitive market, price is equal to both average revenue and marginal revenue.*

Determining the Profit-Maximizing Level of Output

To determine how Farmer Parker can maximize profit, we have to consider his costs as well as his revenue. A wheat farmer has many costs, including seed, fertilizer, and the wages of farm workers. In Table 11-3, we bring together the revenue data from Table 11-1 with cost data for Farmer Parker's farm. Recall from Chapter 10 that a firm's *marginal cost* is the increase in total cost resulting from producing another unit of output.

Average revenue (AR) Total revenue divided by the quantity of the product sold.

Marginal revenue (MR) Change in total revenue from selling one more unit of a product.

TABLE 11-3

Farmer Parker's Profits from Wheat Farming

QUANTITY (BUSHELS) (*Q*)	TOTAL REVENUE (*TR*)	TOTAL COST (*TC*)	PROFIT (*TR–TC*)	MARGINAL REVENUE (*MR*)	MARGINAL COST (*MC*)
0	$0.00	$1.00	–$1.00	—	—
1	4.00	4.00	0.00	$4.00	$3.00
2	8.00	6.00	2.00	4.00	2.00
3	12.00	7.50	4.50	4.00	1.50
4	16.00	9.50	6.50	4.00	2.00
5	20.00	12.00	8.00	4.00	2.50
6	24.00	15.00	9.00	4.00	3.00
7	28.00	19.50	8.50	4.00	4.50
8	32.00	25.50	6.50	4.00	6.00
9	36.00	32.50	3.50	4.00	7.00
10	40.00	40.50	–0.50	4.00	8.00

We calculate profit in the fourth column by subtracting total cost in the third column from total revenue in the second column. The fourth column shows that as long as Farmer Parker produces between 2 and 9 bushels of wheat, he will earn a profit. His maximum profit is $9.00, which he will earn by producing 6 bushels of wheat. Because Farmer Parker wants to maximize his profits, we would expect him to produce 6 bushels of wheat. Producing more than 6 bushels reduces his profit. For example, if he produces 7 bushels of wheat, his profit will decline from $9.00 to $8.50. The values for marginal cost given in the last column of the table help us understand why Farmer Parker's profits will decline if he produces more than 6 bushels of wheat. After the sixth bushel of wheat, rising marginal cost causes Farmer Parker's profits to fall.

In fact, comparing the marginal cost and marginal revenue at each level of output is an alternative method of calculating Farmer Parker's profits. We illustrate the two methods of calculating profits in Figure 11-3 on the next page. We show the total revenue and total cost approach in panel (a) and the marginal revenue and marginal cost approach in panel (b). Total revenue is a straight line on the graph in panel (a) because total revenue increases at a constant rate of $4 for each additional bushel sold. Farmer Parker's profits are maximized when the vertical distance between the line representing total revenue and the total cost curve is as large as possible. Just as we saw in Table 11-3, this occurs at an output of 6 bushels.

The last two columns of Table 11-3 provide information on the marginal revenue (*MR*) Farmer Parker receives from selling another bushel of wheat and his marginal cost (*MC*) of producing another bushel of wheat. Panel (b) is a graph of Farmer Parker's marginal revenue and marginal cost. Because marginal revenue is always equal to $4, it is a horizontal line at the market price. We have already seen that the demand curve for a perfectly competitive firm is also a horizontal line at the market price. *Therefore, the marginal revenue curve for a perfectly competitive firm is the same as its demand curve.* Farmer Parker's marginal cost of producing wheat first falls and then rises, following the usual pattern we discussed in Chapter 10.

We know from panel (a) that profit is at a maximum at 6 bushels of wheat. In panel (b), profit is also at a maximum at 6 bushels of wheat. To understand why profit is maximized at the level of output where marginal revenue equals marginal cost, remember a key economic principle that we discussed in Chapter 1: *Optimal decisions are made at the margin.* Firms use this principle to decide the quantity of a good to produce. For example, in deciding how much wheat to produce, Farmer Parker needs

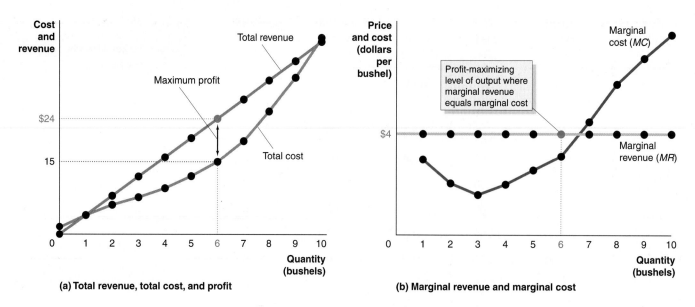

Figure 11-3 | The Profit-Maximizing Level of Output

In panel (a), Farmer Parker maximizes his profit where the vertical distance between total revenue and total cost is the largest. This happens at an output of 6 bushels. Panel (b) shows that Farmer Parker's marginal revenue (*MR*) is equal to a constant $4 per bushel. Farmer Parker maximizes profits by producing wheat up to the point where the marginal revenue of the last bushel produced is equal to its marginal cost, or *MR* = *MC*.

In this case, at no level of output does marginal revenue exactly equal marginal cost. The closest Farmer Parker can come is to produce 6 bushels of wheat. He will not want to continue to produce once marginal cost is greater than marginal revenue because that would reduce his profits. Panels (a) and (b) show alternative ways of thinking about how Farmer Parker can determine the profit-maximizing quantity of wheat to produce.

to compare the marginal revenue he earns from selling another bushel of wheat to the marginal cost of producing that bushel. The difference between the marginal revenue and the marginal cost is the additional profit (or loss) from producing one more bushel. As long as marginal revenue is greater than marginal cost, Farmer Parker's profits are increasing, and he will want to expand production. For example, he will not stop producing at 5 bushels of wheat because producing and selling the sixth bushel adds $4 to his revenue but only $3 to his cost, so his profit increases by $1. He wants to continue producing until the marginal revenue he receives from selling another bushel is equal to the marginal cost of producing it. At that level of output, he will make no *additional* profit by selling another bushel, so he will have maximized his profits.

By inspecting the table, we can see that at no level of output does marginal revenue exactly equal marginal cost. The closest Farmer Parker can come is to produce 6 bushels of wheat. He will not want to continue to produce once marginal cost is greater than marginal revenue because that would reduce his profits. For example, the seventh bushel of wheat adds $4.50 to his cost but only $4.00 to his revenue, so producing the seventh bushel *reduces* his profit by $0.50.

From the information in Table 11-3 and Figure 11-3, we can draw the following conclusions:

1 The profit-maximizing level of output is where the difference between total revenue and total cost is the greatest.

2 The profit-maximizing level of output is also where marginal revenue equals marginal cost, or *MR* = *MC*.

Both these conclusions are true for any firm, whether or not it is in a perfectly competitive industry. We can draw one other conclusion about profit maximization that is true only of firms in perfectly competitive industries: For a firm in a perfectly competitive industry, price is equal to marginal revenue, or *P* = *MR*. So, we can restate the *MR* = *MC* condition as *P* = *MC*.

11.3 | Use graphs to show a firm's profit or loss.

Illustrating Profit or Loss on the Cost Curve Graph

We have seen that profit is the difference between total revenue and total cost. We can also express profit in terms of *average total cost* (*ATC*). This allows us to show profit on the cost curve graph we developed in Chapter 10.

To begin, we need to work through the several steps necessary to determine the relationship between profit and average total cost. Because profit is equal to total revenue minus total cost (*TC*) and total revenue is price times quantity, we can write the following:

$$\text{Profit} = (P \times Q) - TC.$$

If we divide both sides of this equation by Q, we have:

$$\frac{\text{Profit}}{Q} = \frac{(P \times Q)}{Q} - \frac{TC}{Q},$$

or:

$$\frac{\text{Profit}}{Q} = P - ATC,$$

because TC/Q equals ATC. This equation tells us that profit per unit (or average profit) equals price minus average total cost. Finally, we obtain the expression for the relationship between total profit and average total cost by multiplying again by Q:

$$\text{Profit} = (P - ATC) \times Q.$$

This expression tells us that a firm's total profit is equal to the quantity produced multiplied by the difference between price and average total cost.

Showing a Profit on the Graph

Figure 11-4 shows the relationship between a firm's average total cost and its marginal cost that we discussed in Chapter 10. In this figure, we also show the firm's marginal revenue curve (which is the same as its demand curve) and the area representing total profit. Using the relationship between profit and average total cost that we just determined, we can say that the area representing total profit has a height equal to ($P - ATC$) and a base equal to Q. This area is shown by the green-shaded rectangle.

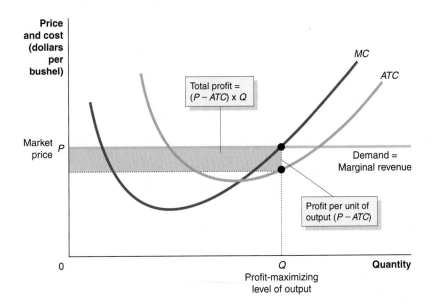

Figure 11-4

The Area of Maximum Profit

A firm maximizes profit at the level of output at which marginal revenue equals marginal cost. The difference between price and average total cost equals profit per unit of output. Total profit equals profit per unit multiplied by the number of units produced. Total profit is represented by the area of the green-shaded rectangle, which has a height equal to ($P - ATC$) and a width equal to Q.

Solved Problem | 11-3

Determining Profit-Maximizing Price and Quantity

Suppose that Andy sells basketballs in the perfectly competitive basketball market. His output per day and his costs are as follows:

OUTPUT PER DAY	TOTAL COST
0	$10.00
1	15.00
2	17.50
3	22.50
4	30.00
5	40.00
6	52.50
7	67.50
8	85.00
9	105.00

a. If the current equilibrium price in the basketball market is $12.50, to maximize profits, how many basketballs will Andy produce, what price will he charge, and how much profit (or loss) will he make? Draw a graph to illustrate your answer. Your graph should be labeled clearly and should include Andy's demand, ATC, AVC, MC, and MR curves; the price he is charging; the quantity he is producing; and the area representing his profit (or loss).

b. Suppose the equilibrium price of basketballs falls to $5.00. Now how many basketballs will Andy produce, what price will he charge, and how much profit (or loss) will he make? Draw a graph to illustrate this situation, using the instructions in question (a).

SOLVING THE PROBLEM:

Step 1: Review the chapter material. This problem is about using cost curve graphs to analyze perfectly competitive firms, so you may want to review the section "Illustrating Profit or Loss on the Cost Curve Graph," which begins on page 385.

Step 2: Calculate Andy's marginal cost, average total cost, and average variable cost. To maximize profits, Andy will produce the level of output where marginal revenue is equal to marginal cost. We can calculate marginal cost from the information given in the table. We can also calculate average total cost and average variable cost in order to draw the required graph. Average total cost (ATC) equals total cost (TC) divided by the level of output (Q). Average variable cost (AVC) equals variable cost (VC) divided by output (Q). To calculate variable cost, recall that total cost equals variable cost plus fixed cost. When output equals zero, total cost equals fixed cost. In this case, fixed cost equals $10.00.

OUTPUT PER DAY (Q)	TOTAL COST (TC)	FIXED COST (FC)	VARIABLE COST (VC)	AVERAGE TOTAL COST (ATC)	AVERAGE VARIABLE COST (AVC)	MARGINAL COST (MC)
0	$10.00	$10.00	$0.00	—	—	—
1	15.00	10.00	5.00	$15.00	$5.00	$5.00
2	17.50	10.00	7.50	8.75	3.75	2.50
3	22.50	10.00	12.50	7.50	4.17	5.00
4	30.00	10.00	20.00	7.50	5.00	7.50
5	40.00	10.00	30.00	8.00	6.00	10.00
6	52.50	10.00	42.50	8.75	7.08	12.50
7	67.50	10.00	57.50	9.64	8.21	15.00
8	85.00	10.00	75.00	10.63	9.38	17.50
9	105.00	10.00	95.00	11.67	10.56	20.00

Step 3: **Use the information from the table in step 2 to calculate how many basketballs Andy will produce, what price he will charge, and how much profit he will earn if the market price of basketballs is $12.50.** Andy's marginal revenue is equal to the market price of $12.50. Marginal revenue equals marginal cost when Andy produces 6 basketballs per day. So, Andy will produce 6 basketballs per day and charge a price of $12.50 per basketball. Andy's profits are equal to his total revenue minus his total costs. His total revenue equals the 6 basketballs he sells multiplied by the $12.50 price, or $75.00. So, his profits equal $75.00 − $52.50 = $22.50.

Step 4: **Use the information from the table in step 2 to illustrate your answer to question (a) with a graph.**

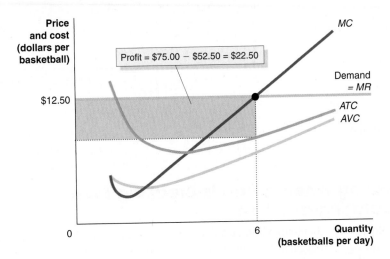

Step 5: **Calculate how many basketballs Andy will produce, what price he will charge, and how much profit he will earn when the market price of basketballs is $5.00.** Referring to the table in step 2, we can see that marginal revenue equals marginal cost when Andy produces 3 basketballs per day. He charges the market price of $5.00 per basketball. His total revenue is only $15.00, while his total costs are $22.50, so he will have a loss of $7.50. (Can we be sure that Andy will continue to produce even though he is operating at a loss? We answer this question in the next section.)

Step 6: **Illustrate your answer to question (b) with a graph.**

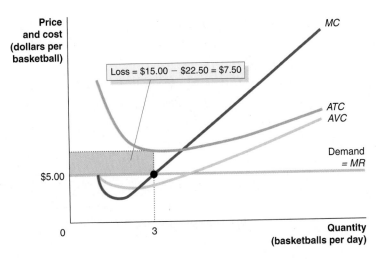

YOUR TURN: For more practice, do related problems 3.3 and 3.4 on page 406 at the end of this chapter.

>> **End Solved Problem 11-3**

Don't Let This Happen to **YOU!**

Remember That Firms Maximize Total Profit, Not Profit per Unit

A student examines the following graph and argues, "I believe that a firm will want to produce at Q_1, not Q_2. At Q_1, the distance between price and average total cost is the greatest. Therefore, at Q_1, the firm will be maximizing its profits per unit." Briefly explain whether you agree with the student's argument.

The student's argument is incorrect because firms are interested in maximizing their *total* profits and not their profits per unit. We know that profits are not maximized at Q_1 because at that level of output, marginal revenue is greater than marginal cost. A firm can always increase its profits by producing any unit that adds more to its revenue than it does to its costs. Only when the firm has expanded production to Q_2 will it have produced every unit for which marginal revenue is greater than marginal cost. At that point, it will have maximized profit.

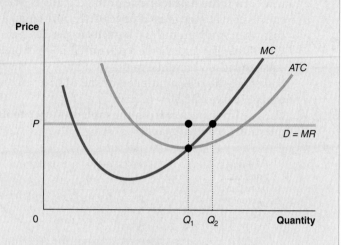

YOUR TURN: Test your understanding by doing related problem 3.5 on page 406 at the end of this chapter.

Illustrating When a Firm Is Breaking Even or Operating at a Loss

We have already seen that to maximize profits, a firm produces the level of output where marginal revenue equals marginal cost. But will the firm actually make a profit at that level of output? It depends on the relationship of price to average total cost. There are three possibilities:

1 $P > ATC$, which means the firm makes a profit.
2 $P = ATC$, which means the firm *breaks even* (its total cost equals its total revenue).
3 $P < ATC$, which means the firm experiences losses.

Figure 11-4 shows the first possibility, where the firm makes a profit. Panels (a) and (b) of Figure 11-5 show the situations where a firm experiences losses or breaks

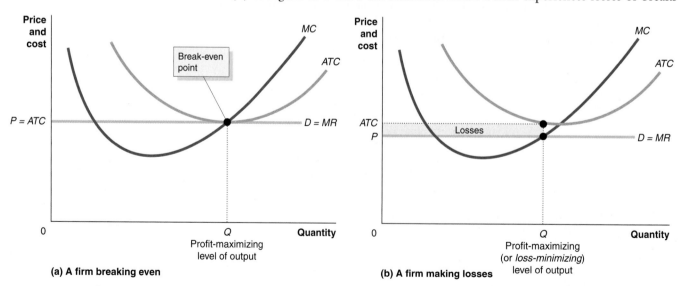

Figure 11-5 | A Firm Breaking Even and a Firm Experiencing Losses

In panel (a), price equals average total cost, and the firm breaks even because its total revenue will be equal to its total cost. In this situation, the firm makes zero economic profit. In panel (b), price is below average total cost, and the firm experiences a loss.

The loss is represented by the area of the red-shaded rectangle, which has a height equal to $(ATC - P)$ and a width equal to Q.

even. In panel (a) of Figure 11-5, at the level of output at which $MR = MC$, price is equal to average total cost. Therefore, total revenue is equal to total cost, and the firm will break even, making zero economic profit. In panel (b), at the level of output at which $MR = MC$, price is less than average total cost. Therefore, total revenue is less than total cost, and the firm has losses. In this case, maximizing profits amounts to *minimizing* losses.

Making the Connection | Losing Money in the Medical Screening Industry

In a market system, a good or service becomes available to consumers only if an entrepreneur brings the product to market. Thousands of new businesses open every week in the United States. Each new business represents an entrepreneur risking his or her funds trying to earn a profit by offering a good or service to consumers. Of course, there are no guarantees of success, and many new businesses experience losses rather than earn the profits their owners hoped for.

In the early 2000s, technological advance reduced the price of computed tomography (CT) scanning equipment. For years, doctors and hospitals have prescribed CT scans to diagnose patients showing symptoms of heart disease, cancer, and other disorders. The declining price of CT scanning equipment convinced many entrepreneurs that it would be profitable to offer preventive body scans to apparently healthy people. The idea was that the scans would provide early detection of diseases before the customers had begun experiencing symptoms. Unfortunately, the new firms offering this service ran into several difficulties: First, because the CT scan was a voluntary procedure, it was not covered under most medical insurance plans. Second, very few consumers used the service more than once, so there was almost no repeat business. Finally, as with any other medical test, some false positives occurred, where the scan appeared to detect a problem that did not actually exist. Negative publicity from people who had expensive additional—and unnecessary—medical procedures as a result of false-positive CT scans also hurt these new businesses.

As a result of these difficulties, the demand for CT scans was less than most of these entrepreneurs had expected, and the new businesses operated at a loss. For example, the owner of California HeartScan would have broken even if the market price had been $495 per heart scan, but it suffered losses because the actual market price was only $250. The following graphs show the owner's situation.

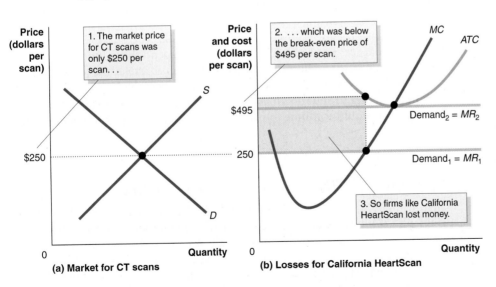

(a) Market for CT scans

(b) Losses for California HeartScan

Why didn't California HeartScan and other medical clinics just raise the price to the level they needed to break even? We have already seen that any firm that tries to raise the price it charges above the market price loses customers to competing firms. By fall 2003, many scanning businesses began to close. Most of the entrepreneurs who had started these businesses lost their investments.

Source: Patricia Callahan, "Scanning for Trouble," *Wall Street Journal*, September 11, 2003, p. B1.

YOUR TURN: Test your understanding by doing related problem 3.8 on page 406 at the end of this chapter.

11.4 LEARNING OBJECTIVE

11.4 | Explain why firms may shut down temporarily.

Deciding Whether to Produce or to Shut Down in the Short Run

In panel (b) of Figure 11-5, we assumed that the firm would continue to produce, even though it was operating at a loss. In fact, in the short run, a firm suffering losses has two choices:

1 Continue to produce

2 Stop production by shutting down temporarily

In many cases, a firm experiencing losses will consider stopping production temporarily. Even during a temporary shutdown, however, a firm must still pay its fixed costs. For example, if the firm has signed a lease for its building, the landlord will expect to receive a monthly rent payment, even if the firm is not producing anything that month. Therefore, if a firm does not produce, it will suffer a loss equal to its fixed costs. This loss is the maximum the firm will accept. If, by producing, the firm would lose an amount greater than its fixed costs, it will shut down.

A firm will be able to reduce its loss below the amount of its total fixed cost by continuing to produce, provided the total revenue it receives is greater than its variable cost. A firm can use the revenue over and above variable cost to cover part of its fixed cost. In this case, the firm will have a smaller loss by continuing to produce than if it shut down.

Sunk cost A cost that has already been paid and that cannot be recovered.

In analyzing the firm's decision to shut down, we are assuming that its fixed costs are *sunk costs*. Remember from Chapter 9 that a **sunk cost** is a cost that has already been paid and cannot be recovered. We assume, as is usually the case, that the firm cannot recover its fixed costs by shutting down. For example, if a farmer has taken out a loan to buy land, the farmer is legally required to make the monthly loan payment whether he grows any wheat that season or not. The farmer has to spend those funds and cannot get them back, so the farmer should treat his sunk costs as irrelevant to his decision making. For any firm, whether total revenue is greater or less than *variable costs* is the key to deciding whether to shut down. As long as a firm's total revenue is greater than its variable costs, it should continue to produce no matter how large or small its fixed costs are.

Making the Connection | When to Close a Laundry

An article in the *Wall Street Journal* describes what happened to Robert Kjelgaard when he quit his job writing software code at Microsoft and bought a laundry by paying the previous owner $80,000. For this payment, he received 76 washers and dryers and the existing lease on the building. The lease had six years remaining and required a monthly payment of $3,300. Unfortunately, Mr. Kjelgaard had difficulty operating the laundry at a profit. His explicit costs were $4,000 per month more than his revenue.

He tried but failed to sell the laundry. As he told a reporter, "It's hard to sell a business that's losing money." He considered closing the laundry, but as a sole proprietor, he would be responsible for the remainder of the lease. At $3,300 per month for six years, he would be responsible for paying almost $200,000 out of his personal savings. Closing the laundry would still seem to be the better choice because his $3,300 per month in sunk costs were less than the $4,000 per month plus the opportunity cost of his time, which he was losing from operating the laundry.

He finally decided to reorganize his business and hire a professional manager. This change allowed him to return to Microsoft and still reduce his losses to $2,000 per month. Because this amount was less than the $3,300 per month he would lose by shutting down, it made sense for him to continue to operate the laundry. But he was still suffering losses and, according to the article, his wife was "counting the days until the lease runs out."

Source: G. Pascal Zachary, "How a Success at Microsoft Washed Out at a Laundry," *Wall Street Journal*, May 30, 1995.

YOUR TURN: Test your understanding by doing related problems 4.5 and 4.6 on page 407 at the end of this chapter.

Keeping a business open even when suffering losses can sometimes be the best decision for an entrepreneur in the short run.

One option not available to a firm with losses in a perfectly competitive market is to raise its price. If the firm did raise its price, it would lose all its customers, and its sales would drop to zero. For example, in a recent year, the price of wheat in the United States was $3.16 per bushel. At that price, the typical U.S. wheat farmer lost $9,500. At a price of about $4.25 per bushel, the typical wheat farmer would have broken even. But any wheat farmer who tried to raise his price to $4.25 per bushel would have seen his sales quickly disappear because buyers could purchase all the wheat they wanted at $3.16 per bushel from the thousands of other wheat farmers.

The Supply Curve of a Firm in the Short Run

Remember that the supply curve for a firm tells us how many units of a product the firm is willing to sell at any given price. Notice that the marginal cost curve for a firm in a perfectly competitive market tells us the same thing. The firm will produce at the level of output where $MR = MC$. Because price equals marginal revenue for a firm in a perfectly competitive market, the firm will produce where $P = MC$. For any given price, we can determine from the marginal cost curve the quantity of output the firm will supply. *Therefore, a perfectly competitive firm's marginal cost curve also is its supply curve.* There is, however, an important qualification to this. We have seen that if a firm is experiencing losses, it will shut down if its total revenue is less than its variable cost:

$$\text{Total revenue} < \text{Variable cost},$$

or, in symbols:

$$P \times Q < VC.$$

If we divide both sides by Q, we have the result that the firm will shut down if:

$$P < AVC.$$

If the price drops below average variable cost, the firm will have a smaller loss if it shuts down and produces no output. *So, the firm's marginal cost curve is its supply curve only for prices at or above average variable cost.* The red line in Figure 11-6 shows the supply curve for the firm in the short run.

Recall that the marginal cost curve intersects the average variable cost where the average variable cost curve is at its minimum point. Therefore, the firm's supply curve is its marginal cost curve above the minimum point of the average variable cost curve. For prices below minimum average variable cost (P_{MIN}), the firm will shut down, and its output will fall to zero. The minimum point on the average variable cost curve is called the **shutdown point** and occurs in Figure 11-6 at output level Q_{SD}.

Shutdown point The minimum point on a firm's average variable cost curve; if the price falls below this point, the firm shuts down production in the short run.

Figure 11-6

The Firm's Short-Run Supply Curve

The firm will produce at the level of output at which $MR = MC$. Because price equals marginal revenue for a firm in a perfectly competitive market, the firm will produce where $P = MC$. For any given price, we can determine the quantity of output the firm will supply from the marginal cost curve. In other words, the marginal cost curve is the firm's supply curve. But remember that the firm will shut down if the price falls below average variable cost. The marginal cost curve crosses the average variable cost at the firm's shutdown point. This point occurs at output level Q_{SD}. For prices below P_{MIN}, the supply curve is a vertical line along the price axis, which shows that the firm will supply zero output at those prices. The red line in the figure is the firm's short-run supply curve.

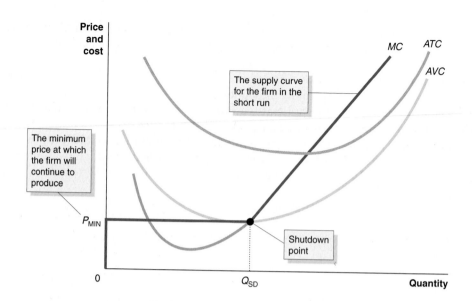

The Market Supply Curve in a Perfectly Competitive Industry

We saw in Chapter 9 that the market demand curve is determined by adding up the quantity demanded by each consumer in the market at each price. Similarly, the market supply curve is determined by adding up the quantity supplied by each firm in the market at each price. Each firm's marginal cost curve tells us how much that firm will supply at each price. So, the market supply curve can be derived directly from the marginal cost curves of the firms in the market. Panel (a) of Figure 11-7 shows the marginal cost curve for one wheat farmer. At a price of $4, this wheat farmer supplies 8,000 bushels of wheat.

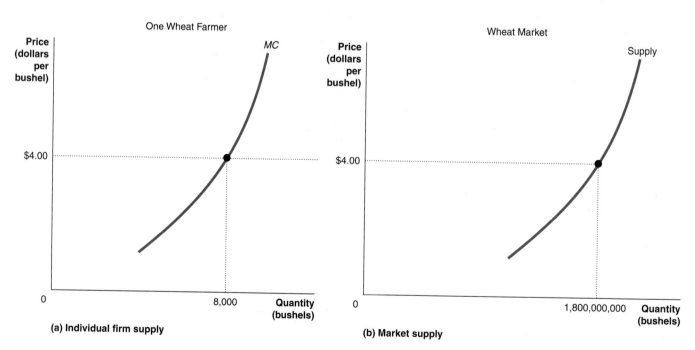

Figure 11-7 | Firm Supply and Market Supply

We can derive the market supply curve by adding up the quantity that each firm in the market is willing to supply at each price. In panel (a), one wheat farmer is willing to supply 8,000 bushels of wheat at a price of $4 per bushel. If every wheat farmer supplies the same amount of wheat at this price and if there are 225,000 wheat farmers, the total amount of wheat supplied at a price of $4 will equal 8,000 bushels per farmer × 225,000 farmers = 1.8 billion bushels of wheat. This is one point on the market supply curve for wheat shown in panel (b). We can find the other points on the market supply curve by seeing how much wheat each farmer is willing to supply at each price.

If every wheat farmer supplies the same amount of wheat at this price and if there are 225,000 wheat farmers, the total amount of wheat supplied at a price of $4 will be:

8,000 bushels per farmer × 225,000 farmers = 1.8 billion bushels of wheat.

Panel (b) shows a price of $4 and a quantity of 1.8 billion bushels as a point on the market supply curve for wheat. In reality, of course, not all wheat farms are alike. Some wheat farms supply more at the market price than the typical farm; other wheat farms supply less. The key point is that we can derive the market supply curve by adding up the quantity that each firm in the market is willing to supply at each price.

11.5 | Explain how entry and exit ensure that perfectly competitive firms earn zero economic profit in the long run.

"If Everyone Can Do It, You Can't Make Money at It": The Entry and Exit of Firms in the Long Run

In the long run, unless a firm can cover all its costs, it will shut down and exit the industry. In a market system, firms continually enter and exit industries. In this section, we will see how profits and losses provide signals to firms that lead to entry and exit.

Economic Profit and the Entry or Exit Decision

To begin, let's look more closely at how economists characterize the profits earned by the owners of a firm. Suppose Anne Moreno decides to start her own business. After considering her interests and preparing a business plan, she decides to start an organic apple farm rather than open a restaurant or gift shop. After 10 years of effort, Anne has saved $100,000 and borrowed another $900,000 from a bank. With these funds, she has bought the land, apple trees, and farm equipment necessary to start her organic apple business. As we saw in Chapter 10, when someone invests her own funds in her firm, the opportunity cost to the firm is the return the funds would have earned in their best alternative use. If Farmer Moreno could have earned a 10 percent return on her $100,000 in savings in their best alternative use—which might have been, for example, to buy a small restaurant—then her apple business incurs a $10,000 opportunity cost. We can also think of this $10,000 as being the minimum amount that Farmer Moreno needs to earn on her $100,000 investment in her farm to remain in the industry in the long run.

Table 11-4 lists Farmer Moreno's costs. In addition to her explicit costs, we assume that she has two implicit costs: the $10,000, which represents the opportunity cost of the

EXPLICIT COSTS	
Water	$10,000
Wages	$15,000
Organic fertilizer	$10,000
Electricity	$5,000
Payment on bank loan	$45,000
IMPLICIT COSTS	
Foregone salary	$30,000
Opportunity cost of the $100,000 she has invested in her farm	$10,000
Total cost	$125,000

TABLE 11-4

Farmer Moreno's Costs per Year

funds she invested in her farm, and the $30,000 salary she could have earned managing someone else's farm instead of her own. Her total costs are $125,000. If the market price of organic apples is $15 per box and Farmer Moreno sells 10,000 boxes, her total revenue will be $150,000 and her economic profit will be $25,000 (total revenue of $150,000 minus total costs of $125,000). Recall from Chapter 7 that **economic profit** equals a firm's revenues minus all of its costs, implicit and explicit. So, Farmer Moreno is covering the $10,000 opportunity cost of the funds invested in her firm, and she is also earning an additional $25,000 in economic profit.

Economic profit A firm's revenues minus all its costs, implicit and explicit.

Economic Profit Leads to Entry of New Firms

Unfortunately, Farmer Moreno is unlikely to earn an economic profit for very long. Suppose other apple farmers are just breaking even by growing apples using conventional methods. In that case, they will have an incentive to convert to organic growing methods so they can begin earning an economic profit. Remember that the more firms there are in an industry, the further to the right the market supply curve is. Panel (a) of Figure 11-8 shows that more farmers entering the market for organically grown apples will cause the market supply curve to shift to the right. Farmers will continue entering the market until the market supply curve has shifted from S_1 to S_2.

With the supply curve at S_2, the market price will have fallen to $10 per box. Panel (b) shows the effect on Farmer Moreno, whom we assume has the same costs as other organic apple farmers. As the market price falls from $15 to $10 per box, Farmer Moreno's demand curve shifts down, from D_1 to D_2. In the new equilibrium, Farmer Moreno is selling 8,000 boxes at a price of $10 per box. She and the other organic apple growers are no longer earning any economic profit. They are just breaking even, and the return on their investment is just covering the opportunity cost of these funds. New farmers will stop entering the market for organic apples because the rate of return is no better than they can earn elsewhere.

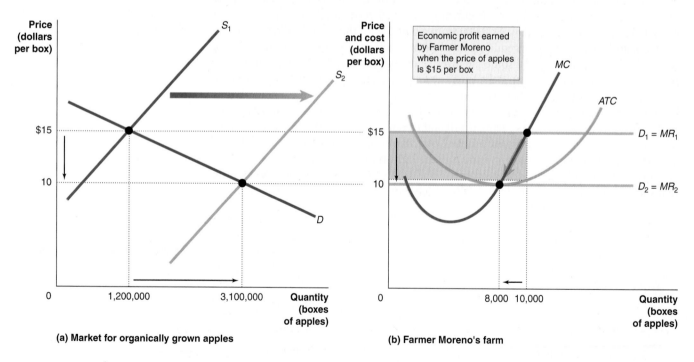

(a) Market for organically grown apples   **(b) Farmer Moreno's farm**

Figure 11-8 | The Effect of Entry on Economic Profits

We assume that Farmer Moreno's costs are the same as the costs of other organic apple growers. Initially, she and other producers of organically grown apples are able to charge $15 per box and earn an economic profit. Farmer Moreno's economic profit is represented by the area of the green box. Panel (a) shows that as other farmers begin to grow apples using organic methods, the market supply curve shifts to the right, from S_1 to S_2, and the market price drops to $10 per box. Panel (b) shows that

the falling price causes Farmer Moreno's demand curve to shift down from D_1 to D_2, and she reduces her output from 10,000 boxes to 8,000. At the new market price of $10 per box, organic apple growers are just breaking even: Their total revenue is equal to their total cost, and their economic profit is zero. Notice the difference in scale between the graph in panel (a) and the graph in panel (b).

Will Farmer Moreno continue to grow organic apples even though she is just breaking even? She will because growing organic apples earns her as high a return on her investment as she could earn elsewhere. It may seem strange that new firms will continue to enter a market until all economic profits are eliminated and that established firms remain in a market despite not earning any economic profit. It only seems strange because we are used to thinking in terms of accounting profits, rather than *economic* profits. Remember that accounting rules generally require that only explicit costs be included on a firm's financial statements. The opportunity cost of the funds Farmer Moreno invested in her firm—$10,000—and her foregone salary—$30,000—are economic costs, but neither is an accounting cost. So, although an accountant would see Farmer Moreno as earning a profit of $40,000, an economist would see her as just breaking even. Farmer Moreno must pay attention to her accounting profit when preparing her financial statements and when paying her income tax. But because economic profit takes into account all her costs, it gives a truer indication of the financial health of her farm.

Economic Losses Lead to Exit of Firms Suppose some consumers decide there are no important benefits from eating organically grown apples and they switch back to buying conventionally grown apples. Panel (a) of Figure 11-9 shows that the demand curve for organically grown apples will shift to the left, from D_1 to D_2, and the market price will fall from $10 per box to $7. Panel (b) shows that as the price falls, a typical organic apple farmer, like Anne Moreno, will move down her marginal cost curve to a lower level of output. At the lower level of output and lower price, she will be suffering an **economic loss** because she will not cover all her costs. As long as price is above average variable cost, she will continue to produce in the short run, even when suffering losses. But in the long run, firms will exit an industry if they are unable to cover all their costs. In this case, some organic apple growers will switch back to growing apples using conventional methods.

Panel (c) of Figure 11-9 shows that firms exiting the organic apple industry will cause the market supply curve to shift to the left. Firms will continue to exit, and the supply curve will continue to shift to the left until the price has risen back to $10 and the market supply curve is at S_2. Panel (d) shows that when the price is back to $10, the remaining firms in the industry will be breaking even.

Economic loss The situation in which a firm's total revenue is less than its total cost, including all implicit costs.

Long-Run Equilibrium in a Perfectly Competitive Market

We have seen that economic profits attract firms to enter an industry. The entry of firms forces down the market price until the typical firm is breaking even. Economic losses cause firms to exit an industry. The exit of firms forces up the equilibrium market price until the typical firm is breaking even. This process of entry and exit results in *long-run competitive equilibrium*. In **long-run competitive equilibrium**, entry and exit have resulted in the typical firm breaking even. The *long-run equilibrium market price* is at a level equal to the minimum point on the typical firm's average total cost curve.

Long-run competitive equilibrium The situation in which the entry and exit of firms has resulted in the typical firm breaking even.

The long run in the organic apple market is three to four years, which is the amount of time it takes farmers to convert from conventional growing methods to organic growing methods. As discussed at the beginning of this chapter, only during the years from 1997 to 2001 was it possible for organic apple farmers to earn economic profits. By 2002, the entry of new firms had eliminated economic profits in the industry.

Firms in perfectly competitive markets are in a constant struggle to stay one step ahead of their competitors. They are always looking for new ways to provide a product, such as growing apples organically. It is possible for firms to find ways to earn an economic profit for a while, but to repeat the quote from a Yakima Valley organic apple farmer at the beginning of this chapter, "It's like anything else in agriculture. If people see an economic opportunity, usually it only lasts for a few years." This observation is not restricted to agriculture. In any perfectly competitive market, an opportunity to make economic profits never lasts long. As Sharon Oster, an economist at Yale University, has put it, "If everyone can do it, you can't make money at it."

at this price because it is at the minimum point on the firm's average total cost curve. We can draw the important conclusion that *in the long run, a perfectly competitive market will supply whatever amount of a good consumers demand at a price determined by the minimum point on the typical firm's average total cost curve.*

Because the position of the long-run supply curve is determined by the minimum point on the typical firm's average total cost curve, anything that raises or lowers the costs of the typical firm in the long run will cause the long-run supply curve to shift. For example, if a disease infects apple trees and the costs of treating the disease adds $2 per box to the cost of producing apples, the long-run supply curve will shift up by $2.

Increasing-Cost and Decreasing-Cost Industries

Any industry in which the typical firm's average costs do not change as the industry expands production will have a horizontal long-run supply curve, like the one in Figure 11-10. Industries, like the apple industry, where this holds true are called *constant-cost industries*. It's possible, however, for the typical firm's average costs to change as an industry expands.

For example, if an input used in producing a good is available in only limited quantities, the cost of the input will rise as the industry expands. If only a limited amount of land is available on which to grow the grapes to make a certain variety of wine, an increase in demand for wine made from these grapes will result in competition for the land and will drive up its price. As a result, more of the wine will be produced in the long run only if the price rises to cover the higher average costs of the typical firm. In this case, the long-run supply curve will slope upward. Industries with upward-sloping long-run supply curves are called *increasing-cost industries*.

Finally, in some cases, the typical firm's costs may fall as the industry expands. Suppose that someone invents a new microwave that uses as an input a specialized memory chip that is currently produced only in small quantities. If demand for the microwave increases, firms that produce microwaves will increase their orders for the memory chip. We saw in Chapter 10 that if there are economies of scale in producing a good, its average cost will decline as output increases. If there are economies of scale in producing this memory chip, the average cost of producing it will fall, and competition will result in its price falling as well. This price decline, in turn, will lower the average cost of producing the new microwave. In the long run, competition will force the price of the microwave to fall to the level of the new lower average cost of the typical firm. In this case, the long-run supply curve will slope downward. Industries with downward-sloping long-run supply curves are called *decreasing-cost industries*.

11.6 LEARNING OBJECTIVE   11.6 | Explain how perfect competition leads to economic efficiency.

Perfect Competition and Efficiency

Notice how powerful consumers are in a market system. If consumers want more organic apples, the market will supply them. This happens not because a government bureaucrat in Washington, DC, or an official in an apple growers' association gives orders. The additional apples are produced because an increase in demand results in higher prices and a higher rate of return on investments in organic growing techniques. Apple growers, trying to get the highest possible return on their investment, begin to switch from using conventional growing methods to using organic growing methods. If consumers lose their taste for organic apples and demand falls, the process works in reverse.

Making
the
Connection

The Decline of Apple Production in New York State

Although New York State is second only to Washington State in production of apples, its production has been declining during the past 20 years. The decline has been particularly steep in counties close to New York City. In 1985, there were more than 11,000 acres of apple orchards in Ulster County, which is 75 miles north of New York City. Today, fewer than 5,000 acres remain. As it became difficult for apple growers in the county to compete with lower-cost producers elsewhere, the resources these entrepreneurs were using to produce apples—particularly land—became more valuable in other uses. Many farmers sold their land to housing developers. As one apple farmer put it, "Over the last ten years or so, [apple] prices have been stagnant or going down. I didn't see a return on the money, and I didn't want to continue."

In a market system, entrepreneurs will not continue to employ economic resources to produce a good or service unless consumers are willing to pay a price at least high enough for them to break even. Consumers were not willing to pay a high enough price for apples for many New York State apple growers to break even on their investments. As a result, resources left apple production in that state.

When apple growers in New York State stopped breaking even, many sold their land to housing developers.

Sources: Lisa W. Foderaro, "Where Apples Don't Pay, Developers Will," *New York Times*, June 23, 2001; and USDA, *2002 Census of Agriculture, Volume 1, Chapter 2*, New York County Level Data, Table 31.

YOUR TURN: Test your understanding by doing related problem 6.7 on page 409 at the end of this chapter.

Productive Efficiency

In the market system, consumers get as many apples as they want, produced at the lowest average cost possible. The forces of competition will drive the market price to the minimum average cost of the typical firm. **Productive efficiency** refers to the situation in which a good or service is produced at the lowest possible cost. As we have seen, perfect competition results in productive efficiency.

The managers of every firm strive to earn an economic profit by reducing costs. But in a perfectly competitive market, other firms quickly copy ways of reducing costs, so that in the long run, only the consumer benefits from cost reductions.

Productive efficiency The situation in which a good or service is produced at the lowest possible cost.

Solved Problem | 11-6

How Productive Efficiency Benefits Consumers

Writing in the *New York Times* on the technology boom of the late 1990s, Michael Lewis argues "The sad truth, for investors, seems to be that most of the benefits of new technologies are passed right through to consumers free of charge."

a. What do you think Lewis means by the benefits of new technology being "passed right through to consumers free of charge"? Use a graph like Figure 11-8 on page 394 to illustrate your answer.

b. Explain why this result is a "sad truth" for investors.

SOLVING THE PROBLEM:

Step 1: **Review the chapter material.** This problem is about perfect competition and efficiency, so you may want to review the section "Perfect Competition and Efficiency," which begins on page 398.

Step 2: **Use the concepts from this chapter to explain what Lewis means.** By "new technologies," Lewis means new products—like cell phones or plasma television sets—or lower-cost ways of producing existing products. In either case, new technologies will allow firms to earn economic profits for a while, but these profits will lead new firms to enter the market in the long run.

Step 3: **Use a graph like Figure 11-8 to illustrate why the benefits of new technologies are "passed right through to consumers free of charge."** Figure 11-8 shows the situation in which a firm is making economic profits in the short run but has these profits eliminated by entry in the long run. We can draw a similar graph to analyze what happens in the long run in the market for plasma televisions:

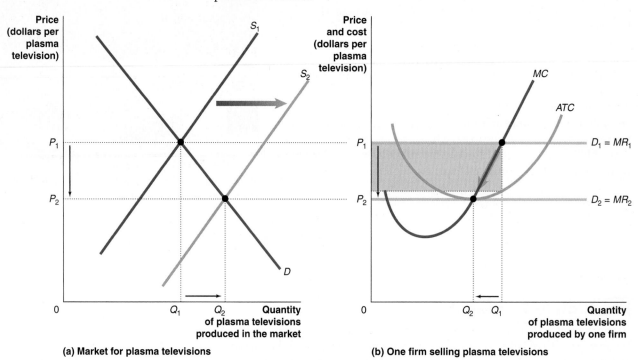

(a) Market for plasma televisions   **(b) One firm selling plasma televisions**

When plasma televisions were first introduced, prices were high, and only a few firms were in the market. Panel (a) shows that the initial equilibrium price in the market for plasma televisions is P_1. Panel (b) shows that at this price, the typical firm in the industry is earning an economic profit, which is shown by the green-shaded box. The economic profit attracts new firms into the industry. This entry shifts the market supply curve from S_1 to S_2 in panel (a) and lowers the equilibrium price from P_1 to P_2. Panel (b) shows that at the new market price, P_2, the typical firm is breaking even. Therefore, plasma televisions are being produced at the lowest possible cost, and productive efficiency is achieved. Consumers receive the new technology "free of charge" in the sense that they only have to pay a price equal to the lowest possible cost of production.

Step 4: **Answer question (b) by explaining why the result in question (a) is a "sad truth" for investors.** We have seen in answering question (a) that in the long run, firms only break even on their investment in producing high-technology goods. That result implies that investors in these firms are also unlikely to earn an economic profit in the long run.

EXTRA CREDIT: Lewis is using a key result from this chapter: In the long run, entry of new firms competes away economic profits. We should notice that, strictly speaking, the high-technology industries Lewis is discussing are not perfectly competitive. Cell phones or plasma televisions, for instance, are not identical, and each cell phone company produces a quantity large enough to affect the market price. However, as we will see in Chapter 12, these deviations from perfect competition do not change the important conclusion that the entry of new firms benefits consumers by forcing prices down to the level of average cost. In fact, the price of plasma televisions dropped by more than 75 percent within five years of their first becoming widely available.

Source: Michael Lewis, "In Defense of the Boom," *New York Times*, October 27, 2002.

YOUR TURN: For more practice, do related problems 6.4, 6.5, and 6.6 on page 409 at the end of this chapter.

>> End Solved Problem 11-6

Allocative Efficiency

Not only do perfectly competitive firms produce goods and services at the lowest possible cost, they also produce the goods and services that consumers value most. Firms will produce a good up to the point where the marginal cost of producing another unit is equal to the marginal benefit consumers receive from consuming that unit. In other words, firms will supply all those goods that provide consumers with a marginal benefit at least as great as the marginal cost of producing them. We know this is true because:

1 The price of a good represents the marginal benefit consumers receive from consuming the last unit of the good sold.

2 Perfectly competitive firms produce up to the point where the price of the good equals the marginal cost of producing the last unit.

3 Therefore, firms produce up to the point where the last unit provides a marginal benefit to consumers equal to the marginal cost of producing it.

These statements are another way of saying that entrepreneurs in a market system efficiently *allocate* labor, machinery, and other inputs to produce the goods and services that best satisfy consumer wants. In this sense, perfect competition achieves **allocative efficiency**. As we will explore in the next few chapters, many goods and services sold in the U.S. economy are not produced in perfectly competitive markets. Nevertheless, productive efficiency and allocative efficiency are useful benchmarks against which to compare the actual performance of the economy.

Allocative efficiency A state of the economy in which production represents consumer preferences; in particular, every good or service is produced up to the point where the last unit provides a marginal benefit to consumers equal to the marginal cost of producing it.

Economics in YOUR Life!

>> Continued from page 377

At the beginning of the chapter, we asked you to think about why you can charge only a relatively low price for performing services such as babysitting or lawn mowing. In the chapter, we saw that firms selling products in competitive markets are unable to charge prices higher than those being charged by competing firms. The market for babysitting and lawn mowing is very competitive. In most neighborhoods, there are a lot of teenagers willing to supply these services. The price you can charge for babysitting may not be worth your while at age 20 but is enough to cover the opportunity cost of a 14-year-old eager to enter the market. (Or, as we put it in Table 11-1 on page 378, the ease of entry into babysitting and lawn mowing is high.) So, in your career as a teenage entrepreneur, you may have become familiar with one of the lessons of this chapter: A firm in a competitive market has no control over price.

Conclusion

The competitive forces of the market impose relentless pressure on firms to produce new and better goods and services at the lowest possible cost. Firms that fail to adequately anticipate changes in consumer tastes or that fail to adopt the latest and most efficient technology do not survive in the long run. In the nineteenth century, the biologist Charles Darwin developed a theory of evolution based on the idea of the "survival of the fittest." Only those plants and animals that are best able to adapt to the demands of their environment are able to survive. Darwin first realized the important role that the struggle for existence plays in the natural world after reading early nineteenth-century economists' descriptions of the role it plays in the economic world. Just as "survival of the fittest" is the rule in nature, so it is in the economic world.

At the start of this chapter, we saw that there are four market structures: perfect competition, monopolistic competition, oligopoly, and monopoly. Now that we have studied perfect competition, in the following chapters we move on to the other three market structures. Before turning to those chapters, read *An Inside Look* on the next page to learn how firms are rushing to enter the market for organic snacks.

Why Are Organic Farmers Worried about Wal-Mart?

BUSINESSWEEK, MARCH 29, 2006

Wal-Mart's Organic Offensive

Richard DeWilde has a long history with organic farming. His grandfather, Nick Hoogshagen, adopted the organic approach five decades ago on his farm in South Dakota, well before it became popular with consumers and fueled the popularity of retailers like Whole Foods Market.

Now, DeWilde, 57 is a working farmer himself, carrying on the family tradition of avoiding pesticides and other chemicals that can contaminate food in favor of a more natural approach. He's co-owner of Harmony Valley Farm, which grows Swiss chard, parsnips, turnips, and kale on 100 acres in the southwestern corner of Wisconsin. So you might think that DeWilde would be overjoyed at the news that Wal-Mart has finally come around to his grandfather's philosophy. The juggernaut retailer said recently that it plans to double its offering of organic product, including produce, dairy, and dry goods.

But DeWilde isn't thrilled. Instead, he's dismayed at the prospect of Wal-Mart becoming a player in the organic market. He fears that the company will use its market strength to drive down prices and hurt U.S. farmers. "Wal-Mart has the reputation of beating up on its suppliers," says DeWilde. "I certainly don't see 'selling at a lower price' as an opportunity."

He's hardly the only one. Many farmers who have benefited from the strong demand and healthy margins for organic goods are fretting that the market's newfound success also brings with it newfound risks. As large companies enter the market, from Kraft and Dean Foods to Wal-Mart, farmers worry that the corporatization of organic foods could have negative consequences.

Large corporations have taken sizable steps into the organic market, even if it isn't always obvious from the brands on store shelves. Silk, the best-selling branded soy milk, is a product from Dean Foods, the $10 billion behemoth that sells the most milk in the country. Cascadian Farms, which makes organic cereal, frozen fruits, and other products, is a brand of cereal giant General Mills. And Kraft owns Boca Burgers. . . .

Organic farmers are straining to meet rising demand, one of the reasons that legislators have been willing to drop certain requirements for organic foods. In the past year, the demand for organic milk outstripped the supply by 10% and created acute shortages. That even prompted organic dairy company Stonyfield Farms to stop producing its fat-free 32-ounce cups of yogurt. Now Stonyfield has resumed its production, but organic milk consumption nationwide is growing 30% annually.

Wal-Mart is making its aggressive move into organics at the same time it's trying to improve its environmental image. Last year, it embarked on a new green policy and has several initiatives to demonstrate how serious it is. The company recently said that it will require that all its wild-caught fresh and frozen fish meet the Marine Stewardship Council's standard for sustainable and well-managed fisheries. Fish accounts for a third of all the chain's seafood sales. . . .

While some farmers are concerned that Wal-Mart may try to squeeze them financially, there could be a more benign impact. Farmers who now use pesticides and other chemicals could turn to organic farming, as they see increased demand. Consider what's happening in California.

Last year, the state showed an increase of 40,000 acres, or 27%, in organic livestock production. The number of acres dedicated to organic vegetable production increased by 5,000 acres, or 12%, according to the California Certified Organic Farmers, an organics trade association. "Strong demand is creating markets here," says Jake Lewin, director of marketing at the organization.

Meanwhile, back in Wisconsin, DeWilde is preparing for warmer weather and the spring planting season. He is worried about how the increasing attention from Wal-Mart and other large companies may change the business of organic foods. Yet he's more convinced than ever of the benefits of the approach his grandfather helped champion. "It's the future of farming," he says.

Source: Pallavi Gogoi, "Wal-Mart's Organic Offensive," BusinessWeek, March 29, 2006.

Key Points in the Article

The increasing popularity of organic food has caught the attention of large food producers, such as Dean Foods, which produces Silk, the best-selling brand of soy milk. Wal-Mart, which is the largest seller of groceries in the United States, has also begun to offer more organic foods for sale. Some farmers who supply organic foods are concerned that Wal-Mart may offer lower prices than they have been receiving from supermarkets. Other farmers believe that if Wal-Mart begins selling more organic foods it may increase the popularity of these products and increase the demand for them.

Analyzing the News

(a) One of the key points of this chapter is that, ultimately, it is *consumers* who decide which goods will be produced. If consumers increase their demand for organic foods, then firms will redirect workers, machines, and natural resources toward producing those goods. One industry analyst (not quoted in the article) observed, "Organic is a niche, but a very profitable niche. Give consumers what they truly want/need and they will dig deeply into their pockets."

In fact, it is those profits that signal to entrepreneurs that demand for organic foods has increased. We know from the analysis in this chapter, though, that these profits will not persist in the long run. Figure 1 shows that an increase in demand for organic food raises the price from P_1 to P_2, which results in the typical firm earning economic profits.

(b) Figure 2 shows the long-run result. The economic profit earned by producing organic foods will attract additional firms to enter the industry. As the article mentions, farmers in California are taking resources out of non-organic farming and putting them into organic farming. The entrance of new firms will eventually cause the market price to fall back to P_1. At a price of P_1, the typical firm is once again breaking even. The increase in consumer demand for organic foods results in the quantity supplied rising in the long run, as new firms enter the industry. In the long run the typical firm in a perfectly competitive industry breaks even, as economic profits are competed away.

Thinking Critically

1. Use a demand and supply graph and a cost curve graph to show what would happen if the government tightened its regulations, making it more difficult for foods to be labeled as "organic."

2. Suppose that farmers who produce organic foods protest to Congress as prices decline. Use a demand and supply graph to show the impact on the market for organic foods if Congress decides to impose a price floor above the equilibrium price. What happens to consumer surplus and producer surplus as a result of the price floor?

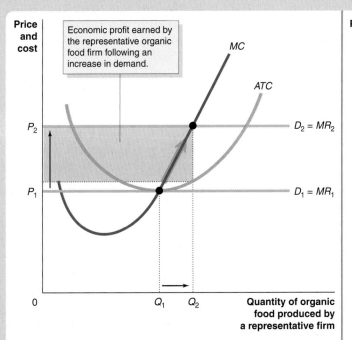

Figure 1. The short-run effects of an increase in demand for organic food.

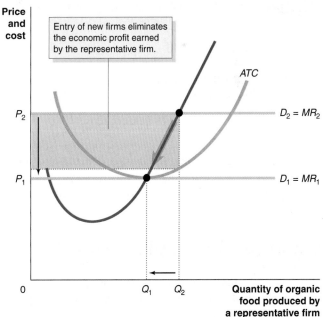

Figure 2. The long-run effects of an increase in demand for organic foods.

403

Key Terms

Allocative efficiency, p. 401

Average revenue (*AR*), p. 382

Economic loss, p. 395

Economic profit, p. 394

Long-run competitive equilibrium, p. 395

Long-run supply curve, p. 397

Marginal revenue (*MR*), p. 382

Perfectly competitive market, p. 379

Price taker, p. 379

Productive efficiency, p. 399

Profit, p. 381

Shutdown point, p. 391

Sunk cost, p. 390

11.1 LEARNING OBJECTIVE 11.1 | Define a perfectly competitive market and explain why a perfect competitor faces a horizontal demand curve, **pages 379–381.**

Perfectly Competitive Markets

Summary

A **perfectly competitive market** must have many buyers and sellers, firms must be producing identical products, and there must be no barriers to entry of new firms. The demand curve for a good or service produced in a perfectly competitive market is downward sloping, but the demand curve for the output of one firm in a perfectly competitive market is a horizontal line at the market price. Firms in perfectly competitive markets are **price takers** and see their sales drop to zero if they attempt to charge more than the market price.

 Visit www.myeconlab.com to complete these exercises online and get instant feedback.

Review Questions

1.1 What are the three conditions for a market to be perfectly competitive?

1.2 What is a price taker? When are firms likely to be price takers?

1.3 Draw a graph showing the market demand and supply for corn and the demand for the corn produced by one corn farmer. Be sure to indicate the market price and the price received by the corn farmer.

Problems and Applications

1.4 Explain whether each of the following is a perfectly competitive market. For each market that is not perfectly competitive, explain why it is not.
   a. Corn farming
   b. Retail bookselling
   c. Automobile manufacturing
   d. New home construction

1.5 Why are consumers usually price takers when they buy most goods and services, while relatively few firms are price takers?

1.6 **(Related to the *Don't Let This Happen to You!* on page 380)** Explain whether you agree or disagree with the following remark:

> According to the model of perfectly competitive markets, the demand for wheat should be a horizontal line. But this can't be true: When the price of wheat rises, the quantity of wheat demanded falls, and when the price of wheat falls, the quantity of wheat demanded rises. Therefore, the demand for wheat is not a horizontal line.

1.7 The financial writer Andrew Tobias has described an incident when he was a student at the Harvard Business School: Each student in the class was given large amounts of information about a particular firm and asked to determine a pricing strategy for the firm. Most of the students spent hours preparing their answers and came to class carrying many sheets of paper with their calculations. Tobias came up with the correct answer after just a few minutes and without having made any calculations. When his professor called on him in class for an answer, Tobias stated, "The case said the XYZ Company was in a very competitive industry . . . and the case said that the company had all the business it could handle." Given this information, what price do you think Tobias argued the company should charge? Briefly explain. (Tobias says the class greeted his answer with "thunderous applause.")

Source: Andrew Tobias, *The Only Investment Guide You'll Ever Need*, San Diego: Harcourt, 2005, pp. 6–8.

>> End Learning Objective 11.1

How a Firm Maximizes Profit in a Perfectly Competitive Market

Summary

Profit is the difference between total revenue (*TR*) and total cost (*TC*). **Average revenue** (*AR*) is total revenue divided by the quantity of the product sold. A firm maximizes profit by producing the level of output where the difference between revenue and cost is the greatest. This is the same level of output where marginal revenue is equal to marginal cost. **Marginal revenue** is the change in total revenue from selling one more unit.

myeconlab Visit www.myeconlab.com to complete these exercises
Get Ahead of the Curve online and get instant feedback.

Review Questions

2.1 Explain why it is true that for a firm in a perfectly competitive market that $P = MR = AR$.

2.2 Explain why it is true that for a firm in a perfectly competitive market, the profit-maximizing condition $MR = MC$ is equivalent to the condition $P = MC$.

Problems and Applications

2.3 A student argues: "To maximize profit, a firm should produce the quantity where the difference between marginal revenue and marginal cost is the greatest. If it produces more than this quantity, then the profit made on each additional unit will be falling." Briefly explain whether you agree with this reasoning.

2.4 Why don't firms maximize revenue rather than profit? If a firm decided to maximize revenue, would it be likely to produce a smaller or a larger quantity than if it were maximizing profit? Briefly explain.

2.5 Refer to Table 11-2 on page 382 and Table 11-3 on page 383. Suppose the price of wheat rises to $6.00 per bushel. How many bushels of wheat will Farmer Parker produce, and how much profit will he make? Briefly explain.

2.6 Refer to Table 11-2 and Table 11-3. Suppose that the marginal cost of wheat is $0.50 higher for every bushel of wheat produced. For example, the marginal cost of producing the eighth bushel of wheat is now $6.50. Assume that the price of wheat remains $4 per bushel. Will this increase in marginal cost change the profit-maximizing level of production for Farmer Parker? Briefly explain. How much profit will Farmer Parker make now?

>> **End Learning Objective 11.2**

Illustrating Profit or Loss on the Cost Curve Graph

Summary

From the definitions of profit and average total cost, we can develop the following expression for the relationship between total profit and average total cost: Profit = $(P − ATC) \times Q$. Using this expression, we can determine the area showing profit or loss on a cost-curve graph: The area of profit or loss is a box with a height equal to price minus average total cost (for profit) or average total cost minus price (for loss) and a base equal to the quantity of output.

myeconlab Visit www.myeconlab.com to complete these exercises
Get Ahead of the Curve online and get instant feedback.

Review Questions

3.1 Draw a graph showing a firm in a perfectly competitive market that is making a profit. Be sure your graph includes the firm's demand curve, marginal revenue curve, marginal cost curve, average total cost curve, and average variable cost curve and make sure to indicate the area representing the firm's profits.

3.2 Draw a graph showing a firm in a perfectly competitive market that is operating at a loss. Be sure your graph includes the firm's demand curve, marginal revenue curve, marginal cost curve, average total cost curve, and average variable cost curve and make sure to indicate the area representing the firm's losses.

Problems and Applications

3.3 (Related to *Solved Problem 11-3* on page 386) Frances sells earrings in the perfectly competitive earring market. Her output per day and costs are as follows:

OUTPUT PER DAY	TOTAL COST
0	$1.00
1	2.50
2	3.50
3	4.20
4	4.50
5	5.20
6	6.80
7	8.70
8	10.70
9	13.00

a. If the current equilibrium price in the earring market is $1.80, how many earrings will Frances produce, what price will she charge, and how much profit (or loss) will she make? Draw a graph to illustrate your answer. Your graph should be clearly labeled and should include Frances's demand, *ATC*, *AVC*, *MC*, and *MR* curves; the price she is charging; the quantity she is producing; and the area representing her profit (or loss).

b. Suppose the equilibrium price of earrings falls to $1.00. Now how many earrings will Frances produce, what price will she charge, and how much profit (or loss) will she make? Show your work. Draw a graph to illustrate this situation, using the instructions in question (a).

c. Suppose the equilibrium price of earrings falls to $0.25. Now how many earrings will Frances produce, what price will she charge, and how much profit (or loss) will she make?

3.4 (Related to *Solved Problem 11-3* on page 386) Review Solved Problem 11-3 and then answer the following: Suppose the equilibrium price of basketballs falls to $2.50. Now how many basketballs will Andy produce? What price will he charge? How much profit (or loss) will he make?

3.5 (Related to the *Don't Let This Happen to You!* on page 388) A student examines the following

graph and argues, "I believe that a firm will want to produce at Q_1, not Q_2. At Q_1, the distance between price and marginal cost is the greatest. Therefore, at Q_1, the firm will be maximizing its profits." Briefly explain whether you agree with the student's argument.

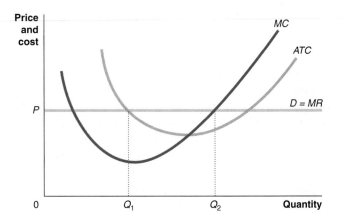

3.6 According to a report in the *Wall Street Journal*, during the fourth quarter of 2003, the profits of British Airways rose to £83 million, from £13 million one year earlier. At the same time, "the average amount the airline makes on each paying passenger fell 0.8%." If profit per passenger fell, how could total profits rise? Illustrate your answer with a graph. Be sure to indicate profit per passenger and total profit on the graph.

Source: Emma Blake, "British Airways Reports Sharp Jump in Net Profits," *Wall Street Journal*, February 9, 2004.

3.7 The following is from an article in the *Los Angeles Times*: "Gerald Lasseigne, a 53-year-old information systems technician in Donaldsonville, La., lost his job last month when steep natural gas prices forced Triad Nitrogen to shut down its fertilizer plant on the banks of the Mississippi River." Draw a graph showing the Triad Nitrogen company earning a profit from its fertilizer plant before the increase in the price of natural gas. Draw a second graph showing why Triad Nitrogen shut down the plant following the increase in the price of natural gas.

Source: Warren Vieth and Aparna Kumar, "Higher Oil Prices Ooze into Economy," *Los Angeles Times*, March 25, 2003, p. C1.

3.8 (Related to the *Making the Connection* on page 389) Suppose the medical screening firms had run an effective advertising campaign which convinced a large number of people that yearly CT scans were critical for good health. How would this have changed the fortunes of these firms? Illustrate your answer with a graph showing the situation for a representative firm in the industry. Be sure your graph includes the firm's demand curve, marginal revenue curve, marginal cost curve, and average total cost curve.

>> **End Learning Objective 11.3**

11.4 | Explain why firms may shut down temporarily, **pages 390–393.**

Deciding Whether to Produce or to Shut Down in the Short Run

Summary

In deciding whether to shut down or produce during a given period, a firm should ignore its *sunk costs*. A **sunk cost** is a cost that has already been paid and that cannot by recovered. In the short run, a firm continues to produce as long as its price is at least equal to its average variable cost. A perfectly competitive firm's **shutdown point** is the minimum point on the firm's average variable cost curve. If price falls below average variable cost, the firm shuts down in the short run. For prices above the shutdown point, a perfectly competitive firm's marginal cost curve is also its supply curve.

myeconlab Visit www.myeconlab.com to complete these exercises
Get Ahead of the Curve online and get instant feedback.

Review Questions

4.1 What is the difference between a firm's shutdown point in the short run and in the long run? Why are firms willing to accept losses in the short run but not in the long run?

4.2 What is the relationship between a perfectly competitive firm's marginal cost curve and its supply curve?

Problems and Applications

4.3 Edward Scahill produces table lamps in the perfectly competitive desk lamp market.
a. Fill in the missing values in the table.

OUTPUT PER WEEK	TOTAL COSTS	AFC	AVC	ATC	MC
0	$100				
1	150				
2	175				
3	190				
4	210				
5	240				
6	280				
7	330				
8	390				
9	460				
10	540				

b. Suppose the equilibrium price in the desk lamp market is $50. How many table lamps should Edward produce, and how much profit will he make?
c. If next week the equilibrium price of desk lamps drops to $30, should Edward shut down? Explain.

4.4 The graph represents the situation of a perfectly competitive firm.

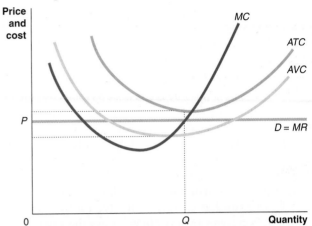

Indicate on the graph the areas that represent the following:
a. Total cost
b. Total revenue
c. Variable cost
d. Profit or loss
   Briefly explain whether the firm will continue to produce in the short run.

4.5 (Related to the *Making the Connection* on page 390) Suppose you decide to open a copy store. You rent store space (signing a one-year lease to do so), and you take out a loan at a local bank and use the money to purchase 10 copiers. Six months later, a large chain opens a copy store two blocks away from yours. As a result, the revenue you receive from your copy store, while sufficient to cover the wages of your employees and the costs of paper and utilities, doesn't cover all your rent and the interest and repayment costs on the loan you took out to purchase the copiers. Should you continue operating your business?

4.6 (Related to the *Making the Connection* on page 390) Club Mediterranee operates 120 Club Med resorts around the world. Following the September 11, 2001, terrorist attacks on the United States, many American tourists were reluctant to travel to foreign resorts. As a result, the prices Club Med could charge visitors to its resorts declined. In November 2001, Club Med decided to temporarily shut down 15 of its resorts. Analyze possible reasons for Club Med's decision. Be sure to discuss the likely relationship between the revenue Club Med received from operating these resorts and the resorts' fixed and variable costs.

Source: Rafer Guzmán, "Club Med Plans to Temporarily Close 15 Resorts," *Wall Street Journal*, November 9, 2001, p. B1.

>> End Learning Objective 11.4

"If Everyone Can Do It, You Can't Make Money at It": The Entry and Exit of Firms in the Long Run

Summary

Economic profit is a firm's revenues minus all its costs, implicit and explicit. **Economic loss** is the situation in which a firm's total revenue is less than its total cost, including all implicit costs. If firms make economic profits in the short run, new firms enter the industry until the market price has fallen enough to wipe out the profits. If firms make economic losses, firms exit the industry until the market price has risen enough to wipe out the losses. **Long-run competitive equilibrium** is the situation in which the entry and exit of firms has resulted in the typical firm breaking even. The **long-run supply curve** shows the relationship between market price and the quantity supplied.

myeconlab Visit www.myeconlab.com to complete these exercises
Get Ahead of the Curve online and get instant feedback.

Review Questions

5.1 When are firms likely to enter an industry? When are they likely to exit an industry?

5.2 Would a firm earning zero economic profit continue to produce, even in the long run?

5.3 Discuss the shape of the long-run supply curve in a perfectly competitive market. Suppose that a perfectly competitive market is initially at long-run equilibrium and then there is a permanent decrease in the demand for the product. Draw a graph showing how the market adjusts in the long run.

Problems and Applications

5.4 Suppose an assistant professor of economics is earning a salary of $65,000 per year. One day she quits her job, sells $100,000 worth of bonds that had been earning 5 percent per year, and uses the funds to open a bookstore. At the end of the year, she shows an accounting profit of $80,000 on her income tax return. What is her economic profit?

5.5 Suppose that you and your sister both decide to open copy stores. Your parents always liked your sister better than you, so they purchase and give to her free of charge the three copiers she needs to operate her store. You, however, have to rent your copiers for $1,500 per month each. Does your sister have lower costs in operating her copy store than you have in operating your copy store because of this? Explain.

5.6 Consider the following statement: "The products for which demand is the greatest will also be the products that are most profitable to produce." Briefly explain whether you agree with this statement.

5.7 In panel (b) of Figure 11-9 on page 396, Anne Moreno reduces her output from 8,000 to 5,000 boxes of apples when the price falls to $7. At this price and this output level, she is operating at a loss. Why doesn't she just continue charging the original $10 and continue producing 8,000 boxes of apples?

5.8 The following statement appeared in a Congressional analysis of the airline industry: "In lean times, airlines can operate for extended periods of time [while making losses] . . . because revenues will cover a large part of their costs (Pan Am lost money for about a decade before finally closing down)." Why would Pan Am—or any other airline—continue losing money for 10 years rather than shut down immediately? In the statement "revenues will cover a large part of their costs," does it matter if the costs being referred to are fixed costs or variable costs? Briefly explain.

Source: Joint Economic Committee, Democratic Staff, *Assessing Losses for the Airline Industry and Its Workers in the Aftermath of the Terrorist Attacks,* October 3, 2001.

5.9 A student in a principles of economics course makes the following remark: "The economic model of perfectly competitive markets is fine in theory but not very realistic. It predicts that in the long run, a firm in a perfectly competitive market will earn no profits. No firm in the real world would stay in business if it earned zero profits." Do you agree with this remark?

5.10 Suppose that the laptop computer industry is perfectly competitive and that the firms that assemble laptops do not also make the displays, or screens, for them. Suppose that the laptop display industry is also perfectly competitive. Finally, suppose that because the demand for laptop displays is currently relatively small, firms in the laptop display industry have not been able to take advantage of all the economies of scale in laptop display production. Use a graph of the laptop computer market to illustrate the long-run effects on equilibrium price and quantity in the laptop computer market of a substantial and sustained increase in the demand for laptop computers. Use another graph to show the impact on the cost curves of a typical firm in the laptop computer industry. Briefly explain your graphs. Do your graphs indicate that the laptop computer industry is a constant-cost industry, an increasing-cost industry, or a decreasing-cost industry?

5.11 (Related to the *Chapter Opener* on page 376) If in the long run apple growers who use organic methods of cultivation make no greater rate of return on their investment than apple growers who use conventional methods, why did a significant number of apple growers switch from conventional to organic methods in the first place?

>> End Learning Objective 11.5

11.6 LEARNING OBJECTIVE 11.6 | Explain how perfect competition leads to economic efficiency, **pages 398–401.**

Perfect Competition and Efficiency

Summary

Perfect competition results in **productive efficiency,** which means that goods and services are produced at the lowest possible cost. Perfect competition also results in **allocative efficiency,** which means the goods and services are produced up to the point where the last unit provides a marginal benefit to consumers equal to the marginal cost of producing it.

myeconlab Visit www.myeconlab.com to complete these exercises *Get Ahead of the Curve* online and get instant feedback.

Review Questions

6.1 What is meant by allocative efficiency? What is meant by productive efficiency? Briefly discuss the difference between these two concepts.

6.2 How does perfect competition lead to allocative and productive efficiency?

Problems and Applications

6.3 The chapter states, "Firms will supply all those goods that provide consumers with a marginal benefit at least as great as the marginal cost of producing them." A student objects to this statement by making the following argument: "I doubt that firms will really do this. After all, firms are in business to make a profit; they don't care about what is best for consumers." Evaluate the student's argument.

6.4 (Related to *Solved Problem 11-6* on page 399) Discuss the following statement: "In a perfectly competitive market, in the long run consumers benefit from reductions in costs, but firms don't." Don't firms also benefit from cost reductions because they are able to earn greater profits?

6.5 (Related to *Solved Problem 11-6* on page 399) Suppose you read the following item in a newspaper article under the headline "Price Gouging Alleged in Pencil Market":

Consumer advocacy groups charged at a press conference yesterday that there is widespread price gouging in the sale of pencils. They released a study showing that whereas the average retail price of pencils was $1.00, the average cost of producing pencils was only $0.50. "Pencils can be produced without complicated machinery or highly skilled workers, so there is no justification for companies charging a price that is twice what it costs them to produce the product. Pencils are too important in the life of every American for us to tolerate this sort of price gouging any longer," said George Grommet, chief spokesperson for the consumer groups. The consumer groups advocate passage of a law that would allow companies selling pencils to charge a price no more than 20 percent greater than their average cost of production.

Do you believe such a law would be advisable in a situation like this? Explain.

6.6 (Related to *Solved Problem 11-6* on page 399) In early 2007, Pioneer and JVC, two Japanese electronics firms, each announced that their profits were going to be lower than expected because they were both forced to cut prices for LCD and plasma television sets. Given the strong consumer demand for plasma television sets, shouldn't firms have been able to raise prices and increase their profits? Briefly explain.

Source: Hiroyuki Kachi, "Pioneer's Net Rises 74%, JVC Posts Loss," *Wall Street Journal,* February 1, 2007.

6.7 (Related to the *Making the Connection* on page 398) Suppose a nutritionist develops a revolutionary new diet that involves eating 10 apples per day. The new diet becomes wildly popular. What effect is the new diet likely to have on the number of apple orchards within 100 miles of New York City? What effect is the diet likely to have on housing prices in New York City?

>> End Learning Objective 11.6

Monopolistic Competition: The Competitive Model in a More Realistic Setting

Starbucks: Growth through Product Differentiation

Starbucks coffee shops seem to be everywhere—in malls, downtown shopping districts, airports, Barnes & Noble bookstores, and practically everywhere else you can imagine. By 2007, Starbucks operated 13,000 stores worldwide, with the company planning to eventually open 40,000. More than 44 million people visit a Starbucks each week.

Like many other firms that are currently large, Starbucks started small. In 1971, entrepreneurs Gordon Bowker, Gerald Baldwin, and Zev Siegl opened the first Starbucks in Seattle. About 10 years later, they hired Howard Schultz to manage the firm's retail sales and marketing. Even though at that point the chain had only five stores, Schultz was determined to make the company first a national chain and then a worldwide chain. By 1993, Starbucks was opening stores on the East Coast, and in 1996, it opened its first store outside North America, in Tokyo, Japan. Today, Starbucks has stores in 38 countries. Schultz had achieved his dream and had become

chairman of the board and chief executive officer of the company.

Of course, fresh-brewed coffee has always been widely available in restaurants, diners, and donut shops. What Howard Schultz and the other Starbucks executives realized, however, was that a significant consumer demand existed for coffeehouses where customers could sit, relax, read newspapers, and drink higher-quality coffee than was typically served in diners or donut shops. The espresso-based coffees served at Starbucks were relatively difficult to find elsewhere during the 1990s, as Starbucks expanded nationally.

Still, Starbucks is *not* unique: You probably know of three or more coffeehouses in your neighborhood. The coffeehouse market is competitive because it is inexpensive to open a new store by leasing store space and buying espresso machines. Hundreds of firms in the United States operate coffeehouses. Some firms are large nationwide chains, such as Caribou Coffee and Diedrich Coffee, which have hundreds of stores. Others are regional chains, such as Dunn Brothers Coffee, which operates 65 stores in four states. Still others are small firms that operate only one store.

In Chapter 11, we discussed the situation of firms in perfectly competitive markets. These markets share three key characteristics:

1. There are many firms.
2. All firms sell identical products.
3. There are no barriers to new firms entering the industry.

The market Starbucks competes in shares two of these characteristics: There are many other coffeehouses—with the number increasing all the time—and the barriers to entering the market are very low. But consumers do not view the products sold by coffeehouses as being identical. The coffee at Starbucks, as well as the muffins and other snacks, are not identical to what competing coffeehouses offer. Selling coffee in coffeehouses is not like selling wheat: The products that Starbucks and its competitors sell are *differentiated* rather than identical. So, the coffeehouse market is *monopolistically competitive* rather than perfectly competitive. **AN INSIDE LOOK** on **page 430** explores one of the ways that businesses like Starbucks and Dunkin' Donuts attempt to differentiate themselves from the competition.

Economics in YOUR Life!

Opening Your Own Restaurant

After you graduate, you plan to realize your dream of opening your own Italian restaurant. You are confident that many people will enjoy the pasta prepared with your grandmother's secret sauce. Although your hometown already has three Italian restaurants, you are convinced that you can enter this market and make a profit.

You have many choices to make in operating your restaurant. Will it be "family style," with sturdy but inexpensive furniture, where families with small—and noisy!—children will feel welcome, or will it be more elegant, with nice furniture, tablecloths, and candles? Will you offer a full menu or concentrate on just pasta dishes that use your grandmother's secret sauce? These and other choices you make will distinguish your restaurant from other competing restaurants. What's likely to happen in the restaurant market in your hometown after you open? How successful are you likely to be? See if you can answer these questions as you read this chapter. You can check your answers against those we provide at the end of the chapter. >> Continued on page 429

411

M any markets in the U.S. economy are similar to the coffeehouse market: They have many buyers and sellers, and the barriers to entry are low, but the goods and services offered for sale are differentiated rather than identical. Examples of these markets include consumer electronics stores, restaurants, movie theaters, supermarkets, and manufacturers of men's and women's clothing. In fact, the majority of the firms you patronize are competing in **monopolistically competitive** markets.

> **Monopolistic competition** A market structure in which barriers to entry are low and many firms compete by selling similar, but not identical, products.

In Chapter 11, we saw how perfect competition benefits consumers and results in economic efficiency. Will these same desirable outcomes also hold for monopolistically competitive markets? This question, which we explore in this chapter, is important because monopolistically competitive markets are so common.

12.1 LEARNING OBJECTIVE

12.1 | Explain why a monopolistically competitive firm has downward-sloping demand and marginal revenue curves.

Demand and Marginal Revenue for a Firm in a Monopolistically Competitive Market

If the Starbucks coffeehouse located one mile from your house raises the price for a caffè latte from $3.00 to $3.25, it will lose some, but not all, of its customers. Some customers will switch to buying their coffee at another store, but other customers will be willing to pay the higher price for a variety of reasons: This store may be closer to them, or they may prefer Starbucks caffè lattes to similar coffees at competing stores. Because changing the price affects the quantity of caffè lattes sold, a Starbucks store will face a downward-sloping demand curve rather than the horizontal demand curve that a wheat farmer faces.

The Demand Curve for a Monopolistically Competitive Firm

Figure 12-1 shows how a change in price affects the quantity of caffè lattes Starbucks sells. The increase in the price from $3.00 to $3.25 decreases the quantity of caffè lattes sold from 3,000 per week to 2,400 per week.

Figure 12-1

The Downward-Sloping Demand for Caffè Lattes at a Starbucks

If a Starbucks increases the price of caffè lattes, it will lose some, but not all, of its customers. In this case, raising the price from $3.00 to $3.25 reduces the quantity of caffè lattes sold from 3,000 to 2,400. Therefore, unlike a perfect competitor, a Starbucks store faces a downward-sloping demand curve.

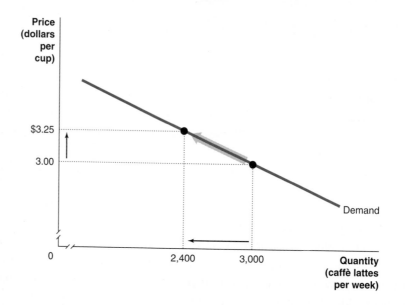

Marginal Revenue for a Firm with a Downward-Sloping Demand Curve

Recall from Chapter 11 that for a firm in a perfectly competitive market, the demand curve and the marginal revenue curve are the same. A perfectly competitive firm faces a horizontal demand curve and does not have to cut the price to sell a larger quantity. A monopolistically competitive firm, however, must cut the price to sell more, so its marginal revenue curve will slope downward and will be below its demand curve.

The data in Table 12-1 illustrate this point. To keep the numbers simple, let's assume that your local Starbucks coffeehouse is very small and sells at most 10 caffè lattes per week. If Starbucks charges a price of $6.00 or more, all of its potential customers will buy their coffee somewhere else. If it charges $5.50, it will sell 1 caffè latte per week. For each additional $0.50 Starbucks reduces the price, it increases the number of caffè lattes it sells by 1. The third column in the table shows how the firm's *total revenue* changes as it sells more caffè lattes. The fourth column shows the firm's revenue per unit, or its *average revenue*. Average revenue is equal to total revenue divided by quantity. Because total revenue equals price multiplied by quantity, dividing by quantity leaves just price. Therefore, *average revenue is always equal to price*. This result will be true for firms selling in any of the four market structures we discussed in Chapter 11.

The last column shows the firm's marginal revenue, or the amount that total revenue changes as the firm sells 1 more caffè latte. For a perfectly competitive firm, the additional revenue received from selling 1 more unit is just equal to the price. That will not be true for Starbucks because to sell another caffè latte, it has to reduce the price. When the firm cuts the price by $0.50, one good thing and one bad thing happen:

- **The good thing.** It sells one more caffè latte; we can call this the *output effect*.

- **The bad thing.** It receives $0.50 less for each caffè latte that it could have sold at the higher price; we can call this the *price effect*.

Figure 12-2 illustrates what happens when the firm cuts the price from $3.50 to $3.00. Selling the sixth caffè latte adds the $3.00 price to the firm's revenue; this is the output effect. But Starbucks now receives a price of $3.00, rather than $3.50, on the first 5 caffè lattes sold; this is the price effect. As a result of the price effect, the firm's revenue

TABLE 12-1

Demand and Marginal Revenue at a Starbucks

CAFFÈ LATTES SOLD PER WEEK (Q)	PRICE (P)	TOTAL REVENUE (TR = P × Q)	AVERAGE REVENUE $\left(AR = \dfrac{TR}{Q} \right)$	MARGINAL REVENUE $\left(MR = \dfrac{\Delta TR}{\Delta Q} \right)$
0	$6.00	$0.00	—	—
1	5.50	5.50	$5.50	$5.50
2	5.00	10.00	5.00	4.50
3	4.50	13.50	4.50	3.50
4	4.00	16.00	4.00	2.50
5	3.50	17.50	3.50	1.50
6	3.00	18.00	3.00	0.50
7	2.50	17.50	2.50	−0.50
8	2.00	16.00	2.00	−1.50
9	1.50	13.50	1.50	−2.50
10	1.00	10.00	1.00	−3.50

Figure 12-2

How a Price Cut Affects a Firm's Revenue

If the local Starbucks reduces the price of a caffè latte from $3.50 to $3.00, the number of caffè lattes it sells per week will increase from 5 to 6. Its marginal revenue from selling the sixth caffè latte will be $0.50, which is equal to the $3.00 additional revenue from selling 1 more caffè latte (the area of the green box) minus the $2.50 loss in revenue from selling the first 5 caffè lattes for $0.50 less each (the area of the red box).

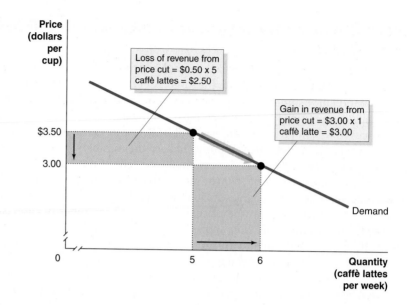

Loss of revenue from price cut = $0.50 x 5 caffè lattes = $2.50

Gain in revenue from price cut = $3.00 x 1 caffè latte = $3.00

on these 5 caffè lattes is $2.50 less than it would have been if the price had remained at $3.50. So, the firm has gained $3.00 in revenue on the sixth caffè latte and lost $2.50 in revenue on the first 5 caffè lattes, for a net change in revenue of $0.50. Marginal revenue is the change in total revenue from selling one more unit. Therefore, the marginal revenue of the sixth caffè latte is $0.50. Notice that the marginal revenue of the sixth unit is far below its price of $3.00. In fact, for each additional caffè latte Starbucks sells, marginal revenue will be less than price. There is an important general point: *Every firm that has the ability to affect the price of the good or service it sells will have a marginal revenue curve that is below its demand curve.* Only firms in perfectly competitive markets, which can sell as many units as they want at the market price, have marginal revenue curves that are the same as their demand curves.

Figure 12-3 shows the relationship between the demand curve and the marginal revenue curve for the local Starbucks. Notice that after the sixth caffè latte, marginal rev-

Figure 12-3

The Demand and Marginal Revenue Curves for a Monopolistically Competitive Firm

Any firm that has the ability to affect the price of the product it sells will have a marginal revenue curve that is below its demand curve. We plot the data from Table 12-1 to create the demand and marginal revenue curves. After the sixth caffè latte, marginal revenue becomes negative because the additional revenue received from selling 1 more caffè latte is smaller than the revenue lost from receiving a lower price on the caffè lattes that could have been sold at the original price.

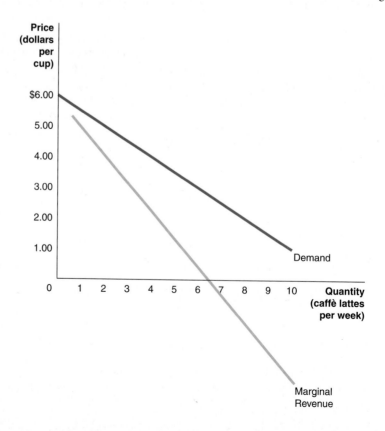

enue becomes negative. Marginal revenue is negative because the additional revenue received from selling 1 more caffè latte is smaller than the revenue lost from receiving a lower price on the caffè lattes that could have been sold at the original price.

12.2 | Explain how a monopolistically competitive firm maximizes profits in the short run.

How a Monopolistically Competitive Firm Maximizes Profits in the Short Run

All firms use the same approach to maximize profits: They produce where marginal revenue is equal to marginal cost. For the local Starbucks, this means selling the quantity of caffè lattes for which the last caffè latte sold adds the same amount to the firm's revenue as to its costs. To begin our discussion of how monopolistically competitive firms maximize profits, let's consider the situation the local Starbucks faces in the short run. Recall from Chapter 10 that in the short run, at least one factor of production is fixed and there is not enough time for new firms to enter the market. A Starbucks has many costs, including the cost of purchasing the ingredients for its caffè lattes and other coffees, the electricity it uses, and the wages of its employees. Recall that a firm's *marginal cost* is the increase in total cost resulting from producing another unit of output. We have seen that for many firms, marginal cost has a U shape. We will assume that the Starbucks marginal cost has this usual shape.

In the table in Figure 12-4, we bring together the revenue data from Table 12-1 with the cost data for Starbucks. The graphs in Figure 12-4 plot the data from the table. In panel (a), we see how Starbucks can determine its profit-maximizing quantity and price. As long as the marginal cost of selling one more caffè latte is less than the marginal revenue, the firm should sell additional caffè lattes. For example, increasing the quantity of caffè lattes sold from 3 per week to 4 per week increases marginal cost by $1.00 but increases marginal revenue by $2.50. So, the firm's profits are increased by $1.50 as a result of selling the fourth caffè latte.

As Starbucks sells more caffè lattes, rising marginal cost eventually equals marginal revenue, and the firm sells the profit-maximizing quantity of caffè lattes. Marginal cost equals marginal revenue with the fifth caffè latte, which adds $1.50 to the firm's costs and $1.50 to its revenues—point *A* in panel (a) of Figure 12-4. The demand curve tells us the price at which the firm is able to sell 5 caffè lattes per week. In Figure 12-4, if we draw a vertical line from 5 caffè lattes up to the demand curve, we can see that the price at which the firm can sell 5 caffè lattes per week is $3.50 (point *B*). We can conclude that for Starbucks the profit-maximizing quantity is 5 caffè lattes, and its profit-maximizing price is $3.50. If the firm sells more than 5 caffè lattes per week, its profits fall. For example, selling a sixth caffè latte adds $2.00 to its costs and only $0.50 to its revenues. So, its profit would fall from $5.00 to $3.50.

Panel (b) adds the average total cost curve for Starbucks. The panel shows that the average total cost of selling 5 caffè lattes is $2.50. Recall from Chapter 11 that:

$$\text{Profit} = (P - ATC) \times Q.$$

In this case, profit = ($3.50 − $2.50) × 5 = $5.00. The green box in panel (b) shows the amount of profit. The box has a base equal to *Q* and a height equal to (*P* − *ATC*), so its area equals profit.

Notice that, unlike a perfectly competitive firm, which produces where $P = MC$, a monopolistically competitive firm produces where $P > MC$. In this case, Starbucks is charging a price of $3.50, although marginal cost is $1.50. For the perfectly competitive firm, price equals marginal revenue, $P = MR$. Therefore, to fulfill the $MR = MC$ condition for profit maximization, a perfectly competitive firm will produce where $P = MC$. Because $P > MR$ for a monopolistically competitive firm—which results from the marginal revenue curve being below the demand curve—a monopolistically competitive firm will maximize profits where $P > MC$.

Caffè Lattes Sold per Week (Q)	Price (P)	Total Revenue (TR)	Marginal Revenue (MR)	Total Cost (TC)	Marginal Cost (MC)	Average Total Cost (ATC)	Profit
0	$6.00	$0.00	–	$5.00	–	–	–$5.00
1	5.50	5.50	$5.50	8.00	$3.00	$8.00	–2.50
2	5.00	10.00	4.50	9.50	1.50	4.75	0.50
3	4.50	13.50	3.50	10.00	0.50	3.33	3.50
4	4.00	16.00	2.50	11.00	1.00	2.75	5.00
5	3.50	17.50	1.50	12.50	1.50	2.50	5.00
6	3.00	18.00	0.50	14.50	2.00	2.42	3.50
7	2.50	17.50	–0.50	17.00	2.50	2.43	0.50
8	2.00	16.00	–1.50	20.00	3.00	2.50	–4.00
9	1.50	13.50	–2.50	23.50	3.50	2.61	–10.00
10	1.00	10.00	–3.50	27.50	4.00	2.75	–17.50

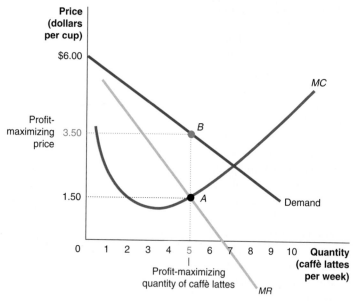

(a) Profit-maximizing quantity and price for a monopolistic competitor

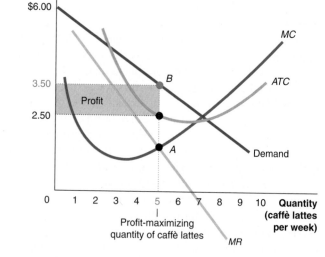

(b) Short-run profits for a monopolistic competitor

Figure 12-4 | Maximizing Profit in a Monopolistically Competitive Market

To maximize profit, a Starbucks coffeehouse wants to sell caffè lattes up to the point where the marginal revenue from selling the last caffè latte is just equal to the marginal cost. As the table shows, this happens with the fifth caffè latte—point A in panel (a)—which adds $1.50 to the firm's costs and $1.50 to its revenues. The firm then uses the demand curve to find the price that will lead consumers to buy this quantity

of caffè lattes (point B). In panel (b), the green box represents the firm's profits. The box has a height equal to $1.00, which is the price of $3.50 minus the average total cost of $2.50, and a base equal to the quantity of 5 caffè lattes. So, this Starbucks profit equals $1 × 5 = $5.00.

Solved Problem | 12-2

How Not to Maximize Profits at a Publishing Company

In an article in the *New York Times*, Virginia Postrel states that when deciding the "question of whether printing another copy of a given, already published book, is a profitable thing

to do," managers at publishing firms begin by calculating the cost of printing one additional copy. But these managers "often fall prey to the mistake of adding up every expense associated with a book, including the overhead like rent and editors' salaries, and then dividing by the number of copies." Will the process described in the previous sentence give an accurate estimate of marginal cost? If you were a manager at a publishing firm, how would you determine whether producing one more copy of a book will increase your profits?

SOLVING THE PROBLEM:

Step 1: **Review the chapter material.** This problem is about how monopolistically competitive firms maximize profits, so you may want to review the section "How a Monopolistically Competitive Firm Maximizes Profits in the Short Run," which begins on page 415.

Step 2: **Analyze the costs described in the problem.** We have seen that to maximize profits, firms should produce up to the point where marginal revenue equals marginal cost. Marginal cost is the increase in total cost that results from producing another unit of output. Rent and editors' salaries are part of a publishing company's fixed costs because they do not change as the company increases its output of books. Therefore, managers at publishing companies should not include them in calculating marginal cost.

Step 3: **Explain how a manager at a publishing firm should decide whether to publish one more copy of a book.** To determine whether producing one more copy of a book will increase your profits, you need to compare the marginal revenue received from selling the book with the marginal cost of producing it. If the marginal revenue is greater than the marginal cost, producing the book will increase your profits.

Source: Virginia Postrel, "Often, Basic Concepts in Economics Are Taken for Granted," *New York Times*, January 3, 2002.

YOUR TURN: For more practice, do related problem 2.9 on pages 433–434 at the end of this chapter.

>> **End Solved Problem 12-2**

12.3 LEARNING OBJECTIVE

12.3 | Analyze the situation of a monopolistically competitive firm in the long run.

What Happens to Profits in the Long Run?

Remember that a firm makes an economic profit when its total revenue is greater than all of its costs, including the opportunity cost of the funds invested in the firm by its owners. Because cost curves include the owners' opportunity costs, the Starbucks coffeehouse represented in Figure 12-4 is making an economic profit. This economic profit gives entrepreneurs an incentive to enter this market and establish new firms. If a Starbucks is earning economic profit selling caffè lattes, new coffeehouses are likely to open in the same area.

How Does the Entry of New Firms Affect the Profits of Existing Firms?

As new coffeehouses open near the local Starbucks, the firm's demand curve will shift to the left. The demand curve will shift because Starbucks will sell fewer caffè lattes at each price when there are additional coffeehouses in the area selling similar drinks. The demand curve will also become more elastic because consumers have additional coffeehouses from which to buy coffee, so Starbucks will lose more sales if it raises its prices. Figure 12-5 shows how the demand curve for the local Starbucks shifts as new firms enter its market.

In panel (a) of Figure 12-5, the short-run demand curve shows the relationship between the price of caffè lattes and the quantity of caffè lattes Starbucks sells per week before the entry of new firms. With this demand curve, Starbucks can charge a price above average total cost—shown as point *A* in panel (a)—and make a profit. But this profit attracts additional coffeehouses to the area and shifts the demand curve for the Starbucks caffè lattes to the left. As long as Starbucks is making an economic profit, there is an incentive for additional coffeehouses to open in the area, and the demand curve will

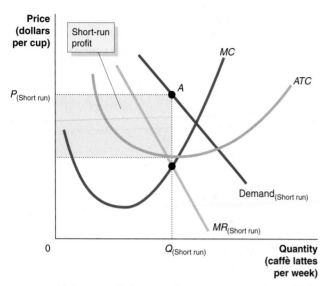

(a) A monopolistic competitor may earn a short-run profit

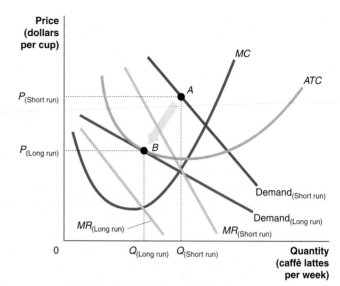

(b) A monopolistic competitor's profits are eliminated in the long run

Figure 12-5 | How Entry of New Firms Eliminates Profits

In the short run—panel (a)—the local Starbucks faces the demand and marginal revenue curves labeled "Short run." With this demand curve, Starbucks can charge a price above average total cost (point *A*) and make a profit, shown by the green rectangle. But this profit attracts new firms to enter the market, which shifts the demand and marginal revenue curves to the ones labeled "Long run" in panel (b). Because price is now equal to average total cost (point *B*), Starbucks breaks even and no longer earns an economic profit.

continue shifting to the left. As panel (b) shows, eventually the demand curve will have shifted to the point where it is just touching—or tangent to—the average cost curve.

In the long run, at the point at which the demand curve is tangent to the average cost curve, price is equal to average total cost (point *B*), the firm is breaking even, and it no longer earns an economic profit. In the long run, the demand curve is also more elastic because the more coffeehouses there are in the area, the more sales Starbucks will lose to other coffeehouses if it raises its price.

Of course, it is possible that a monopolistically competitive firm will suffer economic losses in the short run. As a consequence, the owners of the firm will not be covering the opportunity cost of their investment. We expect that, in the long run, firms will exit an industry if they are suffering economic losses. If firms exit, the demand curve for the output of a remaining firm will shift to the right. This process will continue until the representative firm in the industry is able to charge a price equal to its average cost and break even. Therefore, in the long run, monopolistically competitive firms will experience neither economic profits nor economic losses. Table 12-2 summarizes the short run and the long run for a monopolistically competitive firm.

Don't Let This Happen to **YOU!**

Don't Confuse Zero Economic Profit with Zero Accounting Profit

Remember that economists count the opportunity cost of the owner's investment in a firm as a cost. For example, suppose you invest $200,000 opening a pizza parlor, and the return you could earn on those funds each year in a similar investment—such as opening a sandwich shop—is 10 percent. Therefore, the annual opportunity cost of investing the funds in your own business is 10 percent of $200,000, or $20,000.

This $20,000 is part of your profit in the accounting sense, and you would have to pay taxes on it. But in an economic sense, the $20,000 is a cost. In long-run equilibrium, we would expect that entry of new firms would keep you from earning more than 10 percent on your investment. So, you would end up breaking even and earning zero economic profit, even though you were earning an accounting profit of $20,000.

YOUR TURN: Test your understanding by doing related problem 3.4 on page 435 at the end of this chapter.

TABLE 12-2 | **The Short Run and the Long Run for a Monopolistically Competitive Firm**

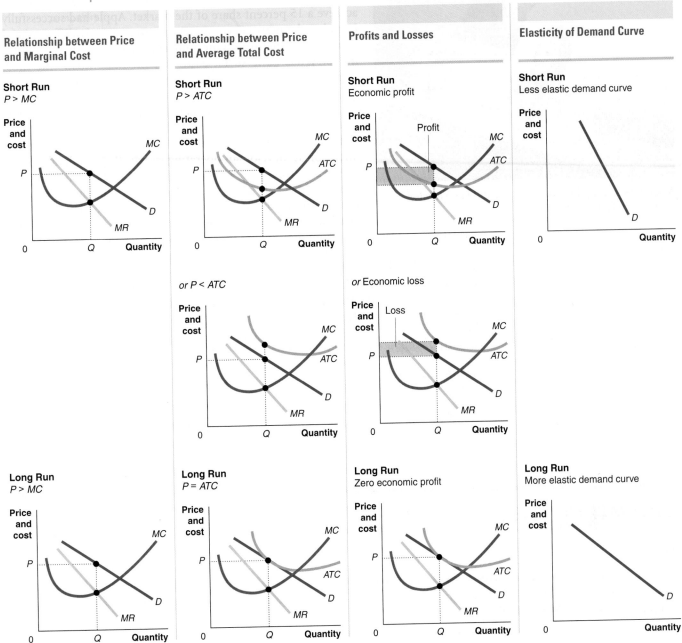

Making the Connection | The Rise and Fall of Apple's Macintosh Computer

In 1983, there were more than 15 firms selling personal computers nationally, as well as many smaller firms in local markets selling computers assembled from purchased components. None of these personal computers operated using the current system of clicking on icons with a mouse. Instead, users had to type in commands to call up word processing, spreadsheet, and other software programs. This awkward system required users to memorize many commands or constantly consult computer manuals. In January 1984, Apple Computer introduced the Macintosh, which used a mouse and could be operated by clicking on icons. The average cost of producing Macintoshes was about $500. Apple sold them for prices between $2,500 and $3,000. This price was more than twice that

In 2007, Howard Schultz, the chairman of Starbucks, was well aware of this fact. In opening thousands of coffeehouses worldwide, he worried that Starbucks had made the customer experience less distinctive and easier for competitors to copy. Starbucks has used various strategies to differentiate itself from competing coffeehouses. Competitors have found it difficult to duplicate the European espresso bar atmosphere of Starbucks, with its large, comfortable chairs; music playing; and groups of friends dropping in and out during the day. Most importantly, Starbucks has continued to be very responsive to its customers' preferences. As one observer put it, "How many retailers could put up with 'I'll have a grande low-fat triple-shot half-caf white-chocolate mocha, extra hot, easy on the whipped cream. And I'm in a rush'?" But Howard Schultz was worried. In a memo sent to employees, he wrote, "Over the past ten years, in order to achieve the growth, development, and scale necessary to go from less than 1,000 stores to 13,000 stores . . . we have had to make a series of decisions that . . . have led to the watering down of the Starbucks experience." Starbucks has begun serving breakfast sandwiches and installing drive-through windows that make its stores appear similar to other fast-food restaurants. Although at one time Starbucks had been able to maintain greater control over the operations of its coffeehouses, because unlike many of its competitors, all of its coffeehouses were company owned, it now has thousands of *franchises*. A franchise is a business with the legal right to sell a good or service in a particular area. When a firm uses franchises, local businesspeople are able to buy and run the stores in their area. This makes it easier for a firm to finance its expansion but forces the firm to give up some control over its stores.

Starbucks experienced great success during the 1990s and the early 2000s, but history shows that in the long run, competitors will be able to duplicate most of what it does. In the face of that competition, it will be very difficult for Starbucks to continue earning economic profits. As Howard Schultz put it, "Competitors of all kinds, small and large coffee companies, fast food operators, and mom and pops, [have positioned] themselves in a way that creates awareness . . . and loyalty of people who previously have been Starbucks customers." He concluded, "I have said for 20 years that our success is not an entitlement and now it's proving to be a reality."

The owner of a competitive firm is in a position similar to that of Ebenezer Scrooge in Charles Dickens's *A Christmas Carol*. When the Ghost of Christmas Yet to Come shows Scrooge visions of his own death, he asks the ghost, "Are these the shadows of the things that Will be, or are they shadows of things that May be, only?" The shadow of the end of their profits haunts owners of every firm. Firms try to avoid losing profits by reducing costs, by improving their products, or by convincing consumers their products are indeed different from what competitors offer. To stay one step ahead of its competitors, a firm has to offer consumers goods or services that they perceive to have greater *value* than those offered by competing firms. Value can take the form of product differentiation that makes the good or service more suited to consumers' preferences, or it can take the form of a lower price.

Making the Connection	## Staying One Step Ahead of the Competition: Eugène Schueller and L'Oréal

Today, L'Oréal, with headquarters in the Paris suburb of Clichy, is the largest seller of perfumes, cosmetics, and hair care products in the world. In addition to L'Oréal, its brands include Lancôme, Maybelline, Soft Sheen/Carson, Garnier, Redken, Ralph Lauren, and Matrix. Like most other large firms, L'Oréal was started by an entrepreneur with an idea. Eugène Schueller was a French chemist who experimented in the evenings trying to find a safe and reliable hair coloring for women. In 1907, he founded the firm that became L'Oréal and began selling his hair coloring preparations to Paris hair salons. Schueller was able to take advantage of changes in fashion. In the early twentieth century, women began to cut their hair much shorter than had been typical in the nineteenth century, and it had become socially acceptable to spend time and money styling it. The number of hair salons in Europe and the United States increased rapidly. By the 1920s and 1930s, the international popularity of Hollywood films, many starring "platinum blonde bombshells" such as Jean Harlow, made it fashionable for women to color their hair. By the late 1920s, L'Oréal was selling its products throughout Europe, the United States, and Japan.

Unlike many monopolistically competitive firms, L'Oréal has earned economic profits for a very long time.

Perfumes, cosmetics, and hair coloring are all products that should be easy for rival firms to duplicate. We would expect, then, that the economic profits L'Oréal earned in its early years would have been competed away in the long run through the entry of new firms. In fact, though, the firm has remained profitable through the decades, following a strategy of developing new products, improving existing products, and expanding into new markets. For example, when French workers first received paid holidays during the 1930s, L'Oréal moved quickly to dominate the new market for suntan lotion. Today, the firm's SoftSheen brand is experiencing rapid sales increases in Africa. When L'Oréal launched a new line of men's skin-care products, including shaving cream, one analyst observed that at L'Oréal, "brands don't stay at home serving the same old clientele. They get spruced up, put in a new set of traveling clothes, and sent abroad to meet new customers." L'Oréal has maintained its ability to innovate by spending more on research and development than do competing firms. The firm has a research staff of more than 1,000.

One reason L'Oréal has been able to follow a focused strategy is that the firm has had only three chairmen in its nearly century of existence: founder Eugène Schueller, François Dalle, and Lindsay Owen-Jones, who became chairman in 1988. Owen-Jones has described the firm's strategy: "Each brand is positioned on a very precise [market] segment, which overlaps as little as possible with the others." The story of L'Oréal shows that it is possible for a firm to stay one step ahead of the competition, but it takes top management committed to an entrepreneurial spirit of continually developing new products.

Source for quotes: Richard Tomlinson, "L'Oréal's Global Makeover," *Fortune*, September 30, 2002.

YOUR TURN: Test your understanding by doing related problem 3.9 on page 436 at the end of this chapter.

12.4 | Compare the efficiency of monopolistic competition and perfect competition.

12.4 LEARNING OBJECTIVE

Comparing Perfect Competition and Monopolistic Competition

We have seen that monopolistic competition and perfect competition share the characteristic that in long-run equilibrium, firms earn zero economic profits. As Figure 12-6 shows, however, there are two important differences between long-run equilibrium in the two markets:

- Monopolistically competitive firms charge a price greater than marginal cost.

- Monopolistically competitive firms do not produce at minimum average total cost.

Excess Capacity under Monopolistic Competition

Recall that a firm in a perfectly competitive market faces a perfectly elastic demand curve that is also its marginal revenue curve. Therefore, the firm maximizes profit by producing where price equals marginal cost. As panel (a) of Figure 12-6 shows, in

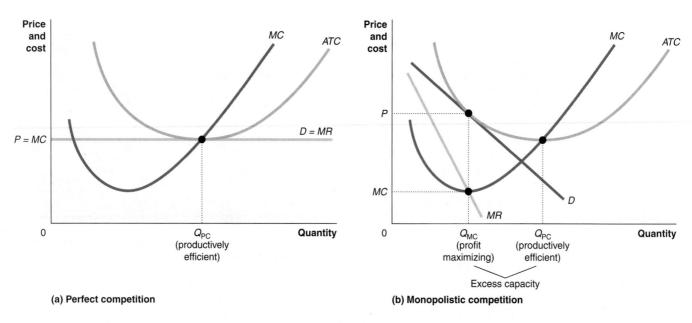

Figure 12-6 | Comparing Long-Run Equilibrium under Perfect Competition and Monopolistic Competition

In panel (a), the perfectly competitive firm in long-run equilibrium produces at Q_{PC}, where price equals marginal cost, and average total cost is at a minimum. The perfectly competitive firm is both allocatively efficient and productively efficient. In panel (b), the monopolistically competitive firm produces at Q_{MC}, where price is greater than marginal cost, and average total cost is not at a minimum. As a result, the monopolistically competitive firm is neither allocatively efficient nor productively efficient. The monopolistically competitive firm has excess capacity equal to the difference between its profit-maximizing level of output and the productively efficient level of output.

long-run equilibrium, a perfectly competitive firm produces at the minimum point of its average total cost curve.

Panel (b) of Figure 12-6 shows that the profit-maximizing level of output for a monopolistically competitive firm comes at a level of output where price is greater than marginal cost and the firm is not at the minimum point of its average total cost curve. A monopolistically competitive firm has *excess capacity*: If it increased its output, it could produce at a lower average cost.

Is Monopolistic Competition Inefficient?

In Chapter 11, we discussed *productive efficiency* and *allocative efficiency*. Productive efficiency refers to the situation where a good is produced at the lowest possible cost. Allocative efficiency refers to the situation where every good or service is produced up to the point where the last unit provides a marginal benefit to consumers equal to the marginal cost of producing it. For productive efficiency to hold, firms must produce at the minimum point of average total cost. For allocative efficiency to hold, firms must charge a price equal to marginal cost. In a perfectly competitive market, both productive efficiency and allocative efficiency are achieved, but in a monopolistically competitive market, neither is achieved. Does it matter? Economists have debated whether monopolistically competitive markets being neither productively nor allocatively efficient results in a significant loss of well-being to society in these markets compared with perfectly competitive markets.

How Consumers Benefit from Monopolistic Competition

Looking again at Figure 12-6, you can see that the only difference between the monopolistically competitive firm and the perfectly competitive firm is that the demand curve for the monopolistically competitive firm slopes downward, whereas the demand curve for the perfectly competitive firm is a horizontal line. The demand curve for the monopolistically competitive firm slopes downward because the good or service the firm is selling is differentiated from the goods or services being sold by competing firms. The perfectly competitive firm is selling a good or service identical to those being sold by its competitors. A key point to remember is that *firms differentiate their products to appeal to consumers.* When Starbucks coffeehouses begin offering new flavors of coffee, when Blockbuster stores begin carrying more HD-DVDs and fewer regular DVDs, when General Mills introduces Apple-Cinnamon Cheerios, or when PepsiCo introduces caffeine-free Diet Pepsi, they are all attempting to attract and retain consumers through product differentiation. The success of these product differentiation strategies indicates that some consumers find these products preferable to the alternatives. Consumers, therefore, are better off than they would have been had these companies not differentiated their products.

We can conclude that consumers face a trade-off when buying the product of a monopolistically competitive firm: They are paying a price that is greater than marginal cost, and the product is not being produced at minimum average cost, but they benefit from being able to purchase a product that is differentiated and more closely suited to their tastes.

Making the Connection	### Abercrombie & Fitch: Can the Product Be Too Differentiated?

Business managers often refer to differentiating their products as finding a "market niche." The larger the niche you have, the greater the potential profit but the more likely that other firms will be able to compete against you. Too small a niche, however, may reduce competition—but also reduce profits. Some analysts believe that the market niche chosen by the managers of the Abercrombie & Fitch clothing stores is too small. The chief executive, Mike Jeffries, argues that his store's target customer is an "18-to-22 [year old] college guy who has a good body and is aspirational." He admits that this is a narrow niche: "If I exclude people—absolutely. Delighted to do so."

But is A&F excluding too many people? One analyst argues "they've . . . pushed a lot of people out of the brand." A&F's sales results seemed to indicate that this analyst may be correct. Managers of retail stores closely monitor "same-store sales," which measures how much sales have increased in the same stores from one year to the next. To offset the effects of inflation—or general increases in prices in the economy—same-store sales need to increase at least 2 percent to 3 percent each year. A firm whose strategy of product differentiation succeeds will experience increases in same-store sales of at least 5 percent to 6 percent each year. For several years in the early 2000s, A&F's 350 stores experienced *negative* same-store results. Although sales increased from 2004 through early 2006, negative changes in same-store sales returned in late 2006 and continued through mid 2007. A&F may have gone too far in narrowing its market niche.

Did Abercrombie and Fitch narrow its target market too much?

Sources: James Covert, "Retail Sales Slide Fuels Concern," *Wall Street Journal*, May 11, 2007; and Shelly Branch, "Maybe Sex Doesn't Sell, A&F Is Discovering," *Wall Street Journal*, December 12, 2003.

YOUR TURN: Test your understanding by doing related problem 4.6 on page 437 at the end of this chapter.

12.5 | Define marketing and explain how firms use it to differentiate their products.

12.5 LEARNING OBJECTIVE

How Marketing Differentiates Products

Firms can differentiate their products through marketing. **Marketing** refers to all the activities necessary for a firm to sell a product to a consumer. Marketing includes activities such as determining which product to produce, designing the product, advertising the product, deciding how to distribute the product—for example, in retail stores or

Marketing All the activities necessary for a firm to sell a product to a consumer.

through a Web site—and monitoring how changes in consumer tastes are affecting the market for the product. Peter F. Drucker, a leading business strategist, describes marketing as follows: "It is the whole business seen from the point of view of its final result, that is, from the consumer's point of view. . . . True marketing . . . does not ask, 'What do we want to sell?' It asks, 'What does the consumer want to buy?'"

As we have seen, for monopolistically competitive firms to earn economic profits and to defend those profits from competitors, they must differentiate their products. Firms use two marketing tools to differentiate their products: brand management and advertising.

Brand Management

Brand management The actions of a firm intended to maintain the differentiation of a product over time.

Once a firm has succeeded in differentiating its product, it must try to maintain that differentiation over time through **brand management**. As we have seen, whenever a firm successfully introduces a new product or a significantly different version of an old product, it earns economic profits in the short run. But the success of the firm inspires competitors to copy the new or improved product and, in the long run, the firm's economic profits will be competed away. Firms use brand management to postpone the time when they will no longer be able to earn economic profits.

Advertising

An innovative advertising campaign can make even long-established and familiar products, such as Coke or McDonald's Big Mac hamburgers, seem more desirable than competing products. When a firm advertises a product, it is trying to shift the demand curve for the product to the right and to make it more inelastic. If the firm is successful, it will sell more of the product at every price, and it will be able to increase the price it charges without losing as many customers. Of course, advertising also increases a firm's costs. If the increase in revenue that results from the advertising is greater than the increase in costs, the firm's profits will rise.

Needless to say, advertising campaigns are not always successful. In 1957, the Ford Motor Company introduced a new car, the Edsel, designed to compete with the Buick from General Motors. Ford set up a new division of the company to produce the Edsel in five different models and hired the advertising firm of Foote, Cone & Belding to direct a massive advertising campaign. Among other things, Ford purchased an hour of prime television time on the CBS network to broadcast *The Edsel Show*, hosted by Frank Sinatra, Bing Crosby, and Louis Armstrong, three of the biggest stars of the 1950s. Ford set a sales goal of 200,000 cars during the first year of production. Unfortunately, most of the car-buying public found the styling of the Edsel, with its oversized headlights and elaborate front grill, unappealing. First-year sales were only about 63,000 cars. During the same period, General Motors sold more than 230,000 Buicks. Ford decided to shift its advertising account for the Edsel from Foote, Cone & Belding to Kenyon & Eckhardt. Despite a revised advertising campaign, sales of the Edsel remained very low. Ford sold fewer than 45,000 Edsels during the car's second year of production. In November 1959, after only two years in production, Ford stopped making the Edsel. Even one of the largest advertising campaigns in history had failed to make the Edsel successful.

Defending a Brand Name

Once a firm has established a successful brand name, it has a strong incentive to defend it. A firm can apply for a *trademark*, which grants legal protection against other firms using its product's name.

One threat to a trademarked name is the possibility that it will become so widely used for a type of product that it will no longer be associated with the product of a specific company. Courts in the United States have ruled that when this happens, a firm is no longer entitled to legal protection of the brand name. For example, "aspirin," "escalator," and "thermos" were originally all brand names of the products of particular firms, but each became so widely used to refer to a type of product that none remains a legally protected brand name. Firms spend substantial amounts of money trying to make sure that this does not happen to them. Coca-Cola, for example, employs workers to travel around the country stopping at restaurants and asking to be served a "Coke" with their meal. If the restaurant serves Pepsi or some other cola, rather than Coke, Coca-Cola's legal department sends the restaurant a letter reminding that "Coke" is a trademarked name and not a generic name for any cola. Similarly, Xerox Corporation spends money on advertising to remind the public that "Xerox" is not a generic term for making photocopies.

Legally enforcing trademarks can be difficult. Estimates are that each year, U.S. firms lose hundreds of billions of dollars in sales worldwide as a result of unauthorized use of their trademarked brand names. U.S. firms often find it difficult to enforce their trademarks in the courts of some foreign countries, although recent international agreements have increased the legal protections for trademarks.

Firms that sell their products through franchises rather than through company-owned stores encounter the problem that if a franchisee does not run his or her business well, the firm's brand may be damaged. Automobile firms send "roadmen" to visit their dealers to make sure the dealerships are clean and well maintained and that the service departments employ competent mechanics and are well equipped with spare parts. Similarly, McDonald's sends employees from corporate headquarters to visit McDonald's franchises to make sure the bathrooms are clean and the French fries are hot.

12.6 | Identify the key factors that determine a firm's success.

12.6 LEARNING OBJECTIVE

What Makes a Firm Successful?

A firm's owners and managers control some of the factors that make a firm successful and allow it to earn economic profits. The most important of these are the firm's ability to differentiate its product and to produce its product at a lower average cost than competing firms. A firm that successfully does these things creates *value* for its customers. Consumers will buy a product if they believe it meets a need not met by competing products or if its price is below that of competitors.

Some factors that affect a firm's profitability are not directly under the firm's control. Certain factors will affect all the firms in a market. For example, rising prices for jet fuel will reduce the profitability of all airlines. If consumers decide that they would rather watch pay-for-view movies delivered to their homes by cable or satellite than buy DVDs, the profitability of all stores selling DVDs will be reduced.

Sheer chance also plays a role in business, as it does in all other aspects of life. A struggling McDonald's franchise may see profits increase dramatically after the county unexpectedly decides to build a new road nearby. Many businesses in New York City, including restaurants, hotels, and theaters, experienced a marked drop in customers and profits following the September 11, 2001, terrorist attacks. Figure 12-7 illustrates the important point that factors within the firm's control and factors outside the firm's control interact to determine the firm's profitability.

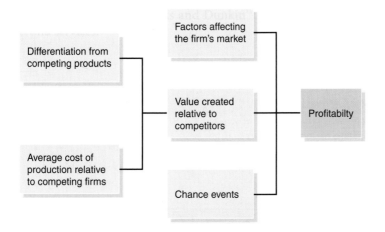

Figure 12-7

What Makes a Firm Successful?

The factors under a firm's control—the ability to differentiate its product and the ability to produce it at lower cost—combine with the factors beyond its control to determine the firm's profitability.

Source: Adapted from Figure 11.3 in David Besanko, David Dranove, Mark Shanley, and Scott Schaefer, *The Economics of Strategy*, 4th ed., New York: Wiley, 2007.

Can Dunkin' Donuts Really Compete with Starbucks?

WALL STREET JOURNAL, APRIL 8, 2006

Brewing Battle: Dunkin' Donuts Tries to Go Upscale, but Not too Far

Dunkin' Donuts last year paid dozens of faithful customers in Phoenix, Chicago and Charlotte, N.C., $100 a week to buy coffee at Starbucks instead. At the same time, the no-frills coffee chain paid Starbucks customers to make the opposite switch.

When it later debriefed the two groups, Dunkin' says it found them so polarized that company researchers dubbed them "tribes"—each of whom loathed the very things that made the other tribe loyal to their coffee shop. Dunkin' fans viewed Starbucks as pretentious and trendy, while Starbucks loyalists saw Dunkin' as austere and unoriginal.

"I don't get it," one Dunkin' regular told researchers after visiting Starbucks. "If I want to sit on a couch, I stay at home."

(a) Bridging some of that divide—but not too much—is key to Dunkin' Donuts' ambitious plan to expand its largely Eastern coffee chain into a national powerhouse that's as synonymous with coffee as Starbucks Corp., the nation's largest coffee chain. Armed with fresh capital from December's $2.43 billion private-equity buyout of Dunkin' Brands Inc., Dunkin' plans to remake its nearly 5,000 U.S. stores over the next three years and have triple that number in less than 15 years. . . .

(b) While executives of Canton, Mass.-based Dunkin' insist they aren't trying to emulate their Seattle rival, Dunkin's store makeovers include some similarities to Starbucks. A prototype Dunkin' store in Euclid, Ohio, outside Cleveland, features rounded granite-style coffee bars where workers make espresso drinks face-to-face with customers. Open-air pastry cases brim with yogurt parfaits and fresh fruit while a carefully orchestrated pop-music soundtrack is piped throughout. . . .

Yet Dunkin' built itself on serving simple fare to working-class customers. Inching upscale without alienating that base is proving tricky. There will be no couches in the new stores. And Dunkin' renamed a new hot sandwich a "stuffed melt" after customers complained that calling it a "panini" was too fancy.

Some customers "have remarked along the lines of 'You're trying to be somebody else,'" says Ryan Humphrey, who oversees Dunkin' franchisees in the Cleveland area. Regina Lewis, the chain's vice president, consumer and brand insights, says, "We're walking that line. The thing about the Dunkin' tribe is, they see through the hype."

Anne Saunders, Starbucks senior vice president, global brand, says Starbucks doesn't focus on Dunkin' Donuts as a competitor. While competitors may use elements of its strategy, they can't recreate Starbucks' "unique and differentiated concept," she says. . . .

Company researchers set out to determine whether Dunkin' could draw consumers in new cities, and how to lure customers from fast-food chains, coffee houses and convenience stores. "Consumers love environments," Mr. Luther (Dunkin's Chief Executive) says. "We have to move our environment where the customer is."

(c) Early research showed customers wanted nicer stores, but revealed a potential problem: the loyal Dunkin' tribe was bewildered and turned off by the atmosphere at Starbucks. They groused that crowds of laptop users made it difficult to find a seat, Dunkin' says. They didn't like Starbucks' "tall," "grande" and "venti" lingo for small, medium and large coffees. And, Dunkin' says, they couldn't understand why anyone would pay as much as $4 for a cup of coffee. . . .

Dunkin' researchers concluded that it wasn't income that set the two tribes apart, as much as an ideal: Dunkin' tribe members wanted to be part of a crowd, while members of the Starbucks tribe had a desire to stand out as individuals. "The Starbucks tribe, they seek out things to make them feel more important," Ms. Lewis says. Members of the Dunkin' Donuts tribe "don't need to be any more important than they are." . . .

Source: Janet Adamy, "Brewing Battle: Dunkin' Donuts Tries to Go Upscale, but Not too Far," Wall Street Journal, April 8, 2006. p. A1. Copyright © 2006 Dow Jones. Reprinted by permission of Dow Jones via Copyright Clearance Center.

Key Points in the Article

This article discusses an attempt by Dunkin' Donuts to appeal to some of Starbucks' customers. As we have seen in this chapter, when a firm successfully differentiates its product, its competitors do their best to copy it. Starbucks has experienced great success by reinventing the coffeehouse. But the article notes that many Starbucks customers see Dunkin' Donuts stores as "austere and unoriginal." As Dunkin' Donuts begins to expand nationwide, it is redesigning its stores to make them more like Starbucks. As this chapter has shown, once consumers show they want a particular good or service, firms will compete to offer it to them.

Analyzing the News

a Currently, upscale coffeehouses like Starbucks are earning an economic profit. This would suggest that an existing firm could be represented by point A in the figure selling Q_1 cups of coffee and charging a price of P_1 dollars. The profit-maximizing quantity is found at the point where the marginal revenue curve MR_1 intersects the marginal cost curve MC. The price is determined by the demand curve. The firm is earning economic profits equal to the shaded area. The economic profits earned by coffeehouses like Starbucks explains why as Dunkin' Donuts expands nationwide, it has been building stores that are more upscale than its older stores.

b Dunkin' Donuts is trying to capture the feel of a Starbucks' store in order to attract customers who may like some of the elements of Starbucks, but who may also like some of the elements of Dunkin' Donuts. Dunkin' Donuts will never attract loyal Starbucks' customers, but they do hope to attract customers who like some features about Starbucks but who may prefer a different environment and food selection. As the figure shows, new entrants in a market will take some demand away from current firms in the market. This causes the demand curve to shift to the left from demand curve D_1 to demand curve D_2. The marginal revenue curve also shifts to the left (from MR_1 to MR_2).

The profit-maximizing level of output is now Q_2, where the new marginal revenue curve intersects the marginal cost curve, MC. The new profit maximizing price is P_2. Notice that at this point the demand curve D_2 is tangent to the average total cost curve ATC and the firm is earning zero profits. At equilibrium, all firms in the market will earn zero profits. This is shown as point E in the figure.

c This section illustrates why product differentiation is important in a market. While customers at Dunkin' Donuts and Starbucks are looking for similar products—coffee and food—there are important differences between the customers that cause them to shop at one coffee shop over another. Those who are in the Starbucks tribe or the Dunkin' Donuts tribe are unlikely to go to another coffee shop. There may, however, be a third tribe looking for a home.

Thinking Critically

1. Suppose the government required a license to open a coffeehouse and that the number of licenses was limited. How would this new requirement affect the equilibrium market price and quantity in the coffeehouse market? Who would gain from this requirement, and who would lose?

2. Suppose that the number of people in the Dunkin' Donuts tribe increases as people begin to prefer donuts with their coffee rather than couches. How would Starbucks likely respond to this change in tastes?

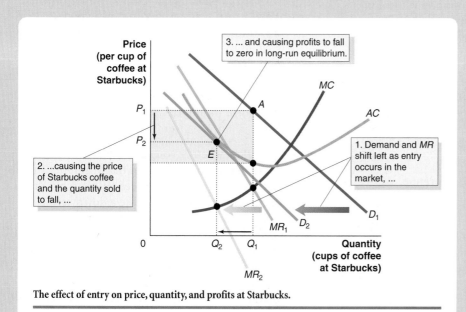

The effect of entry on price, quantity, and profits at Starbucks.

Key Terms

Brand management, p. 426   Monopolistic competition, p. 412

Marketing, p. 425

12.1 LEARNING OBJECTIVE   12.1 | Explain why a monopolistically competitive firm has downward-sloping demand and marginal revenue curves, **pages 412–415.**

Demand and Marginal Revenue for a Firm in a Monopolistically Competitive Market

Summary

A firm competing in a **monopolistically competitive** market sells a differentiated product. Therefore, unlike a firm in a perfectly competitive market, it faces a downward-sloping demand curve. When a monopolistically competitive firm cuts the price of its product, it sells more units but must accept a lower price on the units it could have sold at the higher price. As a result, its marginal revenue curve is downward sloping. Every firm that has the ability to affect the price of the good or service it sells will have a marginal revenue curve that is below its demand curve.

myeconlab Visit www.myeconlab.com to complete these exercises
Get Ahead of the Curve online and get instant feedback.

Review Questions

1.1 What are the most important differences between perfectly competitive markets and monopolistically competitive markets? Give two examples of products sold in perfectly competitive markets and two examples of products sold in monopolistically competitive markets.

1.2 Why does the local McDonald's face a downward-sloping demand curve for Big Macs? If it raises the price it charges for Big Macs above the prices charged by other McDonald's stores, won't it lose all its customers?

1.3 Explain the differences between total revenue, average revenue, and marginal revenue.

Problems and Applications

1.4 Complete the following table:

DVDS RENTED PER WEEK (Q)	PRICE (P)	TOTAL REVENUE (TR = P × Q)	AVERAGE REVENUE (AR = TR/Q)	MARGINAL REVENUE (MR = ΔTR/ΔQ)
0	$8.00			
1	7.50			
2	7.00			
3	6.50			
4	6.00			
5	5.50			
6	5.00			
7	4.50			
8	4.00			

1.5 A student makes the following argument:

> When a firm sells another unit of a good, the additional revenue the firm receives is equal to the price: If the price is $10, then the additional revenue is also $10. Therefore, this chapter is incorrect when it says that marginal revenue is less than price for a monopolistically competitive firm.

Briefly explain whether you agree with this argument.

1.6 There are many wheat farms in the world, but there are also many Starbucks coffeehouses. Why, then, does a Starbucks coffeehouse face a downward-sloping demand curve when a wheat farmer faces a horizontal demand curve?

1.7 Is it possible for marginal revenue to be negative for a firm selling in a perfectly competitive market? Would a firm selling in a monopolistically competitive market ever produce where marginal revenue is negative?

>> **End Learning Objective 12.1**

How a Monopolistically Competitive Firm Maximizes Profits in the Short Run

Summary

A monopolistically competitive firm maximizes profits at the level of output where marginal revenue equals marginal cost. Price equals marginal revenue for a perfectly competitive firm, but price is greater than marginal revenue for a monopolistically competitive firm. Therefore, unlike a perfectly competitive firm, which produces where $P = MC$, a monopolistically competitive firm produces where $P > MC$.

myeconlab Visit www.myeconlab.com to complete these exercises
Get Ahead of the Curve online and get instant feedback.

Review Questions

2.1 Sally runs a McDonald's franchise. She is selling 350 Big Macs per week at a price of $3.25. If she lowers the price to $3.20, she will sell 351 Big Macs. What is the marginal revenue of the 351st Big Mac?

2.2 Sam runs a Hollywood Video store. Sam is currently renting 3,525 DVDs per week. If instead of renting 3,525 DVDs, he rents 3,526 DVDs, he will add $2.95 to his costs and $2.75 to his revenues. What will be the effect on his profits of renting 3,526 DVDs instead of 3,525 DVDs?

2.3 Should a monopolistically competitive firm take into account its fixed costs when deciding how much to produce? Briefly explain.

Problems and Applications

2.4 If Daniel sells 350 Big Macs at a price of $3.25, and his average cost of producing 350 Big Macs is $3.00, what is his profit?

2.5 Alicia manages a Hollywood Video store and has the following information on demand and costs:

DVDS RENTED PER WEEK (Q)	PRICE (P)	TOTAL COST (TC)
0	$6.00	$3.00
1	5.50	7.00
2	5.00	10.00
3	4.50	12.50
4	4.00	14.50
5	3.50	16.00
6	3.00	17.00
7	2.50	18.50
8	2.00	21.00

a. To maximize profit, how many DVDs should Alicia rent, what price should she charge, and how much profit will she make?

b. What is the marginal revenue received by renting the profit-maximizing DVD? What is the marginal cost of renting the profit-maximizing DVD?

2.6 A trucking company investigates the relationship between the gas mileage of its trucks and the average speed at which the trucks are driven on the highway. The company finds the relationship shown in the following graph:

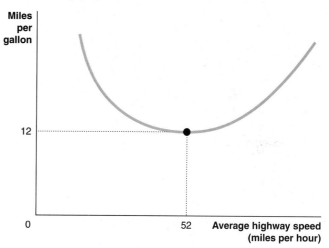

Will the firm maximize profits if it instructs its drivers to maintain an average speed of 52 miles per hour? Briefly explain.

2.7 The following is from an article in the *Wall Street Journal*: "Krispy Kreme Doughnuts Inc. reported its profit fell 56% in its second quarter despite an 11% increase in revenue." Briefly explain how it is possible for a firm's revenue to increase at the same time its profits decrease.

Source: "Krispy Kreme's Net Falls 56%; Company Cuts Sales Forecast," *Wall Street Journal*, August 26, 2004.

2.8 During 2003, General Motors cut the prices of most of its car models. As a result, GM earned a profit of only $184 per car, compared to the profit of $555 per car it had earned in 2002. Does the decline in GM's profits per car indicate that cutting prices was not a profit-maximizing strategy? Briefly explain.

Source: Karen Lundergaard and Sholnn Freeman, "Detroit's Challenge: Weaning Buyers from Years of Deals," *Wall Street Journal*, January 6, 2004.

2.9 (Related to *Solved Problem 12-2* on page 416) William Germano is vice president and publishing director at the Routledge publishing company. He has given the following description of how a publisher might deal with an unexpected increase in the cost of publishing a book:

> It's often asked why the publisher can't simply raise the price [if costs increase]. . . . It's likely that the editor [is already] . . . charging as much as the market will bear. . . . In other words, you might be willing to pay $50.00 for a . . . book on the Brooklyn Bridge, but if . . . production costs [increase] by 25 percent, you might think $62.50 is too much to pay, though that would be what the publisher needs to charge. And indeed the publisher may determine that $50.00 is this book's ceiling—the most you would pay before deciding to rent a movie instead.

According to what you have learned in this chapter, how do firms adjust the price of a good when there is an increase in cost? Use a graph to illustrate your answer. Does the model of monopolistic competition seem to fit Germano's description? If a publisher does not raise the price of a book following an increase in its production cost, what will be the result?

Source: William Germano, *Getting It Published: A Guide to Scholars and Anyone Else Serious about Serious Books*, Chicago: University of Chicago Press, 2001, pp. 110–111.

2.10 The following excerpt is from an article in the *Wall Street Journal*:

> [Amazon.com], whose sales stagnated last year, increased revenue [this quarter] by 21 percent, to $806 million. . . . It attributed the increase to its price-cutting strategy: discounting books that cost more than $15 each and offering free shipping on orders of at least $49.

a. If Amazon.com's revenue increased after it cut the price of books, what must be true about the price elasticity of demand for ordering books online?

b. Suppose that before the price cut, Amazon.com was not selling the profit-maximizing quantity of

books, but after the price cut, it was. Draw a graph that shows Amazon.com's situation before and after the price cut. (For simplicity, assume that Amazon charges the same price for all books.) Be sure your graph includes the price Amazon was charging and the quantity of books it was selling before the price cut; the price and quantity after the price cut; Amazon's demand, marginal revenue, average total cost, and marginal cost curves; and the areas representing Amazon's profits before and after the price cut.

Source: Saul Hansell, "Citing Its Price Strategy, Amazon Pares Loss," *Wall Street Journal*, July 24, 2002.

2.11 In 1916, the Ford Motor Company produced 500,000 Model T Fords at a price of $440 each. The company made a profit of $60 million that year. Henry Ford told a newspaper reporter that he intended to reduce the price of the Model T to $360, and he expected to sell 800,000 cars at that price. Ford said, "Less profit on each car, but more cars, more employment of labor, and in the end we get all the total profit we ought to make."

a. Did Ford expect the total revenue he received from selling Model Ts to rise or fall following the price cut?

b. Use the information given above to calculate the price elasticity of demand for Model Ts. Use the midpoint formula to make your calculation. See Chapter 6, page 176, if you need a refresher on the midpoint formula.

c. What would the average total cost of producing 800,000 Model Ts have to be for Ford to make as much profit selling 800,000 Model Ts as it made selling 500,000 Model Ts? Is this smaller or larger than the average total cost of producing 500,000 Model Ts?

d. Assume that Ford would make the same total profit when selling 800,000 cars as when selling 500,000 cars. Was Henry Ford correct in saying he would make less profit per car when selling 800,000 cars than when selling 500,000 cars?

>> **End Learning Objective 12.2**

12.3 LEARNING OBJECTIVE   12.3 | Analyze the situation of a monopolistically competitive firm in the long run, pages 417–423.

What Happens to Profits in the Long Run?

Summary

If a monopolistically competitive firm is earning economic profits in the short run, entry of new firms will eliminate those profits in the long run. If a monopolistically competi-

tive firm is suffering economic losses in the short run, exit of existing firms will eliminate those losses in the long run. Monopolistically competitive firms continually struggle to find new ways of differentiating their products as they try to stay one step ahead of other firms that are attempting to copy their success.

Visit www.myeconlab.com to complete these exercises
Get Ahead of the Curve online and get instant feedback.

Review Questions

3.1 What effect does the entry of new firms have on the economic profits of existing firms?

3.2 What is the difference between zero accounting profit and zero economic profit.

Problems and Applications

3.3 Use this graph to answer the questions that follow.

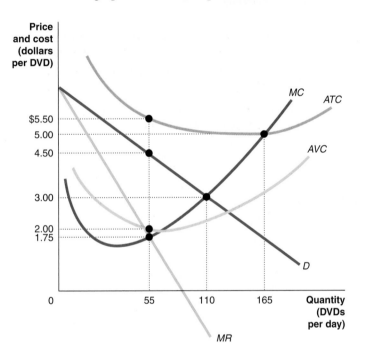

a. If the owner of this video store wants to maximize profits, how many DVDs should she rent per day, and what rental price should she charge? Briefly explain your answer.

b. How much economic profit (or loss) is she making? Briefly explain.

c. Is the owner likely to continue renting this number of DVDs in the long run? Briefly explain.

3.4 **(Related to the *Don't Let This Happen to You!* on page 418)** A student remarks:

> If firms in a monopolistically competitive industry are earning economic profits, new firms will enter the industry. Eventually, the representative firm will find its demand curve has shifted to the left until it is just tangent to its average cost curve and it is earning zero profit. Because firms are earning zero profit at that point, some firms will leave the industry and the representative firm will

find its demand curve will shift to the right. In long-run equilibrium, price will be above average total cost by just enough so that each firm is just breaking even.

Briefly explain whether you agree with this analysis.

3.5 **(Related to the *Making the Connection* on page 419)** Writing in the *Wall Street Journal*, Walter Mossberg argues:

> But the new popularity of the [Macintosh computer] is also partly due to the fact that it can now run Windows along with Apple's superior Mac OS X operating system. That means that if there's a program you need that comes only in a Windows version, you can run it on any current Mac model, speedily and with all its features.

If it is an advantage to Apple that the Macintosh can now run Windows as well as the Mac operating system, would Apple be even better off if it abandoned its own operating system and installed only Windows on the computers it sells?

Source: Walter S. Mossberg, "Fusion is the Latest Way for Macs to Run Windows. PC Software," *Wall Street Journal*, August 2, 2007.

3.6 **(Related to *Solved Problem 12-3* on page 420)** Michael Porter, an economist at Harvard Business School, argues that firms in the U.S. commercial-printing industry have been "investing heavily in the same new equipment, running their presses faster, and reducing crew sizes. But the resulting major productivity gains are being captured by customers and equipment suppliers, not retained in superior profitability." How would consumers gain from these productivity increases? Why haven't the productivity increases made the printing firms more profitable?

Source: Michael E. Porter, "What Is Strategy?" *Harvard Business Review*, November–December 1996, p. 63.

3.7 Michael Korda was, for many years, editor-in-chief at the Simon & Schuster book publishing company. He has written about the many books that have become bestsellers by promising to give readers financial advice that will make them wealthy, by, for example, buying and selling real estate. Korda is very skeptical about the usefulness of the advice in these books because "I have yet to meet anybody who got rich by buying a book, though quite a few people got rich by writing one." On the basis of the analysis in this chapter, discuss why it may be very difficult to become rich by following the advice found in a book.

Source: Michael Korda, *Making the List: A Cultural History of the American Bestseller, 1900–1999*, New York: Barnes & Noble Books, 2001, p. 168.

3.8 **(Related to the *Chapter Opener* on page 410)** According to an article in *Fortune* magazine, "The big question for [Starbucks' chairman] Howard Schultz is whether Starbucks can keep it up. There are those on Wall Street who say that Starbucks' game is almost over." What do you think the article means by "Starbucks' game is almost over"? Why would some people on Wall Street be making this prediction about a firm that was making substantial economic profits at the time the article was written?

Source: Andy Serwer, "Hot Starbucks to Go," *Fortune*, January 12, 2004.

3.9 (Related to the *Making the Connection* on page 422) L'Oreal devotes significant resources to developing new products and differentiating its products from those of its competitors. Suppose it did not do that. What would be the effect on its profits in the short run? What would be the effect on its profits in the long run?

>> **End Learning Objective 12.3**

12.4 LEARNING OBJECTIVE   12.4 | Compare the efficiency of monopolistic competition and perfect competition, **pages 423–425.**

Comparing Perfect Competition and Monopolistic Competition

Summary

Perfectly competitive firms produce where price equals marginal cost and at minimum average total cost. Perfectly competitive firms achieve both allocative and productive efficiency. Monopolistically competitive firms produce where price is greater than marginal cost and above minimum average total cost. Monopolistically competitive firms do not achieve either allocative or productive efficiency. Consumers face a trade-off when buying the product of a monopolistically competitive firm: They are paying a price that is greater than marginal cost, and the product is not being produced at minimum average cost, but they benefit from being able to purchase a product that is differentiated and more closely suited to their tastes.

myeconlab Visit www.myeconlab.com to complete these exercises *Get Ahead of the Curve* online and get instant feedback.

Review Questions

4.1 What are the differences between the long-run equilibrium of a perfectly competitive firm and the long-run equilibrium of a monopolistically competitive firm?

4.2 Does the fact that monopolistically competitive markets are not allocatively or productively efficient mean that there is a significant loss in economic well-being to society in these markets? In your answer, be sure to define what you mean by "economic well-being."

Problems and Applications

4.3 A student asks the following question:

I can understand why a perfectly competitive firm will not earn profits in the long run because a perfectly competitive firm charges a price equal to marginal cost. But

a monopolistically competitive firm can charge a price greater than marginal cost, so why can't it continue to earn profits in the long run?

How would you answer this question?

4.4 Consider the following graph.

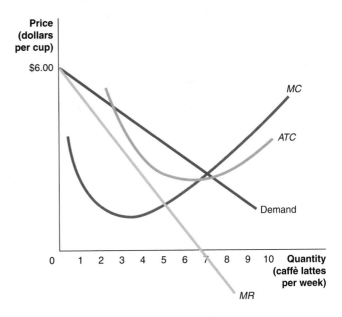

a. Is it possible to say whether this firm is a perfectly competitive firm or a monopolistically competitive firm? If so, explain how you are able to say this.

b. Does the graph show a short-run equilibrium or a long-run equilibrium? Briefly explain.

c. What quantity on the graph represents long-run equilibrium if the firm were perfectly competitive?

4.5 Before the fall of Communism, most basic consumer products in Eastern Europe and the Soviet Union were standardized. For example, government-run stores would offer for sale only one type of bar soap or one type of toothpaste. Soviet economists often argued that this system of standardizing basic consumer products avoided the waste associated with the differentiated goods and services produced in Western Europe and the United States. Do you agree with this argument?

4.6 (Related to the *Making the Connection* on page 425) Juicy Couture has been successful in selling women's clothing using an unusual strategy. According to an article in the *Wall Street Journal* the key to the firm's strategy is to "Limit distribution to maintain the brand's exclusive cachet, even if that means sacrificing sales, a brand-management technique once used only for high-end luxury brands." In 2006, Juicy clothes were sold in only four department stores: Neiman Marcus, Saks, Bloomingdale's, and Nordstrom. Although Juicy was originally known mainly for the fashion tracksuits it sold, "Juicy Couture doesn't just make tracksuits favored by celebrities any more. With its edgy contemporary sportswear and accessories, it has become a lifestyle brand for women, men and kids with estimated annual sales of more than $300 million, up from $47 million in 2002. . . . "

a. Why would limiting the number of stores your product was sold in be a successful strategy for a clothing firm? What would be likely to happen to Juicy's sales if it began to sell its clothes at Wal-Mart and similar stores?

b. Compared with the situation Apple Computer faced during the mid 1980s, is Juicy more or less likely to be able to maintain its product differentiation over a long period of time?

Source: Rachel Dodes, "From Track Suits to Fast Track," *Wall Street Journal*, September 13, 2006.

>> **End Learning Objective 12.4**

12.5 LEARNING OBJECTIVE   12.5 | Define marketing and explain how firms use it to differentiate their products, pages 425–427.

How Marketing Differentiates Products

Summary

Marketing refers to all the activities necessary for a firm to sell a product to a consumer. Firms use two marketing tools to differentiate their products: brand management and advertising. **Brand management** refers to the actions of a firm intended to maintain the differentiation of a product over time. When a firm has established a successful brand name, it has a strong incentive to defend it. A firm can apply for a *trademark*, which grants legal protection against other firms using its product's name.

myeconlab Visit www.myeconlab.com to complete these exercises *Get Ahead of the Curve* online and get instant feedback.

Review Questions

5.1 Define marketing. Is marketing just another name for advertising?

5.2 Why are many companies so concerned about brand management?

Problems and Applications

5.3 Draw a graph that shows the impact on a firm's profits when it increases spending on advertising and the increased advertising has *no* effect on the demand for the firm's product.

5.4 A skeptic says, "Marketing research and brand management are redundant. If a company wants to find out what customers want, it should simply look at what they're already buying." Do you agree with this comment? Explain.

5.5 The National Football League (NFL) has a trademark on the name "Super Bowl" for its championship game. Advertisers can only use the words Super Bowl in their advertising if they pay the NFL a fee. Many companies attempt to get around this trademark by using the phrase "the big game" in their advertising. For example, just before the Super Bowl is to be played a consumer electronics store might have an advertisement with the phrase "Watch the big game on a new HD TV." In 2007, the National Football League indicated that it might attempt legal action to have the phrase "the big game" included in its Super Bowl trademark.

a. Why does the government allow firms to trademark their products?

b. Would consumers gain or lose if the NFL were allowed to trademark the phrase "the big game"? Briefly explain.

5.6 Some companies have done a poor job protecting their products' images. For example, Hormel's Spam brand name is widely ridiculed and has escaped from the company's control in cyberspace. Think of other cases where companies have failed to protect their brand names. What can they do about it now? Should they re-brand their products?

>> **End Learning Objective 12.5**

What Makes a Firm Successful?

Summary

A firm's owners and managers control some of the factors that determine the profitability of the firm. Other factors affect all the firms in the market or are the result of chance, so they are not under the control of the firm's owners. The interactions between factors the firm controls and factors it does not control determine its profitability.

 Visit www.myeconlab.com to complete these exercises *Get Ahead of the Curve* online and get instant feedback.

Review Questions

6.1 What are the key factors that determine the profitability of a firm in a monopolistically competitive market?

6.2 How might a monopolistically competitive firm continually earn economic profit greater than zero?

Problems and Applications

6.3 According to an article in the *Wall Street Journal*:

> In early January last year, after a disappointing Christmas season and amid worries about competition from discount retailers, Zale Corp. decided to shake things up: The self-proclaimed jeweler to Middle America was going to chase upscale customers. . . . The move was a disaster. The Irving, Texas, retailer lost many of its traditional customers without winning the new ones it coveted.

Why would a firm like Zale abandon one market niche for another market niche? We know that in this case the move was not successful. Can you think of other cases where it has been successful?

Source: Ann Zimmerman and Kris Hudson, "Chasing Upscale Customers Tarnishes Mass-Market Jeweler," *Wall Street Journal*, June 26, 2006. p. A1.

6.4 7-Eleven, Inc., operates more than 20,000 convenience stores worldwide. Edward Moneypenny, 7-Eleven's chief financial officer, was asked to name the biggest risk the company faced. He replied, "I would say that the biggest risk that 7-Eleven faces, like all retailers, is competition . . . because that is something that you've got to be aware of in this business." In what sense is competition a "risk" to a business? Why would a company in the retail business need to be particularly aware of competition?

Source: Company Report, CEO Interview: Edward Moneypenny—7-Eleven, Inc., The Wall Street Transcript Corporation.

6.5 In 2006, Wal-Mart closed its stores in South Korea and Germany. According to an article in the *New York Times*:

> Wal-Mart's most successful markets, like Mexico, are those in which it started big. There, the company bought the country's largest and best-run retail chain, Cifra, and has never looked back. This year, Wal-Mart is spending more than $1 billion in Mexico to open 120 new stores.

What advantages does Wal-Mart gain from buying large retail chains, as it did in Mexico, rather than small chains, as it did in its unsuccessful attempts to enter the South Korean and German markets?

Source: Mark Landler and Michael Barbaro, "Wal-Mart Finds That Its Formula Doesn't Fit Every Culture," *New York Times*, August 2, 2006.

6.6 **(Related to the *Making the Connection* on page 428)** A firm that is first to the market with a new product frequently discovers that there are design flaws or problems with the product that were not anticipated. For example, the ballpoint pens made by the Reynolds International Pen Company often leaked. What effect do these problems have on the innovating firm and how do these unexpected problems open up possibilities for other firms to enter the market?

>> **End Learning Objective 12.6**

Chapter 13

Oligopoly: Firms in Less Competitive Markets

Competing with Wal-Mart

Many of the largest corporations in the United States began as small businesses. In 1975, Bill Gates and Paul Allen founded the Microsoft Corporation in Albuquerque, New Mexico, with themselves as the only employees. Michael Dell started the Dell computer company in 1984 from his dorm room at the University of Texas. Sam Walton, founder of Wal-Mart, bought his first store in 1945 with $20,000 borrowed from his father-in-law. Eventually, Wal-Mart would become the largest company in the world. Today, Wal-Mart employs nearly 1.8 million people, which is four times as many as McDonalds, the second largest employer.

When each of these firms was founded, their industries included many more firms than they do now. Today, in the software and computer industries, fewer than 10 firms account for the great majority of sales. Wal-Mart accounts for a large share of several segments of retail sales. In 2007, Wal-Mart was the leading seller of groceries in the United States. It sells more than 25 percent of all the disposable diapers, toothpaste, dog food, and photographic film sold in

the United States. It is also the leading seller of CDs and DVDs, with market shares of 15 to 20 percent. More than 93 percent of U.S. families shop at Wal-Mart at least once per year.

An industry with only a few firms is an *oligopoly*. In an oligopoly, a firm's profitability depends on its interactions with other firms. In these industries, firms must develop *business strategies*, which involve not just deciding what price to charge and how many units to produce but also how much to advertise, which new technologies to adopt, how to manage relations with suppliers, and which new markets to enter.

A key part of Sam Walton's business strategy for Wal-Mart involved placing stores in small towns, where the main competition was from small, locally owned stores. By buying in bulk directly from manufacturers, Walton was able to lower costs, which enabled him to charge lower prices than his competitors. As early as the 1970s, Wal-Mart also made large investments in information technology (IT). Unlike most of its competitors, which had to count unsold goods by hand to find out how many were left in inventory, Wal-Mart had a computerized system for tracking goods. To aid this system, Wal-Mart insisted in the early 1980s that its suppliers use UPC barcodes on

products. This helped spread the use of barcodes to nearly every product sold in the United States. Today, Wal-Mart is pioneering the use of radio frequency identification (RFID) tracking tags that may ultimately replace barcodes. With this system, employees will no longer have to manually scan barcodes. Instead, a radio signal will automatically record the arrival of a product in the warehouse, its shipment to a Wal-Mart store, and its purchase by the consumer. By 2007, many of Wal-Mart's largest suppliers had implemented RFID systems.

In recent years, Wal-Mart has been criticized for several practices, including selling goods produced in foreign factories by low-paid workers, paying low wages to its own workers, providing limited health care benefits, and driving smaller competitors into bankruptcy. As a result, Wal-Mart has run into some difficulty getting local government approvals to open new stores. Wal-Mart's competitors, however, continue to search for ways to successfully compete. **AN INSIDE LOOK** on **page 462** discusses Target's attempts to compete with Wal-Mart in the market for generic prescription drugs.

Source: "The Bulldozer of Bentonville Slows," *Economist*, February 15, 2007.

LEARNING Objectives

After studying this chapter, you should be able to:

13.1 Show how **barriers to entry** explain the existence of **oligopolies**, page 442.

13.2 Use **game theory** to analyze the strategies of oligopolistic firms, page 445.

13.3 Use **sequential games** to analyze business strategies, page 454.

13.4 Use the **five competitive forces model** to analyze competition in an industry, page 457.

Economics in YOUR Life!

Why Can't You Find a Cheap PlayStation 3?

It's the end of finals, and you and your roommate decide to treat yourselves to a PlayStation 3 game system—provided that you can find one that has a relatively low price. First you check Amazon.com and find a price of $499.99. Then you check Best Buy, but the price is also $499.99. Then you check Target; $499.99 again! Finally, you check Wal-Mart, and you find a lower price: $499. *82*, a whopping discount of $0.17. Why isn't one of these big retailers willing to charge a lower price? What happened to price competition? As you read the chapter, see if you can answer these questions. You can check your answers against those we provide at the end of the chapter. **>> Continued on page 461**

441

Oligopoly A market structure in which a small number of interdependent firms compete.

I n Chapters 11 and 12, we studied perfectly competitive and monopolistically competitive industries. Our analysis focused on the determination of a firm's profit-maximizing price and quantity. We concluded that firms maximize profit by producing where marginal revenue equals marginal cost. To determine marginal revenue and marginal cost, we used graphs that included the firm's demand, marginal revenue, and marginal cost curves. In this chapter, we will study **oligopoly**, a market structure in which a small number of interdependent firms compete. In analyzing oligopoly, we cannot rely on the same types of graphs we used in analyzing perfect competition and monopolistic competition—for two reasons.

First, we need to use economic models that allow us to analyze the more complex business strategies of large oligopoly firms. Second, even in determining the profit-maximizing price and output of an oligopoly firm, demand curves and cost curves are not as useful as in the cases of perfect competition and monopolistic competition. We are able to draw the demand curves for competitive firms by assuming that the prices these firms charge have no impact on the prices other firms in their industries charge. This assumption is realistic when each firm is small relative to the market. It is not a realistic assumption, however, for firms that are as large relative to their markets as Microsoft, Dell, or Wal-Mart.

When large firms cut their prices, their rivals in the industry often—but not always—respond by also cutting their prices. Because we don't know for sure how other firms will respond to a price change, we don't know the quantity an oligopolist will sell at a particular price. In other words, it is difficult to know what an oligopolist's demand curve will look like. As we have seen, a firm's marginal revenue curve depends on its demand curve. If we don't know what an oligopolist's demand curve looks like, we also don't know what its marginal revenue curve looks like. Not knowing marginal revenue, we can't calculate the profit-maximizing level of output and the profit-maximizing price the way we did for competitive firms.

The approach we use to analyze competition among oligopolists is called *game theory*. Game theory can be used to analyze any situation in which groups or individuals interact. In the context of economic analysis, game theory is the study of the decisions of firms in industries where the profits of each firm depend on its interactions with other firms. It has been applied to strategies for nuclear war, for international trade negotiations, and for political campaigns, among many other examples. In this chapter, we use game theory to analyze the business strategies of large firms.

13.1 | Show how barriers to entry explain the existence of oligopolies.

Oligopoly and Barriers to Entry

Oligopolies are industries with only a few firms. This market structure lies between the competitive industries we studied in Chapters 11 and 12, which have many firms, and the monopolies we will study in Chapter 14, which have only a single firm. One measure of the extent of competition in an industry is the *concentration ratio*. Every five years, the U.S. Bureau of the Census publishes four-firm concentration ratios that state the fraction of each industry's sales accounted for by its four largest firms. Most economists believe that a four-firm concentration ratio of greater than 40 percent indicates that an industry is an oligopoly.

The concentration ratio has some flaws as a measure of the extent of competition in an industry. For example, concentration ratios do not include sales in the United States by foreign firms. In addition, concentration ratios are calculated for the national market, even though the competition in some industries, such as restaurants or college book-stores, is mainly local. Finally, competition sometimes exists between firms in different industries. For example, Wal-Mart is included in the discount department stores indus-try but also competes with firms in the supermarket industry and the retail toy store industry. As we will see in Chapter 14, some economists prefer another measure of com-petition, known as the *Herfindahl-Hirschman Index*. Despite their shortcomings, con-centration ratios can be useful in providing a general idea of the extent of competition in an industry.

Table 13-1 lists examples of oligopolies in manufacturing and retail trade. Notice that the "Discount Department Stores" industry that includes Wal-Mart is highly con-centrated. Wal-Mart also operates Sam's Club stores, which are in the highly concen-trated "Warehouse Clubs and Supercenters" industry.

Barriers to Entry

Why do oligopolies exist? Why aren't there many more firms in the discount department store industry, the beer industry, or the automobile industry? Recall that new firms will enter industries where existing firms are earning economic profits. But new firms often have difficulty entering an oligopoly. Anything that keeps new firms from entering an industry in which firms are earning economic profits is called a **barrier to entry**. Three barriers to entry are economies of scale, ownership of a key input, and government-imposed barriers.

Economies of Scale The most important barrier to entry is economies of scale. Chapter 10 stated that **economies of scale** exist when a firm's long-run average costs fall as it increases output. The greater the economies of scale, the fewer the number of firms that will be in the industry. Figure 13-1 illustrates this point.

If economies of scale are relatively unimportant in the industry, the typical firm's long-run average cost curve (*LRAC*) will reach a minimum at a level of output (Q_1 in Figure 13-1) that is a small fraction of total industry sales. The industry will have room for a large number of firms and will be competitive. If economies of scale are significant, the typical firm will not reach the minimum point on its long-run average cost curve (Q_2 in Figure 13-1) until it has produced a large fraction of industry sales. Then the industry will have room for only a few firms and will be an oligopoly.

Barrier to entry Anything that keeps new firms from entering an industry in which firms are earning economic profits.

Economies of scale The situation when a firm's long-run average costs fall as it increases output.

TABLE 13-1

Examples of Oligopolies in Retail Trade and Manufacturing

RETAIL TRADE		**MANUFACTURING**	
INDUSTRY	**FOUR-FIRM CONCENTRATION RATIO**	**INDUSTRY**	**FOUR-FIRM CONCENTRATION RATIO**
Discount Department Stores	95%	Cigarettes	95%
Warehouse Clubs and Supercenters	92%	Beer	91%
Hobby, Toy, and Game Stores	72%	Aircraft	81%
Athletic Footwear Stores	71%	Breakfast Cereal	78%
College Bookstores	70%	Automobiles	76%
Radio, Television, and Other Electronic Stores	69%	Computers	76%
Pharmacies and Drugstores	53%	Dog and Cat Food	64%

Source: U.S. Census Bureau, *Concentration Ratios, 2002,* May 2006; and U.S. Census Bureau, *Establishment and Firm Size, 2002,* November 2005.

Figure 13-1

Economies of Scale Help Determine the Extent of Competition in an Industry

An industry will be competitive if the minimum point on the typical firm's long-run average cost curve ($LRAC_1$) occurs at a level of output that is a small fraction of total industry sales, like Q_1. The industry will be an oligopoly if the minimum point comes at a level of output that is a large fraction of industry sales, like Q_2.

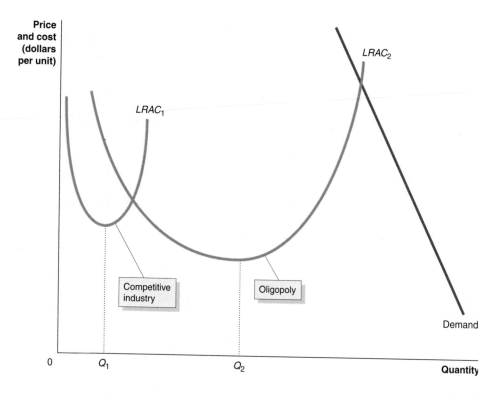

Economies of scale can explain why there is much more competition in the restaurant industry than in the discount department store industry. Because very large restaurants do not have lower average costs than smaller restaurants, the restaurant industry has room for many firms. In contrast, large discount department stores, such as Wal-Mart, have much lower average costs than small discount department stores, for the reasons we discussed in the chapter opener. As a result, just four firms—Wal-Mart, Target, Kmart, and Costco—account for about 95 percent of all sales in this industry.

Ownership of a Key Input If production of a good requires a particular input, then control of that input can be a barrier to entry. For many years, the Aluminum Company of America (Alcoa) controlled most of the world's supply of high-quality bauxite, the mineral needed to produce aluminum. The only way other companies could enter the industry to compete with Alcoa was to recycle aluminum. The De Beers Company of South Africa was able to block competition in the diamond market by controlling the output of most of the world's diamond mines. Until the 1990s, Ocean Spray had very little competition in the market for fresh and frozen cranberries because it controlled almost the entire supply of cranberries. Even today, it controls about 80 percent of the cranberry crop.

Government-Imposed Barriers Firms sometimes try to have the government impose barriers to entry. Many large firms employ *lobbyists* to convince state legislators and members of Congress to pass laws favorable to the economic interests of the firms. There are tens of thousands of lobbyists in Washington, DC, alone. Top lobbyists command annual salaries of $300,000 or more, which indicates the value firms place on their activities. Examples of government-imposed barriers to entry are patents, licensing requirements, and barriers to international trade. A **patent** gives a firm the exclusive right to a new product for a period of 20 years from the date the product is invented. Governments use patents to encourage firms to carry out research and development of new and better products and better ways of producing existing products. Output and living standards increase faster when firms devote resources to research and development, but a firm that spends money to develop a new product may not earn much profit if other firms can copy the product. For example, the pharmaceutical company Merck spends more than $3 billion per year to develop new prescription drugs. If rival compa-

Patent The exclusive right to a product for a period of 20 years from the date the product is invented.

nies could freely produce these new drugs as soon as Merck developed them, most of the firm's investment would be wasted. Because Merck can patent a new drug, the firm can charge higher prices during the years the patent is in force and make an economic profit on its successful innovation.

The government also restricts competition through *occupational licensing*. The United States currently has about 500 occupational licensing laws. For example, doctors and dentists in every state need licenses to practice. The justification for the laws is to protect the public from incompetent practitioners, but by restricting the number of people who can enter the licensed professions, the laws also raise prices. Studies have shown that states that make it harder to earn a dentist's license have prices for dental services that are about 15 percent higher than in other states. Similarly, states that require a license for out-of-state firms to sell contact lenses have higher prices for contact lenses. When state licenses are required for occupations like hair braiding, which was done several years ago in California, restricting competition is the main result.

Government also imposes barriers to entering some industries by imposing tariffs and quotas on foreign competition. As we saw in Chapter 8, a *tariff* is a tax on imports, and a *quota* limits the quantity of a good that can be imported into a country. A quota on foreign sugar imports severely limits competition in the U.S. sugar market. As a result, U.S. sugar companies can charge prices that are more than twice as high as those charged by companies outside the United States.

In summary, to earn economic profits, all firms would like to charge a price well above average cost, but earning economic profits attracts new firms to enter the industry. Eventually, the increased competition forces price down to average cost, and firms just break even. In an oligopoly, barriers to entry prevent—or at least slow down—entry, which allows firms to earn economic profits over a longer period.

13.2 | Use game theory to analyze the strategies of oligopolistic firms.

Using Game Theory to Analyze Oligopoly

As we noted at the beginning of the chapter, economists analyze oligopolies using *game theory*, which was developed during the 1940s by the mathematician John von Neumann and the economist Oskar Morgenstern. **Game theory** is the study of how people make decisions in situations in which attaining their goals depends on their interactions with others. In oligopolies, the interactions among firms are crucial in determining profitability because the firms are large relative to the market.

In all games—whether poker, chess, or Monopoly—the interactions among the players are crucial in determining the outcome. In addition, games share three key characteristics:

1. *Rules* that determine what actions are allowable

2. *Strategies* that players employ to attain their objectives in the game

3. *Payoffs* that are the results of the interaction among the players' strategies

In business situations, the rules of the "game" include not just laws that a firm must obey but also other matters beyond a firm's control—at least in the short run—such as its production function. A **business strategy** is a set of actions that a firm takes to achieve a goal, such as maximizing profits. The *payoffs* are the profits earned as a result of a firm's strategies interacting with the strategies of the other firms. The best way to understand the game theory approach is to look at an example.

Game theory The study of how people make decisions in situations in which attaining their goals depends on their interactions with others; in economics, the study of the decisions of firms in industries where the profits of each firm depend on its interactions with other firms.

Business strategy Actions taken by a firm to achieve a goal, such as maximizing profits.

A Duopoly Game: Price Competition between Two Firms

In this simple example, we use game theory to analyze price competition in a *duopoly*—an oligopoly with two firms. Suppose that an isolated town in Alaska has only two stores: Wal-Mart and Target. Both stores sell the new Sony PlayStation 3. For simplicity, let's

Figure 13-2

A Duopoly Game

Wal-Mart's profits are in blue, and Target's profits are in red. Wal-Mart and Target would each make profits of $10,000 per month on sales of PlayStation 3 if they both charged $600. However, each store manager has an incentive to undercut the other by charging a lower price. If both charge $400, they would each make a profit of only $7,500 per month.

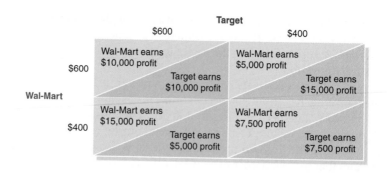

Payoff matrix A table that shows the payoffs that each firm earns from every combination of strategies by the firms.

assume that no other stores stock PlayStation 3 and that consumers in the town can't buy it on the Internet or through mail-order catalogs. The manager of each store decides whether to charge $400 or $600 for the PlayStation. Which price will be more profitable depends on the price the other store charges. The decision regarding what price to charge is an example of a business strategy. In Figure 13-2, we organize the possible outcomes that result from the actions of the two firms into a *payoff matrix*. A **payoff matrix** is a table that shows the payoffs that each firm earns from every combination of strategies by the firms.

Wal-Mart's profits are shown in blue, and Target's profits are shown in red. If Wal-Mart and Target both charge $600 for the PlayStation, each store will make a profit of $10,000 per month from sales of the game console. If Wal-Mart charges the lower price of $400, while Target charges $600, Wal-Mart will gain many of Target's customers. Wal-Mart's profits will be $15,000, and Target's will be only $5,000. Similarly, if Wal-Mart charges $600, while Target is charging $400, Wal-Mart's profits will be only $5,000, while Target's profits will be $15,000. If both stores charge $400, each will earn profits of $7,500 per month.

Collusion An agreement among firms to charge the same price or otherwise not to compete.

Clearly, the stores will be better off if they both charge $600 for the PlayStation. But will they both charge this price? One possibility is that the manager of the Wal-Mart and the manager of the Target will get together and *collude* by agreeing to charge the higher price. **Collusion** is an agreement among firms to charge the same price or otherwise not to compete. Unfortunately, for Wal-Mart and Target—but fortunately for their customers—collusion is against the law in the United States. The government can fine companies that collude and send the managers involved to jail.

The manager of the Wal-Mart store legally can't discuss his pricing decision with the manager of the Target store, so he has to predict what the other manager will do. Suppose the Wal-Mart manager is convinced that the Target manager will charge $600 for the PlayStation. In this case, the Wal-Mart manager will definitely charge $400 because that will increase his profit from $10,000 to $15,000. But suppose instead the Wal-Mart manager is convinced that the Target manager will charge $400. Then the Wal-Mart manager also definitely will charge $400 because that will increase his profit from $5,000 to $7,500. In fact, whichever price the Target manager decides to charge, the Wal-Mart manager is better off charging $400. So, we know that the Wal-Mart manager will choose a price of $400 for the PlayStation.

Dominant strategy A strategy that is the best for a firm, no matter what strategies other firms use.

Now consider the situation of the Target manager. The Target manager is in the identical position to the Wal-Mart manager, so we can expect her to make the same decision to charge $400 for the PlayStation. In this situation, each manager has a *dominant strategy*. A **dominant strategy** is the best strategy for a firm, no matter what strategies other firms use. The result is an equilibrium where both managers charge $400 for the PlayStation. This situation is an equilibrium because each manager is maximizing profits, *given the price chosen by the other manager*. In other words, neither firm can increase its profits by changing its price, given the price chosen by the other firm. An equilibrium where each firm chooses the best strategy, given the strategies chosen by other firms, is called a **Nash equilibrium**, named after Nobel laureate John Nash of Princeton University, a pioneer in the development of game theory.

Nash equilibrium A situation in which each firm chooses the best strategy, given the strategies chosen by other firms.

| Making the Connection | ## A Beautiful Mind: Game Theory Goes to the Movies |

John Nash is the most celebrated game theorist in the world, partly because of his achievements and partly because of his dramatic life. In 1948, at the age of 20, Nash received bachelor's and master's degrees in mathematics from the Carnegie Institute of Technology (now known as Carnegie Mellon University). Two years later, he received a Ph.D. from Princeton for his 27-page dissertation on game theory. It was in this dissertation that he first discussed the concept that became known as the *Nash equilibrium*. Nash appeared to be on his way to a brilliant academic career until he developed schizophrenia in the 1950s. He spent decades in and out of mental hospitals. During these years, he roamed the Princeton campus, covering blackboards in unused classrooms with indecipherable writings. He became known as the "Phantom of Fine Hall." In the 1970s, Nash gradually began to recover. In 1994, he shared the Nobel Prize in Economics with John Harsanyi of the University of California, Berkeley, and Reinhard Selten of Rheinische Friedrich–Wilhelms Universität, Germany, for his work on game theory.

In 1998, Sylvia Nasar of the *New York Times* wrote a biography of Nash, titled *A Beautiful Mind*. Three years later, the book was adapted into an award-winning film starring Russell Crowe. Unfortunately, the (fictitious) scene in the film that shows Nash discovering the idea of Nash equilibrium misstates the concept. In the scene, Nash is in a bar with several friends when four women with brown hair and one with blonde hair walk in. Nash and all of his friends prefer the blonde to the brunettes. One of Nash's friends points out that if they all compete for the blonde, they are unlikely to get her. In competing for the blonde, they will also insult the brunettes, with the result that none of them will end up with a date. Nash then gets a sudden insight. He suggests that they ignore the blonde and each approach one of the brunettes. That is the only way, he argues, that each of them will end up with a date.

Nash immediately claims that this is also an economic insight. He points out that Adam Smith had argued that the best result comes from everyone in the group doing what's best for himself. Nash argues, however, "The best result comes from everyone in the group doing what's best for himself *and* the group." But this is not an accurate description of the Nash equilibrium. As we have seen, in a Nash equilibrium, each player uses a strategy that will make him as well off as possible, *given the strategies of the other players*. The bar situation would not be a Nash equilibrium. Once the other men have chosen a brunette, each man will have an incentive to switch from the brunette he initially chose to the blonde.

In the film A Beautiful Mind, *Russell Crowe played John Nash, winner of the Nobel Prize in Economics.*

YOUR TURN: Test your understanding by doing related problem 2.11 on page 466 at the end of this chapter.

Don't Let This Happen to **YOU!**

Don't Misunderstand Why Each Manager Ends Up Charging a Price of $400

It is tempting to think that the Wal-Mart manager and the Target manager would each charge $400 rather than $600 for the PlayStation because each is afraid that the other manager will charge $400. In fact, fear of being undercut by the other firm's charging a lower price is not the key to understanding each manager's pricing strategy. Notice that charging $400 is the most profitable strategy for each man-

ager, no matter which price the other manager decides to charge. For example, even if the Wal-Mart manager somehow knew for sure that the Target manager intended to charge $600, he would still charge $400 because his profits would be $15,000 instead of $10,000. The Target manager is in the same situation. That is why charging $400 is a dominant strategy for both managers.

YOUR TURN: Test your understanding by doing related problem 2.15 on page 467 at the end of the chapter.

Firm Behavior and the Prisoners' Dilemma

Notice that the equilibrium in Figure 13-2 is not very satisfactory for either firm. The firms earn $7,500 profit each month by charging $400, but they could have earned $10,000 profit if they had both charged $600. By "cooperating" and charging the higher price, they would have achieved a *cooperative equilibrium*. In a **cooperative equilibrium**, players cooperate to increase their mutual payoff. We have seen, though, that the outcome of this game is likely to be a **noncooperative equilibrium**, in which each firm pursues its own self-interest.

A situation like this, in which pursuing dominant strategies results in noncooperation that leaves everyone worse off, is called a **prisoners' dilemma**. The game gets its name from the problem faced by two suspects the police arrest for a crime. If the police lack other evidence, they may separate the suspects and offer each a reduced prison sentence in exchange for confessing to the crime and testifying against the other criminal. Because each suspect has a dominant strategy to confess to the crime, they will both confess and serve a jail term, even though they would have gone free if they had both remained silent.

Cooperative equilibrium An equilibrium in a game in which players cooperate to increase their mutual payoff.

Noncooperative equilibrium An equilibrium in a game in which players do not cooperate but pursue their own self-interest.

Prisoners' dilemma A game in which pursuing dominant strategies results in noncooperation that leaves everyone worse off.

Solved Problem | 13-2

Is Advertising a Prisoners' Dilemma for Coca-Cola and Pepsi?

Coca-Cola and Pepsi both advertise aggressively, but would they be better off if they didn't? Their commercials are not designed to convey new information about the products. Instead, they are designed to capture each other's customers. Construct a payoff matrix using the following hypothetical information:

- If neither firm advertises, Coca-Cola and Pepsi both earn profits of $750 million per year.

- If both firms advertise, Coca-Cola and Pepsi both earn profits of $500 million per year.

- If Coca-Cola advertises and Pepsi doesn't, Coca-Cola earns profits of $900 million and Pepsi earns profits of $400 million.

- If Pepsi advertises and Coca-Cola doesn't, Pepsi earns profits of $900 million and Coca-Cola earns profits of $400 million.

a. If Coca-Cola wants to maximize profit, will it advertise? Briefly explain.

b. If Pepsi wants to maximize profit, will it advertise? Briefly explain.

c. Is there a Nash equilibrium to this advertising game? If so, what is it?

SOLVING THE PROBLEM:

Step 1: **Review the chapter material.** This problem uses payoff matrixes to analyze a business situation, so you may want to review the section "A Duopoly Game: Price Competition between Two Firms," which begins on page 445.

Step 2: **Construct the payoff matrix.**

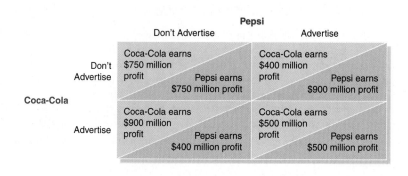

Step 3: Answer question (a) by showing that Coca-Cola has a dominant strategy of advertising. If Pepsi doesn't advertise, then Coca-Cola will make $900 million if it advertises but only $750 million if it doesn't. If Pepsi advertises, then Coca-Cola will make $500 million if it advertises but only $400 million if it doesn't. Therefore, advertising is a dominant strategy for Coca-Cola.

Step 4: Answer question (b) by showing that Pepsi has a dominant strategy of advertising. Pepsi is in the same position as Coca-Cola, so it also has a dominant strategy of advertising.

Step 5: Answer question (c) by showing that there is a Nash equilibrium for this game. Both firms advertising is a Nash equilibrium. Given that Pepsi is advertising, Coca-Cola's best strategy is to advertise. Given that Coca-Cola is advertising, Pepsi's best strategy is to advertise. Therefore, advertising is the optimal decision for both firms, *given the decision by the other firm.*

EXTRA CREDIT: This is another example of the prisoners' dilemma game. Coca-Cola and Pepsi would be more profitable if they both refrained from advertising, thereby saving the enormous expense of television and radio commercials and newspaper and magazine ads. Each firm's dominant strategy is to advertise, however, so they end up in an equilibrium where both advertise, and their profits are reduced.

YOUR TURN: For more practice, do related problems 2.12, 2.13, and 2.14 on pages 466–467 at the end of this chapter.

>> **End Solved Problem 13-2**

Making the Connection | **Is There a Dominant Strategy for Bidding on eBay?**

An auction is a game in which bidders compete to buy a product. The payoff in winning an auction is equal to the difference between the subjective value you place on the product being auctioned and the amount of the winning bid. On the online auction site eBay, more than 200 million items valued at more than $10 billion are auctioned each year.

eBay is run as a *second-price auction*, where the winning bidder pays the price of the second-highest bidder. If the high bidder on a DVD of *Spider-Man 3* bids $15, and the second bidder bids $10, the high bidder wins the auction and pays $10. It may seem that your best strategy when bidding on eBay is to place a bid well below the subjective value you place on the item in the hope of winning it at a low price. In fact, bidders on eBay have a dominant strategy of entering a bid equal to the maximum value they place on the item. For instance, suppose you are looking for a present for your parents' anniversary. They are Rolling Stones fans, and someone is auctioning a pair of Stones concert tickets. If the maximum value you place on the tickets is $200, that should be your bid. To see why, consider the results of strategies of bidding more or less than $200.

There are two possible outcomes of the auction: Either someone else bids more than you do, or you are the high bidder. First, suppose you bid $200 but someone else bids more than you do. If you had bid less than

On eBay, bidding the maximum value you place on an item is a dominant strategy.

$200, you would still have lost. If you had bid more than $200, you might have been the high bidder, but because your bid would be for more than the value you place on the tickets, you would have a negative payoff. Second, suppose you bid $200 and you are the high bidder. If you had bid less than $200, you would have run the risk of losing the tickets to someone whose bid you would have beaten by bidding $200. You would be worse off than if you had bid $200 and won. If you had bid more than $200, you would not have affected the price you ended up paying—which, remember, is equal to the amount bid by the second-highest bidder. Therefore, a strategy of bidding $200—the maximum value you place on the tickets—dominates bidding more or less than $200.

Even though making your first bid your highest bid is a dominant strategy on eBay, many bidders don't use it. After an auction is over, a link leads to a Web page showing all the bids. In many auctions, the same bidder bids several times, showing that the bidder had not understood his or her dominant strategy.

YOUR TURN: Test your understanding by doing related problem 2.16 on page 467 at the end of this chapter.

▬▬▬▬▬

Can Firms Escape the Prisoners' Dilemma?

Although the prisoners' dilemma game seems to show that cooperative behavior always breaks down, we know it doesn't. People often cooperate to achieve their goals, and firms find ways to cooperate by not competing on price. The reason the basic prisoners' dilemma story is not always applicable is that it assumes the game will be played only once. Most business situations, however, are repeated over and over. Each month, the Target and Wal-Mart managers will decide again what price they will charge for PlayStation 3. In the language of game theory, the managers are playing a *repeated game*. In a repeated game, the losses from not cooperating are greater than in a game played once, and players can also employ *retaliation strategies* against those who don't cooperate. As a result, we are more likely to see cooperative behavior.

Figure 13-2 on page 446 shows that Wal-Mart and Target are earning $2,500 less per month by both charging $400 instead of $600 for the PlayStation 3. Every month that passes with both stores charging $400 increases the total amount lost: Two years of charging $400 will cause each store to lose $60,000 in profit. This lost profit increases the incentive for the store managers to cooperate by *implicitly* colluding. Remember that *explicit* collusion—such as the managers meeting and agreeing to charge $600—is illegal. But if the managers can find a way to signal each other that they will charge $600, they may be within the law.

Suppose, for example, that Wal-Mart and Target both advertise that they will match the lowest price offered by any competitor—in our simple example, they are each other's only competitor. These advertisements are signals to each other that they intend to charge $600 for the PlayStation. The signal is clear because each store knows that if it charges $400, the other store will automatically retaliate by also lowering its price to $400. The offer to match prices is a good *enforcement mechanism* because it guarantees that if either store fails to cooperate and charges the lower price, the competing store will automatically punish that store by also charging the lower price. As Figure 13-3 shows, the stores have changed the payoff matrix they face.

With the original payoff matrix (a), there is no matching offer, and each store makes more profit if it charges $400 when the other charges $600. The matching offer changes the payoff matrix to (b). Now the stores can charge $600 and receive a profit of $10,000 per month, or they can charge $400 and receive a profit of $7,500 per month. The equilibrium shifts from the prisoners' dilemma result of both stores charging the low price and receiving low profits to a result where both stores charge the high price and receive high profits. An offer to match competitors' prices might seem to benefit consumers, but game theory shows that it actually may hurt consumers by helping to keep prices high.

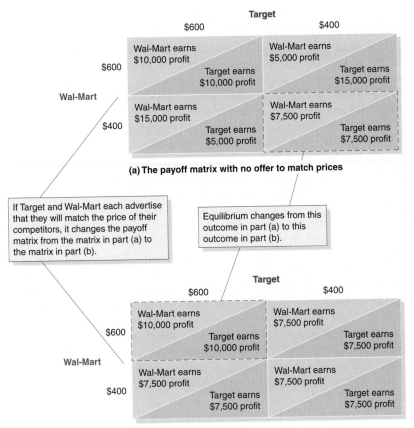

(a) The payoff matrix with no offer to match prices

If Target and Wal-Mart each advertise that they will match the price of their competitors, it changes the payoff matrix from the matrix in part (a) to the matrix in part (b).

Equilibrium changes from this outcome in part (a) to this outcome in part (b).

(b) The payoff matrix with an offer to match prices

Figure 13-3

Changing the Payoff Matrix in a Repeated Game

Wal-Mart and Target can change the payoff matrix by advertising that they will match their competitor's price. This retaliation strategy provides a signal that one store charging a lower price will be met automatically by the other store charging a lower price. In payoff matrix (a), there is no matching offer, and each store benefits if it charges $400 when the other charges $600. In payoff matrix (b), with the matching offer, the companies have only two choices: They can charge $600 and receive a profit of $10,000 per month, or they can charge $400 and receive a profit of $7,500 per month. The equilibrium shifts from the prisoners' dilemma result of both stores charging the low price and receiving low profits to both stores charging the high price and receiving high profits.

One form of implicit collusion occurs as a result of *price leadership*. With **price leadership**, one firm takes the lead in announcing a price change, which is then matched by the other firms in the industry. For example, through the 1970s, General Motors would announce a price change at the beginning of a model year and Ford and Chrysler would match GM's price change. In some cases, such as the airline industry, firms have attempted to act as price leaders, but failed when other firms in the industry declined to cooperate.

Price leadership A form of implicit collusion where one firm in an oligopoly announces a price change, which is matched by the other firms in the industry.

| Making the Connection | **American Airlines and Northwest Airlines Fail to Cooperate on a Price Increase** |

Coordinating prices is easier in some industries than in others. Fixed costs in the airline industry are very large, and marginal costs are very small. The marginal cost of flying one more passenger from New York to Chicago is no more than a few dollars: the cost of another snack served and a small amount of additional jet fuel. As a result, airlines often engage in last-minute price cutting to fill the remaining empty seats on a flight. Even a low-price ticket will increase marginal revenue more than marginal cost. As with other oligopolies, if all airlines cut prices, industry profits will decline. Airlines therefore continually adjust their prices while at the same time monitoring their rivals' prices and retaliating against them either for cutting prices or failing to go along with price increases.

The airlines have trouble raising the price this business traveler pays for a ticket.

Consider the following fairly typical events from the spring of 2002. American Airlines decided to raise some of its ticket prices in a roundabout way. Business travelers are usually willing to pay higher prices for airline tickets than are leisure travelers. Business travelers also often must make their flight plans only a few days before they leave. Airlines take advantage of this fact by requiring 10- to 14-day advance reservations to get a fully discounted ticket. A smaller discount is available with a 3-day advance reservation. This smaller discount is aimed at business travelers. American decided to increase to 7 days the advance purchase requirement for the business travel discount. Because many business travelers cannot make their reservations that far in advance, they would have to buy full-fare tickets.

Continental Airlines matched American's change, but the other airlines refused to go along. They hoped that by not matching American's price increase, they would gain some of its customers. American then retaliated by offering very low $99 one-way tickets in 10 markets where Northwest Airlines, United Airlines, Delta Air Lines, and US Airways offered nonstop service. American did not offer the $99 fares in the markets where Continental offered nonstop service. An airline industry consultant observed that "American is trying to slap the hands of people who wouldn't go along with its increase."

Northwest immediately responded by offering $99 fares in 20 markets where American offers nonstop service. American retaliated by offering the low fare in 10 additional markets served by Northwest. Northwest then further retaliated by offering the low fare in a total of 160 markets served by American. After several days of very low fares and lost profits, American and Northwest restored their normal fares, and American went back to a 3-day advance reservation requirement for discounted business-travel tickets.

Did American's aggressive retaliation make it easier for airlines to agree on ticket price increases in the future? Apparently not. A few weeks later, Continental raised its prices for round-trip discounted tickets by $20. Every airline but Northwest matched the price increase. Rather than lose customers to Northwest, Continental and the other airlines rolled back the price increase.

Sources: Scott McCartney, "Airfare Wars Show Why Deals Arrive and Depart," *Wall Street Journal*, March 19, 2002; and Scott McCartney, "Airlines Drop $20 Fare Increase after Northwest Fails to Join In," *Wall Street Journal*, April 16, 2002.

YOUR TURN: Test your understanding by doing related problems 2.18, 2.19, and 2.20 on pages 467–468 at the end of this chapter.

Cartels: The Case of OPEC

In the United States, firms cannot legally meet to agree on what prices to charge and how much to produce. But suppose they could. Would this be enough to guarantee that their collusion would be successful? The example of the Organization of Petroleum Exporting Countries (OPEC) indicates that the answer to this question is "no." OPEC has 11 members, including Saudi Arabia, Kuwait, and other Arab countries, as well as Iran, Venezuela, Nigeria, and Indonesia. Together, these countries own 75 percent of the world's proven oil reserves, although they pump a smaller share of the total oil sold each year. OPEC operates as a **cartel**, which is a group of firms that collude to restrict output to increase prices and profits. The members of OPEC meet periodically and agree on quotas, quantities of oil that each country agrees to produce. The quotas are intended to reduce oil production well below the competitive level, to force up the price of oil, and to increase the profits of member countries.

Figure 13-4 shows world oil prices from 1972 to 2006. The blue line shows the price of a barrel of oil in each year. Prices in general have risen since 1972, which has reduced the amount of goods and services that consumers can purchase with a dollar. The red line corrects for general price increases by measuring oil prices in terms of the dollar's purchasing power in 2006. Although political unrest in the Middle East and other factors also affect the price of oil, the figure shows that OPEC had considerable success in raising the price of oil during the mid-1970s and early 1980s. Oil prices, which had been below $3 per barrel in 1972, rose to more than $35 per barrel in 1981, which was almost

Cartel A group of firms that collude by agreeing to restrict output to increase prices and profits.

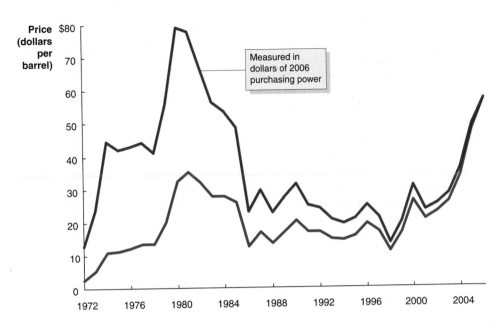

Figure 13-4

World Oil Prices, 1972–2006

The blue line shows the price of a barrel of oil in each year. The red line measures the price of a barrel of oil in terms of the purchasing power of the dollar in 2006. By reducing oil production, the Organization of Petroleum Exporting Countries (OPEC) was able to raise the world price of oil in the mid-1970s and early 1980s. Sustaining high prices has been difficult over the long run, however, because members often exceed their output quotas.
Source: U.S. Energy Information Agency, *Monthly Energy Review*, March 2007, Table 9.1.

$78 measured in dollars of 2006 purchasing power. The figure also shows that OPEC has had difficulty sustaining the high prices of 1981 in later years, although beginning in 2004, oil prices rose, in part due to increasing demand from China and India.

Game theory helps us understand why oil prices have fluctuated. If every member of OPEC cooperates and produces the low output level dictated by its quota, prices will be high, and the cartel will earn large profits. Once the price has been driven up, however, each member has an incentive to stop cooperating and to earn even higher profits by increasing output beyond its quota. But if no country sticks to its quota, total oil output will increase, and profits will decline. In other words, OPEC is caught in a prisoners' dilemma.

If the members of OPEC always exceeded their production quotas, the cartel would have no effect on world oil prices. In fact, the members of OPEC periodically meet and assign new quotas that, at least for a while, enable them to restrict output enough to raise prices. OPEC's occasional success at behaving as a cartel can be explained by two factors. First, the members of OPEC are participating in a repeated game. As we have seen, this increases the likelihood of a cooperative outcome. Second, Saudi Arabia has far larger oil reserves than any other member of OPEC. Therefore, it has the most to gain from high oil prices and a greater incentive to cooperate. To see this, consider the payoff matrix shown in Figure 13-5. To keep things simple, let's assume that OPEC has only two members:

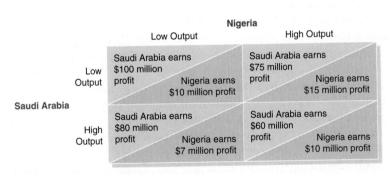

Figure 13-5 | The OPEC Cartel with Unequal Members

Because Saudi Arabia can produce so much more oil than Nigeria, its output decisions have a much larger effect on the price of oil. In the figure, "low output" corresponds to cooperating with the OPEC-assigned output quota, and "high output" corresponds to producing at maximum capacity. Saudi Arabia has a dominant strategy to cooperate and produce a low output. Nigeria, however, has a dominant strategy not to cooperate and produce a high output. Therefore, the equilibrium of this game will occur with Saudi Arabia producing a low output and Nigeria producing a high output.

Saudi Arabia and Nigeria. In Figure 13-5, "low output" corresponds to cooperating with the OPEC-assigned output quota, and "high output" corresponds to producing at maximum capacity. The payoff matrix shows the profits received per day by each country.

We can see that Saudi Arabia has a strong incentive to cooperate and maintain its low output quota. By keeping output low, Saudi Arabia can by itself significantly raise the world price of oil, increasing its own profits as well as those of other members of OPEC. Therefore, Saudi Arabia has a dominant strategy of cooperating with the quota and producing a low output. Nigeria, however, cannot by itself have much effect on the price of oil. Therefore, Nigeria has a dominant strategy of not cooperating and producing a high output. The equilibrium of this game will occur with Saudi Arabia producing a low output and Nigeria producing a high output. In fact, OPEC often operates in just this way. Saudi Arabia will cooperate with the quota, while the other 10 members produce at capacity. Because this is a repeated game, however, Saudi Arabia will occasionally produce more oil than its quota to intentionally drive down the price and retaliate against the other members for not cooperating.

13.3 LEARNING OBJECTIVE

13.3 | Use sequential games to analyze business strategies.

Sequential Games and Business Strategy

We have been analyzing games in which both players move simultaneously. In many business situations, however, one firm will act first, and then other firms will respond. These situations can be analyzed using *sequential games*. We will use sequential games to analyze two business strategies: deterring entry and bargaining between firms. To keep things simple, we consider situations that involve only two firms.

Deterring Entry

We saw earlier that barriers to entry are a key to firms continuing to earn economic profits. Can firms create barriers to deter new firms from entering an industry? Some recent research in game theory has focused on this question. To take a simple example, suppose a town in South Dakota currently has no discount department stores. Executives at Wal-Mart decide to enter the market and are considering what size store to build. To break even by covering the opportunity cost of the funds involved, the store must provide a minimum rate of return of 15 percent on the firm's investment. If Wal-Mart builds a small store in the town, it will earn economic profits by receiving a return of 30 percent. If Wal-Mart builds a large store, its costs will be somewhat higher, and it will receive a return of only 22 percent.

It seems clear that Wal-Mart should build the small store, but the executives are worried that Target may also build a store in this market. If Wal-Mart builds a small store and Target enters the market, both firms will earn an 18 percent return on their investment in this market. If Wal-Mart builds a large store and Target enters, the stores will have to cut prices, and the firms will each earn only 10 percent return on their investments, which is below the 15 percent return necessary for either firm to break even.

We can analyze a sequential game by using a *decision tree*, like the one shown in Figure 13-6. The boxes in the figure represent *decision nodes*, which are points when the firms must make the decisions contained in the boxes. At the left, Wal-Mart makes the initial decision of what size store to build, and then Target responds by either entering the market or not. The decisions made are shown beside the arrows. The *terminal nodes* at the right side of the figure show the resulting rates of return.

Let's start with Wal-Mart's initial decision. If Wal-Mart builds a large store, then the arrow directs us to the upper red decision node for Target. If Target decides to enter, it will earn only a 10 percent rate of return on its investment, which represents an economic loss because it is below the opportunity cost of the funds involved. If Target doesn't enter, Wal-Mart will earn 22 percent, and Target will not earn anything in this

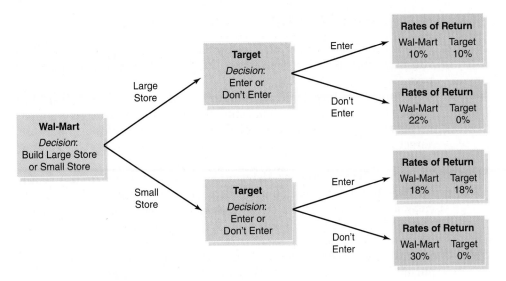

Figure 13-6

The Decision Tree for an Entry Game

Wal-Mart earns its highest return if it builds a small store and Target doesn't enter the market. If Wal-Mart builds a small store, Target will enter because it will earn economic profit by receiving an 18 percent return on its investment. Therefore, the best decision for Wal-Mart is to build a large store to deter Target's entry. Once Wal-Mart has built a large store, Target knows that if it enters this market, it will earn only 10 percent on its investment, which represents an economic loss, so it won't enter the market.

market. Wal-Mart executives can conclude that if they build a large store, Target will not enter, and Wal-Mart will earn 22 percent on its investment.

If Wal-Mart decides to build a small store, then the arrow directs us to the lower red decision node for Target. If Target decides to enter, it will earn an 18 percent rate of return. If it doesn't enter, Wal-Mart will earn 30 percent, and Target will not earn anything in this market. Wal-Mart executives can conclude that if they build a small store, Target will enter, and Wal-Mart will earn 18 percent on its investment.

This analysis should lead Wal-Mart executives to conclude that they can build a small store and earn 18 percent—because Target will enter—or they can build a large store and earn 22 percent by deterring Target's entry.

Solved Problem | 13-3

Is Deterring Entry Always a Good Idea?

Whether deterring entry makes sense depends on how costly it is to the firm doing the deterring. Use the following decision tree to decide whether Wal-Mart should deter Target from entering this market. Assume that each firm must earn a 15 percent return on its investment to break even.

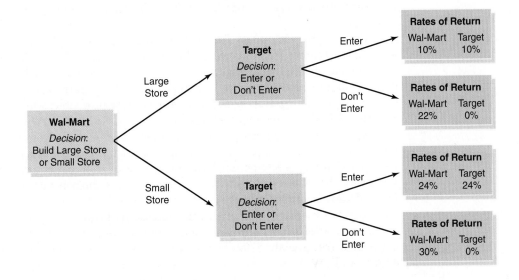

SOLVING THE PROBLEM:

Step 1: **Review the chapter material.** This problem is about sequential games, so you may want to review the section "Deterring Entry," which begins on page 454.

Step 2: **Determine how Target will respond to Wal-Mart's decision.** If Wal-Mart builds a large store, Target will not enter this market because the return on its investment represents an economic loss. If Wal-Mart builds a small store, Target will enter because it will earn a return that represents an economic profit.

Step 3: **Given how Target will react, determine which strategy maximizes profits for Wal-Mart.** If Wal-Mart builds the large store, it will have deterred Target's entry, and the rate of return on its investment will be 22 percent. If it builds the small store, Target will enter, but Wal-Mart will actually earn a higher return of 24 percent.

Step 4: **State your conclusion.** Like any other business strategy, deterrence is worth pursuing only if its costs are not too high. In this case, the high cost of building a large store lowers Wal-Mart's economic profits below what it earns by building a small store, even given that Target will enter the market.

>> **End Solved Problem 13-3**

YOUR TURN: For more practice, do related problem 3.3 on page 469 at the end of this chapter.

Bargaining

The success of many firms depends on how well they bargain with other firms. For example, firms often must bargain with their suppliers over the prices they pay for inputs. Suppose that TruImage is a small firm that has developed software that improves how pictures from a digital camera are displayed on computer screens. TruImage currently sells its software only on its Web site and earns profits of $2 million per year. Dell Computer informs TruImage that it is considering installing the software on every new computer Dell sells. Dell expects to sell more computers at a higher price if it can install TruImage's software on its computers. The two firms begin bargaining over what price Dell will pay TruImage for its software.

The decision tree in Figure 13-7 illustrates this bargaining game. At the left, Dell makes the initial decision on what price to offer TruImage for its software, and then TruImage responds by either accepting or rejecting the contract offer. First, suppose that Dell offers TruImage a contract price of $30 per copy for its software. If TruImage accepts this contract, its profits will be $5 million per year, and Dell will earn $10 million in additional profits. If TruImage rejects the contract, its profits will be the $2 million per year it earns selling its software on its Web site, and Dell will earn zero additional profits.

Now, suppose Dell offers TruImage a contract price of $20 per copy. If TruImage accepts this contract, its profits will be $3 million per year, and Dell will earn $15 million in additional profits. If TruImage rejects this contract, its profits will be the $2 million it earns selling its software on its Web site, and Dell will earn zero additional profits. Clearly, for Dell, a contract of $20 per copy is more profitable, while for TruImage, a contract of $30 per copy is more profitable.

Suppose TruImage attempts to obtain a favorable outcome from the bargaining by telling Dell that it will reject a $20-per-copy contract. If Dell believes this threat, then it will offer TruImage a $30-per-copy contract because Dell is better off with the $10 million profit that will result from TruImage's accepting the contract than with the zero profits Dell will earn if TruImage rejects the $20-per-copy contract. This result is a Nash equilibrium because neither firm can increase its profits by changing its choice—*provided that Dell believes TruImage's threat.* But is TruImage's threat credible? Once Dell has offered TruImage the $20 contract, TruImage's choices are to accept the contract and earn $3 million or reject the contract and earn only $2 million. Because rejecting the

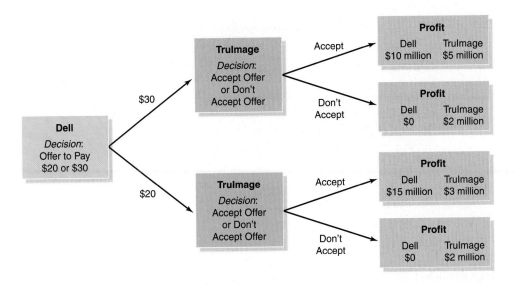

Figure 13-7 | The Decision Tree for a Bargaining Game

Dell earns the highest profit if it offers a contract price of $20 per copy and TruImage accepts the contract. TruImage earns the highest profit if Dell offers it a contract of $30 per copy and it accepts the contract. TruImage may attempt to bargain by threatening to reject a $20-per-copy contract. But Dell knows this threat is not credible because once Dell has offered a $20-per-copy contract, TruImage's profits are higher if it accepts the contract than if it rejects it.

contract reduces TruImage's profits, TruImage's threat to reject the contract is not credible, and Dell should ignore it.

As a result, we would expect Dell to use the strategy of offering TruImage a $20-per-copy contract and TruImage to use the strategy of accepting the contract. Dell will earn additional profits of $15 million per year, and TruImage will earn profits of $3 million per year. This outcome is called a *subgame-perfect equilibrium*. A subgame-perfect equilibrium is a Nash equilibrium in which no player can make himself better off by changing his decision at any decision node. In our simple bargaining game, each player has only one decision to make. As we have seen, Dell's profits are highest if it offers the $20-per-copy contract, and TruImage's profits are highest if it accepts the contract. Typically, in sequential games of this type, there is only one subgame-perfect equilibrium.

Managers use decision trees like those in Figures 13-6 and 13-7 in business planning because they provide a systematic way of thinking through the implications of a strategy and of predicting the reactions of rivals. We can see the benefits of decision trees in the simple examples we considered here. In the first example, Wal-Mart managers can conclude that building a large store is more profitable than building a smaller store. In the second example, Dell managers can conclude that TruImage's threat to reject a $20-per-copy contract is not credible.

13.4 LEARNING OBJECTIVE

13.4 | Use the five competitive forces model to analyze competition in an industry.

The Five Competitive Forces Model

We have seen that the number of competitors in an industry affects a firm's ability to charge a price above average cost and earn an economic profit. The number of firms is not the only determinant of the level of competition in an industry, however. Michael Porter of Harvard Business School has drawn on the research of a number of economists to develop a model that shows how five competitive forces determine the overall level of competition in an industry. Figure 13-8 illustrates Porter's model.

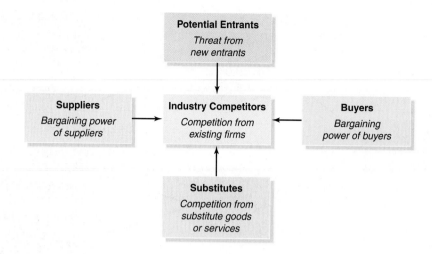

Figure 13-8 | The Five Competitive Forces Model

Michael Porter's model identifies five forces that determine the level of competition in an industry: (1) competition from existing firms, (2) the threat from new entrants, (3) competition from substitute goods or services, (4) the bargaining power of buyers, and (5) the bargaining power of suppliers.

Source: Reprinted with the permission of The Free Press, a Division of Simon & Schuster Adult Publishing Group, from Michael E. Porter, *Competitive Strategy: Techniques for Analyzing Industries and Competitors.* Copyright © 1980, 1998 by The Free Press. All rights reserved.

We now look at each of the five competitive forces: (1) competition from existing firms, (2) the threat from potential entrants, (3) competition from substitute goods or services, (4) the bargaining power of buyers, and (5) the bargaining power of suppliers.

Competition from Existing Firms

We have already seen that competition among firms in an industry can lower prices and profits. To take another example: The Educational Testing Service (ETS) produces the Scholastic Aptitude Test (SAT) and the Graduate Record Exam (GRE). The GRE is taken by students applying to graduate school. In 2007, the Educational Testing Service charged a price of $43 to take the SAT, but $140 to take the GRE. Part of the explanation for these large price differences is that ETS faces competition in the market for tests given to high school seniors applying to college, where the SAT competes with the ACT Assessment, produced by ACT, Inc. But there is no competition for the GRE test. As we saw earlier in this chapter, when there are only a few firms in a market, it is easier for them to implicitly collude and to charge a price close to the monopoly price. In this case, however, competition from a single firm was enough to cause ETS to keep the price of the SAT near the competition level.

Competition in the form of advertising, better customer service, or longer warranties can also reduce profits by raising costs. For example, online booksellers Amazon.com, BarnesandNoble.com, and Buy.com have competed by offering low-cost—or free—shipping, by increasing their customer service staffs, and by building more warehouses to provide faster deliveries. These activities have raised the booksellers' costs and reduced their profits.

The Threat from Potential Entrants

Firms face competition from companies that currently are not in the market but might enter. We have already seen how actions taken to deter entry can reduce profits. In our hypothetical example in the previous section, Wal-Mart built a larger store and earned less profit to deter Target's entry. Business managers often take actions aimed at deterring entry. Some of these actions include advertising to create product loyalty, introducing new products—such as slightly different cereals or toothpastes—to fill market niches, and setting lower prices to keep profits at a level that would make entry less attractive.

Competition from Substitute Goods or Services

Firms are always vulnerable to competitors introducing a new product that fills a consumer need better than their current product does. Consider the encyclopedia business. For decades, many parents bought expensive and bulky encyclopedias for their children attending high school or college. By the 1990s, computer software companies were offering electronic encyclopedias that sold for a small fraction of the price of the printed encyclopedias. Encyclopedia Britannica and the other encyclopedia publishers responded by cutting prices and launching advertising campaigns aimed at showing the superiority of printed encyclopedias. Still, profits continued to decline, and by the end of the 1990s, most printed encyclopedias had disappeared.

The Bargaining Power of Buyers

If buyers have enough bargaining power, they can insist on lower prices, higher-quality products, or additional services. Automobile companies, for example, have significant bargaining power in the tire market, which tends to lower tire prices and limit the profitability of tire manufacturers. Some retailers have significant buying power over their suppliers. For instance, Wal-Mart has required many of its suppliers to alter their distribution systems to accommodate Wal-Mart's need to control the stocks of goods in its stores.

The Bargaining Power of Suppliers

If many firms can supply an input and the input is not specialized, the suppliers are unlikely to have the bargaining power to limit a firm's profits. For instance, suppliers of paper napkins to McDonald's restaurants have very little bargaining power. With only a single or a few suppliers of an input, the purchasing firm may face a high price. During the 1930s and 1940s, for example, the Technicolor Company was the only producer of the cameras and film that studios needed to produce color movies. Technicolor charged the studios high prices to use its cameras, and it had the power to insist that only its technicians could operate the cameras. The only alternative for the movie studios was to make black-and-white movies.

As with other competitive forces, the bargaining power of suppliers can change over time. For instance, when IBM chose Microsoft to supply the operating system for its personal computers, Microsoft was a small company with very limited bargaining power. As Microsoft's Windows operating system became standard in more than 90 percent of personal computers, this large market share increased Microsoft's bargaining power.

Making
the
Connection

Is Southwest's Business Strategy More Important Than the Structure of the Airline Industry?

For years, economists and business strategists believed that market structure was the most important factor in explaining the ability of some firms to continue earning economic profits. For example, most economists argued

Southwest's business strategy allowed it to remain profitable when many other airlines faced heavy losses.

that during the first few decades after World War II, steel companies in the United States earned economic profits because barriers to entry were high, there were few firms in the industry, and competition among firms was low. In contrast, restaurants were seen as less profitable because barriers to entry were low and the industry was intensely competitive. One problem with this approach to analyzing the profitability of firms is that it does not explain how firms in the same industry can have very different levels of profit.

Today, economists and business strategists put greater emphasis on the characteristics of individual firms and the strategies their managements use to continue to earn economic profits. This approach helps explain why Nucor continues to be a profitable steel company while Bethlehem Steel, at one time the second-largest steel producer in the United States, was forced into bankruptcy. It also explains why Dell, which began as a small company run by Michael Dell from his dorm room at the University of Texas, went on to become extremely profitable and an industry leader, while other computer companies have disappeared.

Many economists argue that the best strategy for a company is to identify a segment of the market and then shape the company to fit that segment. This strategy makes it more difficult for rivals to compete in that part of the market. For example, Southwest Airlines concentrates on customers who fly relatively short distances and who want a low-price, no-frills airline flight. Every aspect of the company is focused on this goal. Southwest's planes have no first-class or business sections—only coach seats are available. By flying primarily between midsize cities, Southwest can avoid the delays at the crowded airports near big cities and can keep its planes at the airport gate for only 15 minutes—much less time than other airlines. This lowers its costs by allowing it to keep its planes in the air longer and to offer more flights with fewer planes. Southwest also lowers costs by not serving meals, flying only Boeing 737s to standardize maintenance, not assigning passengers to particular seats, and not checking luggage through to connecting flights.

It is very difficult for the other full-service airlines, such as Delta, American, and United, to compete with Southwest. Because they fly out of larger, more congested airports, those airlines have no hope of turning around their planes at the gate as quickly as Southwest does. Because many of their passengers are flying longer distances—often using connecting flights—they have to serve meals and check luggage through. Many of the other airlines' customers want upgraded seats and service, so those airlines must offer first-class and business-class seats. Even when Delta, American, and United have tried to offer stripped-down service on certain routes in direct competition with Southwest, they have not been successful. Southwest's complete focus on providing low-cost, low-price service has proven very difficult for the other airlines to copy. While other airlines suffered heavy losses in 2003–2004 as fuel prices rose and demand declined as a result of the war in Iraq and the spread of the disease SARS (severe acute respiratory syndrome), Southwest continued to earn profits. In 2006, it remained the leading airline in on-time arrivals and fewest customer complaints.

Southwest's corporate strategy, rather than the structure of the airline industry, explains why Southwest earns economic profits.

Source: Scott McCartney, "A Report Card on the Nation's Airlines," *Wall Street Journal*, February 6, 2007, p. D1.

YOUR TURN: Test your understanding by doing related problem 4.5 on page 470 at the end of this chapter.

Economics in YOUR Life!

≫ Continued from page 441

At the beginning of this chapter, we asked you to consider why the price of the PlayStation 3 game system is almost the same at every large retailer, from Amazon.com to Wal-Mart. Why don't these retailers seem to compete on price for this type of product? In this chapter, we have seen that if big retailers were engaged in a one-time game of pricing PlayStations, they would be in a prisoner's dilemma and probably all charge a low price. However, we have also seen that pricing PlayStations is actually a repeated game because the retailers will be selling the game system in competition over a long period of time. In this situation, it is more likely that a cooperative equilibrium will be arrived at in which the retailers will all charge a high price. This is good news for the profits of the retailers but bad news for consumers! This is one of many insights that game theory provides into the business strategies of oligopolists.

Conclusion

Firms are locked in a never-ending struggle to earn economic profits. As noted in the two preceding chapters, competition erodes economic profits. Even in the oligopolies discussed in this chapter, firms have difficulty earning economic profits in the long run. We have seen that firms attempt to avoid the effects of competition in various ways. For example, they can stake out a secure niche in the market, they can engage in implicit collusion with competing firms, or they can attempt to have the government impose barriers to entry. Read *An Inside Look* on the next page for a discussion of the business strategy Target uses to compete with Wal-Mart in the market for generic prescription drugs.

Can Target Compete with Wal-Mart in the Market for Generic Drugs?

USA TODAY, SEPTEMBER 23, 2006

Target Says It Will Match Wal-Mart's $4 Generic Drug Price

(a) Chain store Target said late Thursday that it will match rival Wal-Mart's $4 price on 150 generic drug prescriptions in the Tampa Bay area. Target's brief press release didn't say whether it would keep pace with Wal-Mart's plan to take the lower prices nationwide, but it did say it has a "long-standing practice to be price competitive with Wal-Mart."

Wal-Mart, the nation's third-largest seller of prescription drugs, said earlier Thursday that it will offer the $4 price on about 150 generic drugs to the insured and uninsured alike, starting immediately in the Tampa area, and will take the program statewide by January.

"We intend to take it nationwide (b) next year," says Bill Simon, Wal-Mart's executive vice president of the Professional Services Division. For uninsured consumers, the $4 price for some generics is below what they would pay at most pharmacy counters and is less than typical $10 to $15 co-payments on generics offered by many insurance plans.

Wal-Mart's move could save modest amounts for some consumers. It may also draw more customers to its stores or prompt a price war with other pharmacies. Savings could be less than $1 per prescription to more than $20, depending on the drug and pharmacy where customers shop, according to information from Wal-Mart and prices of other retailers posted at MyFloridarx.com, a state-run website.

That could draw more customers to Wal-Mart, already the largest seller of groceries and toys, possibly forcing other chain drugstores to cut their prices, says Ed Kaplan of the Segal Co., a benefits consulting firm. "Customers who take five or seven medications a month and can save $10 on each might switch," says Kaplan.

The move caused share prices for generic drug and pharmacy companies to drop Thursday.

Wal-Mart says the $4 for 30-day (c) supply price would save customers $7.98 a month for blood-pressure drug Lisinopril, $3.85 for diabetes drug metformin and 80 cents for blood-pressure drug atenolol.

Simon says the $4 generics are not expected to be a "loss leader," meaning Wal-Mart doesn't expect to lose money on the drugs in hopes of attracting more customers to buy other products. That's because the drugs offered are longtime generics that have multiple manufacturers and they are already inexpensive on the wholesale market. Large companies such as Wal-Mart can often buy in bulk for less than the $4 cost.

Wal-Mart's press release said 291 drugs will be covered, a total that includes different dosage strengths of the same drugs. When the differing dosage strengths are taken out, the list includes fewer than 150 products, including treatments for high blood pressure, infection and diabetes, along with some vitamins and painkiller ibuprofen. That's a fraction of the estimated 2,100 generic products available.

"This is a much narrower list than they're giving the impression it is," says drug-industry expert Stephen Schondelmeyer at the University of Minnesota. Simon says the drugs chosen for the list represent 20% of the prescriptions Wal-Mart currently fills and cover a wide range of medical needs. More products may be added, he says.

The move comes as Wal-Mart works to counter critics who say the firm doesn't make health insurance affordable for many of its workers. "Providing low-cost drugs is a good thing. But not providing affordable health care to workers is not a good thing. Why can't Wal-Mart address the serious health care crisis in its own stores?" says Chris Kofinis, with Wake-UpWalmart.com.

Some praised Wal-Mart's move. "That's a great price for a 30-day supply of drugs and will be a tremendous boon for seniors," says Devon Herrick, economist at the National Center for Policy Analysis.

Source: Julie Appley, "Target Says It Will Match Wal-Mart's $4 Generic Drug Price," USA Today, September 23, 2006. Reprinted by permission of USA Today.

Key Points in the Article

This article illustrates Target's plan to match Wal-Mart's low price on generic prescription drugs. As we have seen in this chapter, when a market is an oligopoly, there are only a few firms. So, each firm must take into account the actions of its competitors. When a competitor changes the price it charges, the other firms in the industry must decide how to react. In this case, Target determined that its profits would be higher by matching Wal-Mart's price.

Analyzing the News

(a) In an oligopoly market, a firm's profits depend not only on the price it chooses, but on the price its rivals choose. In this case, Target had to choose how to respond to Wal-Mart's pricing decision. From Target's action, we can assume that it believes its profits will be higher with a low price, given that Wal-Mart is charging a low price. The figure is helpful in analyzing whether Wal-Mart can profitably sell generic

drugs at a price of $4. In both panel (a) and panel (b), the rate of return by Wal-Mart is higher when it offers generics at $4 regardless of what Target does. So, Wal-Mart has a dominant strategy of charging $4.

Target faces the choice of whether to match this price. In panel (a), if Target matches the price it earns an 8 percent return, while if it does not match the price it will earn a return of 0 percent. Target prefers the 8 percent return and will choose to match Wal-Mart's $4 generic drug price.

But suppose that Target determines that given its competitive position relative to Wal-Mart the situation is actually that shown in panel (b). Wal-Mart still has a dominant strategy of charging $4 for generic prescription, but now Target faces the choice of a 3 percent return if it matches Wal-Mart's price, or a 5 percent return if it does not match Wal-Mart's price. In this case, Target would be better off not matching the $4 generic price.

(b) Larger stores sometimes cut the price of a product even if this means they will take a loss on sales of the product, if the store manager believes the low price will attract new customers. If low prescription prices attract more customers to Wal-Mart stores, we would expect that Wal-Mart would earn additional profits from the other goods those customers purchased while in Wal-Mart.

(c) As mentioned in the chapter opener, Wal-Mart is facing increased criticism over its corporate policies. Just as Wal-Mart has to decide how to respond to the market behavior of its rivals, such as pricing, it must also decide how to respond to the behavior of its critics.

Thinking Critically

1. Suppose that you manage a small pharmacy in a local town. How will you decide whether to match the lower generic drug prices of Wal-Mart and Target?

2. Suppose that Congress passes legislation that places a price floor on generic drugs. Who would likely gain from such a law? Who would likely lose? Use a graph to show changes in producer surplus and consumer surplus.

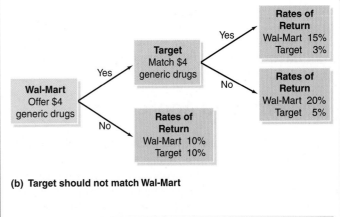
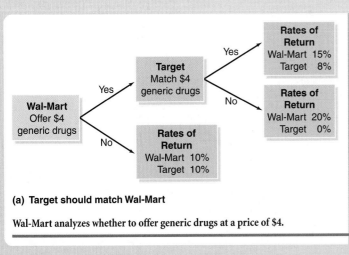

(a) Target should match Wal-Mart

(b) Target should not match Wal-Mart

Wal-Mart analyzes whether to offer generic drugs at a price of $4.

Key Terms

Barrier to entry, p. 443

Business strategy, p. 445

Cartel, p. 452

Collusion, p. 446

Cooperative equilibrium, p. 448

Dominant strategy, p. 446

Economies of scale, p. 443

Game theory, p. 445

Nash equilibrium, p. 446

Noncooperative equilibrium, p. 448

Oligopoly, p. 442

Patent, p. 444

Payoff matrix, p. 446

Price leadership, p. 451

Prisoners' dilemma, p. 448

13.1 LEARNING OBJECTIVE   13.1 | Show how barriers to entry explain the existence of oligopolies, **pages 442–445.**

Oligopoly and Barriers to Entry

Summary

An **oligopoly** is a market structure in which a small number of interdependent firms compete. **Barriers to entry** keep new firms from entering an industry. The three most important barriers to entry are economies of scale, ownership of a key input or raw material, and government barriers. Economies of scale are the most important barrier to entry. **Economies of scale** exist when a firm's long-run average costs fall as it increases output. Government barriers include patents, licensing, and barriers to international trade. A **patent** is the exclusive right to a product for a period of 20 years from the date the product is invented.

 Visit www.myeconlab.com to complete these exercises *Get Ahead of the Curve* online and get instant feedback.

Review Questions

1.1 What is an oligopoly? Give three examples of oligopolistic industries in the United States.

1.2 What do barriers to entry have to do with the extent of competition, or lack thereof, in an industry? What are the most important barriers to entry?

1.3 Give an example of a government-imposed barrier to entry. Why would the government be willing to erect barriers to entering an industry?

Problems and Applications

1.4 Michael Porter has argued, "The intensity of competition in an industry is neither a matter of coincidence nor bad luck. Rather, competition in an industry is rooted in its underlying economic structure." What does Porter mean by "economic structure"? What factors, other than economic structure, might be expected to determine the intensity of competition in an industry?

Source: Michael Porter, *Competitive Strategy: Techniques for Analyzing Industries and Competitors,* New York: The Free Press, 1980, p. 3.

1.5 "Less-than-truckload" trucking companies include goods from several shippers in their highway trailers. According to an article in the *Wall Street Journal:* "Unlike [the truckload industry, which is] a fiercely

competitive business it is relatively easy to enter, less-than-truckload companies face a higher entry barrier due to the cost of an extensive network of terminals to consolidate shipments." Would you expect truckload companies or less-than-truckload companies to charge higher prices to ship freight? Which companies are likely to earn economic profits? Briefly explain.

Source: Daniel Machalaba, "Yellow Freight to Raise Rates 4.9% on Bet about Lower Inventory Costs," *Wall Street Journal,* July 5, 2001.

1.6 Thomas McCraw, a professor at Harvard Business School, has written the following: "Throughout American history, entrepreneurs have tried, sometimes desperately, to create big businesses out of naturally small-scale operations. It has not worked." What advantage would entrepreneurs expect to gain from creating "big businesses"? Why would entrepreneurs fail to create big businesses with "naturally small-scale operations"? Illustrate your answer with a graph showing long-run average costs.

Source: Thomas K. McCraw, ed., *Creating Modern Capitalism,* Cambridge, MA: Harvard University Press, 1997, p. 323.

1.7 The graph below illustrates the average total cost curves for two automobile manufacturing firms: Little Auto and Big Auto. Under which of the follow-

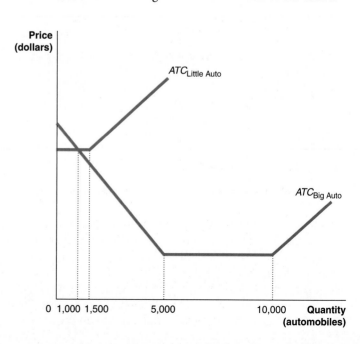

ing conditions would you expect to see the market composed of firms like Little Auto, and under which conditions would you expect to see the market dominated by firms like Big Auto?

a. When the market demand curve intersects the quantity axis at less than 1,000 units

b. When the market demand curve intersects the quantity axis at more than 1,000 units but less than 10,000 units

c. When the market demand curve intersects the quantity axis at more than 10,000 units

1.8 The following graph contains two long-run average cost curves. Briefly explain which cost curve would most likely be associated with an oligopoly and which would most likely be associated with a perfectly competitive industry.

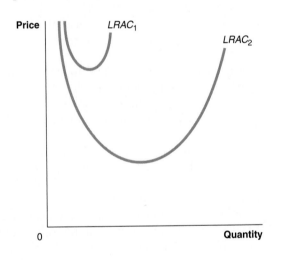

1.9 Alfred Chandler, who was a professor at Harvard Business School, observed, "Imagine the diseconomies of scale—the great increase in unit costs—that would result from placing close to one-fourth of the world's production of shoes, or textiles, or lumber into three factories or mills!" The shoe, textiles, and lumber industries are very competitive, with many firms producing each of these products. Briefly explain whether Chandler's observation helps us explain why.

Source: Alfred D. Chandler, Jr., "The Emergence of Managerial Capitalism," in Alfred D. Chandler, Jr., and Richard S. Tedlow, *The Coming of Managerial Capitalism*, New York: Irwin, 1985, p. 406.

1.10 A historical account of the development of the cotton textile industry in England argues the following:

> The cotton textile industry was shaped by ruthless competition. Rapid growth in demand, low barriers to entry, frequent technological innovations, and a high rate of firm bankruptcy all combined to form an environment in which . . . oligopolistic competition became almost impossible.

Explain how each of the factors described here would contribute to making the cotton textile industry competitive rather than oligopolistic.

Source: Thomas K. McCraw, ed., *Creating Modern Capitalism*, Cambridge, MA: Harvard University Press, pp. 61–62.

> **>> End Learning Objective 13.1**

13.2 LEARNING OBJECTIVE 13.2 | Use game theory to analyze the strategies of oligopolistic firms, **pages 445–454.**

Using Game Theory to Analyze Oligopoly

Summary

Because an oligopoly has only a few firms, interactions among those firms are particularly important. **Game theory** is the study of how people make decisions in situations in which attaining their goals depends on their interactions with others; in economics, it is the study of the decisions of firms in industries where the profits of each firm depend on its interactions with other firms. A **business strategy** refers to actions taken by a firm to achieve a goal, such as maximizing profits. Oligopoly games can be illustrated with a **payoff matrix**, which is a table that shows the payoffs that each firm earns from every combination of strategies by the firms. One possible outcome in oligopoly is **collusion**, which is an agreement among firms to charge the same price or otherwise not to compete. A **cartel** is a group of firms that collude by agreeing to restrict output to increase prices and profits. In a **cooperative equilibrium**, firms cooperate to increase their mutual payoff. In a **noncooperative equilibrium**, firms do not cooperate but pursue their own self-interest. A **dominant strategy** is a strategy that is the best for a firm, no matter what strategies other firms use. A **Nash equilibrium** is a situation in which each firm chooses the best strategy, given the strategies chosen by other firms. A situation in which pursuing dominant strategies results in noncooperation that leaves everyone worse off is called a **prisoners' dilemma**. Because many business situations are repeated games, firms may end up implicitly colluding to keep prices high. With **price leadership**, one firm takes the lead in announcing a price change, which is then matched by the other firms in the industry.

Visit www.myeconlab.com to complete these exercises online and get instant feedback.

Review Questions

2.1 Give brief definitions of the following concepts.
  a. Game theory
  b. Cooperative equilibrium
  c. Noncooperative equilibrium
  d. Dominant strategy
  e. Nash equilibrium

2.2 Why do economists refer to the methodology for analyzing oligopolies as game theory?

2.3 Why do economists refer to the pricing strategies of oligopoly firms as a prisoners' dilemma game?

2.4 What is the difference between explicit collusion and implicit collusion? Give an example of each.

2.5 How is the prisoners' dilemma result changed in a repeated game?

Problems and Applications

2.6 Bob and Tom are two criminals who have been arrested for burglary. The police put Tom and Bob in separate cells. They offer to let Bob go free if he confesses to the crime and testifies against Tom. Bob also is told that he will serve a 15-year sentence if he remains silent while Tom confesses. If he confesses and Tom also confesses, they will each serve a 10-year sentence. Separately, the police make the same offer to Tom. Assume that if Bob and Tom both remain silent, the police have only enough evidence to convict them of a lesser crime, and they will both serve 3-year sentences.
  a. Use the information provided to write a payoff matrix for Bob and Tom.
  b. Does Bob have a dominant strategy? If so, what is it?
  c. Does Tom have a dominant strategy? If so, what is it?
  d. What sentences do Bob and Tom serve? How might they have avoided this outcome?

2.7 Explain how collusion makes firms better off. Given the incentives to collude, briefly explain why every industry doesn't become a cartel.

2.8 Under "early decision" college admission plans, students apply to a college in the fall and, if they are accepted, they must enroll in that college. According to an article in *BusinessWeek*, Yale president Richard Levin argues that early decision plans put too much pressure on students to decide early in their senior years which college they wish to attend. Levin has proposed abolishing early decision plans. But the author of the article is doubtful that this will succeed because "as long as some big-name schools offer early admissions, the others feel they must, too, or lose out

on the best talent." Do you agree with this conclusion? How can game theory help us analyze this situation?

2.9 Baseball players who hit the most home runs *relative to other players* usually receive the highest pay. Beginning in the mid-1990s, the typical baseball player became significantly stronger and more muscular. As one baseball announcer put it, "The players of 20 years ago look like stick figures compared with the players of today." As a result, the average number of home runs hit each year increased dramatically. Some of the increased strength that baseball players gained came from more weight training and better conditioning and diet. As some players admitted, though, some of the increased strength came from taking steroids and other illegal drugs. Taking steroids can significantly increase the risk of developing cancer and other medical problems.
  a. In these circumstances, are baseball players in a prisoners' dilemma? Carefully explain.
  b. Suppose that Major League Baseball begins testing players for steroids and firing players who are caught using them (or other illegal muscle-building drugs). Will this testing make baseball players as a group better off or worse off? Briefly explain.

2.10 Soldiers in battle may face a prisoners' dilemma. If all soldiers stand and fight, the chance that the soldiers, as a unit, will survive is maximized. If there is a significant chance that the soldiers will lose the battle, an individual soldier may maximize his chance of survival by running away while the other soldiers hold off the enemy by fighting. If all soldiers run away, however, many of them are likely to be killed or captured by the enemy because no one is left to hold off the enemy. In ancient times, the Roman army practiced "decimation." If a unit of soldiers was guilty of running away during a battle or committing other cowardly acts, all would be lined up, and every tenth soldier would be killed by being run through with a sword. No attempt was made to distinguish between soldiers in the unit who had fought well and those who had been cowardly. Briefly explain under what condition the Roman system of decimation was likely to have solved the prisoners' dilemma of soldiers running away in battle.

2.11 (Related to the *Making the Connection* on page 447) Convert the scene from the bar into a game. There are two players John and Steve. They each have the same possible strategies: "approach the blonde" or "approach the brunette." Think of the payoffs in the matrices as measures of utility. Choose payoffs so that there is no Nash equilibrium.

2.12 (Related to *Solved Problem 13-2* on page 448) Would a ban on advertising beer on television be likely to increase or decrease the profits of beer companies? Briefly explain.

2.13 (Related to *Solved Problem 13-2* on page 448) Beginning in 2003, the U.S. government spent billions of dollars rebuilding the infrastructure damaged by the war in Iraq. Much of the work was carried out by construction and engineering firms that had to bid for the business. Suppose, hypothetically, that only two companies—Bechtel and Halliburton—enter the bidding and that each firm is deciding whether to bid either $4 billion or $5 billion. (Remember that in this type of bidding, the winning bid is the *low* bid because the bid represents the amount the government will have to pay to have the work done.) Each firm will have costs of $2.5 billion to do the work. If they both make the same bid, they will both be hired and will split the work and the profits. If one makes a low bid and one makes a high bid, only the low bidder will be hired, and it will receive all the profits. The result is the following payoff matrix.

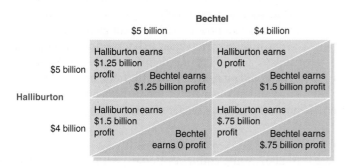

a. Is there a Nash equilibrium in this game? Briefly explain.

b. How might the situation be changed if the two companies expect to be bidding on many similar projects in future years?

2.14 (Related to *Solved Problem 13-2* on page 448 and the *Chapter Opener* on page 440) Suppose that Wal-Mart and Target are independently deciding whether to stick with bar codes or switch to RFID tags to monitor the flow of products. Because many suppliers sell to both Wal-Mart and Target, it is much less costly for suppliers to use one system or the other rather than to use both. The following payoff matrix shows the profits per year for each company resulting from the interaction of their strategies.

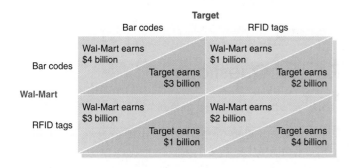

a. Briefly explain whether Wal-Mart has a dominant strategy.

b. Briefly explain whether Target has a dominant strategy.

c. Briefly explain whether there is a Nash equilibrium in this game.

2.15 (Related to the *Don't Let This Happen to You!* on page 447) A student argues, "The prisoners' dilemma game is unrealistic. Each player's strategy is based on the assumption that the other player won't cooperate. But if each player assumes that the other player *will* cooperate, the 'dilemma' disappears." Briefly explain whether you agree with this argument.

2.16 (Related to the *Making the Connection* on page 449) We made that argument that a bidder on an eBay auction has a dominant strategy of bidding only once, with that bid being the maximum the bidder would be willing to pay.

a. Is it possible that a bidder might receive useful information during the auction, particularly from the dollar amounts other bidders are bidding? If so, how does that change a bidder's optimal strategy?

b. Many people recommend the practice of "sniping," or placing your bid at the last second before the auction ends. Is there connection between sniping and your answer to part a.?

2.17 Consider two oligopolistic industries. In the first industry, firms always match price changes by any other firm in the industry. In the second industry, firms always ignore price changes by any other firm. In which industry are firms likely to charge higher prices? Briefly explain.

2.18 (Related to the *Making the Connection* on page 451) Airlines often find themselves in price wars. Consider the following game: Northwest and Continental are the only two airlines flying the route from Houston to Omaha. Each firm has two strategies: charge a high price or charge a low price.

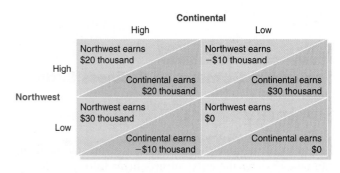

a. What (if any) is the dominant strategy for each firm?

b. Is this game a prisoner's dilemma?

c. How could repeated playing of the game change the strategy each firm uses?

2.19 (Related to the *Making the Connection* on page 451) Consider the following two excerpts from articles in the *Wall Street Journal*:

> [From February 2003] An attempt by major airlines to raise fares $20 per round-trip ticket fell apart over the weekend as Northwest Airlines, the fourth-largest carrier, refused to go along. . . . By yesterday morning, all airlines had rolled back prices.

> [From August 2003] Northwest Airlines triggered a major round of discounting last week when it launched a fare sale for late summer and early fall travel—setting off a chain reaction in the industry. During the course of one day, airlines cut fares on nearly 35,881 routes.

Briefly explain why airlines might be more likely to match price cuts than price increases.

Sources: Scott McCartney and Susan Carey, "Airlines' Move to Raise Fares Falls Apart as Northwest Balks," *Wall Street Journal*, February 18, 2003; and Eleena De Lisser, "Fall Travel Deals Arrive Early," *Wall Street Journal*, August 14, 2003.

2.20 (Related to the *Making the Connection* on page 451) Until the late 1990s, airlines would post proposed changes in ticket prices on computer reservations systems several days before the new ticket prices went into effect. Then the federal government took action to end the practice. Now airlines can only post prices on their reservations systems for tickets that are immediately available for sale. Why would the federal government object to the old system of posting prices before they went into effect?

Source: Scott McCartney, "Airfare Wars Show Why Deals Arrive and Depart," *Wall Street Journal*, March 19, 2002.

2.21 Finding dominant strategies is often a very effective way of analyzing a game. Consider the following

game: Microsoft and Apple are the two firms in the market for operating systems. Each firm has two strategies: charge a high price or charge a low price.

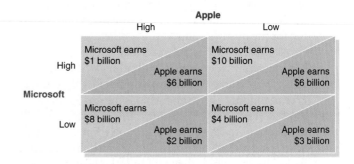

a. What (if any) is the dominant strategy for each firm?
b. Is there a Nash equilibrium? Briefly explain.

2.22 One day in October 2006, oil prices dropped 93 cents per barrel, to their lowest level in almost one year. As an article in the *Wall Street Journal* noted: "The drop Wednesday came even as the Organization of Petroleum Exporting Countries said it will cut global production by one million barrels a day to boost prices, Nigerian oil minister and OPEC president Edmund Daukoru said." Why would oil prices drop at the same time that OPEC was announcing a cut in production. Shouldn't lower production lead to higher prices?

Source: Worth Civils, "Stocks Decline Amid Fed Minutes, Alcoa Earnings, Lower Oil Prices," *Wall Street Jurnal*, October 11, 2006.

2.23 In 2007, some countries that export natural gas discussed forming a cartel, modeled on the OPEC oil cartel. The head of Libya's energy sector was quoted as saying: "We are trying to strengthen the cooperation among gas producers to avoid harmful competition."
a. What is a cartel?
b. What is "harmful competition"? Is competition typically harmful to consumers?
c. What factors would help the cartel succeed? What factors would reduce the cartels chances for success?

Source: Ayesha Daya and James Herron, "Gas Exporters to Study Cartel," *Wall Street Journal*, April 10, 2007, p. A6.

>> End Learning Objective 13.2

13.3 LEARNING OBJECTIVE   13.3 | Use sequential games to analyze business strategies, **pages 454–457.**

Sequential Games and Business Strategy

Summary

Recent work in game theory has focused on actions firms can take to deter the entry of new firms into an industry. Deterring entry can be analyzed using a sequential game, where first one firm makes a decision and then another firm reacts to that decision. Sequential games can be illustrated using decision trees.

 Visit www.myeconlab.com to complete these exercises *Get Ahead of the Curve* online and get instant feedback.

Review Questions

3.1 What is a sequential game?

3.2 How are decision trees used to analyze sequential games?

Problems and Applications

3.3 (Related to *Solved Problem 13-3* on page 455) Bradford is a small town that currently has no fast-food restaurants. McDonald's and Burger King are both considering entering this market. Burger King will wait until McDonald's has made its decision before deciding whether to enter. Use the following decision tree to decide the optimal strategy for each company. Does your answer depend on the rate of return that owners of fast-food restaurants must earn on their investments in order to break even? Briefly explain.

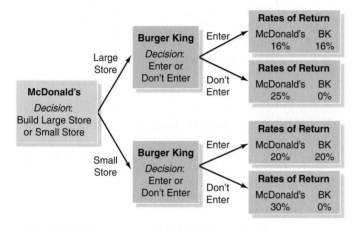

3.4 Suppose that in the situation shown in Figure 13-7 on page 457, TruImage's profits are $1.5 million if the firm accepts Dell's contract offer of $20 per copy. Now will Dell offer TruImage a contract of $20 per copy or a contract of $30 per copy? Briefly explain.

3.5 Refer to Figure 13-5 on page 453. Consider the entries in the row of the payoff matrix that correspond to Saudi Arabia choosing "low output." Suppose the numbers change so that Nigeria's profit is $15 million when Nigeria chooses "low output" and $10 million when it chooses "high output."

a. Create the payoff matrix for this new situation, assuming that Saudi Arabia and Nigeria choose their output levels simultaneously. Is there a Nash equilibrium to this game? If so, what is it?

b. Now draw the decision tree for this situation, (using the values from the payoff matrix you created in part a), assuming that Saudi Arabia and Nigeria make their decisions sequentially: First Saudi Arabia chooses its output level, and then Nigeria responds by choosing its output level. Is there a Nash equilibrium to this game? If so, what is it?

c. Compare your answers to parts a and b. Briefly explain the reason for any differences in the outcomes of these two games.

>> End Learning Objective 13.3

13.4 LEARNING OBJECTIVE   13.4 | Use the five competitive forces model to analyze competition in an industry,
pages 457–460.

The Five Competitive Forces Model

Summary

Michael Porter of Harvard Business School argues that the state of competition in an industry is determined by five competitive forces: the degree of competition among existing firms, the threat from new entrants, competition from substitute goods or services, the bargaining power of buyers, and the bargaining power of suppliers.

myeconlab Visit www.myeconlab.com to complete these exercises
Get Ahead of the Curve online and get instant feedback.

Review Questions

4.1 List the competitive forces in the five competitive forces model.

4.2 Does the strength of each of the five competitive forces remain constant over time? Briefly explain.

Problems and Applications

4.3 Michael Porter has argued that in many industries, "strategies converge and competition becomes a series of races down identical paths that no one can win." Briefly explain whether firms in these industries likely will earn economic profits.

Source: Michael E. Porter, "What Is Strategy?" *Harvard Business Review*, November–December 1996, p. 64.

4.4 According to an article in the *Wall Street Journal*:

The big car makers are pushing a wide array of new technology into production, responding to relentless competitive pressure, rising energy prices and consumer demand for better safety. Once, side-curtain airbags were rare. Now they're becoming standard equipment on a growing number of vehicles. Car makers are racing to deploy fuel-saving technologies such as cylinder shutdown (variously known as "active fuel management" or "multi-displacement system"), six-speed transmissions and, of course, various kinds of gas-electric hybrid drives.

a. What does the article mean by "relentless competitive pressure"? Which of the five competitive forces is being referred to?

b. In the long run, will the car maker who first successfully incorporates these new technologies in its cars earn economic profits? Which group is likely to benefit the most from these innovations: the car companies or consumers?

Source: Joseph B. White, "Ford, GM Eye Shift in Buying Habits," *Wall Street Journal*, May 22, 2006.

4.5 **(Related to *Making the Connection* on page 459)** An article in the *Wall Street Journal* argues, "Finally, American [Airlines] has figured out what Southwest Airlines and others have known for some time: There is a cost to complexity." What does the author mean by a "cost to complexity"? How does Southwest Airlines avoid this cost?

Source: Scott McCartney, "Large Carriers Are Beginning to Discover the Benefits of Simplicity," *Wall Street Journal*, August 15, 2002, p. D4.

4.6 In early 2004, Yahoo was set to challenge Google as the leading online search engine. According to an article in the *Wall Street Journal*, Yahoo's strategy was "not simply to match what Google does now but to add features its rival can't easily match." The article quoted a senior vice president at Yahoo as stating, "We're not going to beat the competition by being the competition." Briefly explain what the Yahoo executive means by "being the competition." Briefly discuss whether the strategy of "being the competition" ever makes sense.

Source: Mylene Mangalindan, "Yahoo Gets Set to Give Google a Run for Its Money," *Wall Street Journal*, January 6, 2004.

4.7 The following is from an article in the *Wall Street Journal*:

As U.S. car makers continue to offer generous cash discounts and cut-rate financing to woo buyers, top Japanese manufacturers are taking a different pricing approach that seems to be working: Hold sticker prices steady but pack cars with alluring new features.

What happens to the profit a car company makes on each car sold if it cuts the price while holding the car's features constant? What happens to the company's profit per car if the company adds new features while holding the price constant? Briefly discuss how a car company might decide which of these strategies to use.

Source: Todd Zaun, "Japanese Battle U.S. Discounts with Extras," *Wall Street Journal*, January 6, 2004.

>> End Learning Objective 13.4

Chapter 14

Monopoly and Antitrust Policy

Time Warner Rules Manhattan

Today most people can hardly imagine life without cable television. In fact, almost 80 percent of U.S. homes have cable television: a larger fraction than have clothes dryers, dishwashers, air conditioning, or personal computers. The first cable systems were established in the 1940s in cities that were too small to support broadcast stations. Those systems consisted of large antennas set up on hills to receive broadcasts from television stations within range. The signals were then transmitted by cable to individual houses.

The cable industry grew slowly because the technology did not exist to rebroadcast the signals of distant stations, so cable systems offered just a few channels. By 1970, only about 7 percent of households had cable television. In addition, the Federal Communications Commission (FCC)—the U.S. government agency that regulates the television industry—placed restrictions on both rebroadcasting the signals of distant stations and the fees that could be charged for "premium channels" that would show movies or sporting events. In the

two key developments occurred: First, satellite relay technology made it feasible for local cable systems to receive signals relayed by satellite from distant broadcast stations. Second, Congress loosened regulations on rebroadcasting distant stations and premium channels. The result of these developments was the growth of both "superstations," which are local broadcast stations in large cities—such as New York, Chicago, and Atlanta—whose programming is sent by satellite to cable systems around the country, and premium channels, such as Home Box Office (HBO).

One of the most successful of the superstations was WTBS, started by Atlanta entrepreneur Robert Edward "Ted" Turner III. Turner went on to found the Turner Broadcasting System (TBS), which included the Cable News Network (CNN), the first 24-hour news network. In 2001, Turner was involved in the largest merger of entertainment companies in history, when AOL Time Warner was formed. The company—now known as Time Warner—was made up of leading firms from four segments of the entertainment industry: Warner Brothers (movie making), *Time* (magazine publishing), TBS (cable television),

and AOL (Internet). Today, Time Warner operates cable systems in 22 states through Time Warner Cable.

A firm needs a license from the city government to enter a local cable television market. If you live in Manhattan and you want cable television, you have to purchase it from Time Warner Cable. Other cable companies could ask the New York City government for licenses to compete against Time Warner Cable in Manhattan, but none have. This is not an unusual situation for a cable television system: Of the nearly 9,000 markets for cable television in the United States, fewer than 400 have competing cable systems.

As the only provider of cable TV in Manhattan, Time Warner has a *monopoly*. Few firms in the United States are monopolies because in a market system, whenever a firm earns economic profits, other firms will enter its market. Therefore, it is very difficult for a firm to remain the only provider of a good or service. In this chapter, we will develop an economic model of monopoly that can help us analyze how such firms affect the economy. **AN INSIDE LOOK AT POLICY** on **page 496** explores how legislation in California is lowering barriers to entry in the cable TV market.

LEARNING Objectives

After studying this chapter, you should be able to:

14.1 Define **monopoly**, page 474.

14.2 Explain the four main **reasons monopolies arise**, page 475.

14.3 Explain how a monopoly chooses **price** and **output**, page 481.

14.4 Use a graph to illustrate how a monopoly affects **economic efficiency**, page 485.

14.5 Discuss **government policies** toward monopoly, page 488.

Economics in YOUR Life!

Why Can't I Watch the NFL Network?

Are you a fan of the National Football League? Would you like to see more NFL-related programming on television? If so, you're not alone. The NFL felt there was so much demand for more football programming that it began its own football network, the NFL Network.

Unfortunately for many football fans, the NFL Network is not available to most households with cable television. Why are some of the largest cable TV systems unwilling to include the NFL Network in their channel lineups? Why are some systems requiring customers who want the NFL Network to upgrade to more expensive channel packages or digital service? As you read this chapter, see if you can answer these questions. You can check your answers against those we provide at the end of the chapter. **>> Continued on page 495**

Although few firms are monopolies, the economic model of monopoly can still be quite useful. As we saw in Chapter 11, even though perfectly competitive markets are rare, this market model provides a benchmark for how a firm acts in the most competitive situation possible: when it is in an industry with many firms that all supply the same product. Monopoly provides a benchmark for the other extreme, where a firm is the only one in its market and, therefore, faces no competition from other firms supplying its product. The monopoly model is also useful in analyzing situations in which firms agree to *collude*, or not compete, and act together as if they were a monopoly. As we will discuss in this chapter, collusion is illegal in the United States, but it occasionally happens.

Monopolies also pose a dilemma for the government. Should the government allow monopolies to exist? Are there circumstances in which the government should actually promote the existence of monopolies? Should the government regulate the prices monopolies charge? If so, will such price regulation increase economic efficiency? In this chapter, we will explore these public policy issues.

14.1 LEARNING OBJECTIVE

14.1 | Define monopoly.

Is Any Firm Ever Really a Monopoly?

Monopoly A firm that is the only seller of a good or service that does not have a close substitute.

A **monopoly** is a firm that is the only seller of a good or service that does not have a close substitute. Because substitutes of some kind exist for just about every product, can any firm really be a monopoly? The answer is "yes," provided that the substitutes are not "close" substitutes. But how do we decide whether a substitute is a close substitute? A narrow definition of monopoly that some economists use is that a firm has a monopoly if it can ignore the actions of all other firms. In other words, other firms must not be producing close substitutes if the monopolist can ignore the other firms' prices. For example, candles are a substitute for electric lights, but your local electric company can ignore candle prices because however low the price of candles falls, almost no customers will give up using electric lights and switch to candles. Therefore, your local electric company is clearly a monopoly.

Many economists, however, use a broader definition of monopoly. For example, suppose Joe Santos owns the only pizza parlor in a small town. (We will consider later the question of *why* a market may have only a single firm.) Does Joe have a monopoly? Substitutes for pizzas certainly exist. If the price of pizza is too high, people will switch to hamburgers or fried chicken or some other food instead. People do not have to eat at Joe's or starve. Joe is in competition with the local McDonald's and Kentucky Fried Chicken, among other firms. So, Joe does not meet the narrow definition of a monopoly. But many economists would still argue that it is useful to think of Joe as having a monopoly.

Although hamburgers and fried chicken are substitutes for pizza, competition from firms selling them is not enough to keep Joe from earning economic profits. We saw in Chapter 11 that when firms earn economic profits, we can expect new firms to enter the industry, and in the long run, the economic profits are competed away. Joe's profits will not be competed away as long as he is the *only* seller of pizza. Using the broader definition, Joe has a monopoly because there are no other firms selling a substitute close enough that his economic profits are competed away in the long run.

Making the Connection | Is Xbox 360 a Close Substitute for PlayStation 3?

In the early 2000s, Microsoft's Xbox and Sony's PlayStation 2 (PS2) were the best-selling video game consoles. When the two companies began work on the next generation of consoles, they had important decisions to make. In developing the Xbox, Microsoft had decided to include a hard disk and a version of the Windows computer operating system. As a result, the cost of producing the Xbox was much higher than the cost to Sony of producing the PlayStation 2. Microsoft was not concerned by the higher production cost because it believed it would be able to charge a higher price for Xbox than Sony charged for PlayStation 2. Unfortunately for Microsoft, consumers considered the Sony PS2 a close substitute for the Xbox. Microsoft was forced to charge the same price for the Xbox that Sony charged for the PS2. So, while Sony was able to make a substantial profit at that price, Microsoft initially lost money on the Xbox because of its higher costs.

To many gamers, PlayStation 3 is a close substitute for Xbox.

In developing the next generation of video game consoles, both companies hoped to produce devices that could serve as multipurpose home-entertainment systems. To achieve this goal, the new systems needed to play DVDs as well as games. Sony developed a new type of DVD called Blu-ray. Blu-ray DVDs can store five times as much data as conventional DVDs and can play back high-definition (HD) video. Sony's decision to give the new PlayStation 3 (PS3) the capability to play Blu-ray DVDs was risky in two ways: First, it raised the cost of producing the consoles. Second, because there is a competing second-generation standard for DVDs, called HD-DVD, the PlayStation 3 would not be capable of playing all available second-generation DVDs, thereby reducing its appeal to some consumers. Microsoft decided to sell its Xbox 360 with only the capability of playing older-format DVDs, while making available an add-on component that would play HD-DVDs.

Early indications were that Microsoft may have made the better decision. Consumers seemed to consider the PS3 and the Xbox to be close substitutes. In that case, the fact that the PS3's price was $200 higher than the Xbox 360's price was a significant problem for Sony. Ironically, Sony made the same mistake Microsoft made several years before when it launched the Xbox to compete with PS2.

Sources: Stephen H, Wildstrom, "PlayStation 3: It's Got Game," *BusinessWeek*, December 4, 2006; and "Sony: Playing a Long Game," *Economist*, November 16, 2006.

YOUR TURN: Test your understanding by doing related problem 1.7 on page 498 at the end of this chapter.

14.2 | Explain the four main reasons monopolies arise.

14.2 LEARNING OBJECTIVE

Where Do Monopolies Come From?

Because monopolies do not face competition, every firm would like to have a monopoly. But to have a monopoly, barriers to entering the market must be so high that no other firms can enter. *Barriers to entry* may be high enough to keep out competing firms for four main reasons:

1 Government blocks the entry of more than one firm into a market.

2 One firm has control of a key resource necessary to produce a good.

3 There are important *network externalities* in supplying the good or service.

4 Economies of scale are so large that one firm has a *natural monopoly*.

Entry Blocked by Government Action

As we will discuss later in this chapter, governments ordinarily try to promote competition in markets, but sometimes governments take action to block entry into a market. In the United States, government blocks entry in two main ways:

1 By granting a *patent* or *copyright* to an individual or firm, giving it the exclusive right to produce a product.

2 By granting a firm a *public franchise*, making it the exclusive legal provider of a good or service.

Patent The exclusive right to a product for a period of 20 years from the date the product is invented.

Patents and Copyrights The U.S. government grants patents to firms that develop new products or new ways of making existing products. A **patent** gives a firm the exclusive right to a new product for a period of 20 years from the date the product is invented. Because Microsoft has a patent on the Windows operating system, other firms cannot sell their own versions of Windows. The government grants patents to encourage firms to spend money on the research and development necessary to create new products. If other firms could have freely copied Windows, Microsoft is unlikely to have spent the money necessary to develop it. Sometimes firms are able to maintain a monopoly in the production of a good without patent protection, provided that they can keep secret how the product is made.

Patent protection is of vital importance to pharmaceutical firms as they develop new prescription drugs. Pharmaceutical firms start research and development work on a new prescription drug an average of 12 years before the drug is available for sale. A firm applies for a patent about 10 years before it begins to sell the product. The average 10-year delay between the government granting a patent and the firm actually selling the drug is due to the federal Food and Drug Administration's requirements that the firm demonstrate that the drug is both safe and effective. Therefore, during the period before the drug can be sold, the firm will have substantial costs to develop and test the drug. If the drug does not make it successfully to market, the firm will have a substantial loss.

Once a drug is available for sale, the profits the firm earns from the drug will increase throughout the period of patent protection—which is usually about 10 years—as the drug becomes more widely known to doctors and patients. After the patent has expired, other firms are free to legally produce chemically identical drugs called *generic drugs*. Gradually, competition from generic drugs will eliminate the profits the original firm had been earning. For example, when patent protection expired for Glucophage, a diabetes drug manufactured by Bristol-Myers Squibb, sales of the drug declined by more than $1.5 billion in the first year due to competition from 12 generic versions of the drug produced by other firms. When the patent expired on Prozac, an antidepressant drug manufactured by Eli Lilly, sales dropped by more than 80 percent. Most economic profits from selling a prescription drug are eliminated 20 years after the drug is first offered for sale.

Making the Connection | The End of the Christmas Plant Monopoly

In December, the poinsettia plant seems to be almost everywhere, decorating stores, restaurants, and houses. Although it may seem strange that anyone can have a monopoly on the production of a plant, for many years the Paul Ecke Ranch in Encinitas, California, had a monopoly on poinsettias.

The poinsettia is a wildflower native to Mexico. It was almost unknown in the United States before Albert Ecke, a German immigrant, began selling it in the early twentieth century at his flower stand in Hollywood, California. Unlike almost every other flowering plant, the poinsettia blossoms in the winter. This timing, along with the plant's striking red and green colors, makes the Poinsettia ideal for Christmas decorating.

Albert Ecke's son, Paul, discovered that by grafting together two varieties of poinsettias, it was possible to have multiple branches grow from one stem. The result was a plant that had more leaves and was much more colorful than conventional poinsettias. Paul Ecke did not attempt to patent his new technique for growing poinsettias. But because the Ecke family kept the technique secret for decades, it was able to maintain a monopoly on the commercial production of the plants. Unfortunately for the Ecke family—but fortunately for consumers—a university researcher discovered the technique and published it in an academic journal.

New firms quickly entered the industry, and the price of poinsettias plummeted. Soon consumers could purchase them for as little as three for $10. At those prices, the Ecke's firm was unable to earn economic profits. Eventually, Paul Ecke III, the owner of the firm, decided to sell off more than half the firm's land to fund new state-of-the-art

At one time, the Ecke family had a monopoly on growing poinsettias, but many new firms entered the industry.

greenhouses and research into new varieties of plants that he hoped would earn the firm economic profits once again. One of the firm's new products was a variety of white poinsettias that could be spray-painted in different colors and sold for $10 or more—double the price of plain poinsettias.

Sources: Bart Ziegler, "What Color Is Your Poinsettia?" *Wall Street Journal*, December 14, 2006; Cynthia Crossen, "Holiday's Ubiquitous Houseplant," *Wall Street Journal*, December 19, 2000; and Mike Freeman and David E. Graham, "Ecke Ranch Plans to Sell Most of Its Remaining Land," *San Diego Union-Tribune*, December 11, 2003.

YOUR TURN: Test your understanding by doing related problem 2.9 on page 499 at the end of this chapter.

Just as the government grants a new product patent protection, books, films, and software receive **copyright** protection. U.S. law grants the creator of a book, film, or piece of music the exclusive right to use the creation during the creator's lifetime. The creator's heirs retain this exclusive right for 70 years after the creator's death. In effect, copyrights create monopolies for the copyrighted items. Without copyrights, individuals and firms would be less likely to invest in creating new books, films, and software.

Copyright A government-granted exclusive right to produce and sell a creation.

Public Franchises In some cases, the government grants a firm a **public franchise** that allows it to be the only legal provider of a good or service. For example, state and local governments often designate one company as the sole provider of electricity, natural gas, or water.

Public franchise A designation by the government that a firm is the only legal provider of a good or service.

Occasionally, the government may decide to provide certain services directly to consumers through a *public enterprise*. This is much more common in Europe than in the United States. For example, the governments in most European countries own the railroad systems. In the United States, many city governments provide water and sewage service themselves rather than rely on private firms.

Control of a Key Resource

Another way for a firm to become a monopoly is by controlling a key resource. This happens infrequently because most resources, including raw materials such as oil or iron ore, are widely available from a variety of suppliers. There are, however, a few prominent examples of monopolies based on control of a key resource, such as the Aluminum Company of America (Alcoa) and the International Nickel Company of Canada.

For many years until the 1940s, Alcoa either owned or had long-term contracts to buy nearly all of the available bauxite, the mineral needed to produce aluminum. Without access to bauxite, competing firms had to use recycled aluminum, which limited the amount of aluminum they could produce. Similarly, the International Nickel Company of Canada controlled more than 90 percent of available nickel supplies. Competition in the nickel market increased when the Petsamo nickel fields in northern Russia were developed after World War II.

In the United States, a key resource for a professional sports team is a large stadium. The teams that make up the major professional sports leagues—Major League Baseball, the National Football League, and the National Basketball Association—usually have long-term leases with the stadiums in major cities. Control of these stadiums is a major barrier to new professional baseball, football, or basketball leagues forming.

Making the Connection | **Are Diamond Profits Forever? The De Beers Diamond Monopoly**

The most famous monopoly based on control of a raw material is the De Beers diamond mining and marketing company of South Africa. Before the 1860s, diamonds were extremely rare. Only a few pounds of diamonds were produced each year, primarily from Brazil and India. Then in 1870,

De Beers promoted the sentimental value of diamonds as a way to maintain its position in the diamond market.

enormous deposits of diamonds were discovered along the Orange River in South Africa. It became possible to produce thousands of pounds of diamonds per year, and the owners of the new mines feared that the price of diamonds would plummet. To avoid financial disaster, the mine owners decided in 1888 to merge and form De Beers Consolidated Mines, Ltd.

De Beers became one of the most profitable and longest-lived monopolies in history. The company has carefully controlled the supply of diamonds to keep prices high. As new diamond deposits were discovered in Russia and Zaire, De Beers was able to maintain prices by buying most of the new supplies.

Because diamonds are rarely destroyed, De Beers has always worried about competition from the resale of stones. Heavily promoting diamond engagement and wedding rings with the slogan "A Diamond Is Forever" was a way around this problem. Because engagement and wedding rings have great sentimental value, they are seldom resold, even by the heirs of the original recipients. De Beers advertising has been successful even in some countries, such as Japan, that have had no custom of giving diamond engagement rings. As the populations in De Beers's key markets age, its advertising in recent years has focused on middle-aged men presenting diamond rings to their wives as symbols of financial success and continuing love and on professional women buying "right-hand rings" for themselves.

In the past few years, competition has finally come to the diamond business. By 2000, De Beers directly controlled only about 40 percent of world diamond production. The company became concerned about the amount it was spending to buy diamonds from other sources to keep them off the market. It decided to adopt a strategy of differentiating its diamonds by relying on its name recognition. Each De Beers diamond is now marked with a microscopic brand—a "Forevermark"—to reassure consumers of its high quality. Other firms, such as BHP Billiton, which owns mines in northern Canada, have followed suit by branding their diamonds. Sellers of Canadian diamonds stress that they are "mined under ethical, environmentally friendly conditions," as opposed to "blood diamonds," which are supposedly "mined under armed force in war-torn African countries and exported to finance military campaigns." Whether consumers will pay attention to brands on diamonds remains to be seen, although through 2006, the branding strategy had helped De Beers maintain its 40 percent share of the diamond market.

Sources: Edward Jay Epstein, "Have You Ever Tried to Sell a Diamond?" *Atlantic Monthly*, February 1982; Donna J. Bergenstock, Mary E. Deily, and Larry W. Taylor, "A Cartel's Response to Cheating: An Empirical Investigation of the De Beers Diamond Empire," *Southern Economic Journal*, Vol. 73, No. 1, July 2006, pp. 173–189; Bernard Simon, "Adding Brand Names to Nameless Stones," *New York Times*, June 27, 2002; Blythe Yee, "Ads Remind Women They Have Two Hands," *Wall Street Journal*, August 14, 2003; quote in last paragraph from Joel Baglole, "Political Correctness by the Carat," *Wall Street Journal*, April 17, 2003.

YOUR TURN: Test your understanding by doing related problem 2.10 on page 499 at the end of this chapter.

Network Externalities

Network externalities The situation where the usefulness of a product increases with the number of consumers who use it.

There are **network externalities** in the consumption of a product if the usefulness of the product increases with the number of people who use it. If you owned the only cell phone in the world, for example, it would not be very valuable. The more cell phones there are in use, the more valuable they become to consumers.

Some economists argue that network externalities can serve as barriers to entry. For example, in the early 1980s, Microsoft gained an advantage over other software companies by developing MS-DOS, the operating system for the first IBM personal computers. Because IBM sold more computers than any other company, software developers wrote many application programs for MS-DOS. The more people who used MS-DOS–based programs, the greater the usefulness to a consumer of using an MS-DOS–based program. Today, Windows, the program Microsoft developed to succeed MS-DOS, has a 95 percent share in the market for personal computer operating systems (although

Windows has a much lower share in the market for operating systems for servers). If another firm introduced a competing operating system, some economists argue that relatively few people would use it initially, and few applications would run on it, which would limit the operating system's value to other consumers.

eBay was the first Internet site to attract a significant number of people to its online auctions. Once a large number of people began to use eBay to buy and sell collectibles, antiques, and many other products, it became a more valuable place to buy and sell. Yahoo.com, Amazon.com, and other Internet sites eventually started online auctions, but they found it difficult to attract buyers and sellers. On eBay, a buyer expects to find more sellers, and a seller expects to find more potential buyers than on Amazon or other auction sites.

As these examples show, network externalities can set off a *virtuous cycle*: If a firm can attract enough customers initially, it can attract additional customers because its product's value has been increased by more people using it, which attracts even more customers, and so on. With products such as computer operating systems and online auctions, it might be difficult for new firms to enter the market and compete away the profits being earned by the first firm in the market.

Economists engage in considerable debate, however, about the extent to which network externalities are important barriers to entry in the business world. Some economists argue that the dominant positions of Microsoft and eBay reflect the efficiency of those firms in offering products that satisfy consumer preferences more than the effects of network externalities. In this view, the advantages existing firms gain from network externalities would not be enough to protect them from competing firms offering better products. In other words, a firm entering the operating system market with a program better than Windows or a firm offering an Internet auction site better than eBay would be successful despite the effects of network externalities. (We discussed this point in more detail in Chapter 9.)

Natural Monopoly

We saw in Chapter 10 that economies of scale exist when a firm's long-run average costs fall as it increases the quantity of output it produces. A **natural monopoly** occurs when economies of scale are so large that one firm can supply the entire market at a lower average total cost than two or more firms. In that case, there is really "room" in the market for only one firm.

Figure 14-1 shows the average total cost curve for a firm producing electricity and the total demand for electricity in the firm's market. Notice that the average total cost

Natural monopoly A situation in which economies of scale are so large that one firm can supply the entire market at a lower average total cost than can two or more firms.

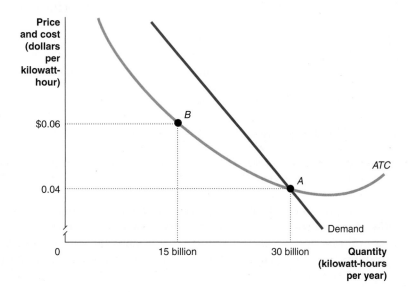

Figure 14-1

Average Total Cost Curve for a Natural Monopoly

With a natural monopoly, the average total cost curve is still falling when it crosses the demand curve (point *A*). If only one firm is producing electric power in the market and it produces where average cost intersects the demand curve, average total cost will equal $0.04 per kilowatt-hour of electricity produced. If the market is divided between two firms, each producing 15 billion kilowatt-hours, the average cost of producing electricity rises to $0.06 per kilowatt-hour (point *B*). In this case, if one firm expands production, it can move down the average total cost curve, lower its price, and drive the other firm out of business.

curve is still falling when it crosses the demand curve at point *A*. If the firm is a monopoly and produces 30 billion kilowatt-hours of electricity per year, its average total cost of production will be $0.04 per kilowatt-hour. Suppose instead that two firms are in the market, each producing half of the market output, or 15 billion kilowatt-hours per year. Assume that each firm has the same average total cost curve. The figure shows that producing 15 billion kilowatt-hours would move each firm back up its average cost curve so that the average cost of producing electricity would rise to $0.06 per kilowatt-hour (point *B*). In this case, if one of the firms expands production, it will move down the average total cost curve. With lower average costs, it will be able to offer electricity at a lower price than the other firm can. Eventually, the other firm will be driven out of business, and the remaining firm will have a monopoly. Because a monopoly would develop automatically—or *naturally*—in this market, it is a natural monopoly.

Natural monopolies are most likely to occur in markets where fixed costs are very large relative to variable costs. For example, a firm that produces electricity must make a substantial investment in machinery and equipment necessary to generate the electricity and in wires and cables necessary to distribute it. Once the initial investment has been made, however, the marginal cost of producing another kilowatt-hour of electricity is relatively small.

Solved Problem | 14-2

Is the "Proxy Business" a Natural Monopoly?

A corporation is owned by its shareholders, who elect members of the corporation's board of directors and who also vote on particularly important issues of corporate policy. The shareholders of large corporations are spread around the country, and relatively few of them are present at the annual meetings at which elections take place. Before each meeting, corporations must provide shareholders with annual reports and forms that allow them to vote by mail. Voting by mail is referred to as "proxy voting." People who work on Wall Street refer to providing annual reports and ballots to shareholders as the "proxy business." Currently, one company, Broadridge, controls almost all of the proxy business.

According to the *Wall Street Journal*, Don Kittell of the Securities Industry Association has explained Broadridge's virtual monopoly by arguing that, "The economies of scale and the efficiencies achieved by Broadridge handling all the brokerage business—rather than multiple companies—resulted in savings to [corporations]."

a. Assuming that Kittell is correct, draw a graph showing the market for handling proxy materials. Be sure that the graph contains the demand for proxy materials and Broadridge's average total cost curve. Explain why cost savings result from having the proxy business handled by a single firm.

b. According to a spokesperson for Broadridge, the proxy business produces a profit rate of about 7 percent, which is lower than the profit rate the company receives from any of its other businesses. Does this information support or undermine Kittell's analysis? Explain.

SOLVING THE PROBLEM:

Step 1: **Review the chapter material.** This problem is about natural monopoly, so you may want to review the section "Natural Monopoly," which begins on page 479.

Step 2: **Answer question (a) by drawing a natural monopoly graph and discussing the potential cost savings in this industry.** Kittell describes a situation of natural monopoly. Otherwise, the entry of another firm into the market would not raise average cost. Draw a natural monopoly graph, like the one in Figure 14-1:

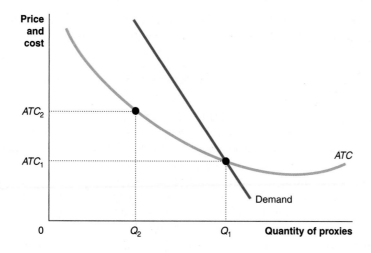

Make sure your average total cost curve is still declining when it crosses the demand curve. If one firm can supply Q_1 proxies at an average total cost of ATC_1, then dividing the business equally between two firms each supplying Q_2 proxies would raise average total cost to ATC_2.

Step 3: **Answer question (b) by discussing the implications of Broadridge's low profit rate in the proxy business.** If Broadridge earns a low profit rate on its investment in this business even though it has a monopoly, Kittell probably is correct that the proxy business is a natural monopoly.

EXTRA CREDIT: Keep in mind that competition is not good for its own sake. It is good because it can lead to lower costs, lower prices, and better products. In certain markets, however, cost conditions are such that competition is likely to lead to higher costs and higher prices. These markets are natural monopolies that are best served by one firm.

Source: Phyllis Plitch, "Competition Remains Issue in Proxy-Mailing Costs," *Wall Street Journal*, January 16, 2002.

YOUR TURN: For more practice, do related problem 2.11 on page 499 at the end of this chapter.

>> **End Solved Problem 14-2**

14.3 | Explain how a monopoly chooses price and output.   **14.3 LEARNING** OBJECTIVE

How Does a Monopoly Choose Price and Output?

Like every other firm, a monopoly maximizes profit by producing where marginal revenue equals marginal cost. A monopoly differs from other firms in that *a monopoly's demand curve is the same as the demand curve for the product.* We emphasized in Chapter 11 that the market demand curve for wheat was very different from the demand curve for the wheat produced by any one farmer. If, however, one farmer had a monopoly on wheat production, the two demand curves would be exactly the same.

Marginal Revenue Once Again

Recall from Chapter 11 that firms in perfectly competitive markets—such as a farmer in the wheat market—face horizontal demand curves. They are *price takers.* All other firms, including monopolies, are *price makers.* If price makers raise their prices, they will lose some, but not all, of their customers. Therefore, they face a downward-sloping demand curve and a downward-sloping marginal revenue curve as well. Let's review why a firm's marginal revenue curve slopes downward if its demand curve slopes downward.

Remember that when a firm cuts the price of a product, one good thing happens, and one bad thing happens:

- **The good thing.** It sells more units of the product.

- **The bad thing.** It receives less revenue from each unit than it would have received at the higher price.

For example, consider the table in Figure 14-2, which shows the demand curve for Time Warner Cable's basic cable package. For simplicity, we assume that the market has only 10 potential subscribers instead of the millions it actually has. If Time Warner charges a price of $60 per month, it won't have any subscribers. If it charges a price of $57, it sells 1 subscription. At $54, it sells 2, and so on. Time Warner's total revenue is equal to the number of subscriptions sold per month multiplied by the price. The firm's average revenue—or revenue per subscription sold—is equal to its total revenue divided by the quantity of subscriptions sold. Time Warner is particularly interested in marginal revenue because marginal revenue tells the firm how much revenue will increase if it cuts the price to sell one more subscription.

Notice that Time Warner's marginal revenue is less than the price for every subscription sold after the first subscription. To see why, think about what happens if Time Warner cuts the price of its basic cable package from $42 to $39, which increases its subscriptions sold from 6 to 7. Time Warner increases its revenue by the $39 it receives for the seventh subscription. But it also loses revenue of $3 per subscription on the first 6 subscriptions because it could have sold them at the old price of $42. So, its marginal

Figure 14-2

Calculating a Monopoly's Revenue

Time Warner Cable faces a downward-sloping demand curve for subscriptions to basic cable. To sell more subscriptions, it must cut the price. When this happens, it gains the revenue from selling more subscriptions but loses revenue from selling at a lower price the subscriptions that it could have sold at a higher price. The firm's marginal revenue is the change in revenue from selling another subscription. We can calculate marginal revenue by subtracting the revenue lost as a result of a price cut from the revenue gained. The table shows that Time Warner's marginal revenue is less than the price for every subscription sold after the first subscription. Therefore, Time Warner's marginal revenue curve will be below its demand curve.

Subscribers per Month (Q)	Price (P)	Total Revenue (TR = P x Q)	Average Revenue (AR = TR/Q)	Marginal Revenue (MR = ΔTR/ΔQ)
0	$60	$0	–	–
1	57	57	$57	$57
2	54	108	54	51
3	51	153	51	45
4	48	192	48	39
5	45	225	45	33
6	42	252	42	27
7	39	273	39	21
8	36	288	36	15
9	33	297	33	9
10	30	300	30	3

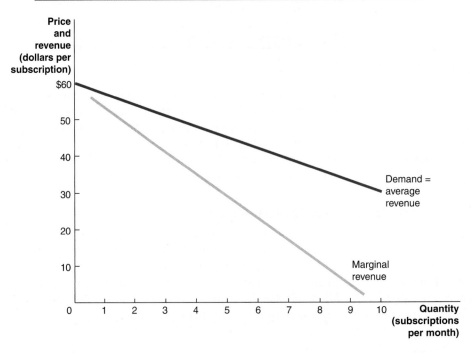

revenue on the seventh subscription is $39 − $18 = $21, which is the value shown in the table. The graph in Figure 14-2 plots Time Warner's demand and marginal revenue curves, based on the information given in the table.

Profit Maximization for a Monopolist

Figure 14-3 shows how Time Warner combines the information on demand and marginal revenue with information on average and marginal costs to decide how many subscriptions to sell and what price to charge. We assume that the firm's marginal cost and average total cost curves have the usual U shapes we encountered in Chapters 10 and 11. In panel (a), we see how Time Warner can calculate its profit-maximizing quantity and price. As long as the marginal cost of selling one more subscription is less than the marginal revenue, the firm should sell additional subscriptions because it is adding to its profits. As Time Warner sells more cable subscriptions, rising marginal cost will eventually equal marginal revenue, and the firm will be selling the profit-maximizing quantity of subscriptions. This happens with the sixth subscription, which adds $27 to the firm's costs and $27 to its revenues (point A in panel (a) of Figure 14-3). The demand curve tells us that Time Warner can sell 6 subscriptions for a price of $42 per month. We can conclude that Time Warner's profit-maximizing quantity of subscriptions is 6 and its profit-maximizing price is $42.

Panel (b) shows that the average total cost of 6 subscriptions is $30 and that Time Warner can sell 6 subscriptions at a price of $42 per month (point B on the demand curve). Time Warner is making a profit of $12 per subscription—the price of $42 minus the average cost of $30. Its total profit is $72 (6 subscriptions × $12 profit per subscription), which is shown by the area of the green-shaded rectangle in the figure. We could also have calculated Time Warner's total profit as the difference between its total revenue and its total cost. Its total revenue from selling 6 subscriptions is $252. Its total cost equals its average cost multiplied by the number of subscriptions sold, or $30 × 6 = $180. So, its profit is $252 − $180 = $72.

It's important to note that even though Time Warner is earning economic profits, new firms will *not* enter the market. Because Time Warner has a monopoly, it will not face competition from other cable operators. Therefore, if other factors remain unchanged, Time Warner will be able to continue to earn economic profits, even in the long run.

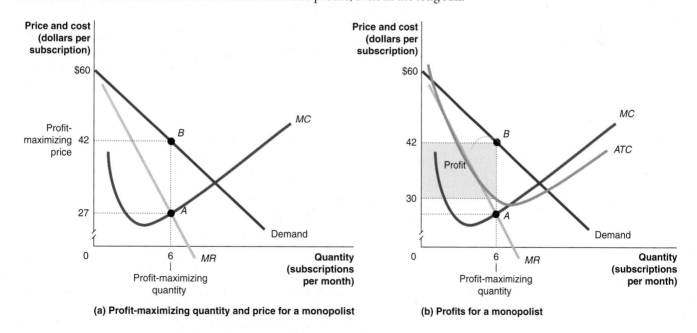

(a) Profit-maximizing quantity and price for a monopolist

(b) Profits for a monopolist

Figure 14-3 | Profit-Maximizing Price and Output for a Monopoly

Panel (a) shows that to maximize profit, Time Warner should sell subscriptions up to the point that the marginal revenue from selling the last subscription equals its marginal cost (point A). In this case, the marginal revenue from selling the sixth subscription and the marginal cost are both $27. Time Warner maximizes profit by selling 6

subscriptions per month and charging a price of $42 (point B). In panel (b), the green box represents Time Warner's profits. The box has a height equal to $12, which is the price of $42 minus the average total cost of $30, and a base equal to the quantity of 6 cable subscriptions. Time Warner's profit equals $12 × 6 = $72.

Solved Problem | 14-3

Finding the Profit-Maximizing Price and Output for a Monopolist

Suppose that Comcast has a cable monopoly in Philadelphia. The following table gives Comcast's demand and costs per month for subscriptions to basic cable (for simplicity, we once again keep the number of subscribers artificially small).

PRICE	QUANTITY	TOTAL REVENUE	MARGINAL REVENUE $(MR = \Delta TR/\Delta Q)$	TOTAL COST	MARGINAL COST $(MC = \Delta TC/\Delta Q)$
$17	3			$56	
16	4			63	
15	5			71	
14	6			80	
13	7			90	
12	8			101	

a. Fill in the missing values in the table.

b. If Comcast wants to maximize profits, what price should it charge and how many cable subscriptions per month should it sell? How much profit will Comcast make? Briefly explain.

c. Suppose the local government imposes a $2.50 per month tax on cable companies. Now what price should Comcast charge, how many subscriptions should it sell, and what will its profits be?

SOLVING THE PROBLEM:

Step 1: **Review the chapter material.** This problem is about finding the profit-maximizing quantity and price for a monopolist, so you may want to review the section "Profit Maximization for a Monopolist," which begins on page 483.

Step 2: **Answer question (a) by filling in the missing values in the table.** Remember that to calculate marginal revenue and marginal cost, you must divide the change in total revenue or total cost by the change in quantity.

PRICE	QUANTITY	TOTAL REVENUE	MARGINAL REVENUE $(MR = \Delta TR/\Delta Q)$	TOTAL COST	MARGINAL COST $(MC = \Delta TC/\Delta Q)$
$17	3	$51	—	$56	—
16	4	64	$13	63	$7
15	5	75	11	71	8
14	6	84	9	80	9
13	7	91	7	90	10
12	8	96	5	101	11

We don't have enough information from the table to fill in the values for marginal revenue or marginal cost in the first row.

Step 3: **Answer question (b) by determining the profit-maximizing quantity and price.** We know that Comcast will maximize profits by selling subscriptions up to the point where marginal cost equals marginal revenue. In this case, that means selling 6 subscriptions per month. From the information in the first two columns, we know Comcast can sell 6 subscriptions at a price of $14 each. Comcast's profits are equal to the difference between its total revenue and its total cost: Profit = $84 − $80 = $4 per month.

Step 4: **Answer question (c) by analyzing the impact of the tax.** This tax is a fixed cost to Comcast because it is a flat $2.50, no matter how many subscriptions it sells. Because the tax has no impact on Comcast's marginal revenue or marginal cost, the profit-maximizing level of output has not changed. So, Comcast will still sell 6 subscriptions per month at a price of $14, but its profits will fall by the amount of the tax from $4.00 per month to $1.50.

YOUR TURN: For more practice, do related problems 3.3 and 3.4 on page 500 at the end of this chapter.

>> **End Solved Problem 14-3**

14.4 | Use a graph to illustrate how a monopoly affects economic efficiency.

14.4 LEARNING OBJECTIVE

Does Monopoly Reduce Economic Efficiency?

We saw in Chapter 11 that a perfectly competitive market is economically efficient. How would economic efficiency be affected if instead of being perfectly competitive, a market were a monopoly? In Chapter 4, we developed the idea of *economic surplus*. Economic surplus provides a way of characterizing the economic efficiency of a perfectly competitive market: *Equilibrium in a perfectly competitive market results in the greatest amount of economic surplus, or total benefit to society, from the production of a good or service.* What happens to economic surplus under monopoly? We can begin the analysis by considering the hypothetical case of what would happen if the market for television sets begins as perfectly competitive and then becomes a monopoly. (In reality, the market for television sets is not perfectly competitive, but assuming that it is simplifies our analysis.)

Comparing Monopoly and Perfect Competition

Panel (a) in Figure 14-4 illustrates the situation if the market for televisions is perfectly competitive. Price and quantity are determined by the intersection of the demand and supply curves. Remember that none of the individual firms in a perfectly competitive industry has any control over price. Each firm must accept the price determined by the market. Panel (b) shows what happens if the television industry becomes a monopoly. We know that the monopoly will maximize profits by producing where marginal revenue equals marginal cost. To do this, the monopoly reduces the quantity of televisions

---

Don't Let This Happen to **YOU!**

Don't Assume That Charging a Higher Price Is Always More Profitable for a Monopolist

In answering question (c) of Solved Problem 14-3, it's tempting to argue that Comcast should increase its price to make up for the tax. After all, Comcast is a monopolist, so why can't it just pass along the tax to its customers? The reason it can't is that Comcast, like any other monopolist, must pay attention to demand. Comcast is not interested in charging high prices for the sake of charging high prices; it is interested in maximizing profits. Charging a price of $1,000 for a basic cable subscription sounds nice, but if no one will buy at that price, Comcast would hardly be maximizing profits.

To look at it another way, before the tax is imposed, Comcast has already determined $14 is the price that will maximize its profits. After the tax is imposed, it must determine whether $14 is still the profit-maximizing price. Because the tax has not affected Comcast's marginal revenue or marginal cost (or had any effect on consumer demand), $14 is still the profit-maximizing price, and Comcast should continue to charge it. The tax cuts into Comcast's profits but doesn't cause it to increase the price of cable subscriptions.

YOUR TURN: Test your understanding by doing related problems 3.7 and 3.8 on page 500 at the end of this chapter.

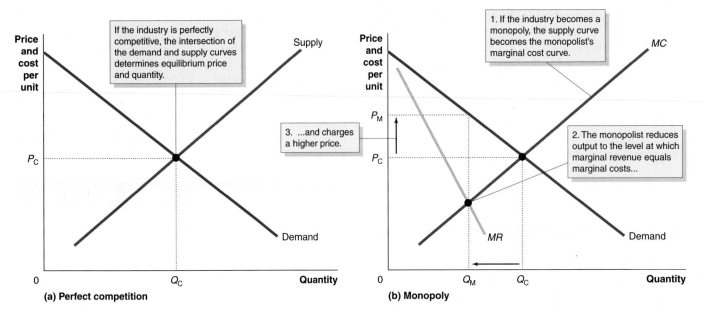

Figure 14-4 | What Happens If a Perfectly Competitive Industry Becomes a Monopoly?

In panel (a), the market for television sets is perfectly competitive, and price and quantity are determined by the intersection of the demand and supply curves. In panel (b), the perfectly competitive television industry became a monopoly. As a result, the equilibrium quantity falls, and the equilibrium price rises.

1. The industry supply curve becomes the monopolist's marginal cost curve.
2. The monopolist reduces output to where marginal revenue equals marginal cost, Q_M.
3. The monopolist raises the price from P_C to P_M.

that would have been produced if the industry were perfectly competitive and increases the price. Panel (b) illustrates an important conclusion: *A monopoly will produce less and charge a higher price than would a perfectly competitive industry producing the same good.*

Measuring the Efficiency Losses from Monopoly

Figure 14-5 uses panel (b) from Figure 14-4 to illustrate how monopoly affects consumers, producers, and the efficiency of the economy. Recall from Chapter 4 that *consumer surplus* measures the net benefit received by consumers from purchasing a good or service. We measure consumer surplus as the area below the demand curve and above the market price. The higher the price, the smaller the consumer surplus. Because a monopoly raises the market price, it reduces consumer surplus. In Figure 14-5, the loss of consumer surplus is equal to rectangle *A* plus triangle *B*. Remember that *producer surplus* measures the net benefit to producers from selling a good or service. We measure producer surplus as the area above the supply curve and below the market price. The increase in price due to monopoly increases producer surplus by an amount equal to rectangle *A* and reduces it by an amount equal to triangle *C*. Because rectangle *A* is larger than triangle *C*, we know that a monopoly increases producer surplus compared with perfect competition.

Economic surplus is equal to the sum of consumer surplus plus producer surplus. By increasing price and reducing the quantity produced, the monopolist has reduced economic surplus by an amount equal to the areas of triangles *B* and *C*. This reduction in economic surplus is called *deadweight loss* and represents the loss of economic efficiency due to monopoly.

The best way to understand how a monopoly causes a loss of economic efficiency is to recall that price is equal to marginal cost in a perfectly competitive market. As a result, a consumer in a perfectly competitive market is always able to buy a good if she is willing to pay a price equal to the marginal cost of producing it. As Figure 14-5 shows, the monopolist stops producing at a point where the price is well above marginal cost. Consumers are unable to buy some units of the good for which they would be willing to pay a price greater

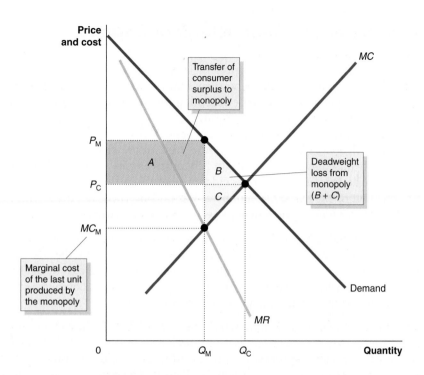

Figure 14-5

The Inefficiency of Monopoly

A monopoly charges a higher price, P_M, and produces a smaller quantity, Q_M, than a perfectly competitive industry, which charges a price of P_C and produces at Q_C. The higher price reduces consumer surplus by the area equal to the rectangle A and the triangle B. Some of the reduction in consumer surplus is captured by the monopoly as producer surplus, and some becomes deadweight loss, which is the area equal to triangles B and C.

than the marginal cost of producing them. Why doesn't the monopolist produce this additional output? Because the monopolist's profits are greater if it restricts output and forces up the price. A monopoly produces the profit-maximizing level of output but fails to produce the efficient level of output from the point of view of society.

We can summarize the effects of monopoly as follows:

1 Monopoly causes a reduction in consumer surplus.

2 Monopoly causes an increase in producer surplus.

3 Monopoly causes a deadweight loss, which represents a reduction in economic efficiency.

How Large Are the Efficiency Losses Due to Monopoly?

We know that there are relatively few monopolies, so the loss of economic efficiency due to monopoly must be small. Many firms, though, have **market power**, which is the ability of a firm to charge a price greater than marginal cost. The analysis we just completed shows that some loss of economic efficiency will occur whenever a firm has market power and can charge a price greater than marginal cost, even if the firm is not a monopoly. The only firms that do *not* have market power are firms in perfectly competitive markets, who must charge a price equal to marginal cost. Because few markets are perfectly competitive, *some loss of economic efficiency occurs in the market for nearly every good or service.*

Is the total loss of economic efficiency due to market power large or small? It is possible to put a dollar value on the loss of economic efficiency by estimating for every industry the size of the deadweight loss triangle, as in Figure 14-5. The first economist to do this was Arnold Harberger of the University of Chicago. His estimates—largely confirmed by later researchers—indicated that the total loss of economic efficiency in the U.S. economy due to market power is small. According to his estimates, if every industry in the economy were perfectly competitive, so that price were equal to marginal cost in every market, the gain in economic efficiency would equal less than 1 percent of the value of total production in the United States, or about $450 per person.

The loss of economic efficiency is this small primarily because true monopolies are very rare. In most industries, competition keeps price much closer to marginal cost than would be the case in a monopoly. The closer price is to marginal cost, the smaller the size of the deadweight loss.

Market power The ability of a firm to charge a price greater than marginal cost.

Market Power and Technological Change

Some economists have raised the possibility that the economy may actually benefit from firms having market power. This argument is most closely identified with Joseph Schumpeter, an Austrian economist who spent many years as a professor of economics at Harvard. Schumpeter argued that economic progress depended on technological change in the form of new products. For example, the replacement of horse-drawn carriages by automobiles, the replacement of ice boxes by refrigerators, and the replacement of mechanical calculators by electronic computers all represent technological changes that significantly raised living standards. In Schumpeter's view, new products unleash a "gale of creative destruction" that drives older products—and, often, the firms that produced them—out of the market. Schumpeter was unconcerned that firms with market power would charge higher prices than perfectly competitive firms:

> It is not that kind of [price] competition which counts but the competition from the new commodity, the new technology, the new source of supply, the new type of organization . . . competition which commands a decisive cost or quality advantage and which strikes not at the margins of the profits and outputs of the existing firms but at their foundations and their very lives.

Economists who support Schumpeter's view argue that the introduction of new products requires firms to spend funds on research and development. It is possible for firms to raise this money by borrowing from investors or from banks. But investors and banks are usually skeptical of ideas for new products that have not yet passed the test of consumer acceptance in the market. As a result, firms are often forced to rely on their profits to finance the research and development needed for new products. Because firms with market power are more likely to earn economic profits than are perfectly competitive firms, they are also more likely to carry out research and development and introduce new products. In this view, the higher prices firms with market power charge are unimportant compared with the benefits from the new products these firms introduce to the market.

Some economists disagree with Schumpeter's views. These economists point to the number of new products developed by smaller firms, including, for example, Steve Jobs and Steve Wozniak inventing the first Apple computer in Wozniak's garage, and Larry Page and Sergey Brin inventing the Google search engine as graduate students at Stanford. As we will see in the next section, government policymakers continue to struggle with the issue of whether, on balance, large firms with market power are good or bad for the economy.

14.5 LEARNING OBJECTIVE

14.5 | Discuss government policies toward monopoly.

Government Policy toward Monopoly

Collusion An agreement among firms to charge the same price or otherwise not to compete.

Because monopolies reduce consumer surplus and economic efficiency, most governments have policies that regulate their behavior. Recall from Chapter 13 that **collusion** refers to an agreement among firms to charge the same price or otherwise not to compete. In the United States, government policies with respect to monopolies and collusion are embodied in the *antitrust laws*. These laws make illegal any attempts to form a monopoly or to collude. Governments also regulate firms that are natural monopolies, often by controlling the prices they charge.

Antitrust Laws and Antitrust Enforcement

The first important law regulating monopolies in the United States was the Sherman Act, which Congress passed in 1890 to promote competition and prevent the formation of monopolies. Section 1 of the Sherman Act outlaws "every contract, combination in the form of trust or otherwise, or conspiracy in restraint of trade." Section 2 states that "every person who shall monopolize, or attempt to monopolize, or combine or conspire with any other person or persons, to monopolize any part of the trade or commerce . . . shall be deemed guilty of a felony."

The Sherman Act targeted firms in several industries that had combined together during the 1870s and 1880s to form "trusts." In a trust, the firms were operated independently but gave voting control to a board of trustees. The board enforced collusive agreements for the firms to charge the same price and not to compete for each other's customers. The most notorious of the trusts was the Standard Oil Trust, organized by John D. Rockefeller. After the Sherman Act was passed, trusts disappeared, but the term **antitrust laws** has lived on to refer to the laws aimed at eliminating collusion and promoting competition among firms.

The Sherman Act prohibited trusts and collusive agreements, but it left several loopholes. For example, it was not clear whether it would be legal for two or more firms to merge to form a new, larger firm that would have substantial market power. A series of Supreme Court decisions interpreted the Sherman Act narrowly, and the result was a wave of mergers at the turn of the twentieth century. Included in these mergers was the U.S. Steel Corporation, which was formed from dozens of smaller companies. U.S. Steel, organized by J. P. Morgan, was the first billion-dollar corporation, and it controlled two-thirds of steel production in the United States. The Sherman Act also left unclear whether any business practices short of outright collusion were illegal.

To address the loopholes in the Sherman Act, in 1914, Congress passed the Clayton Act and the Federal Trade Commission Act. Under the Clayton Act, a merger was illegal if its effect was "substantially to lessen competition, or to tend to create a monopoly." The Federal Trade Commission Act set up the Federal Trade Commission (FTC), which was given the power to police unfair business practices. The FTC has brought lawsuits against firms employing a variety of business practices, including deceptive advertising. In setting up the FTC, however, Congress divided the authority to police mergers. Currently, both the Antitrust Division of the U.S. Department of Justice and the FTC are responsible for merger policy. Table 14-1 lists the most important U.S. antitrust laws and the purpose of each.

Antitrust laws Laws aimed at eliminating collusion and promoting competition among firms.

Mergers: The Trade-off between Market Power and Efficiency

The federal government regulates business mergers because it knows that if firms gain market power by merging, they may use that market power to raise prices and reduce output. As a result, the government is most concerned with **horizontal mergers**, or mergers between firms in the same industry. Horizontal mergers are more likely to increase market power than **vertical mergers**, which are mergers between firms at different stages of the production of a good. An example of a vertical merger would be a merger between a company making personal computers and a company making computer hard drives.

Horizontal merger A merger between firms in the same industry.

Vertical merger A merger between firms at different stages of production of a good.

LAW	DATE	PURPOSE
Sherman Act	1890	Prohibited "restraint of trade," including price fixing and collusion. Also outlawed monopolization.
Clayton Act	1914	Prohibited firms from buying stock in competitors and from having directors serve on the boards of competing firms.
Federal Trade Commission Act	1914	Established the Federal Trade Commission (FTC) to help administer antitrust laws.
Robinson–Patman Act	1936	Prohibited charging buyers different prices if the result would reduce competition.
Cellar–Kefauver Act	1950	Toughened restrictions on mergers by prohibiting any mergers that would reduce competition.

TABLE 14-1

Important U.S. Antitrust Laws

Regulating horizontal mergers can be complicated by two factors. First, the "market" that firms are in is not always clear. For example, if Hershey Foods wants to merge with Mars, Inc., maker of M&Ms, Snickers, and other candies, what is the relevant market? If the government looks just at the candy market, the newly merged company would have more than 70 percent of the market, a level at which the government would likely oppose the merger. What if the government looks at the broader market for "snacks"? In this market, Hershey and Mars compete with makers of potato chips, pretzels, peanuts, and, perhaps, even producers of fresh fruit. Of course, if the government looked at the very broad market for "food," then both Hershey and Mars have very small market shares, and there would be no reason to oppose their merger. In practice, the government defines the relevant market on the basis of whether there are close substitutes for the products being made by the merging firms. In this case, potato chips and the other snack foods mentioned are not close substitutes for candy. So, the government would consider the candy market to be the relevant market and would oppose the merger on the grounds that the new firm would have too much market power.

The second factor that complicates merger policy is the possibility that the newly merged firm might be more efficient than the merging firms were individually. For example, one firm might have an excellent product but a poor distribution system for getting the product into the hands of consumers. A competing firm might have built a great distribution system but have an inferior product. Allowing these firms to merge might be good for both the firms and consumers. Or, two competing firms might each have an extensive system of warehouses that are only half full, but if the firms merged, they could consolidate their warehouses and significantly reduce their costs.

An example of the government dealing with the issue of greater efficiency versus reduced competition occurred in early 2000, when Time Warner—which owns cable systems with more than 20 million subscribers—and America Online (AOL)—which was the country's largest Internet service provider (ISP), with more than 26 million subscribers—announced plans to merge. The firms argued that the merger would speed the development of high-speed (or "broadband") Internet access and would lead to more rapid growth of services such as interactive television. Some competing firms complained that the new firm created by the merger would have excessive market power. In particular, other ISPs were worried that they would be denied access to the cable systems owned by Time Warner. After more than a year of study, the FTC finally approved the merger, subject to certain conditions. One key condition was that Time Warner was required to allow AOL's competitors to offer their services over Time Warner's high-speed cable lines before AOL would be permitted to offer its services over those lines.

Most of the mergers that come under scrutiny by the Department of Justice and the FTC are between large firms. For simplicity, let's consider a case where all the firms in a perfectly competitive industry want to merge to form a monopoly. As we saw in Figure 14-5, as a result of this merger, prices will rise and output will fall, leading to a decline in consumer surplus and economic efficiency. But what if the larger, newly merged firm actually is more efficient than the smaller firms had been? Figure 14-6 shows a possible result.

If costs are unaffected by the merger, we get the same result as in Figure 14-5: Price rises from P_C to P_M, quantity falls from Q_C to Q_M, consumer surplus is lower, and a loss of economic efficiency results. If the monopoly has lower costs than the competitive firms, it is possible for price to decline and quantity to increase. In Figure 14-6, to find the new profit-maximizing quantity, note where MR crosses MC after the merger. This new profit-maximizing quantity is Q_{Merge}. The demand curve shows that the monopolist can sell this quantity at a price of P_{Merge}. Therefore, the price declines after the merger from P_C to P_{Merge} and quantity increases from Q_C to Q_{Merge}. We have the following seemingly paradoxical result: *Although the newly merged firm has a great deal of market power, because it is more efficient, consumers are better off and economic efficiency is improved.* Of course, sometimes a merged firm will be more efficient and have lower costs, and other times it won't. Even if a merged firm is more efficient and has lower costs, that may not offset the increased market power of the firm enough to increase consumer surplus and economic efficiency.

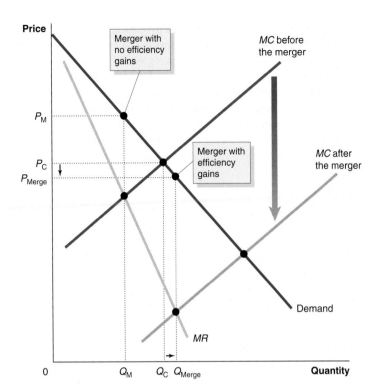

Figure 14-6

A Merger That Makes Consumers Better Off

This figure shows the result of all the firms in a perfectly competitive industry merging to form a monopoly. If costs are unaffected by the merger, the result is the same as in Figure 14-5 on page 487: Price rises from P_C to P_M, quantity falls from Q_C to Q_M, consumer surplus declines, and a loss of economic efficiency results. If, however, the monopoly has lower costs than the perfectly competitive firms, as shown by the marginal cost curve shifting to *MC* after the merger, it is possible that the price will actually decline from P_C to P_{Merge} and output will increase from Q_C to Q_{Merge} following the merger.

As you might expect, whenever large firms propose a merger, they claim that the newly merged firm will be more efficient and have lower costs. They realize that without these claims, it is unlikely their merger will be approved. It is up to the Department of Justice and the FTC, along with the court system, to evaluate the merits of these claims.

The Department of Justice and Federal Trade Commission Merger Guidelines

For many years after the passage of the Sherman Antitrust Act in 1890, lawyers from the Department of Justice enforced the antitrust laws. They rarely considered economic arguments, such as the possibility that consumers might be made better off by a merger if economic efficiency were significantly improved. This began to change in 1965, when Donald Turner became the first Ph.D. economist to head the Antitrust Division of the Department of Justice. Under Turner and his successors, economic analysis shaped antitrust policy. In 1973, the Economics Section of the Antitrust Division was established and staffed with economists who evaluate the economic consequences of proposed mergers.

Economists played a major role in the development of merger guidelines by the Department of Justice and the FTC in 1982. The guidelines made it easier for firms considering a merger to understand whether the government was likely to allow the merger or to oppose it. The guidelines have three main parts:

1 Market definition

2 Measure of concentration

3 Merger standards

Market Definition A market consists of all firms making products that consumers view as close substitutes. We can identify close substitutes by looking at the effect of a price increase. If our definition of a market is too narrow, a price increase will cause firms to experience a significant decline in sales—and profits—as consumers switch to buying close substitutes.

Identifying the relevant market involved in a proposed merger begins with a narrow definition of the industry. For the hypothetical merger of Hershey Foods and Mars, Inc., discussed previously in this chapter, we might start with the candy industry. If all firms in the candy industry increased price by 5 percent, would their profits increase or decrease? If profits would increase, the market is defined as being just these firms. If profits would decrease, we would try a broader definition—say, by adding in potato chips and other snacks. Would a price increase of 5 percent by all firms in the broader market raise profits? If profits increase, the relevant market has been identified. If profits decrease, we consider a broader definition. We continue this procedure until a market has been identified.

Measure of Concentration A market is *concentrated* if a relatively small number of firms have a large share of total sales in the market. A merger between firms in a market that is already highly concentrated is very likely to increase market power. A merger between firms in an industry that has a very low concentration is unlikely to increase market power and can be ignored. The guidelines use the *Herfindahl-Hirschman Index (HHI)* of concentration, which squares the market shares of each firm in the industry and adds up the values of the squares. The following are some examples of calculating a Herfindahl-Hirschman Index:

- 1 firm, with 100% market share (a monopoly):

$$HHI = 100^2 = 10,000$$

- 2 firms, each with a 50% market share:

$$HHI = 50^2 + 50^2 = 5,000$$

- 4 firms, with market shares of 30%, 30%, 20%, and 20%:

$$HHI = 30^2 + 30^2 + 20^2 + 20^2 = 2,600$$

- 10 firms, each with market shares of 10%:

$$HHI = 10\,(10^2) = 1,000$$

Merger Standards The Department of Justice and the FTC use the HHI calculation for a market to evaluate proposed horizontal mergers according to these standards:

- *Post-merger HHI below 1,000.* These markets are not concentrated, so mergers in them are not challenged.

- *Post-merger HHI between 1,000 and 1,800.* These markets are moderately concentrated. Mergers that raise the HHI by less than 100 probably will not be challenged. Mergers that raise the HHI by more than 100 may be challenged.

- *Post-merger HHI above 1,800.* These markets are highly concentrated. Mergers that increase the HHI by less than 50 points will not be challenged. Mergers that increase the HHI by 50 to 100 points may be challenged. Mergers that increase the HHI by more than 100 points will be challenged.

Increases in economic efficiency will be taken into account and can lead to approval of a merger that otherwise would be opposed, but the burden of showing that the efficiencies exist lies with the merging firms:

> The merging firms must substantiate efficiency claims so that the [Department of Justice and the FTC] can verify by reasonable means the likelihood and magnitude of each asserted efficiency. . . . Efficiency claims will not be considered if they are vague or speculative or otherwise cannot be verified by reasonable means.

Making the Connection

Should the Government Prevent Banks from Becoming Too Big?

For many years, state and federal regulations kept banks small. Until the 1990s, federal regulations required a bank to operate in only a single state. This restriction on interstate banking meant that there were no nationwide banks. As recently as the 1980s, some states—including Illinois and Texas—did not allow banks to have branches. So, if a bank opened in Chicago, it could not have branches in other cities in Illinois. Today, these regulations have been repealed, and banks are free to have as many branches as they choose and can operate nationwide. Many economists believe that the old regulations on banks reduced economic efficiency. If there are significant economies of scale in banking, then keeping banks artificially small by not allowing them to operate in more than one state will drive up their average cost of providing banking services. As a result, consumers will have to pay higher interest rates on loans and will receive lower interest rates on deposits.

The elimination of government regulations on nationwide banking and on branch banking led to a sharp decline in the number of banks. In the early 1980s, there were 14,500 banks in the United States; today there are fewer than 7,500. Smaller, less efficient banks were acquired by larger banks or went out of business, and some large banks merged with other large banks. There is, however, still one limit on the size of banks. In 1994, when Congress removed restrictions on interstate banking, it wrote into the law a restriction that no bank mergers would be allowed if they resulted in one bank having more than 10 percent of all bank deposits. This provision was included because some smaller, community-based banks were afraid that they would be unable to compete against large, nationwide banks.

The Top-Five U.S. Banks by Domestic Deposits, Through Sept. 30 of Each Year

2006	Dometic deposits, in billions	Percentage of all U.S. deposits	1994	Dometic deposits, in billions	Percentage of all U.S. deposits
Bank of America	$584.33	**9.0%**	Bank of America	$125.59	**4.0%**
J.P. Morgan Chase	447.30	**6.9**	NationsBank	87.44	**2.8**
Wachovia/Golden West Financial*	375.61	**5.8**	Chemical Banking	66.86	**2.1**
Wells Fargo	295.14	**4.6**	Banc One	64.74	**2.1**
Citigroup	226.26	**3.5**	First Union	52.54	**1.7**

Note: Deposit share information is based on FDIC quarterly reports. The Federal Reserve, which approves acquisitions, uses a slightly different definition of deposits.
* Figures are combined to reflect merger which took place Oct. 1, 2006
Source: FDIC call reports

As the chart shows, at the time the government removed restrictions on interstate banking, no bank was near the 10 percent limit. But by the end of 2006, Bank of America had 9 percent of all U.S. deposits and was considering mergers that would have brought its share above 10 percent. Bank of America Chairman and Chief Executive Kenneth D. Lewis began to push for Congress to remove the 10 percent limit. He argued that because other countries did not have limits on the size of banks, foreign banks were able to take advantage of economies of scale beyond what was possible for U.S. banks. In a position paper, Bank of America argued, "In time, the mega-foreign banks will be positioned to acquire the largest U.S. banks." Many community banks, though, remained opposed to lifting the 10 percent limit. Some consumer groups also argued that very large banks would have enough market power to raise interest rates on loans and lower interest rates on deposits because they would have less competition. Members of Congress considering the possibility of changing the law had to face the usual question raised by antitrust policy: Will a potential increase in monopoly power made possible by lifting the 10-percent limit be offset by gains in economic efficiency?

Source: Valerie Bauerlein and Damian Paletta, "Bank of America Quietly Targets Barrier to Growth," *Wall Street Journal*, January 16, 2007, p. A1.

YOUR TURN: Test your understanding by doing related problem 5.16 on page 504 at the end of this chapter.

Regulating Natural Monopolies

If a firm is a natural monopoly, competition from other firms will not play its usual role of forcing price down to the level where the company earns zero economic profit. As a result, local or state *regulatory commissions* usually set the prices for natural monopolies, such as firms selling natural gas or electricity. What price should these commissions set? Recall from Chapter 11 that economic efficiency requires the last unit of a good or service produced to provide an additional benefit to consumers equal to the additional cost of producing it. We can measure the additional benefit consumers receive from the last unit by the price and the additional cost to the monopoly of producing the last unit by marginal cost. Therefore, to achieve economic efficiency, regulators should require that the monopoly charge a price equal to its marginal cost. There is, however, an important drawback to doing so, which is illustrated in Figure 14-7. This figure shows the situation of a typical regulated natural monopoly.

Remember that with a natural monopoly, the average total cost curve is still falling when it crosses the demand curve. If unregulated, the monopoly will charge a price equal to P_M and produce Q_M. To achieve economic efficiency, regulators should require the monopoly to charge a price equal to P_E. The monopoly will then produce Q_E. But here is the drawback: P_E is less than average total cost, so the monopoly will be suffering a loss, shown by the area of the red-shaded rectangle. In the long run, the owners of the monopoly will not continue in business if they are experiencing losses. Realizing this, most regulators will set the regulated price, P_R, equal to the level of average total cost at which the demand curve intersects the *ATC* curve. At that price, the owners of the monopoly are able to break even on their investment by producing the quantity Q_R.

Figure 14-7

Regulating a Natural Monopoly

A natural monopoly that is not subject to government regulation will charge a price equal to P_M and produce Q_M. If government regulators want to achieve economic efficiency, they will set the regulated price equal to P_E, and the monopoly will produce Q_E. Unfortunately, P_E is below average cost, and the monopoly will suffer a loss, shown by the shaded rectangle. Because the monopoly will not continue to produce in the long run if it suffers a loss, government regulators set a price equal to average cost, which is P_R in the figure.

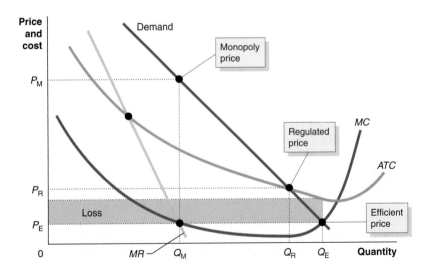

Economics in YOUR Life

>> Continued from page 473

At the beginning of the chapter, we asked why many cable systems won't carry the NFL Network. You might think that the cable systems would want to televise one of the most popular sports in the nation. In most cities, a customer of a cable system can't switch to a competing cable system, so many areas cable systems can be the sole source of many programs. (Although some consumers have the option of switching to satellite television.) As a result, a cable system can increase its profits by, for example, not offering popular programming such as the NFL Network as part of its normal programming package, requiring instead that consumers upgrade to digital programming at a higher price.

Conclusion

The more intense the level of competition among firms, the better a market works. In this chapter, we have seen that with monopoly—where competition is entirely absent—price is higher, output is lower, and consumer surplus and economic efficiency decline compared with perfect competition. Fortunately, true monopolies are rare. Even though most firms resemble monopolies in being able to charge a price above marginal cost, most markets have enough competition to keep the efficiency losses from market power quite low.

We've seen that barriers to entry are an important source of market power. Read *An Inside Look at Policy* on the next page for a discussion of how legislation in California is lowering barriers to entry into the cable TV market.

As Barriers Fall, Will Cable TV Competition Rise?

WALL STREET JOURNAL, SEPTEMBER 28, 2006

Cable Guys

In an era of partisan nastiness and gridlock, the California legislature did something on Aug. 31 that was shockingly harmonious, reasonable and beneficial to consumers. Both parties voted overwhelmingly to allow competition into a sector—cable television—where prices have been elevated and service depressed by the most pernicious monopoly in America.

When Gov. Arnold Schwarzenegger signs the bill, as expected, companies that want a statewide video franchise can go straight to the Public Utility Commission and get approval to operate within 44 days. In the past, in California, as in other states, cable companies had to make separate deals with America's 33,760 municipal units—a process that can take years. . . .

The effect was to create cable monopolies that often infuriated captive customers. According to a 2004 study by the Government Accountability Office, "cable subscribers in about 2% of all markets have the opportunity to choose between two or more wire-based operators." As cable rates rose in the 1980s, the federal government tried to fix the market with more regulation. That attempt, of course, failed. For the five years ending January 2004, the Federal Communications Commission reports that average cable rates increased 7.8% annually, compared with a 2.1% increase in the Consumer Price Index.

Very quietly, things are changing. Seven states, comprising about one-third of the U.S. population, have now passed video franchise laws, which will not only lower monthly subscriber costs but also create new technology jobs—10,000 in California alone, according to one estimate—as Verizon and AT&T, along with cable overbuilders like RCN, jump in with both feet. To bring high-quality video to the home over a technology called Internet protocol, the telcos will make major investments to drive the fiber—which carries the data—much more deeply into their networks. Broadband service will improve; state and local governments will still get their franchise fees. All that will end is a monopoly that drives consumers nuts. . . .

With a national election coming up, you would expect Congress to get on the bandwagon and embrace a version of the state bills, killing the monopoly and taking the credit. Instead, federal legislation is slowed down by measures promoting "net neutrality"—the concept that telecom companies should be barred from asking content providers, like Amazon, to pay extra for higher-speed service the telcos develop—the way that an airline asks more for a first-class seat. . . .

How much will consumers save? A 2004 study by the GAO looked at six markets with cable competition and found that rates were 15% to 41% below similar markets with no competition. Annual savings for U.S. households through competition will total $8 billion, says the Phoenix Center for Advanced Legal and Economic Public Policy.

In Texas, where a statewide franchising law went into effect last year, a study by the American Consumer Institute surveyed consumers and found that 22% switched cable providers and saved an average of $22.30 per month. Subscribers who stayed with incumbent providers saved $26.83 per month because of the downward pressure on prices. Verizon rolled out a service in Keller, Plano and Lewisville, charging $43.95 a month for 180 video and music channels. "Shortly thereafter," writes the Heartland Institute's Steven Titch, Charter, the erstwhile monopoly cable provider, "began offering a bundle of 240 channels and fast Internet service for $50 a month, compared to $68.99 Charter had been charging for the TV package alone." Savings in Texas this year alone will total $599 million, according to the Phoenix Center. Yale Braunstein, an economist at the University of California at Berkeley, estimates that Californians will save between $692 million and $1 billion a year.

Yes, Americans can choose satellite TV, but, for reasons of convenience and service, many find it an inadequate substitute. There's a reason that cable families far outnumber satellite families. "Overall customer satisfaction among satellite subscribers has declined," says Steve Kirkeby, senior director of telecommunication research for J.D. Power and Associates. . . .

Source: James K. Glassman, "Cable Guys," Wall Street Journal, September 28, 2006. Copyright © 2006 Dow Jones. Reprinted by permission of Dow Jones via Copyright Clearance Center.

Key Points in the Article

This article discusses a change in regulatory policy toward cable television in California. The change should make it easier for new cable firms to enter the market. As a result, prices for cable TV should fall, and we should see more firms offering cable TV in California cities. This article indicates that an increase in quantity and a decrease in price occurs as policy makes entry into the cable TV market easier.

Analyzing the News

(a) In California, the state government's requirement that a cable provider buy

a franchise in each jurisdiction was a barrier to entry because of the high cost of franchises. By allowing firms a statewide license, California has made it easier for them to enter the cable TV market in a given jurisdiction, making competition more likely. In fact, the relative lack of competition in many local cable television markets was partly the result of technology—laying more than one set of cables to an individual home would be very expensive—and partly the result of government regulations, which often allowed only one firm to be in the market.

(b) Entry, of course, will reduce the economic profit existing firms earn. The figure illustrates what happens as entry occurs and the market becomes competitive. For simplicity, we assume that the marginal cost of providing cable services is constant, so the marginal cost curve is a horizontal line. Notice that output increases from Q_M to Q_C, and price falls from P_M to

P_C. You can also see that consumer surplus increases from areas $A + E$ to areas $A + E + B + C + D$, and the deadweight loss in the market (area D) disappears and becomes consumer surplus. In this figure, what were profits to the monopoly (areas $B + C$) are redistributed to consumers as consumer surplus. Economic profits fall to zero.

(c) One of the benefits of competition is that firms compete not just by cutting prices, but also by improving the services they offer. Here, we see cable systems competing by providing more services and channels to their customers.

Thinking Critically
About Policy

1. What is the most a firm would be willing to spend to remain the sole provider of cable television in a market?
2. Even with a statewide franchise, what might prevent new cable TV firms from entering local markets?

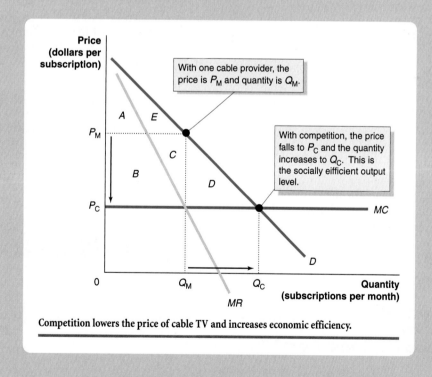

Competition lowers the price of cable TV and increases economic efficiency.

Key Terms

Antitrust laws, p. 489

Collusion, p. 488

Copyright, p. 477

Horizontal merger, p. 489

Market power, p. 487

Monopoly, p. 474

Natural monopoly, p. 479

Network externalities, p. 478

Patent, p. 476

Public franchise, p. 477

Vertical merger, p. 489

14.1 LEARNING OBJECTIVE   14.1 | Define monopoly, **pages 474–475.**

Is Any Firm Ever Really a Monopoly?

Summary

A **monopoly** exists only in the rare situation in which a firm is producing a good or service for which there are no close substitutes. A narrow definition of monopoly that some economists use is that a firm has a monopoly if it can ignore the actions of all other firms. Many economists favor a broader definition of monopoly. Under the broader definition, a firm has a monopoly if no other firms are selling a substitute close enough that the firm's economic profits are competed away in the long run.

 Visit www.myeconlab.com to complete these exercises online and get instant feedback.

Review Questions

1.1 What is a monopoly? Can a firm be a monopoly if close substitutes for its product exist?

1.2 If you own the only hardware store in a small town, do you have a monopoly?

Problems and Applications

1.3 Is "monopoly" a good name for the game *Monopoly*? What aspects of the game involve monopoly? Explain briefly, using the definition of monopoly.

1.4 (Related to the *Chapter Opener* on page 472) Some observers say that changes in the past few years have eroded the monopoly power of local cable TV companies, even though no other cable firms have entered their markets. What are these changes? Do these "monopoly" firms still have monopoly power?

1.5 Are there any products for which there are no substitutes? Are these the only products for which it would be possible to have a monopoly? Briefly explain.

1.6 An economist argues, "No firm can remain a monopoly for long in the face of technological change." Do you agree?

1.7 (Related to the *Making the Connection* on page 474) Microsoft thought that the initial Xbox was sufficiently different from PS2 that it could charge a significantly higher price for the Xbox than Sony could charge for PS2. As it turns out, Microsoft was wrong. Draw the average total cost and marginal cost curves for Microsoft's Xbox. Now draw the demand curve Microsoft thought would exist for Xbox and the demand curve that actually existed. Why were the two demand curves different? Show on your graph the profits Microsoft would earn with each demand curve.

>> **End Learning Objective 14.1**

14.2 LEARNING OBJECTIVE   14.2 | Explain the four main reasons monopolies arise, **pages 475–481.**

Where Do Monopolies Come From?

Summary

To have a monopoly, barriers to entering the market must be so high that no other firms can enter. Barriers to entry may be high enough to keep out competing firms for four main reasons: (1) government blocks the entry of more than one firm into a market by issuing a **patent**, which is the exclusive right to a product for 20 years, or a **copyright**, which is the exclusive right to produce and sell a creation, or giving a firm a **public franchise**, which is the right to be the only legal provider of a good or service (2) one firm has control of a key raw material necessary to produce a good, (3) there are important *network externalities* in supplying the good or service, or (4) economies of scale are so large that one firm has a *natural monopoly*. **Network externalities** refer to the situation where the usefulness of a product increases with the number of consumers who use it. A **natural monopoly** is a situation in which economies of scale are so large that one firm can supply the entire market at a lower average cost than two or more firms.

 Visit www.myeconlab.com to complete these exercises *Get Ahead of the Curve* online and get instant feedback.

Review Questions

2.1 What are the four most important ways a firm becomes a monopoly?

2.2 If patents reduce competition, why does the federal government grant them?

2.3 What is a public franchise? Are all public franchises natural monopolies?

2.4 What is "natural" about a natural monopoly?

Problems and Applications

2.5 The U.S. Postal Service (USPS) is a monopoly because the federal government has blocked entry into the market for delivering first-class mail. Is it also a natural monopoly? How can we tell? What would happen if the law preventing competition in this market were removed?

2.6 Patents are granted for 20 years, but pharmaceutical companies can't use their patent-guaranteed monopoly powers for anywhere near this long because it takes several years to acquire FDA approval of drugs. Should the life of drug patents be extended to 20 years *after* FDA approval? What would be the costs and benefits of this extension?

2.7 Just as a new product or a new method of making a product receives patent protection from the government, books, articles, and essays receive copyright protection. Under U.S. law, authors have the exclusive right to their writings during their lifetimes—unless they sell this right, as most authors do to their

publishers—and their heirs retain this exclusive right for 50 years after their death. The historian Thomas Macaulay once described the copyright law as "a tax on readers to give a bounty to authors." In what sense does the existence of the copyright law impose a tax on readers? What "bounty" do copyright laws give authors? Discuss whether the government would be doing readers a favor by abolishing the copyright law.

Source of quote: Thomas Mallon, *Stolen Words: The Classic Book on Plagiarism*, San Diego: Harcourt, 2001 (original ed. 1989), p. 59.

2.8 The German company Koenig & Bauer has 90 percent of the world market for presses that print currency. Discuss the factors that would make it difficult for new companies to enter this market.

2.9 (Related to the *Making the Connection* on page 476) Would the Ecke's have been better off if they had patented their process for growing poinsettias? Briefly explain.

2.10 (Related to the *Making the Connection* on page 477) Why was De Beers worried that people might resell their old diamonds? How did De Beers attempt to convince consumers that used diamonds were not good substitutes for new diamonds? How did De Beers' strategy affect the demand curve for new diamonds? How were De Beers' profits affected?

2.11 (Related to *Solved Problem 14-2* on page 480) Suppose that the quantity demanded per day for a product is 90 when the price is $35. The following table shows costs for a firm with a monopoly in this market:

QUANTITY (PER DAY)	TOTAL COST
30	$1,200
40	1,400
50	2,250
60	3,000

Briefly explain whether this firm has a natural monopoly in this market.

>> **End Learning Objective 14.2**

14.3 LEARNING OBJECTIVE 14.3 | Explain how a monopoly chooses price and output, **pages 481–485.**

How Does a Monopoly Choose Price and Output?

Summary

Monopolists face downward-sloping demand and marginal revenue curves and, like all other firms, maximize profit by producing where marginal revenue equals marginal cost.

Unlike a perfect competitor, a monopolist that earns economic profits does not face the entry of new firms into the market. Therefore, a monopolist can earn economic profits, even in the long run.

Visit www.myeconlab.com to complete these exercises
Get Ahead of the Curve online and get instant feedback.

Review Questions

3.1 What is the relationship between a monopolist's demand curve and the market demand curve? What is the relationship between a monopolist's demand curve and its marginal revenue curve?

3.2 Draw a graph that shows a monopolist that is earning a profit. Be sure your graph includes the monopolist's demand, marginal revenue, average total cost, and marginal cost curves. Be sure to indicate the profit-maximizing level of output and price.

Problems and Applications

3.3 **(Related to** *Solved Problem 14-3* **on page 484)** Ed Scahill has acquired a monopoly on the production of baseballs (don't ask how), and faces the demand and cost situation given in the following table:

PRICE	QUANTITY (PER WEEK)	TOTAL REVENUE	MARGINAL REVENUE	TOTAL COST	MARGINAL COST
$20	15,000			$330,000	
19	20,000			365,000	
18	25,000			405,000	
17	30,000			450,000	
16	35,000			500,000	
15	40,000			555,000	

a. Fill in the remaining values in the table.
b. If Ed wants to maximize profits, what price should he charge and how many baseballs should he sell? How much profit will he make?
c. Suppose the government imposes a tax of $50,000 per week on baseball production. Now what price should Ed charge, how many baseballs should he sell, and what will his profits be?

3.4 **(Related to** *Solved Problem 14-3* **on page 484)** Use the information in Solved Problem 14-3 to answer the following questions.
a. What will Comcast do if the tax is $6.00 per month instead of $2.50? (*Hint:* Will its decision be different in the long run than in the short run?)
b. Suppose that the flat per-month tax is replaced with a tax on the firm of $0.50 per cable subscriber. Now how many subscriptions should Comcast sell if it wants to maximize profit? What

price does it charge? What are its profits? (Assume that Comcast will sell only the quantities listed in the table.)

3.5 Before inexpensive pocket calculators were developed, many science and engineering students used slide rules to make numeric calculations. Slide rules are no longer produced, which means nothing prevents you from establishing a monopoly in the slide rule market. Draw a graph showing the situation your slide rule firm would be in. Be sure to include on your graph your demand, marginal revenue, average total cost, and marginal cost curves. Indicate the price you would charge and the quantity you would produce. Are you likely to make a profit or a loss? Show this area on your graph.

3.6 Does a monopolist have a supply curve? Briefly explain. (*Hint:* Look again at the definition of a supply curve in Chapter 3 and consider whether this applies to a monopolist.)

3.7 **(Related to the** *Don't Let This Happen to You!* **on page 485)** A student argues, "If a monopolist finds a way of producing a good at lower cost, he will not lower his price. Because he is a monopolist, he will keep the price and the quantity the same and just increase his profit." Do you agree? Use a graph to illustrate your answer.

3.8 **(Related to the** *Don't Let This Happen to You!* **on page 485)** Discuss whether you agree or disagree with the following statement: "A monopolist maximizes profit by charging the highest price at which it can sell any of the good at all."

3.9 When home builders construct a new housing development, they usually sell the rights to lay cable to a single cable television company. As a result, anyone buying a home in that development is not able to choose between competing cable companies. Some cities have begun to ban such exclusive agreements. Williams Township, Pennsylvania, decided to allow any cable company to lay cable in the utility trenches of new housing developments. The head of the township board of supervisors argued, "What I would like to see and do is give the consumers a choice. If there's no choice, then the price [of cable] is at the whim of the provider." In a situation in which the consumers in a housing development have only one cable company available, is the price really at the whim of the company? Would a company in this situation be likely to charge, say, $500 per month for basic cable services? Briefly explain why or why not.

Source: Sam Kennedy, "Williams Township May Ban Exclusive Cable Provider Pacts," (Allentown, Pennsylvania) *Morning Call*, November 5, 2004, p. D1.

3.10 Will a monopoly that maximizes profit also be maximizing revenue? Will it be maximizing production? Briefly explain.

Does Monopoly Reduce Economic Efficiency?

Summary

Compared with a perfectly competitive industry, a monopoly charges a higher price and produces less, which reduces consumer surplus and economic efficiency. Some loss of economic efficiency will occur whenever firms have **market power** and can charge a price greater than marginal cost. The total loss of economic efficiency in the U.S. economy due to market power is small, however, because true monopolies are very rare. In most industries, competition will keep price much closer to marginal cost than would be the case in a monopoly.

myeconlab Visit www.myeconlab.com to complete these exercises *Get Ahead of the Curve* online and get instant feedback.

Review Questions

4.1 Suppose that a perfectly competitive industry becomes a monopoly. Describe the effects of this change on consumer surplus, producer surplus, and deadweight loss.

4.2 Explain why market power leads to a deadweight loss. Is the total deadweight loss from market power for the economy large or small?

Problems and Applications

4.3 Review Figure 14-5 on page 487 on the inefficiency of monopoly. Will the deadweight loss due to monopoly

be larger if the demand is elastic or if it is inelastic? Briefly explain.

4.4 Economist Harvey Leibenstein argued that the loss of economic efficiency in industries that are not perfectly competitive has been understated. He argues that when competition is weak, firms are under less pressure to adopt the best techniques or to hold down their costs. He refers to this effect as "x-inefficiency." If x-inefficiency causes a firm's marginal costs to rise, show that the deadweight loss in Figure 14-5 understates the true deadweight loss caused by a monopoly.

4.5 In most cities, the city owns the water system that provides water to homes and businesses. Some cities charge a flat monthly fee, while other cities charge by the gallon. Which method of pricing is more likely to result in economic efficiency in the water market? Be sure to refer to the definition of economic efficiency in your answer. Why do you think the same method of pricing isn't used by all cities?

4.6 Review the concept of externalities on page 138 in Chapter 5. If a market is a monopoly, will a negative externality in production always lead to production beyond the level of economic efficiency? Use a graph to illustrate your answer.

>> **End Learning Objective 14.4**

Government Policy toward Monopoly

Summary

Because monopolies reduce consumer surplus and economic efficiency, most governments regulate monopolies. Firms that are not monopolies have an incentive to avoid competition by **colluding**, or agreeing to charge the same price, or otherwise not to compete. In the United States, **antitrust laws** are aimed at deterring monopoly, eliminating collusion, and promoting competition among firms. The Antitrust Division of the U.S. Department of Justice and the Federal Trade Commission share responsibility for enforcing the antitrust laws including regulating mergers between firms. A **horizontal merger** is a merger between firms in the same industry. A **vertical merger** is a merger between firms at different stages of production of a good. Local

governments regulate the prices charged by natural monopolies.

myeconlab Visit www.myeconlab.com to complete these exercises *Get Ahead of the Curve* online and get instant feedback.

Review Questions

5.1 What is the purpose of the antitrust laws? Who is in charge of enforcing them?

5.2 What is the difference between a horizontal merger and a vertical merger? Which type of merger is more likely to increase the market power of a newly merged firm?

5.3 Why would it be economically efficient to require a natural monopoly to charge a price equal to marginal cost? Why do most regulatory agencies require natural monopolies to charge a price equal to average cost instead?

Problems and Applications

5.4 Use the following graph for a monopoly to answer the questions.

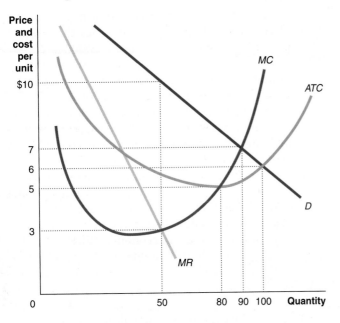

a. What quantity will the monopoly produce, and what price will the monopoly charge?

b. Suppose the monopoly is regulated. If the regulatory agency wants to achieve economic efficiency, what price should it require the monopoly to charge? How much output will the monopoly produce at this price? Will the monopoly make a profit if it charges this price? Briefly explain.

5.5 Use the following graph for a monopoly to answer the questions.

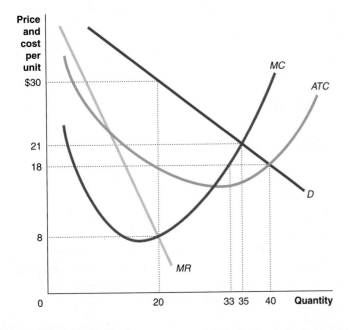

a. What quantity will the monopoly produce, and what price will the monopoly charge?

b. Suppose the government decides to regulate this monopoly and imposes a price ceiling of $18 (in other words, the monopoly can charge less than $18 but can't charge more). Now what quantity will the monopoly produce, and what price will the monopoly charge? Will every consumer who is willing to pay this price be able to buy the product? Briefly explain.

5.6 The following is from an article in the *New York Times*: "United Airlines and US Airways announced today that they had called off their proposed merger after the Justice Department threatened to file a lawsuit to block the $4.2 billion deal, calling it anticompetitive." Why would the Justice Department care if two airlines merge? What is "anticompetitive" about two airlines merging?

Source: Kenneth N. Gilpin and Jack Lynch, "United and US Airways Call Off Merger after U.S. Opposes It," *New York Times*, July 27, 2001.

5.7 A marketing textbook observes, "Pricing actions that violate laws can land executives in jail." Why would executives be thrown in jail because of the prices they charge? Which laws are they likely to have violated?

Source: David W. Cravens, *Strategic Marketing*, 5th ed., Boston: Irwin McGraw-Hill, 1997, p. 343.

5.8 Draw a graph like Figure 14-6 on page 491. On your graph, show producer surplus and consumer surplus before a merger and consumer surplus and producer surplus after a merger.

5.9 The following phone call took place in February 1982 between Robert Crandall, the chief executive officer of American Airlines, and Howard Putnam, the chief executive officer of Braniff Airways. Although Crandall didn't know it, Putnam was recording the call:

> ***Crandall:*** I think it's dumb . . . to sit here and pound the (obscenity) out of each other and neither one of us making a (obscenity) dime . . .
>
> ***Putnam:*** Do you have a suggestion for me?
>
> ***Crandall:*** Yes, I have a suggestion for you. Raise your . . . fares 20 percent. I'll raise mine the next morning.
>
> ***Putnam:*** Robert, we . . .
>
> ***Crandall:*** You'll make more money and I will, too.
>
> ***Putnam:*** We can't talk about pricing.
>
> ***Crandall:*** Oh (obscenity), Howard. We can talk about any . . . thing we want to talk about.

Who had a better understanding of antitrust law, Crandall or Putnam? Briefly explain.

Source: Mark Potts, "American Airlines Charged with Seeking a Monopoly," *Washington Post*, February 24, 1983; "Blunt Talk on the Phone," *New York Times*, February 24, 1983; and Thomas Petzinger Jr., *Hard Landing: The Epic Contest for Power and Profits that Plunged the Airline Industry into Chaos*, New York: Random House, 1995, pp. 149–150.

5.10 Look again at the section "The Department of Justice and Federal Trade Commission Merger Guidelines," which begins on page 491. Evaluate the following situations.

a. A market initially has 20 firms, each with a 5 percent market share. Of the firms, 4 propose to merge, leaving a total of 17 firms in the industry. Are the Department of Justice and the Federal Trade Commission likely to oppose the merger? Briefly explain.

b. A market initially has 5 firms, each with a 20 percent market share. Of the firms, 2 propose to merge, leaving a total of 4 firms in the industry. Are the Department of Justice and the Federal Trade Commission likely to oppose the merger? Briefly explain.

5.11 In 2007, Sirius Satellite Radio and XM Satellite Radio, the only two satellite radio firms, announced that they would attempt to merge. Maurice McKenzie, an analyst for Signal Hill investment bank, was quoted in the *Wall Street Journal* as arguing, "We believe that governmental approval could hinge on the market definition surrounding radio competition, which we expect to be narrowly defined to include terrestrial and satellite radio operators. . . . " What is a "terrestrial" radio operator? Why would government approval depend on how it defines the relevant market? What other firms—apart from terrestrial radio operators—might the government consider competitors to a newly merged Sirius-XM firm?

Source: "Analysts Like Sirius-XM Merger, but Note Regulatory Difficulties," *Wall Street Journal*, February 20, 2007.

5.12 In a column in the *Wall Street Journal*, David Henderson, an economist at the Hoover Institution, argued that it was possible to judge whether the proposed merger between Sirius and XM would make consumers better or worse off by looking at how owners of "free," or broadcast, radio stations reacted:

> Look at what the "free" broadcasters are saying about the XM-Sirius merger. As this newspaper recently reported, "The radio industry has loudly opposed the deal since it was announced, and broadcasters cite satellite-radio operators as major competitors in securities filings." Traditional radio broadcasters understand that they are competing with satellite radio. And they oppose the merger.

Why would "free" radio broadcasters oppose the merger? If the newly merged Sirius-XM charged higher prices, wouldn't that be good news to "free" radio broadcasters? Does the reaction of the "free" radio broadcasters indicate that consumers would be made better or worse off by the Sirius-XM merger?

Source: David R. Henderson, "Sirius Business," *Wall Street Journal*, February 28, 2007.

5.13 Industrial gases are used in the electronics industry. For example, nitrogen trifluoride is used for cleaning semiconductor wafers. The following table shows the market shares for the companies in this industry.

COMPANY	MARKET SHARE
Air Products	29%
Air Liquide	22
BOC Gases	21
Nippon Sanso	17
Praxzir	8
Other	3

In 2000, Air Products discussed a merger with BOC Gases. Use the information in the section "The Department of Justice and Federal Trade Commission Merger Guidelines" that begins on page 491 to predict whether the Department of Justice and the Federal Trade Commission opposed this merger. Assume that "Other" in the table consists of three firms, each of which has a 1 percent share of the market.

Source for market share data: Dan Shope, "Air Products Turns a Corner," (Allentown, Pennsylvania) *Morning Call*, July 29, 2001.

5.14 The following table gives the market shares of the companies in the U.S. carbonated soft drink industry.

COMPANY	MARKET SHARE
Coca-Cola	37%
PepsiCo	35
Cadbury Schweppes	17
Other	11

Use the information in the section "The Department of Justice and Federal Trade Commission Merger Guidelines" that begins on page 491 to predict whether the Department of Justice and the Federal Trade Commission would be likely to approve a merger between any two of the first three companies listed. Does your answer depend on how many companies are included in the "Other" category? Briefly explain.

Source: Pepsico *Annual Report, 2003.*

5.15 According to a column in the *New York Times* by Austan Goolsbee of the University of Chicago, the French National Assembly approved a bill:

> . . . that would require Apple Computer to crack open the software codes of its iTunes music store and let the files work on players other than the iPod. . . . If the French gave away the codes, Apple would lose much of its rationale for improving iTunes.

a. Why would Apple no longer want to improve iTunes if its software codes were no longer secret?

b. Why would the French government believe it was a good idea to require Apple to make the codes public?

Source: Austan Goolsbee, "In iTunes War, France Has Met the Enemy. Perhaps It Is France," *New York Times*, April 27, 2006.

5.16 **(Related to the *Making the Connection* on page 493)** Bank of America has attempted to convince Congress to eliminate the rule that banks may not merge if the newly merged bank would have more than a 10 percent share of U.S. deposits. In 2007, Bank of America was expanding its banking activities by, among other things, offering checking accounts and credit cards to illegal immigrants and other people who lacked Social Security numbers. An article in the *Wall Street Journal* observed:

> Unorthodox initiatives like the new credit-card program may be crucial to Bank of America's long-term success. In the past

the bank, which operates in 31 states and the District of Columbia, grew mostly by buying up other banks. Now, however, it is bumping up against a regulatory cap that bars any U.S. bank from an acquisition that would give it more than 10% of the nation's total bank deposits. That means Bank of America's only way to grow domestically is to sell more products to existing customers and to attract new ones.

Should the government take this information into account in evaluating the policy of limiting mergers among large banks? The *Wall Street Journal* article also notes, "Illegal immigrants have typically relied on loan sharks and neighborhood finance shops [which charge very high interest rates] for credit." Should the government consider this additional piece of information when formulating policy on bank mergers?

Source: Miriam Jordan and Valerie Bauerlein, "Bank of America Casts Wider Net for Hispanics," *Wall Street Journal*, February 13, 2007, p. A1.

>> **End Learning Objective 14.5**

Chapter 15

Pricing Strategy

Getting into Walt Disney World: One Price Does Not Fit All

When you visit Walt Disney World in Florida, your age, home address, and occupation can determine how much you pay for admission. In the summer of 2007, the price for a one-day ticket for an adult was $71.36. The same ticket for a child, aged three to nine, was $59.64. Children under three were free. Florida residents paid $64.22. Florida residents who were also members of Auto Club South paid $60.30. Active members of the military paid $69. Why does Disney charge so many different prices for the same product?

In previous chapters, we assumed that firms charge all consumers the same price for a given product. In reality, many firms charge customers different prices, based on differences in their willingness to pay for the product. Firms often face complicated pricing problems. For example, the Walt Disney Company faces the problem of determining the profit-maximizing prices to charge different groups of consumers for admission to its Disneyland and Walt Disney World theme parks.

The Walt Disney Company was founded in 1923 by Walt Disney and his brother Roy O. Disney. Several times, the Disney brothers risked financial ruin by investing most of the company's funds in innovative entertainment ideas. In 1927, they released *Steamboat Willie* starring Mickey Mouse, the first cartoon to feature synchronized sound. The profits from *Steamboat Willie* and other short cartoons helped finance production of *Snow White and the Seven Dwarfs*. Released in 1937, this was the first full-length Technicolor cartoon.

In the early 1950s, Walt Disney began to believe there was a market for theme parks. At that time, amusement parks—like Coney Island in New York—were usually collections of unrelated rides, such as roller coasters and Ferris wheels. The parks often had rowdy reputations and appealed more to teenagers and young adults than to families with children. Disney believed that a theme park, with attractions that emphasized storytelling over thrills, would be more attractive to families than were amusement parks. Disney had trouble raising the funds necessary to build his new park, however, because it was so strikingly different from existing parks. Disney hired an economist to evaluate the feasibility of the park. Managers of existing parks gave this advice to the economist: "Tell your boss to save his money. Tell him to stick to what he knows and leave the amusement business to people who know it."

Eventually, Disney convinced the ABC television network to provide funding in exchange for his providing them with a weekly television program.

When Disneyland opened in Anaheim, California, in July 1955, the Disney company had to set ticket prices. Should the company charge for entry into the park—which most amusements parks did not—and also charge for each ride within the park? Disney decided to charge a low price—$1 for adults and $0.50 for children—for admission into the park and also to charge for tickets to the rides. This system of separate charges for admission and for the rides continued until the early 1980s, when Disney decided to switch to a very different pricing strategy. Today, there is a high price for admission to Disneyland and Walt Disney World, but once a customer is in the park, the rides are free. Why did Disney change its pricing strategy? In this chapter, we will study some common pricing strategies, and we will see how Disney and other firms use these strategies to increase their profits. **AN INSIDE LOOK** on **page 526** discusses how colleges also charge different prices to different students.

Sources: Harrison Price, *Walt's Revolution! By the Numbers*, Ripley Entertainment, Inc., 2004, p. 31; and Bruce Gordon and David Mumford, *Disneyland: The Nickel Tour*, Santa Clarita, CA: Camphor Tree Publishers, 2000, pp. 174–175.

LEARNING Objectives

After studying this chapter, you should be able to:

15.1 Define the **law of one price** and explain the role of **arbitrage**, page 508.

15.2 Explain how a firm can increase its profits through **price discrimination**, page 510.

15.3 Explain how some firms increase their profits through the use of **odd pricing, cost-plus pricing**, and **two-part tariffs**, page 519.

Economics in YOUR Life!

Why So Many Prices to See a Movie?

Think about the movie theaters in your area. How much do you, as a student, pay to get into a theater? Would your parents pay the same amount? What about your grandparents? How about your little brother or sister? Is the price the same at night as in the afternoon? Why do you suppose movie theaters charge different prices to different groups of consumers?

If you buy popcorn at the movie theater, you pay the same price as everyone else. Why do you suppose people in certain age groups get a discount on movie admission but not on movie popcorn? As you read the chapter, see if you can answer these questions. You can check your answers against those we provide at the end of the chapter. **>> Continued on page 525**

I n previous chapters, we saw that entrepreneurs continually seek out economic profit. Pricing strategies are one way firms can attempt to increase their economic profit. One of these strategies is called *price discrimination*. It involves firms setting different prices for the same good or service, as Disney does when setting admission prices at Disney World. In Chapter 14, we analyzed the situation of a monopolist who sets a single price for its product. In this chapter, we will see how a firm can increase its profits by charging a higher price to consumers who value the good more and a lower price to consumers who value the good less.

We will also analyze the widely used strategies of *odd pricing* and *cost-plus pricing*. Finally, we will analyze situations in which firms are able to charge consumers one price for the right to buy a good and a second price for each unit of the good purchased. The ability of Disney to charge for admission to Disney World and also to charge for each ride is an example of this situation, which economists call a *two-part tariff*.

15.1 | Define the law of one price and explain the role of arbitrage.

Pricing Strategy, the Law of One Price, and Arbitrage

We saw in the opening to this chapter that sometimes firms can increase their profits by charging different prices for the same good. In fact, many firms rely on economic analysis to practice *price discrimination* by charging higher prices to some customers and lower prices to others. Firms use technology to gather information on the preferences of consumers and their responsiveness to changes in prices. Managers use the information to rapidly adjust the prices of their goods and services. This practice of rapidly adjusting prices, called *yield management*, has been particularly important to airlines and hotels. There are limits, though, to the ability of firms to charge different prices for the same product. The key limit is the possibility in some circumstances that consumers who can buy a good at a low price will resell it to consumers who would otherwise have to buy at a high price.

Arbitrage

According to the *law of one price*, identical products should sell for the same price everywhere. Let's explore why the law of one price usually holds true. Suppose that a Sony PlayStation Portable (PSP) handheld video game player sells for $249 in stores in Atlanta and for $199 in stores in San Francisco. Anyone who lives in San Francisco could buy PSPs for $199 and resell them for $249 in Atlanta. They could sell them on eBay or ship them to someone they know in Atlanta who could sell them in local flea markets. Buying a product in one market at a low price and reselling it in another market at a high price is referred to as *arbitrage*. The profits received from engaging in arbitrage are referred to as *arbitrage profits*.

As the supply of PSPs in Atlanta increases, the price of PSPs in Atlanta will decline, and as the supply of PSPs in San Francisco decreases, the price of PSPs in San Francisco will rise. Eventually the arbitrage process will eliminate most, but not all, of the price difference. Some price difference will remain because sellers must pay to list PSPs on eBay and to ship them to Atlanta. The costs of carrying out a transaction—by, for example, listing items on eBay and shipping them across the country—are called **transactions costs**. The law of one price holds exactly *only if transactions costs are zero*. As we will soon see, in cases in which it is impossible to resell a product, the law of one price will not hold, and firms will be able to price discriminate. Apart from this important qualification, we expect that arbitrage will result in a product selling for the same price everywhere.

Transactions costs The costs in time and other resources that parties incur in the process of agreeing to and carrying out an exchange of goods or services.

Solved Problem | 15-1

Is Arbitrage Just a Rip-off?

People are often suspicious of arbitrage. Buying something at a low price and reselling it at a high price exploits the person buying at the high price. Or does it? Is this view correct? If so, do the auctions on eBay serve any useful economic purpose?

SOLVING THE PROBLEM:

Step 1: **Review the chapter material.** This problem is about arbitrage, so you may want to review the section "Arbitrage," which begins on page 508. If necessary, also review the discussion of the benefits from trade in Chapters 2 and 8.

Step 2: **Use the discussion of arbitrage and the discussion in earlier chapters of the benefits from trade to answer the questions.** Many of the goods on eBay have been bought at a low price and are being resold at a higher price. In fact, some people supplement their incomes by buying collectibles and other goods at garage sales and reselling them on eBay. Does eBay serve a useful economic purpose? Economists would say that it does. Consider the case of Lou, who buys collectible movie posters and resells them on eBay. Suppose Lou buys a *Spider-Man 3* poster at a garage sale for $30 and resells it on eBay for $60. Both the person who sold to Lou at the garage sale and the person who bought from him on eBay must have been made better off by the deals *or they would not have made them.* Lou has performed the useful service of locating the poster and making it available for sale on eBay. In carrying out this service, Lou has incurred costs, including the opportunity cost of his time spent searching garage sales, the opportunity cost of the funds he has tied up in posters he has purchased but not yet sold, and the cost of the fees eBay charges him. It is easy to sell goods on eBay, so over time, competition among Lou and other movie poster dealers should cause the difference between the prices of posters sold at garage sales and the prices on eBay to shrink until they are equal to the dealers' costs of reselling the posters.

YOUR TURN: For more practice, do related problems 1.5 and 1.6 on page 528 at the end of this chapter.

>> End Solved Problem 15-1

Why Don't All Firms Charge the Same Price?

The law of one price may appear to be violated even where transactions costs are zero and a product can be resold. For example, different Internet Web sites may sell what seem to be identical products for different prices. We can resolve this apparent contradiction if we look more closely at what "product" an Internet Web site—or other business—actually offers for sale.

Suppose you want to buy a copy of the book *Harry Potter and the Deathly Hallows.* You use mySimon.com or some other search engine to compare the book's price at various Web sites. You get the results shown in Table 15-1.

Would you automatically buy the book from one of the last two sites listed rather than from Amazon.com or BarnesandNoble.com? We can think about why you might not. Consider what product is being offered for sale. Amazon.com is not just offering *Harry Potter and the Deathly Hallows*; it is offering *Harry Potter and the Deathly Hallows* delivered quickly to your home, well packaged so it's not damaged in the mail, and charged to your credit card using a secure method that keeps your credit card number safe from computer hackers. As we discussed in Chapter 12, firms differentiate the products they sell in many ways. One way is by providing faster and more reliable delivery than competitors.

TABLE 15-1

Which Internet Bookseller Would You Buy From?

PRODUCT: *HARRY POTTER AND THE DEATHLY HALLOWS*	
COMPANY	PRICE
Amazon.com	$18.89
BarnesandNoble.com	18.89
WaitForeverForYourOrder.com	17.50
JustStartedinBusinessLastWednesday.com	16.75

Amazon.com and BarnesandNoble.com have built reputations for fast and reliable service. New Internet booksellers who lack that reputation will have to differentiate their products on the basis of price, as the two fictitious firms listed in the table have done. So, the difference in the prices of products offered on Web sites does *not* violate the law of one price. A book Amazon.com offers for sale is not the same product as a book JustStartedinBusinessLastWednesday.com offers for sale.

15.2 LEARNING OBJECTIVE

15.2 | Explain how a firm can increase its profits through price discrimination.

Price Discrimination: Charging Different Prices for the Same Product

Price discrimination Charging different prices to different customers for the same product when the price differences are not due to differences in cost.

We saw at the beginning of this chapter that the Walt Disney Company charges different prices for the same product: admission to Disney World. Charging different prices to different customers for the same good or service when the price differences are not due to differences in cost is called **price discrimination**. But doesn't price discrimination

Don't Let This Happen to **YOU!**

Don't Confuse Price Discrimination with Other Types of Discrimination

Don't confuse price discrimination with discrimination based on race or gender. Discriminating on the basis of arbitrary characteristics, like race or gender, is illegal under the civil rights laws. Price discrimination is legal because it involves charging people different prices on the basis of their willingness to pay rather than on the basis of arbitrary characteristics. There is a gray area, however, when companies charge different prices on the basis of race or gender. For example, insurance companies usually charge women lower prices than men for automobile insurance. The courts have ruled that this is not illegal discrimination under the civil rights laws because women, on average, have better driving records than men. Because the costs of insuring men are higher than the costs of insuring women, insurance companies are allowed to charge them higher prices. Notice that this is not actually price discrimination as we have defined it here. Price discrimination involves charging different prices for the same product *where the price differences are not due to differences in cost.*

Insurance companies have been less successful in defending the practice of charging black people higher life insurance prices than white people. The insurance companies had claimed that this practice, which continued into the 1960s, was based on the shorter average life span of black people. Even though most insurance companies stopped the practice in the 1960s for new policies, most companies continued to collect the higher prices on policies that were already in effect. When this became widely known, several state insurance commissions launched investigations. Eventually, most companies reimbursed policyholders for the higher prices and paid substantial fines to the government. MetLife, the largest publicly held life insurance company in the United States, paid $250 million to settle a lawsuit by policyholders and to pay fines imposed by the New York State Insurance Department.

YOUR TURN: Test your understanding by doing related problem 2.18 on page 531 at the end of this chapter.

contradict the law of one price? Why doesn't the possibility of arbitrage profits lead people to buy at the low price and resell at the high price?

The Requirements for Successful Price Discrimination

A successful strategy of price discrimination has three requirements:

1 A firm must possess market power.

2 Some consumers must have a greater willingness to pay for the product than other consumers, and the firm must be able to know what prices customers are willing to pay.

3 The firm must be able to divide up—or *segment*—the market for the product so that consumers who buy the product at a low price are not able to resell it at a high price. In other words, price discrimination will not work if arbitrage is possible.

Note that a firm selling in a perfectly competitive market cannot practice price discrimination because it can only charge the market price. But because most firms do not sell in perfectly competitive markets, they have market power and can set the price of the good they sell. Many firms may also be able to determine that some customers have a greater willingness to pay for the product than others. However, the third requirement—that markets be segmented so that customers buying at a low price will not be able to resell the product—can be difficult to fulfill. For example, some people really love Big Macs and would be willing to pay $10 rather than do without one. Other people would not be willing to pay a penny more than $1 for one. Even if McDonald's could identify differences in the willingness of its customers to pay for Big Macs, it would not be able to charge them different prices. Suppose McDonald's knows that Joe is willing to pay $10, whereas Jill will pay only $1. If McDonald's tries to charge Joe $10, he will just have Jill buy his Big Mac for him.

Only firms that can keep consumers from reselling a product are able to practice price discrimination. Because buyers cannot resell the product, the law of one price does not hold. For example, movie theaters know that many people are willing to pay more to see a movie at night than during the afternoon. As a result, theaters usually charge higher prices for tickets to night showings than for tickets to afternoon showings. They keep these markets separate by making the tickets to afternoon showings a different color or by having the time printed on them, and by having a ticket taker examine the tickets. That makes it difficult for someone to buy a lower-priced ticket in the afternoon and use the ticket to gain admission to an evening showing.

Figure 15-1 illustrates how the owners of movie theaters use price discrimination to increase their profits. The marginal cost to the movie theater owner from another person attending a showing is very small: a little more wear on a theater seat and a few more kernels of popcorn to be swept from the floor. In previous chapters, we assumed that marginal cost has a U shape. In Figure 15-1, we assume for simplicity that marginal cost is a constant $0.50, shown as a horizontal line. Panel (a) shows the demand for afternoon showings. In this segment of its market, the theater should maximize profit by selling the number of tickets for which marginal revenue equals marginal cost, or 450 tickets. We know from the demand curve that the theater can sell 450 tickets at a price of $4.50 per ticket. Panel (b) shows the demand for night showings. Notice that charging $4.50 per ticket would *not* be profit maximizing in this market. At a price of $4.50, the theater sells 850 tickets, which is 225 more tickets than the profit-maximizing number of 625. By charging $4.50 for tickets to afternoon showings and $6.75 for tickets to night showings, the theater has maximized profits.

Figure 15-1 also illustrates another important point about price discrimination: When firms can price discriminate, they will charge customers who are less sensitive to price—those whose demand for the product is *less elastic*—a higher price and charge customers who are more sensitive to price—those whose demand is *more elastic*—a lower price. In this case, the demand for tickets to night showings is less elastic, so the price charged is higher, and the demand for tickets to afternoon showings is more elastic, so the price charged is lower.

Airlines divide their customers into two main categories: business travelers and leisure travelers. Business travelers often have inflexible schedules, can't commit until the last minute to traveling on a particular day, and, most importantly, are not very sensitive to changes in price. The opposite is true for leisure travelers: They are flexible about when they travel, willing to buy their tickets well in advance, and sensitive to changes in price. Based on what we discussed earlier in this chapter, you can see that airlines will maximize profits by charging business travelers higher ticket prices than leisure travelers, but they need to determine who is a business traveler and who is a leisure traveler. Some airlines do this by requiring people who want to buy a ticket at the leisure price to buy 14 days in advance and to stay at their destination over a Saturday night. Anyone unable to meet these requirements must pay a much higher price. Because business travelers often cannot make their plans 14 days in advance of their flight and don't want to stay over a weekend, they end up paying the higher ticket price. The gap between leisure fares and business fares is often very substantial. For example, in April 2007, the price of a leisure-fare ticket between New York and San Francisco on United Airlines was $308. The price of a business-fare ticket was $1,198.

The airlines go well beyond a single leisure fare and a single business fare in their pricing strategies. Although they ordinarily charge high prices for tickets sold only a few days in advance, they are willing to reduce prices for seats that they expect will not be sold at existing prices. Since the late 1980s, airlines have employed economists and mathematicians to construct computer models of the market for airline tickets. To calculate a suggested price each day for each seat, these models take into account factors that affect the demand for tickets, such as the season of the year, the length of the route, the day of the week, and whether the flight typically attracts primarily business or leisure travelers. This practice of continually adjusting prices to take into account fluctuations in demand is called *yield management*.

Since the late 1990s, Internet sites such as Priceline.com have helped the airlines to implement yield management. On Priceline.com, buyers commit to paying a price of their choosing for a ticket on a particular day and agree that they will fly at any time on that day. This gives airlines the opportunity to fill seats that otherwise would have gone empty, particularly on late night or early morning flights, even though the price may be well below the normal leisure fare. In 2001, several airlines combined to form the Internet site Orbitz, which became another means of filling seats at discount prices. In fact, in the past few years, the chance that you paid the same price for your airline ticket as the person sitting next to you has become quite small. Figure 15-2 shows an actual

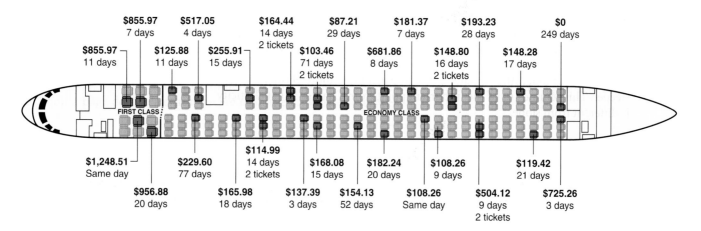

Figure 15-2 | 33 Customers and 27 Different Prices

To fill as many seats on a flight as possible, airlines charge many different ticket prices. The 33 passengers on this United Airlines flight from Chicago to Los Angeles paid 27 different prices for their tickets, including one passenger who used frequent flyer miles to obtain a free ticket. The first number in the figure is the price paid for the ticket; the second number is the number of days in advance that the ticket was purchased.

Source: Matthew L. Wald, "So, How Much Did You Pay for Your Ticket?" *New York Times*, April 12, 1998. Used with permission of New York Times Agency.

United Airlines flight from Chicago to Los Angeles. The 33 passengers on the flight paid 27 different prices for their tickets, including one passenger who used frequent flyer miles to obtain a free ticket.

Making the Connection | How Colleges Use Yield Management

Some colleges use yield management techniques to determine financial aid.

Traditionally, colleges have based financial aid decisions only on the incomes of prospective students. In recent years, however, many colleges have started using yield management techniques, first developed for the airlines, to determine the amount of financial aid they offer different students. Colleges typically use a name like "financial aid engineering" or "student enrollment management" rather than "yield management" to describe what they are doing. There is an important difference between the airlines and colleges: Colleges are interested not just in maximizing the revenue they receive from student tuition but also in increasing the academic quality of the students who enroll.

The "price" of a college education equals the tuition charged minus any financial aid received. When colleges use yield management techniques, they increase financial aid offers to students likely to be more price sensitive, and they reduce financial aid offers to students likely to be less price sensitive. As Stanford economist Caroline Hoxby puts it, "Universities are trying to find the people whose decisions will be changed by these [financial aid] grants." Some of the factors colleges use to judge how sensitive to price students are likely to be include whether they applied for early admission, whether they came for an on-campus interview, their intended major, their home state, and the level of their family's income. Focusing on one of these factors, William F. Elliot, vice president for enrollment management at Carnegie Mellon University, advises, "If finances are a concern, you shouldn't be applying any place [for] early decision" because you are less likely to receive a large financial aid offer.

Many students (and their parents) are critical of colleges that use yield management techniques in allocating financial aid. Some colleges, such as those in the Ivy League, have large enough endowments to meet all of their students' financial aid needs, so they don't practice yield management. Less well-endowed colleges defend the practice on the grounds that it allows them to recruit the best students at a lower cost in financial aid.

Sources: Jane J. Kim and Anjali Athavaley, "Colleges Seek to Address Affordability," *Wall Street Journal*, May 3, 2007; and Albert B. Crenshaw, "Price Wars on Campus: Colleges Use Discounts to Draw Best Mix of Top Students, Paying Customers," *Washington Post*, October 15, 2002; and Steve Stecklow, "Expensive Lesson: Colleges Manipulate Financial-Aid Offers, *Wall Street Journal*, April 1, 1996.

YOUR TURN: Test your understanding by doing related problem 2.14 on page 530 at the end of this chapter.

Perfect Price Discrimination

If a firm knew every consumer's willingness to pay—and could keep consumers who bought a product at a low price from reselling it—the firm could charge every consumer a different price. In this case of *perfect price discrimination*—also known as *first-degree price discrimination*—each consumer would have to pay a price equal to the consumer's willingness to pay and, therefore, would receive no consumer surplus. To see why, remember that consumer surplus is the difference between the highest price a consumer is willing to pay for a product and the price the consumer actually pays. But if the price the consumer pays is the maximum the consumer would be willing to pay, there is no consumer surplus.

Figure 15-3 shows the effects of perfect price discrimination. To simplify the discussion, we assume that the firm is a monopoly and that it has constant marginal and average costs. Panel (a) should be familiar from Chapter 14. It shows the case of a monopolist who cannot price discriminate and, therefore, can charge only a single price for its product. The monopolist maximizes profits by producing the level of output where marginal revenue equals marginal cost. Recall that the economically efficient level of output occurs where price is equal to marginal cost, which is the level of output in a perfectly competitive market. Because the monopolist produces where price is greater than marginal cost, it causes a loss of economic efficiency equal to the area of the deadweight loss triangle in the figure.

Panel (b) shows the situation of a monopolist practicing perfect price discrimination. Because the firm can now charge each consumer the maximum the consumer is willing to pay, its marginal revenue from selling one more unit is equal to the price of that unit. Therefore, the monopolist's marginal revenue curve becomes equal to its demand curve, and the firm will continue to produce up to the point where price is equal to marginal cost. It may seem like a paradox, but the ability to perfectly price discriminate causes the monopolist to produce the efficient level of output. By doing so, it converts into profits what in panel (a) had been consumer surplus *and* what had been deadweight loss. In both panel (a) and panel (b), the profit shown is also producer surplus.

Even though the result in panel (b) is more economically efficient than the result in panel (a), consumers clearly are worse off because the amount of consumer surplus has been reduced to zero. We probably will never see a case of perfect price discrimination in the real world because firms typically do not know how much each consumer is willing to pay and therefore cannot charge each consumer a different price. Still, this extreme case helps us to see the two key results of price discrimination:

1 Profits increase.

2 Consumer surplus decreases.

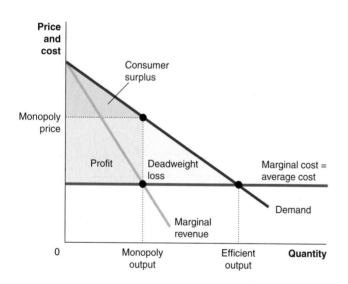

(a) A monopolist who cannot practice price discrimination

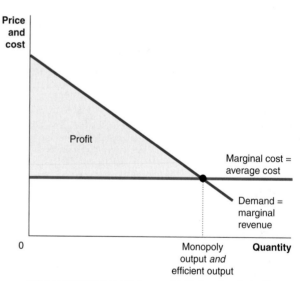

(b) A monopolist practicing perfect price discrimination

Figure 15-3 | Perfect Price Discrimination

Panel (a) shows the case of a monopolist who cannot price discriminate and, therefore, can charge only a single price for its product. The graph, like those in Chapter 14, shows that to maximize profits, the monopolist will produce the level of output where marginal revenue equals marginal cost. The resulting profit is shown by the area of the green rectangle. Given the monopoly price, the amount of consumer surplus in this market is shown by the area of the blue triangle. The economically efficient level of output occurs where price equals marginal cost. Because the monopolist stops production at a level of output where price is above marginal cost, there is a deadweight loss equal to the area of the yellow triangle. In panel (b), the monopolist is able to perfectly price discriminate by charging a different price to each consumer. The result is to convert both the consumer surplus *and* the deadweight loss from panel (a) into profit.

With perfect price discrimination, economic efficiency is improved. Can we also say that this will be the case if price discrimination is less than perfect? Often, less-than-perfect price discrimination will improve economic efficiency. But under certain circumstances, it may actually reduce economic efficiency, so we can't draw a general conclusion.

Price Discrimination across Time

Firms are sometimes able to engage in price discrimination over time. With this strategy, firms charge a higher price for a product when it is first introduced and a lower price later. Some consumers are *early adopters* who will pay a high price to be among the first to own certain new products. This pattern helps explain why DVD players, digital cameras, and flat-screen plasma televisions all sold for very high prices when they were first introduced. After the demand of the early adopters was satisfied, the companies reduced prices to attract more price-sensitive customers. For example, the price of DVD players dropped by 95 percent within five years of their introduction. Some of the price reductions over time for these products was also due to falling costs as companies took advantage of economies of scale, but some represented price discrimination across time.

Book publishers routinely use price discrimination across time to increase profits. Hardcover editions of novels have much higher prices and are published months before paperback editions. For example, the hardcover edition of Stephen King's novel *Lisey's Story* was published in October 2006 at a price of $28. The paperback edition was published in June 2007 for $9.99. Although this difference in price might seem to reflect the higher costs of hardcover books, in fact, it does not. The marginal cost of printing another copy of the hardcover is about $1.50. The marginal cost of printing another copy of the paperback edition is only slightly less, about $1.25. So, the difference in price between the hardcover and paperback is driven primarily by differences in demand. Stephen King's most devoted fans want to read his next book at the earliest possible moment and are not too sensitive to price. Many casual readers are also interested in King's books but will read something else if the price is too high.

As Figure 15-4 shows, a publisher will maximize profits by segmenting the market—in this case across time—and by charging a higher price to the less elastic market segment and a lower price to the more elastic segment. (This example is similar to our earlier analysis of movie tickets in Figure 15-1 on page 512.) If the publisher had skipped the hardcover and issued only the paperback version at a price of $9.99 when the book was first published in October, its revenue would have dropped by the number of readers who bought the hardcover multiplied by the difference between the price of the hardcover and the price of the paperback, or 500,000 × ($28 − 9.99) = $9,005,000.

Can Price Discrimination Be Illegal?

In Chapter 14, we saw that Congress has passed *antitrust laws* to promote competition. Price discrimination may be illegal if its effect is to reduce competition in an industry. In 1936, Congress passed the Robinson–Patman Act, which outlawed price discrimination that reduced competition, but which also contained language that could be interpreted as making illegal *all* price discrimination not based on differences in cost. In the 1960s, the Federal Trade Commission sued the Borden company under this act because Borden was selling the same evaporated milk for two different prices. Cans with the Borden label were sold for a high price, and cans sold to supermarkets to be repackaged as the supermarkets' private brands were sold for a much lower price. The courts ultimately ruled that Borden had not violated the law because the price differences increased, rather than reduced, competition in the market

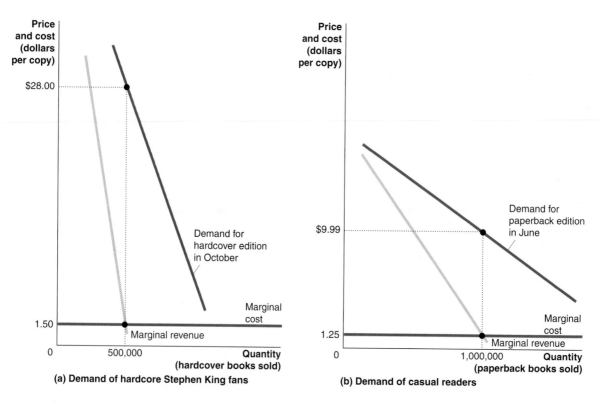

Figure 15-4 | Price Discrimination across Time

Publishers issue most novels in hardcover at high prices to satisfy the demand of the novelists' most devoted fans. Later, they publish paperback editions at much lower prices to capture sales from casual readers. In panel (a), with a marginal cost of $1.50 per copy for a hardcover, the profit-maximizing level of output is 500,000 copies, which can be sold at a price of $28. In panel (b), the more elastic demand of casual readers and the slightly lower marginal cost result in a profit-maximizing output of 1,000,000 for the paperback edition, which can be sold at a price of $9.99.

for evaporated milk. In recent years, the courts have interpreted Robinson–Patman narrowly, allowing firms to use the types of price discrimination described in this chapter.

Why does renting only a few movies get you better service on Netflix?

Making the **Connection**

Price Discrimination with a Twist at Netflix

Price discrimination usually refers to charging different prices to different consumers for the same good or service. But price discrimination can also involve charging the same price for goods or services of different quality. Netflix, an online DVD rental service, has apparently engaged in this second form of price discrimination. According to a newspaper story, "Netflix customers who pay the same price for the same service are often treated differently, depending on their rental patterns." Netflix subscribers pay a fixed monthly fee to rent a given number of DVDs. For instance, in 2007, Netflix was charging $17.99 per month to rent three DVDs at a time. After a subscriber returns a DVD, Netflix mails that subscriber a new DVD. Subscribers can rent an unlimited number of DVDs per month, although they can have no more than three at any one time. Netflix has become very popular, with more than seven million subscribers by 2007.

But does every Netflix subscriber receive service of the same quality? In particular, does every subscriber have an equal chance of receiving the latest movie released on DVD? Apparently not. Although Netflix does not emphasize it in its advertising, subscribers who rent the fewest movies per month have the best chance of receiving the latest releases and will typically receive their DVDs faster. According to Netflix's Terms of Use (the "fine print" that most subscribers don't read):

> In determining priority for shipping and inventory allocation, we may utilize many different factors. . . . For example, if all other factors are the same, we give priority to those members who receive the fewest DVDs through our service. . . . Also . . . [the service you experience] may be different from the service we provide to other members on the same membership plan.

One Netflix subscriber was quoted in a newspaper article as saying, "Sometimes it would be two or three months before I got [a movie] once it came out on DVD. The longer I was a customer, the worse it got."

Why would Netflix provide better service to subscribers who rent only a few DVDs per month and poorer service to subscribers who rent many DVDs per month? Subscribers who rent many DVDs per month are likely to have less elastic demand—they really like watching movies—than subscribers who rent only a few DVDs per month. As we have seen in this chapter, firms can increase their profits by charging higher prices to consumers with less elastic demand and lower prices to consumers with more elastic demand. But this strategy works only if firms have a way of reliably separating consumers into groups on the basis of how elastic their demand is. When they first subscribe, Netflix has no way of separating their consumers on the basis of how elastic their demand is, so it has to charge the same price to everyone. But after a few months of observing a subscriber's pattern of rentals, Netflix has enough information to determine whether the subscriber's demand is more or less elastic. By reducing the level of service to subscribers with less elastic demand, Netflix is, in effect, raising the price these consumers pay relative to consumers who receive better service. In effect, Netflix is engaging in price discrimination and increasing its profits over what they would be if every subscriber received the same service at the same price.

Sources: Alina Tugend, "Getting Movies from a Store or a Mailbox (or Just a Box)," *New York Times*, August 5, 2006; and "Netflix Critics Slam 'Throttling,'" Associated Press, February 10, 2006.

YOUR TURN: Test your understanding by doing related problem 2.17 on page 531 at the end of this chapter.

15.3 LEARNING OBJECTIVE

15.3 | Explain how some firms increase their profits through the use of odd pricing, cost-plus pricing, and two-part tariffs.

Other Pricing Strategies

In addition to price discrimination, firms use many different pricing strategies, depending on the nature of their products, the level of competition in their markets, and the characteristics of their customers. In this section, we consider three important strategies: odd pricing, cost-plus pricing, and two-part tariffs.

Odd Pricing: Why Is the Price $2.99 Instead of $3.00?

Many firms use what is called *odd pricing*—for example, charging $4.95 instead of $5.00, or $199 instead of $200. Surveys show that 80 percent to 90 percent of the products sold in supermarkets have prices ending in "9" or "5" rather than "0." Odd pricing has a long history. In the early nineteenth century, most goods in the United States were sold in general stores and did not have fixed prices. Instead, prices were often determined by haggling, much as prices of new cars are often determined today by haggling on dealers'

that cost-plus pricing may be the best way to determine the optimal price in two situations:

1 When marginal cost and average cost are roughly equal

2 When the firm has difficulty estimating its demand curve

In fact, most large firms that use cost-plus pricing do not just mechanically apply a markup to their estimate of average cost. Instead, they adjust the markup to reflect their best estimate of current demand. At General Motors, for example, a pricing policy committee adjusts prices to reflect its views of the current state of competition in the industry and the current state of the economy. If competition is strong in a weak economy, the pricing committee may decide to set price significantly below the cost-plus price—perhaps by offering buyers a rebate.

In general, firms that take demand into account will charge lower markups on products that are more price elastic and higher markups on products that are less elastic. Supermarkets, where cost-plus pricing is widely used, have markups in the 5 percent to 10 percent range for products with more elastic demand, such as soft drinks and breakfast cereals, and markups in the 50 percent range for products with less elastic demand, such as fresh fruits and vegetables.

Pricing with Two-Part Tariffs

Some firms can require consumers to pay an initial fee for the right to buy their product and an additional fee for each unit of the product purchased. For example, many golf and tennis clubs require members to buy an annual membership in addition to paying a fee each time they use the tennis court or golf course. Sam's Club requires consumers to pay a membership fee before shopping at its stores. Cellular phone companies charge a monthly fee and then have a per-minute charge after a certain number of minutes have been used. Economists refer to this situation as a **two-part tariff**.

Two-part tariff A situation in which consumers pay one price (or tariff) for the right to buy as much of a related good as they want at a second price.

The Walt Disney Company is in a position to use a two-part tariff by charging consumers for admission to Walt Disney World or Disneyland and also charging them to use the rides in the parks. As mentioned at the beginning of this chapter, at one time, the admission price to Disneyland was low, but people had to purchase tickets to go on the rides. Today, you must pay a high price for admission to Disneyland or Disney World, but the rides are free once you're in the park. Figure 15-5 helps us understand which of these pricing strategies is more profitable for Disney. The numbers in the figure are simplified to make the calculations easier.

Once visitors are inside the park, Disney is in the position of a monopolist—no other firm is operating rides in Disney World. So, we can draw panel (a) in Figure 15-5 to represent the market for rides at Disney World. This graph looks like the standard monopoly graph from Chapter 14. (Note that the marginal cost of another rider is quite low. We can assume that it is a constant $2 and equal to the average cost.) It seems obvious—but it will turn out to be wrong!—that Disney should determine the profit-maximizing quantity of ride tickets by setting marginal revenue equal to marginal cost. In this case, that would lead to 20,000 ride tickets sold per day at a price of $26 per ride. Disney's profit from selling *ride tickets* is shown by the area of the light-green rectangle, *B*. It equals the difference between the $26 price and the average cost of $2, multiplied by the 20,000 tickets sold, or ($26 − $2) × 20,000 = $480,000. Disney also has a second source of profit from selling *admission tickets* to the park. Given the $26 price for ride tickets, what price would Disney be able to charge for admission tickets?

Let's assume the following for simplicity: The only reason people want admission to Disney World is to go on the rides, all consumers have the same individual demand curve for rides, and Disney knows what this demand curve is. This last assumption allows Disney to be able to practice perfect price discrimination. More realistic assumptions would make the outcome of the analysis somewhat different but would not affect

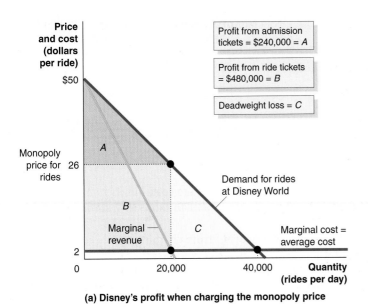

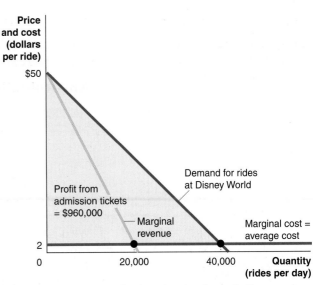

(a) Disney's profit when charging the monopoly price

(b) Disney's profit when charging the perfectly competitive price

Figure 15-5 | A Two-Part Tariff at Disney World

In panel (a), Disney charges the monopoly price of $26 per ride ticket and sells 20,000 ride tickets. Its profit from *ride tickets* is shown by the area of the light-green rectangle, *B*, $480,000. If Disney is in the position of knowing every consumer's willingness to pay, it can also charge a price for *admission tickets* that would result in the total amount paid for admission tickets being equal to total consumer surplus from the rides. Total consumer surplus from the rides equals the area of the dark-green trian-

gle, *A*, or $240,000. So, when charging the monopoly price, Disney's total profit equals $480,000 + $240,000, or $720,000. In panel (b), Disney charges the perfectly competitive price of $2, where marginal revenue equals marginal cost, and sells 40,000 ride tickets. At the lower ride ticket price, Disney can charge a higher price for admission tickets, which will increase its total profits from operating the park to the area of the light-green triangle, or $960,000.

the main point of how Disney uses a two-part tariff to increase its profits. With these assumptions, we can use the concept of consumer surplus to calculate the maximum total amount consumers would be willing to pay for admission. Remember that consumer surplus is equal to the area below the demand curve and above the price line, shown by the dark-green triangle, *A*, in panel (a). The area represents the benefit to buyers from consuming the product. In this case, consumers would not be willing to pay more for admission to the park than the consumer surplus they receive from the rides. In panel (a) of Figure 15-5, the total consumer surplus when Disney charges a price of $26 per ride is $240,000. (This number is easy to calculate if you remember that the formula for the area of a triangle is ½ × base × height, or ½ × 20,000 × $24.) Disney can set the price of admission tickets so that the *total* amount spent by buyers would be $240,000. In other words, Disney can set the price of admission to capture the entire consumer surplus from the rides. So, Disney's total profit from Disney World would be the $240,000 it receives from admission tickets plus the $480,000 in profit from the rides, or $720,000 per day.

Is this the most profit Disney can earn from selling admission tickets and ride tickets? The answer is "no." The key to seeing why is to notice that *the lower the price Disney charges for ride tickets, the higher the price it can charge for admission tickets.* Lower-priced ride tickets increase consumer surplus from the rides and, therefore, increase the willingness of buyers to pay a higher price for admission tickets. In panel (b) of Figure 15-5, we assume that Disney acts as it would in a perfectly competitive market and charges a price for ride tickets that is equal to marginal cost, or $2. Charging this price increases consumer surplus— *and the maximum total amount that Disney can charge for admission tickets*—from $240,000 to $960,000. (Once again, we use the formula for the area of a triangle to calculate the light-green area in panel (b): ½ × 40,000 × 48 × $960,000) Disney's profits from the rides will decline to

TABLE 15-2

Disney's Profits per Day from Different Pricing Strategies

	MONOPOLY PRICE FOR RIDES	COMPETITIVE PRICE FOR RIDES
PROFITS FROM ADMISSION TICKETS	$240,000	$960,000
PROFITS FROM RIDE TICKETS	480,000	0
TOTAL PROFIT	720,000	960,000

zero because it is now charging a price equal to average cost, *but its total profit from Disney World will rise from $720,000 per day to $960,000*. Table 15-2 summarizes this result.

What is the source of Disney's increased profit from charging a price equal to marginal cost? The answer is that Disney has converted what was deadweight loss when the monopoly price was charged—the area of triangle *C* in panel (a)—into consumer surplus. It then turns this consumer surplus into profit by increasing the price of admission tickets.

It is important to note the following about the outcome of a firm using an optimal two-part tariff:

1. Because price equals marginal cost at the level of output supplied, the outcome is economically efficient.

2. All of consumer surplus is transformed into profit.

Notice that, in effect, Disney is practicing perfect price discrimination. As we noted in our discussion of perfect price discrimination on page 515, Disney's use of a two-part tariff has increased the amount of the product—in this case, rides at Disney World—consumers are able to purchase, but has eliminated consumer surplus. Although it may seem paradoxical, consumer surplus was actually higher when consumers were being charged the monopoly price for the rides. The solution to the paradox is that although consumers pay a lower price for the rides when Disney employs a two-part tariff, the overall amount they pay to be at Disney World increases.

Disney actually does follow the profit-maximizing strategy of charging a high price for admission to the park and a very low price—zero—for the rides. It seems that Disney could increase its profits by raising the price for the rides from zero to the marginal cost of the rides. But the marginal cost is so low that it would not be worth the expense of printing ride tickets and hiring additional workers to sell the tickets and collect them at each ride. Finally, note that because the demand curves of Disney's customers are not all the same, and because Disney does not actually know precisely what these demand curves are, Disney is not able to convert all of consumer surplus into profit.

The rides at Disney World are free—once you have paid to get into the park.

Economics in YOUR Life!

Continued from page 507

At the beginning of the chapter, we asked you to think about what you pay for a movie ticket and what people in other age groups pay. A movie theater will try to charge different prices to different consumers based on their willingness to pay. If you have two otherwise identical people, one a student and one not, you might assume that the student has less income, and thus a lower willingness to pay, than the non-student, and the movie theater would like to charge the student a lower price. The movie theater employee can ask to see a student ID to ensure that the theater is giving the discount to a student.

But why don't theaters practice price discrimination at the concession stand? It is likely that a student will also have a lower willingness to pay for popcorn, and the theater can check for a student ID at the time of purchase, but unlike the case of the entry ticket, the theater would have a hard time preventing the student from giving the popcorn to a non-student once inside the theater. Since it is easier to limit resale in movie admissions, we often see different prices for different groups. Since it is difficult to limit resale of popcorn and other movie concessions, all groups will typically pay the same price.

Conclusion

Firms in perfectly competitive industries must sell their products at the market price. For firms in other industries—which means, of course, the vast majority of firms—pricing is an important part of the strategy used to maximize profits. We have seen in this chapter, for example, that if firms can successfully segment their customers into different groups on the basis of willingness to pay, they can increase their profits by charging different segments different prices.

Read *An Inside Look* on the next page for a discussion of why colleges do not charge all students the same tuition.

College Tuition: One Price Does Not Fit All

WALL STREET JOURNAL, OCTOBER 11, 2006

Amid Rising Costs and Criticism, Some Colleges Cut Back Merit Aid

As colleges and universities consider whether to join Harvard and Princeton in abandoning early-admissions programs, some are also trying to roll back another popular recruiting tool: merit aid.

Colleges offer merit aid, which is typically awarded on the basis of grades, class rank and test scores, to students who ordinarily wouldn't qualify for financial help. Because merit aid can be a deciding factor in these students' choice of schools, it has become a major weapon in the bidding wars among colleges for high achievers who can help boost their national rankings. . . .

But the cost of such programs has mounted as their use has expanded and tuition has risen. Meanwhile, criticism has grown that they disproportionately benefit students from wealthier communities with better school systems, siphoning resources away from lower-income students with greater financial need. In some cases, students who qualify for neither need- nor merit-based aid end up paying even more to cover a college's costs. As a result, a small but growing number of schools and university systems are trying to reduce their merit offerings. The University of Florida recently slashed the value of its four-year scholarships for in-state scholars who qualified under the National Merit program by 79% to a total of $5,000. . . .

Allegheny College, in Meadville, Pa., where annual tuition and fees total about $28,300, gave its $15,000-a-year merit scholarships to 15% of this year's freshmen, down from about 33% three years ago. To free up funding for more need-based aid, Rhode Island's Providence College scuttled its smaller merit scholarships and raised the eligibility requirements for its larger ones: A grade-point average of about 3.7 on a 4.0 scale used to be good enough; now it takes around a 3.83. Providence's merit scholarships can run as high as full tuition, which is $26,780 this year. . . .

Efforts to cut back on merit aid also risk setting off a backlash from middle- and upper-income families who don't qualify for need-based aid but are finding the rising cost of a college to be a daunting stretch. "Family income isn't keeping pace with the things driving higher-education costs," says Jim Scannell, a partner at Scannell & Kurz Inc., a Pittsford, N.Y., consulting firm that works with colleges on enrollment issues.

Some high-achieving applicants target schools that have merit-aid programs, hoping to win a tuition break. With tuition and fees at many private schools surpassing $40,000 a year, small private liberal-arts colleges that lack the cachet of the Ivy League but whose tuitions far exceed those of state colleges could have the most to lose from any cutbacks in merit aid. . . .

Many institutions have no intention of cutting back on merit aid. Baylor University, a Baptist college in Waco, Texas, recently increased the value of the merit awards it gives to all incoming freshmen who score at least 1,300 points out of a possible 1,600 on SAT reading and math exams. The awards, which rise in value in tandem with a student's SAT scores, range from $2,000 to $4,000 a year. . . .

For some smaller schools, merit aid is less about boosting rankings than adding revenue by swelling enrollment. In most cases, students are still paying substantial sums for tuition even after receiving a scholarship. "I think in many cases it's misleading to call it merit aid," says Michael McPherson, president of the Spencer Foundation, a Chicago-based educational research group. "It's 'get 'em in the door' aid."

At private Wilkes University, Wilkes Barre, Pa., where tuition and fees are about $23,000 a year, only 81 of this year's 580 incoming freshmen didn't get merit aid. To land a scholarship, which starts at $6,000 a year, students have to have graduated in the top half of their high-school class and to have scored a combined total of at least a 900 on the SAT reading and math exams, not much above average. . . .

Although families with earnings of $100,000 or more might qualify for need-based aid, depending on factors such as how many college-aged children they have, college administrators say many such families usually don't bother to apply for need-based aid because they presume they won't get it. . . .

Source: Robert Tomsho, "Amid Rising Costs and Criticism, Some Colleges Cut Back Merit Aid," Wall Street Journal, October 11, 2006.

Key Points in the Article

This article highlights a change in the scholarships offered by universities and colleges. In particular, colleges are reducing merit aid and increasing the amount of need-based financial aid. Because many students receive scholarships and other types of aid, they pay a variety of actual tuition prices, which may be very different from the posted tuition price.

Analyzing the News

(a) High-achieving students are typically offered admission by a number of different universities, many of which are good substitutes for each other. As a result, talented high school seniors would have a relatively elastic demand for attending any particular college. Consumers with more elastic demands tend to pay lower prices for goods.

(b) Need-based aid can be thought of as a form of price discrimination, separating the market into high-income students (with high demand) and low-income students (with low demand). Panel (a) in the figure below shows two demand curves for

college education: one for high-income students and the other for low-income students. Notice that for any quantity, high-income students have a higher willingness to pay for education. So for Q_1 of each type of student to be enrolled, the school could charge P_1 dollars to high-income students but only P_2 dollars to low-income students. Need-based aid makes it possible to charge a lower price to low-income students without changing the tuition price charged to high-income students. You can see in panel (a) that if the school had to charge P_1 to both types of students, it would still enroll Q_1 high-income students but only Q_2 low-income students, so it would not maximize revenue.

(c) An additional student adds very little to the cost of running a college or university. As a result, offering merit aid is usually not the difference between a student paying full tuition or reduced tuition; it is the difference between a student enrolling and paying some tuition or not enrolling and paying $0 to the school. Panel (b) in the figure below shows the demand curve for enrollment at a school. Notice that in this example as the price drops from P_1 to P_2,

there is a large increase in quantity, from Q_1 to Q_2 students. If the demand for education at a particular college is elastic, as it likely is, tuition revenues will increase as the school lowers its price. At the higher price, P_1, with Q_1 students, revenue is shown as areas $A + B$. If tuition drops, revenue at price P_2 with Q_2 students will be areas $B + C$. The school will be better off if the increased revenue from additional students is (area C) greater than the lost revenue from the lower price now charged to the original Q_1 students (area A). In this example, area C is greater than area A, so the college's revenues increase when it cuts its tuition.

Thinking Critically

1. If lowering the tuition to some students increases a university's revenue, why don't universities just lower the tuition for everyone?
2. If customers with less elastic demands will pay more for a product when firms can price discriminate, would you expect to see freshmen or seniors pay higher tuition at your college? How might a college charge different classes different levels of tuition?

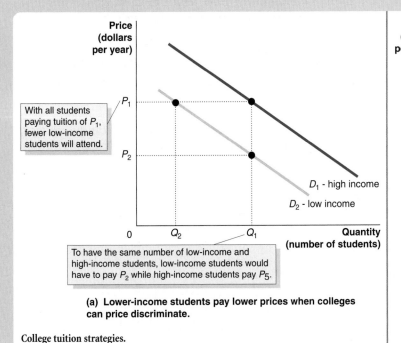

(a) Lower-income students pay lower prices when colleges can price discriminate.

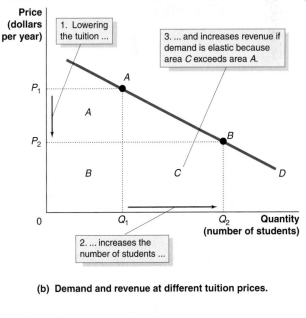

(b) Demand and revenue at different tuition prices.

College tuition strategies.

Key Terms

Price discrimination, p. 510   Two-part tariff, p. 522

Transactions costs, p. 508

15.1 LEARNING OBJECTIVE   15.1 | Define the law of one price and explain the role of arbitrage, **pages 508–510.**

Pricing Strategy, the Law of One Price, and Arbitrage

Summary

According to the *law of one price*, identical products should sell for the same price everywhere. If a product sells for different prices, it will be possible to make a profit through *arbitrage*: buying a product at a low price and reselling it at a high price. The law of one price will hold as long as arbitrage is possible. Arbitrage is sometimes blocked by high **transactions costs**, which are the costs in time and other resources incurred to carry out an exchange, or because the product cannot be resold. Another apparent exception to the law of one price occurs when companies offset the higher price they charge for a product by providing superior or more reliable service to customers.

 Visit www.myeconlab.com to complete these exercises *Get Ahead of the Curve* online and get instant feedback.

Review Questions

1.1 What is the law of one price? What is arbitrage?

1.2 Does a product always have to sell for the same price everywhere? Briefly explain.

Problems and Applications

1.3 A newspaper article contains the following description:

> For years, shoppers from New York City have played a game of retail arbitrage, traveling to the many malls in northern New Jersey, a state where there is no tax on clothing and shoes. Even accounting for tolls, gas and time, shoppers could save money by visiting the Westfield Garden State Plaza and other malls here, escaping the 8.375 percent sales tax they must pay in New York City on clothing and shoes that cost more than $110 per item.

Does this article use the word *arbitrage* correctly? Briefly explain.

Source: Ken Belson and Nate Schweber, "Sales Tax Cut in City May Dim Allure of Stores Across Hudson," *New York Times*, January 18, 2007.

1.4 The following table contains the actual prices charged by four Web sites for a DVD of the movie *Borat* in March 2007.

Amazon.com	$15.99
Wal-Mart	$15.87
DeepDiscount	$17.21
CDUniverse	$22.19

Briefly explain whether the information in this table contradicts the law of one price.

1.5 (Related to *Solved Problem 15-1* on page 509) Suppose California has many apple trees, and the price of apples there is low. Nevada has few apple trees, and the price of apples there is high. Abner buys low-priced California apples and ships them to Nevada, where he resells them at a high price. Is Abner exploiting Nevada consumers by doing this? Is he likely to earn economic profits in the long run? Briefly explain.

1.6 (Related to *Solved Problem 15-1* on page 509) Suspicions of arbitrage have a long history. For example, Valerian of Cimiez, a Catholic bishop who lived during the fifth century, wrote, "When something is bought cheaply only so it can be retailed dearly, doing business always means cheating." What might Valerian think of eBay? Do you agree with his conclusion? Explain.

Source for quote: Michael McCormick, *The Origins of the European Economy: Communications and Commerce, A.D. 300–900*, New York: Cambridge University Press, 2001, p. 85.

>> End Learning Objective 15.1

Price Discrimination: Charging Different Prices for the Same Product

Summary

Price discrimination occurs if a firm charges different prices for the same product when the price differences are not due to differences in cost. Three requirements must be met for a firm to successfully price discriminate: (1) A firm must possess market power. (2) Some consumers must have a greater willingness to pay for the product than other consumers, and firms must be able to know what customers are willing to pay. (3) Firms must be able to divide up—or segment—the market for the product so that consumers who buy the product at a low price cannot resell it a high price. In the case of *perfect price discrimination*, each consumer pays a price equal to the consumer's willingness to pay.

myeconlab Visit www.myeconlab.com to complete these exercises
Get Ahead of the Curve online and get instant feedback.

Review Questions

2.1 What is price discrimination? Under what circumstances can a firm successfully practice price discrimination?

2.2 During a particular week, America West charged $218 for a round-trip ticket on a flight from New York to San Francisco, provided that the ticket was purchased at least 10 days in advance and the ticket buyer was willing to stay over a Saturday night. If the buyer did not meet these conditions, the price for the ticket was $1,361. Why does America West use this pricing strategy?

2.3 What is yield management? Give an example of a firm using yield management to increase profits.

2.4 What is perfect price discrimination? Is it likely to ever occur? Explain. Is perfect price discrimination economically efficient? Explain.

2.5 Is it possible to price discriminate across time? Briefly explain.

Problems and Applications

2.6 An article on the AMC movie theater chain contained the following:

In July, [AMC] announced plans to offer steeply discounted movie tickets to shows on Friday, Saturday and Sunday mornings. "Seventy-five percent of the revenue comes from the weekend," Mr. Brown [AMC's CEO] said. His recent initiatives

are attempts to address the question: "Is there a way with price that you can create opportunity, a new market?"

Why would it be profitable for AMC to sell "steeply discounted" movie tickets for movies being shown on weekend mornings? Wouldn't the firm's revenues be higher if it charged the regular—higher—price for these showings? Briefly explain.

Source: Kate Kelly, "Box-Office Bounty Stirs Theater Deals," *Wall Street Journal*, August 10, 2006, p. C1.

2.7 According to an article in the *Wall Street Journal*, the average price of Ford Explorers sold in Dallas, Texas, was $30,142. During the same period, the average price of identically equipped Explorers in Oklahoma was only $27,939. Briefly explain whether this is an example of price discrimination.

Source: Karen Lundegaard, "How to Buy Your Next Car: First, Get a Plane Ticket," *Wall Street Journal*, April 30, 2002.

2.8 An article on how prices in South Bend, Indiana rise during Notre Dame home football games contained the following:

[Notre Dame football fan Anthony] Gallis ended up reserving a suite at a Hampton Inn and Suites in South Bend, which normally goes for $129 a night, for $400 a night, with a three-night minimum. "It's just insane," says the 42-year-old owner of a State Farm Insurance agency back in Pennsylvania. . . . Indeed, rates for many of the 4,015 hotel rooms in the South Bend area are skyrocketing. Two weeks before the start of the season, the Comfort Suites here was asking $245 a night, with a two-night minimum, for the Penn State weekend. That's up from $109 a night on non-football weekends. For the Sept. 16 game against the University of Michigan, the South Bend Marriott is charging $649 a night for a double room. That's more than the price of a room at the Waldorf-Astoria Hotel in New York. The Marriott's regular weekend price is $149 a night.

Is this an example of price discrimination? Briefly explain.

Source: Ilan Brat, "Notre Dame Football Introduces Its Fans To Inflationary Spiral, *Wall Street Journal*, September 7, 2006, p. A1.

2.9 Political columnist Michael Kinsley writes, "The infuriating [airline] rules about Saturday night stayovers and so on are a crude alternative to administering truth serum and asking, 'So how much are you really willing to pay?'" Would a truth serum—or some other way of knowing how much people would be willing to pay for an airline ticket—really be all the airlines need to price discriminate? Briefly explain.

Source: Michael Kinsley, "Consuming Gets More Complicated," *Slate*, November 21, 2001.

2.10 In a column in the *Wall Street Journal*, Walter Mossberg offered the following opinion:

> There's a sucker in the software business today, and if you're in an average family with a couple of PCs, that sucker is you. . . . Families constitute the only significant customer group not getting a discount on [Microsoft] Office when upgrading multiple PCs. Big corporations, organizations and government agencies get a discount, called a "site license." College students get a discount. Small and medium-size businesses get a discount. But not families.

Why might Microsoft charge families a higher price for Office than it charges the other groups Mossberg mentions?

Source: Walter Mossberg, "Microsoft Should Offer Families a Deal with Its Office Program," *Wall Street Journal*, July 18, 2002.

2.11 According to an article in the *Economist*, "The PS3 [PlayStation 3] is available in two configurations, costing $500 and $600 in America, and ¥50,000 ($425) and ¥60,000 ($510) in Japan." Based on this information, does Sony consider the demand of U.S. consumers for the PS3 to be more elastic or less elastic than the demand of Japanese consumers? Briefly explain.

Source: "Playing a Long Game," *Economist*, November 16, 2006.

2.12 (Related to *Solved Problem 15-2* on page 512) Use the graphs at the bottom of the page to answer the following questions.
   a. If the firm wants to maximize profits, what price will it charge in Market 1, and what quantity will it sell?
   b. If the firm wants to maximize profits, what price will it charge in Market 2, and what quantity will it sell?

2.13 When a firm offers a rebate on a product, the buyer normally has to fill out a form and mail it in to receive a rebate check in the mail. A financial columnist argues:

> When a manufacturer offers a rebate, you needn't be too suspicious. The manufacturer wants to lower the price temporarily (to move an old product or combat a competitor's new low price), but doesn't have faith that the retailer will pass on the savings.

But suppose that a manufacturer wants to engage in price discrimination. Would offering rebates be a way of doing this? Briefly explain.

Source: Carol Vinzant, "The Great Rebate Scam," *Slate*, June 10, 2003.

2.14 (Related to the *Making the Connection* on page 515) Assume that the marginal cost of admitting one more student is constant for every university. Also assume that the demand for places in the freshmen class is downward sloping at every university. Now suppose that the public becomes upset that universities charge different prices to different students. Responding to these concerns, the federal government requires universities to charge the same price to each student. Who would gain and who would lose?

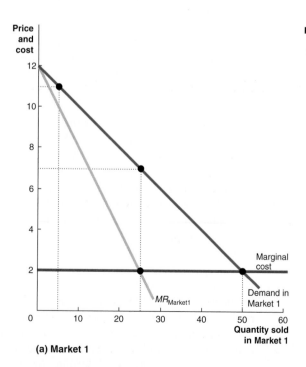

(a) Market 1

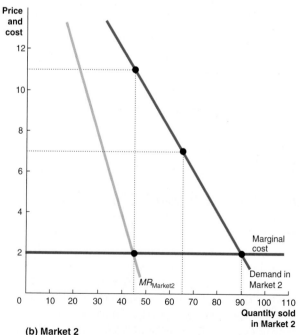

(b) Market 2

2.15 (Related to the *Chapter Opener* on page 506) Why does Walt Disney World charge a lower admission price for children aged 3 to 9 than for adults? Why does it categorize a 10-year-old as an adult for this purpose? Why does it admit children under 3 for free? Why does it charge residents of Florida a lower price than residents of other states?

2.16 Are supermarket coupons a form of price discrimination? Briefly explain why or why not.

2.17 (Related to the *Making the Connection* on page 518) Netflix offers subscriptions. Some have a higher price and allow more—or unlimited—movies to be rented per month. Others have a lower price and allow fewer movies to be rented per month. Is Netflix practicing price discrimination by offering these different subscriptions? Briefly explain.

2.18 (Related to the *Don't Let This Happen to You!* on page 510) Beginning in 2002, a state law in California made it illegal for businesses to charge men and women different prices for dry cleaning, laundry, tailoring, or hair grooming. The state legislator who proposed the law did so after a dry cleaner charged her more to have her shirts dry-cleaned than to have her husband's shirts dry-cleaned: "They charged me $1.50 for each of his, and he wears an extra large. They charged $3.50 for each of mine, and I wear a small." According to a newspaper article, "the dry cleaning proprietor told her that the price difference stemmed from the need for hand ironing her shirts because automatic presses are not made to handle small-sized women's garments."

    a. Was the dry cleaner practicing price discrimination, as defined in this chapter? Briefly explain.

    b. Do you support laws like this one? Briefly explain.

Source: Harry Brooks, "Law Mandates Equality in Dry Cleaning, Hair Styling," *North County (California) Times*, October 7, 2001.

2.19 Eric Orkin, the president of Opus 2 Revenue Technologies, Inc., which sells yield management systems to hotels, argues, "The price-sensitive person gets what he wants as long as he's willing to have some flexibility." Why would a yield management system for hotels result in lower prices for "price-sensitive" customers than the alternative of charging one price for all customers? Why would a price-sensitive person need to be "flexible" to receive a lower price?

Source: Neal Templin, "Property Report: Your Room Costs $250 . . . No! $200 . . . No . . . ," *Wall Street Journal*, May 5, 1999.

2.20 Draw a graph that shows producer surplus, consumer surplus, and deadweight loss (if any) in a market where the seller practices perfect price discrimination. Profit-maximizing firms select an output at which marginal cost equals marginal revenue. Where is the marginal revenue curve in this graph?

> **>> End Learning Objective 15.2**

15.3 | Explain how some firms increase their profits through the use of odd pricing, cost-plus pricing, and two-part tariffs, **pages 519–524.**

Other Pricing Strategies

Summary

In addition to price discrimination, firms also use odd pricing, cost-plus pricing, and two-part tariffs as pricing strategies. Firms use *odd pricing*—for example, charging $1.99 rather than $2.00—because consumers tend to buy more at odd prices than would be predicted from estimated demand curves. With *cost-plus pricing*, firms set the price for a product by adding a percentage markup to average cost. Cost-plus pricing may be a good way to come close to the profit-maximizing price when marginal revenue or marginal cost is difficult to measure. Some firms can require consumers to pay an initial fee for the right to buy their product and an additional fee for each unit of the product purchased. Economists refer to this situation as a **two-part tariff**. Sam's Club, cell phone companies, and many golf and tennis clubs use two-part tariffs in pricing their products.

 Visit www.myeconlab.com to complete these exercises online and get instant feedback.

Review Questions

3.1 What is odd pricing?

3.2 What is cost-plus pricing? Is using cost-plus pricing consistent with a firm maximizing profits?

3.3 Give an example of a firm using a two-part tariff as part of its pricing strategy.

3.4 Why did the Walt Disney Company switch from charging for admission to Disneyland and charging for the rides to charging for admission and *not* charging for the rides?

Problems and Applications

3.5 One leading explanation for odd pricing is that it allows firms to trick buyers into the illusion that they're paying less than they really are. If this is true, in what types of markets and among what groups of consumers would you be mostly likely to find odd pricing? Should the government ban this practice and force companies to round up their prices to the nearest dollar?

3.6 Emerson Electric Company of St. Louis makes industrial equipment. Jerry Bernstein, the director of its price improvement team, describes how the company previously determined the prices of its products: "You developed a product, worked at the costs, and said, 'I need to make X [profit],' and you marked it up accordingly." Using this approach, Emerson arrived at a cost of $2,650 for a compact sensor used in pharmaceutical factories. In recent years, Emerson has moved away from a policy of cost-plus pricing, so it ended up charging $3,150, rather than $2,650, for the sensor. Discuss the factors that would lead Emerson to charge a price higher than the cost-plus price.

Source: Timothy Aeppel, "Amid Weak Inflation, Firms Turn Creative to Boost Prices," *Wall Street Journal*, September 18, 2002.

3.7 An article in the *Wall Street Journal* gives the following explanation of how products were traditionally priced at Parker-Hannifin Corporation:

> For as long as anyone at the 89-year-old company could recall, Parker used the same simple formula to determine prices of its 800,000 parts—from heat-resistant seals for jet engines to steel valves that hoist buckets on cherry pickers. Company managers would calculate how much it cost to make and deliver each product and add a flat percentage on top, usually aiming for about 35%. Many managers liked the method because it was straightforward. . . .

Is it likely that this system of pricing maximized the firm's profits? Briefly explain.

Source: Timothy Aeppel, "Changing the Formula: Seeking Perfect Prices, CEO Tears Up the Rules," *Wall Street Journal*, March 27, 2007, p. A1.

3.8 **(Related to the *Making the Connection* on page 520)** Would you expect a publishing company to use a strict cost-plus pricing system for all of its books? How might you find some indication whether a publishing company actually was using cost-pull pricing for all of its books?

3.9 Some professional sports teams charge fans a one-time lump sum for a "personal seat license." The personal seat license allows a fan the right to buy season tickets each year. No one without a personal seat license can buy season tickets. After the original purchase from the team, the personal seat licenses usually can be bought and sold by fans—whoever owns the seat license in a given year can buy season tickets—but the team does not earn any additional revenue from this buying and selling. Suppose a new sports stadium has been built, and the team is trying to decide on the price to charge for season tickets.

  a. Will the team make more profit from the combination of selling personal seat licenses and season tickets if it keeps the prices of the season tickets low or if it charges the monopoly price? Briefly explain.

  b. After the first year, is the team's strategy for pricing season tickets likely to change?

  c. Will it make a difference in the team's pricing strategy for season tickets if all the personal seat licenses are sold in the first year?

3.10 During the nineteenth century, the U.S. Congress encouraged railroad companies to build transcontinental railways across the Great Plains by giving them land grants. At that time, the federal government owned most of the land on the Great Plains. The land grants consisted of the land on which the railway was built and alternating sections of 1 square mile each on either side of the railway to a distance of 6 to 40 miles, depending on the location. The railroad companies were free to sell this land to farmers or anyone else who wanted to buy it. The process of selling the land took decades. Some economic historians have argued that the railroad companies charged lower prices to ship freight because they owned so much land along the tracks. Briefly explain the reasoning of these economic historians.

3.11 Thomas Kinnaman, an economist at Bucknell University, has analyzed the pricing of garbage collection:

> Setting the appropriate fee for garbage collection can be tricky when there are both fixed and marginal costs of garbage collection. . . . A curbside price set equal to the average total cost of collection would have high garbage generators partially subsidizing the fixed costs of low garbage generators. For example, if the time that a truck idles outside a one-can household and a two-can household is the same, and the fees are set to cover the total cost of garbage collection, then the two-can household paying twice that of the one-can household has subsidized a portion of the collection costs of the one-can household.

Briefly explain how a city might solve this pricing problem by using a two-part tariff in setting the garbage collection fees households are charged.

Source: Thomas C. Kinnaman, "Examining the Justification for Residential Recycling," *Journal of Economic Perspectives*, Vol. 20, No. 4, Fall 2006, p. 224.

>> **End Learning Objective 15.3**

Chapter 16

The **Markets** for **Labor** and **Other Factors** of **Production**

Why Are the Chicago Cubs Paying Alfonso Soriano $18 Million per Year?

Few businesses arouse in their customers the level of passion that sports teams do. Unlike most other industries, the sports industry has an entire section devoted to it in most newspapers. Jerry Jones made a fortune in the oil and gas exploration business in Oklahoma, but few people knew who he was until he bought the Dallas Cowboys football team. Of course, the best-known people in sports are not the owners of teams but some of their employees—the players.

Sports fans admire the skills of star athletes, but many are also fascinated by their high salaries. How is it, fans often wonder, that some athletes are paid salaries in the millions of dollars "just for playing a game"? Many baseball fans also wonder why a few teams, such as the New York Yankees, Boston Red Sox, and Chicago Cubs, are able to pay higher salaries than other teams. For example, before the 2007 baseball season, the Chicago Cubs signed Alfonso Soriano to a contract worth an average of $18 million per season. This represented a significant raise from the $10 million the Washington Nationals, his previous team, had paid him the year before.

The University of Illinois, Chicago pays professors on its faculty an average salary of $80,000. Why are the Cubs willing to pay a baseball player so much more than the University of Illinois, Chicago is willing to pay a professor?

The key to answering these questions is to understand that wages are determined in the labor market by the demand and supply of labor, just as the price of apples is determined by the demand and supply of apples and the price of DVDs is determined by the demand and supply of DVDs. In Chapter 3, we developed a model for analyzing the demand and supply of goods and services. We will use some of the same concepts in this chapter to analyze the demand and supply of labor and other factors of production. But there are important ways in which the markets for factors of production are not like markets for goods. The most obvious difference is that in factor markets, firms are deman-ders, and households are suppliers.

Another difference between the labor market and the markets for goods and services is that concepts of fairness arise more frequently in labor markets. When an athlete like Alfonso Soriano signs a contract for millions of dollars, people often wonder "Why should someone playing a game get paid so much more than teachers, nurses, and other people

doing more important jobs?" Because people typically earn most of their income from wages and salaries, they often view the labor market as being the most important market they participate in. **AN INSIDE LOOK** on **page 564** discusses the salaries of ex-college athletes who work for NASCAR pit crews.

Economics in YOUR Life!

Why Is It So Hard to Get a Raise?

Imagine that you have worked for a local sandwich shop for over a year and are preparing to ask for a raise. You might tell the manager that you are a good employee, with a good attitude and work ethic. You might also explain that you have learned more about your job and are now able to make sandwiches quicker, track inventory more accurately, and work the cash register more effectively than when you were first hired. Will this be enough to convince your manager to give you a raise? How can you convince your manager that you are worth more money than you are currently being paid? As you read this chapter, see if you can answer these questions. You can check your answers against those we provide at the end of the chapter. >> Continued on page 563

Factors of production Labor, capital, natural resources, and other inputs used to produce goods and services.

Firms use **factors of production**—such as labor, capital, and natural resources—to produce goods and services. For example, the Chicago Cubs use labor (baseball players), capital (Wrigley Field), and natural resources (the land on which Wrigley Field sits) to produce baseball games. In this chapter, we will explore how firms choose the profit-maximizing quantity of labor and other factors of production. The interaction between firm demand for labor and household supply of labor determines the equilibrium wage rate.

Because there are many different types of labor, there are many different labor markets. The equilibrium wage in the market for baseball players is much higher than the equilibrium wage in the market for college professors. We will explore why this is true. We will also explore how factors such as discrimination, unions, and compensation for dangerous or unpleasant jobs help explain differences among wages. We will then look at *personnel economics*, which is concerned with how firms can use economic analysis to design their employee compensation plans. Finally, we will analyze the markets for other factors of production.

16.1 LEARNING OBJECTIVE

16.1 | Explain how firms choose the profit-maximizing quantity of labor to employ.

The Demand for Labor

Up until now we have concentrated on consumer demand for final goods and services. The demand for labor is different from the demand for final goods and services because it is a *derived demand*. A **derived demand** is the demand for a factor of production that is based on the demand for the good the factor produces. You demand an Apple iPod because of the utility you receive from listening to music. Apple's demand for the labor to make iPods is derived from the underlying consumer demand for iPods. As a result, we can say that Apple's demand for labor depends primarily on two factors:

Derived demand The demand for a factor of production that is derived from the demand for the good the factor produces.

1 The additional iPods Apple will be able to produce if it hires one more worker

2 The additional revenue Apple receives from selling the additional iPods

The Marginal Revenue Product of Labor

Consider the following example. To keep the main point clear, let's assume that in the short run, Apple can increase production of iPods only by increasing the quantity of labor it employs. The table in Figure 16-1 shows the relationship between the quantity of workers Apple hires, the quantity of iPods it produces, the additional revenue from selling the additional iPods, and the additional profit from hiring each additional worker.

For simplicity, we are keeping the scale of Apple's factory very small. We will also assume that Apple is a perfect competitor both in the market for selling digital music players and in the market for hiring labor. This means that Apple is a *price taker* in both markets. Although this is not realistic, the basic analysis would not change if we assumed that Apple can affect the price of digital music players and the wage paid to workers. Given these assumptions, suppose that Apple can sell as many iPods as it wants at a price of $200 and can hire as many workers as it wants at a wage of $600 per week. Remember from Chapter 10 that the additional output a firm produces as a result of hiring one more worker is called the **marginal product of labor**. In the table, we calculate the marginal product of labor as the change in total output as each additional worker is hired. As we saw in Chapter 10, because of *the law of diminishing returns*, the marginal product of labor declines as a firm hires more workers.

Marginal product of labor The additional output a firm produces as a result of hiring one more worker.

When deciding how many workers to hire, a firm is not interested in how much *output* will increase as it hires another worker but in how much *revenue* will increase as it hires another worker. In other words, what matters is how much the firm's revenue will rise when it sells the additional output it can produce by hiring one more worker.

Number of Workers	Output of iPods per Week	Marginal Product of Labor (iPods per week)	Product Price	Marginal Revenue Product of Labor (dollars per week)	Wage (dollars per week)	Additional Profit from Hiring One More Worker (dollars per week)
L	Q	MP	P	$MRP = P \times MP$	W	$MRP - W$
0	0	—	$200	—	$600	—
1	6	6	200	$1,200	600	$600
2	11	5	200	1,000	600	400
3	15	4	200	800	600	200
4	18	3	200	600	600	0
5	20	2	200	400	600	−200
6	21	1	200	200	600	−400

Figure 16-1

The Marginal Revenue Product of Labor and the Demand for Labor

The marginal revenue product of labor equals the marginal product of labor multiplied by the price of the good. The marginal revenue product curve slopes downward because diminishing returns cause the marginal product of labor to decline as more workers are hired. A firm maximizes profits by hiring workers up to the point where the wage equals the marginal revenue product of labor. The marginal revenue product of labor curve is the firm's demand curve for labor because it tells the firm the profit-maximizing quantity of workers to hire at each wage. For example, using the demand curve shown in this figure, if the wage is $600, the firm will hire 4 workers.

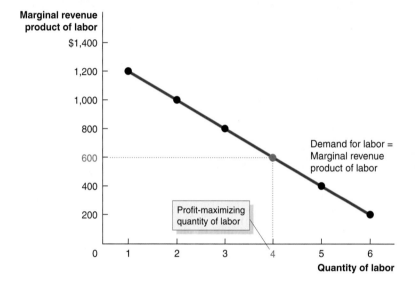

We can calculate this amount by multiplying the additional output produced by the product price. This amount is called the **marginal revenue product of labor** (*MRP*). For example, consider what happens if Apple increases the number of workers hired from 2 to 3. The table in Figure 16-1 shows that hiring the third worker allows Apple to increase its weekly output of iPods from 11 to 15, so the marginal product of labor is 4 iPods. The price of the iPods is $200, so the marginal revenue product of the third worker is 4 × $200, or $800. In other words, Apple adds $800 to its revenue as a result of hiring the third worker. In the graph, we plot the values of the marginal revenue product of labor at each quantity of labor.

To decide how many workers to hire, Apple must compare the additional revenue it earns from hiring another worker to the increase in its costs from paying that worker. The difference between the additional revenue and the additional cost is the additional profit (or loss) from hiring one more worker. This additional profit is shown in the last column of the table in Figure 16-1 and is calculated by subtracting the wage from the marginal revenue product of labor. As long as the marginal revenue product of labor is greater than the wage, Apple's profits are increasing, and it should continue to hire more workers. When the marginal revenue product of labor is less than the wage, Apple's profits are falling, and it should hire fewer workers. When the marginal revenue product of labor is equal to the wage, Apple has maximized its profits by hiring the optimal number of workers. The values in the table show that Apple should hire 4 workers. If the company hires a fifth worker, the marginal revenue product of $400 will be less than the wage of $600, and its profits will fall by $200. Table 16-1 summarizes the relationship between the marginal revenue product of labor and the wage.

Marginal revenue product of labor (*MRP*) The change in a firm's revenue as a result of hiring one more worker.

TABLE 16-1

The Relationship between the Marginal Revenue Product of Labor and the Wage

WHEN . . .	THEN THE FIRM . . .
MRP > W,	should hire more workers to increase profits.
MRP < W,	should hire fewer workers to increase profits.
MRP = W,	is hiring the optimal number of workers and is maximizing profits.

We can see from Figure 16-1 that if Apple has to pay a wage of $600 per week, it should hire 4 workers. If the wage were to rise to $1,000, then applying the rule that profits are maximized where the marginal revenue product of labor equals the wage, Apple should hire only 2 workers. Similarly, if the wage is only $400 per week, Apple should hire 5 workers. In fact, the marginal revenue product curve tells a firm how many workers it should hire at any wage rate. In other words, *the marginal revenue product of labor curve is the demand curve for labor.*

Solved Problem | 16-1

Hiring Decisions by a Firm That Is a Price Maker

We have assumed that Apple can sell as many iPods as it wants without having to cut the price. Recall from Chapter 11 that this is the case for firms in perfectly competitive markets. These firms are *price takers.* Suppose instead that a firm has market power and is a *price maker,* so that to increase sales, it must reduce the price.

Suppose Apple faces the situation shown in the following table. Fill in the blanks and then determine the profit-maximizing number of workers for Apple to hire. Briefly explain why hiring this number of workers is profit maximizing.

(1) QUANTITY OF LABOR	(2) OUTPUT OF iPODS PER WEEK	(3) MARGINAL PRODUCT OF LABOR	(4) PRODUCT PRICE	(5) TOTAL REVENUE	(6) MARGINAL REVENUE PRODUCT OF LABOR	(7) WAGE	(8) ADDITIONAL PROFIT FROM HIRING ONE ADDITIONAL WORKER
0	0	—	$200		—	$500	—
1	6	6	180			500	
2	11	5	160			500	
3	15	4	140			500	
4	18	3	120			500	
5	20	2	100			500	
6	21	1	80			500	

SOLVING THE PROBLEM:

Step 1: Review the chapter material. This problem is about determining the profit-maximizing quantity of labor for a firm to hire, so you may want to review the section "The Demand for Labor," which begins on page 536.

Step 2: Fill in the blanks in the table. As Apple hires more workers, it sells more iPods and earns more revenue. You can calculate how revenue increases by multiplying the number of iPods produced—shown in column 2—by the price—shown in column 4. Then you can calculate the marginal revenue product of labor as the change in revenue as each additional worker is hired. (Notice that in this case marginal revenue product is *not* calculated by multiplying the marginal product by the product price. Because Apple is a price maker, its marginal revenue from selling additional iPods is less than the price of iPods.) Finally, you can calculate the additional profit from hiring one more worker by subtracting the wage—shown in column 7—from each worker's marginal revenue product.

(1) QUANTITY OF LABOR	(2) OUTPUT OF iPODS PER WEEK	(3) MARGINAL PRODUCT OF LABOR	(4) PRODUCT PRICE	(5) TOTAL REVENUE	(6) MARGINAL REVENUE PRODUCT OF LABOR	(7) WAGE	(8) ADDITIONAL PROFIT FROM HIRING ONE ADDITIONAL WORKER
0	0	—	$200	$0	—	$500	—
1	6	6	180	1,080	$1,080	500	$580
2	11	5	160	1,760	680	500	180
3	15	4	140	2,100	340	500	−160
4	18	3	120	2,160	60	500	−440
5	20	2	100	2,000	−160	500	−660
6	21	1	80	1,680	−320	500	−820

Step 3: **Use the information in the table to determine the profit-maximizing quantity of workers to hire.** To determine the profit-maximizing quantity of workers to hire, you need to compare the marginal revenue product of labor with the wage. Column 8 does this by subtracting the wage from the marginal revenue product. As long as the values in column 8 are positive, the firm should continue to hire workers. The marginal revenue product of the second worker is $680, and the wage is $500, so column 8 shows that hiring the second worker will add $180 to Apple's profits. The marginal revenue product of the third worker is $340, and the wage is $500, so hiring the third worker would reduce Apple's profits by $160. Therefore, Apple will maximize profits by hiring 2 workers.

YOUR TURN: For more practice, do problem 1.5 on page 566 at the end of this chapter.

>> End Solved Problem 16-1

The Market Demand Curve for Labor

We can determine the market demand curve for labor in the same way we determine a market demand curve for a good. We saw in Chapter 9 that the market demand curve for a good is determined by adding up the quantity of the good demanded by each consumer at each price. Similarly, the market demand curve for labor is determined by adding up the quantity of labor demanded by each firm at each wage, holding constant all other variables that might affect the willingness of firms to hire workers.

Factors That Shift the Market Demand Curve for Labor

In constructing the demand curve for labor, we held constant all variables that would affect the willingness of firms to demand labor—except for the wage. An increase or a decrease in the wage causes *an increase or a decrease in the quantity of labor demanded*, which we show by a movement along the demand curve. If any variable other than the wage changes, the result is *an increase or a decrease in the demand for labor*, which we show by a shift of the demand curve. The five most important variables that cause the labor demand curve to shift are the following:

- *Increases in human capital.* **Human capital** represents the accumulated training and skills that workers possess. For example, a worker with a college education generally has more skills and is more productive than a worker who has only a high school diploma. If workers become more educated and are therefore able to produce

Human capital The accumulated training and skills that workers possess.

demand for animators much faster than the supply of animators was increasing. The annual salary for a top animator rose from about $125,000 in 1994 to $550,000 in 1999. These high salaries led more people with artistic ability to choose to get training as film animators, causing the supply of animators to increase after 1999. Several of the animated films released between 1999 and 2001 failed to earn profits, which caused some companies to stop making these films, thereby decreasing the demand for animators. The decrease in demand for animators and the increase in supply caused the salaries of top animators to fall from $550,000 in 1999 to $225,000 in 2002.

Making the Connection | Immigration and Wages, Then and Now

The flower industry is one of many industries in the United States that rely on immigrant workers.

Between 1900 and the outbreak of World War I in 1914, about 13.4 million immigrants arrived in the United States. Relative to the U.S. population—which was about 76 million in 1900—this was the largest wave of immigration in the history of the world. Many commentators at the time predicted that this great increase in the U.S. labor supply would cause a sharp fall in wages. Figure 16-6 shows that this is a reasonable prediction of the effect of an increase in labor supply on the equilibrium wage, *but only if the demand for labor remains unchanged*. In fact, the demand for labor increased rapidly during these years as technological progress, such as electrification and the development of mass-production techniques, increased the productivity of labor.

As a result, the demand for labor shifted to the right faster than the supply of labor, and wages rose. The following figure shows the situation in manufacturing. Both demand and supply increased, but because the shift in demand was greater than the shift in supply, average hourly earnings rose from less than $0.18 in 1900 to $0.22 in 1914, or by almost 25 percent. (The data for both years use 1914 prices to correct for the effects of inflation.) During the same years, employment in manufacturing rose from about 5.5 million workers to almost 9 million.

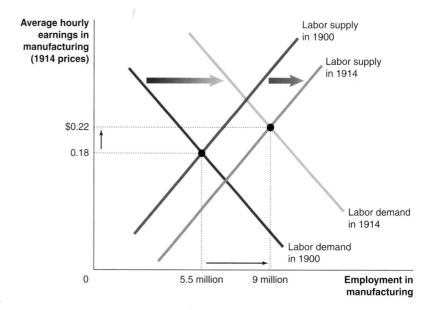

In 2007, the economics of immigration was once again in the forefront during the debate over a proposal by President George W. Bush to revise the immigration laws. President Bush proposed allowing the approximately 12 million illegal immigrants in the United States to enter a process that would allow them to become legal permanent residents. He also proposed strengthening security at the country's borders to reduce future illegal immigration. The figure below shows estimates by the Pew Hispanic Center indicating that illegal immigrants had become a substantial part of the labor supply in a number of industries.

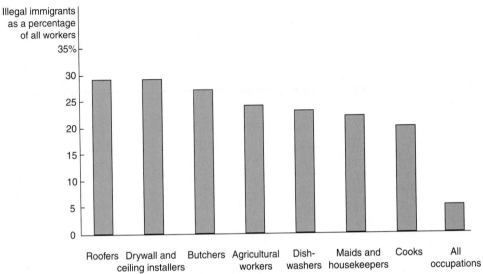

Source: Jeffrey S. Passel, "The Size and Characteristics of the Unauthorized Migrant Population in the U.S.," Pew Hispanic Center Research Report, March 7, 2006, Table 1, p. 12.

Economists have debated the impact of illegal immigrants on the wages of unskilled workers. As the figure indicates, illegal immigrants have substantially increased the supply of labor in some occupations. Some economists argue that illegal immigration may have significantly contributed to the distribution of income becoming more unequal in recent years. Illegal immigration increases income inequality if the supply of illegal workers reduces the wages of low-income workers relative to high-income workers. Claudia Goldin and Lawrence Katz, economists at Harvard University, have recently estimated that immigration—both legal and illegal—can explain only about 10 percent of the increase in the gap between the wages of college-educated workers and the wages of high school-educated workers during the years between 1980 and 2005. George Borjas, of Harvard, Jeffrey Grogger, of the University of Chicago, and Gordon Hanson, of the University of California, San Diego, find a significant impact of immigration on the employment opportunities of African Americans. They find that if as a result of immigration there is a 10 percent increase in the supply of labor with a particular skill, the wages of African Americans with that skill fall by 4 percent, the employment rate of African Americans falls by 3.5 percentage points, and the fraction of African Americans in jail increases by 1 percentage point.

The economic impact of immigration is certain to remain a hotly debated issue for the foreseeable future.

Source: U.S. Department of Commerce, *Historical Statistics of the United States*, Washington, DC: USGPO, 1976; Jeffrey S. Passel, "The Size and Characteristics of the Unauthorized Migrant Population in the U.S.," Pew Hispanic Center Research Report, March 7, 2006; Claudia Goldin and Lawrence F. Katz, "The Race Between Education and Technology," NBER Working Paper, No. 12984, March 2007; and George J. Borjas, Jeffrey Grogger, and Gordon H. Hanson, "Immigration and African-American Employment Opportunties," NBER Working Paper No. 12518, May 2007.

YOUR TURN: Test your understanding by doing related problems 3.5, 3.6, 3.7, and 3.8 on page 568 at the end of this chapter.

16.4 | Use demand and supply analysis to explain how compensating differentials, discrimination, and labor unions cause wages to differ.

Explaining Differences in Wages

A key conclusion of our discussion of the labor market is that the equilibrium wage equals the marginal revenue product of labor. The more productive workers are and the higher the price workers' output can be sold for, the higher the wages workers will receive. At the beginning of the chapter, we raised the question of why major league baseball players are paid so much more than college professors. We are now ready to use demand and supply analysis to answer this question. Figure 16-7 shows the demand and supply curves for major league baseball players and the demand and supply curves for college professors.

Consider first the marginal revenue product of baseball players, which is the additional revenue a team owner will receive from hiring one more player. Baseball players are hired to produce baseball games that are then sold to fans who pay admission to baseball stadiums and to radio and television stations that broadcast the games. Because a major league baseball team can sell each baseball game for a large amount, the marginal revenue product of baseball players is high. The supply of people with the ability to play major league baseball is also very limited. As a result, the average annual salary of the 750 major league baseball players is about $2,700,000.

The marginal revenue product of college professors is much lower than for baseball players. College professors are hired to produce college educations that are then sold to students and their parents. Although one year's college tuition is quite high at many colleges, hiring one more professor allows a college to admit at most a few more students. So, the marginal revenue product of a college professor is much lower than the marginal revenue product of a baseball player. There are also many more people who possess the skills to be a college professor than possess the skills to be a major league baseball player. As a result, the country's 663,000 college professors are paid an average salary of about $73,000.

This still leaves unanswered the question raised at the beginning of this chapter: Why are the Chicago Cubs willing to pay Alfonso Soriano more than the Washington Nationals were? Soriano's marginal product—which we can think of as the extra games a

Figure 16-7

Baseball Players Are Paid More Than College Professors

The marginal revenue product of baseball players is very high, and the supply of people with the ability to play major league baseball is low. The result is that the 750 major league baseball players receive an average wage of $2,700,000. The marginal revenue product of college professors is much lower, and the supply of people with the ability to be college professors is much higher. The result is that the 663,000 college professors in the United States receive an average wage of $73,000, far below that of baseball players.

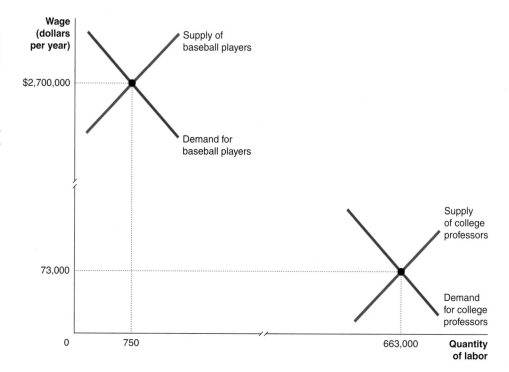

Don't Let This Happen to **YOU!**

Remember That Prices and Wages Are Determined at the Margin

You have probably heard some variation of the following remark: "We could live without baseball, but we can't live without the garbage being hauled away. In a more rational world, garbage collectors would be paid more than baseball players." This remark seems logical: The total value to society of having the garbage hauled away certainly is greater than the total value of baseball games. But wages—like prices—do not depend on total value but on *marginal* value. The *additional* baseball games the Chicago Cubs expect to win by signing Alfonso Soriano will result in millions of dollars in increased revenue. The supply of people with the ability to play major league baseball is very limited. The supply of people with the ability to be trash haulers is much greater. If a trash-hauling firm hires another worker, the *additional* trash-hauling services it can now offer will bring in a relatively small amount of revenue. The *total* value of baseball games and the *total* value of trash hauling are not relevant in determining the relative salaries of baseball players and garbage collectors.

This point is related to the diamond and water paradox first noted by Adam Smith. On the one hand, water is very valuable—we literally couldn't live without it—but its price is very low. On the other hand, apart from a few industrial uses, diamonds are used only for jewelry, yet their prices are quite high. We resolve the paradox by noting that the price of water is low because the supply is very large and the additional benefit consumers receive from the last gallon purchased is low. The price of diamonds is high because the supply is very small, and the additional benefit consumers receive from the last diamond purchased is high.

YOUR TURN: Test your understanding by doing related problem 4.6 on page 569 at the end of this chapter.

team will win by employing him—should be about the same in Chicago as it was in Washington, DC. But his *marginal revenue product* will be higher in Chicago. Because the population of the Chicago metropolitan area is about twice as large as the population of the Washington metropolitan area, winning more games will result in a greater increase in attendance at Chicago Cubs games than it would at Washington Nationals games. It will also result in a greater increase in viewers for Cubs games on television. Therefore, the Cubs are able to sell the extra wins that Soriano produces for much more than the Washington Nationals can. This difference explains why the Cubs were willing to pay Soriano $18 million per year when he had made "only" $10 million with the Nationals.

Making the Connection | Technology and the Earnings of "Superstars"

The gap between Alfonso Soriano's salary and the salary of the lowest-paid baseball players is much greater than the gap between the salaries paid during the 1950s and 1960s to top players such as Mickey Mantle and Willie Mays and the salaries of the lowest-paid players. Similarly, the gap between the $20 million Julia Roberts is paid to star in a movie and the salary paid to an actor in a minor role is much greater than the gap between the salaries paid during the 1930s and 1940s to stars such as Clark Gable and Cary Grant and the salaries paid to bit players. In fact, in most areas of sports and entertainment, the highest-paid performers—the "superstars"—now have much higher incomes relative to other members of their professions than was true a few decades ago.

The increase in the relative incomes of superstars is mainly due to technological advances. The spread of cable television has increased the number of potential viewers of Cubs games, but many of those viewers will watch only if the Cubs are winning. This increases the value to the Cubs of winning games and, therefore, increases Soriano's marginal revenue product and the salary he can earn.

With DVDs, Internet streaming video, and pay-per-view cable, the value to movie studios of producing a hit movie has risen greatly. Not surprisingly, movie studios have also increased their willingness to pay large salaries to stars like Julia Roberts or Brad Pitt because they think these superstars will significantly raise the chances of a film being successful.

Why does Julia Roberts earn more today relative to the typical actor than stars did in the 1940s?

This process has been going on for a long time. For instance, before the invention of the motion picture, anyone who wanted to see a play had to attend the theater and see a live performance. Limits on the number of people who could see the best actors and actresses perform created an opportunity for many more people to succeed in the acting profession, and the gap between the salaries earned by the best actors and the salaries earned by average actors was relatively small. Today, when a hit movie starring Julia Roberts appears on DVD, millions of people will buy or rent it, and they will not be forced to spend money to see a lesser actress, as their great-great-grandparents might have been.

YOUR TURN: Test your understanding by doing related problems 4.9 and 4.10 on page 569 at the end of this chapter.

▬▬▬▬▬▬▬▬▬

Differences in marginal revenue products are the most important factor in explaining differences in wages, but they are not the whole story. To provide a more complete explanation for differences in wages, we must take into account three important aspects of labor markets: compensating differentials, discrimination, and labor unions. We begin with compensating differentials.

Compensating Differentials

Suppose Paul runs a video rental store and acquires a reputation for being a bad boss who yells at his workers and is generally unpleasant. Two blocks away, Brendan also runs a video rental store, but Brendan is always very polite to his workers. We would expect in these circumstances that Paul will have to pay a higher wage than Brendan to attract and retain workers. Higher wages that compensate workers for unpleasant aspects of a job are called **compensating differentials**.

If working in a dynamite factory requires the same degree of training and education as working in a semiconductor factory but is much more dangerous, a larger number of workers will want to work making semiconductors than will want to work making dynamite. As a consequence, the wages of dynamite workers will be higher than the wages of semiconductor workers. We can think of the difference in wages as being the price of risk. As each worker decides on his or her willingness to assume risk and decides how much higher the wage must be to compensate for assuming more risk, wages will adjust so that dynamite factories will end up paying wages that are just high enough to compensate workers who choose to work there for the extra risk they assume. Only when workers in dynamite factories have been fully compensated with higher wages for the additional risk they assume will dynamite companies be able to attract enough workers.

One surprising implication of compensating differentials is that *laws protecting the health and safety of workers may not make workers better off*. To see this, suppose that dynamite factories pay wages of $25 per hour, and semiconductor factories pay wages of $20 per hour, with the $5 difference in wages being a compensating differential for the greater risk of working in a dynamite factory. Suppose that the government passes a law regulating the manufacture of dynamite in order to improve safety in dynamite factories. As a result of this law, dynamite factories are no longer any more dangerous than semiconductor factories. Once this happens, the wages in dynamite factories will decline to $20 per hour, the same as in semiconductor factories. Are workers in dynamite factories any better or worse off? Before the law was passed, their wages were $25 per hour, but $5 per hour was a compensating differential for the extra risk they were exposed to. Now their wages are only $20 per hour, but the extra risk has been eliminated. The conclusion seems to be that dynamite workers are no better off as a result of the safety legislation.

This conclusion is only true, though, if the compensating differential actually does compensate workers fully for the additional risk. George Akerlof of the University of California, Berkeley, and William Dickens of the Brookings Institution have argued that the psychological principle known as *cognitive dissonance* might cause workers to underestimate the true risk of their jobs. According to this principle, people prefer to think of

Compensating differentials Higher wages that compensate workers for unpleasant aspects of a job.

themselves as intelligent and rational and tend to reject evidence that seems to contradict this image. Because working in a very hazardous job may seem irrational, workers in such jobs may refuse to believe that the jobs really are hazardous. Akerlof and Dickens present evidence that workers in chemical plants producing benzene and workers in nuclear power plants underestimate the hazards of their jobs. If this is true, the wages of these workers will not be high enough to compensate them fully for the risk they have assumed. So, in this situation, safety legislation may make workers better off.

Discrimination

Table 16-2 shows that in the United States, white males on average earn more than other groups. One possible explanation for this is **economic discrimination**, which involves paying a person a lower wage or excluding a person from an occupation on the basis of an irrelevant characteristic such as race or gender.

Economic discrimination Paying a person a lower wage or excluding a person from an occupation on the basis of an irrelevant characteristic such as race or gender.

If employers discriminate by hiring only white males for high-paying jobs or by paying white males higher wages than other groups working the same jobs, white males would have higher earnings, as Table 16-2 shows. However, excluding groups from certain jobs or paying one group more than another has been illegal in the United States since the passage of the Equal Pay Act of 1963 and the Civil Rights Act of 1964. Nevertheless, it is possible that employers are ignoring the law and practicing economic discrimination.

Most economists believe that only a small amount of the gap between the wages of white males and the wages of other groups is due to discrimination. Instead, most of the gap is explained by three main factors:

1 Differences in education

2 Differences in experience

3 Differing preferences for jobs

Differences in Education Some of the difference between the incomes of whites and the incomes of blacks can be explained by differences in education. Historically, African Americans have had less schooling than whites. Although the gap has closed significantly over the years, 90 percent of adult non-Hispanic white males in 2005 had graduated from high school, but only 80 percent of adult African American males had. Whereas 33 percent of white males had graduated from college, only 17 percent of African American males had. These statistics understate the true gap in education between blacks and whites because many blacks receive a substandard education in inner-city schools. Not surprisingly, studies have shown that differing levels of education can account for a significant part of the gap between the earnings of white and black males.

GROUP	ANNUAL EARNINGS
White males	$46,746
White females	34,464
Black males	33,248
Black females	29,749
Hispanic males	26,769
Hispanic females	24,402

Note: The values are median annual earnings for persons who worked full time, year round in 2005. Persons of Hispanic origin can be of any race.

Source: U.S. Bureau of the Census, Table PINC-10, Current Population Survey, *Annual Social and Economic Supplement,* March 2006.

TABLE 16-2

Why Do White Males Earn More Than Other Groups?

hired is L_1. Setting the wage for dental technicians above equilibrium at $550 increases the quantity of labor supplied in this occupation from L_1 to L_3 but reduces the quantity of labor demanded by employers from L_1 to L_2. The result is a surplus of dental technicians equal to $L_3 - L_2$, as shown by the bracket in the graph.

EXTRA CREDIT: Most economists are skeptical of government attempts to set wages and prices, as comparable-worth legislation would require. Supporters of comparable-worth legislation, by contrast, see differences between men's and women's wages as being mainly due to discrimination and are looking to government legislation as a solution.

YOUR TURN: For more practice, do related problems 4.15 and 4.16 on page 570 at the end of this chapter.

>> **End Solved Problem 16-4**

The Difficulty of Measuring Discrimination When two people are paid different wages, discrimination may be the explanation. But differences in productivity or preferences may also be an explanation. Labor economists have attempted to measure what part of differences in wages between blacks and whites and between men and women is due to discrimination and what part is due to other factors. Unfortunately, it is difficult to measure precisely differences in productivity or in worker preferences. As a result, we can't know exactly the extent of economic discrimination in the United States today. Most economists do believe, however, that most of the differences in wages between different groups are due to factors other than discrimination.

Does It Pay to Discriminate? Many economists argue that economic discrimination is no longer a major factor in labor markets in the United States. One reason is that *employers who discriminate pay an economic penalty.* To see why this is true, let's consider a simplified example. Suppose that men and women are equally qualified to be airline pilots and that, initially, airlines do not discriminate. In Figure 16-8, we divide the airlines

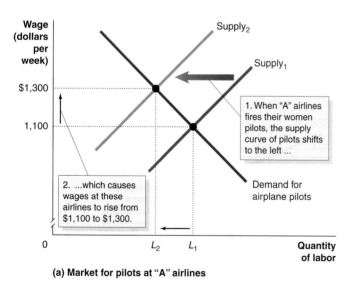

(a) Market for pilots at "A" airlines

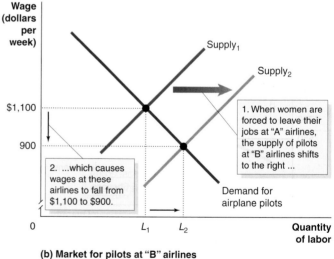

(b) Market for pilots at "B" airlines

Figure 16-8 | Discrimination and Wages

In this hypothetical example, we assume that initially neither "A" airlines nor "B" airlines discriminate. As a result, men and women pilots receive the same wage of $1,100 per week at both groups of airlines. We then assume that "A" airlines discriminates by firing all their women pilots. Panel (a) shows that this reduces the supply of pilots to "A" airlines and raises the wage paid by these airlines from $1,100 to $1,300. Panel (b) shows that this increases the supply of pilots to "B" airlines and lowers the wage paid by these airlines from $1,100 to $900. All the women pilots will end up being employed at the nondiscriminating airlines and will be paid a lower wage than the men who are employed by the discriminating airlines.

into two groups: "A" airlines and "B" airlines. If neither group of airlines discriminates, we would expect them to pay an equal wage of $1,100 per week to both men and women pilots. Now suppose that "A" airlines decide to discriminate and to fire all their women pilots. This action will reduce the supply of pilots to these airlines and, as shown in panel (a), that will force up the wage from $1,100 to $1,300. At the same time, as women fired from the jobs with "A" airlines apply for jobs with "B" airlines, the supply of pilots to "B" airlines will increase, and the equilibrium wage will fall from $1,100 to $900. All the women pilots will end up being employed at the nondiscriminating airlines and be paid a lower wage than the men who are employed by the discriminating airlines.

But this situation cannot persist for two reasons. First, male pilots employed by "B" airlines will also receive the lower wage. This lower wage gives them an incentive to quit their jobs at "B" airlines and apply at "A" airlines, which will shift the labor supply curve for "B" airlines to the left and the labor supply curve for "A" airlines to the right. Second, "A" airlines are paying $1,300 per week to hire pilots who are no more productive than the pilots being paid $900 per week by "B" airlines. As a result, "B" airlines will have lower costs and will be able to charge lower prices. Eventually, "A" airlines will lose their customers to "B" airlines and be driven out of business. The market will have imposed an economic penalty on the discriminating airlines. So, discrimination will not persist, and the wages of men and women pilots will become equal.

Can we conclude from this analysis that competition in markets will eliminate all economic discrimination? Unfortunately, this optimistic conclusion is not completely accurate. We know that until the Civil Rights Act of 1964 was passed, many firms in the United States refused to hire blacks. Even though this practice had persisted for decades, nondiscriminating competitors did not drive these firms out of business. Why not? There were three important factors:

1   ***Worker discrimination.*** In many cases, white workers refused to work alongside black workers. As a result, some industries—such as the important cotton textile industry in the South—were all white. Because of discrimination by white workers, a businessperson who wanted to use low-cost black labor might need to hire an all-black workforce. Some businesspeople tried this, but because blacks had been excluded from these industries, they often lacked the skills and experience to form an effective workforce.

2   ***Customer discrimination.*** Some white consumers were unwilling to buy from companies in certain industries if they employed black workers. This was not a significant barrier in manufacturing industries, where customers would not know the race of the workers producing the good. It was, however, a problem for firms in industries in which workers came into direct contact with the public.

3   ***Negative feedback loops.*** Our analysis in Figure 16-8 assumed that men and women pilots were equally qualified. However, if discrimination makes it difficult for a member of a group to find employment in a particular occupation, his or her incentive to be trained to enter that occupation is reduced. Consider the legal profession as an example. In 1952, future Supreme Court Justice Sandra Day O'Connor graduated third in her class at Stanford University Law School and was an editor of the *Stanford Law Review*, but for some time she was unable to find a job as a lawyer because in those years, many law firms would not hire women. Facing such bleak job prospects, it's not surprising that relatively few women entered law school. As a result, a law firm that did not discriminate would have been unable to act like the nondiscriminating airlines in our example by hiring women lawyers at a lower salary and using this cost advantage to drive discriminating law firms out of business. In this situation, an unfortunate feedback loop was in place: Few women prepared to become lawyers because many law firms discriminated against women, and nondiscriminating law firms were unable to drive discriminating law firms out of business because there were too few women lawyers available.

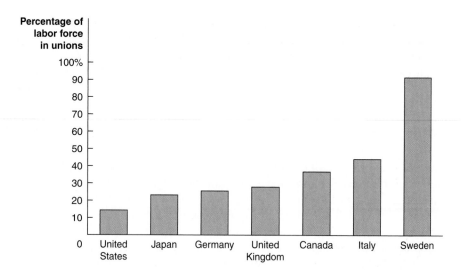

Figure 16-9 │ The United States Is Less Unionized Than Most Industrial Countries

In 2006, the percentage of the labor force belonging to unions was lower in the United States than in most other industrial countries.
Source: International Labour Organization.

Most economists agree that the market imposes an economic penalty on firms that discriminate, but because of the factors just discussed, it may take the market a very long time to eliminate discrimination entirely. The passage of the Civil Rights Act of 1964, which outlawed hiring discrimination on the basis of race and sex, greatly sped up the process of reducing economic discrimination in the United States.

Labor Unions

Labor union An organization of employees that has the legal right to bargain with employers about wages and working conditions.

Workers' wages can differ depending on whether the workers are members of labor unions. **Labor unions** are organizations of employees that have the legal right to bargain with employers about wages and working conditions. If a union is unable to reach an agreement with a company, it has the legal right to call a *strike*, which means its members refuse to work until a satisfactory agreement has been reached. As Figure 16-9 shows, a smaller fraction of the U.S. labor force is unionized than in most other industrial countries.

As Table 16-4 shows, in the United States, workers in unions receive higher wages than workers who are not in unions. Do union members earn more than nonunion members because they are in unions? The answer might seem to be "yes," but many union workers are in industries, such as automobile manufacturing, in which their marginal revenue products are high, so their wages would be high even if they were not unionized. Economists who have attempted to estimate statistically the impact of unionization on wages have concluded that being in a union increases a worker's wages about 10 percent, holding constant other factors, such as the industry the worker is in. A

TABLE 16-4

Union Workers Earn More Than Nonunion Workers

	AVERAGE WEEKLY EARNINGS
UNION WORKERS	$833
NONUNION WORKERS	642

Note: "Union workers" includes union members as well as workers who are represented by unions but who are not members of them.
Source: U.S. Bureau of Labor Statistics, *Union Members Summary*, January 25, 2007.

related question is whether unions raise the total amount of wages received by all workers, whether unionized or not. Because the share of national income received by workers has remained roughly constant over many years, most economists do not believe that unions have raised the total amount of wages received by workers.

16.5 | Discuss the role personnel economics can play in helping firms deal with human resources issues.

Personnel Economics

Traditionally, labor economists have focused on issues such as the effects of labor unions on wages or the determinants of changes in average wages over time. They have spent less time analyzing *human resources issues*, which address how firms hire, train, and promote workers and set their wages and benefits. In recent years, some labor economists, including Edward Lazear of Stanford University and William Neilson of Texas A&M University, have begun exploring the application of economic analysis to human resources issues. This new focus has become known as **personnel economics**.

Personnel economics analyzes the link between differences among jobs and differences in the way workers are paid. Jobs have different skill requirements, require more or less interaction with other workers, have to be performed in more or less unpleasant environments, and so on. Firms need to design compensation policies that take into account these differences. Personnel economics also analyzes policies related to other human resources issues, such as promotions, training, and pensions. In this brief overview, we look only at compensation policies.

Personnel economics The application of economic analysis to human resources issues.

Should Workers' Pay Depend on How Much They Work or on How Much They Produce?

One issue personnel economics addresses is when workers should receive *straight-time pay*—a certain wage per hour or salary per week or month—and when they should receive *commission* or *piece-rate pay*—a wage based on how much output they produce.

Suppose, for example, that Anne owns a car dealership and is trying to decide whether to pay her salespeople a salary of $800 per week or a commission of $200 on each car they sell. Figure 16-10 compares the compensation a salesperson would receive under the two systems, according to the number of cars the salesperson sells.

With a straight salary, the salesperson receives $800 per week, no matter how many cars she sells. This outcome is shown by the horizontal line in Figure 16-10. If she receives a commission of $200 per car, her compensation will increase with every car she sells. This outcome is shown by the upward-sloping line. A salesperson who sells fewer than 4 cars per week would earn more by receiving a straight salary of $800 per week. A salesperson who sells more than 4 cars per week would be better off receiving the $200-per-car commission. We can identify two advantages Anne would receive from paying her salespeople commissions rather than salaries: She would attract and retain the most productive employees, and she would provide an incentive to her employees to sell more cars.

Suppose that other car dealerships were all paying salaries of $800 per week. If Anne pays her employees on commission, any of her employees who are unable to sell at least 4 cars per week can improve their pay by going to work for one of her competitors. By the same token, any salespeople at Anne's competitors who can sell more than 4 cars per week can raise their pay by quitting and coming to work for Anne. Over time, Anne will find her least productive employees leaving, while she is able to hire new employees who are more productive.

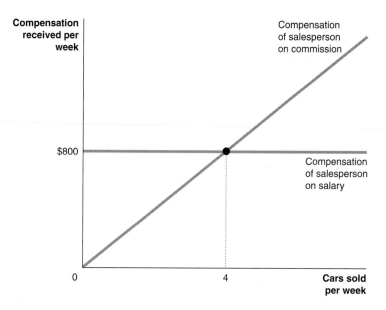

Figure 16-10 | Paying Car Salespeople by Salary or by Commission

This figure compares the compensation a car salesperson receives if she is on a straight salary of $800 per week or if she receives a commission of $200 for each car she sells. With a straight salary, she receives $800 per week, no matter how many cars she sells. This outcome is shown by the horizontal line in the figure. If she receives a commission of $200 per car, her compensation will increase with every car she sells. This outcome is shown by the upward-sloping line. If she sells fewer than 4 cars per week, she would be better off with the $800 salary. If she sells more than 4 cars per week, she would be better off with the $200-per-car commission.

Paying a commission also increases the incentive Anne's salespeople have to sell more cars. If Anne paid a salary, her employees would receive the same amount no matter how few cars they sold. An employee on salary might decide on a particularly hot or cold day that it was less trouble to stay inside the building than to go out on the car lot to greet potential customers. An employee on commission would know that the additional effort expended on selling more cars would be rewarded with additional compensation.

A piece-rate system at Safelite AutoGlass led to increased worker wages and firm profits.

Making the Connection | **Raising Pay, Productivity, and Profits at Safelite AutoGlass**

Safelite Group, headquartered in Columbus, Ohio, is the parent company of Safelite AutoGlass, the nation's largest installer of auto glass, with 600 repair shops. In the mid-1990s, Safelite shifted from paying its glass installers hourly wages to paying them on the basis of how many windows they installed. Safelite already had in place a computer system that allowed it to track easily how many windows each worker installed per day. To make sure quality did not suffer, Safelite added a rule that if a workmanship-related defect occurred with the installed windshield, the worker would have to install a new windshield and would not be paid for the additional work.

Edward Lazear analyzed data provided by the firm and discovered that under the new piece-rate system, the number of windows installed per worker jumped 44 percent. Lazear estimates that half of this increase was due to increased productivity from workers who continued with the company and half was due to new hires being more productive than the workers they replaced who had left the company. Worker pay rose on average by about 9.9 percent. Ninety-two percent of workers experienced a pay increase, and one-quarter received an increase of at least 28 percent. Safelite's profits also increased as the cost to the company per window installed fell from \$44.43 under the hourly wage system to \$35.24 under the piece-rate system.

Sociologists sometimes question whether worker productivity can be increased through the use of monetary incentives. The experience of Safelite AutoGlass provides a clear example of workers reacting favorably to the opportunity to increase output in exchange for higher compensation.

Source: Edward P. Lazear, "Performance Pay and Productivity," *American Economic Review*, Vol. 90, No. 5, December 2000, pp. 1346–1361.

YOUR TURN: Test your understanding by doing related problem 5.7 on page 572 at the end of this chapter.

Other Considerations in Setting Compensation Systems

The discussion so far indicates that companies will find it more profitable to use a commission or piece-rate system of compensation rather than a salary system. In fact, many firms continue to pay their workers salaries, which means they are paying their workers on the basis of how long they work rather than on the basis of how much they produce. Firms may choose a salary system for several good reasons:

- *Difficulty in measuring output.* Often it is difficult to attribute output to any particular worker. For example, projects carried out by an engineering firm may involve teams of workers whose individual contributions are difficult to distinguish. On assembly lines, such as those used in the automobile industry, the amount produced by each worker is determined by the speed of the line, which is set by managers rather than by workers. Managers at many firms perform such a wide variety of tasks that measuring their output would be costly, if it could be done at all.

- *Concerns about quality.* If workers are paid on the basis of the number of units produced, they may become less concerned about quality. An office assistant who is paid on the basis of the quantity of letters typed may become careless about how many typos the letters contain. In some cases, there are ways around this problem; for example, the assistant may be required to correct the mistakes on his or her own time without pay.

- *Worker dislike of risk.* Piece-rate or commission systems of compensation increase the risk to workers because sometimes output declines for reasons not connected to the worker's effort. For example, if there is a very snowy winter, few customers may show up at Anne's auto dealership. Through no fault of their own, her salespeople may have great difficulty selling any cars. If they are paid a salary, their income will not be affected, but if they are on commission, their incomes may drop to low levels. The flip side of this is that by paying salaries, Anne assumes a greater risk. During a snowy winter, her payroll expenses will remain high even though her sales are low. With a commission system of compensation, her payroll expenses will decline along with her sales. But owners of firms are typically better able to bear risk than are workers. As a result, some firms may find that workers who would earn more under a commission system will prefer to receive a salary to reduce their risk. In these situations, paying a lower salary may reduce the firm's payroll expenses compared with what they would have been under a commission or piece-rate system.

Personnel economics is a relatively new field, but it holds great potential for helping firms deal more efficiently with human relations issues.

16.6 | Show how equilibrium prices are determined in the markets for capital and natural resources.

The Markets for Capital and Natural Resources

The approach we have used to analyze the market for labor can also be used to analyze the markets for other factors of production. We have seen that the demand for labor is determined by the marginal revenue product of labor because the value to a firm from hiring another worker equals the increase in the firm's revenue from selling the additional output it can produce by hiring the worker. The demand for capital and natural resources is determined in a similar way.

The Market for Capital

Physical capital includes machines, equipment, and buildings. Firms sometimes buy capital, but we will focus on situations in which firms rent capital. A chocolate manufacturer renting a warehouse and an airline leasing a plane are examples of firms renting capital. Like the demand for labor, the demand for capital is a derived demand. When a firm is considering increasing its capital by, for example, employing another machine, the value it receives equals the increase in the firm's revenue from selling the additional output it can produce by employing the machine. The *marginal revenue product of capital* is the change in the firm's revenue as a result of employing one more unit of capital, such as a machine. We have seen that the marginal revenue product of labor curve is the demand curve for labor. Similarly, the marginal revenue product of capital curve is also the demand curve for capital.

Firms producing capital goods face increasing marginal costs, so the supply curve of capital goods is upward sloping, as are the supply curves for other goods and services. Figure 16-11 shows equilibrium in the market for capital. In equilibrium,

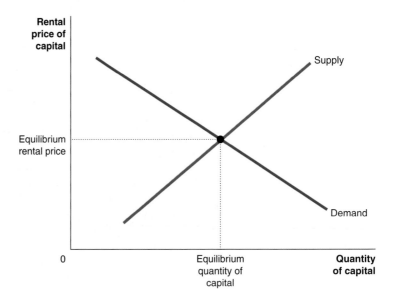

Figure 16-11 | Equilibrium in the Market for Capital

The rental price of capital is determined by equilibrium in the market for capital. In equilibrium, the rental price of capital is equal to the marginal revenue product of capital.

suppliers of capital receive a rental price equal to the marginal revenue product of capital, just as suppliers of labor receive a wage equal to the marginal revenue product of labor.

The Market for Natural Resources

The market for natural resources can be analyzed in the same way as the markets for labor and capital. When a firm is considering employing more natural resources, the value it receives equals the increase in the firm's revenue from selling the additional output it can produce by buying the natural resources. So, the demand for natural resources is also a derived demand. The *marginal revenue product of natural resources* is the change in the firm's revenue as a result of employing one more unit of natural resources, such as a barrel of oil. The marginal revenue product of natural resources curve is also the demand curve for natural resources.

Although the total quantity of most natural resources is ultimately fixed—as the humorist Will Rogers once remarked, "Buy land; They ain't making any more of it"—in many cases, the quantity supplied still responds to the price. For example, although the total quantity of oil deposits in the world is fixed, an increase in the price of oil will result in an increase in the quantity of oil supplied during a particular period. The result, as shown in panel (a) of Figure 16-12, is an upward-sloping supply curve. In some cases, however, the quantity of a natural resource that will be supplied is fixed and will not change as the price changes. The land available at a busy intersection is fixed, for example. In panel (b) of Figure 16-12, we illustrate this situation with a supply curve that is a vertical line, or perfectly inelastic. The price received by a factor of production that is in fixed supply is called an **economic rent** (or **pure rent**) because, in this case, the price of the factor is determined only by demand. For example, if a new highway diverts much of the traffic from a previously busy intersection, the

Economic rent (or **pure rent**) The price of a factor of production that is in fixed supply.

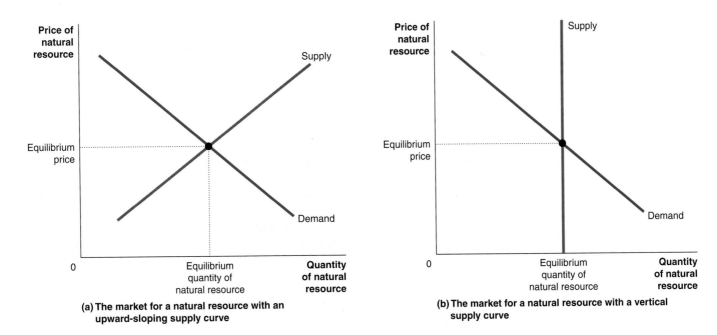

(a) The market for a natural resource with an upward-sloping supply curve

(b) The market for a natural resource with a vertical supply curve

Figure 16-12 | Equilibrium in the Market for Natural Resources

In panel (a), the supply curve of a natural resource is upward sloping. The price of the natural resource is determined by the interaction of demand and supply. In panel (b), the supply curve of the natural resource is a vertical line, indicating that the quantity supplied does not respond to changes in price. In this case, the price of the natural resource is determined only by demand. The price of a factor of production with a vertical supply curve is called an *economic rent* or a *pure rent*.

demand for the land will decline and the price of the land will fall, but the quantity of the land will not change.

Monopsony

Monopsony The sole buyer of a factor of production.

In Chapter 14, we analyzed the case of *monopoly*, where a firm is the sole *seller* of a good or service. What happens if a firm is the sole *buyer* of a factor of production? This case, which is known as **monopsony**, is comparatively rare. An example is a firm in an isolated town—perhaps a lumber mill in a small town in Washington or Oregon—that is the sole employer of labor in that location. In the nineteenth and early twentieth centuries, some coal mining firms were the sole employers in certain small towns in West Virginia and some pineapple plantations were the sole employers on certain small islands in Hawaii. In these cases, not only would the firm own the mill, mine, or plantation, but it would also own the stores and other businesses in the town. Workers would have the choice of working for the sole employer in the town or moving to another town.

With only one lumber mill in town, the wages of these loggers won't be as high.

We know that a firm with a monopoly in an output market takes advantage of its market power to reduce the quantity supplied to force up the market price and increase its profits. A firm that has a monopsony in a factor market would employ a similar strategy: It would restrict the quantity of the factor demanded to force down the price of the factor and increase profits. A firm with a monopsony in a labor market will hire fewer workers and pay lower wages than would be the case in a competitive market. Because fewer workers are hired than would be true in a competitive market, monopsony results in a deadweight loss. Monopoly and monopsony have similar effects on the economy: In both cases a firm's market power results in a lower equilibrium quantity, a deadweight loss, and a reduction in economic efficiency compared with a competitive market.

In some cases, monopsony in labor markets is offset by worker membership in a labor union. A notable example of this is professional sports. For instance, Major League Baseball (MLB) effectively has a monopsony on employing professional baseball players. (Although independent baseball leagues exist, none of the best players play for these teams, and the teams pay salaries that are a small fraction of those paid by MLB teams.) The monopsony power of the owners of MLB teams is offset by the power of the Major League Baseball Players Association, the union that represents baseball players. Bargaining between the representatives of MLB and the players union has resulted in baseball players being paid something close to what they would be receiving in a competitive market.

The Marginal Productivity Theory of Income Distribution

We have seen that in equilibrium, each factor of production receives a price equal to its marginal revenue product. We can use this fact to explain the distribution of income. Marginal revenue product represents the value of a factor's marginal contribution to producing goods and services. Therefore, individuals will receive income equal to the marginal contributions to production from the factors of production they own, including their labor. The more factors of production an individual owns and the more productive those factors are, the higher the individual's income will be. This approach to explaining the distribution of income is called the **marginal productivity theory of income distribution**. The marginal productivity theory of income distribution was developed by John Bates Clark, who taught at Columbia University in the late nineteenth and early twentieth centuries.

Marginal productivity theory of income distribution The theory that the distribution of income is determined by the marginal productivity of the factors of production that individuals own.

Economics in YOUR Life!

>> Continued from page 535

At the beginning of the chapter, we asked you to imagine that you work at a local sandwich shop and that you plan to ask your manager for a raise. One way to show the manager your worth is to demonstrate how many dollars your work earns for the sandwich shop: your marginal revenue product. You could certainly suggest that as you have become better at your job and have gained new skills that you are a more productive employee, but more importantly, that your productivity results in increased revenue to the sandwich shop. By showing how your employment contributes to higher revenue and profit for the shop, you may be able to convince your manager to raise your pay.

Conclusion

In this chapter, we used the demand and supply model from Chapter 3 to explain why wages differ among workers. The demand for workers depends on their productivity and on the price that firms receive for the output the workers produce. The supply of workers to an occupation depends on the wages and working conditions offered by employers and on the skills required. The demand and supply for labor can also help us analyze such issues as economic discrimination and the impact of labor unions.

Read *An Inside Look* on the next page to see how demand and supply determine the salaries of ex-college athletes who work for NASCAR pit crews.

Are Race Car Drivers Athletes? We Don't Know, but the Pit-Crew Members Are

WALL STREET JOURNAL, JUNE 16, 2005

Racing Teams Recruit Athletes and Train Them Hard; The $60,000 Tire Carrier

After Bob Dowens finished playing college football, he turned pro. But not in the NFL—in the National Association for Stock Car Auto Racing.

Once a defensive back at Fairleigh Dickinson University, the 28-year-old Mr. Dowens is now a professional tire carrier in a Nascar pit crew. At Evernham Motorsports, the stock-car racing team for which Mr. Dowens works, pit-crew members practice five days a week. A pit coach studies videos to hone their footwork and hand speed. A trainer has them lift weights and run sprints.

Years ago, mechanics who worked on race cars during the week simply did double duty on Sundays in the pits. Nobody thought about athletic fitness, and beer bellies were OK. The crew was too busy during the week welding and machining to practice pit stops.

Today, teams like Evernham look increasingly for college jocks whose strength and speed can save precious tenths of a second in a race. One of Mr. Dowens's teammates, jack-man Ed Watkins, was a 300-pound offensive lineman at East Carolina University. The Chip Ganassi Racing team's pit crew includes baseball players from Wake Forest University; football players from Wake, the University of Kentucky and the University of North Carolina; and a hockey player from Dartmouth.

Top tire-changers—the guys who air-wrench lug nuts off and on—can make $100,000 a year. The average at Evernham is about $60,000. Mr. Dowens figures he'll be a bit over that, with bonuses, this year.

Big money is what drives the demand for world-class tire-changers. In the 1990s, Nascar's popularity exploded, bringing hundreds of millions of dollars in television and sponsorship revenue into the sport. With more money at stake, competition intensified, and pit stops often affected the outcome of a race. Twenty years ago, pit crews were doing pretty well to change four tires in less than 30 seconds. Today, taking more than 16 seconds can be disastrous.

"These guys are serious athletes," says Evernham's pit coach, Greg Miller, 33. A car going 200 miles per hour covers nearly 300 feet in a second, so a half-second advantage in the pit can put a driver ahead two or three spots. "In our world, two seconds is a lifetime." . . .

That brought Mr. Dowens under the tutelage of Evernham's coach, Mr. Miller. A former fitness trainer with a master's degree in physiology, he thought he could combine his profession with his love of Nascar and joined a team in 1998. At Evernham, Mr. Miller keeps a thick binder with details of every practice and race-day pit stop of the three crews he coaches, with times of each man's tasks, the car's position entering and leaving the pit.

Last year, Mr. Miller got approval to add a full-time strength coach. It started badly: The first running drill left the former East Carolina lineman, Mr. Watkins, with torn tendons in both knees. Now it's paying off. At

5 feet 10 inches, Mr. Dowens weighs 190 pounds, 20 pounds less than in his football days. The 6-foot-3-inch Mr. Watkins is a buff 230. In May, an Evernham crew came in second in a Nascar pit competition. Two weeks later, a different Evernham pit crew took the title and shared $75,000 in bonus money. . . .

On Sunday at the race, the Coca-Cola 600 in Charlotte, fans strolled the pit area seeking autographs and souvenir lug nuts. . . .

On this day Mr. Dowens was carrying for the No. 19 car driven by Jeremy Mayfield. Early in the 600-mile race, Mr. Mayfield's Charger screamed into the pit; 14.32 seconds later, it was gone. On the next stop, a tire changer slipped on an air hose. The time: 15.39. Mr. Miller grimaced.

As the 600-mile race wore on, the pit times edged below 14 seconds. Mr. Dowens was doing well, indexing tires at under seven-tenths of a second. With their car hanging on in a crash-filled race, Mr. Miller shouted, "Need a good one, boys." With 59 laps to go, the car pulled in for four tires and two cans of gas. It was out in 13.95 seconds, a time that helped Mr. Mayfield leap from 14th to ninth. With that momentum, he finished the race in fourth place, tying his best finish this year.

The pit crew did well, too. "We can do better, but no major problems," Mr. Miller said. "All it takes is one to screw up the race."

Source: Neal E. Boudette, "Racing Teams Recruit Athletes and Train Them Hard; The $60,000 Tire Carrier," Wall Street Journal, June 16, 2005, p. A1. Copyright © 2005 Dow Jones. Reprinted by permission of Dow Jones via Copyright Clearance.

Key Points in the Article

This article highlights college athletes who have found a career working on pit crews for NASCAR races. Productivity and the value of the output produced are the two key factors that determine the wages of these pit-crew workers.

Analyzing the News

(a) Changes in marginal product will shift the demand for labor. You can see this in the figure as the demand curve shifts to the right from D_1 to D_2. Because labor demand is based on the marginal revenue product of labor, as the marginal product increases, so too will the demand for labor. For race teams, faster pit times would represent an increase in productivity. By hiring athletes, a race team hopes that the speed of its pit stops will fall, which will improve its finishing spot in the race. Holding the value

of winning a NASCAR race constant, this would increase the demand for labor.

(b) As NASCAR has become more popular, sponsors are willing to pay more money to place logos on the cars, and prize money for races has increased. Sponsors will pay more money for cars with better finishing positions. If a pit crew can improve the finishing position of a team, the value of the output increases. As the value of the output increases, the value of the marginal product of labor increases, holding productivity constant. This will also increase the demand for labor, as shown in the figure as the demand curve shifts from D_1 to D_2. So, the article indicates that the demand for pit crews has increased for two reasons: pit crews have become more productive and the value of winning a NASCAR race has increased. As labor demand increases, the wages paid to pit-crew workers increases from W_1 to W_2.

(c) How can we measure the value of a pit crew? A quick pit stop allowed Jeremy Mayfield to advance five spots in the field. The additional prize money—not only per race but over the 36-race season—adds a large amount of revenue to the race team. The value of a better pit crew could be measured by the additional prize money and sponsorship money the team receives from higher race finishes.

Thinking Critically

1. Suppose NASCAR loses popularity over the next few years. What do you suppose will happen to the wages offered to pit-crew members?
2. The United Auto Workers labor union and an automotive company, such as Ford or General Motors, will sometimes jointly sponsor a NASCAR race. Why would a labor union want to help a company sell more cars?

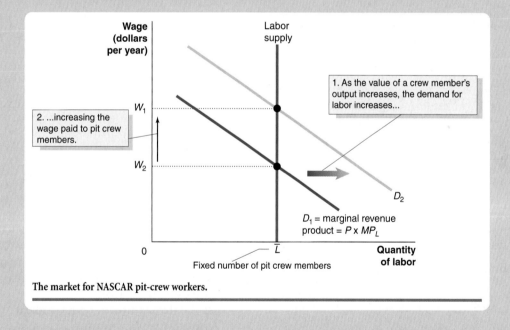

The market for NASCAR pit-crew workers.

Key Terms

16.1 LEARNING OBJECTIVE   16.1 | Explain how firms choose the profit-maximizing quantity of labor to employ.
pages 536–540.

The Demand for Labor

Summary

The demand for labor is a **derived demand** because it depends on the demand consumers have for goods and services. The additional output produced by a firm as a result of hiring another worker is called the **marginal product of labor**. The amount by which the firm's revenue will increase as a result of hiring one more worker is called the **marginal revenue product of labor** (*MRP*). A firm's marginal revenue product of labor curve is its demand curve for labor. Firms maximize profit by hiring workers up to the point where the wage is equal to the marginal revenue product of labor. The market demand curve for labor is determined by adding up the quantity of labor demanded by each firm at each wage, holding constant all other variables that might affect the willingness of firms to hire workers. The most important variables that shift the labor demand curve are changes in human capital, technology, the price of the product, the quantity of other inputs, and the number of firms in the market. **Human capital** is the accumulated training and skills that workers possess.

 Visit www.myeconlab.com to complete these exercises online and get instant feedback.

Review Questions

1.1 What is the difference between the marginal product of labor and the marginal revenue product of labor?

1.2 Why is the demand curve for labor downward sloping?

1.3 What are the five most important variables that cause the market demand curve for labor to shift?

Problems and Applications

1.4 Frank Gunter owns an apple orchard. He employs 87 apple pickers and pays them each $8 per hour to pick apples, which he sells for $1.60 per box. If Frank is maximizing profits, what is the marginal revenue product of the last worker he hired? What is that worker's marginal product?

1.5 **(Related to *Solved Problem 16-1* on page 538)** Fill in the blanks in the following table for Tommy's Televisions:

NUMBER OF WORKERS (L)	OUTPUT OF TELEVISIONS PER WEEK (Q)	MARGINAL PRODUCT OF LABOR (TELEVISION SETS PER WEEK) (MP)	PRODUCT PRICE (P)	MARGINAL REVENUE PRODUCT OF LABOR (DOLLARS PER WEEK)	WAGE (DOLLARS PER WEEK) (W)	ADDITIONAL PROFIT FROM HIRING ONE MORE WORKER (DOLLARS PER WEEK)
0	0	—	$300	—	$1,800	—
1	8	—	300	—	1,800	—
2	15	—	300	—	1,800	—
3	21	—	300	—	1,800	—
4	26	—	300	—	1,800	—
5	30	—	300	—	1,800	—
6	33	—	300	—	1,800	—

a. From the information in the table, can you determine whether this firm is a price taker or a price maker? Briefly explain.

b. Use the information in the table to draw a graph like Figure 16-1 on page 537 that shows the demand for labor by this firm. Be sure to indicate the profit-maximizing quantity of labor on your graph.

1.6 State whether each of the following events will result in a movement along the market demand curve for labor in electronics factories in Japan or whether it will cause the market demand curve for labor to shift. If the demand curve shifts, indicate whether it will shift to the left or to the right and draw a graph to illustrate the shift.

a. The wage rate declines.

b. The price of televisions declines.

c. Several firms exit the television market in Japan.

d. Japanese high schools introduce new vocational courses in assembling electronic products.

1.7 Under what circumstances would a firm's demand curve for labor be a horizontal line?

>> **End Learning Objective 16.1**

The Supply of Labor

Summary

As the wage increases, the opportunity cost of leisure increases, causing individuals to supply a greater quantity of labor. Normally, the labor supply curve is upward sloping, but it is possible that at very high wage levels, the supply curve might be backward bending. This outcome occurs when someone with a high income is willing to accept a somewhat lower income in exchange for more leisure. The market labor supply curve is determined by adding up the quantity of labor supplied by each worker at each wage, holding constant all other variables that might affect the willingness of workers to supply labor. The most important variables that shift the labor supply curve are increases in population, changing demographics, and changing alternatives.

myeconlab Visit www.myeconlab.com to complete these exercises
Get Ahead of the Curve online and get instant feedback.

Review Questions

2.1   How can we measure the opportunity cost of leisure? Why is the supply curve of labor usually upward sloping?

2.2   What are the three most important variables that cause the market supply curve of labor to shift?

Problems and Applications

2.3   Daniel had been earning $65 per hour and working 45 hours per week. Then Daniel's wage rose to $75 per hour, and as a result, he now works 40 hours per week.

What can we conclude from this information about the income effect and the substitution effect of a wage change for Daniel?

2.4   Most labor economists believe that many adult males are on the vertical section of their labor supply curves. Explain when and why someone's supply of labor curve would be vertical, using the concepts of income and substitution effects.

Source: Robert Whaples, "Is There Consensus among American Labor Economists: Survey Results on Forty Propositions," *Journal of Labor Research*, Vol. 17, No. 4, Fall 1996.

2.5   Suppose that a large oil field is discovered in Michigan. By imposing a tax on the oil, the state government is able to eliminate the state income tax on wages. What is likely to be the effect on the labor supply curve in Michigan?

2.6   State whether each of the following events will result in a movement along the market supply curve of agricultural labor in the United States or whether it will cause the market supply curve of labor to shift. If the supply curve shifts, indicate whether it will shift to the left or to the right and draw a graph to illustrate the shift.
   a.   The agricultural wage rate declines.
   b.   Wages outside of agriculture increase.
   c.   The law is changed to allow for unlimited immigration into the United States.

>> **End Learning Objective 16.2**

Equilibrium in the Labor Market

Summary

The intersection between labor supply and labor demand determines the equilibrium wage and the equilibrium level of employment. If labor supply is unchanged, an increase in labor demand will increase both the equilibrium wage and the number of workers employed. If labor demand is unchanged, an increase in labor supply will lower the equilibrium wage and increase the number of workers employed.

myeconlab Visit www.myeconlab.com to complete these exercises
Get Ahead of the Curve online and get instant feedback.

Review Questions

3.1   If the labor demand curve shifts to the left and the labor supply curve remains unchanged, what will happen to the equilibrium wage and the equilibrium level of employment? Illustrate your answer with a graph.

3.2   If the labor supply curve shifts to the left and the labor demand curve remains unchanged, what will happen to the equilibrium wage and the equilibrium level of employment? Illustrate your answer with a graph.

Problems and Applications

3.3 (Related to the *Making the Connection* on page 544) Over time, the gap between the wages of workers with a college degree and the wages of workers without a college degree has been increasing. Shouldn't this gap have increased the incentive for workers to earn a college degree, thereby increasing the supply of college-educated workers, and reducing the size of the gap?

3.4 Reread the discussion on page 545 of changes in the salaries of film animators. Use a graph to illustrate this situation. Make sure your graph has labor demand and supply curves for 1994, 1999, and 2002 and that the equilibrium point for each year is clearly indicated.

3.5 (Related to the *Making the Connection* on page 546) Francis Walker served as commissioner general of the U.S. Immigration Service and as first president of the American Economic Association. In 1896, he wrote the following:

> The question today is protecting the American rate of wages, the American standard of living, and the quality of American citizenship from degradation through the tumultuous access of vast throngs of ignorant and brutalized peasantry from the countries of Eastern and Southern Europe.
>
> Why would Walker have feared that immigration to the United States would drive down wages? Did wages, in fact, fall as he predicted? Briefly explain.

Source: Quoted in Julian L. Simon and Rita James Simon, "Do We Really Need All These Immigrants?" in D. N. McCloskey, *Second Thoughts: Myths and Morals of U.S. Economic History*, New York: Oxford University Press, 1993, p. 20.

3.6 (Related to the *Making the Connection* on page 546) Suppose the United States had not allowed any immigration between 1900 and 1914. Which groups would have benefited from prohibiting immigration and which groups would have lost?

3.7 (Related to the *Making the Connection* on page 546) Former presidential candidate Patrick J. Buchanan has argued, "The U.S. labor supply has grown by more tens of millions in the past twenty-five years than in any other period in history. How could the price of labor *not* fall?" Answer Buchanan's question: If there is an increase in labor supply, does the equilibrium wage have to fall?

Source: Patrick J. Buchanan, *The Great Betrayal: How American Sovereignty and Social Justice Are Being Sacrificed to the Gods of the Global Economy*, Boston: Little, Brown, 1998, p. 16.

3.8 (Related to the *Making the Connection* on page 546) According to an article in the *Wall Street Journal*:

> Through the 1990s, U.S.-bound immigration was split between the poor fleeing hunger or oppression and wealthy elites seeking high-paying jobs. Now, more middle-class, middle-skilled emigrants are heading to the U.S.
>
> Most of the "middle-class, middle-skilled emigrants" referred to in the article were legal immigrants to the United States. Suppose that more effective border control measures reduce the number of low-skilled, illegal immigrants to the United States and the fraction of immigrants who are "middle-skilled" increases significantly. What difference would this change make in the economic impact of immigration? Would it be likely to affect the political debate over immigration?

Source: Joel Millman, "Tidy Business: Immigrant Group Puts a New Spin On Cleaning Niche, *Wall Street Journal*, February 16, 2006, p. A1.

3.9 In 541 A.D., an outbreak of bubonic plague hit the Byzantine Empire. Because the plague was spread by flea-infested rats that often lived on ships, ports were hit particularly hard. In some ports, more than 40 percent of the population died. The emperor, Justinian, was concerned that the wages of sailors were rising very rapidly as a result of the plague. In 544 A.D., he placed a ceiling on the wages of sailors. Use a demand and supply graph of the market for sailors to show the effect of the plague on the wages of sailors. Use the same graph to show the effect of Justinian's wage ceiling. Briefly explain what is happening in your graph.

Source: Michael McCormick, *The Origins of the European Economy: Communications and Commerce, A.D., 300–900*, New York: Cambridge University Press, 2001, p. 109.

> **>> End Learning Objective 16.3**

16.4 LEARNING OBJECTIVE   16.4 | Use demand and supply analysis to explain how compensating differentials, discrimination, and labor unions cause wages to differ, **pages 548–557.**

Explaining Differences in Wages

Summary

The equilibrium wage is determined by the intersection of the labor demand and labor supply curves. Some differences in wages are explained by **compensating differentials**, which are higher wages that compensate workers for unpleasant aspects of a job. Wages can also differ because of **economic discrimination**, which involves paying a person a lower wage or excluding a person from an occupation on the basis of irrelevant characteristics, such as race or gender. **Labor unions** are organizations of employees that have the legal right to bargain with employers about wages and working conditions. Being in a union increases a worker's wages about 10 percent, holding constant other factors, such as the industry in question.

 Visit www.myeconlab.com to complete these exercises online and get instant feedback.

Review Questions

4.1 What is a compensating differential? Give an example.

4.2 Define economic discrimination. Is the fact that one group in the population has higher earnings than other groups evidence of economic discrimination? Briefly explain.

4.3 Is the fraction of U.S. workers in labor unions larger or smaller than in other countries?

Problems and Applications

4.4 The journalist Michael Kinsley has argued, "Free-market capitalism . . . works well for almost all by rewarding some people more than others." Discuss whether you agree.

Source: Michael Kinsley, "Curse You, Robert Caro!" *Slate*, November 21, 2002.

4.5 **(Related to the *Chapter Opener* on page 534)** A student remarks, "I don't think the idea of marginal revenue product really helps explain differences in wages. After all, a ticket to a baseball game costs much less than college tuition, yet baseball players are paid much more than college professors." Do you agree with the student's reasoning?

4.6 **(Related to the *Don't Let This Happen to You!* on page 549)** Joe Morgan is a sportscaster and former baseball player. After he stated that he thought the salaries of major league baseball players were justified, a baseball fan wrote the following to ESPN.com columnist, Rob Neyer:

> Mr. Neyer,
>
> What are your feelings about Joe Morgan's comment that players are justified in being paid what they're being paid? How is it ok for A-Rod [New York Yankees infielder Alex Rodriguez] to earn $115,000 per GAME while my boss works 80 hour weeks and earns $30,000 per year?
>
> How would you answer this fan's questions?

Source: ESPN.com, August 30, 2002.

4.7 Buster Olney, a columnist for ESPN.com, wonders why baseball teams pay the teams' managers and general managers less than they pay most baseball players:

> About two-thirds of the players on the [New York] Mets' roster will make more money than [manager Willie] Randolph; Willie will get somewhere in the neighborhood of half of an average major league salary for 2007. But Randolph's deal is right in line with what other managers are making, and right in the range of what the highest-paid general managers are making. . . . I have a hard time believing that Randolph or general manager Omar Minaya will have less impact on the Mets than left-handed reliever Scott Schoeneweis, who will get paid more than either the manager or GM.

Provide an economic explanation of why baseball managers and general managers are generally paid less than baseball players.

Source: Buster Olney, "Managers Low on Pay Scale," ESPN.com, January 25, 2007.

4.8 In early 2007, Nick Saban agreed to leave his job as head coach of the Miami Dolphins National Football League team to take a job as head football coach at the University of Alabama at a salary of $4 million per year for eight years. Ivan Maisel, a columnist for ESPN.com, wondered whether Saban was worth such a large salary: "Is Saban eight times better than the coach who outmaneuvered Bob Stoops of Oklahoma on Monday night? Boise State paid Chris Petersen $500,000 this season—and he still hasn't lost a game." Might Saban still be a worth a salary of $4 million per year to Alabama even if he is not "eight times better" than a coach being paid $500,000 at another school? In your answer, be sure to refer to the difference between the marginal product of labor and the marginal revenue product of labor.

Source: Ivan Maisel, "Saban Will Find Crowded Pond in Tuscaloosa," ESPN.com, January 3, 2007.

4.9 **(Related to the *Making the Connection* on page 549)** According to Alan Krueger, an economist at Princeton University, the share of concert ticket revenue received by the top 1 percent of all acts rose from 26 percent in 1982 to 56 percent in 2003. Does this information indicate that the top acts in 2003 must have been much better performers relative to other acts than was the case in 1982? If not, can you think of another explanation?

Source: Eduardo Porter, "More Than Ever, It Pays to Be the Top Executive," *New York Times*, May 25, 2007.

4.10 **(Related to the *Making the Connection* on page 549)** Why are there superstar basketball players but no superstar automobile mechanics?

4.11 Tennis stars Venus Williams and Serena Williams do not play for teams. They enter tennis tournaments as individuals. Is the concept of marginal revenue product as important in explaining their earnings as it is in explaining the earnings of major league baseball players? Briefly explain.

4.12 (Related to the *Chapter Opener* on page 534) The number of players on each major league baseball team is determined by negotiation between the players' union and the owners of major league teams. How does this fact affect the explanation given in the text of why baseball players are paid more than college professors? Briefly explain.

4.13 Prior to the early twentieth century, a worker who was injured on the job could collect damages only by suing his employer. To sue successfully, the worker—or his family, if the worker had been killed—had to show that the injury was due to the employer's negligence, that the worker did not know the job was hazardous, and that the worker's own negligence had not contributed to the accident. These lawsuits were difficult for workers to win, and even workers who had been seriously injured on the job often were unable to collect any damages from their employers. Beginning in 1910, most states passed "workers' compensation" laws that required employers to purchase insurance that would compensate workers for injuries suffered on the job. A study by Price Fishback and Shawn Kantor of the University of Arizona shows that after the passage of workers' compensation laws, wages received by workers in the coal and lumber industries fell. Briefly explain why passage of workers' compensation laws would lead to a fall in wages in some industries.

Source: Price V. Fishback and Shawn Everett Kantor, "Did Workers Pay for the Passage of Workers' Compensation Laws?" *Quarterly Journal of Economics*, Vol. 100, No. 3, August 1995, pp. 713–742.

4.14 The following table is similar to Table 16-2 on page 551, except that it includes the earnings of Asian males and females. Does the fact that Asian males are the highest-earning group in the table affect the likelihood that economic discrimination is the best explanation for why earnings differ among the groups listed in the table? Briefly explain your argument.

GROUP	ANNUAL EARNINGS
Asian males	$48,103
White males	46,746
Asian females	36,549
White females	34,464
Black males	33,248
Black females	29,749
Hispanic males	26,769
Hispanic females	24,402

Source: U.S. Bureau of the Census, Current Population Survey, *Annual Social and Economic Supplement*, Table PINC-10, March 2006.

4.15 (Related to *Solved Problem 16-4* on page 553) Use the following graphs to answer the questions.

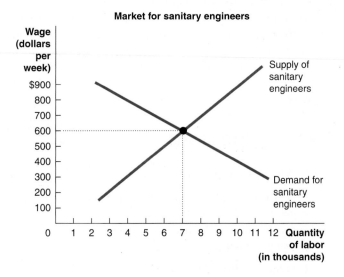

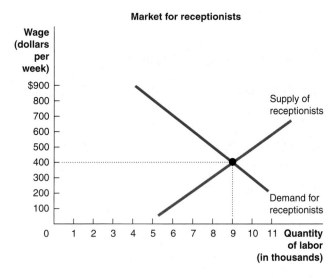

a. What is the equilibrium quantity of sanitary engineers hired, and what is the equilibrium wage?

b. What is the equilibrium quantity of receptionists hired, and what is the equilibrium wage?

c. Briefly discuss why sanitary engineers might earn a higher weekly wage than receptionists.

d. Suppose that comparable-worth legislation is passed and the government requires that sanitary engineers and receptionists must be paid the same wage of $500 per week. Now how many sanitary engineers will be hired and how many receptionists will be hired?

4.16 (Related to *Solved Problem 16-4* on page 553) In most universities, economics professors receive larger salaries than English professors. Suppose that the government requires that from now on, all universities must pay economics professors the same salaries as English professors. Use demand and supply graphs to analyze the effect of this requirement.

4.17 During the 1970s, many women changed their minds about whether they would leave the labor force after marrying and having children or whether they would be in the labor force most of their adult lives. In 1968, the National Longitudinal Survey asked a representative sample of women aged 14 to 24 whether they expected to be in the labor force at age 35. Twenty-nine percent of white women and 59 percent of black women responded that they expected to be in the labor force at that age. In fact, when these women were 35, 60 percent of those who were married and 80 percent of those who were unmarried were in the labor force. In other words, many more women ended up being in the labor force than expected to be when they were of high school and college age. What impact did this fact have on the earnings of these women? Briefly explain.

Source: Claudia Goldin, *Explaining the Gender Gap: An Economic History of American Women*, New York: Oxford University Press, 1990, p. 155.

4.18 In the early twentieth century, black people in the U.S. South were excluded from some occupations, but in jobs such as agriculture that employed both white and black workers, black workers received about the same wages as white workers. Briefly discuss why economic discrimination in the South took this form.

>> **End Learning Objective 16.4**

16.5 LEARNING OBJECTIVE 16.5 | Discuss the role personnel economics can play in helping firms deal with human resources issues, **pages 557–559.**

Personnel Economics

Summary

Personnel economics is the application of economic analysis to human resources issues. One insight of personnel economics is that the productivity of workers often can be increased if firms move from straight-time pay to commission or piece-rate pay.

 Visit www.myeconlab.com to complete these exercises online and get instant feedback.

Review Questions

5.1 What is personnel economics?

5.2 If piece-rate or commission systems of compensating workers have important advantages for firms, why don't more firms use them?

Problems and Applications

5.3 According to a recent economic study, the number of jobs in which firms used bonuses, commission, or piece rates to tie workers' pay to their performance increased from an estimated 30 percent of all jobs in the 1970s to 40 percent in the 1990s. Why would systems that tie workers pay to how much they produce have become increasingly popular with firms? The same study found that these pay systems were more common in higher-paid jobs than in lower-paid jobs. What explains this result?

Source: Thomas Lemieux, W. Bentley MacLeod, and Daniel Parent, "Performance Pay and Wage Inequality," NBER Working Paper No. 13128, May 2007.

5.4 Many companies that pay workers an hourly wage require some minimum level of acceptable output. Suppose a company that has been using this system decides to switch to a piece-rate system under which workers are compensated on the basis of how much output they produce but under which they are also free to choose how much to produce. Is it likely that workers under a piece-rate system will end up choosing to produce less than the minimum output required under the hourly wage system? Briefly explain.

5.5 In most jobs, the harder you work, the more you earn. Some workers would rather work harder and earn more; others would rather work less hard, even though as a result they earn less. Suppose, though, that all workers at a company fall into the "work harder and earn more" group. Suppose, also, that the workers all have the same abilities. In these circumstances, would output per worker be the same under an hourly wage compensation system as under a piece-rate system? Briefly explain.

5.6 For years, the Goodyear Tire & Rubber Company compensated its sales force by paying a salesperson a salary plus a bonus based on the number of tires he or she sold. In early 2002, Goodyear made two changes to this policy: (1) The basis for the bonus was changed from the *quantity* of tires sold to the *revenue* from the tires sold, and (2) salespeople were required to get approval from corporate headquarters in Akron, Ohio, before offering to sell tires to customers at reduced prices. Explain why these changes were likely to increase Goodyear's profits.

Source: Timothy Aeppel, "Amid Weak Inflation, Firms Turn Creative to Boost Prices," *Wall Street Journal*, September 18, 2002.

5.7 (Related to the *Making the Connection* on page 558) What affect did the incentive pay system have on Safelite's marginal cost of installing replacement car windows? If all firms that replace car windows adopted an incentive pay system, what would happen to the price of replacing automobile glass? Who ultimately would benefit?

>> End Learning Objective 16.5

16.6 LEARNING OBJECTIVE   16.6 | Show how equilibrium prices are determined in the markets for capital and natural resources, **pages 560–563.**

The Markets for Capital and Natural Resources

Summary

The approach used to analyze the market for labor can also be used to analyze the markets for other factors of production. In equilibrium, the price of capital is equal to the marginal revenue product of capital, and the price of natural resources is equal to the marginal revenue product of natural resources. The price received by a factor that is in fixed supply is called an *economic rent*, or pure rent. A **monopsony** is the sole buyer of a factor of production. According to the **marginal productivity theory of income distribution**, the distribution of income is determined by the marginal productivity of the factors of production individuals own.

myeconlab Visit www.myeconlab.com to complete these exercises online and get instant feedback.
Get Ahead of the Curve

Review Questions

6.1 In equilibrium, what determines the price of capital? What determines the price of natural resources? What is the marginal productivity theory of income distribution?

6.2 What is an economic rent? What is a monopsony?

Problems and Applications

6.3 Adam operates a pin factory. Suppose Adam faces the situation shown in the following table and the cost of renting a machine is $550 per week.

NUMBER OF MACHINES	OUTPUT OF PINS (BOXES PER WEEK)	MARGINAL PRODUCT OF CAPITAL	PRODUCT PRICE (DOLLARS PER BOX)	TOTAL REVENUE	MARGINAL REVENUE PRODUCT OF CAPITAL	RENTAL COST PER MACHINE	ADDITIONAL PROFIT FROM RENTING ONE ADDITIONAL MACHINE
0	0	—	$100		—	$550	
1	12		100			550	
2	21		100			550	
3	28		100			550	
4	34		100			550	
5	39		100			550	
6	43		100			550	

a. Fill in the blanks in the table and determine the profit-maximizing number of machines for Adam to rent. Briefly explain why renting this number of machines is profit maximizing.
b. Draw Adam's demand curve for capital.

6.4 Many people have predicted, using a model like the one in panel (b) of Figure 16-12 on page 561, that the price of natural resources should rise consistently over time in comparison with the prices of other goods because the demand curve for natural resources is continually shifting to the right while the supply curve must be shifting to the left as natural resources are used up. However, the relative prices of most natural resources have not been increasing. Draw a graph that shows the demand and supply for natural resources that can explain why prices haven't risen even though demand has.

6.5 In 1879, economist Henry George published *Progress and Poverty*, which became one of the best-selling books of the nineteenth century. In this book, George argued that all existing taxes should be replaced with a single tax on land. In Chapter 4, we discussed the concept of tax incidence, or the actual division of the burden of a tax between buyers and sellers in a market. If land is taxed, how will the burden of the tax be divided between the sellers of land and the buyers of land? Illustrate your answer with a graph of the market for land.

6.6 The total amount of oil in the earth is not increasing. Does this mean that in the market for oil, the supply curve is perfectly inelastic? Briefly explain.

6.7 In a competitive labor market, imposing a minimum wage should reduce the equilibrium level of employment. Will this also be true if the labor market is a monopsony? Briefly explain.

>> End Learning Objective 16.6

Chapter 17

The Economics of Information

Why Does State Farm Charge Young Men So Much More Than Young Women for Auto Insurance?

In 2006, if you were a 21-year-old male in Denver, Colorado, driving a car of average value an average number of miles per year, you had to pay State Farm Insurance $1,069 for automobile insurance. If you were a 21-year-old female, you paid only $879. A 35-year-old male paid $625, and a 68-year-old female paid just $444. Was State Farm practicing age and sex discrimination? Was the company practicing price discrimination of the type we discussed in Chapter 15? Actually, State Farm was attempting to match up the prices they charged for automobile insurance with the costs they were likely to incur on each policy. Young males are involved in many more auto accidents than young females, or middle-aged males, so they cost State Farm more to insure.

With corporate headquarters in Bloomington, Illinois, State Farm is the largest automobile insurance company in the United States, insuring one out of five automobiles. State Farm was founded in 1922 by George J. Mecherle. Mecherle had started life as a farmer, but later took a job selling insurance. The company he worked for charged the same price for automobile

insurance to people living in the city of Bloomington as it did to farmers living outside town. Mecherle realized that farmers had far fewer accidents than did city drivers. So he started the State Farm Mutual Automobile Insurance Company to offer farmers automobile insurance polices at lower prices.

Mecherle's success highlights the importance to insurance companies of correctly pricing policies. A key difficulty facing insurance companies is that drivers know more about how likely they are to have accidents than do the companies. As a result, insurance companies may charge safe drivers prices that are too high—causing these drivers to buy policies from other companies—and charge risky drivers prices that are too low. The difficulties insurance companies face in pricing their policies are caused by *asymmetric information*, which exists when one party to an economic transaction has less information than the other party. In the market for insurance, asymmetric information leads to two problems: *adverse selection* and *moral hazard*. Adverse selection can result in an insurance company attracting more high-risk drivers than it would like, given the prices of its policies. Moral hazard occurs when people change their behavior *after* purchasing insurance. Whether drivers have an accident depends partly on how safely they drive. If drivers did not have insurance to pay for the repairs needed after accidents, they would be likely to drive more cautiously.

In recent years, insurance companies have changed how they price policies. Insurance companies have always aimed at charging high prices to drivers likely to have more accidents and file more claims and lower prices to safer drivers. Usually, though, companies had divided drivers into just a few categories, based on their ages and driving records. Today, many companies use sophisticated computer models that employ thousands of variables to predict the chance that a driver will have an accident. The result has been an increase in the different prices being charged to drivers. For example, until recently, most companies lumped all drivers aged 21 to 70 into one category. But more sophisticated analysis of accident data shows that more categories would be better. As one executive of an insurance company put it, "Now we know a 22-year-old married woman is not as good a driving risk as a 45-year-old married woman." The differing prices State Farm charges drivers in Denver were the result of implementing the new pricing models.

AN INSIDE LOOK on **page 590** examines how insurance companies use credit reports to decide who is likely to be a risky driver.

Sources: Information on State Farm pricing from the Colorado State Department of Regulatory Agencies, Division of Insurance Web site; Denise Trowbridge, "State Farm to Lower Auto Rates," *The Columbus (Ohio) Dispatch*, March 23, 2007, p. 01H; and Christopher Oster, "Auto Insurers Cut Rates—For Some," *Wall Street Journal*, April 22, 2004, p. D1.

LEARNING Objectives

After studying this chapter, you should be able to:

17.1 Define **asymmetric information** and distinguish between **adverse selection** and **moral hazard** page 576.

17.2 Apply the concepts of adverse selection and moral hazard to **financial markets** page 581.

17.3 Apply the concepts of adverse selection and moral hazard to **labor markets** page 583.

17.4 Explain the **winner's curse** and why it occurs, page 585.

Economics in YOUR Life!

Have You Ever Tried to Sell a Car?

The classified sections of newspapers are filled with ads from people trying to sell cars. Many colleges also have online bulletin boards where students can list cars for sale. Some people also list cars for sale on eBay. Car buyers choose between buying from individual sellers or buying from used car dealers. If you have tried to sell a car through a newspaper or an online ad, you have probably had trouble selling at a price as high as car dealers receive.

Why are used car buyers only willing to pay relatively low prices for cars they buy from individual sellers? If you found two seemingly identical cars, one at a local car dealer and the other for sale by an individual on eBay, would you be willing to pay the same amount for the two cars? As you read this chapter, see if you can answer these questions. You can check your answers against those we provide at the end of the chapter. **>> Continued on page 589**

I
n previous chapters, we assumed that buyers and sellers in a market possess the same amount of information. In the market for insurance, as we have seen, buyers often have more information than sellers. Later in this chapter, we will see that the reverse is often true in financial markets: Firms selling stocks and bonds usually have more information than buyers. In other markets, buyers and sellers may both lack complete information. For example, when an oil company bids for the right to drill on tracts of government land, neither the company nor the government has complete information on how much oil the tracts contain. When telecommunications companies bid in U.S. Federal Communications Commission auctions for licenses to provide mobile phone services, they don't have complete information on how valuable the licenses may be.

In this chapter, we discuss the economics of information and how imperfect information can affect the decisions of both households and firms. After reading this chapter, you will better understand situations such as auctions and the markets for insurance and stocks and bonds, in which the role of imperfect information is particularly important.

17.1 LEARNING OBJECTIVE

17.1 | Define asymmetric information and distinguish between adverse selection and moral hazard.

Asymmetric Information

Asymmetric information A situation in which one party to an economic transaction has less information than the other party.

The difficulty in correctly pricing insurance policies arises from the problem of **asymmetric information**, which occurs when one party to an economic transaction has less information than the other party. As we will see, in some markets, it is difficult to understand the actions of buyers and sellers without understanding the effects of asymmetric information. In fact, guarding against the effects of asymmetric information is a major objective of sellers in the insurance market and of buyers in financial markets. The market for used automobiles was the first in which economists began to carefully study the problem of asymmetric information.

Adverse Selection and the Market for "Lemons"

The study of asymmetric information began with an analysis of the used car market by Nobel laureate George Akerlof, of the University of California, Berkeley. Akerlof pointed out that the seller of a used car will always have more information on the true condition of the car than will potential buyers. A car that has been poorly maintained—by, for instance, not having its oil changed regularly—may have damage that could be difficult to detect even by a trained mechanic.

If potential buyers of used cars know that they will have difficulty separating the good used cars from the bad used cars, or "lemons," they will take this into account in the prices they are willing to pay. Consider the following simple example: Suppose that half of the 2006 Volkswagen Jettas offered for sale have been well maintained and are good, reliable used cars. The other half have been poorly maintained and are lemons that will be unreliable. Suppose that potential buyers of 2006 Jettas would be willing to pay $10,000 for a reliable one but only $5,000 for an unreliable one. The sellers know how well they have maintained their cars and whether they are reliable, but the buyers do not have this information and so have no way of telling the reliable cars from the unreliable ones.

In this situation, buyers will generally offer a price somewhere between the price they would be willing to pay for a good car and the price they would be willing to pay for a lemon. In this case, with a 50–50 chance of buying a good car or a lemon, buyers might offer $7,500, which is halfway between the price they would pay if they knew for certain the car was a good one and the price they would pay if they knew it was a lemon.

Unfortunately for used car buyers, a major glitch arises at this point. From the buyers' perspective, given that they don't know whether any particular car offered for sale is a good car or a lemon, an offer of $7,500 seems reasonable. But the sellers *do* know whether the cars they are offering are good cars or lemons. To a seller of a good car, an offer of $7,500 is $2,500 below the true value of the car, and the seller will be reluctant to sell. But to a seller of a lemon, an offer of $7,500 is $2,500 *above* the true value of the car, and the seller will be quite happy to sell. As sellers of lemons take advantage of knowing more about the cars they are selling than buyers do, the used car market will fall victim to **adverse selection**: Most used cars offered for sale will be lemons. In other words, because of asymmetric information, the market has selected adversely the cars that will be offered for sale. Notice as well that the problem of adverse selection reduces the total quantity of used cars bought and sold in the market because few good cars are offered for sale. From this example we can conclude that information problems reduce economic efficiency in a market.

Adverse selection The situation in which one party to a transaction takes advantage of knowing more than the other party to the transaction.

Reducing Adverse Selection in the Car Market: Warranties and Reputations

There are ways of reducing the adverse selection problem in the used car market. Car manufacturers provide warranties when cars are sold new. These warranties cover the costs of major repairs and can be transferred to a new owner when a car is resold. Warranties give prospective buyers some assurance that they will not be stuck with all the cost of repairs. In addition, used car dealers take steps to assure buyers that the cars they are selling are not lemons. They do this by building a reputation for selling reliable used cars and by offering their own warranties if the manufacturer's warranty has expired or can't be transferred. If a used car dealer can convince buyers that the dealer is selling reliable cars, then, using the numbers from our earlier example, buyers would be willing to pay $10,000 rather than $7,500 for a used Jetta.

Some states have passed "lemon laws" to help reduce information problems in the car market. Most lemon laws have two main provisions:

1 New cars that need several major repairs during the first year or two after the date of the original purchase may be returned to the manufacturer for a full refund.

2 Car manufacturers must indicate whether a used car they are offering for sale was repurchased from the original owner as a lemon.

Although lemon laws are popular with consumers, opposition from manufacturers has resulted in these laws being enacted in fewer than 20 states.

Asymmetric Information in the Market for Insurance

Asymmetric information problems are particularly severe in the market for insurance. Buyers of insurance policies will always know more about the likelihood of the event being insured against happening than will insurance companies. For example, buyers of health insurance policies know more about the state of their health—and, therefore, how likely they are to submit medical bills to the insurance company—than will the insurance company that sells them the policies. Similarly, drivers know more about whether they are reckless drivers, homeowners know more about potential fire hazards in their homes, and so on than do the insurance companies selling them policies. Insurance companies will cover their costs, including the opportunity cost of funds invested in them by their owners, only if they set the prices—or *premiums*—of policies at levels that cover the claims for payment insured people are likely to submit.

Reducing Adverse Selection in the Insurance Market

Adverse selection problems arise because sick people are more likely to want health insurance than are healthy people, reckless drivers are more likely to want automobile insurance than are careful drivers, and people living in homes that are fire hazards are more likely to want fire insurance than are people living in safe homes. If insurance companies have trouble determining who is healthy and who is sick or who is a reckless driver and who is a safe driver, they will end up setting their premiums too low and will fail to cover their costs. To reduce the problem of adverse selection, insurance companies gather as much information as they can on people applying for policies. For example, people applying for individual health insurance policies or life insurance policies usually need to submit their medical records to the insurance company. Insurance companies usually also carry out their own medical examinations. People applying for automobile insurance have their driving record reviewed. Insurance companies charge higher premiums to people who have caused accidents or who have speeding tickets. As we saw in the chapter opener, insurance companies like State Farm will remain profitable only if they succeed in identifying the riskiest drivers so as to charge them higher premiums.

Sometimes the adverse selection problem leads insurance companies simply to refuse to offer insurance policies to certain people at any price. Someone with a terminal or chronic illness, for example, may find it difficult to buy an individual health insurance or life insurance policy. The owner of a home or warehouse in an area that is prone to arson fires may have difficulty getting fire insurance. An alternative to refusing to sell policies to these people would be for insurance companies to charge very high premiums for coverage. This may make the adverse selection problem worse, however. When premiums are very high, only people who are almost certain to make a claim will purchase a policy.

The adverse selection problem can also be reduced if people are automatically covered by insurance. For example, state governments require that every driver buy automobile insurance. This policy reduces the problem of insurance being purchased primarily by bad drivers. As we saw at the beginning of the chapter, however, State Farm and other insurance companies still face the problem of determining the profit-maximizing prices to charge for their policies.

Insurance companies can reduce adverse selection problems in selling health insurance and life insurance by offering *group coverage* to large firms—including colleges and universities—or to alliances of smaller firms. With group coverage, everyone employed by a firm is automatically covered. As long as the group is large enough, the coverage is likely to represent the proportions of healthy and unhealthy people found in the general population. As a result of this *risk pooling*, it is much easier for insurance companies to estimate the average number of claims likely to be filed under a group health insurance or life insurance policy than it would be to predict the number of claims likely to be filed under an individual policy. Because everyone in the group must pay the premium—or have it paid for them by their employer—insurance companies avoid the problem of only sick people buying the insurance. Group coverage that allows healthy people not to participate is still subject to adverse selection problems, however. If healthy people don't participate, the number of claims filed per participating employee is likely to be high. This level of claims may cause the insurance company to raise the price it charges to the firm for the group policy. If the firm then raises the monthly payment required of employees, the higher price will discourage additional numbers of healthy employees from participating.

Making the Connection | Does Adverse Selection Explain Why Some People Do Not Have Health Insurance?

More that 45 million people in the United States do not have health insurance. As the chart shows, more than two-thirds of Americans are covered by private health insurance plans—primarily plans provided by firms to their employees—and more than one-quarter of people are covered by government health insurance plans—such as the Medicare program for people over age 65 or the Medicaid program for poor people. But about 16 percent of people are not covered by health insurance. (Note that the percentages in the chart sum to more than 100 because some people are covered by both private health insurance and government health insurance.)

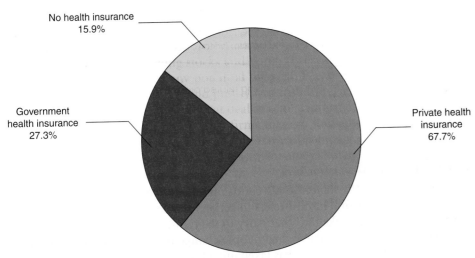

Source: U.S. Bureau of the Census, *Income, Poverty and Health Insurance in the United States, 2005*, P60–231, Figure 6, August 2006. www.census.gov/prod/2006pubs/p60-231.pdf.

There are number of reasons people may not have health insurance. Some healthy young adults don't expect to need medical care and so do not want to pay the monthly premiums to buy insurance they don't expect to need. As a result, although 15.9 percent of the total population lacks health insurance, the proportion of people between the ages of 18 and 24 who do not have insurance is almost twice as large, at 30.6 percent. And more than one-quarter of those between the ages of 25 and 34 do not have insurance. Many low-income people qualify for government health insurance through the Medicaid program. But some low-income people either do not take advantage of Medicaid or are not eligible for it. For these people, their low incomes may be the main reason that they do not have insurance. However, only about 20 percent of the uninsured have incomes below the official U.S. poverty line; more than 30 percent of the uninsured have incomes more than three times greater than the poverty line. Kate Bundorf of Stanford University and Mark Pauly of the University of Pennsylvania have estimated that as many as three-quarters of the uninsured can afford to buy health insurance.

Some economists have argued that adverse selection may be an important explanation for the significant percentage of people lacking health insurance in the United States. We have seen that one effect of adverse selection in a market is that the equilibrium quantity of the good or service may be smaller than it would have been if there were no information problems. Because insurance companies are aware of the adverse selection problem, they may sometimes offer health insurance policies at prices higher than young, healthy consumers are willing to pay. Similarly, as we have already seen, insurance companies will sometimes refuse to offer insurance to people with chronic illnesses.

In recent years, state governments may have unintentionally made the adverse selection problem worse by regulating the terms of the policies insurance companies are allowed to offer small firms. These state regulations generally restrict the ability of insurance companies to offer policies that charge higher premiums to employees with existing health conditions. Research by Kosali Ilayperuma Simon of Cornell University

about which they had relatively little information. As investors became more focused on stock prices during those years, pressure increased for firms to report that they had earned profits at least as high as investment analysts were forecasting. Firms reporting profits that were lower than analysts had forecast could experience a sharp decline in the price of their stock. As we discussed in Chapter 7, the managers of some firms gave in to the temptation to "cook the books" by falsely reporting that their profits were much higher than they really were. This cheating could not be concealed forever. During 2002, a number of scandals involving the reporting of inflated profits came to light. These scandals served as a reminder to investors of the difficulty of overcoming adverse selection and moral hazard problems in financial markets.

| Making the Connection | **Using Government Policy to Reduce Moral Hazard in Investments** |

The basic information on the financial condition of a company is contained in its *financial statements*, particularly its income statement and balance sheet. A firm's income statement reports its profits over a period of time, and its balance sheet shows the net value of the firm, based on the value of everything it owns minus the value of everything it owes. (For more on financial statements, see the appendix to Chapter 7.) Investment analysts at brokerage firms and individual investors rely on this information when evaluating firms. All firms that issue stock to the public have their statements *audited* by certified public accountants (CPAs). A CPA is an employee of an accounting firm, *not* of the company being audited. The audit is intended to provide investors with an independent opinion as to whether the company's financial statements reflect the true financial condition of the firm.

Unfortunately, a series of spectacular scandals during 2002 revealed that the financial statements of even some very large firms were not reliable. In July 2002, WorldCom, the second-largest provider of long-distance telephone service in the United States, filed for bankruptcy. In June, WorldCom executives had admitted to misstating more than $3.8 billion in expenses on WorldCom's financial statements. As a result, instead of the profit it initially reported earning during 2001 and the first quarter of 2002, it had actually lost

The government has intervened to increase the confidence of investors in the securities traded on the New York Stock Exchange and in other financial markets.

$1.2 billion. Investors saw the value of the 3 billion shares of stock issued by WorldCom drop to zero. Enron, an energy trading company, had managed to keep much of its debt from being included on its balance sheet. Eventually, it too had to declare bankruptcy. Members of the Rigas family, which controlled Adelphia Communications, one of the largest cable television companies in the United States, were accused of using more than $250 million of the firm's money for personal expenses—a striking example of moral hazard. The firm also filed for bankruptcy, and two Rigas family members were convicted of looting the company and are serving prison terms of 15 to 20 years.

The news that these and other firms had "cooked the books" illustrates the difficulty that moral hazard poses for investors. The management of a firm knows far more about the firm's finances than any outside investor can. If investors believe they cannot rely on the firm's financial statements to represent the true financial condition of the firm, they will be extremely reluctant to invest in the firm. Many observers have argued that a general loss of confidence in the reliability of financial statements was behind the wave of selling that hit U.S. stock markets in the summer of 2002.

To help restore confidence in financial statements, Congress passed and President George W. Bush signed into law the Sarbanes-Oxley Act of 2002, which is aimed at strengthening the country's security laws. The bill authorizes the SEC to set up a government board to oversee the auditing of financial statements. The role of the board was to address the problem of outside auditors who failed to ensure the accuracy of corporate financial statements. Under the provisions of the bill, auditors who willfully violate accounting rules face five-year prison sentences. The bill also requires chief executive officers and chief financial officers to personally certify the accuracy of financial statements. The maximum prison term for violating the securities laws was raised to 25 years.

YOUR TURN: Test your understanding by doing related problem 2.7 on page 594 at the end of this chapter.

Adverse Selection and Moral Hazard in Labor Markets

We saw in Chapter 7 that economists refer to the conflict between the interests of shareholders and the interests of top management as a **principal–agent problem**. This problem occurs when agents—in this case, a firm's top management—pursue their own interests rather than the interests of the principal—in this case, the shareholders of the corporation—who hired them. There is also the potential for a principal–agent problem between the managers of a firm and its workers. The moral hazard behind the principal–agent problem is that workers, once hired, may shirk their obligations and not work hard.

Employers can ensure that workers are doing their jobs by closely monitoring them. Telemarketing firms, for example, can monitor their employees electronically to ensure that they make the required number of telephone calls per hour. Not all firms, however, can monitor their employees so closely. Often firms must rely on workers being sufficiently motivated so they do not shirk their responsibilities. One way to motivate workers is to increase the value to them of their current jobs, relative to other jobs they might have. If you consider your current job to be more valuable than the alternatives, you will be reluctant to shirk because you won't want to risk being fired. Firms have several ways to make a worker's job seem more valuable:

Principal–agent problem A problem caused by agents pursuing their own interests rather than the interests of the principals who hired them.

- *Efficiency wages.* There is a market for every kind of labor, just as there is a market for every good and service. A firm's demand for labor is determined by how much output workers can produce for the firm—the workers' *productivity*—and by the price the firm receives when it sells the output the workers produce. The supply of labor is determined by the willingness of workers to supply a given amount of work at a particular wage. The equilibrium wage equates the quantity of labor demanded to the quantity of labor supplied. If a firm offers to pay a wage above the equilibrium wage, a worker will consider the job to be valuable and will be less likely to shirk and risk losing the job. An *efficiency wage* is a higher-than-equilibrium wage firms pay to give workers an incentive to work harder.

- *Seniority system.* Many firms use a seniority system under which workers who have been with the firm longer receive higher pay and other benefits, such as the choice of better or more interesting jobs. A worker who early in his career at a firm is fired for shirking will give up the possibility of participating in the benefits of seniority. A seniority system can have an effect similar to that of an efficiency wage in giving workers an incentive to work harder.

high given the amount of oil that was likely to actually be in the tract. Capen, Clapp, and Campbell came to two conclusions:

1 "In competitive bidding, the winner tends to be the player who most overestimates true tract value."

2 "He who bids on a parcel what he thinks it is worth will, in the long run, be taken to the cleaners."

These conclusions became known as the *winner's curse* because they indicate that the winner of an auction may end up worse off than the losers. In fact, Capen, Clapp, and Campbell concluded that the oil companies would have made a greater return on their investments if they had taken the funds and put them in a savings account in a bank rather than using them to bid on oil tracts.

Making the Connection | Is There a Winner's Curse in the Marriage Market?

In the United States, about 43 percent of all marriages end in divorce. Why the divorce rate is so high is a complicated question. But economics can provide some insight, even if it can't provide a full explanation. Economists have proposed thinking of the interactions of men and women looking for marriage partners as a *marriage market*. Of course, the marriage market is not a typical market in which a good or service is bought and sold for money. But like participants in other markets, the men and women in the marriage market are trying to make themselves as well off as possible, and they are competing against each other to find the best partners.

It's hard to tell how good a marriage partner someone will make until you are actually married to him or her. Like oil companies trying to estimate the amount of oil in a tract of land, men and women use all the information they can to estimate how good a spouse someone will be. But which potential mate are you likely to pursue most strongly? And which potential mate is most likely to find your romantic ardor greater than that of other potential marriage partners? The answer to both questions is the person whose value as a marriage partner you have most greatly overestimated. In other words, if your estimate of how desirable someone is as a marriage partner is much higher than other people's estimates, you have a good chance of marrying that person—but also a good chance of discovering later that your estimate was wrong. The idea of the winner's curse can help explain not only why oil companies can be dissatisfied with the profits from winning oil field auctions but also why many people are apparently dissatisfied with their marriages.

A life of bliss or the winner's curse?

YOUR TURN: Test your understanding by doing related problem 4.7 on page 595 at the end of this chapter.

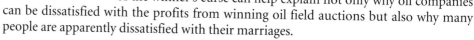

When Does the Winner's Curse Apply?

Does the winner's curse indicate that the winner of every auction would have been better off losing? No, because the winner's curse applies only to auctions of *common-value* assets—such as oil fields—that would be given the same value by all bidders if they had perfect information. The winner's curse does not apply to auctions of *private-value* assets where the value to each bidder depends on the bidder's own preferences. For example, if you win an auction on eBay for a DVD player, you are not subject to the winner's curse if the DVD player is new and the auction described it completely. You had all the information you needed to evaluate the DVD player, and your bid was based on your preference for a DVD player relative to other things you could have purchased.

Solved Problem | 17-4

Auctions, Available Information, and the Winner's Curse

Suppose that the government has decided to auction off oil fields in Alaska. Suppose, also, that advances in geology have increased the accuracy with which oil companies can pre- dict how much oil will be found in a tract of land. Are these advances likely to increase or decrease the amount of revenue the government receives from the auction?

SOLVING THE PROBLEM:

Step 1: **Review the chapter material.** This problem is about the winner's curse, so you may want to review the section "The Winner's Curse: When Is It Bad to Win an Auction?" which begins on page 585.

Step 2: **Use the information on the winner's curse to answer the problem.** This is an example of a common-value auction where the bidders lack full information about what is being auctioned. We've already seen that oil companies run the risk of the winner's curse when they do not know exactly how much oil is in each tract being auctioned. As shown in Figure 17-1, the winning bidder may significantly overestimate the true amount of oil and end up earning little, if any profit, from its investment.

If the oil companies knew with certainty how much oil was in each tract, the bids would all be close together and close to the true value of the tract. The amount of revenue received by the government would be lower in this case because the highest bid would be lower. In this problem, however, some uncertainty remains about how much oil is in each tract, so the winner's curse may still arise. Because advances in geology have allowed the companies to make more accurate estimates, the highest bid is likely to be lower than it would have been. Therefore, the advances in geology are likely to *decrease* the amount of revenue the government receives from the auction.

YOUR TURN: For more practice, do related problem 4.5 on page 595 at the end of this chapter.   **>> End Solved Problem 17-4**

Pacific Telesis Uses the Winner's Curse to Its Own Advantage

In late 1994, the Federal Communications Commission began auctioning 99 licenses that would allow firms to operate wireless communication networks—for mobile phones and similar devices—in specific geographic areas. Pacific Telesis (now part of AT&T) was the local telephone provider in California at that time. It was determined to win the FCC auctions to provide wireless ser- vice in California.

Pacific Telesis hired several economists to help plan its bidding strategy. There was no doubt that the licenses being auctioned were valuable, but given the rapid evolution of the market for mobile phones and other wireless devices, no firm had enough informa- tion to determine exactly how valuable. In these circumstances, the Pacific Telesis economists knew that the problem of the winner's curse meant that the firm ran the risk of either overpaying or losing the auction to another firm that would overpay. To avoid this out- come, Pacific Telesis launched a campaign to warn other firms that it was far more knowledgeable about this market than they were and that to win the auction, another firm would have to pay more than the licenses were worth. Pacific Telesis took out full-page ads in newspapers in the cities where the corporate headquarters of

Fear of the winner's curse affected the bidding in auctions for wireless service in California.

Should Bad Credit Increase Your Car Insurance Rate?

USA TODAY, JUNE 11, 2007

Your Money: Bad Credit Can Inflate Car Insurance Premiums

You always use your turn signal and observe the speed limit. The only ticket you've ever gotten was for an expired parking meter. You should be eligible for lower car-insurance premiums than that bozo who cut you off this morning is, right? Not necessarily.

If your credit report is blemished, you might not get the lowest insurance rates, despite your spotless driving record. And as a result of a Supreme Court decision last week, your insurer doesn't have to tell you that you're not getting the best rates.

The high court overturned a 9th Circuit Court of Appeals ruling that said the federal Fair Credit Reporting Act requires insurers to notify customers whenever their credit history prevents them from getting the best available rate.

Insurers argued that credit histories are just one of many factors they use to set rates. They also contended that the ruling would have required insurers to send out millions of notices to customers to avoid costly class-action lawsuits.

For about a decade, most insurers have considered a customer's credit history when setting rates, says Joseph Annotti, a spokesman for the Property Casualty Insurers Association of America. Annotti says research has shown that drivers with poor credit are more likely to file insurance claims.

A credit report "is a solid predictor of risk," Annotti says. "People can get tickets taken off their record, DUIs get changed into running a stop sign—there are lots of ways to play with your motor vehicle record. It's less likely for a person who is inherently financial irresponsible to, all of a sudden overnight, change their behavior."

Consumer groups disagree. The insurance industry's contention that people with damaged credit are high-risk drivers is a "pretty disturbing moral hypothesis," says Chi Chi Wu, of the National Consumer Law Center. Many people have poor credit because of divorce, job loss or serious illness, she says. "They're not bad people. They're people who have fallen on hard times."

In addition, credit reports are "notorious for errors," Wu says. Identity theft could also damage an individual's record, she notes.

In November, Oregon voters defeated a measure that would have barred insurers from using credit histories to set auto and home insurance rates. Still, 26 states have adopted a model law that requires insurers to notify consumers that their credit history might affect their rates. The law also bars insurers from refusing to insure someone based solely on the individual's credit history.

The model law also encourages insurers to take into account "extraordinary life events," such as a catastrophic illness or the loss of a spouse, when evaluating a consumer's credit history.

Know Your Score

Consumer groups contend that a notification requirement would encourage people to check their credit reports more frequently. Most consumers aren't aware that their credit histories can affect their insurance rates, says Scott Shorr, a lawyer in Portland, Ore., who represented the plaintiffs in the insurance case.

Now, though, "If you want to know whether there's some inaccuracy in your credit report that's resulting in your paying more for insurance or credit generally, then you're going to have to check your credit report yourself," says Scott Nelson, an attorney for Public Citizen, a consumer-advocacy group.

How to protect yourself:

- When applying for insurance, ask the insurer what factors will be considered in determining your rates. Insurers won't tell you how they weigh them, but the company might tell you the factors it considers when reviewing a potential customer's credit report, Annotti says.

  For example, he says, some insurers are interested only in major credit events, such as foreclosures and bankruptcies. . . .

- Monitor your credit reports regularly for errors. You're entitled to a free copy of a credit report from the three credit-reporting agencies—TransUnion, Equifax and Experian—once a year. . . .

  If you find errors in your credit report, contact the credit agency that issued the report. The agencies are required by law to investigate disputed items.

- Beware of companies that claim they can "repair" your credit report.

Source: Sandra Block, "Your Money: Bad Credit Can Inflate Car Insurance Premiums," USA Today, June 11, 2007. Reprinted by permission of USA Today.

Key Points in the Article

This article discusses the controversy over insurance companies using credit records to set the policy premiums they charge their customers. Because the buyers of insurance know more about their driving habits and risk-taking than do the sellers of insurance, sellers are looking for some signal that will indicate which buyers are likely to be good risks and which are likely to be bad risks.

Analyzing the News

a In markets where one side of the market has more information than the other, the less informed party will seek ways to gain information. Because credit records can provide information about how responsible a person acts, insurance companies may find it valuable to use credit records to separate consumers who are likely to be safe drivers from those who are more likely to have accidents. Insurance companies are using credit histories both to decide whether or not to offer insurance to a particular applicant,

but also to decide what premiums to charge.

b When a firm uses a credit report to determine whether a person is a good or bad insurance risk, the firm is relying on the statistical correlation between a person's credit history and the likelihood that the person will have an accident. Having bad credit does not cause a person to be a bad driver, but bad credit may be a signal that a person has some unobservable characteristic that results in the person making bad decisions. A person's credit history may be a good signal that reveals to the insurance companies information that is relevant to setting insurance premiums. When insurance companies have better information about the risks they face from different consumers, the companies will be better able to judge the profitability of the policies, and the supply of insurance in the market should increase. You can see the increase in the figure as the supply curve shifts from S_1 to S_2. When this occurs, the market price of insurance falls from P_1 to P_2, and the quantity of insurance sold in the market increases from Q_1 to Q_2.

c How does the information insurance companies obtain from credit histories affect the market for insurance? Suppose that there are only two types of consumers: good risks and bad risks. A good risk will have insurance claims of $100 per year, and

a bad risk will have insurance claims of $5,000 per year. If the insurance company believes that half of its customers are of each type, the expected payout for the insurance company is $2,550 per year, calculated as 0.5($100) + 0.5($5,000). If the company charged that premium, bad risks would happily seek coverage, and good risks would not. Suppose instead that the insurance company could use credit records to identify which customers are likely to be good risks and charge them close to $100 per year, and which are likely to be bad risks and charge them close to $5,000 per year. This would make it less likely that only bad risks would seek insurance. The insurance companies would be more likely to cover their costs (which they must do to stay in business) and encourage drivers who are good risks to purchase insurance.

Thinking Critically About Policy

1. Suppose states banned the use of credit checks by insurance companies in setting premiums. What would happen to the price and quantity of insurance offered in those states? Who would benefit from this change?

2. What would be the benefits and the costs of states requiring that insurance companies charge all drivers the same premium?

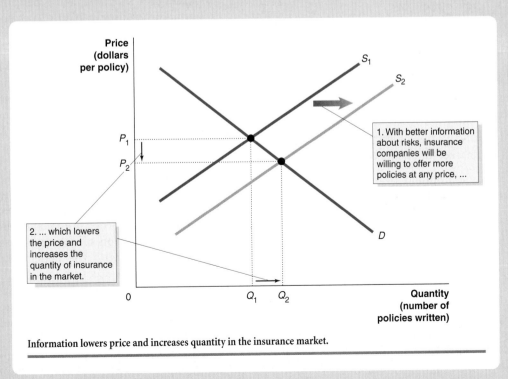

Information lowers price and increases quantity in the insurance market.

Key Terms

17.1 LEARNING OBJECTIVE   17.1 | Define asymmetric information and distinguish between adverse selection and moral hazard, **pages 576–580.**

Asymmetric Information

Summary

Asymmetric information is a situation in which one party to an economic transaction has less information than the other party. Asymmetric information can lead to **adverse selection**, which occurs when one party to a transaction takes advantage of knowing more than the other party to the transaction. An example is the "lemons" problem, where adverse selection may lead to only unreliable used cars being offered for sale. Asymmetric information can also lead to **moral hazard**, which refers to actions people take after they have entered into a transaction that make the other party to the transaction worse off. For example, a firm that has taken out a fire insurance policy on a warehouse may be less careful in the future about avoiding fire hazards. Information problems result in the equilibrium quantity in markets being smaller than it would be if these problems did not exist. Therefore, there is a reduction in economic efficiency.

myeconlab Visit www.myeconlab.com to complete these exercises online and get instant feedback.
Get Ahead of the Curve

Review Questions

1.1 What is asymmetric information? How does asymmetric information show up in the market for used cars?

1.2 What is the difference between adverse selection and moral hazard? Which is a bigger problem for consumers in the market for used cars?

1.3 Briefly discuss how adverse selection and moral hazard affect the market for insurance.

1.4 What methods do insurance companies use to reduce adverse selection and moral hazard?

Problems and Applications

1.5 Suppose you see a 2006 Volkswagen Jetta GLS Turbo Sedan advertised in the campus newspaper for $10,000. If you knew the car was reliable, you would be willing to pay $12,000 for it. If you knew the car was unreliable, you would only be willing to pay $8,000 for it. Under what circumstances should you buy the car?

1.6 Why are there lemon laws for the car market but not for the television market or the toothbrush market?

1.7 Michael Kinsley, a political columnist, observes that, "The idea of insurance is to share the risks of bad outcomes." In what sense does insurance involve sharing risks? How does the problem of adverse selection affect the ability of insurance to provide the benefit of sharing risk?

Source: Michael Kinsley, "Congress on Drugs," *Slate*, August 1, 2002.

1.8 Under the Social Security retirement system, the federal government collects a tax on most people's wage income and makes payments to retired workers above a certain age who are covered by the system. (The age to receive full Social Security retirement benefits varies based on the year the worker was born.) The Social Security retirement system is sometimes referred to as a program of social insurance. Is Social Security an insurance program in the same sense as a group life insurance or health insurance policy that a company provides to its workers? Briefly explain.

1.9 There are 10,000 houses in Lawrence. Suppose that houses cost $100,000, and 5 percent of the houses burn down each year. Which 5 percent of houses will burn down in any particular year is impossible for anyone, including the owners, to predict. There is no fire insurance available to Lawrence residents, so you decide to start an insurance company and begin offering policies. Your policy will pay the purchaser $100,000 if his or her house burns down. You charge a premium of $22,000 per year.

a. Are the residents of Lawrence likely to buy your policies? Briefly explain.

b. Now suppose that 5 percent of the owners know with certainty that their houses will burn down and that the other 95 percent of the owners know with certainty that their houses will not burn down. You offer everyone the same insurance policy with the same $22,000 premium. What is your accounting profit likely to be for the year? Assume that you have no explicit costs except for the payments you make to people who bought your policies and had their houses burn down.

c. Now suppose that people do not know with certainty whether their houses will burn down and that some houses are significantly more likely to burn down than others. Unfortunately, the owners of the houses that are significantly more likely to burn down know it, but you do not. Is it possible for you to restructure the insurance policies you offer—that is, change the terms of how much you pay out and the premium you charge—in order to deal with this problem?

1.10 Every state requires that drivers have an automobile insurance policy that covers any car they own and operate. Some people have such bad driving records that they are unable to find any insurance company willing to sell them a policy. These drivers are placed in an "assigned risk pool." Every insurance company that sells automobile insurance in the state is required to insure some drivers from the assigned risk pool. The state government usually sets the rates these drivers pay for insurance. Why is this system necessary? Why don't insurance companies voluntarily insure these bad drivers and charge them very high rates? Why does the state government have to force insurance companies to insure bad drivers?

1.11 (Related to the *Making the Connection* on page 578) Suppose a large firm allows its employees to choose whether to participate in its health insurance plan. The firm is trying to decide whether to offer a plan with a high deductible, but a low monthly premium, or one with a low deductible, but a high monthly premium. Under which plan is adverse selection likely to be a bigger problem? Briefly explain.

1.12 (Related to the *Making the Connection* on page 578) An editorial in the *Wall Street Journal* argues that regulations imposed by state governments

are responsible for making health insurance "so expensive to buy." The editorial singles out "'community rating' (insurers can't price based on differing risk factors such as age) and 'guaranteed issue' (you can wait until you're sick to buy insurance)." What problems do these regulations cause for insurance companies? How might insurance companies respond to these regulations? Do these regulations make consumers better off? The editorial concludes:

> The real scandal in American health insurance isn't that some people lack coverage for this or that treatment, but that tens of millions of Americans risk financial ruin because of [government] policies that make basic insurance difficult or impossible to buy.

Briefly explain whether you agree or disagree with this conclusion.

Source: "Why Can't You Buy Insurance?" *Wall Street Journal,* October 1, 2002.

1.13 (Related to the *Chapter Opener* on page 574) Why have auto insurers like State Farm started collecting more information on drivers and using computer models that employ thousands of variables to predict the chance that a driver will have an accident? Why didn't these firms do this sooner if these differences among drivers always existed?

1.14 (Related to the *Don't Let This Happen to You!* on page 580) Briefly explain whether you agree with the following statement: "The reluctance of healthy young adults to buy medical insurance creates a moral hazard problem for insurance companies."

>> End Learning Objective 17.1

17.2 LEARNING OBJECTIVE   17.2 | Apply the concepts of adverse selection and moral hazard to financial markets, pages 581–583.

Adverse Selection and Moral Hazard in Financial Markets

Summary

Adverse selection and moral hazard are serious problems in financial markets. When firms sell stocks and bonds, they know much more about their true financial condition than do potential investors. Investors are reluctant to buy stocks and bonds issued by small and medium-sized firms because they lack sufficient information about these firms. Investors also worry about the moral hazard problem of firms misusing the funds they raise through the sale of stocks and bonds. The Securities and Exchange Commission (SEC) has the authority to regulate the stock and bond markets and attempts to reduce adverse selection and moral hazard problems. The scandals of 2002 that involved the top managers in a number of corporations misusing funds and

reporting inflated profits indicate the extent of information problems in financial markets.

 Visit www.myeconlab.com to complete these exercises online and get instant feedback.

Review Questions

2.1 Explain why asymmetric information makes it difficult for small firms to sell stocks and bonds.

2.2 What is the Securities and Exchange Commission? Why was it founded?

2.3 What additional responsibility did the SEC receive in 2002? Why did Congress and the president decide that the SEC needed to take on this additional responsibility?

Problems and Applications

2.4 In an article in the *New York Times*, Warren Buffett, one of the most successful investors of the past 30 years, wrote, "For many years, I've had little confidence in the earnings reported by corporations." Why might he be suspicious that firms were not reporting their profits accurately?

Source: Warren Buffett, "Who Really Cooks the Books?" *New York Times*, July 24, 2002.

2.5 Many firms provide information about their plans and financial health to investment analysts who have no stake in the firm. Why would firms divulge such secrets?

2.6 After the countries of Eastern Europe converted from Communism to the market system, they tried to set up stock and bond markets. Most of these markets have remained very small, with few firms being able to find buyers for their stocks or bonds. One economist remarked that the reason these financial markets have been unsuccessful is that "the lemons problem has been too great." Explain what the economist meant.

2.7 **(Related to the *Making the Connection* on page 582)** In 2002, Congress prohibited firms from making loans to members of their boards of directors or to their top managers. Do you think this prohibition is meant to reduce asymmetric information problems? Briefly explain.

>> **End Learning Objective 17.2**

17.3 LEARNING OBJECTIVE | 17.3 | Apply the concepts of adverse selection and moral hazard to labor markets, pages 583–584.

Adverse Selection and Moral Hazard in Labor Markets

Summary

The potential for a **principal–agent problem** exists between employers and workers. This problem is caused by agents—workers—pursuing their own interests rather than the interests of the principals who hired them. When workers are not monitored, they may have no incentive to work hard. Employers try to avoid this moral hazard problem by increasing the value to a worker of the worker's current job. Three ways to increase the value of a worker's job are offering efficiency wages, using a seniority system, and offering profit sharing.

 Visit www.myeconlab.com to complete these exercises online and get instant feedback.

Review Questions

3.1 What problems can adverse selection and moral hazard cause in labor markets? What steps do firms take to deal with these problems?

3.2 What are efficiency wages? What role can they play in reducing the principal-agent problem?

Problems and Applications

3.3 **(Related to the *Don't Let This Happen to You!* on page 580)** Briefly explain whether you agree with the following:

From an employer's point of view, the moral hazard problem in labor markets is that the potential employees who don't intend to work hard are the ones who are most eager for you to hire them. The adverse selection problem is that once you have hired a worker, he or she has an incentive to work hard only if monitored.

3.4 **(Related to *Solved Problem 17-3* on page 584)** What role do tips play in dealing with the principal–agent problem in the market for restaurant servers? Suppose that a law is passed that outlaws tips, so that now restaurant servers just receive a wage, instead of a wage plus tips. Is the total income of servers likely to rise or fall? Briefly explain.

3.5 Colleges and universities grant tenure to many professors, making it virtually impossible to fire them after they've worked there for six or seven years. Analyze this labor market strategy in light of asymmetric information, adverse selection, and moral hazard.

3.6 The going wage for janitors is $6 per hour. The Executive Building decides to pay its janitors $10 per hour. Will this higher wage increase or decrease the firm's profits? Or could it go either way? In your answer, discuss asymmetric information and efficiency wages.

>> **End Learning Objective 17.3**

The Winner's Curse: When Is It Bad to Win an Auction?

Summary

In auctions where bidders do not know the true value of what is being auctioned, the winner, by overestimating the value of what is being bid for, can end up worse off than the losers. This is known as the **winner's curse**, and it occurs in auctions of common-value assets that would be given the same value by all bidders if they had perfect information.

Review Questions

4.1 What is the winner's curse? Is it a problem for the winner of every auction? Briefly explain why or why not.

4.2 Briefly explain whether you agree or disagree with the following statement: "The more information bidders have on the true value of what is being auctioned, the less likely they are to fall victim to the winner's curse."

Problems and Applications

4.3 Suppose you are advising one of the oil companies involved in the oil field bidding shown in Figure 17-1 on page 585. What bidding strategy would you recommend to the company so it could avoid the winner's curse?

4.4 After playing for six years in the major leagues, baseball players are free to sign a contract to play for any team. (Before that time, they are obligated to play for the team that first signed them.) In this situation, players often sign a contract to play for several years with the team that offers them the highest salary. Consider two players: Joe is a minor star who performs at about the same level each year. Sam's performance has been more uneven: Some years, he seems like one of the best players in baseball, but in other years, his performance has not been very good. Suppose Joe signs with the Cleveland Indians and Sam signs with the Cincinnati Reds. Three years later, is Cleveland or Cincinnati likely to be most satisfied that the player they signed played well enough to justify his salary? Briefly explain.

4.5 **(Related to Solved Problem 17-4 on page 587)** Suppose that everyone in an auction has perfect information about the value of whatever is being auctioned. Will the winner's curse still apply? Briefly explain.

4.6 A corporate takeover occurs when one firm—or a group of outside investors—buys up a majority of the stock in another firm. The usual aim of a takeover is to take advantage of the efficiencies possible with the newly merged firm or to bring in new management and run the acquired firm more profitably. In either case, the investors taking over the acquired firm are expecting to profit from the takeover. However, studies of corporate takeovers by Richard Roll of UCLA show that although the stockholders of the firm being taken over receive substantial gains—because the acquiring firm or investors bid up the price of the stock of the acquired firm as they try to take it over—the firm or investors carrying out the takeover earn small gains, if any. Relate Roll's finding to the problem of the winner's curse.

Source: Richard Roll, "The Hubris Hypothesis of Corporate Takeovers," *Journal of Business*, Vol. 59, No. 2, Pt. 1, April 1986, pp. 197–216.

4.7 **(Related to the Making the Connection on page 586)** The winner's curse may apply to the marriage market. The winner's curse usually applies in markets with common-value assets but not in markets with private-value assets. Discuss whether it is more accurate to think of the marriage market as a market with common-value assets, private-value assets, or some combination of the two.

4.8 Well-known novelists often auction off the rights to publish their latest books. John Dessauer has described the process:

> Major books are often "auctioned off" among publishers, *i.e.*, literally sold to the highest bidder. . . . The problem is, simply, that most of the auctioned books are not earning [the amounts paid for them]. In fact, very often such books have turned out to be dismal failures whose value was more perceived than real and which benefited from the ability of a plausible agent to sell the big sizzle on a small, tough steak.

Why do publishers who win auctions for books often end up paying more than the book turns out to be worth?

Source: John P. Dessauer, *Book Publishing: What It Is, What It Does*, 2nd ed., New York: Bowker, 1981, pp. 34–35.

4.9 In ancient Rome, the Praetorian Guards were the personal bodyguards of the emperor. The guard was made up of thousands of troops, and occasionally an emperor would lose control over them. In 193 A.D., the Praetorian Guard revolted and murdered Emperor

Pertinax. The guard then decided to auction off the office of emperor. The ancient historian Dio described the situation:

> Then ensued a most disgraceful business and one unworthy of Rome. For, just as if it had been in some market or auction-room, both the City and its entire empire were auctioned off. The sellers were the ones who had slain their emperor, and the would-be buyers were Sulpicianus and Julianus.

Didius Julianus won the auction with a bid that would be the equivalent of more than $1 billion today. Unfortunately, he greatly overestimated the value of becoming emperor in this way. His reign was very short. The general Septimius Severus brought his army from the Danube to Rome, deposed Didius Julianus, and was proclaimed emperor. In the words of the historian Edward Gibbon, Didius Julianus was "beheaded as a common criminal, after having purchased, with an immense treasure, an anxious and precarious reign of only sixty-six days." Does the analysis in this chapter help you understand what happened to Didius Julianus?

Source: Paul Klemperer and Peter Temin, "An Early Example of the 'Winner's Curse' in an Auction," *Journal of Political Economy,* December 2001.

4.10 **(Related to the *Making the Connection* on page 588)** Suppose that a $100 bill is auctioned off instead of a jar containing an unknown number of coins. Will the winner's curse still apply? Briefly explain.

>> **End Learning Objective 17.4**

Chapter 18

Public Choice, Taxes, and the **Distribution** of **Income**

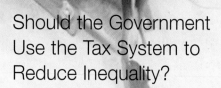

Should the Government Use the Tax System to Reduce Inequality?

Taxes can have a large effect on business decisions. When the federal government cut the tax on dividends—payments corporations make to stockholders—many companies responded in a big way. Before the tax cut, Microsoft, for instance, had never paid a dividend. After the tax cut, in one year alone, Microsoft paid out more than $40 billion in dividends, with Bill Gates, Microsoft's chair and largest share-holder, receiving a $3 billion divi-dend check. (Gates donated his divi-dend to the Bill and Melinda Gates Foundation.) Supporters of cutting the tax on dividends argued that cor-porate profits are taxed once under corporate income tax; if shareholders have to pay taxes on dividends, then the same income is taxed twice. Reducing the tax on dividends reduces this "double taxation." Opponents of cutting the tax pointed out that high-income people are more likely to receive dividends than are low-income people. If high-income people, like Bill Gates, received the largest immediate gain from the tax cut, then the distri-bution of income would be made more unequal.

How should we evaluate tax laws? Tax laws affect economic incentives and economic activity and can also affect fairness. The questions raised by the debate over the tax cut on divi-dends are not new. Presidents John F. Kennedy and Ronald Reagan proposed significant cuts in income taxes that they claimed would enhance eco-nomic efficiency, while their oppo-nents claimed that the tax cuts rewarded high-income taxpayers.

The debate over the tax system was particularly heated during the 2008 presidential election campaign. Senator Barack Obama, while running for the Democratic nomination for president, argued that major changes were needed in the U.S. tax system. According to Obama, the tax cut on dividends, as well as other tax cuts enacted during the early 2000s, had increased the burden on individuals with low and moderate incomes, while the burden on the wealthy and on corporations had been reduced, resulting in the highest level of income inequality since 1928. He advocated raising taxes on the wealthy to pay for a system of universal health care. In contrast, former New York Mayor Rudolph Giuliani, while run-ning for the Republican nomination, argued that the individuals with the highest incomes were paying the majority of the federal individual income tax and that many of those individuals were businesspeople who used the tax cuts to fund investments in their firms. Giuliani doubted that changes in taxes had had much effect on the distribution of income.

Putting aside the particulars of the political debate of 2008, the design of the tax system and the criteria to use in evaluating it are important questions. Has the tax code improved economic efficiency? Has the government, through its tax and other policies, had much impact on the distribution of income?

AN INSIDE LOOK AT POLICY on **page 624** examines a speech by Federal Reserve Chairman Ben Bernanke in which he discusses sources of income inequality in the United States.

Sources: Bret Hayworth, "Obama Touts Renewed Role," *Sioux City Journal*, April 1, 2007; and Deborah Solomon, "Republican Hopefuls Vie for Tax Cutters' Support," *Wall Street Journal*, March 29, 2007.

LEARNING Objectives

After studying this chapter, you should be able to:

18.1 Define the **public choice model** and explain how it is used to analyze **government decision making**, page 600.

18.2 Understand the **tax system** in the United States, including the principles that governments use to create **tax policy**, page 604.

18.3 Understand the effect of price **elasticity** on **tax incidence**, page 612.

18.4 Discuss the **distribution of income** in the United States and understand the extent of **income mobility**, page 615.

Economics in YOUR Life!

How Much Tax Should You Pay?

Government is ever present in your life. Just today, you likely drove on roads that the government paid for. You may attend a public college or university, paid for, at least in part, by government. Where does a government get its money? By taxing citizens. Think of the different taxes you pay. Do you think you pay more than, less than, or just about your fair share in taxes? How do you determine what your fair share is? As you read this chapter, see if you can answer these questions. You can check your answers against those we provide at the end of the chapter. > Continued on page 623

Figure 18-1

The Median Voter Theorem

The median voter theorem states that the outcome of a majority vote is likely to represent the preferences of the voter who is in the political middle. In this case, David is in the political middle because two voters want to spend more on breast cancer research than he does and two voters want to spend less. In any vote between a proposal to spend $2 billion and a proposal to spend a different amount, a proposal to spend $2 billion will win.

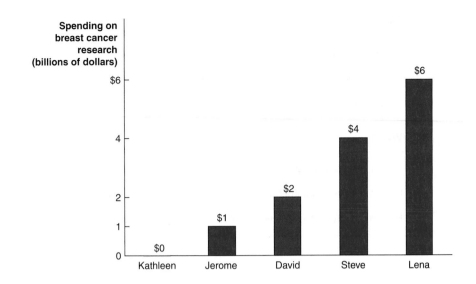

research—preferring the funds to be spent on other programs or for federal spending to be reduced and taxes lowered— to Lena, who prefers to spend $6 billion.

In this case, David is the median voter because he is in the political middle; two voters would prefer to spend less than David wants to and two would prefer to spend more. To see why the median voter's preferences are likely to prevail, consider first a vote between David's preferred outcome of spending $2 billion and a proposal to spend $6 billion. Because only Lena favors $6 billion and the other voters all prefer spending less, the proposal to spend $2 billion would win four votes to one. Similarly, consider a vote between spending $2 billion and spending $1 billion. Three voters prefer spending more than $1 billion and only two prefer spending $1 billion or less, so the proposal to spend $2 billion will win three votes to two. Only the proposal to spend $2 billion will have the support of a majority when paired with proposals to spend a different amount. Notice also that the amount spent as a result of the voting is less than the amount that would result from taking the simple average of the voter's preferences—$2 billion versus $2.6 billion.

One implication of the median voter theorem is that the political process tends to serve individuals whose preferences are in the middle, but not those individuals whose preferences are far away from the median. There is an important contrast between the political process, which results in collective actions in which everyone is obliged to participate, and the market process in which individuals are free to participate or not. For instance, even though Kathleen would prefer not to spend government funds on breast cancer research, once a majority has voted to spend $2 billion, Kathleen is obliged to go along with the spending—and the taxes required to fund the research. This is in contrast with the market for goods and services where if, for instance, Kathleen disagrees with the majority of consumers who like iPods, she is under no obligation to buy one. Similarly, even though Lena and Steve might prefer to pay significantly higher taxes to fund additional spending on breast cancer research, they are obligated to go along with the lower level of spending the majority approved. If Lena would like to have her iPod gold plated, she can choose to do so, even if the vast majority of consumers would consider such spending a waste of money.

Government Failure?

The voting models we have just looked at indicate that individuals are less likely to see their preferences represented in the outcomes of government policies than in the outcomes of markets. The public choice model goes beyond this observation to question whether the self-interest of policymakers is likely to cause them to take actions that are inconsistent with the preferences of voters, even where those preferences are clear. There are several aspects of how the political process works that might lead to this outcome.

Rent seeking Economists usually focus on analyzing the actions of individuals and firms as they attempt to make themselves better off by interacting in markets. The public choice model shifts the focus to attempts by individuals and firms to engage in **rent seeking**, which is the use of government action to make themselves better off at the expense of others. One of the benefits of the market system is that it channels self-interested behavior in a way that benefits society as a whole. Although Apple developed the iPod to make profits, its actions increased the well-being of millions of consumers. When Microsoft introduced the Zune to compete with the iPod, it also was motivated by the desire for profit, but it further increased consumer well-being by expanding the choice of digital music players available. Rent seeking, in contrast, can benefit a few individuals or firms at the expense of all other individuals and firms. For example, we saw in Chapter 8 that U.S. sugar firms have successfully convinced Congress to impose a quota on imports of sugar. The quota has benefited the owners of U.S. sugar firms and the people who work for them but has reduced consumer surplus, hurt U.S. candy companies and their workers, and reduced economic efficiency.

Because firms can benefit from government intervention in the economy, as the sugar companies benefited from the sugar quota, they are willing to spend resources attempting to secure these interventions. Members of Congress, state legislators, governors, and presidents need funds to finance their election campaigns. So, these policymakers may accept campaign contributions from rent-seeking firms and be willing to introduce *special interest legislation* in their behalf.

Logrolling and Rational Ignorance Two other factors help explain why rent-seeking behavior can sometimes succeed. It may seem puzzling that the sugar quota has been enacted when the number of workers and firms helped by it is so small. Why would members of Congress vote for the sugar quota if they do not have sugar producers in their districts? One possibility is *logrolling*. Logrolling refers to the situation where a member of Congress votes to approve a bill in exchange for favorable votes from other members on other bills. For example, a member of Congress from Texas might vote for the sugar quota, even though none of the member's constituents will benefit from it. In exchange, members of Congress from districts where sugar producers are located will vote for legislation the member of Congress from Texas would like to see passed. This vote trading may result in a majority of Congress supporting legislation that benefits the economic interests of a few, while harming the economic interests of a much larger group.

But if the majority of voters is harmed by rent-seeking legislation, how does it get passed, even given the effects of logrolling? In Chapter 8, we discussed one possible explanation with respect to the sugar quota. Although, collectively, consumer surplus declines by $2.2 billion per year because of the sugar quota, spread across a population of 300 million, the loss per person is only $7.50. Because the loss is so small, most people do not take it into account when deciding how to vote in elections, and many people are not even aware that the sugar quota exists. Other voters may be convinced to support restrictions on trade because the jobs saved by tariffs and quotas are visible and often highly publicized, while the jobs lost because of these restrictions and the reductions in consumer surplus are harder to detect. Because becoming informed on an issue may require time and effort and the economic payoff is often low, some economists argue that many voters are *rationally ignorant* of the effect of rent-seeking legislation. In this view, because voters frequently lack an economic incentive to become informed about pending legislation, the voters' preferences do not act as a constraint on legislators voting for rent-seeking legislation.

Regulatory Capture One way in which the government intervenes in the economy is by establishing a regulatory agency or commission that is given authority over a particular industry or type of product. For example, no firm is allowed to sell prescription drugs in the United States without receiving authorization from the Food and Drug Administration (FDA). Ideally, regulatory agencies will make decisions in the public interest. The FDA should weigh the benefits to patients from quickly approving a new drug against the costs that the agency may overlook potentially dangerous side effects of the drug if approval is too rapid. However, because the firms being regulated are

Rent seeking The attempts by individuals and firms to use government action to make themselves better off at the expense of others.

significantly affected by the regulatory agency's actions, the firms have an incentive to try to influence those actions. In extreme cases, this influence may lead the agency to make decisions that are in the best interests of the firms being regulated, even if these actions are not in the public interest. In that case, the agency has been subject to *regulatory capture* by the industry being regulated. Some economists point to the Interstate Commerce Commission (ICC) as an example of regulatory capture. Although it has since been abolished by Congress, for decades the ICC determined the prices that railroads and long-distance trucking firms could charge to haul freight. Congress originally established the ICC to safeguard the interests of consumers, but some economists have argued that for many years the ICC operated to suppress competition, which was in the interests of the railroads and trucking firms. Economists debate the extent to which regulatory capture explains the decision of some government agencies.

In Chapter 5, we saw how the presence of externalities can lead to market failure, which is the situation where the market does not supply the economically efficient quantity of a good or service. Public choice analysis indicates that *government failure* can also occur. For the reasons we have discussed in this section, it is possible that government intervention in the economy may reduce economic efficiency rather than increase it. Economists differ over the extent to which they believe government failure results in serious economic inefficiency in the U.S. economy. Most economists, though, accept the basic argument of the public choice model that policymakers may have incentives to intervene in the economy in ways that do not promote efficiency and that proposals for such intervention should be evaluated with care.

Is Government Regulation Necessary?

The public choice model raises important questions about the effect of government regulation on economic efficiency. But can we conclude that Congress should abolish agencies such as the Food and Drug Administration (FDA), the Environmental Protection Agency (EPA), and the Federal Trade Commission (FTC)? In fact, most economists agree that these agencies can serve a very useful purpose. For instance, in Chapter 5 we discussed how the EPA can help correct the effects of production externalities, such as pollution. Regulatory agencies can also improve economic efficiency in markets where consumers have difficulty obtaining the information needed for informed purchases. For example, consumers have no easy way of detecting bacteria and other contaminants in food or determining whether prescription drugs are safe and effective. The FDA was established in the early twentieth century to monitor the nation's food supply following newspaper accounts of unsanitary practices in many meatpacking plants.

Although government regulation can clearly provide important benefits to consumers, we need to take the costs of regulations into account. Recent estimates indicate that the costs of federal regulations may be several thousand dollars per taxpayer. Economics can help policymakers devise regulations that provide benefits to consumers that exceed their costs.

18.2 LEARNING OBJECTIVE

18.2 | Understand the tax system in the United States, including the principles that governments use to create tax policy.

The Tax System

However the size of government and the types of activities it engages in are determined, government spending has to be financed. The government primarily relies on taxes to raise the revenue it needs. Some taxes, though, such as those on cigarettes or alcohol, are intended more to discourage what society views as undesirable behavior than to raise revenue. These are the most widely used taxes:

- *Individual income taxes.* The federal government, most state governments, and some local governments tax the wages, salaries, and other income of households and the profits of firms. The individual income tax is the largest source of revenue for the federal government. In 2005, the average U.S. taxpayer earned about $55,019 and paid federal personal income taxes of $7,219.

- **Social insurance taxes.** The federal government taxes wages and salaries to raise revenue for the Social Security and Medicare systems. *Social Security* makes payments to retired workers and to the disabled. *Medicare* helps pay the medical expenses of people over age 65. The Social Security and Medicare taxes are often referred to as "payroll taxes." As the U.S. population has aged, payroll taxes have increased. By 2007, 75 percent of taxpayers paid more in payroll taxes than in federal income taxes. The federal government and state governments also tax wages and salaries to raise revenue for the unemployment insurance system, which makes payments to workers who have lost their jobs.

- **Sales taxes.** Most state and local governments tax retail sales of most products. More than half the states exempt food from the sales tax, and a few states also exempt clothing.

- **Property taxes.** Most local governments tax homes, offices, factories, and the land they are built on. In the United States, the property tax is the largest source of funds for public schools.

- **Excise taxes.** The federal government and some state governments levy excise taxes on specific goods, such as gasoline, cigarettes, and beer.

An Overview of the U.S. Tax System

Panels (a) and (b) of Figure 18-2 show the revenue sources of the federal, state, and local governments. Panel (a) shows that the federal government raises almost 80 percent of its revenue from the individual income tax and from social insurance taxes. Corporate

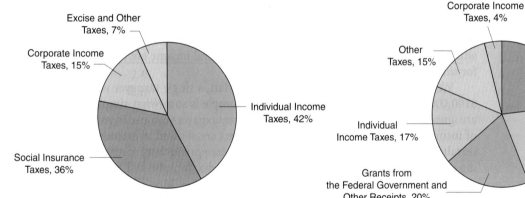

Tax	Amount (billions)	Amount per Person	Percentage of Total Tax Receipts
Individual Income Taxes	$1,060	$3,533	42%
Social Insurance Taxes	920	3,067	36
Corporate Income Taxes	389	1,297	15
Excise and Other Taxes	169	563	7
Total	$2,538	$8,460	100%

Tax	Amount (billions)	Amount per Person	Percentage of Total Tax Receipts
Sales Taxes	$414	$1,380	23%
Property Taxes	369	1,230	21
Grants from the Federal Government and Other Receipts	358	1,193	20
Individual Income Taxes	301	1,003	17
Other Taxes	277	923	15
Corporate Income Taxes	69	230	4
Total	$1,788	$5,959	100%

(a) Sources of federal govenment revenue, 2006

(b) Sources of state and local government revenue, 2006

Figure 18-2 | Federal, State, and Local Sources of Revenue, 2006

Individual income taxes are the most important source of revenue for the federal government, with social insurance taxes being the second most important source. State and local governments receive the most revenue from sales taxes. State and local governments also receive large transfers from the federal government, in part to help pay

for federally mandated programs. Many local governments depend on property taxes to raise most of their tax revenue.

Source: U.S. Department of Commerce, Bureau of Economic Analysis, *National Income and Product Accounts of the United States,* Tables 3.2 and 3.3, March 29, 2007.

Figure 18-3

The Efficiency Loss from a Sales Tax

This figure reviews the discussion from Chapter 4 on the efficiency loss from a tax. A sales tax increases the cost of supplying a good, which causes the supply curve to shift up from S_1 to S_2. Without the tax, the equilibrium price of the good is P_1, and the equilibrium quantity is Q_1. After the tax is imposed, the equilibrium price rises to P_2, and the equilibrium quantity falls to Q_2. After paying the tax, producers receive P_3. The government receives tax revenue equal to the green-shaded rectangle. Some consumer surplus and some producer surplus become tax revenue for the government, and some become deadweight loss, shown by the yellow-shaded triangle. The deadweight loss is the *excess burden* of the tax.

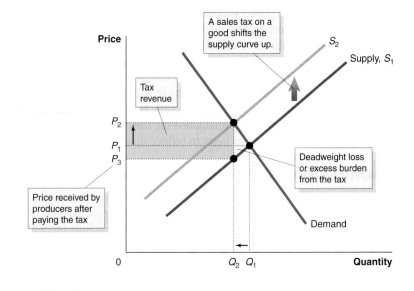

Excess burden The efficiency loss to the economy that results from a tax causing a reduction in the quantity of a good produced; also known as the deadweight loss.

occur. Figure 18-3 uses a demand and supply graph to illustrate this point for a sales tax. As we saw in Chapter 4, a sales tax increases the cost of supplying a good, which causes the supply curve to shift up by the amount of the tax. In the figure, the equilibrium price rises from P_1 to P_2, and the equilibrium quantity falls from Q_1 to Q_2. When a good is taxed, less of it is produced.

The government collects tax revenue equal to the tax per unit multiplied by the number of units sold. The green-shaded rectangle in Figure 18-3 represents the government's tax revenue. Although sellers appear to receive a higher price for the good—P_2—the price they receive after paying the tax falls to P_3. Because the price consumers pay has risen, consumer surplus has fallen. Because the price producers receive has also fallen, producer surplus has fallen. Some of the reduction in consumer surplus and producer surplus becomes tax revenue for the government. The rest of the reduction in consumer surplus and producer surplus is equal to the deadweight loss from the tax and is shown in the figure by the yellow-shaded triangle. The deadweight loss from a tax is known as the **excess burden** of the tax. The excess burden measures the efficiency loss to the economy that results from the tax having reduced the quantity of the good produced. *A tax is efficient if it imposes a small excess burden relative to the tax revenue it raises.*

To improve the economic efficiency of a tax system, economists argue that the government should reduce its reliance on taxes that have a high deadweight loss relative to the revenue raised. The tax on interest earned from savings is an example of a tax with a high deadweight loss because savings often comes from income already taxed once. Therefore, taxing interest earned on savings from income that has already been taxed amounts to double taxation.

There are other examples of significant deadweight losses of taxation. High taxes on work can reduce the number of hours an individual works, as well as how hard the individual works or whether the individual starts a business. In each case, the reduction in the taxed activity—here, work—generates less government revenue, and individuals are worse off because the tax encourages them to change their behavior.

Taxation can have substantial effects on economic efficiency by altering incentives to work, save, or invest. A good illustration of this effect can be seen in the large differences between annual hours worked in Europe and in the United States. It is well known that Europeans now work fewer hours than do Americans. According to a recent analysis by Nobel laureate Edward Prescott of Arizona State University, this difference was not always present. In the early 1970s, when European and U.S. tax rates on income were comparable, European and U.S. hours worked per employee were also comparable. Prescott finds that virtually all of the difference between labor supply in the United States and labor supply in France and Germany since that time is due to differences in their tax systems.

Making the Connection

Should the United States Shift from an Income Tax to a Consumption Tax?

A key issue in recent debates over tax policy is whether the federal government should shift from relying on an income tax to relying on a *consumption tax*. Under the income tax, households pay taxes on all income earned. Under a consumption tax, households pay taxes only on the part of income they spend. Households pay taxes on saved income only if they spend the money at a later time.

To see how a shift from an income tax to a consumption tax can affect the economic incentives individuals face, consider the following example: Suppose a 20-year-old is deciding whether to save a $1,000 bonus paid by her employer. If she saves the $1,000 by putting it in a bank certificate of deposit (CD), the $1,000 *and* the interest she earns will both be taxed under the income tax, but neither will be taxed if the income tax is replaced by a consumption tax. Suppose she earns 6 percent per year on the CD and keeps it until she retires at age 70. With interest compounding tax-free over 50 years, she will have accumulated $18,420 at age 70. Now suppose that under the income tax she is taxed at a rate of 33 percent. As a result, she will only have $670 of her bonus left after paying the tax. In addition, if she saves the money in a CD, her after-tax return each year is only 6 percent $\times$ (1 − 0.33) = 4 percent. Now saving her bonus in a CD at age 20 yields only $4,761 at age 70. This big difference in accumulation—$13,659—is the tax burden on saving, a burden that makes saving less attractive.

Many economists argue that a taxpayer's well-being is better measured by his or her consumption (how much he or she spends) than by his or her income (how much he or she earns). Taxing consumption may therefore be more appropriate than taxing income. Also, because the income tax taxes interest and other returns to saving, it taxes *future* consumption—which is what current saving is for—more heavily than *present* consumption. That is, under an income tax, current consumption is taxed more favorably than future consumption, reducing households' willingness to save, as in the preceding example.

Would a consumption tax be more efficient than an income tax?

Some economists oppose a shift from an income tax to a consumption tax because they believe a consumption tax will be more regressive than an income tax. These economists argue that people with very low incomes are able to save little or nothing and so would not be able to benefit from the increased incentives for saving that exist under a consumption tax.

Would a shift to a consumption tax be a radical change in the tax system? For many households, the answer is, perhaps surprisingly, "no." Most taxpayers can already put part of their savings into accounts where the funds deposited and the interest received are not taxed until the funds are withdrawn for retirement spending—for example, 401(k) plans and certain types of Individual Retirement Accounts (IRAs). In effect, individuals whose savings are mainly in these retirement accounts are already paying a consumption tax rather than an income tax. And recent reductions in tax rates on dividends and capital gains—which are both returns to savings—and proposals to expand saving incentives will further increase the role of consumption taxation.

YOUR TURN: Test your understanding by doing related problem 2.11 on page 628 at the end of this chapter.

The administrative burden of a tax represents another example of the deadweight loss of taxation. Individuals spend many hours during the year keeping records for income tax purposes, and they spend many more hours prior to April 15 preparing their tax returns. The opportunity cost of this time is tens of billions of dollars each year and represents an administrative burden of the federal income tax. For corporations, complexity in tax planning arises in many areas. The federal government also has to devote resources to enforcing the tax laws. Although the government collects the revenue from taxation, the resources spent on administrative burdens benefit neither taxpayers nor the government.

Wouldn't tax simplification reduce the administrative burden and the deadweight loss of taxation? Yes. So why is the tax code complicated? In part, complexity arises because the political process has resulted in different types of income being taxed at different rates, requiring rules to limit taxpayers' ability to avoid taxes. In addition, interest groups seek benefits, while the majority of taxpayers, who do not benefit, find it difficult to organize a drive for a simpler tax system.

The Ability-to-Pay Principle The *ability-to-pay principle* holds that when the government raises revenue through taxes, it is fair to expect a greater share of the tax burden to be borne by people who have a greater ability to pay. Usually this principle means raising more taxes from people with high incomes than from people with low incomes, which is sometimes referred to as *vertical equity*. The federal income tax is consistent with the ability-to-pay principle. The sales tax, in contrast, is not consistent with the ability-to-pay principle because low-income people tend to spend a larger fraction of their income than do high-income people. As a result, low-income people will pay a greater fraction of their income in sales taxes than will high-income people.

The Horizontal-Equity Principle The *horizontal-equity principle* states that people in the same economic situation should be treated equally. Although this principle seems desirable, it is not easy to use in practice because it is sometimes difficult to determine whether two people are in the same economic situation. For example, two people with the same income are not necessarily in the same economic situation. Suppose one person does not work but receives an income of $50,000 per year entirely from interest received on bonds and another person receives an income of $50,000 per year from working at two jobs 16 hours a day. In this case, we could argue that the two people are in different economic situations and should not pay the same tax. Although policymakers and economists usually consider horizontal equity when evaluating proposals to change the tax system, it is not a principle that they can follow easily.

The Benefits-Received Principle According to the *benefits-received principle*, those people who receive the benefits from a government program should pay the taxes that support the program. For example, if a city operates a marina used by private boat owners, the government can raise the revenue to operate the marina by levying a tax on the boat owners. Raising the revenue through a general income tax paid both by boat owners and non–boat owners would be inconsistent with the benefits-received principle. Because the government has many programs, however, it would be impractical to identify and tax the beneficiaries of every program.

The Goal of Attaining Social Objectives Taxes are sometimes used to attain social objectives. For example, the government may want to discourage smoking and drinking alcohol. Taxing cigarettes and alcoholic beverages is one way to help achieve this objective. Taxes intended to discourage certain activities are sometimes referred to as "sin taxes."

18.3 LEARNING OBJECTIVE

18.3 | Understand the effect of price elasticity on tax incidence.

Tax Incidence Revisited: The Effect of Price Elasticity

In Chapter 4, we saw the difference between who is legally required to send a tax payment to the government and who actually bears the burden of a tax. Recall that the actual division of the burden of a tax between buyers and sellers in a market is known as **tax incidence**. We can go beyond the basic analysis of tax incidence by considering how the price elasticity of demand and price elasticity of supply affect how the burden of a tax is shared between consumers and firms.

Tax incidence The actual division of the burden of a tax between buyers and sellers in a market.

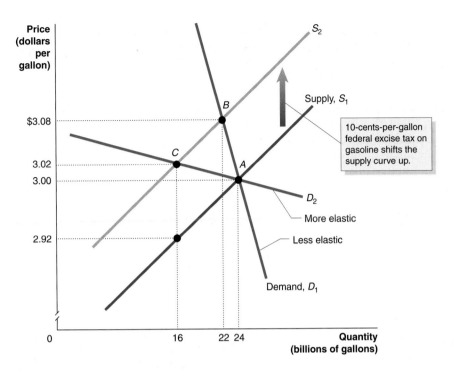

Figure 18-4

The Effect of Elasticity on Tax Incidence

When demand is more elastic than supply, consumers bear less of the burden of a tax. When supply is more elastic than demand, firms bear less of the burden of a tax. D_1 is inelastic between point A and point B, and D_2 is elastic between point A and point C. With demand curve D_1, a 10-cents-per-gallon tax raises the equilibrium price from \$3.00 (point A) to \$3.08 (point B), so consumers pay 8 cents of the tax, and firms pay 2 cents. With D_2, a 10-cents-per-gallon tax on gasoline raises the equilibrium price only from \$3.00 (point A) to \$3.02 (point C), so consumers pay 2 cents of the tax. Because in this case producers receive \$2.92 per gallon after paying the tax, their share of the tax is 8 cents per gallon.

In Chapter 4, we discussed whether consumers or firms bear the larger share of a 10-cents-per-gallon federal excise tax on gasoline. We saw that consumers paid the majority of the tax. We can expand on this conclusion by stating that consumers of gasoline pay a larger fraction of gasoline taxes than do sellers because the elasticity of demand for gasoline is smaller than the elasticity of supply. In fact, we can draw a general conclusion: *When the demand for a product is less elastic than the supply, consumers pay the majority of the tax on the product. When demand for a product is more elastic than the supply, firms pay the majority of the tax on the product.*

We can see why this conclusion is correct with the aid of Figure 18-4. In Figure 18-4, D_1 is inelastic between points A and B, and D_2 is elastic between points A and C. With demand curve D_1, the 10-cents-per-gallon tax raises the market price of gasoline from \$3.00 (point A) to \$3.08 (point B) per gallon, so consumers pay 8 cents of the tax, and firms pay 2 cents. With D_2, the market price rises only to \$3.02 (point C) per gallon, and consumers pay only 2 cents of the tax. With demand curve D_2, sellers of gasoline receive only \$2.92 per gallon after paying the tax. So, the amount they receive per gallon after taxes falls from \$3.00 to \$2.92 per gallon, and they pay 8 cents of the tax.

Don't Let This Happen to **YOU!**

Remember Not to Confuse Who Pays the Tax with Who Bears the Burden of the Tax

Consider the following statement: "Of course I bear the burden of the sales tax on everything I buy. I can show you my sales receipts with the 6 percent sales tax clearly labeled. The seller doesn't bear that tax. I do."

The statement is incorrect. To understand why it is incorrect, think about what would happen to the price of a product if the sales tax on it were eliminated. Figure 18-4 shows that the price of the product would fall because the supply curve would shift down by the amount of the tax. The equilibrium price, however, would fall by less than the amount of the tax. (If you doubt that this is true, draw the

graph to convince yourself.) So, the gain from eliminating the tax would be received partly by consumers in the form of a lower price but also partly by sellers in the form of a new price that is higher than the amount they received from the old price minus the tax. Therefore, the burden from imposing a sales tax is borne partly by consumers and partly by sellers.

In determining the burden of a tax, what counts is not what is printed on the receipt for a product but what happens to the price of a product as a result of the tax.

YOUR TURN: Test your understanding by doing related problem 3.9 on page 629 at the end of this chapter.

Making
the
Connection

Do Corporations Really Bear the Burden of the Federal Corporate Income Tax?

The incidence of the corporate income tax is one of the most controversial questions in the economics of tax policy. It is straightforward to determine the incidence of the gasoline tax using demand and supply analysis. Determining the incidence of the corporate income tax is more complicated because economists disagree over how corporations respond to the tax.

As a study by the Congressional Budget Office puts it:

> A corporation may write its check to the Internal Revenue Service for payment of the corporate income tax, but the money must come from somewhere: from reduced returns to investors in the company, lower wages to its workers, or higher prices that consumers pay for the products the company produces.

Most economists agree that some of the burden of the corporate income tax is passed on to consumers in the form of higher prices. There is also some agreement that because

Who really bears the burden of the taxes Apple pays?

the corporate income tax reduces the rates of return received by investors, it results in less investment in corporations. This reduced investment means workers have less capital available to them. As we discussed in Chapter 16, when workers have less capital, their productivity and their wages both fall. In this way, some of the burden of the corporate income tax is shifted from corporations to workers in the form of lower wages. The deadweight loss or excess burden from the corporate income tax is substantial. A study by the Congressional Budget Office estimated that this excess burden could be equal to more than half of the revenues raised by the tax. This estimate would make the corporate income tax one of the most inefficient taxes imposed by the federal government.

As a consequence, economists have long argued for reform of the system of double taxing income earned on investments that corporations finance by issuing stock. This income is taxed once by the corporate income tax and again by the individual income tax as profits are distributed to shareholders. Tax rates on dividends and capital gains were reduced in 2003, but whether to reduce double taxation further remains the subject of vigorous political debate.

Source: Congressional Budget Office, "The Incidence of the Corporate Income Tax," CBO paper, March 1996.

YOUR TURN: Test your understanding by doing related problem 3.7 on page 629 at the end of this chapter.

Solved Problem | 18-3

The Effect of Price Elasticity on the Excess Burden of a Tax

Explain whether you agree or disagree with the following statement: "For a given supply curve, the excess burden of a tax will be greater when demand is less elastic than when it is more elastic." Illustrate your answer with a demand and supply graph.

SOLVING THE PROBLEM:

Step 1: **Review the chapter material.** This problem is about both excess burden and tax incidence, so you may want to review the section "Evaluating Taxes," which begins on page 609, and the section "Tax Incidence Revisited: The Effect of Price Elasticity," which begins on page 612.

Step 2: **Draw a graph to illustrate the relationship between tax incidence and excess burden.** Figure 18-4 provides a good example of the type of graph to draw. Be sure to indicate the areas representing excess burden.

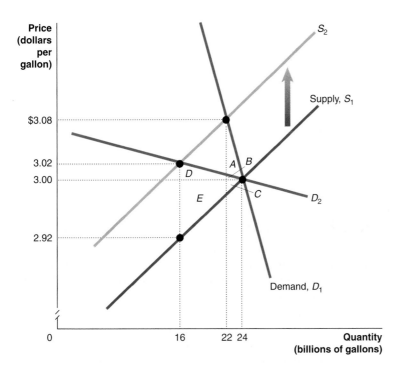

Step 3: **Use the graph to evaluate the statement.** The graph above is the same as Figure 18-4. As we have seen, for a given supply curve, when demand is more elastic, as with demand curve D_2, the fall in equilibrium quantity is greater than when demand is less elastic, as with demand curve D_1. The deadweight loss when demand is less elastic is shown by the area of the triangle made up of A, B, and C. The deadweight loss when demand is more elastic is shown by the area of the triangle made up of B, C, D, and E. The area of the deadweight loss is clearly larger when demand is more elastic than when it is less elastic. Recall that the excess burden of a tax is measured by the deadweight loss. Therefore, when demand is less elastic, the excess burden of a tax is *smaller* than when demand is more elastic. We can conclude that the statement is incorrect.

YOUR TURN: For more practice, do related problems 3.5 and 3.6 on pages 628–629 at the end of this chapter.

>> **End Solved Problem 18-3**

18.4 | Discuss the distribution of income in the United States and understand the extent of income mobility.

18.4 LEARNING OBJECTIVE

Income Distribution and Poverty

In practice, in most economies, some individuals will have very high incomes, and some individuals will have very low incomes. But how unequal is the distribution of income in the United States today? How does this compare with the distribution of income in the United States in the past or with the distribution of income in other countries today? What determines the distribution of income? And, to return to an issue raised at the beginning of this chapter, what impact does the tax system have on the distribution of income? These are questions we will explore in the remainder of this chapter.

For most people, of course, the most important factor of production they own is their labor. Therefore, the income they earn depends on how productive they are and on the prices of the goods and services their labor helps produce. Baseball player Alfonso Soriano earns $18 million per year because he is a very productive player, and his employer, the Chicago Cubs, can sell tickets and television rights to the baseball games Soriano plays in for a high price. Individuals who help to produce goods and services that can be sold for only a low price earn lower incomes.

Many people own other factors of production as well. For example, many people own capital by owning stock in corporations or by owning shares in mutual funds that buy the stock of corporations. Ownership of capital is not equally distributed, and income earned from capital is more unequally distributed than income earned from labor. Some people supply entrepreneurial skills by starting and managing businesses. Their income is increased by the profits from these businesses.

We saw in Table 18-6 that income inequality has increased somewhat during the past 25 years. Two factors that appear to have contributed to this increase are technological change and expanding international trade. Rapid technological change, particularly the development of information technology, has led to the substitution of computers and other machines for unskilled labor. This substitution has caused a decline in the wages of unskilled workers relative to other workers. Expanding international trade has put U.S. workers in competition with foreign workers to a greater extent than in the past. This competition has caused the wages of unskilled workers to be depressed relative to the wages of other workers. Some economists have also argued that the incomes of low-income workers have been depressed by competition with workers who are in the United States illegally.

Most economists believe that changes in tax laws have not played a major role in recent changes in income inequality. Federal income tax rates have changed dramatically during the years covered in Table 18-6. For example, the top marginal income tax rate was 91 percent in the 1950s, declining to 70 percent in the 1960s and to 28 percent in the 1980s. It then rose to 39.6 percent in the 1990s, before declining to 35 percent in 2003. Because tax rates changed significantly but the distribution of income has changed relatively little, it is unlikely that changes in tax rates have had a large impact on the distribution of income.

Finally, like everything else in life, earning an income is also subject to good and bad fortune. A poor person who becomes a millionaire by winning the state lottery is an obvious example, as is a person whose earning power drastically declines after a debilitating illness or accident. So, we can say that as a group, the people with high incomes are likely to have greater-than-average productivity and own greater-than-average amounts of capital. They are also likely to have experienced good fortune. As a group, poor people are likely to have lower-than-average productivity and own lower-than-average amounts of capital. They are also likely to have been less fortunate.

Showing the Income Distribution with a Lorenz Curve

Lorenz curve A curve that shows the distribution of income by arraying incomes from lowest to highest on the horizontal axis and indicating the cumulative fraction of income earned by each fraction of households on the vertical axis.

Figure 18-6 presents the distribution of income using a *Lorenz curve*. A **Lorenz curve** shows the distribution of income by arraying incomes from lowest to highest on the horizontal axis and indicating the cumulative fraction of income earned by each fraction of households on the vertical axis. If the distribution of income were perfectly equal, a Lorenz curve would be a straight line because the first 20 percent of households would earn 20 percent of total income, the first 40 percent of households would earn 40 percent of total income, and so on. Panel (a) of Figure 18-6 shows a Lorenz curve for the actual distribution of income in the United States in 1980 and another curve for the distribution of income in 2005, using the data in Table 18-6. We know that income was distributed more unequally in 2005 than in 1980 because the Lorenz curve for 2005 is farther away from the line of equal distribution than is the Lorenz curve for 1980.

Panel (b) illustrates how to calculate the *Gini coefficient*, which is one way of summarizing the information provided by a Lorenz curve. The Gini coefficient is equal to

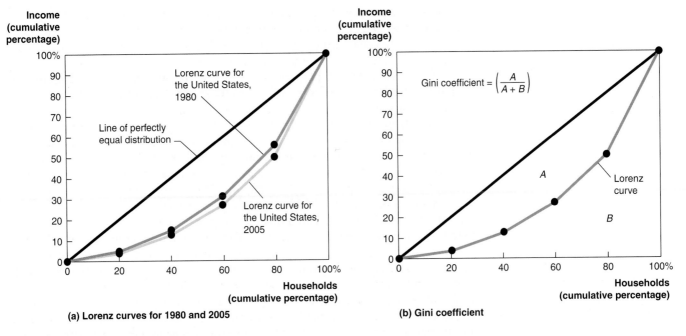

Figure 18-6 | The Lorenz Curve and Gini Coefficient

In panel (a), the Lorenz curves show the distribution of income by arraying incomes from the lowest to the highest on the horizontal axis and indicating the cumulative fraction of income by each fraction of households on the vertical axis. The straight line represents perfect income equality. Because the Lorenz curve for 1980 is closer to the line of perfect equality than the Lorenz curve for 2005, we know that income was more equally distributed in 1980 than in 2005. In panel (b), we show the Gini coefficient, which is equal to the area between the line of perfect income equality and the Lorenz curve—area A—divided by the whole area below the line of perfect equality—area A plus area B. The closer the Gini coefficient is to 1, the more unequal the income distribution.

the area between the line of perfect income equality and the Lorenz curve—area A in panel (b)—divided by the whole area below the line of perfect equality—area A plus area B in panel (b). Or:

$$\text{Gini coefficient} = \left(\frac{A}{A + B}\right).$$

If the income distribution were completely *equal*, the Lorenz curve would be the same as the line of perfect income equality, area A would be zero, and the Gini coefficient would be zero. If the income distribution were completely *unequal*, area B would be zero, and the Gini coefficient would equal 1. Therefore, the greater the degree of income inequality, the greater the value of the Gini coefficient. In 1980, the Gini coefficient for the United States was 0.403. In 2005, it was 0.469, which tells us again that income inequality increased between 1980 and 2005.

Problems in Measuring Poverty and the Distribution of Income

The measures of poverty and the distribution of income that we have discussed to this point may be misleading for two reasons. First, these measures are snapshots in time that do not take into account *income mobility*. Second, they ignore the effects of government programs meant to reduce poverty.

Income Mobility in the United States We expect to see some income mobility. When you graduate from college, your income will rise as you assume a new job. A family may be below the poverty line one year because the main wage earner is unemployed but may rise well above the poverty line the next year when that wage earner finds a job.

A medical student may have a very low income for several years but a very high income after graduating and establishing a medical practice. It is also true that someone might have a high income one year—perhaps from making a killing on the stock market—and have a much lower income in future years.

Statistics on income mobility are more difficult to collect than statistics on income during a particular year because they involve following the same individuals over a number of years. A study by the U.S. Census Bureau tracked the incomes of the same households for each year from 1996 to 1999. Figure 18-7 shows the results of the study. Each column represents one quintile—or 20 percent—of households, arranged by their incomes in 1996. Reading up the column, we can see where the households that started in that quintile in 1996 ended up in 1999. For example, the bottom quintile (the first column) consists of households with incomes of $16,220 or less in 1996 (all values are measured in 1999 dollars to correct for the effects of inflation). Only 62 percent of these households were still in the bottom quintile in 1999. Only a small number—1.2 percent—had moved all the way to the top quintile, but more than one-third had moved into either the second quintile or the middle quintile. At the other end of the income distribution, of those households in the top income quintile—with incomes of $68,649 or more—in 1996, only two-thirds were still in the top quintile in 1999. Given the relatively short time period involved, this study indicates that there is significant income mobility in the United States over time.

It should be noted that the U.S. economy experienced rapid growth between 1996 and 1999, which may have increased the degree of income mobility. However, an earlier study by Peter Gottschalk of Boston College and Sheldon Danziger of the University of Michigan also provides evidence of significant income mobility. In that study, only 47 percent of those people who were in the lowest 20 percent of incomes in 1968 were still in the lowest bracket in 1991. More than 25 percent had incomes in 1991 that put them in the middle or higher-income brackets. Of those people who were in the highest-income bracket in 1968, only 42 percent were still in the highest bracket in 1991. Almost 8 percent of this group had fallen to the lowest-income bracket.

Another study by the U.S. Census Bureau showed that of the people who were in poverty in 1996, only 50.5 percent remained in poverty in 1999. The same study indicated that of the people who were in poverty at any time during 1996, 51.1 percent were in poverty for four months or less. Only 20.4 percent were in poverty for more than one year.

Figure 18-7

Income Mobility in the United States, 1996–1999

Each column represents one quintile—or 20 percent—of households, arranged by their incomes in 1996. Reading up the column, we can see where the households that started in that quintile in 1996 ended up in 1999. Only 62 percent of the households that were in the bottom quintile of income in 1996 were still in the bottom quintile in 1999. Only 66 percent of the households that were in the top quintile of income in 1996 were still in the top quintile in 1999.

Note: Incomes are in 1999 dollars to correct for the effects of inflation.

Source: U.S. Census Bureau, "Dynamics of Economic Well-Being: Movements in the U.S. Income Distribution, 1996–1999," *Current Population Reports*, P70–95, July 2004.

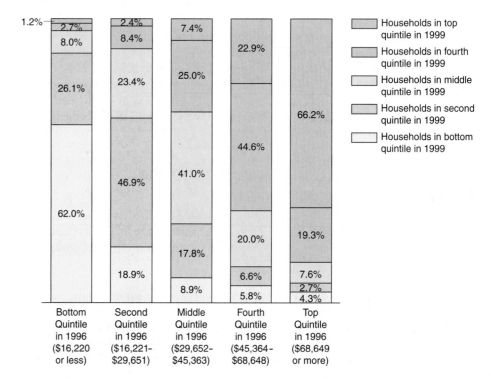

Solved Problem | 18-4

Are Many Individuals Stuck in Poverty?

Evaluate the following statement:

Government statistics indicate that 12 percent of the population is below the poverty line. The fraction of the population in poverty has never dropped below 10 percent. Therefore, more than 10 percent of the population must cope with very low incomes year after year.

SOLVING THE PROBLEM:

Step 1: **Review the chapter material.** This problem is about income mobility, so you may want to review the section "Income Mobility in the United States," which begins on page 619.

Step 2: **Use the discussion in this chapter to evaluate the statement.** Although it is true that the poverty rate in the United States is never below 10 percent, it is not the same 10 percent of the population that is in poverty each year. This chapter discusses a U.S. Census Bureau study that showed that only about half of the people who were in poverty in 1996 were still in poverty in 1999. Poverty remains a problem in the United States, but fortunately, the number of people who remain in poverty for many years is much smaller than the number who are in poverty during any one year.

YOUR TURN: For more practice, do related problem 4.7 on page 630 at the end of this chapter.

>> **End Solved Problem 18-4**

The Effect of Taxes and Transfers A second reason the conventional statistics on poverty and income distribution may be misleading is that they omit the effects of government programs. Because of government programs, there is a difference between the income people earn and the income they actually have available to spend. The data in Tables 18-5 and 18-6 show the distribution of income before taxes are paid. We have seen that at the federal level, taxes are progressive, meaning people with high incomes pay a larger share of their incomes in taxes than do people with low incomes. Therefore, income remaining after taxes is more equally distributed than is income before taxes. The tables also do not include income from *transfer payments* individuals receive from the government, such as Social Security payments to retired and disabled people. The Social Security system has been very effective in reducing the poverty rate among people older than 65. In 1960, 35 percent of people in the United States over age 65 had incomes below the poverty line. By 2005, only about 10 percent of people over 65 had incomes below the poverty line.

Individuals with low incomes also receive noncash benefits, such as food stamps, free school lunches, and rent subsidies. The *food stamp program* has been a particularly important noncash benefit. Under this program, individuals with low incomes can buy, at a discount, coupons to purchase food in supermarkets. During 2005, more than 25 million people participated in this program at a cost to the federal government of $28.6 billion. Because individuals with low incomes are more likely to receive transfer payments and other benefits from the government than are individuals with high incomes, the distribution of income is more equal if we take these benefits into account. For example, in 2005, 12.6 percent of the U.S. population was below the poverty line using the official definition of income. Taking into account taxes paid and benefits received from government programs raises the incomes of enough people to reduce the poverty rate to 10.3 percent.

Income Distribution and Poverty around the World

How does income inequality in the United States compare with income inequality in other countries? Table 18-8 compares the ratio of total income received by the 20 percent of the population with the lowest incomes and the 20 percent with the highest incomes

TABLE 18-8

Income Inequality around
the World

	LOWEST 20%	HIGHEST 20%	RATIO
BOLIVIA	1.5%	63.0%	42.0
BOTSWANA	2.2	70.3	32.0
BRAZIL	2.6	62.1	23.9
CHILE	3.3	62.2	18.8
UNITED STATES	3.4	50.4	14.8
THAILAND	6.3	49.0	7.8
UNITED KINGDOM	6.1	44.0	7.2
IRELAND	7.4	42.0	5.7
FRANCE	7.2	40.2	5.6
CANADA	7.2	39.9	5.5
SOUTH KOREA	7.9	37.5	4.7
GERMANY	8.5	36.9	4.3
NORWAY	9.6	37.2	3.9
JAPAN	10.6	35.7	3.4

Note: Data for most countries are from the early 2000s; U.S. data are from 2005.

Source: Adapted from United Nations, *Human Development Report, 2006*, New York: Palgrave Macmillan, 2006, Table 15.

in several countries. The countries are ranked from most unequal to least unequal. In Bolivia, for example, the highest-income group has 63.0/1.5 = 42.0 times the income of the lowest-income group. In Japan, by contrast, the highest-income group has only 35.7/10.6 = 3.4 times the income of the lowest-income group. As the table shows, poor countries, such as Bolivia and Botswana, typically have more unequal distributions of income than does the United States. The distribution of income in the United States is more equal than some moderate-income countries, such as Brazil and Chile, but less equal than other moderate-income countries, such as Thailand. The United States has the most unequal distribution of income of any high-income country in the world. Of course, one must be careful with such comparisons because transfer payments are not counted in income. For example, the Social Security and Medicare systems in the United States are much more generous than the corresponding systems in Japan but less generous than those in France and Germany.

Although poverty remains a problem in high-income countries, it is a much larger problem in poor countries. The level of poverty in much of Sub-Saharan Africa, in particular, is a human catastrophe. In 2006, the poverty line in the United States for a family of four was an annual income of $20,444, but economists often use a much lower threshold income of $570 per person per year (or about $1.50 per day) when calculating the rate of poverty in poor countries. As Table 18-9 shows, by this measure, poverty declined from about 20 percent of the world population in 1970 to 7 percent in 2000, the most recent year for which statistics are available. The greatest reduction in poverty has taken place in Asia. In China, the poverty rate dropped spectacularly from 32 percent in 1970 to 3.1 percent in 2000. In south Asia, which includes India, poverty rates dropped from 30.3 percent to 2.5 percent. By contrast, the poverty rate in Sub-Saharan Africa *increased* from 35.1 percent in 1970 to 48.8 percent in 2000. Why has poverty fallen dramatically in Asia but risen in Africa? The key explanation is that the countries of Asia have had higher rates of economic growth than have the countries of Sub-Saharan Africa. Recent economic research demonstrates a positive relationship between economic growth and the incomes of lower-income people.

	PERCENTAGE OF THE POPULATION IN POVERTY	
REGION	**1970**	**2000**
World	20.2%	7.0%
East Asia	32.7	2.4
China	32.0	3.1
South Asia	30.3	2.5
Middle East and North Africa	10.7	0.6
Latin America	10.3	4.2
Sub-Saharan Africa	35.1	48.8

TABLE 18-9

Poverty in Sub-Saharan Africa Is Much Greater Than Elsewhere in the World

Source: Xavier Sala-i-Martin, "The World Distribution of Income: Falling Poverty and Convergence, Period," *Quarterly Journal of Economics*, Vol. 121, No. 2 (May 2006), pp. 351–397.

Economics in YOUR Life!

>> Continued from page 599

At the beginning of the chapter, we asked you to think about where government gets the money to provide goods and services and about whether you pay your fair share of taxes. After reading this chapter, you should see that you pay taxes in many different forms. When you work, you pay taxes on your income, both for individual income taxes and social insurance taxes. When you buy gasoline, you pay an excise tax, which, in part, pays for highways. When you buy goods at a local store, you pay state and local sales taxes the government uses to fund education and other services. Whether you are paying your fair share of taxes is a normative question. The U.S. tax system is progressive, so higher-income individuals pay more in taxes than do lower-income individuals. In fact, as we saw in the *Making the Connection* on page 607, people in the lowest 40 percent of the income distribution pay no federal income taxes at all. You may find that you will not pay much in federal income taxes in your first job after college. But as your income grows during your career, so will the percentage of your income you pay in taxes.

Conclusion

The public choice model provides insights into how government decisions are made. The decisions of policymakers will not necessarily reflect the preferences of voters. Attempts by government to intervene in the economy may increase economic efficiency, as we saw in Chapter 5, but also lead to government failure and a reduction in economic efficiency.

A saying attributed to Benjamin Franklin states that "nothing in this world is certain but death and taxes." But which taxes? As we saw at the beginning of this chapter, politicians continue to debate whether the government should use the tax system and other programs to reduce the level of income inequality in the United States. The tax system represents a balance among the objectives of economic efficiency, ability to pay, paying for benefits received, and achieving social objectives. Those favoring government intervention to reduce inequality argue that it is unfair for some people to have much higher incomes than others. Others argue that income inequality largely reflects higher incomes resulting from greater skills and from entrepreneurial ability and that higher taxes reduce work, saving, and investment.

Many economists are skeptical of tax policy proposals to reduce income inequality very significantly. They argue that a market system relies on individuals being willing to work hard and take risks with the promise of high incomes if they are successful. If some of those incomes are taken from them in the name of reducing income inequality, the incentives to work hard and take risks are reduced. Ultimately, whether policies to reduce income inequality should be pursued is a normative question. Economics alone cannot decide the issue.

Read *An Inside Look at Policy* on the next page for a discussion of the views of Federal Reserve Chairman Ben Bernanke on sources of income inequality in the United States.

Balancing Flexible Markets and a Government Safety Net

WASHINGTON POST, FEBRUARY 7, 2007

The Grand Bargainer

(a) With President Bush having finally acknowledged the problem of growing income inequality, and Democratic leaders tripping over each other to do something about it, we desperately need a trustworthy moderator for this national debate.

Now we may have one, in Federal Reserve Chairman Ben Bernanke. In a speech yesterday to the Greater Omaha Chamber of Commerce, the former Princeton University professor cut through all the usual cant of the left and right and drew on the best and latest research to quantify just how much inequality has increased over the past 30 years. He gently, but deftly, dismissed the favorite conservative arguments that the story is not one of greater inequality so much as one of greater mobility. At the same time, Bernanke exposed as myth all those overblown fears about the broad decline in standard of living and the death of the American middle class.

The causes of rising inequality are well known: technological change that has reduced demand for unskilled labor and increased it for skilled labor; increased trade and immigration, which march under the now-tainted banner of globalization; the winner-take-all dynamic of certain labor markets that produces superstar salaries for professional athletes, entertainers and chief executives; and changing "institutional arrangements," from the declining power of unions to deregulation.

(b) Much effort has gone into figuring out the relative importance of these factors, driven in part because how you define the problem often dictates how you craft a solution. Bernanke tends to side with those who credit new technologies, like computers, that have increased the demand—and thus the relative pay—for educated workers. This analysis suggests the answer lies in more education, which appeals to market-oriented conservatives who are anxious to avoid solutions that might throw sand in the gears of globalization. It also appeals to academic economists, who have a natural preference for anything that involves hiring more college professors. . . .

One reason the U.S. economy is the most productive, the most dynamic, the most innovative in the world, Bernanke explained, is that we offer the biggest rewards to skill, effort and ingenuity. We also have an economic framework that not only allows companies and individuals the flexibility to adapt to changes in technology or consumer tastes or competition, but rewards them handsomely when they do.

Bernanke says the flip side of this dynamism has been to generate not only a higher level of inequality, but also a higher level of economic insecurity. Now, he says, the only way to make these politically acceptable is to "put some limits on the downside risks to individuals affected by economic change."

(c) One way to limit those risks, of course, would be to restrict trade, impose new regulations on labor and product markets, or use the tax code to massively redistribute incomes. For Bernanke, the costs in terms of slower growth and higher unemployment would be too high.

The better alternative, he argued, is to preserve the political consensus for open and flexible markets by offering Americans a stronger economic safety net—one that might include more portable and affordable health insurance and pensions, some expansion of income support in the event of a job loss and a big new investment in education and training, from early childhood through adulthood.

Source: Steven Pearlstein, "The Grand Bargainer," Washington Post, February 7, 2007, p. D1. Copyright © 2007 The Washington Post Company. Reprinted by permission.

Key Points in the Article

This article highlights the political problem of growing income inequality. Most agree that growing income inequality is a problem. Popular solutions to the problem involve limiting trade and using the tax code to redistribute income. Ben Bernanke suggests that the cost of these approaches is too high and that we should instead explore strengthening the economic safety net while investing in education and training. The U.S. economy rewards skill, innovation, and effort. The article suggests that we need to continue to make progress in these areas, while taking steps to reduce the economic insecurity caused by the dynamic nature of the U.S. economy.

Analyzing the News

(a) U.S. politicians of both parties see income inequality in the United States as a growing problem. Some of the concern is the growing gap between the very rich and the simply rich. Some of the concern is the sense that the standard of living of middle-income earners is staying constant, while the upper-income earners are enjoying higher-income and wealth. While many agree on the existence of the problem, as we saw in the chapter, the way to reduce income inequality is far less certain.

(b) Recall from Chapter 16 that a worker is paid the worker's marginal revenue product, or the value of the additional output that the worker produces. Higher-skilled workers will not only be able to produce more output—that is, have a higher marginal product—but will also be able to produce more valuable output. Both higher marginal product and a higher value of output will lead to higher wages.

(c) The government already uses the tax code to redistribute income. The nature of a progressive tax system distributes income by taxing high-income people at higher rates than low-income people. In addition, programs such as the Earned Income Tax Credit give money to lower-income working families with children. The following table shows the distribution of individual income tax payments by adjusted gross income (AGI), range from 1999 to 2004. Since 1999, the share of federal income taxes paid by the bottom 50 percent of the income distribution has fallen while that of top income earners has increased. For 2004, the top 10 percent of tax filers claimed 44.35 percent of AGI and paid 68.19 percent of income taxes. Making the income tax system more progressive would require placing a larger tax burden on those in the top of the income distribution.

The article points out that this may be costly in terms of economic growth.

It should be noted that parts of the tax system are not very progressive at all. For example, in 2007, the payroll tax for Social Security is not paid on labor earnings above $97,500 per year, and the Medicare tax is a constant rate of labor earnings, regardless of income.

Thinking Critically
About Policy

1. It is often claimed that recent tax cuts have provided more tax relief for those in the upper ranges of the income distribution than those in the lower ranges. Evaluate this claim in light of the tax shares given in the table.

2. While they may pay little individual income taxes, all low-income families with earned income are subject to the payroll taxes for Social Security and Medicare. Some policymakers have proposed abolishing the payroll taxes and funding Social Security and Medicare by increasing the personal income tax. What potential benefits and drawbacks are there to this proposal?

PERCENTAGE OF FEDERAL INCOME TAX PAID

PERCENTILES BY AGI	1999	2000	2001	2002	2003	2004	2004 SHARE OF AGI EARNED BY TAXPAYERS IN THIS CATEGORY	2004 AGI LEVEL FOR THIS CATEGORY
Top 1%	36.18	37.42	33.89	33.71	34.27	36.89	19.00	$328,049
Top 5	55.45	56.47	53.25	53.80	54.36	57.13	33.45	137,056
Top 10	66.45	67.33	64.89	65.73	65.84	68.19	44.35	99,112
Top 25	83.54	84.01	82.90	83.90	83.88	84.86	66.13	60,041
Top 50	96.00	96.09	96.03	96.50	96.54	96.70	86.58	30,122
Bottom 50	4.00	3.91	3.97	3.50	3.46	3.30	13.42	<30,122

Sources: Gerald Prante, Tax Foundation, *Summary of Latest Federal Individual Income Tax Data*, Fiscal Fact No. 66; National Taxpayers Union, *Who Pays Income Taxes? See Who Pays What*, www.ntu.org/main/page.php?PageID=6; and Internal Revenue Service, *Statistics of Income*, various years.

Key Terms

Arrow impossibility theorem, p. 601	Lorenz curve, p. 618	Poverty rate, p. 617	Rent seeking, p. 603
	Marginal tax rate, p. 608	Progressive tax, p. 606	Tax incidence, p. 612
Average tax rate, p. 608	Median voter theorem, p. 601	Public choice model, p. 600	Voting paradox, p. 601
Excess burden, p. 610	Poverty line, p. 616	Regressive tax, p. 606	

18.1 LEARNING OBJECTIVE   18.1 | Define the public choice model and explain how it is used to analyze government decision making, **pages 600–604.**

Public Choice

Summary

The **public choice model** applies economic analysis to government decision making. The observation that majority voting may not always result in consistent choices is called the **voting paradox**. The **Arrow impossibility theorem** states that no system of voting can be devised that will consistently represent the underlying preferences of voters. The **median voter theorem** states that the outcome of a majority vote is likely to represent the preferences of the voter who is in the political middle. Individuals and firms sometimes engage in **rent seeking**, which is the use of government action to make themselves better off at the expense of others. Although government intervention can sometimes improve economic efficiency, public choice analysis indicates that *government failure* can also occur reducing economic efficiency.

myeconlab   Visit www.myeconlab.com to complete these exercises
Get Ahead of the Curve online and get instant feedback.

Review Questions

1.1 What is the public choice model?

1.2 What is the difference between the voting paradox and the Arrow impossibility theorem?

1.3 What is rent seeking and what relation does it have to regulatory capture?

1.4 What is the relationship between market failure and government failure?

Problems and Applications

1.5 Will the preferences shown in the following table lead to a voting paradox? Briefly explain.

POLICY	LENA	DAVID	KATHLEEN
Cancer research	1st	2nd	3rd
Mass transit	2nd	1st	1st
Border security	3rd	3rd	2nd

1.6 Many political observers have noted that Republican presidential candidates tend to emphasize their conservative positions on policy issues while running for their party's nomination, and Democratic presidential candidates tend to emphasize their liberal positions on policy issues while running for their party's nomination. In the general election, though, Republican candidates tend to downplay their conservative positions and Democratic candidates tend to downplay their liberal positions. Can the median voter theorem help explain this pattern? Briefly explain.

1.7 Briefly explain whether you agree with the following argument: "The median voter theorem will be an accurate predicator of the outcomes of elections when a majority of voters have preferences very similar to those of the median voter. When the majority of voters have preferences very different from those of the median voter, then the median voter theorem will not lead to accurate predictions of the outcomes of elections."

1.8 An article in the *Economist* magazine makes the following observation:

> People often complain that it is simplistic for economics to assume that individuals are rational and self-interested. Of course this is a simplification, but it is an enlightening one, and not flatly contradicted in the real world. The corresponding assumption about government—that the state aims to maximize social welfare—is contradicted by the real world about as flatly as you could wish.

What does it mean for the state to "maximize the social welfare"? If policymakers are not attempting to maximize the social welfare, what are they attempting to do?

Source: "The Grabbing Hand," *Economist*, February 11, 1999.

1.9 Is the typical person likely to gather more information when buying a new car or when voting for a member of the House of Representatives? Briefly explain.

1.10 James Buchanan, who is one of the key figures in developing the public choice model, has written that:

"The relevant difference between markets and politics does not lie in the kinds of values/interests that persons pursue, but in the conditions under which they pursue their various interests."

Do you agree with this statement? Are there significant ways in which the business marketplace differs from the political marketplace?

Source: James M. Buchanan, "The Constitution of Economic Policy," *American Economic Review*, Vol. 77, No. 3, June 1987, p. 246.

>> **End Learning Objective 18.1**

18.2 LEARNING OBJECTIVE | 18.2 | Understand the tax system in the United States, including the principles that governments use to create tax policy, **pages 604–612.**

The Tax System

Summary

Governments raise the funds they need through taxes. The most widely used taxes are income taxes, social insurance taxes, sales taxes, property taxes, and excise taxes. Governments take into account several important objectives when deciding which taxes to use: efficiency, ability to pay, horizontal equity, benefits received, and attaining social objectives. A **regressive tax** is a tax for which people with lower incomes pay a higher percentage of their incomes in tax than do people with higher incomes. A **progressive tax** is a tax for which people with lower incomes pay a lower percentage of their incomes in tax than do people with higher incomes. The **marginal tax rate** is the fraction of each additional dollar of income that must be paid in taxes. The **average tax rate** is the total tax paid divided by total income. When analyzing the impact of taxes on how much people are willing to work or save or invest, economists focus on the marginal tax rate rather than the average tax rate. The **excess burden** of a tax is the efficiency loss to the economy that results from a tax causing a reduction in the quantity of a good produced.

myeconlab Visit www.myeconlab.com to complete these exercises *Get Ahead of the Curve* online and get instant feedback.

Review Questions

2.1 Which type of tax raises the most revenue for the federal government?

2.2 A study showed that, on average, a family in Pennsylvania earning $40,000 per year paid 6 percent of its income in state taxes. A family earning $100,000 paid 5.6 percent of its income in taxes. Are state taxes in Pennsylvania progressive or regressive? Be sure to

explain the difference between a progressive tax and a regressive tax.

2.3 What is the difference between a marginal tax rate and an average tax rate? Which is more important in determining the impact of the tax system on economic behavior?

2.4 Briefly discuss each of the principles governments consider when deciding which taxes to use.

Problems and Applications

2.5 Why does the federal government raise more tax revenue from taxes on individuals than from taxes on businesses?

2.6 According to an article in the *New York Times*, "the poor and middle class . . . spend a greater portion of their income on cigarettes than the wealthy do." Assuming that this observation is correct, is a sales tax on cigarettes likely to be regressive or progressive? Be sure to define regressive and progressive taxes in your answer.

Source: David Leonhardt, "How a Tax on Cigarettes Can Help the Taxed," *New York Times*, April 14, 2002.

2.7 Many state governments have begun using lotteries to raise revenue. If we think of a lottery as a type of tax, is a lottery likely to be progressive or regressive? What data would you need to determine whether the burden of a lottery is progressive or regressive?

2.8 Use the information in Table 18-2 on page 606 to calculate the total federal income tax paid, the marginal tax rate, and the average tax rate for people with the following incomes. (For simplicity, assume that these people have no exemptions or deductions from their incomes.)
   a. $25,000
   b. $125,000
   c. $300,000

2.9 (Related to the *Making the Connection* on page 607) The following table shows the distribution of federal taxes in 2000.

INCOME CATEGORY	PERCENTAGE OF FEDERAL INDIVIDUAL INCOME TAXES PAID	PERCENTAGE OF TOTAL FEDERAL TAXES PAID
Lowest 20%	–0.6	0.7
Second 20%	0.5	3.9
Third 20%	6.9	10.2
Fourth 20%	16.3	19.9
Highest 20%	76.6	65.1
Total	**100.0**	**100.0**
Highest 1%	29.5	20.1

Source: Department of the Treasury: Office of Tax Analysis Working Paper #85, "U.S. Treasury Distributional Methodology" by Julie-Anne Cronin (September 1999)

Taxes were cut several times under the administration of George W. Bush. The table shows the distribution of federal taxes paid for the year before the first Bush administration tax cut. How did the tax cuts influence the distribution of federal taxes?

2.10 Almost all states levy sales taxes on retail products, but about half of them exempt purchases of food. In addition, virtually all services are exempt from state sales taxes. Evaluate these tax rate differences, using the goals and principles of taxation on pages 609 to 612.

2.11 (Related to the *Making the Connection* on page 611) Suppose the government eliminates the income tax and replaces it with a consumption tax. Think about the effect of this on the market for automobiles. Can you necessarily tell what will happen to the price and quantity of automobiles? Briefly explain.

>> End Learning Objective 18.2

18.3 LEARNING OBJECTIVE   18.3 | Understand the effect of price elasticity on tax incidence, **pages 612–615.**

Tax Incidence Revisited: The Effect of Price Elasticity

Summary

Tax incidence is the actual division of the burden of a tax. In most cases, buyers and sellers share the burden of a tax levied on a good or service. When the elasticity of demand for a product is smaller than the elasticity of supply, consumers pay the majority of the tax on the product. When the elasticity of demand for a product is larger than the elasticity of supply, sellers pay the majority of the tax on the product.

 Visit www.myeconlab.com to complete these exercises *Get Ahead of the Curve* online and get instant feedback.

Review Questions

3.1 What is meant by tax incidence?

3.2 Briefly discuss the effect of price elasticity of supply and demand on tax incidence.

Problems and Applications

3.3 According to the 2004 *Economic Report of the President,* "The actual incidence of a tax may have little to do with the legal specification of its incidence." Briefly explain what this statement means and discuss whether you agree or disagree with it.

3.4 According to the 2004 *Economic Report of the President,* "Another crucial principle [of tax incidence] is that

only people can pay taxes. Businesses and other artificial entities cannot pay taxes." Do you agree that businesses cannot pay taxes? Don't businesses pay the federal corporate income tax? Briefly explain.

3.5 (Related to *Solved Problem 18-3* on page 614) Use the following graph of the market for cigarettes to answer the following questions.

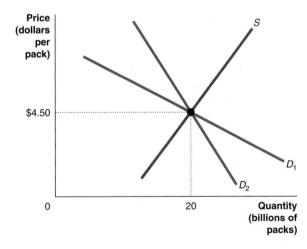

a. If the government imposes a 10-cents-per-pack tax on cigarettes, will the price consumers pay rise more if the demand curve is D_1 or if the demand curve is D_2? Briefly explain.

b. If the government imposes a 10-cents-per-pack tax on cigarettes, will the revenue to the government be greater if the demand curve is D_1 or if the demand curve is D_2? Briefly explain.

c. If the government imposes a 10-cents-per-pack tax on cigarettes, will the excess burden from the tax be greater if the demand curve is D_1 or if the demand curve is D_2? Briefly explain.

3.6 (Related to *Solved Problem 18-3* on page 614) Explain whether you agree or disagree with the following statement: "For a given demand curve, the excess burden of a tax will be greater when supply is less elastic than when it is more elastic." Illustrate your answer with a demand and supply graph.

3.7 (Related to the *Making the Connection* on page 614) Use a demand and supply model for the labor market to show the effect of the corporate income tax on workers. What factors would make the deadweight loss or excess burden from the tax larger or smaller?

3.8 Governments often have multiple objectives in imposing a tax. In each part of this question, use a demand and supply graph to illustrate your answer.

a. If the government wants to minimize the excess burden from excise taxes, should these taxes be imposed on goods that are elastic or goods that are inelastic?

b. Suppose that rather than minimizing excess burden, the government is most interested in maximizing the revenue it receives from the tax. In this situation, should the government impose excise taxes on goods that are elastic or on goods that are inelastic?

c. Suppose that the government wishes to discourage smoking and drinking alcohol. Will a tax be more effective in achieving this objective if the demand for these goods is elastic or if the demand is inelastic?

3.9 (Related to the *Don't Let This Happen to You!* on page 613) Evaluate the following statement: "I just bought a television set that was priced at $300. Because there was a 5 percent sales tax, the total amount I paid was $315. If my state didn't have a sales tax, I would have paid only $300."

>> **End Learning Objective 18.3**

18.4 LEARNING OBJECTIVE 18.4 | Discuss the distribution of income in the United States and understand the extent of income mobility, **pages 615–623.**

Income Distribution and Poverty

Summary

No dramatic changes in the distribution of income have occurred over the past 70 years, although there was some decline in inequality between 1936 and 1980, as well as some increase in inequality between 1980 and today. A **Lorenz curve** shows the distribution of income by arraying incomes from lowest to highest on the horizontal axis and indicating the cumulative fraction of income earned by each fraction of households on the vertical axis. About 12 percent of Americans are below the **poverty line**, which is defined as the annual income equal to three times the amount necessary to purchase the minimal quantity of food required for adequate nutrition. Over time, there has been significant income mobility in the United States. The United States has a more unequal distribution of income than do other high-income countries. **Poverty rates**, the percentage of the population that is poor, have been declining in most countries around the world, with the important exception of Africa. The *marginal productivity theory of income distribution* states that in equilibrium, each factor of production receives a payment equal to its marginal revenue product. The more

factors of production an individual owns and the more productive those factors are, the higher the individual's income will be.

myeconlab Visit www.myeconlab.com to complete these exercises
Get Ahead of the Curve online and get instant feedback.

Review Questions

4.1 Discuss the extent of income inequality in the United States. Has inequality in the distribution of income in the United States increased or decreased over time? Briefly explain.

4.2 Define poverty line and poverty rate. How has the poverty rate changed in the United States since 1960?

4.3 What is a Lorenz curve? What is a Gini coefficient? If a country had a Gini coefficient of 0.48 in 1960 and 0.44 in 2009, would income inequality in the country have increased or decreased?

4.4 Describe the main factors economists believe cause inequality of income.

4.5 Compare the distribution of income in the United States with the distribution of income in other high-income countries.

4.6 Describe the trend in global poverty rates.

Problems and Applications

4.7 (Related to *Solved Problem 18-4* on page 621) Evaluate the following statement: "Policies to redistribute income are desperately needed in the United States. Without such policies, the more than 12 percent of the population that is currently poor has no hope of ever climbing above the poverty line."

4.8 (Related to the *Chapter Opener* on page 598) In his column on MSNBC.com, Robert J. Samuelson wrote, "As for what's caused greater inequality, we're also in the dark. The Reagan and Bush tax cuts are weak explanations, because gains have occurred in pretax incomes. . . . Up to a point, inequality is inevitable and desirable."
   a. What are pretax incomes?
   b. Evaluate Samuelson's argument that tax cuts are unlikely to have been the cause of greater income inequality in the United States.
   c. Do you agree with Samuelson's argument that income inequality may be inevitable and desirable?

   Source: Robert J. Samuelson, "The Rich and the Rest," MSNBC.com, April 18, 2007.

4.9 Use the following Lorenz curve graph to answer the questions.

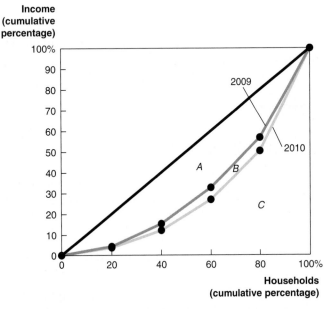

   a. Did the distribution become more equal in 2010 than it was in 2009, or did it become less equal? Briefly explain.
   b. If area A = 2,150, area B = 250, and area C = 2,600, calculate the Gini coefficient for 2009 and the Gini coefficient for 2010.

4.10 Draw a Lorenz curve showing the distribution of income for the five people in the following table.

NAME	ANNUAL EARNINGS
Lena	$70,000
David	60,000
Steve	50,000
Jerome	40,000
Sharon	30,000

4.11 Why do economists often use a lower poverty threshold for poor countries than for high-income countries such as the United States? Is there a difference between *relative* poverty and *absolute* poverty?

4.12 Suppose the Congress and the president decide on a policy of bringing about a perfectly equal distribution of income. What factors might make this policy difficult to achieve? If it were possible to achieve the goal of this policy, would this be desirable?

4.13 If everyone had the same income, would everyone have the same level of well-being?

4.14 Suppose that a country has 20 million households. Ten million are poor households that each have labor market earnings of $20,000 per year, and 10 million are rich households that each have labor market earnings of $80,000 per year. If the government enacted a marginal tax of 10 percent on all labor market earnings above $20,000 and transferred this money to households earning $20,000 or less, would the incomes of the poor rise by $6,000 per year? Explain.

4.15 A U.S. Census Bureau report showed that 46 percent of households living below the poverty line owned their own homes, 76 percent lived in dwellings with air-conditioning, about 75 percent owned cars, and 62 percent had cable or satellite TV reception. All these levels are considerably higher than they were for households below the poverty line a generation ago, but the official poverty rate is virtually unchanged over this period, as Figure 18-5 on page 617 shows. Going back to the official definition of poverty, how could ownership and purchases of these goods by the poor become more common while the poverty rate stayed the same?

4.16 In the speech cited in the *Inside Look* on page 624, Federal Reserve Chairman Ben Bernanke made the following observation: "Although we Americans strive to provide equality of economic opportunity, we do not guarantee equality of economic outcomes, nor should we." Suppose the federal government wanted to "guarantee equality of economic outcomes," how would it do it? If the government succeeded in making the distribution of income completely equal, what would be the benefits and what would be the costs?

   Source: "Remarks by Chairman Ben S. Bernanke Before the Greater Omaha Chamber of Commerce, Omaha, Nebraska," February 6, 2007.

4.17 In an article in the *Wall Street Journal*, Edward Lazear of Stanford University was quoted as saying: "There is some good news . . . most of the inequality reflects an increase in returns to 'investing in skills.' " Why would it be good news if it were true that most of the income inequality in the United States reflected an increase to returns in investing in skills?

Source: Greg Ip and John D. McKinnon, "Bush Reorients Rhetoric, Acknowledges Income Gap," *Wall Street Journal*, March 26, 2007, p. A2.

>> **End Learning Objective 18.4**

Glossary

A

Absolute advantage The ability of an individual, a firm, or a country to produce more of a good or service than competitors, using the same amount of resources.

Accounting profit A firm's net income measured by revenue minus operating expenses and taxes paid.

Adverse selection The situation in which one party to a transaction takes advantage of knowing more than the other party to the transaction.

Aggregate demand and aggregate supply model A model that explains short-run fluctuations in real GDP and the price level.

Aggregate demand curve A curve that shows the relationship between the price level and the quantity of real GDP demanded by households, firms, and the government.

Aggregate expenditure (AE) The total amount of spending in the economy: the sum of consumption, planned investment, government purchases, and net exports.

Aggregate expenditure model A macroeconomic model that focuses on the relationship between total spending and real GDP, assuming that the price level is constant.

Allocative efficiency A state of the economy in which production represents consumer preferences; in particular, every good or service is produced up to the point where the last unit provides a marginal benefit to consumers equal to the marginal cost of producing it.

Antitrust laws Laws aimed at eliminating collusion and promoting competition among firms.

Arrow impossibility theorem A mathematical theorem that holds that no system of voting can be devised that will consistently represent the underlying preferences of voters.

Asset Anything of value owned by a person or a firm.

Asymmetric information A situation in which one party to an economic transaction has less information than the other party.

Autarky A situation in which a country does not trade with other countries.

Automatic stabilizers Government spending and taxes that automatically increase or decrease along with the business cycle.

Autonomous expenditure An expenditure that does not depend on the level of GDP.

Average fixed cost Fixed cost divided by the quantity of output produced.

Average product of labor The total output produced by a firm divided by the quantity of workers.

Average revenue (AR) Total revenue divided by the quantity of the product sold.

Average tax rate Total tax paid divided by total income.

Average total cost Total cost divided by the quantity of output produced.

Average variable cost Variable cost divided by the quantity of output produced.

B

Balance of payments The record of a country's trade with other countries in goods, services, and assets.

Balance of trade The difference between the value of the goods a country exports and the value of the goods a country imports.

Balance sheet A financial statement that sums up a firm's financial position on a particular day, usually the end of a quarter or year.

Bank panic A situation in which many banks experience runs at the same time.

Bank run A situation in which many depositors simultaneously decide to withdraw money from a bank.

Barrier to entry Anything that keeps new firms from entering an industry in which firms are earning economic profits.

Behavioral economics The study of situations in which people make choices that do not appear to be economically rational.

Black market A market in which buying and selling take place at prices that violate government price regulations.

Bond A financial security that represents a promise to repay a fixed amount of funds.

Brand management The actions of a firm intended to maintain the differentiation of a product over time.

Bretton Woods System An exchange rate system that lasted from 1944 to 1971, under which countries pledged to buy and sell their currencies at a fixed rate against the dollar.

Budget constraint The limited amount of income available to consumers to spend on goods and services.

Budget deficit The situation in which the government's expenditures are greater than its tax revenue.

Budget surplus The situation in which the government's expenditures are less than its tax revenue.

Business cycle Alternating periods of economic expansion and economic recession.

Business strategy Actions taken by a firm to achieve a goal, such as maximizing profits.

C

Capital account The part of the balance of payments that records relatively minor transactions, such as migrants' transfers, and

sales and purchases of nonproduced, nonfinancial assets.

Capital controls Limits on the flow of foreign exchange and financial investment across countries.

Capital Manufactured goods that are used to produce other goods and services.

Cartel A group of firms that collude by agreeing to restrict output to increase prices and profits.

Cash flow The difference between the cash revenues received by a firm and the cash spending by the firm.

Catch-up The prediction that the level of GDP per capita (or income per capita) in poor countries will grow faster than in rich countries.

Centrally planned economy An economy in which the government decides how economic resources will be allocated.

***Ceteris paribus* ("all else equal")** The requirement that when analyzing the relationship between two variables—such as price and quantity demanded—other variables must be held constant.

Circular-flow diagram A model that illustrates how participants in markets are linked.

Closed economy An economy that has no interactions in trade or finance with other countries.

Coase theorem The argument of economist Ronald Coase that if transactions costs are low, private bargaining will result in an efficient solution to the problem of externalities.

Collusion An agreement among firms to charge the same price or otherwise not to compete.

Command and control approach An approach that involves the government imposing quantitative limits on the amount of pollution firms are allowed to emit or requiring firms to install specific pollution control devices.

Commodity money   A good used as money that also has value independent of its use as money.

Common resource   A good that is rival but not excludable.

Comparative advantage   The ability of an individual, a firm, or a country to produce a good or service at a lower opportunity cost than competitors.

Compensating differentials   Higher wages that compensate workers for unpleasant aspects of a job.

Competitive market equilibrium   A market equilibrium with many buyers and many sellers.

Complements   Goods and services that are used together.

Constant returns to scale   The situation when a firm's long-run average costs remain unchanged as it increases output.

Consumer price index (CPI)   An average of the prices of the goods and services purchased by the typical urban family of four.

Consumer surplus   The difference between the highest price a consumer is willing to pay and the price the consumer actually pays.

Consumption function   The relationship between consumption spending and disposable income.

Consumption   Spending by households on goods and services, not including spending on new houses.

Contractionary monetary policy   The Federal Reserve's adjusting the money supply to increase interest rates to reduce inflation.

Cooperative equilibrium   An equilibrium in a game in which players cooperate to increase their mutual payoff.

Copyright   A government-granted exclusive right to produce and sell a creation.

Corporate governance   The way in which a corporation is structured and the effect a corporation's structure has on the firm's behavior.

Corporation   A legal form of business that provides the owners with limited liability.

Coupon payment   An interest payment on a bond.

Cross-price elasticity of demand   The percentage change in quantity demanded of one good divided by the percentage change in the price of another good.

Crowding out   A decline in private expenditures as a result of an increase in government purchases.

Currency appreciation   An increase in the market value of one currency relative to another currency.

Currency depreciation   A decrease in the market value of one currency relative to another currency.

Current account   The part of the balance of payments that records a country's net exports, net investment income, and net transfers.

Cyclical unemployment   Unemployment caused by a business cycle recession.

Cyclically adjusted budget deficit or surplus   The deficit or surplus in the federal government's budget if the economy were at potential GDP.

D

Deadweight loss   The reduction in economic surplus resulting from a market not being in competitive equilibrium.

Deflation   A decline in the price level.

Demand curve   A curve that shows the relationship between the price of a product and the quantity of the product demanded.

Demand schedule   A table showing the relationship between the price of a product and the quantity of the product demanded.

Demographics   The characteristics of a population with respect to age, race, and gender.

Derived demand   The demand for a factor of production that is derived from the demand for the good the factor produces.

Devaluation   A reduction in a fixed exchange rate.

Direct finance   A flow of funds from savers to firms through financial markets, such as the New York Stock Exchange.

Discount loans   Loans the Federal Reserve makes to banks.

Discount rate   The interest rate the Federal Reserve charges on discount loans.

Discouraged workers   People who are available for work but have not looked for a job during the previous four weeks because they believe no jobs are available for them.

Diseconomies of scale   The situation when a firm's long-run average costs rise as the firm increases output.

Disinflation   A significant reduction in the inflation rate.

Dividends   Payments by a corporation to its shareholders.

Dominant strategy   A strategy that is the best for a firm, no matter what strategies other firms use.

Dumping   Selling a product for a price below its cost of production.

E

Economic discrimination   Paying a person a lower wage or excluding a person from an occupation on the basis of an irrelevant characteristic such as race or gender.

Economic efficiency   A market outcome in which the marginal benefit to consumers of the last unit produced is equal to its marginal cost of production and in which the sum of consumer surplus and producer surplus is at a maximum.

Economic growth   The ability of an economy to produce increasing quantities of goods and services.

Economic growth model   A model that explains growth rate changes in real GDP per capita in the long run.

Economic loss   The situation in which a firm's total revenue is less than its total cost, including all implicit costs.

Economic model   A simplified version of reality used to analyze real-world economic situations.

Economic profit   A firm's revenues minus all its costs, implicit and explicit.

Economic rent (or pure rent)   The price of a factor of production that is in fixed supply.

Economic surplus   The sum of consumer surplus and producer surplus.

Economic variable   Something measurable that can have different values, such as the wages of software programmers.

Economics   The study of the choices people make to attain their goals, given their scarce resources.

Economies of scale   The situation when a firm's long-run average costs fall as it increases output.

Efficiency wage   A higher-than-market wage that a firm pays to increase worker productivity.

Elastic demand   Demand is elastic when the percentage change in quantity demanded is *greater* than the percentage change in price, so the price elasticity is *greater* than 1 in absolute value.

Elasticity   A measure of how much one economic variable responds to changes in another economic variable.

Endowment effect   The tendency of people to be unwilling to sell a good they already own even if they are offered a price that is greater than the price they would be willing to pay to buy the good if they didn't already own it.

Entrepreneur   Someone who operates a business, bringing together the factors of production—labor, capital, and natural resources—to produce goods and services.

Equity   The fair distribution of economic benefits.

Euro   The common currency of many European countries.

Excess burden   The efficiency loss to the economy that results from a tax causing a reduction in the quantity of a good produced; also known as the deadweight loss.

Excess reserves   Reserves that banks hold over and above the legal requirement.

Exchange rate system   An agreement among countries on how exchange rates should be determined.

Excludability   The situation in which anyone who does not pay for a good cannot consume it.

Expansion path   A curve that shows a firm's cost-minimizing combination of inputs for every level of output.

Expansion   The period of a business cycle during which total production and total employment are increasing.

Expansionary monetary policy The Federal Reserve's increasing the money supply and decreasing interest rates to increase real GDP.

Explicit cost   A cost that involves spending money.

Exports   Goods and services produced domestically but sold to other countries.

External economies   Reductions in a firm's costs that result from an increase in the size of an industry.

Externality   A benefit or cost that affects someone who is not directly involved in the production or consumption of a good or service.

F

Factor markets   Markets for the factors of production, such as labor, capital, natural resources, and entrepreneurial ability.

Factors of production   Labor, capital, natural resources, and other inputs used to produce goods and services.

Federal funds rate   The interest rate banks charge each other for overnight loans.

Federal Open Market Committee (FOMC)   The Federal Reserve committee responsible for open market

operations and managing the money supply in the United States.

Federal Reserve System   The central bank of the United States.

Fiat money   Money, such as paper currency, that is authorized by a central bank or governmental body and that does not have to be exchanged by the central bank for gold or some other commodity money.

Final good or service   A good or service purchased by a final user.

Financial account   The part of the balance of payments that records purchases of assets a country has made abroad and foreign purchases of assets in the country.

Financial intermediaries   Firms, such as banks, mutual funds, pension funds, and insurance companies, that borrow funds from savers and lend them to borrowers.

Financial markets   Markets where financial securities, such as stocks and bonds, are bought and sold.

Financial system   The system of financial markets and financial intermediaries through which firms acquire funds from households.

Fiscal policy   Changes in federal taxes and purchases that are intended to achieve macroeconomic policy objectives, such as high employment, price stability, and high rates of economic growth.

Fixed costs   Costs that remain constant as output changes.

Fixed exchange rate system   A system under which countries agree to keep the exchange rates among their currencies fixed.

Floating currency   The outcome of a country allowing its currency's exchange rate to be determined by demand and supply.

Foreign direct investment (FDI) The purchase or building by a corporation of a facility in a foreign country.

Foreign portfolio investment The purchase by an individual or

a firm of stocks or bonds issued in another country.

Fractional reserve banking system   A banking system in which banks keep less than 100 percent of deposits as reserves.

Free market   A market with few government restrictions on how a good or service can be produced or sold or on how a factor of production can be employed.

Free riding   Benefiting from a good without paying for it.

Free trade   Trade between countries that is without government restrictions.

Frictional unemployment Short-term unemployment that arises from the process of matching workers with jobs.

G

Game theory   The study of how people make decisions in situations in which attaining their goals depends on their interactions with others; in economics, the study of the decisions of firms in industries where the profits of each firm depend on its interactions with other firms.

GDP deflator   A measure of the price level, calculated by dividing nominal GDP by real GDP and multiplying by 100.

Globalization   The process of countries becoming more open to foreign trade and investment.

Government purchases Spending by federal, state, and local governments on goods and services.

Gross domestic product (GDP) The market value of all final goods and services produced in a country during a period of time, typically one year.

H

Horizontal merger   A merger between firms in the same industry.

Human capital   The accumulated knowledge and skills that workers acquire from education and training or from their life experiences.

I

Implicit cost   A nonmonetary opportunity cost.

Imports   Goods and services bought domestically but produced in other countries.

Income effect   The change in the quantity demanded of a good that results from the effect of a change in price on consumer purchasing power, holding all other factors constant.

Income elasticity of demand   A measure of the responsiveness of quantity demanded to changes in income, measured by the percentage change in quantity demanded divided by the percentage change in income.

Income statement   A financial statement that sums up a firm's revenues, costs, and profit over a period of time.

Indifference curve   A curve that shows the combinations of consumption bundles that give the consumer the same utility.

Indirect finance   A flow of funds from savers to borrowers through financial intermediaries such as banks. Intermediaries raise funds from savers to lend to firms (and other borrowers).

Industrial Revolution   The application of mechanical power to the production of goods, beginning in England around 1750.

Inelastic demand   Demand is inelastic when the percentage change in quantity demanded is *less* than the percentage change in price, so the price elasticity is *less* than 1 in absolute value.

Inferior good   A good for which the demand increases as income falls and decreases as income rises.

Inflation targeting   Conducting monetary policy so as to commit the central bank to achieving a publicly announced level of inflation.

Interest rate   The cost of borrowing funds, usually expressed as a percentage of the amount borrowed.

Intermediate good or service   A good or service that is an input into another good or service, such as a tire on a truck.

International Monetary Fund (IMF) An international organization that provides foreign currency loans to central banks and oversees the operation of the international monetary system.

Inventories Goods that have been produced but not yet sold.

Investment Spending by firms on new factories, office buildings, machinery, and additions to inventories, and spending by households on new houses.

Isocost line All the combinations of two inputs, such as capital and labor, that have the same total cost.

Isoquant A curve that shows all the combinations of two inputs, such as capital and labor, that will produce the same level of output.

K

Keynesian revolution The name given to the widespread acceptance during the 1930s and 1940s of John Maynard Keynes's macroeconomic model.

L

Labor force The sum of employed and unemployed workers in the economy.

Labor force participation rate The percentage of the working-age population in the labor force.

Labor productivity The quantity of goods and services that can be produced by one worker or by one hour of work.

Labor union An organization of employees that has the legal right to bargain with employers about wages and working conditions.

Law of demand The rule that, holding everything else constant, when the price of a product falls, the quantity demanded of the product will increase, and when the price of a product rises, the quantity demanded of the product will decrease.

Law of diminishing marginal utility The principle that con-

sumers experience diminishing additional satisfaction as they consume more of a good or service during a given period of time.

Law of diminishing returns The principle that, at some point, adding more of a variable input, such as labor, to the same amount of a fixed input, such as capital, will cause the marginal product of the variable input to decline.

Law of supply The rule that, holding everything else constant, increases in price cause increases in the quantity supplied, and decreases in price cause decreases in the quantity supplied.

Liability Anything owed by a person or a firm.

Limited liability The legal provision that shields owners of a corporation from losing more than they have invested in the firm.

Long run The period of time in which a firm can vary all its inputs, adopt new technology, and increase or decrease the size of its physical plant.

Long-run aggregate supply curve A curve that shows the relationship in the long run between the price level and the quantity of real GDP supplied.

Long-run average cost curve A curve showing the lowest cost at which a firm is able to produce a given quantity of output in the long run, when no inputs are fixed.

Long-run competitive equilibrium The situation in which the entry and exit of firms has resulted in the typical firm breaking even.

Long-run economic growth The process by which rising productivity increases the average standard of living.

Long-run supply curve A curve that shows the relationship in the long run between market price and the quantity supplied.

Lorenz curve A curve that shows the distribution of income by arraying incomes from lowest to highest on the horizontal axis and indicating the cumulative fraction of income earned by

each fraction of households on the vertical axis.

M

M1 The narrowest definition of the money supply: The sum of currency in circulation, checking account deposits in banks, and holdings of traveler's checks.

M2 A broader definition of the money supply: M1 plus savings account balances, small-denomination time deposits, balances in money market deposit accounts in banks, and noninstitutional money market fund shares.

Macroeconomics The study of the economy as a whole, including topics such as inflation, unemployment, and economic growth.

Managed float exchange rate system The current exchange rate system, under which the value of most currencies is determined by demand and supply, with occasional government intervention.

Marginal analysis Analysis that involves comparing marginal benefits and marginal costs.

Marginal benefit The additional benefit to a consumer from consuming one more unit of a good or service.

Marginal cost The change in a firm's total cost from producing one more unit of a good or service.

Marginal product of labor The additional output a firm produces as a result of hiring one more worker.

Marginal productivity theory of income distribution The theory that the distribution of income is determined by the marginal productivity of the factors of production that individuals own.

Marginal propensity to consume (MPC) The slope of the consumption function: The amount by which consumption spending changes when disposable income changes.

Marginal propensity to save (MPS) The change in saving divided by the change in disposable income.

Marginal rate of substitution (MRS) The slope of an indifference curve, which represents the rate at which a consumer would be willing to trade off one good for another.

Marginal rate of technical substitution (MRTS) The slope of an isoquant, or the rate at which a firm is able to substitute one input for another while keeping the level of output constant.

Marginal revenue (MR) Change in total revenue from selling one more unit of a product.

Marginal revenue product of labor (MRP) The change in a firm's revenue as a result of hiring one more worker.

Marginal tax rate The fraction of each additional dollar of income that must be paid in taxes.

Marginal utility (MU) The change in total utility a person receives from consuming one additional unit of a good or service.

Market A group of buyers and sellers of a good or service and the institution or arrangement by which they come together to trade.

Market demand The demand by all the consumers of a given good or service.

Market economy An economy in which the decisions of households and firms interacting in markets allocate economic resources.

Market equilibrium A situation in which quantity demanded equals quantity supplied.

Market failure A situation in which the market fails to produce the efficient level of output.

Market for loanable funds The interaction of borrowers and lenders that determines the market interest rate and the quantity of loanable funds exchanged.

Market power The ability of a firm to charge a price greater than marginal cost.

Marketing All the activities necessary for a firm to sell a product to a consumer.

Median voter theorem The proposition that the outcome of a majority vote is likely to represent the preferences of the voter who is in the political middle.

Menu costs The costs to firms of changing prices.

Microeconomics The study of how households and firms make choices, how they interact in markets, and how the government attempts to influence their choices.

Minimum efficient scale The level of output at which all economies of scale are exhausted.

Mixed economy An economy in which most economic decisions result from the interaction of buyers and sellers in markets but in which the government plays a significant role in the allocation of resources.

Monetarism The macroeconomic theories of Milton Friedman and his followers; particularly the idea that the quantity of money should be increased at a constant rate.

Monetary growth rule A plan for increasing the quantity of money at a fixed rate that does not respond to changes in economic conditions.

Monetary policy The actions the Federal Reserve takes to manage the money supply and interest rates to pursue macroeconomic policy objectives.

Money Assets that people are generally willing to accept in exchange for goods and services or for payment of debts.

Monopolistic competition A market structure in which barriers to entry are low and many firms compete by selling similar, but not identical, products.

Monopoly A firm that is the only seller of a good or service that does not have a close substitute.

Monopsony The sole buyer of a factor of production.

Moral hazard The actions people take after they have entered into a transaction that make the other party to the transaction worse off.

Multinational enterprise A firm that conducts operations in more than one country.

Multiplier effect The series of induced increases in consumption spending that results from an initial increase in autonomous expenditure.

Multiplier The increase in equilibrium real GDP divided by the increase in autonomous expenditure.

N

Nash equilibrium A situation in which each firm chooses the best strategy, given the strategies chosen by other firms.

Natural monopoly A situation in which economies of scale are so large that one firm can supply the entire market at a lower average total cost than can two or more firms.

Natural rate of unemployment The normal rate of unemployment, consisting of frictional unemployment plus structural unemployment.

Net exports Exports minus imports.

Net foreign investment The difference between capital outflows from a country and capital inflows, also equal to net foreign direct investment plus net foreign portfolio investment.

Network externalities The situation where the usefulness of a product increases with the number of consumers who use it.

New classical macroeconomics The macroeconomic theories of Robert Lucas and others, particularly the idea that workers and firms have rational expectations.

New growth theory A model of long-run economic growth which emphasizes that technological change is influenced by economic incentives and so is determined by the working of the market system.

Nominal exchange rate The value of one country's currency in terms of another country's currency.

Nominal GDP The value of final goods and services evaluated at current-year prices.

Nominal interest rate The stated interest rate on a loan.

Nonaccelerating inflation rate of unemployment (NAIRU) The unemployment rate at which the inflation rate has no tendency to increase or decrease.

Noncooperative equilibrium An equilibrium in a game in which players do not cooperate but pursue their own self-interest.

Normal good A good for which the demand increases as income rises and decreases as income falls.

Normative analysis Analysis concerned with what ought to be.

O

Oligopoly A market structure in which a small number of interdependent firms compete.

Open economy An economy that has interactions in trade or finance with other countries.

Open market operations The buying and selling of Treasury securities by the Federal Reserve in order to control the money supply.

Opportunity cost The highest-valued alternative that must be given up to engage in an activity.

P

Partnership A firm owned jointly by two or more persons and not organized as a corporation.

Patent The exclusive right to a product for a period of 20 years from the date the product is invented.

Payoff matrix A table that shows the payoffs that each firm earns from every combination of strategies by the firms.

Pegging The decision by a country to keep the exchange rate fixed between its currency and another currency.

Perfectly competitive market A market that meets the conditions of (1) many buyers and sellers, (2) all firms selling identical products, and (3) no barriers to new firms entering the market.

Perfectly elastic demand The case where the quantity demanded is infinitely responsive to price, and the price elasticity of demand equals infinity.

Perfectly inelastic demand The case where the quantity demanded is completely unresponsive to price, and the price elasticity of demand equals zero.

Personnel economics The application of economic analysis to human resources issues.

Per-worker production function The relationship between real GDP per hour worked and capital per hour worked, holding the level of technology constant.

Phillips curve A curve showing the short-run relationship between the unemployment rate and the inflation rate.

Pigovian taxes and subsidies Government taxes and subsidies intended to bring about an efficient level of output in the presence of externalities.

Positive analysis Analysis concerned with what is.

Potential GDP The level of GDP attained when all firms are producing at capacity.

Poverty line A level of annual income equal to three times the amount of money necessary to purchase the minimal quantity of food required for adequate nutrition.

Poverty rate The percentage of the population that is poor according to the federal government's definition.

Present value The value in today's dollars of funds to be paid or received in the future.

Price ceiling A legally determined maximum price that sellers may charge.

Price discrimination Charging different prices to different customers for the same product when the price differences are not due to differences in cost.

Price elasticity of demand The responsiveness of the quantity demanded to a change in price, measured by dividing the percentage change in the quantity demanded of a product by the percentage change in the product's price.

Price elasticity of supply The responsiveness of the quantity supplied to a change in price, measured by dividing the percentage change in the quantity supplied of a product by the percentage change in the product's price.

Price floor A legally determined minimum price that sellers may receive.

Price leadership A form of implicit collusion where one firm in an oligopoly announces a price change, which is matched by the other firms in the industry.

Price level A measure of the average prices of goods and services in the economy.

Price taker A buyer or seller that is unable to affect the market price.

Principal–agent problem A problem caused by an agent pursuing his own interests rather than the interests of the principal who hired him.

Prisoners' dilemma A game in which pursuing dominant strategies results in noncooperation that leaves everyone worse off.

Private benefit The benefit received by the consumer of a good or service.

Private cost The cost borne by the producer of a good or service.

Private good A good that is both rival and excludable.

Producer price index (PPI) An average of the prices received by producers of goods and services at all stages of the production process.

Producer surplus The difference between the lowest price a firm would be willing to accept and the price it actually receives.

Product markets Markets for goods—such as computers—

and services—such as medical treatment.

Production function The relationship between the inputs employed by a firm and the maximum output it can produce with those inputs.

Production possibilities frontier (PPF) A curve showing the maximum attainable combinations of two products that may be produced with available resources and current technology.

Productive efficiency The situation in which a good or service is produced at the lowest possible cost.

Profit Total revenue minus total cost.

Progressive tax A tax for which people with lower incomes pay a lower percentage of their income in tax than do people with higher incomes.

Protectionism The use of trade barriers to shield domestic firms from foreign competition.

Public choice model A model that applies economic analysis to government decision making.

Public franchise A designation by the government that a firm is the only legal provider of a good or service.

Public good A good that is both nonrivalrous and nonexcludable.

Purchasing power parity The theory that in the long run, exchange rates move to equalize the purchasing powers of different currencies.

Q

Quantity demanded The amount of a good or service that a consumer is willing and able to purchase at a given price.

Quantity supplied The amount of a good or service that a firm is willing and able to supply at a given price.

Quantity theory of money A theory of the connection between money and prices that assumes that the velocity of money is constant.

Quota A numeric limit imposed by a government on the quantity of a good that can be imported into the country.

R

Rational expectations Expectations formed by using all available information about an economic variable.

Real business cycle model A macroeconomic model that focuses on real, rather than monetary, causes of the business cycle.

Real exchange rate The price of domestic goods in terms of foreign goods.

Real GDP The value of final goods and services evaluated at base-year prices.

Real interest rate The nominal interest rate minus the inflation rate.

Recession The period of a business cycle during which total production and total employment are decreasing.

Regressive tax A tax for which people with lower incomes pay a higher percentage of their income in tax than do people with higher incomes.

Rent seeking The attempts by individuals and firms to use government action to make themselves better off at the expense of others.

Required reserve ratio The minimum fraction of deposits banks are required by law to keep as reserves.

Required reserves Reserves that a bank is legally required to hold, based on its checking account deposits.

Reserves Deposits that a bank keeps as cash in its vault or on deposit with the Federal Reserve.

Revaluation An increase in a fixed exchange rate.

Rivalry The situation that occurs when one person's consuming a unit of a good means no one else can consume it.

Rule of law The ability of a government to enforce the laws of the country, particularly with

respect to protecting private property and enforcing contracts.

S

Saving and investment equation An equation that shows that national saving is equal to domestic investment plus net foreign investment.

Scarcity The situation in which unlimited wants exceed the limited resources available to fulfill those wants.

Separation of ownership from control A situation in a corporation in which the top management, rather than the shareholders, control day-to-day operations.

Short run The period of time during which at least one of a firm's inputs is fixed.

Shortage A situation in which the quantity demanded is greater than the quantity supplied.

Short-run aggregate supply curve A curve that shows the relationship in the short run between the price level and the quantity of real GDP supplied by firms.

Shutdown point The minimum point on a firm's average variable cost curve; if the price falls below this point, the firm shuts down production in the short run.

Simple deposit multiplier The ratio of the amount of deposits created by banks to the amount of new reserves.

Social benefit The total benefit from consuming a good or service, including both the private benefit and any external benefit.

Social cost The total cost of producing a good or service, including both the private cost and any external cost.

Sole proprietorship A firm owned by a single individual and not organized as a corporation.

Speculators Currency traders who buy and sell foreign exchange in an attempt to profit from changes in exchange rates.

Stagflation A combination of inflation and recession, usually resulting from a supply shock.

Stock A financial security that represents partial ownership of a firm.

Stockholders' equity The difference between the value of a corporation's assets and the value of its liabilities; also known as net worth.

Structural relationship A relationship that depends on the basic behavior of consumers and firms and remains unchanged over long periods.

Structural unemployment Unemployment arising from a persistent mismatch between the skills and characteristics of workers and the requirements of jobs.

Substitutes Goods and services that can be used for the same purpose.

Substitution effect The change in the quantity demanded of a good that results from a change in price making the good more or less expensive relative to other goods, holding constant the effect of the price change on consumer purchasing power.

Sunk cost A cost that has already been paid and cannot be recovered.

Supply curve A curve that shows the relationship between the price of a product and the quantity of the product supplied.

Supply schedule A table that shows the relationship between the price of a product and the quantity of the product supplied.

Supply shock An unexpected event that causes the short-run aggregate supply curve to shift.

Surplus A situation in which the quantity supplied is greater than the quantity demanded.

T

Tariff A tax imposed by a government on imports.

Tax incidence The actual division of the burden of a tax between buyers and sellers in a market.

Tax wedge The difference between the pretax and posttax return to an economic activity.

Taylor rule A rule developed by John Taylor that links the Fed's target for the federal funds rate to economic variables.

Technological change A change in the quantity of output a firm can produce using a given quantity of inputs.

Technology The processes a firm uses to turn inputs into outputs of goods and services.

Terms of trade The ratio at which a country can trade its exports for imports from other countries.

Total cost The cost of all the inputs a firm uses in production.

Total revenue The total amount of funds received by a seller of a good or service, calculated by multiplying price per unit by the number of units sold.

Trade The act of buying or selling.

Trade-off The idea that because of scarcity, producing more of one good or service means producing less of another good or service.

Tragedy of the commons The tendency for a common resource to be overused.

Transactions costs The costs in time and other resources that parties incur in the process of agreeing to and carrying out an exchange of goods or services.

Transfer payments Payments by the government to individuals for which the government does not receive a new good or service in return.

Two-part tariff A situation in which consumers pay one price (or tariff) for the right to buy as much of a related good as they want at a second price.

U

Underground economy Buying and selling of goods and services that is concealed from the government to avoid taxes or regulations or because the goods and services are illegal.

Unemployment rate The percentage of the labor force that is unemployed.

Unit-elastic demand Demand is unit-elastic when the percentage change in quantity demanded is *equal to* the percentage change in price, so the price elasticity is equal to 1 in absolute value.

Utility The enjoyment or satisfaction people receive from consuming goods and services.

V

Value added The market value a firm adds to a product.

Variable costs Costs that change as output changes.

Velocity of money The average number of times each dollar in the money supply is used to purchase goods and services included in GDP.

Vertical merger A merger between firms at different stages of production of a good.

Voluntary exchange The situation that occurs in markets when both the buyer and seller of a product are made better off by the transaction.

Voluntary export restraint (VER) An agreement negotiated between two countries that places a numeric limit on the quantity of a good that can be imported by one country from the other country.

Voting paradox The failure of majority voting to always result in consistent choices.

W

Winner's curse The idea that the winner in certain auctions may have overestimated the value of the good, thus ending up worse off than the losers.

World Trade Organization (WTO) An international organization that oversees international trade agreements.

Company Index

Subject Index

Key Terms and the page number on which they are defined appear in **boldface**.

Credits

Photo

Chapter 1, *pages 2, 3, 19*, © Phototex/Sipa Press/0501050124; *page 13*, Brian Lee, CORBIS–NY.

Chapter 2, *pages 36, 37, 59*, © Car Culture/CORBIS, All Rights Reserved; *page 41*, Getty Images, Inc.; *page 51 top*, Jupiter Images Picturequest–Royalty Free; *right*, Dan Lim, Masterfile Corporation; *bottom*, Photolibrary.com; *left*, David Young Wolff, Getty Images Inc.–Stone Allstock; *page 53*, © Apple Computer/Court Mast/Handout/Reuters/Corbis; *page 55*, Imagination Photo Design.

Chapter 3, *pages 66, 67, 91*, © Glow Images/Alamy; *page 72*, Getty Images, Inc; *page 75*, Getty Images, Inc.

Chapter 4, *pages 98, 99, 123*, © Ambient Images Inc./Alamy; *page 113*, Neil Guegan, Corbis Zefa Collection; *page 119*, Bill Aron, PhotoEdit, Inc.

Chapter 5, *pages 136, 137, 165*, Mariusz Szachowski, Shutterstock; *page 146*, AP Wide World Photos; *page*, Paul A. Souders, Corbis/Bettmann.

Chapter 6, *pages 172, 173, 199*, Getty Images, Inc.; *page 181*, Michelle D. Bridwell PhotoEdit Inc.; *page 186*, Getty Images, Inc.

Chapter 7, *pages 208, 209, 227*, AP Wide World Photos; *page 211*, Ed Pritchard, Getty Images Inc.–Stone Allstock; *page 219*, David McIntyre, Black Star.

Chapter 8, *pages 242, 243*, David R. Frazier, Photolibrary, Inc., Alamy Images; *page 246*, © Chung Sung-Jun/Getty Images; *page 254*, Ron Sherman, Photographer; *page 263*, Pallava Bagla, Corbis/Sygma; *page 265*, AP Wide World Photos; *page 280*,

Michael Newman, PhotoEdit Inc.

Chapter 9, *pages 284, 285, 311*, © Frank Micelotta/Getty Images; *page 298*, Chris Carlson, AP Wide World Photos; *page 302*, Getty Images, Inc.; *page 305*, Janet Bailey, Masterfile Stock Image Library; *page 307*, Larry Kolvoord, The Image Works.

Chapter 10, *pages 332, 333, 355*, Yoshikazu Tsuno/AFP/Getty Images; *page 334*, Getty Images, Inc.; *page 336*, Getty Images–Stockbyte; *page 340*, © Indranil Mukherjee/AFP/Getty Images; *page 350*, Keystone, Getty Images Inc.–Hulton Archive Photos; *page 372*, © Chris McGrath/Getty Images.

Chapter 11, *pages 376, 377, 403*, © Bob Daemmrich/The Image Works; *page 391*, Raymond Forbes, SuperStock, Inc.; *page 399*, Richard Heinzen, SuperStock, Inc.

Chapter 12, *pages 410, 411, 431*, Bernard Boutrit, Woodfin Camp & Associates; *page 420*, © Up The Resolution (uptheres)/Alamy; *page 423*, © Adam Berry/Bloomberg News/Landov; *page 425*, James A. Finley, AP Wide World Photos; *page 428*, Courtesy of BIC Corporation.

Chapter 13, *pages 440, 441, 463*, Ralf-Finn Hestoft, Corbis/Bettmann; *page 447*, Dreamworks/Universal/Eli Reed, Picture Desk, Inc./Kobal Collection; *page 449*, These materials have been reproduced with the permission of eBay Inc. Copyright © 2006 EBAY INC. All Rights Reserved; *page 451*, Ken Reid, Getty Images, Inc.–Taxi; *page 460*, David Frazier, The Image Works.

Chapter 14, *pages 472, 473, 497*, Getty Images, Inc.; *page 475*,

REUTERS/Toshiyuki Aizawa/Landov; *page 476*, Sean Cayton, The Image Works; *page 478*, Niall McDiarmid, Alamy Images.

Chapter 15, *pages 506, 507*, John M. Greim/CreativeEye/MIRA.com. Disney characters © Disney Enterprises, Inc. Used by permission from Disney Enterprises, Inc.; *page 515*, Bruce Newman, AP Wide World Photos; *page 518*, David Young-Wolff, PhotoEdit Inc.; *page 524*, Gerd Ludwig, The Image Works.

Chapter 16, *pages 534, 535*, Getty Images, Inc.; *page 546*, Getty Images, Inc.; *page 549*, The Kobal Collection/Columbia Pictures; *page 558*, Safelite Group; *page 562*, Willard Culver/National Geographic Image Collection.

Chapter 17, *pages 574, 575, 591*, © Bubbles Photolibrary/Alamy; *page 582*, Getty Images, Inc.; *page 586*, www.indexopen.com; *page 587*, Bruce Laurance/Image Bank/Getty Images; *page 588*, © 2005 Kristen Brochmann/Fundamental Photographs.

Chapter 18, *pages 598, 599*, Anthony P. Bolante, Corbis/Bettmann; *page 611*, Spencer Grant, PhotoEdit Inc.; *page 614*, Paul Sakuma, AP Wide World Photos.

Text

Chapter 1, *page 5*, "In Estonia, Paying Women to Have Babies Is Paying Off" by Marcus Walker from *Wall Street Journal*, October 20, 2006, p. A1. Copyright © 2006 Dow Jones. Reprinted by permission of Dow Jones via Copyright Clearance Center; *page 18*, "Nightmare Scenarios" from *The Economist*, October 7, 2006. Copyright © 2006 *The*

Economist. Reprinted by permission of *The Economist* via Copyright Clearance Center.

Chapter 2, *page 58*, Jim Duplessis, "BMW Expects Turnaround," *Knight Ridder Tribune Business News*, January 25, 2007, p. 1. Reprinted by permission of The Permissions Group.

Chapter 3, *page 90*, "Apple Coup: How Steve Jobs Played Hardball in iPhone Birth" by Armol Sharma, Nick Wingfield, and Li Yuan from *Wall Street Journal*, February 17, 2007, p. A1. Copyright © 2007 Dow Jones. Reprinted by permission of Dow Jones via Copyright Clearance Center.

Chapter 4, *page 122*, Diane Wedner, "The Landlords: Two Sides of a Coin," *Los Angeles Times*, Jan. 14, 2007, p. K1. Copyright © 2007 Los Angeles Times. Reprinted by permission.

Chapter 5, *page 164*, Kevin Morrison, "Next Carbon Trading Phase Promises to Clean Up Anomalies," *Financial Times*, Feb. 7, 2007, p. 38. Reprinted by permission.

Chapter 6, *page 181*, Jerry A. Hausman, "The Price Elasticity of Demand for Breakfast Cereal," in *The Economics of New Goods*, TF Bresnahan & RJ Gordon, eds. Used with permission of The University of Chicago Press; *page 198*, "Borders Slashes Buyer Rewards, Cuts Discounts," by Jeffrey Trachtenberg from *Wall Street Journal*, March 28, 2007, p. D1. Copyright © 2007 Dow Jones. Reprinted by permission of Dow Jones via Copyright Clearance Center.

Chapter 7, *page 217*, "Stock Prices from Abercrombie and Fitch" from *The Wall Street Journal*, March 6, 2007. Copyright © 2007 Dow Jones. Reprinted by permission of Dow Jones via Copyright Clearance Center; *page 226*, Michael Liedtke, "Google CEO, Co-Founders Get $1 Salary," Associated Press, April 4, 2007, 4:52PM ET version. Available at: http://hosted.ap.org/dynamic/stories/G/GOOGLE_APRIL_FOOLS?SITE=TXKER&SECTION=HOME&TEMPLATE=DEFAULT&CTIME=2007-04-02-09-57-41. Reprinted by permission of Associated Press via Reprint Management Services.

Chapter 8, *page 265*, Gordon H. Hanson, "What Has Happened to Wages in Mexico Since NAFTA? Implications for Hemispheric Free Trade" in Toni Estevadeordal, Dani Rodrick, Alan Taylor Andres Velasco, eds., *FTAA and Beyond: Prospects for Integration in the Americas*, Cambridge: Harvard University Press, 2004; *page 278*, The Top 25 Multinational Corporations 2006 from "Fortune Global 500"

Fortune, July 24, 2006. © 2007 Time Inc. All rights reserved. Reprinted by permission.

Chapter 9, *page 284*, Can Jay-Z Get You to Drink Cherry Coke? from Kenneth Hein, "Cherry Coke Gets Fresh Jay-Z Remix," *Brandweek*, January 29, 2007, p. 4; *page 310*, "Mariah Signs Scent Deal with Arden" by Julie Naughton from *WWD*, April 7, 2006, Vol. 191, No. 74, p. 11. Copyright © 2006 Conde Nast Publications. All rights reserved. Reprinted by permission.

Chapter 10, *page 354*, "Flat-Panel TVs, Long Touted, Finally are Becoming the Norm" by Evan Ranstad from *Wall Street Journal Online*, April 15, 2006. Copyright © 2006 Dow Jones. Reprinted by permission of Dow Jones via Copyright Clearance Center.

Chapter 11, *page 402*, Pallavi Gogoi, "Wal-Mart's Organic

Offensive," *BusinessWeek*, March 29, 2006 (from *BusinessWeek* Online).

Chapter 12, *page 430*, "Brewing Battle: Dunkin' Donuts Tries to Go Upscale, But Not Too Far," by Janet Adamy from *Wall Street Journal*, April 8, 2006. p. A1. Copyright © 2006 Dow Jones. Reprinted by permission of Dow Jones via Copyright Clearance Center.

Chapter 13, *page 462*, "Savings, Shakeup Seen in $4 Drug Plan; Wal-Mart May 'Take It Nationwide Next Year' " by Julie Appleby from *USA TODAY*, September 22, 2006, p. 1A. Reprinted by permission of *USA TODAY*.

Chapter 14, *page 496*, James K. Glassman, "Cable Guys," *Wall Street Journal Online*, September 28, 2006. Copyright © 2006 Dow Jones. Reprinted by permission

of Dow Jones via Copyright Clearance Center.

Chapter 16, *page 564*, "Racing Teams Recruit Athletes and Train Them Hard; The $60,000 Tire Carrier" by Neal E. Boudette, Staff Reporter of *Wall Street Journal*, June 16, 2005, p. A1. Copyright © 2005 Dow Jones. Reprinted by permission of Dow Jones via Copyright Clearance Center.

Chapter 17, *page 590*, "Your Money: Bad Credit Can Inflate Car Insurance Premiums" by Sandra Block from *USA TODAY*, June 11, 2007. Reprinted by permission *USA TODAY*.

Chapter 18, *page 624*, "The Grand Bargainer" by Steven Pearlstein from *Washington Post*, Wednesday, February 7, 2007, p. D1. Copyright © 2007 Dow Jones. Reprinted with permission of Dow Jones via Copyright Clearance Center.

We use **business examples** to explain economic concepts. This table highlights the topic and **real-world** company introduced in the chapter-opening vignette and revisited throughout the chapter. This table also lists the companies that appear in our *Making the Connection* and *An Inside Look* features.

Chapter Title	Chapter Opener	Making the Connection	An Inside Look
CHAPTER 1			
Economics: Foundations and Models	What Happens When U.S. High-Technology Firms Move to China?	Will Women Have More Babies if the Government Pays Them To? • When Economists Disagree: A Debate over Outsourcing	Should the United States Worry about High-Tech Competition from India and China? Source: Economist
CHAPTER 2			
Trade-offs, Comparative Advantage, and the Market System	Managers Making Choices at BMW	Trade-offs: Hurricane Katrina, Tsunami Relief, and Charitable Giving • A Story of the Market System in Action: How Do You Make an iPod? • Property Rights in Cyberspace: YouTube and MySpace	BMW Managers Change Production Strategy Source: Knight Ridder Tribune Business News
CHAPTER 3			
Where Prices Come From: The Interaction of Demand and Supply	Apple and the Demand for iPods	Why Supermarkets Need to Understand Substitutes and Complements • Companies Respond to a Growing Hispanic Population • Apple Forecasts the Demand for iPhones and other Consumer Electronics • The Falling Price of LCD Televisions	How Does the iPhone Help Apple and AT&T? Source: WSJ
CHAPTER 4			
Economic Efficiency, Government Price Setting, and Taxes	Should the Government Control Apartment Rents?	The Consumer Surplus from Satellite Television • Price Floors in Labor Markets: The Debate over Minimum Wage Policy • Does Holiday Gift Giving Have a Deadweight Loss? • Is the Burden of the Social Security Tax Really Shared Equally between Workers and Firms?	Is Rent Control a Lifeline or Stranglehold? Source: Los Angeles Times
CHAPTER 5			
Externalities, Environmental Policy, and Public Goods	Economic Policy and the Environment	The Clean Air Act: How a Government Policy Reduced Infant Mortality • The Fable of the Bees • Can Tradable Permits Reduce Global Warming? • Should the Government Run the Health Care System?	Problems with Carbon Trading Source: Financial Times
CHAPTER 6			
Elasticity: The Responsiveness of Demand and Supply	Do People Care about the Prices of Books?	The Price Elasticity of Demand for Breakfast Cereal • Determining the Price Elasticity of Demand for DVDs by Market Experiment • Price Elasticity, Cross-Price Elasticity, and Income Elasticity in the Market for Alcoholic Beverages • Why Are Oil Prices So Unstable?	Borders Changes Its Rewards Program Source: WSJ